The College Writer's
Handbook

Randall VanderMey
Westmont College

Verne Meyer
Dordt College

John Van Rys
Redeemer University
College

Pat Sebranek

HOUGHTON MIFFLIN COMPANY

BOSTON   NEW YORK

Publisher: Pat Coryell

Editor in Chief: Suzanne Phelps Weir

Senior Development Editor: Judith Fifer

Assistant Editor: Anne Leung

Editorial Associate: John McHugh

Senior Project Editor: Aileen Mason

Editorial Assistant: Susan Miscio

Manufacturing Manager: Karen B. Fawcett

Senior Marketing Manager: Cindy Graff Cohen

Marketing Assistant: Kelly Kunert

Cover Design and Interior Design: Tammy Hintz and Van Mua

Illustrations: Chris Krenzke

CD: Chris Erickson, Steve Augustyn, Jason Reynolds, Mark Fairweather

Editorial: J. Robert King, Claire Ziffer, Steven E. Schend, Stephen D. Sullivan, Janae Sebranek, Laura Bachman, Linda Presto, Joyce Becker Lee, Mariellen Hanrahan, Betsy Rasmussen, Lester Smith

Production: April Barrons, Christine Rieker, Julie Spicuzza, Susan Boehm, Kathleen Strom, Kevin Nelson, Colleen Belmont, Mark Lalumondier

Printed in the U.S.A.

Library of Congress Control Number: 2005938039

ISBN 13: 978-0-618-49169-8
ISBN 10: 0-618-49169-4

1 2 3 4 5 6 7 8 9-DOC-10 09 08 07 06

Preface

We want your students to succeed as writers, and this book will help them do so. To that end, we have used a coaching tone in *The College Writer's Handbook* to encourage students to see good writing as tough but doable—and worth doing in a world where good writing matters.

As co-authors, we are seasoned writers with a combined 60 years in college teaching and two dozen books on writing, along with 30 years of practical writing experience in the publishing business. We know from our writing, teaching, and work experience that writing is a process, that learning to write takes time, and that every writer needs a colleague to help him or her improve.

This book can be your students' writing colleague. These pages provide complete instuction for every writing challenge in academia and the workplace. The book introduces each topic briefly, lays out the key issues, and then follows up with practical writing strategies that help students produce their best writing. And because some students might have special challenges such as little writing experience, limited reading proficiency, weak grammar skills, or difficulty with the English language, this handbook continually offers tips that will help students address those challenges.

The College Writer's Handbook was specially designed for today's busy and diverse student population. The book includes everything students need to write well in composition courses, in other courses across the curriculum, and in the workplace, from practical writing-process instruction to guidelines for documenting sources in research writing. You'll find guidelines and samples for twenty common forms of college writing; assistance for nonnative English learners; and focused instruction on thinking critically through reading, viewing, and writing. Coverage of visual rhetoric is particularly helpful for today's students who learn through a variety of media, including television, movies, and the Internet.

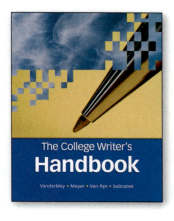

Written in an engaging tone, jam-packed with practical information, colorfully designed for ease of use, and tabbed for fingertip access, *The College Writer's Handbook* is your students' writing colleague.

Features

A focus on critical thinking. Critical thinking skills are essential for college-level work, including strong writing. *The College Writer's Handbook* helps students develop their critical thinking skills through strategies for active, engaged reading of texts; attentive viewing of images; and logically patterned writing. In addition, the first part introduces key principles for persuasion and argumentation, principles students will use in a variety of reading, viewing, and writing tasks. The handbook also stresses rhetorical analysis for writing—a sensitivity to audience, purpose, and context. Finally, woven into the book are periodic ethics tips that press students to consider critically the ethical dimension of their writing.

A focus on writing across the curriculum. Part 9, "Writing Across the Curriculum" (WAC), explains and models how to develop common forms of writing required in college, including personal essays, analytical essays, persuasive essays, literary analyses, business writing, oral presentations, and essay tests. Each form is presented with an overview, student models, guidelines, and a checklist—practical instruction that allows students to take charge of their own writing assignments. In addition, many chapters include WAC Link and Workplace Link boxes, each of which explains how a chapter's ideas are applied across the curriculum and in the workplace. In this way, students are encouraged to see the role of writing in college and beyond.

A focus on writing assessment. *The College Writer's Handbook* explains how and why writing assessment is a crucial part of the writing process, whether self-assessment or peer assessment. Chapter 5, "Assessing Writing," explains how to evaluate writing using "seven traits of good writing." Chapters 6 through 11 explain how to develop these qualities throughout the writing process. And for every form of writing addressed in the book (including research writing), guidelines, checklists, and annotated sample papers show how these seven qualities are relevant for that form. This consistent focus on qualities of good writing offers instructors and students a common vocabulary and a flexible set of tools for strengthening virtually any form of writing.

Thorough coverage of research and documentation. With an eye to contemporary research expectations of college instructors and current practices of college students, Part 10 carefully covers all stages of the research process. Instruction includes planning a research project, taking organized and effective notes, engaging and evaluating both print and electronic sources, conducting primary or field research, using the modern college library, and doing reliable Internet research. The handbook also includes specific instruction on avoiding plagiarism and effectively integrating and documenting source material. Throughout the discussion, instruction is backed up with examples and models, student-friendly coverage of MLA and APA, and overviews of Chicago and CSE formats.

Exceptional ESL coverage. Special assistance is provided to nonnative English speakers through the handbook's design. Its succinct presentations, clear headings, bulleted lists, tables, diagrams, and photographs help ESL learners read and understand the book's contents. Chapters on style, word choice, and sentence structure point out nuances of the English language and help ESL learners identify and learn them. Chapters in Part 8 address special challenges faced by ESL students and provide targeted help with college orientation, sentence structure, word choice, grammar, count and noncount nouns, academic conventions, and more. Also, ESL tips throughout the book provide students help when and where they need it.

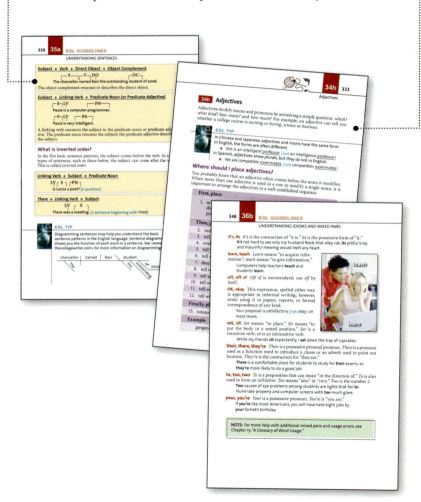

Strong coverage of style and design. *The College Writer's Handbook* treats style and design as key (even related) elements of college writing, not as peripheral, add-on issues of adornment and appearance. In other words, this handbook treats style and design as important rhetorical considerations. Whether students are seeking to write strong paragraphs, shape sentences with impact, or choose the best words, the style chapters will guide them toward more mature language use, including avoiding biased language and using the right word. Similarly, the design chapters help students make rhetorically sound choices for all types of writing, including designing documents through careful attention to format, page layout, and typography; designing and using visuals ranging from numerical tables to line drawings; and writing and designing for the web.

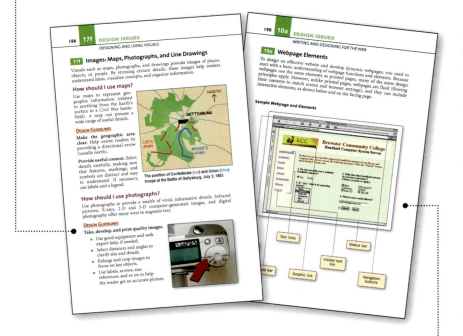

Up-to-date coverage of technology in writing and research. *The College Writer's Handbook* integrates strong coverage of technology in all writing processes, including electronic note taking (while avoiding copy-and-paste plagiarism), using document-design software, writing and designing for the web, searching electronic databases, and conducting reliable Internet research. The text is enhanced with a coordinated package of both print and electronic supplements that reinforce and extend the text with additional models, exercises, and tutorials.

Supplements for the Student

The Technology Resource for **The College Writer's Handbook** provides access to all of the supplemental tools for your students' success. Included in this 16-page booklet is the companion **CD-ROM** as well as directions for accessing *The College Writer's Handbook* Online, WriteSpace Online Interactive Program, and the Online Study Center. Interactive exercises, tests, models, and tutorials can be accessed through the CD or online.

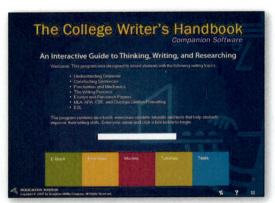

The Exercise Booklet provides numerous editing exercises that cover style, grammar, sentences, punctuation, mechanics, and ESL issues. Additionally, students can find interactive exercises on the companion CD, on *The College Writer's Handbook* Online, on the Online Study Center, and in WriteSpace.

The Online Study Center at <**www.thecollegewriter.com**> offers handy guidelines and checklists for students to review before class, web links from the text, additional sample papers to help students improve their writing, and interactive exercises that can be used as self-tests.

Plagiarism Prevention Zone has critical instruction on how and when to quote, paraphrase, and summarize, as well as how to take notes and cite sources.

A Student Guide to Authoring Your Own Work: Understanding Plagiarism, by Rosemarie Menager-Beeley and Lyn Paulos, is a brief student supplement that will help students avoid the pitfalls of plagiarism. There are sections where students can check their knowledge, including a quiz at the end.

Internet Research Guide has helpful advice and practice for your students on how to conduct research, evaluate sources, build an argument with Internet research, and document papers properly.

SMARTHINKING® links students to experienced writing instructors for one-on-one online tutoring during peak study hours. Please consult your Houghton Mifflin sales representative for more details.

THEA and CLAST Preparation Manuals include practice tests to help students pass the Texas Higher Education Assessment Test and Florida's College Level Academic Skills Test.

The American Heritage College Dictionary, **Fourth Edition** is an indispensable tool and desk reference for college and beyond.

The American Heritage English as a Second Language Dictionary is specially designed with additional sample sentences to suit the needs of intermediate to advanced ESL students.

Supplements for the Instructor

Instructor's Resource Manual, available in print on the Online Teaching Center, provides sample syllabi, chapter summaries, teaching suggestions, and a list of resources.

The Online Teaching Center at <www.thecollegewriter.com> has a downloadable version of the *Instructor's Resource Manual* as well as access to all materials in the Online Study Center.

WriteSpace is an integrated, customizable online writing program with classroom management provided by Blackboard®. In addition to writing tutorials, it has a variety of content that can be administered as self-paced exercises or as gradable exams and assignments. WriteSpace also offers online tutoring and plagiarism detection services. Please consult your Houghton Mifflin sales representative for more details.

Teaching Writing with Computers: An Introduction, edited by Pamela Takayoshi and Brian Huot, is an up-to-date resource on integrating technology into writing instruction.

Finding Our Way: A Writing Teacher's Sourcebook, edited by Wendy Bishop and Deborah Coxwell Teague, is a unique and powerful collection of essays for new or relatively new composition instructors.

The Essentials of Tutoring: Helping College Students Develop Their Writing Skills, by Paul Gary Phillips and Joyce B. Phillips, is a comprehensive guide for writing tutors.

Acknowledgments

The authors wish to express their gratitude to the following people who have contributed their valuable time, energy, and ideas to the development of *The College Writer's Handbook* and its supplements.

Instructors: Shelley Aley, *James Madison University;* Marty Ambrose, *Edison College;* Jan Bone, *Roosevelt University* and *William Rainey Harper College;* Deborah Brothers, *Lincoln Land Community College;* Tracy Constantine, *Durham Technical Community College;* Annette Cozzi, *DePaul University;* Erika Deiters, *Moraine Valley Community College;* Ernest Enchelmayer, *Troy State University;* Joseph Essid, *University of Richmond;* Sandra L. Eubanks, *Jefferson Community and Technical College;* Sam Fiorenza, *Highland Community College;* Kevin Grauke, *LaSalle University;* Kathryn Hamilton, *Columbus State University;* Dick Harrrington, *Piedmont Virginia Community College;* Karen Helbling, *Valley Forge Military Academy and College;* Allan Johnston, *Columbia College;* Ted E. Johnston, *El Paso Community College;* Julie Lumpkins, *Columbia State Community College;* Gina Maranto, *University of Miami;* Susan Martin, *Lord Fairfax Community College;* Lauri Mattenson, *University of California, Los Angeles;* Mark D. Merritt, *University of San Francisco;* Amanda Putnam, *Roosevelt University;* Dave Reinheimer, *Southeast Missouri State University;* Danny Robinson, *Bloomsburg University;* Susan Rosen, *Anne Arundel Community College;* Timothy A. Shonk, *Eastern Illinois University;* William Shute, *San Antonio College;* Kristine Swenson, *University of Missouri, Rolla;* Monica Parish Trent, *Montgomery College;* Martha Vertreace-Doody, *Kennedy King College;* Julie Wakeman-Linn, *Montgomery College;* Ted Walkup, *Clayton College and State University;* Teri Waters, *Waubonsee Community College;* Debbie J. Williams, *Abilene Christian University;* Robbin Zeff, *George Washington University.*

Students: Ryan Bis, *Boston University;* Angie Brewster, *Boston College;* Danielle Gagnon, *Boston University;* Travis Keltner, *Boston College;* Lindsey Lambalot, *Northeastern University;* Sarah Marith, *Boston University.*

Special Thanks: A special thanks goes to Maureen Fitzsimmons of *Syracuse University* for her work on the *Instructor's Resource Manual.* Also thanks to Vici Casana and Janet Young.

Randall VanderMey

Verne Meyer

John Van Rys

Pat Sebranek

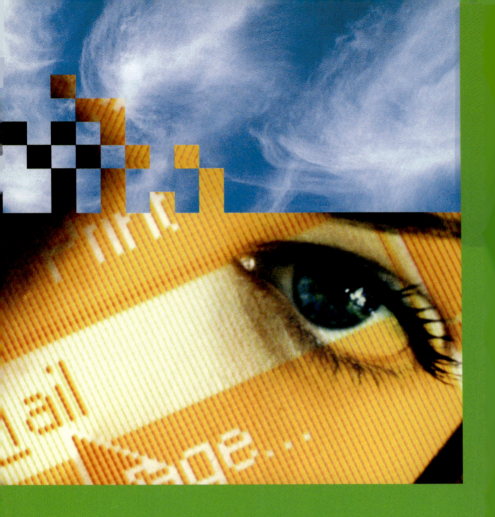

Critical Thinking, Reading, Writing, and Viewing

Critical Thinking, Reading, Writing, and Viewing

Critical Thinking Through Reading

Reading is basic to writing, the way that eating is basic to cooking. Just as creating food worth eating is the goal of cooking, making words worth reading lies at the heart of writing. And while the cook plans the meal around the tastes of his or her guests, the writer must always develop his or her text with the needs or interests of the reader in mind. To appeal to a reader, the writer has to know what good reading is.

Reading is also basic to critical thinking—the process of logically examining ideas and drawing reasonable conclusions based on evidence. In college, at work, and in life, careful reading lies at the heart of such critical thinking and feeds into thoughtful writing.

How can reading improve my writing?

Thoughtful reading is essential to thoughtful writing. As you prepare to write, reading supplies you with facts and ideas, shows you what others have said about your topic, and helps you sort through your own ideas. Moreover, reading teaches by example, showing how you can shape your own sentences, paragraphs, essays, and other forms of writing. Follow these reading principles.

- **Read systematically.** With any reading task or assignment, have a plan. Know why you're reading, what you're looking for, and how you'll use the reading.

- **Read actively.** Pay close attention to what you read so that you can draw understanding or inspiration from it. In fact, such active reading often involves writing.

- **Read critically.** Don't just absorb—examine, reflect, evaluate, and respond. Read "between the lines" for the unstated message.

What's Ahead

CRITICAL THINKING THROUGH READING

1a   Reading Actively

Truly active reading requires more than highlighting every line in yellow or pink. Active reading is really interactive, a kind of mental dialogue with the writer. Certain practical techniques will help you stay alert for active reading:

- **Pace yourself.** Read in stretches of thirty to forty-five minutes, followed by short breaks. As you read, slow down in tough spots, respond to the text, ask questions, and write down your reactions.
- **Predict.** Based on where you have been and where you are in the text, anticipate what will come next and why.
- **Speak the text.** Read difficult parts aloud, or take turns reading aloud with a partner.
- **Track the text.** Record your dialogue with the text through writing strategies like note taking, annotating, mapping, and outlining.

Web Link: Note that the active-reading and critical-reading techniques addressed in this chapter are tied to a sample essay by Leigh Turner, "The Media and the Ethics of Cloning." The full text of this article is available on our website. <www.thecollegewriter.com>

How should I take notes?

First find a note-taking system that suits you. Your system should allow you to distinguish clearly between facts, quotations, paraphrases, summaries, and personal remarks. It is also a good idea to include a reference number or topic word at the top of each note to help you organize your notes later.

While effective note taking is crucial for typical reading assignments in your courses, it's especially important for any research-based writing. In Chapter 46, you'll find more instruction on the following systems: paper or electronic note cards, annotated text, the research log, and the double-entry notebook.

WRITER'S TIP

One critical-reading strategy used by many instructors is SQ3R.
- **Survey** the text, noting its organization: introduction, body, conclusion, headings, illustrations, and so forth.
- **Question** the material, turning headings into questions and posing the five W's (*who, what, where, when,* and *why*).
- **Read** the material, keeping track of main points and details.
- **Recite** the key points out loud, or list them in a summary.
- **Review** the material, perhaps even explaining it to someone else.

How should I annotate texts?

Annotating involves marking up the text itself. If you own the book you're reading or if you are reading a photocopy, write notes in the margins. Writing activates your thinking and records your insights. Try the techniques shown in the sample passage below:

- **Write a question**—or a simple "?"—next to anything that concerns or puzzles you. See whether the text eventually answers your question.
- **Link related passages** by drawing circles, lines, or arrows, or by making notes such as "see page 36."
- **Add personal thoughts.** Keep track of your reactions without worrying about them initially. You can analyze these reactions, whether positive or negative, later.
- **Create a marginal index.** Write key words in the margin or at the top of the page to identify important themes, names, or patterns. For books, list these key words (with page numbers) on a blank page at the end. By doing so, you'll create an index for future use.

ANNOTATING IN ACTION

The following article by Leigh Turner was written in the wake of the first successful animal cloning. This reading might be used in communication, philosophy, ethics, biotechnology, environmental studies, or political science for class discussion.

The excerpt below shows how a student reader engages the text and comments on key ideas. To retrieve the full article and practice annotating the rest of it, go to <www.thecollegewriter.com>, where you'll also find tutorials on active reading strategies.

What's the connection?

The Media and the Ethics of Cloning

Who is he? Check

If the contemporary debate on cloning has a patron saint, surely it is Andy Warhol. Not only did Warhol assert that everyone would have 15 minutes of fame—witness the lawyers, philosophers, theologians, and bioethicists who found their expertise in hot demand on the nightly morality plays of network television following Ian Wilmut's cloning of the sheep Dolly—but he also placed "clones," multiple copies of the same phenomenon, at the heart of popular culture. Instead of multiple images of Marilyn Monroe and Campbell's soup cans, we now have cloned sheep. Regrettably, it is Warhol's capacity for hyperbole rather than his intelligence and ironic vision that permeates the current debate on cloning.

See textbook p. 375

Good definition of cloning

Means extreme exaggeration

It would be unfair to judge hastily written op-ed pieces, popular talk shows, and late-night radio programs by the same standards that one would apply to a sustained piece of philosophical or legal analysis. But the popular media could do more to foster thoughtful public debate on the legal, moral, political, medical, and scientific dimensions of the cloning of humans and nonhuman animals.

Media needs to consider cloning thoughtfully.

As did many of my colleagues at the Hastings Center, I participated in several interviews with the media following Ian Wilmut's announcement in

CRITICAL THINKING THROUGH READING

How can I map texts?

Graphically, one way to map a text is by "clustering." Start by naming the main topic in a circle at the center of the page. Then branch out using lines and "balloons," where each balloon contains a word or phrase for one major subtopic. Branch out in additional layers of balloons to show subordinated points. Add graphics, arrows, drawings—anything that helps you visualize the relationships between ideas.

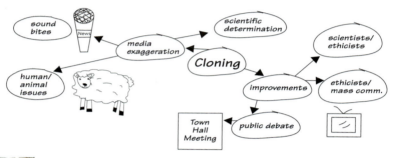

WRITER'S TIP

If the text follows a conventional method of organization such as cause/effect, classification, comparison, process, or problem/solution, use one of the graphic organizers at **7d** to map it.

How can I outline texts?

You can use an outline to show all the major parts, points, and subpoints in a text. An outline uses parallel structure to show coordinated points and indented structure to show subordinated points. Some outlines use only phrases; in full outlines, each item is a complete sentence.

SAMPLE OUTLINE FOR "THE MEDIA AND THE ETHICS OF CLONING"

1. **Introduction:** The current debate about cloning is filled with exaggeration.

2. **Ideas:** The mass media have confused the debate:

   Bombarding the public with sound bites . . . Focusing on human cloning and ignoring animal cloning . . . Saying people are solely products of their genes . . . Promoting scientific determinism

3. **Thesis:** The discussion can be improved in three ways:

   Scientists and ethicists must learn to understand one another's work. Ethicists need to improve how they communicate to the mass media. Public debate about scientific topics must be expanded.

4. **Conclusion:** We need more intelligent discussions so that the public is not misled by the mass media.

1b Evaluating a Text

Critical reading means thoughtfully inspecting and evaluating the writer's ideas. Critical reading requires that you have thoughts of your own and that you submit both your thoughts and the writer's thoughts to the tests of reason and value. As such, critical reading already is a kind of composition, a first step in the writing process. Consider these strategies, noting how they might be used to evaluate Leigh Turner's "The Media and the Ethics of Cloning." (See <www.thecollegewriter.com>.)

1. **Judge the reading's credibility.** Where was it published? How reliable is the author? How current is the information? How accurate and complete does it seem to be? In addition, consider the author's tone of voice, attitude, and apparent biases.

   Discussion: Leigh Turner says that he is a member of the Hastings Center, a nonprofit research institute. How does this information build or break his credibility? Within the article, how does he try to build credibility?

2. **Put the reading in a larger context.** How do the text's ideas match what you know from other sources? What details of background, history, and social context help you understand its perspective? How have things changed or remained the same since the text's publication? What allusions does the writer use? Why?

   Discussion: The topic of cloning is part of the broader subjects of genetic research and ethics. The topic also relates to the debate over the nature of human identity. As for allusions, Turner refers to the artist Andy Warhol and the cloning of the sheep Dolly.

3. **Evaluate the reasoning and support.** Is the reasoning clear and logical? Are the examples and other supporting details appropriate and enlightening? Are inferences (what the text implies) consistent with the tone and message? (Look especially for hidden logic and irony.)

   Discussion: In his article, Turner uses examples and illustrations extensively. He analyzes the problem by breaking it down, and he systematically presents a three-part solution. Is the reasoning sound?

4. **Reflect on how the reading challenges you.** Which of your beliefs and values does the reading call into question? What discomfort does it create? Does your own perspective skew your evaluation?

   Discussion: The article may make us feel uncomfortable about several issues: our lack of concern for animals, our inability to see past the media's treatment of cloning, or the application of cloning to several areas of life. What other challenges does the article raise?

CRITICAL THINKING THROUGH READING

1c Writing a Response to a Text

In a sense, when you read a text, you enter into a dialogue with it. Your response expresses your turn in the dialogue. Obviously, this response can take different forms, from a journal entry to a blog to a discussion-group posting.

How should I respond to a text?

On the surface, responding to a text seems perfectly natural—just let it happen. In reality, it can be a bit more complicated. Typically, a written response is not the same as a private diary entry but is instead shared with other readers, whether your instructor, a peer group, or a class. You develop your response while keeping your instructor's requirements in mind. Follow these guidelines:

- **Be honest.** While you want to remain sensitive to the context in which you will share your response, be bold enough to be honest about your reaction to the text—what it makes you think, feel, and question. To that end, a response usually allows you to express yourself directly using the pronoun "I."
- **Be fluid.** Let the flow of your thoughts and feelings guide you in what you write. Don't stop to worry about grammar, punctuation, mechanics, and spelling.
- **Be reflective.** Generally, the goal of a response is to offer a thoughtful reflection as opposed to a knee-jerk reaction. Show that you are weighing the text's ideas and relating them to your own experience. Avoid a shallow reaction that comes from skimming the text or misreading it.
- **Be selective.** By nature, a response must limit its focus; it cannot cover all your reactions to the text. Zero in on one or two elements to see where they take you in your dialogue with the text.

SAMPLE RESPONSE

Here is part of a student's response to Leigh Turner's "The Media and the Ethics of Cloning." (See <www.thecollegewriter.com>.) Note the personal pronouns, the informality, and the exploratory tone.

> Turner seems dead right about the treatment of cloning in the media, based on some news stories I've recently heard about food from cloned cows. The media just don't go very deep, especially on science issues, which most people find too tough to understand anyway.
>
> Like most people, I've focused on the idea of human cloning, afraid of what it could lead to, but I'm also curious about it. Cloning animals is an issue that hasn't been on my radar screen much. Is it right to clone animals just for the benefit of people? Would I approve of human cloning if it benefited me, if it helped someone I loved or saved my own life?

1d   Writing a Summary of a Text

One way to engage a text is to summarize it. By doing so, you not only create a brief record of its contents but also exercise your ability to comprehend, analyze, and synthesize information—all important thinking skills.

How should I write a summary?

Writing a summary requires sifting out the least important points, sorting the essential ones to show their logical relationships, and putting those points in your own words. Follow these guidelines:

- **Skim first; then read closely.** First, get a sense of the whole, including the main idea and strategies for support. Then read carefully, taking notes as you do.

- **Capture the logic and argument of the text.** Review your notes and annotations, looking for main parts, main points, and clear connections. State these briefly and clearly in your own words. Include only what is essential, excluding most examples and details. Don't say simply that the text talks about its subject; identify what it says about that subject.

- **Test your summary.** Aim to objectively capture the heart of the text; avoid interjecting your own opinions. Similarly, don't confuse an objective summary of a text with a response to it (shown at **1c**). Finally, check your summary against the original text for accuracy and consistency.

SAMPLE SUMMARY

Below is a sample student summary of Leigh Turner's article, "The Media and the Ethics of Cloning." (Go to <www.thecollegewriter.com.) Note how the summary writer includes only main points, using her own words. She departs from the precise order of ideas in the original writing but communicates their sense accurately.

Popular media cover the topic of cloning inadequately. They offer unfocused and one-sided coverage, typically ignoring animal cloning, especially the ethics of cloning animals to create "pharmaceutical factories." By stressing "genetic essentialism," the idea that people are simply products of their genes, they ignore the complexity of growth. And last, the media make it sound as though the advance of cloning is unstoppable. How can this problem be resolved? First, training is needed so that scientists and ethicists can understand one another's work better. Second, ethicists need to be better communicators in the media, especially by publishing in journals that nonscientists can understand. Finally, public institutions need to sponsor debates so that views can be expressed at the grassroots level.

1e   Checklist: Critical Thinking Through Reading

Use this checklist as a reminder of how to improve your thinking and reading skills.

____ How can I improve my active reading skills and strategies?
Which strategies do I already use?
Which ones should I learn and use?

____ How can I use active reading to improve my writing? (See **1a**.)

____ How can I better evaluate the texts that I read? (See **1b**.)

____ How can I strengthen my response writing? (See **1c**.)

____ How can I write stronger summaries of texts? (See **1d**.)

LINKS

WAC Link: While this chapter focuses on critical reading for better writing, it's often important in your college work to read imaginatively—and not just in a literature class. When you read, you can harness the power of imagination, even in "rational" fields such as biology, sociology, or engineering.

Consider these common beliefs:

1. Imagination is childish, so all college-level thinking should be logical.
2. Imagination is for creative writers, actors, and artists—not scientists, social scientists, and philosophers.
3. Reading is not imaginative because a reader just receives what someone else has made.

NOTE: All three statements are false. In any field, imagination is essential to active reading. Consider these examples:

• A history student reading accounts by Holocaust survivors imagines suffering she herself has never experienced.

• A political science student analyzing proposed legislation that could make it tougher to get a driver's license imagines the forces that prompted politicians to draft it.

• An astronomy student reading about the shift from a Ptolemaic to a Copernican model of the universe imagines the effect of such a shift on people's beliefs.

Critical Thinking in Writing

Read the title of this chapter again. Notice that you can read it two ways: (1) thinking critically to write, and (2) writing to improve your critical thinking. Both meanings are intended, because thinking and writing are a revolving process. That is why so much writing is required in college courses: One of the central goals of a college education is teaching students to think.

Chapter 1, "Critical Thinking Through Reading," looked at ways to be a more active, critical, and imaginative reader. This chapter looks at what it means to think both critically and imaginatively in writing. You will develop the following skills:

- **Learn critical thinking moves.** The modes of thinking are like gears on a bicycle—different gears for different slopes. Some thinking is good for generalizing and some for making distinctions, some for detailing and some for condensing, some for asking and some for explaining.

- **Develop critical habits.** Certain habits of mind, such as asking probing questions or remaining open to opposing viewpoints, produce careful thinking. These are valuable throughout your life but are especially valuable when you write.

- **Employ logical reasoning.** This chapter shows how to use inductive and deductive reasoning and how to analyze, synthesize, and evaluate. In Chapter 4, "Understanding Argument and Persuasion," you will see how to build logical and persuasive arguments and how to avoid logical fallacies.

What's Ahead

CRITICAL THINKING IN WRITING

2a Learning Critical Thinking Moves

Critical thinking is clear, thorough, and logical. Critical thinking examines issues fully, weighs competing views objectively, and reaches rational conclusions. Such thinking is demanding: It requires awareness of one's own mind, knowledge of the subject, avoidance of logical pitfalls, and habits that nurture sound reasoning. To hone your critical-thinking skills, practice the following approaches to life and learning:

1. **Be curious.** Ask, "Why?" Kids do it all the time. Get some of that spirit back in your life.

2. **Be creative.** Look at things in a fresh way, asking "What if" questions such as, "What if the Earth's axis tipped at 25 degrees instead of 23.5?"

3. **Be open to new ideas.** Approach thinking as you would approach a road trip—looking for the unexpected along the way.

4. **Value other points of view.** Look at issues from another person's perspective and weigh other ideas against your own. Honestly imagine having a different belief system.

5. **Get involved.** Read books, journals, and newspapers. Join book clubs, film clubs, or social-action activities. Watch documentaries.

6. **Focus.** Sharpen your concentration. Look for details that distinguish a topic and reveal key points related to its nature, function, and impact.

7. **Be rational.** Choose logical thinking patterns like those discussed in this chapter, and then work through the steps to develop and deepen your understanding of a topic.

8. **Make connections.** Use writing to explore how and why topics or issues are related. Use comparisons, analogies, or metaphors to identify and name these relationships.

9. **Tolerate ambiguity.** Consider conflicting ideas and suspend judgment when your position requires further research.

10. **Test the evidence.** Be properly skeptical about all claims. (See **4e**.) Look for verification in other sources.

ESL TIP

Most importantly, expect your writing to produce results. When you focus on the job your writing is meant to accomplish, you understand the *purpose* of your work. All thinking and writing should be purposeful.

2b   Developing Critical Reasoning Skills

Every field uses questions to trigger critical thinking. For example, scientific questions generate hypotheses, mathematical questions call for proofs, and literary critical questions call for interpretations. A good question opens up a problem and guides you all the way to its solution. But not all questions are created equal. Consider the differences:

What dead-end questions should I use cautiously?

Don't limit yourself to the following types of questions.

- **"Rhetorical" questions** aren't meant to be answered. They're asked for effect.
  Example: Who would want to be caught in an earthquake?

- **Closed questions** seek a limited response and can be answered with a yes, a no, or a simple fact.
  Example: Are earthquakes caused by plate tectonics?

How can I use questions to improve my critical thinking?

To improve the critical thinking in your writing, ask better questions.

- **Ask open questions.** Closed questions choke off thinking. Use open questions to trigger a flow of ideas.
  Example: How might a major earthquake affect this urban area?

- **Ask theoretical questions.** These questions call for in-depth explanations rooted in a field of knowledge.
  Example: What causes sudden fracturing along fault lines?

- **Ask "educated" questions.** Compare questions A and B below:
  A. What's wrong with television?
  B. Does the 16.3 percent rise in televised acts of violence during the past three years signal a rising tolerance for violence in the viewing audience? (This question is clearer and suggests debatable issues.)

- **Keep a question journal.** Divide a blank notebook page or split a computer screen. On one side, write down any questions that come to mind regarding the topic that you want to explore. On the other side, write down answers and any thoughts that flow from them.

WRITER'S TIP

Questions can also drive the drafting process. Turn the main idea into a question and write freely to answer it in as many ways as possible. Return to your work and refine it with more questions.

CRITICAL THINKING IN WRITING

2c   Thinking Inductively and Deductively

Questions invite reasoning, and reasoning responds either inductively or deductively.

- **Inductive reasoning** begins with specific information and develops general conclusions. It is sometimes called *bottom-up thinking* because it starts with discrete details and moves "up" to broader ideas.
- **Deductive reasoning** begins with general principles and develops specific applications. It is sometimes called *top-down thinking* because it starts with big-picture principles and works "down" to specific details.

How can I use induction and deduction in writing?

Use induction when you want to postpone your conclusions, as if they lie at the end of a quest. Use deduction for directness, strength, and clarity, or to apply what is already agreed upon to what is still under dispute. Sentences, paragraphs, and entire essays can be organized either inductively or deductively.

Narrative and personal essays tend toward inductive organization, whereas analytical essays (particularly those written in the social or natural sciences) typically use both induction and deduction.

Example: The paragraphs below, from "If We Are What We Wear . . ." (see **40b**), demonstrate both induction and deduction. Note how each approach affects the message.

Deduction: general principles to specific details

The American excuse for owning multiples is that clothing styles change so rapidly. At the end of the 1980s, trends in high fashion changed every two and half months (During 95). Even for those of us who don't keep up with high fashion, styles change often enough that our clothing itself lasts much longer than the current trend. Perhaps this is one of the reasons the average American spent $997 on clothing in 1996 (U.S. Department of Commerce). 1

Induction: specific details to general principles

While Americans are spending a thousand dollars on clothing a year, people in Ethiopia make an average of only $96 a year, those in Bangladesh $280, and the average Filipino worker makes $1,052 (United Nations Statistics Division). I, on the other hand, made over $5,000 last year, and that job was only part-time. When an American college student can earn more money at her part-time job than three billion people each make for a living, it's time to question our culture and ask, as Alan During did, "How much is enough?" 2

2d Thinking by Analysis

The word *analyze* literally means "to loosen or undo." When you analyze something, you break it down into parts and examine each part separately. You classify information, compare objects, trace a process, or explain causes.

What strategies can I use to analyze?

As you analyze, use different types of thinking, each with its own questions. Remember that an analysis often requires two or more different types of thinking that support one another.

Composition:	What elements does the topic contain? What is not part of it?
Categories:	How are things grouped, divided, or classified?
Structure:	What are the parts and how are they related?
Comparison/contrast:	How are things similar? How are they different?
Cause/effect:	Why did this happen? What are the results?
Process:	How does it work or happen? What are the stages?

Example: Read through the passage below from "A Fear Born of Sorrow" (see **39f**). Note how the writer compares and contrasts feelings about the September 11, 2001, attack on the World Trade Center with the Oklahoma City bombing in 1995, and then analyzes the causes and effects of those feelings.

The Oklahoma City bombing was grievous and alarming, but localized. The bomber was soon arrested, his motives deduced, and justice served. While lives were changed and a nation was shaken, the world community remained composed. However, the September 11 attack unsettled us more, in part because the World Trade Center stood for so much more than the Oklahoma City Federal Building did. The twin towers symbolized American domination of world finances: They were a major center for the Internet, a hub for international business, and an emblem of American life. The fall of the towers struck violently at the nation's psyche, and the manner in which they were destroyed—with America's own airplanes filled with passengers—has raised questions about America's security and future. Threatened to the core, Americans have demanded retaliation—but against whom? The terrorists' identity is not clear, and evidence seems elusive. In a sense, an unknown offender has injured Americans, and they beat the air in the dark. In such a case, terrorism is aptly named, for America's outcry expresses more than sorrow—it also expresses fear.

> The writer develops contrasts signaled by "However." While doing so, she also analyzes causes and explains effects.

CRITICAL THINKING IN WRITING

2e   Thinking by Synthesis

Synthesis is the opposite of analysis. Where analysis breaks down elements into parts, synthesis combines elements into a new whole. In your writing, when you pull things together that are normally separate, you are synthesizing. Common ways of synthesizing are predicting, inventing, redesigning, and imagining.

What strategies can I use to synthesize?

When you synthesize, use both reason and imagination. Start by looking closely at two or more items that you want to synthesize, and then think of fresh ways that they can be related. Don't be afraid to see your subjects in a new light or to approach them in a creative way.

The following kinds of questions may get you started:

Applying: What can I do with both? What will be the outcome?

Bridging: How can I build a connection between these two?

Combining: How can I connect, associate, or blend the two?

Conflicting: What strength does each offer the other?

Inventing: How could both things work together?

Sequencing: Which comes first? Is one an extension of the other?

Example: Read through the passage below in which a student imagines life during the Peloponnesian War. He uses a journal entry to combine his knowledge of the war and ancient Greek religion in a personal point of view.

The writer uses his imagination to write a journal entry.

I spent several hours today at the shrine to Athena praying for an end to this war. How long has it been that we have been living in the midst of constant fighting? My father tells me that he can remember a time when we Athenians were the strongest of all the Greeks. Now, no doubt, it is just a matter of time before the Spartans enter our city. Has Athena forsaken the city that was named after her? Maybe we have done something to anger the gods. I remember my uncle telling horrible stories of what the soldiers did to our neighbors to the north when they were out collecting the taxes Athens demanded. That money helped build our fleet of ships. We were truly the lords of the sea! Maybe the gods resented that.

2f Thinking by Evaluation

Evaluation measures the purpose and worth of things. For example, when you express your judgment about an issue or discuss the weak and strong points of an idea, you are evaluating. Many kinds of writing involve evaluation.

What strategies can I use to evaluate?

To evaluate a topic, start by learning as much about it as possible. Then consider how you will evaluate the topic (which standards you will use). Next, judge how the topic measures up to those standards. You can compare the topic (such as a movie based on a book) to a standard (the movie carefully follows the book) or compare the topic to another thing (whether the book and the movie each have their own qualities). Along the way, support your judgment with concrete details, examples, illustrations, and comparisons.

Questions like these will help you evaluate ideas and topics in writing:

Aspects:	Which aspects or elements of the topic will I evaluate?
Vantage Point:	What is my experience and point of view?
Criteria:	On which standards will I base my judgment?
Assessment:	How does the topic measure up to those standards?
Comparison:	How does it compare and contrast with similar things?
Recommendation:	Based on my evaluation, what do I advise?

Example: Read the paragraphs below from Jennifer Berkompas's film review "Wonder of Wonders: *The Lord of the Rings.*" Note how she supports her evaluation by comparing the films with the trilogy.

1   Tolkien fans, be warned: The movies don't try to follow the books scene by scene or character by character. If you are fond of Tom Bombadil or elf lord Glorfindel, you won't find them. But the movies do stay close in spirit to the books. Director Peter Jackson read the books often to prepare for filming, reading key scenes several times as he shot them. The martial power of Numenoreans, the rustic naivete of the Shire, the peace and beauty of Rivendell and Lothlorien, the presence of evil, the persistence of good and camaraderie, the pain, the power—it's all there.

2   Having read the books and seen the movies many times, I recommend that you look at the films with an open mind. Admire the halls of Moria, the bridge of Khazad-dum, the river of Rivendell, the towering kings, the Argonath—all incredible . . .

> Comparing the trilogy and the films, the writer assesses the films' strengths and recommends them using her evaluation criteria.

2g   Checklist: Critical Thinking in Writing

As **2b** shows, questions can spark thoughts, open up problems, and lead to solutions. This checklist can help you understand how thinking shapes your writing and how writing deepens your thinking.

—— Which of the thinking moves in **2a** do I excel at? Which do I need to develop?

—— When do I naturally think inductively? When do I naturally think deductively?

—— When does my major or career require me to analyze? To synthesize? To evaluate?

—— Which activities or habits most improve my critical-thinking skills? Which most hamper my critical-thinking skills?

—— Which writing strategies (researching, revising, editing) would deepen the ideas in my writing?

—— Which thinking techniques could improve the quality of my writing?

—— Which resources (library, writing center, tutoring, internship) does my college or department offer that could help me develop my thinking and writing skills?

WAC Link: Use thinking strategies to answer essay questions and conduct research. When answering an essay question in any discipline, consider using the synthesis questions on **2e** to strengthen and deepen your thinking.

Read "How can I gather good research questions?" on **45b**. Then use strategies in this chapter (thinking by analysis, thinking by synthesis, or thinking by evaluation) to develop probing research questions and form an effective thesis.

Service-Learning Link: In their job advertisements, employers commonly list a job's required duties and skills, including thinking skills. For a service-learning project, you could help job seekers by (1) discussing help-wanted ads with them, (2) helping them assess their skills, and (3) helping them develop their skills.

Workplace Link: If you have an internship, look for opportunities to develop job-related thinking skills. For example, if a job requires written analyses of processes or products, offer to write, edit, or evaluate such documents.

Critical Thinking Through Visual Images

Every day, we are flooded with visual images on magazine covers, movie trailers, and cell phone video screens. Images quicken our work, provoke ideas, and often trigger our emotions. Images in written texts offer some real advantages. They can grab viewers' attention, convey persuasive ideas, simplify complex concepts, and dramatize important points.

But images have some drawbacks, too. They can distort facts, manipulate emotions, and shortcut reasoning. Therefore, writers must learn how to understand, interpret, evaluate, and use visuals—including pictures, tables, charts, and other graphics. For more information, see the following:

- Chapter 16, "Designing Documents"
- Chapter 17, "Designing and Using Visuals"
- Chapter 18, "Writing and Designing for the Web"

How can I better understand visual images?

To begin with, slow down. Though the modern vogue is to process visuals instantaneously, to truly understand an image, you need to take time with it.

- **Read images actively.** Reading visual images takes as much active involvement as reading written texts.
- **Read images knowledgeably.** Consider the relationships between designer and reader, medium and message, image and text, images and other images—in short, the "rhetoric" of images.
- **Interpret what is meant as well as what is shown.** Determine what the image indicates, what message it conveys, and what the basis of its appeal is. Weigh the image for fairness, authenticity, and importance.
- **Evaluate the image in its context.** Consider its purpose, its quality, and its value to the implied reader. (See "Visuals Tip" in **3d**.)

What's Ahead

3a   Reading an Image
3b   Interpreting an Image
3c   Evaluating an Image
3d   Checklist: Visual Images

CRITICAL THINKING THROUGH VISUAL IMAGES

3a Reading an Image

Modern society bombards us with images, and we process most of them very quickly, without actually *reading* them. The first step in reading an image is slowing down. Once you have done that, follow the guidelines below.

1. **Read actively.** Engage your brain, and inspect the whole image.
   - Think about the overall shape and size of the image.
   - Consider its use of light and shadow as well as color.
   - Consider the overall composition of the image.
   - Notice the way your eye moves across the image.

2. **Read with a purpose.** Understand why the image was created and how it is used. Then read appropriately. If the image is meant to
   - **Inform,** then search for information, but note what is left out.
   - **Illustrate,** then decide whether the image clarifies the idea.
   - **Persuade,** then critique the appeal and watch for manipulation.
   - **Summarize,** then look for the main point to remember.

3. **Read with a plan.** Here is a suggested plan for reading and responding to a visual image. (See the sample response on the facing page.)

   Step 1: **Survey it.** Consider the whole, the parts, and the purpose.

   Step 2: **Question it.** Ask the five W's: *Who* created the image? *What* does it show? *When* was it made? *Where* does the image appear? *Why* is it placed here?

   Step 3: **Relate parts to parts.** Understand what each part contributes and how it connects with other parts.

   Step 4: **Relate the image to its context.** Relate it to the text, to other images, and to the world as you know it.

   Step 5: **Respond to it.** Decide what (if anything) you will do with the ideas contained in the image.

Web Link: Suppose you are reading a webpage and up pops a desktop ad saying: "Get rid of annoying pop-ups now!" How should you respond? Though your first impulse might be to toss the computer out the window, instead, do the following:

- **Stay focused.** Even critiquing the ad may be a waste of your time.
- **Be smart.** Know how pop-up ads use images or flashy movement to attract attention. Realize when you are falling into a visual trap.

NOTE: You can protect yourself and your time with software that screens out most pop-ups.

An image to read

DISCUSSION

The drawing "Stopping by Woods on a Snowy Evening" by Chris Krenzke fits perfectly with the poem it illustrates. The illustration depicts a man on a farm wagon pausing on a country lane to stare out into snow-covered pines. The overall shape of the illustration is circular, a shape that gives the piece a serene feeling. The artist repeats this circular pattern elsewhere in the composition—in the distant snowy hills, in the wagon wheels, even in the pair of milk cans he hauls. The top of the illustration is blue-black, with faint snowflakes wafting downward. The middle region of the drawing contains subtle shades of brown, green, and gray. The lowest part of the illustration bleeds into white snow, extending the visual circle down into the page. The drawing has a clear directionality, from the back of the wagon on the left toward the little village crouched on the hill in the far right, suggesting the farmer's return home.

Krenzke uses the postures of the farmer and the horse to tell the story. Both of these travelers are turned away from the viewer, both with their hearts pointed toward the snowy houses in the distance. Their heads, though, look to the woods beside the road. Simply by turning their heads in partial profile, Krenzke has paused the motion of the wagon and captured this moment of gentle reflection.

Perhaps the greatest success of this illustration, however, is its poeticism. It captures in line, texture, and color the same serene moment that Robert Frost captures in words. The houses and the trees all rhyme in shape, much like the wheels, the canisters, and the overall form of the illustration. This drawing does more than illustrate the poem—it transfigures it.

CRITICAL THINKING THROUGH VISUAL IMAGES

3b Interpreting an Image

Interpreting means figuring out what the visual image or graphic design is really meant to do, say, or show. If the meaning were fixed, like the number of jellybeans in a jar, interpreting would be easy. But the meaning is something you have to gather for yourself by considering all the details.

What elements should I consider?

As you interpret an image, consider the following elements.

Designer: The creator (cartoonist, painter, photographer, webpage editor)

Medium: The physical form (photograph, sketch, sculpture)

Subject: The person, place, event, thing, or idea in the image

Message: The thought the designer wants to convey about the subject

Context: The connection of the image to its surroundings (such as text on the page, other images on the wall, or current thoughts and trends)

Viewer: The intended audience and the actual audience

What complications might I find?

Sometimes, an image itself is strange, deceiving, highly technical, or very detailed, making interpretation difficult. Here are some complications to interpretation.

Designer: Unknown, pseudonymous, corporate

Medium: Unusual, outdated, degraded by time (faded, damaged)

Subject: Vague, unfamiliar, complex, technical, disturbing

Message: Mixed, implied, ironic, unwelcome, distorted

Context: Changing, unknown, disconnected, multilayered

Viewer: Uninterested, unfamiliar, biased

VISUALS TIP

Like words, visuals can be misleading. For example, TV ads for weight-loss drugs commonly picture scantily clad, fit young people, incorrectly suggesting that using the drugs produces fit, youthful bodies.

An image to interpret

©2006 Getty Images/David Perry

Discussion

The words "Beauty Shop" contrast starkly with the building's tired appearance. The photo evokes the old saying, "Beauty is only skin deep," and in this case, the skin of the building has certainly lost its beauty. Dingy stucco, peeling paint, weed-filled alleys, cracked sidewalks—these details mock the shop's name.

Designer:	Unknown photographer
Medium:	Black-and-white photograph
Subject:	A rundown beauty shop
Message:	Beauty fades
Context:	A writing handbook
Viewer:	The reader

This irony creates opposite feelings in the viewer: amusement and sadness. The viewer is amused that the beauty shop has so little beauty. However, the cracks and grime tell the viewer that the ugliness results from a battle against age and the mean streets. The further irony is that this shop once was beautiful. Perhaps it was a local gathering point, though all of that loveliness now is gone.

The photographer apparently intends to create this feeling. The black-and-white medium creates a grave appearance, and the darkened corners make the photo itself seem older than it is. The formal symmetry of the shot suggests that the photographer wants the viewer to pause, to think, and to feel just slightly haunted by the message: Beauty fades.

3c Evaluating an Image

When you encounter an image, you must do more than read and interpret it: You have to decide whether it is worth your time and attention. In other words, you have to evaluate it. When you have performed that task well, you can fairly say you have thought it through. The following questions will guide you.

What purpose does the image have?

- **Ornamentation** makes the page more pleasing to the eye.
- **Illustration** supports points made in the accompanying text.
- **Revelation** gives an inside look at something or presents new data.
- **Explanation** uses imagery or graphics to clarify a complex subject.
- **Instruction** guides the viewer through a complex process.
- **Persuasion** influences feelings or beliefs.
- **Entertainment** amuses the reader.

VISUALS TIP

Use no more visuals in your writing than you need to convey your message effectively. Too many images may overwhelm readers and detract from the main message.

What quality does this image have?

To evaluate quality, ask yourself the following questions:

Does the image meet quality standards? See Chapter 17, "Designing and Using Visuals," for design tips for a variety of graphics and visuals. These can serve as standards for quality.

Is it backed by authority? Does the designer have a good reputation? Does the publication or institution have good credentials?

How does the image compare to other images like it? Are clearer or more accurate images available?

What are its shortcomings? Are there gaps in its coverage? Does it twist the evidence? Does it convey clichéd or misleading information?

What value does the image have?

The following questions will help you judge the value of an image:

Is the visual worth viewing? Does it enrich the document by clarifying or otherwise enhancing its message?

Does the visual appeal to you? Listen to other viewers, but also consider your own perspective.

An image to evaluate

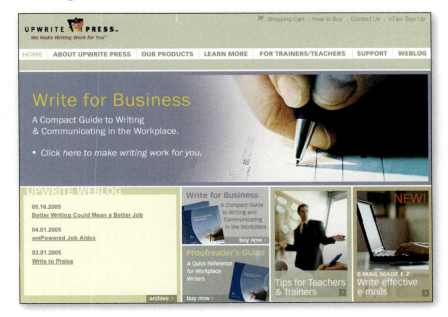

DISCUSSION

The images in the webpage above create a "storefront" for the company UpWrite Press. Below the company logo, a large rectangular image promotes a product—*Write for Business.* The text on the left of this image tells the viewer about the book and encourages clicking to find out more. The image on the right shows a hand writing with a pen—the same image that appears on the cover of the book. This business has wisely connected the cover graphic to the title to create product recognition.

The choice of showing pen-and-paper writing is interesting, especially given that most business writing takes place on the computer. UpWrite Press seems to be using this traditional type of writing to create the impression of stability. The images below the main one help to balance out the traditional writing model. One image shows a man giving a presentation, and it shows a hand in the foreground, holding a pen much like the one above. The implication is that *Write for Business* can help with presentations. Rounding out the set of images is an open laptop with more writing hands and the word "NEW!" emblazoned in red on the picture. While the main image connotes stability and tradition, this image connotes modern technology and innovation.

By connecting these three disparate images, UpWrite Press creates an immediate impression of respectability, adaptability, and applicability to different business environments. Visually, this is a storefront worth exploring.

CRITICAL THINKING THROUGH VISUAL IMAGES

3d   Checklist: Visual Images

Use this checklist to help you read, interpret, and evaluate visual images.

Image

___ What type of image is it, and what are its features? (See **3a–3b**.)

___ How is it organized? Consider framing, focus, foreground and background, and control of the viewer's eye movement.

Designer

___ What is the designer's style and point of view?

___ Do I share the designer's perspective or point of view? Why or why not?

Viewer

___ What experience have I had with images like this?

___ How do my eyes move as I read the image?

Subject

___ What subject and topic does the image address?

___ What does it refer to (implicitly or explicitly)?

Message

___ What is the image's point, appeal, impact, and logic?

___ What complicates the message: irony, ambiguity, a subtext?

Context

___ How and why does the image allude to or reference other images?

___ How does the image relate to nearby words? To what effect?

Medium

___ Has the designer used the medium effectively? How and why?

___ How has the medium affected the making of the image?

VISUALS TIP

The text and visuals in your writing should present one fluent, unified message. To achieve that goal, do the following:

- Plan both the text and visuals for your document (see "Planning Your Document's Design," **16a**), making sure that both fit your purpose, situation, and audience.

- Use color (see **16b**) that fits the document's content, style, and tone.

- Create page designs (see **16d**) that lead readers easily.

- Integrate a visual into the text (see **17a**) by introducing the visual and placing it close to related information.

- Choose types of visuals (tables, graphs, charts, photos) that complement the content, style, and tone of the text. (See **17c**.)

Understanding Argument and Persuasion

"**P**eople generally quarrel," said English author G. K. Chesterton, "because they cannot argue." Both quarreling and arguing are contests of opinion, but while quarreling is careless, good arguing is careful of feelings and ideas. Effective argument is, in fact, quite important to intellectual and public life.

How can I improve my argumentation?

Once you understand the structure of arguments, you'll become a clearer thinker and a better writer. To get started, reflect on these principles:

- **Understand persuasion.** Argument is one form of persuasion among many, from appeals to character to appeals to emotion. Be aware: Some methods of persuasion are more ethical than others.
- **Know how to shape an argument.** A formal argument presents evidence in a logical sequence to support a claim—with the goal of influencing readers' thoughts, feelings, or actions. To argue effectively, you need to know how to find evidence, reason with it, make a supportable claim, and apply the reasoning to your claim.
- **Know how to reason soundly.** Reasoning soundly means making statements that follow logically from one another and lead all the way to an acceptable conclusion. Sound reasoning also avoids logical fallacies—illegal shortcuts on the road of reason.

What's Ahead

UNDERSTANDING ARGUMENT AND PERSUASION

4a Persuading Through Argument

To persuade means to influence someone to think, feel, or decide the way you do. Logical argument is one way to persuade, but there are other ways as well—showing examples, citing authorities, offering rewards, and so on.

What are the elements of persuasion?

Persuasion has four elements: (1) a claim about an issue, (2) a persuader and an audience, (3) a message delivered in a specific way with specific appeals, and (4) an outcome. Here is an example:

> A military recruiter tells a high school student that it would be both wise and good to enlist in the service: wise because the student would draw an income and learn career skills; good because the student would show courage, fulfill personal potential, and show love of country. The outcome will depend on whether the student trusts the recruiter and whether the student accepts the reasoning supporting the claim as valid and emotionally satisfying.

What are the three types of appeal?

Ever since Aristotle's *Rhetoric*, persuasive appeals have usually been broken down into three main types, treated more fully on the pages that follow:

- **An appeal to character** (Greek term *ethos*) calls on the audience's perception of the one making the appeal. Does he or she seem trustworthy, authoritative, intelligent, fair, respected, wise?
- **An appeal to reason** (Greek term *logos*) calls on common sense, logic, well-grounded opinion, and relevant, accurate information.
- **An appeal to emotion** (Greek term *pathos*) works on the audience's feelings, using emotionally charged language, examples, stories, symbols, and descriptions.

ETHICS TIP

Persuasion can be done ethically, but some forms of persuasion use unethical means: offering bribes, creating false impressions, and so on. Unethical persuasion is deceptive: The persuader's interests are at odds with the audience's, and the message masks the persuader's true intention.

In ethical persuasion, the issue is in the open, the appeal of the message is undisguised and genuine, and the outcome is mutually beneficial. To adhere to this ethical standard for persuasion, see Chapter 28 for instructions on writing persuasive essays. Test other texts for this standard—texts as different as ads, webpages, and academic books. (See "Critical Thinking Through Reading," 1a–1e, and "Critical Thinking Through Visual Images," 3a–3d.)

4b Appealing to Character

Have you seen the famous "milk mustache" advertisements? If you have, you probably realize that persuasion appeals not only to logic but also to character, or *ethos*. The people in the ads are popular, successful, and respected. The implication is that (1) you respect their opinions, (2) you want to be like them, (3) they like milk, and, therefore, (4) if you drink milk, you will be like them. Logically, of course, that's a stretch. Here are two ways to appeal to character.

How can I project a good character?

To be persuasive in your writing, you need to project a favorable image of yourself. You need to be seen as

- **Admirable:** Decent, courageous, moral, generous, well liked
- **Authoritative:** Up-to-date, well informed, expert, knowledgeable
- **Careful:** Thorough, accurate
- **Credible:** Well educated, intelligent, experienced
- **Fair:** Objective, nonpartisan
- **Safe:** Open, nonthreatening, friendly

How can I connect with my audience?

Your audience must believe that you actually have the character you project. To build credibility, cultivate these habits:

- **Be honest.** Don't falsify data, spin evidence, or ignore pertinent facts.
- **Use a fitting tone.** Make sure your tone is appropriate for the topic, purpose, situation, and audience. Show tact, respect, and understanding. Focus on issues, not personalities.
- **Be positive.** Appeal to your readers' better nature, to their sense of honor, justice, social commitment, and enlightened self-interest.
- **Be realistic.** Avoid emotionally charged statements, pie-in-the-sky forecasts, and undeliverable deals.
- **Be trustworthy.** Earn trust by your attitude toward the topic, your treatment of readers and others, and your openness.
- **Show respect for opposing viewpoints.** Admit others' strengths.
- **Motivate, don't manipulate.** Avoid bullying, guilt-tripping, and exaggerated tugs on heartstrings. Avoid appeals geared toward ignorance, prejudice, selfishness, or fear.
- **Be clear.** If readers find your thinking too complex, too simple, or too strange, you've lost them.

 ETHICS TIP

The way your audience perceives you has much to do with its own attitudes. If your audience is cynical or rebellious against "the system," your decency might be seen as "out of touch." Building good ethos requires engaging the reader without compromising yourself.

UNDERSTANDING ARGUMENT AND PERSUASION

4c Appealing to Reason

What makes reasoning reasonable? It passes certain tests, at least informally, for logical proof. An argument may stand on any of six major bases for logical proof: induction, deduction, cause and effect, indicators, analogy, and definition.

Induction: Inductive reasoning leads from specific information toward a general conclusion.

> **Example:** Specific Information: Escaped parakeets have been appearing in the treetops of my neighborhood for twenty years. Conclusion: The parakeets have adapted successfully to life in the wild.

SPECIFIC INFORMATION

GENERAL CONCLUSION

> **Testing Inductive Arguments: Is the conclusion the best fit for the facts? Have any facts been left out that would lead to a different conclusion?**

Deduction: Deductive reasoning leads from general principles toward a specific conclusion.

> **Example:** Principle 1: Antibiotics cannot kill viruses. Principle 2: My cold is caused by a virus. Conclusion: Antibiotics cannot cure my cold.

GENERAL PRINCIPLES

SPECIFIC CONCLUSION

> **Testing Deductive Arguments: Are the premises true? Does the conclusion follow from the premises? Is the conclusion properly limited?**

Cause. Reasoning from a cause means predicting or explaining an outcome based on proven cause/effect relationships.

> **Example:** Ice packs and anti-inflammatory medicine reduce swelling. Because your pain is caused by swelling, ice and anti-inflammatory medicine will ease your pain.

CAUSE

EFFECT

> **Testing Causal Arguments: Is the causal claim true? Does the cause match the observed effect? Is the cause necessary to the effect? Is it sufficient? Are there more important causes? Would any conditions keep the cause from having this effect?**

Indicator. Reasoning from an indicator means concluding that something is or is not true based on some visual sign (or lack of one).

> **Example:** A fish must be on my hook: The bobber has gone under and stayed there.

> **Testing Arguments from Indicators: Is the indicator definite? Does it always signify the same thing? Might any other conclusion be indicated by the same sign? Have you interpreted the indicator correctly?**

Analogy. Reasoning by using an analogy means claiming that if something is true of one thing, it is likely to be true of something similar to it.

Some analogies are **literal.** For instance, a scale model race car is literally the same—proportionately—as the full-sized race car.

> **Example:** Because the race car has a spoiler on the back, the model will have a spoiler.

Some analogies are **figurative.** It takes a stretch of imagination, for instance, to see that a legislative assembly is analogous to a rugby team.

> **Example:** A rugby team locks up in a scrum before the ball pops loose, so the legislature may have to reach a deadlock before it can pass the tax bill.

Some analogies are **geographical** or **historical:**

> **Example:** Racism will not be completely eliminated in post-apartheid South Africa just as it was not eliminated in the United States by the 1960s Civil Rights Movement.

Testing Analogies: Is the analogy appropriate, or "apt"? Are the points of comparison relevant? Does the analogy actually support the claim? Is the analogy biased? Where does the analogy break down?

Definition. Reasoning from definition means defining a term and showing that the definition applies in a significant way to a given situation.

> **Example:** According to state law, regional drought conditions must trigger a set of water conservation measures in cities and towns. Drought is defined as three successive years of less than the thirty-year average for rainfall. We have just completed the third year of subaverage rainfall in our state, according to official meteorological measurements. Therefore, our city must soon enforce water conservation measures.

Testing Arguments Based on Definition: Is the definition generally agreed upon? Is the definition clear? Does the definition apply to the situation? Have exceptions been properly considered?

4d Appealing to Emotion

While appeals to character prompt readers to connect with the author and appeals to reason prompt readers to think, persuasion is not complete until the audience is prompted to act. To prompt readers to act, the author must often appeal to emotion. *Emotion, motivation, movement*—all of these terms come from the same root, which means "to push." To push an audience from a standstill is persuasion. The best persuasion makes that movement agreeable.

How can I connect with readers' needs and values?

Begin by understanding who your readers are—peers, professors, co-workers, the general public. Picture them as resistant, needing to be convinced. Think of them as alert, cautious, and demanding—but also interested. You'll need to tap into their emotions—their hopes, fears, needs, and values—either to challenge or to support those emotions. To appeal persuasively to readers' emotions, do the following:

- Show that you understand your readers' needs and values.
- Stress a benefit, an advantage, or an outcome that readers can expect if they accept your claim.

To understand human needs and values, study the lists below, adapted from the hierarchy of needs developed by psychologist Abraham Maslow. Maslow ranks people's needs on a scale from basic to elevated. The list begins with a reader's need for survival and ends with the need for self-fulfillment.

Reader needs . . .	Writer appeals to need for . . .
To survive	Food, water, shelter, sleep, clothing
To be safe	Safety, security, home, order, law
To love and be loved	Acceptance, friendship, belonging, satisfaction, fun, romance
To be esteemed	Self-esteem, reputation, recognition, appreciation, status
To find fulfillment	Self-actualization, peace, unity, spiritual quest, service to others

ETHICS TIP

Arguments sometimes appeal to emotions in a hidden or devious way, possibly by playing on irrational desires and fears (for example, an argument to limit immigration that appeals to citizens' fears of other cultures). When arguments do so, they cross over into hype or propaganda. Well-written arguments appeal to emotions in an honorable and explicit way (for example, by acknowledging such fears and exploring their source).

4e   Developing Your Claim

A claim is the thesis of your argument. Your purpose is to explain and defend it so well that readers agree with it. A strong claim is

- **Clear:** It is a single, understandable assertion, not double or fuzzy.
- **Debatable:** More than one reasonable view of it can be imagined.
- **Defendable:** It can be supported with arguments and evidence.
- **Responsible:** The author has considered its consequences.
- **Interesting:** It is challenging (worth discussing) rather than trivial.

How can I distinguish claims from facts and opinions?

A claim can be established by evidence and reasoning. Conversely, facts and opinions cannot be debated. While facts can be checked for accuracy, opinions tend to express gut-level attitudes, tastes, and preferences.

Fact:	John Lennon was one of the Beatles.
Opinion:	Paul McCartney's songs are better than John Lennon's.
Claim:	The Beatles were a product of, rather than a cause of, social change.

THREE TYPES OF CLAIMS

Truth, value, and policy—the differences between these types of claims are important because of their distinct persuasive goals.

Claims of truth state that something questionable is or is not the case.

Examples:	The Arctic ice cap will begin to disappear as early as 2050.
	The cholesterol in eggs is not as dangerous as previously feared.

Avoid claims that are obviously true or easily verifiable. Consider, too, that some truth claims can have serious consequences, if accepted, and some cannot be proven but only established as probabilities.

Claims of value state that something does or does not have worth.

Examples:	Campus writing centers provide an indispensable service.
	Many music videos are not worth watching because they fail to present positive images of women.

Claims of value should not be simply statements of preference or taste. Note, too, that value is relative to people's feelings of need. Measure each value claim against the hierarchy of needs on **4d**.

Claims of policy state that something ought or ought not to be done.

Examples:	Mileage standards for cars should also apply to SUVs.
	Developers should not be allowed to fill in the pond.

Policy claims often rest upon prior arguments or precedents. To support the policy claim, you must first win the prior arguments. In addition, policy claims are usually meant to add to policies that are already in place, so the whole body of policies needs to be considered.

UNDERSTANDING ARGUMENT AND PERSUASION

REFINING YOUR CLAIM

As you develop an argument, don't be surprised if your central claim evolves. Changing the claim is good if such change reflects deeper thinking, sharper focus, and more exact handling of language.

A basic claim names something, and it claims something.

> **Example:**
>
> Children's toys (name) ⟶ reinforce gender stereotypes (claim).

> **NOTE:** As you research, you might have to adjust the claim to fit the facts, your special interest, or the state of popular culture. Here is the preceding claim transformed with modifiers, defining details, and qualifiers:
>
> - Traditional children's toys such as baby dolls and dump trucks can have a complex influence on a child's psychological development.

An effective claim balances confidence with common sense. Its success stems from its stability in that balance.

Avoid extreme, all-or-nothing claims. Statements containing superlatives such as *all, best, never,* and *worst* may be difficult to support and wide open to attack.

- **Extreme claim:** People charged with a DUI should never drive again.
- **Moderated claim:** Drivers charged with a first-offense DUI should automatically have their driver's licenses suspended for one year.

Make meaningful claims. Avoid claims that are obvious, vague, trivial, or unsupportable.

- **Obvious claim:** College athletes sometimes receive special treatment.
- **Vague claim:** Exercise is great for you.
- **Trivial claim:** The gym is a good place to get fit.
- **Unsupportable claim:** Athletics are irrelevant to college life.
- **Meaningful claim:** In the last thirty years, Title IX regulations have not eliminated discrimination against female athletes on college campuses.

Use qualifiers to temper your claims. Qualifiers are words or phrases that make claims more reasonable.

- **Unqualified:** Star athletes take academic shortcuts.
- **Qualified:** Some star athletes at the state university are allowed to take improper academic shortcuts to get through their courses.

4f   Developing Your Line of Reasoning

Once you have established your claim, you need to develop a line of reasoning to support it. Start by finding strong evidence and becoming aware of your basic assumptions (warrants) that connect the evidence to the claim. Then you are ready to design an overall argument that logically builds your case.

Should I use inductive or deductive logic?

The type of logic you use depends on your purpose in writing. (See **4c**.)

- **Inductive reasoning** works from particular details toward general conclusions. A persuasive essay using induction begins with facts, finds a pattern in them, and then leads the reader to conclusions.

- **Deductive reasoning** starts from general principles and applies them to specific situations. Analyses and reports are often deductive. For deduction to be sound, the starting principles or facts must be accepted as true, the situation must be accurately described, and the application must be logical.

What are valid warrants?

According to British philosopher Stephen Toulmin, every argument includes warrants, which are unstated assumptions that connect evidence to a claim. Consider the following claim, evidence, and warrants:

Claim: Emeryville should shut down its public swimming pools.

Evidence: If current trends in water usage continue, the reservoir will be empty in two years.

Warrants: The following assumptions connect the claim and the evidence.

- It is not good for the reservoir to be empty.
- The swimming pools draw significant amounts of water from the reservoir.
- Emptying the public pools would help preserve the level of the reservoir.
- No other action would better preserve this level.
- It is worse to have an empty reservoir than empty swimming pools.

An argument is no stronger than its warrants. An argument that has solid warrants convinces readers and holds up against opposing viewpoints. An argument with faulty warrants crumbles quickly in the face of opposition.

WRITER'S TIP

As you build your argument, examine your assumptions about the claim and the evidence you have gathered. Also, examine the warrants of others before being persuaded by their arguments.

UNDERSTANDING ARGUMENT AND PERSUASION

How can I support my claims with solid evidence?

Strengthen your support by selecting carefully from the evidence available and by using that evidence effectively to bolster your claim. Consider the following choices.

OBSERVATIONS AND ANECDOTES

These firsthand accounts share what people (including you) have seen, heard, smelled, touched, tasted, and experienced.

- Most of us have closets full of clothes: jeans, sweaters, khakis, T-shirts, and shoes for every occasion.

Benefits: "Eyewitness" perspective can be powerful.
Objections: The observer's viewpoint may be narrow, subjective, or based on hearsay.

STATISTICS

Reasoning with statistical evidence means using amounts and proportions gathered through surveys, studies, and analysis to explain, compare, or predict.

- Pennsylvania spends $30 million annually in deer-related costs. Wisconsin has an annual loss of $37 million for crop damage alone.

Benefits: Statistics look scientific and provide "hard" facts.
Objections: Numbers don't always "speak for themselves." They need to be up-to-date, relevant, and accurate, and they must be interpreted properly—not slanted or taken out of context.

TESTS AND EXPERIMENTS

These sources provide hard data discovered through scientific methods.

- According to the two scientists, the rats with unlimited access to the functional running wheel ran each day and gradually increased the amount of running; in addition, they started to eat less.

Benefits: Well-designed experiments can provide strong cause/effect evidence that supports or disproves a hypothesis; they can also point to practical applications and project likely outcomes.
Objections: Some tests are not well designed or not relevant to the claim, or they may conflict with other tests and evidence.

VISUALS

Various graphics present information and perspectives in visual form, from simple tables to complex charts, maps, and photographs. See the sample visuals in Chapter 3, "Critical Thinking Through Visual Images," and Chapter 17, "Designing and Using Visuals."

Benefits: Visuals offer fast and easy ways to convey complex information.
Objections: When sloppy or biased, graphics can distort the truth.

EXPERT TESTIMONY

This form of evidence offers insights from recognized authorities on the topic.

■ One specialist opposed to drilling is David Klein, a professor at the Institute of Arctic Biology at the University of Alaska–Fairbanks. Klein argues that if the oil industry drills in the ANWR, the number of caribou will likely decrease because calving locations will change.

Benefits: Experts have certification, training, and experience.
Objections: Experts sometimes disagree. Their findings may be shaded by personal interests and distinct perspectives.

ILLUSTRATIONS, EXAMPLES, AND DEMONSTRATIONS

This form of evidence supports general claims with specific instances.

■ American parochialism sometimes hurts Americans most. For example, a resident of New Mexico called to get tickets to the 1996 Summer Olympics in Atlanta but was told he had to call the Mexican Olympic Committee. When the man pointed out he was from *New* Mexico, the operator said, "New Mexico, old Mexico: It doesn't matter. You still have to go through your country's Olympic Committee."

Benefits: These details can make general ideas concrete, vivid, and alive.
Objections: What is presented can be misleading; a single case, by itself insufficient to prove a general idea, may deflect attention from several examples against the claim.

ANALYSES

Such evidence examines subpoints in relation to each other by breaking down a topic through conventional thought patterns.

■ A girl's interest in romance is no more Barbie's fault than the fault of books like *On the Shores of Silver Lake*. Fashion magazines targeted at adolescents are the cause of far more anorexia cases than is Barbie.

Benefits: An analysis can go into details of cause/effect, comparison/contrast, classification, or narrative design—making sense of complexity.
Objections: An analysis can "fail to see the forest for the trees"—muddling the topic when poorly done.

PREDICTIONS

Predictions are forecasts of what might happen under certain conditions—outcomes, consequences, effects, results.

■ While agroterrorist diseases would have little direct effect on people's health, they would be devastating to the agricultural economy, in part because of the many different diseases that could be used in an attack.

Benefits: Predictions make it possible to apply ideas hypothetically.
Objections: Predictions must be backed by logical analysis of facts.

UNDERSTANDING ARGUMENT AND PERSUASION

4g Engaging the Opposition

Think of an argument as an intelligent dialogue with an opponent. Anticipate questions, concerns, objections, and counterarguments.

How should I make concessions?

Offer concessions by recognizing points scored by the other side. In this way, you admit your argument's limits. Such concessions strengthen your argument by keeping it on solid ground. Concede points graciously, using words like these: *admittedly, granted, I concede that, I cannot argue with, it is true that, you're right, I accept, no doubt, of course.*

> Supporters of barbed fishing hooks say that banning the hooks would decrease the number of fish they are able to land. They claim that enjoyment of the sport would be limited by the increased difficulty of keeping fish on the line. They are at least partially correct: Playing a fish is difficult without a barb. However, this does not have to limit the enjoyment of the sport.

How should I develop rebuttals or refutations?

Develop a rebuttal or refutation by tactfully arguing about a weak spot in a counterargument or an objection. Try these strategies:

- **Point out the counterargument's limits** by putting the opposing point in a larger context. Show that the counterargument leaves out something important.
- **Tell the other side of the story.** Offer an opposing interpretation of the evidence, or counter with stronger, more reliable, more convincing evidence.
- **Address logical fallacies** in the counterargument (see the most common fallacies listed at **4i**). Check for faulty reasoning, invalid warrants, or emotional manipulation. Show that other options exist.

How can I consolidate my claim?

After addressing objections, restate your claim carefully so that the weight of your entire argument can rest on it. This is the time and place to sort out the main points for emphasis, letting the supporting arguments take their proper position in the back seat.

How can I apply my argument?

To show how your successful argument will apply to the reader's life, ask yourself, "So what? Why should my reader care about my conclusions? How have I addressed his or her chief concerns about the issue?"

4h   Designing Your Argument

Use one of the following outlines to help you design your argument.

How can I build an inductive argument?

Present a general claim, build arguments, and refine your claim.

Introduction: Question or concern followed by general claim
1. Argument supporting claim
   - Discussion and support
2. Still stronger arguments supporting claim
   - Discussion of and support for each argument
3. Objections, concerns, and counterarguments
   - Discussion, concessions, answers, and rebuttals
4. Strongest argument supporting claim
   - Discussion and support

Conclusion: Argument consolidated—claim refined and reinforced

How can I build an interactive argument?

Address the arguments and counterarguments point by point.

Introduction: Question or concern followed by central claim
1. Strong argument supporting claim
   - Support and discussion
   - Counterarguments, concessions, and rebuttals
2. Other arguments supporting claim
   - For each argument, support and discussion
   - For each argument, counterarguments, concessions, rebuttals
3. Strongest argument supporting claim
   - Support and discussion
   - Counterarguments, concessions, and rebuttals

Conclusion: Argument consolidated—claim reinforced and reaffirmed

How can I build a deductive argument?

Establish premises at the outset; apply them to reach a conclusion.

Introduction: Question or concern followed by claim
1. Principles and premises
2. Description of a situation, case, or issue
3. Application of the principles or premises to the situation

Conclusion: Argument consolidated—claim shown in context
   - Discussion of strengths and weaknesses of the argument
   - Clarifications and counterarguments, concessions, and rebuttals

UNDERSTANDING ARGUMENT AND PERSUASION

4i   Avoiding Logical Fallacies

Fallacies are false arguments—bits of fuzzy, dishonest, or incomplete thinking. They may crop up in your own thinking, in your opposition's thinking, or in such public "arguments" as ads, political appeals, and talk shows. Fallacies are dangerous because they may sway an unsuspecting audience. On the following pages, fallacies are grouped according to how they falsify an argument.

What fallacies distort the issue?

The following fallacies misrepresent the basic question being argued.

Begging the Question A form of circular reasoning, this fallacy arises from assuming in your claim the very point you should be trying to prove.

> "We don't need a useless film series because students can see movies on their laptops." [Objection: The word *useless* begs the question.]

Oversimplification This fallacy treats complex issues in a simplistic way.

> "Capital punishment is simply a question of protecting society."
> [Objection: This statement overlooks questions of religion, moral codes, justice, human rights, and so forth.]

Either-Or Thinking Also known as black-and-white thinking, this fallacy reduces all options to two extremes. Frequently, it derives from a clear bias.

> "Either this community develops light-rail transportation or the community will be impossible to grow in the future." [Objection: Growth might occur through other means.]

Complex Question A question's phrasing may cover up a more basic question.

> "Why can't we bring down the prices that corrupt gas stations are charging?" [Objection: The more basic question is "Are gas stations really corrupt?"]

Straw Man In this fallacy the writer purposely sets up a claim that is easy to knock down—like a scarecrow.

> "Those who oppose euthanasia must believe that the terminally ill deserve to suffer." [Objection: This statement probably misrepresents the thinking of the opposition.]

ETHICS TIP

Sometimes logical fallacies result from incomplete or sloppy thinking. Sometimes they result from an intentional attempt to deceive or manipulate. Whether people are misled by incompetence or by design, they are misled. Remember that the word *ethics* comes from the root word *ethos,* which means "character." Using logical fallacies for whatever reason reflects badly on the user's character.

What fallacies sabotage the argument?

The fallacies below undercut the argument by twisting it and distorting it.

Misusing Humor Jokes, satire, and sarcasm can lighten the mood and highlight truths, but when they distract or insult, they undercut the argument.

> "If we send so many jobs overseas, why don't we just send them our children, too?" [Objection: The statement, based on sarcasm, insults the reader's intelligence.]

Appeal to Pity Rather than using measured emotional appeals, this fallacy tugs on the heartstrings to get the audience to agree.

> "Racially biased admission policies ruined this young man's career. And now he has cancer." [Objection: Admission policies have nothing to do with cancer.]

Red Herring An irrelevant hot-button issue may distract the reader from the real argument. Suppose the real argument is about drilling for oil in Alaska:

> "In 1989, the infamous oil spill of the *Exxon Valdez* led to massive numbers of animal deaths and enormous environmental degradation of the coastline." [Objection: Introducing this ocean oil spill distracts from the real issue— how oil drilling will affect the Alaskan tundra.]

Using Threats Although a threat might *end* an argument, it can't *win* the argument. Usually, a threat is merely implied:

> "If you bring up the issue of money, I'm going to make you regret it." [Objection: Threats are unethical and in some situations illegal.]

Bandwagon Mentality This fallacy implies that if "everyone" believes something, you should, too. Such an appeal manipulates people's desire to belong.

> "Try the celery diet. Millions have done so already with great success." [Objection: History shows that people in the minority have often had the better argument.]

Appeal to Prejudice This fallacy calls upon false assumptions that are harmful to others.

> "Cockroaches live only in the apartments of immigrants." [Objection: The claim ignores scientific evidence about cockroaches and reflects prejudice against immigrants.]

Appeal to Popular Sentiment This fallacy consists of associating your position with something that is popularly loved: the national flag, football, motherhood. Appeals to popular sentiment sidestep thought to play on feelings.

> "Anyone who has seen *Bambi* could never condone hunting deer." [Objection: *Bambi* is an animated film that has nothing to do with the reasons for or against hunting real animals.]

UNDERSTANDING ARGUMENT AND PERSUASION

What fallacies draw faulty conclusions from the evidence?

This group of fallacies is marked by logical missteps.

Appeal to Ignorance This fallacy suggests that because no one has proved a particular claim, it must be false; or, because no one has disproved a claim, it must be true.

> "Flying saucers must be real. No scientific explanation has ruled them out." [Objection: Such an appeal unfairly shifts the burden of proof onto someone else.]

Hasty Generalization Such a claim is based on too little evidence or allows no exceptions. In jumping to a conclusion, the writer may use terms like *all, every,* or *never.*

> "Today's voters are all being taken in by thirty-second sound bites." [Objection: The generalization is unfair. Many may read about politics in other sources.]

False Cause This well-known fallacy implies, illogically, that "If B comes after A, A must have caused B." However, A may be one of several causes, or A and B may be only loosely related, or the connection between A and B may be entirely coincidental.

> "Since that new school opened, drug use among young people has sky-rocketed. Better that the school had never been built." [Objection: Drug use may have increased for entirely unrelated reasons.]

Slippery Slope This fallacy argues that a single step will start an unstoppable chain of events. While such a slide may occur, the prediction lacks real substance.

> "If we legalize marijuana, it's only a matter of time before our country becomes a nation of junkies and addicts." [Objection: Such a drastic outcome cannot be predicted through any verifiable evidence.]

What fallacies misuse evidence?

These fallacies falsify the argument by abusing or distorting the evidence.

Impressing with Numbers In this fallacy, the writer uses big numbers or many numbers to stun readers into agreement.

> "At 35 ppm, CO levels factory-wide are only 10 ppm above the OSHA recommendation of 25 ppm. Clearly, that 10 ppm is insignificant in the big picture, and the occasional readings in some areas of between 40 and 80 ppm are aberrations that can safely be ignored." [Objection: The numbers need analysis. The 10 ppm may be significant, and higher readings may indicate real danger.]

Half-Truths A half-truth leaves out "the rest of the story," so it is both true and false.

> "The new welfare bill is good because it will get people off the public dole." [Objection: Perhaps, but the bill may also hurt some truly needy people.]

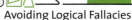

Unreliable Testimony In this fallacy, the argument looks for authority to someone who has no expertise in the field. Such testimony is irrelevant.

"The league's leading home run hitter says that most pork sold today is tainted." [Objection: Fame and success in one field do not confer expertise in another.]

Attack Against the Person This fallacy, known as the *ad hominem* fallacy, directs attention to a person's character, lifestyle, or beliefs rather than to the issue.

"When it comes to economic policies, would you accept the opinion of a candidate who experimented with drugs in college?" [Objection: The allegation might be untrue; regardless, it's irrelevant to the issue.]

Hypothesis Contrary to Fact This fallacy relies on "if only" thinking. It bases the claim on an assumption of what would have happened if something else had, or had not, happened. Pure speculation cannot be tested.

"If only the labors unions had supported affirmative action legislation, the United States would be a united nation." [Objection: This outcome is anything but certain.]

False Analogy Sometimes a person will argue that *X* is good (or bad) because it is like *Y*. If the analogy itself is weak, reasoning based on it is also weak.

"Don't bother voting in this election; it's a stinking quagmire." [Objection: Comparing the election to a "stinking quagmire" is unclear.]

What fallacies misuse language?

These fallacies falsify the argument by the misleading use of words.

Obfuscation This fallacy involves using terms that muddy the issue. These words may make shallow ideas sound profound or false ideas sound true.

"Through the fully functional developmental process of a streamlined target refractory system, the military will successfully reprioritize armor throughputs." [Objection: Impressive sounding, but this sentence means nothing.]

Ambiguity Ambiguous statements can be interpreted in two or more contradictory ways. Ambiguity can be unintentional, but writers sometimes use it purposely to hide a position.

"He struck the teacher as one who acted out his hostility." [Objection: We can't tell if this sentence is about a teacher's perception or a student's physical assault on a teacher.]

Slanted Language The philosopher Bertrand Russell illustrated this fallacy:

"*I* am firm. *You* are obstinate. *He* is pigheaded."
[Objection: The language is loaded with emotional bias.]

Another example shows Oscar Levant's feelings for a certain politician:

"*He'll double-cross that bridge when he gets to it.*"

4j Checklist: Argument and Persuasion

Refer to this checklist when you want either to construct your own argument or to size up someone else's.

___ Does the argument make a claim of fact, value, or policy?

___ How convincingly does the arguer project good character? (See **4b**.)

___ In what ways does the argument appeal to reason? (See **4c**.)

___ In what ways does the argument appeal to emotion? (See **4d**.) Does it show any emotional bias?

___ How is the central claim refined? (See **4e**.)

___ How strong and varied is the evidence? (See **4f**.)

___ How solid are the warrants (assumptions) that connect the evidence to the argument? (See **4f**.)

___ How would you outline the overall design of the argument? (See **4h**.)

___ Is the argument free of logical fallacies? (See **4i**.)

LINKS

WAC Link: Every discipline makes use of argument. In fact, each tends to focus on a distinctive set of debatable, contested issues, valuing specific strategies for argumentation and specific forms of argumentative writing.

English: An essay claims that Shakespeare's *The Tempest* can be read as a critique of European colonial expansion.

Political science: An analysis of poll results suggests the rising influence of women voters.

Art history: A study of letters concludes that André Breton should be considered the "father" of Cubism.

Physics: An article on sunspots predicts disruptions in telecommunications.

Workplace Link: Think of a job you have had or would like to have. Decide how each of the following skills might be put to the test:

- Checking a presentation or report for logical weakness or bias
- Reaching a conclusion about the causes of a problem—and the best solution
- Checking the validity of statistics
- Testing the strength of an analogy
- Assessing the needs of a client, colleague, or supervisor
- Considering the strength of an opposing position
- Distinguishing fact from opinion

REMEMBER: The best argument is one that sounds like an explanation.

Assessing Writing

To *assess* simply means to judge or appraise something. You need to assess your writing throughout the process, particularly as you revise, edit, and proofread. By evaluating the quality of your writing, you determine how to improve it.

You could evaluate the quality of your writing simply by asking yourself questions like these: Do I like the writing? Is it good? Will my audience appreciate it? However, these questions are too general to help you identify the document's specific strengths and weaknesses. They also fail to provide specific strategies for revising or editing your work. This chapter offers you a more structured, trait-based approach to writing assessment.

What is a trait-based approach to writing assessment?

A trait-based approach allows you to assess the quality of a piece of writing by evaluating the following basic traits:

Ideas · Organization · Voice · Words · Sentences · Correctness · Page Design

Study this chapter to learn how you, your instructor, and your classmates can use the seven traits as a common vocabulary for discussing and assessing a piece of writing. Later chapters will give you additional information. For example, Chapters 6–11 will explain how to use the traits to work efficiently through the writing process, and Chapters 25–32 will show how the traits can help you write a broad range of college assignments.

What's Ahead

ASSESSING WRITING

5a　Seven Traits of Good Writing

While writing standards often differ between academic departments—or even between professors within a department—all good writing has the following traits or features: **ideas, organization, voice, word choice, sentence formation, correctness,** and **page design.**

IDEAS

When assessing the **ideas** in a piece of writing, focus on what makes the writing substantial and meaningful in content and development:

- What is the writing's social and scholarly context?
- Does the writing have a clear, worthwhile purpose?
- What is its topic and its central idea, thesis, or thrust?
- Does the writing strengthen and clarify its ideas with details, illustrations (**3a–3d**), examples, appeals (**4b–4d**), reasoning, argument (**4e–4j**), or commentary?
- Does the writing seem original, creative, clear, accurate, logical, and insightful?

ORGANIZATION

When assessing the **organization,** focus on structure and flow:

- Do the parts of the writing fit together into a unified whole?
- Does the order of parts put the main ideas in focus?
- Are the parts coherent, thanks to effective transitions and to structural patterns such as repetition (**12c**) and parallelism (**13e**)?
- Does the writing offer an interesting start and a satisfying closing (**8c**)?
- Is the writing broken into helpful, coherent paragraphs and sections?
- Do the parts flow in a consistent direction?

VOICE

When assessing the **voice,** focus on how the writing "sounds" to readers—the attitude, pacing, and personality that come through:

- Does the voice sound authentic, sincere, and natural, like one person talking to another person?
- Does the person behind the voice seem energetic, enthusiastic, and engaged in the topic?
- Does the writing speak with a consistent purpose?
- Does the voice sound informed, trustworthy, and respectful (**14e**)?
- Is the tone of voice—serious, playful, sarcastic—appropriate for the kind of writing and the intended readers?
- Does the writing take chances—successfully?

WORDS

When assessing the **words,** focus on specific word choices:

- Is the writer's vocabulary appropriate for the academic discipline, topic, audience, and purpose?
- Are the words interesting, engaging, energetic, and powerful?
- Are they accurate, concise, economical, concrete, and vivid?
- Does the writer define technical terms?
- Does the writer avoid jargon, clichés, and redundancies (**14b–14c**)?

SENTENCES

When assessing **sentences,** focus on whether and how the writer expresses complete thoughts:

- Do the sentences have informative subjects and predicates? Are they complete—that is, not fragments or run-ons (**26a–26c**)?
- Do they present information in a natural order?
- Do they use modifying words, phrases, and clauses in clear, logical, and expressive ways? Are the sentences concise and economical?
- Are they energetic and engaging? Do they have appropriate emphasis?
- Do they flow gracefully from one to the next? Do they hang together, or cohere, within their paragraphs?

CORRECTNESS

When assessing the **correctness,** focus on the conventions of language:

- Are the parts of speech used correctly?
- Is the syntax—the order of parts in each sentence—understandable and correct?
- Does the writer make correct use of parallel form?
- Do sentences show correct punctuation and capitalization (**27–30**)?
- Are all words spelled correctly?
- Has the writer followed the rules for proper documentation (**51–58**)?
- Is the writing edited, proofread, and ready for publication?

PAGE DESIGN

When assessing **page design,** focus on the appearance on the page (**16a–16f**):

- Are the margins, indentations, page numbers, titles, subheads, bullets, and the like correctly formatted?
- Are the font types and sizes fitting and consistent?
- Are blocks of text and images balanced, and is white space used well?
- Has the writer carefully integrated written text with any illustrations, photos, tables, and graphics (**17a**)?
- Are tables and graphs correctly formatted and numbered (**17b–17e**)?
- Do design elements focus the reader's eye?

ASSESSING WRITING

5b **Good Writing: A Sample Essay of Definition**

Spurred on by a funny experience, student Mary Beth Bruins researched the word *gullible* and wrote the definition essay below. Study the seven-traits sidenotes and identify the strengths within the paper.

Bruins 1

Mary Beth Bruins

Dr. John Van Rys

English 101

January 20, 2006

The Gullible Family

    The other day, my friend Loris fell for the oldest trick   1
in the book: "Hey, somebody wrote 'gullible' on the ceiling!"
Shortly after mocking "Gullible Loris" for looking up, I
swallowed the news that Wal-Mart sells popcorn that pops
into the shapes of cartoon characters. And so, as "Gullible
Mary," I decided to explore what our name means, and who
else belongs to our Gullible family. What I learned is that the
family includes both people and birds, related to each other
by our willingness to "swallow."

    A gullible person will swallow an idea or argument   2
without questioning its truth. Similarly, the gull (a long-
winged, web-footed bird) will swallow just about anything
thrown to it. In fact, the word *gullible* comes from *gull*, and
this word can be traced back to the Germanic word *gwel* (to
swallow). Both *gull* and *gwel* are linked to the modern word
gulp, which means "to swallow greedily or rapidly in large
amounts." It's not surprising, then, that Loris and I, sisters in
the Gullible family, both eagerly gulped (like gulls) the false
statements thrown to us.

    Swallowing things this quickly isn't too bright, and *gull*   3
(when referring to a bird or person) implies that the swal-
lower is immature and foolish. For example, *gull* refers to
an "unfledged" fowl, which the *Grolier Encyclopedia* describes
as either "an immature bird still lacking flight feathers,"
or something that is "inexperienced, immature, or untried."
These words describe someone who is fooled easily, and
that's why *gull*, when referring to a human, means "dupe" or
"simpleton." In fact, since 1550, *gullet*, which means "throat,"
has also meant "fooled."

Ideas
Clear purpose and thesis; interesting details presented logically

Organization
A lively beginning, well-structured middle, and whimsical closing

Voice
An informed, honest voice and an engaging tone

Words
Precise, lively, and clear words

Sentences
Smooth, varied, graceful, and complete sentences

Bruins 2

4   To illustrate this usage, the *Oxford English Dictionary* quotes two authors who use *gull* as a verb meaning to fool. "Nothing is so easy as to *gull* the public, if you only set up a prodigy," writes Washington Irving. William Dean Howells uses the word similarly when he writes, "You are perfectly safe to go on and *gull* imbeciles to the end of time, for all I care."

5   Both of these authors are pretty critical of gullible people, but does *gullible* have only negative connotations? Is there no hope for Gullibles like Loris and me? C. O. Sylvester Marson's comments about *gullible* may give us some comfort. He links *gullible* to "credulous, confiding, and easily deceived." At first, these adjectives also sound negative, but *credulous* does mean "to follow implicitly." And the word *credit* comes from the Latin word *credo* (meaning "I believe"). So what's bad about that? In other words, isn't *wanting to believe* other people a good thing? Why shouldn't Loris and I be proud of at least that aspect of our gull blood? We want to be positive—and we don't want . . .

Correctness

Correct mechanics, usage, and grammar

Page Design

Attractive format, page layout, and typography; appropriate for the assignment, audience, and purpose

LINKS

WAC Link: Writing well takes practice, but as in any skilled activity—practice makes "perfect" only if you know which skills you need to master. Otherwise, practice is wasted—it may even be damaging. The writing criteria on this and the previous pages are universal. To learn what writing skills are peculiar to your field, do the following:

- Read the literature in your field, noting how it practices the seven traits.
- Visit the campus writing center and ask a peer tutor to assess your writing.
- Search online for OWLs (online writing labs) that post writing samples, rubrics, and instructional material for writing in your discipline. You could start with Purdue University's OWL: <www.owl.english.purdue.edu/webloc>.
- Ask a professor in your field to assess your writing and offer tips.

ASSESSING WRITING

5c Poor Writing: A Sample Essay

Read the poor writing sample shown below. Use the trait-based sidenotes to find specific weaknesses and errors in the writing.

So Whose Gullible?

Ideas
Little development

Organization
No clear thesis

Voice
Informal street language

Words
Repetitive

Sentences
Incomplete or redundant

Correctness
Incorrect conventions

Page Design
Short paragraphs

In today's society, many people are gullible. But what does gullible mean? According to Webster, it means that a guy is willing to swallow just about anything that somebody gives him, like bad ideas or bad sales pitches or whatever. These people just can't think outside the box and the results are terrible.

For example, my dictionary says that "gullible means easily persuaded to believe something; credulous." Now what that means is that a gullible person is incredulous and swallows an idea or something even if it's not true.

One article I read said that gullible comes from birds like gulls. They swallow just bout any thing without thinking, even if it hurts them or even kills them. Sometime people swallow ideas that hurt them or kill them to. Like the Germans during world war 2 swallowed everything Hitlur told them and it killed a lot of them!

In conclusion, gullible comes from birds like gulls and it means to believe things without thinking about them and deciding weather their true or not. So if you're a gullible person, well you better be warned and know that its time to wake up and smell the coffee, learn more about the things that you here, and then think for yourself!!!

5d Checklist: Seven Traits of Good Writing

This checklist will help you reflect on your use of the seven traits.

____ Are my ideas interesting and fully developed?

____ Is the beginning, middle, or ending hardest for me to create? Why?

____ Which adjectives would I use to describe my writing voice?

____ How would I describe my word choice, and how could I improve it?

____ How do I use long, medium, and short sentences?

____ Which aspect of correctness—capitalization, punctuation, spelling, or grammar—gives me the most trouble?

____ Which elements of design could I most improve upon? How?

The Writing Process

The Writing Process

Getting Started

College instructors assign writing often because they know that the activity will help you (1) learn course content, (2) show what you've learned, and (3) polish your writing skills. To do your work well, you must take the time to learn the writing process—a series of six steps that are listed below and described fully in the following chapters.

What are the steps in the writing process?

1. Getting Started	■ Understanding the assignment ■ Selecting a topic ■ Collecting information
2. Planning	■ Forming and developing a thesis ■ Designing a plan or an outline
3. Drafting	■ Opening the draft ■ Developing the middle ■ Ending the draft
4. Revising	■ Improving ideas, organization, and voice ■ Revising collaboratively
5. Editing and Proofreading	■ Editing for word choice and sentence fluency ■ Proofreading for correctness
6. Designing and Publishing	■ Preparing a paper for submission ■ Checking for page design and documentation

> **NOTE:** Writing rarely follows a straight path. As a result, you will often move back and forth between the six steps outlined above. Also, each writer works differently. As you work with the writing process, your personal approach will develop naturally.

What's Ahead

6a Understanding the Assignment
6b Selecting a Topic
6c Exploring a Topic
6d Collecting Information
6e Checklist: Getting Started

GETTING STARTED

6a Understanding the Assignment

While different instructors may shape writing assignments differently, most instructors will spell out (1) the subject, (2) the purpose, (3) the audience, (4) the form, and (5) the parameters for assessment. Your first step, therefore, is to read the assignment carefully, looking for this basic information.

What is the subject?

The subject of a writing assignment is a general path that leaves you free to explore branching trails to find a specific topic. In doing so, you must understand the subject options and restrictions. Consider this assignment:

> **Reflect on the way that a natural disaster has altered your understanding of religion or government.**

Options

- You may choose any natural disaster.
- You may focus on religion or government.
- You may examine any kind of alteration.

Restrictions

- You must reflect on a change in your religious or political understanding.
- The disaster must be natural.

What is the purpose?

Key verbs identify the purpose of the assignment. The purpose is what you are trying to accomplish in your writing. Watch for words such as the following:

- **Analyze:** Break a topic into parts, showing how those parts relate.
- **Apply:** Use information in a new context.
- **Argue:** Defend a claim with logical points and valid support.
- **Classify:** Divide a large group into well-defined subgroups.
- **Compare/contrast:** Point out similarities and/or differences.
- **Convince/persuade:** Use reasoning to get the reader to agree or take action.
- **Define:** Give a clear explanation of what something means.
- **Describe:** Show in detail what something is like.
- **Evaluate:** Weigh the truth, quality, or usefulness of something.
- **Explain:** Give reasons, list steps, or discuss the causes of something.
- **Interpret:** Tell in your own words what something means.
- **Reflect:** Share your well-considered thoughts about a subject.
- **Summarize:** Restate someone else's ideas briefly in your own words.
- **Synthesize:** Connect facts or ideas to create something new.

Who is my audience?

Your audience is the person or group to whom you are writing. Ask yourself the following questions:

- Who are my readers: my instructor? my classmates? others?
- What do the readers know about the subject, what may they want to know, and what should they know?
- What attitude does the audience have: skeptical, accepting, curious, bored, defiant?

What form should my writing take?

The form of the assignment includes the practical elements of the writing. Ask yourself the following questions:

- What type of writing should I produce: an essay, a position paper, a research report, an editorial, a literary analysis, a personal narrative?
- What length (in pages or words) should my work have?
- What formatting requirements does the instructor have?
- Do I need to document any sources? If so, what system of documentation (MLA, APA, CSE, CMS) should I use?

How will my writing be assessed?

It is also crucial to understand the way in which your work will be graded. Ask yourself the following questions:

- Who will evaluate my work?
- Will the evaluator use a writing rubric, and can I get a copy of it?
- How much value (percentage of my grade) has the instructor given to this assignment?
- How does this assignment build on previous assignments or prepare me for following assignments?
- What benefit does the instructor want me to gain: Understand course content more fully? Improve my research skills? Refine my ability to describe, explain, or persuade? Learn how the topic is connected to issues in the workplace?

WRITER'S TIP

Although the assignment may specify a subject, purpose, audience, form, and parameters for assessment, these are merely the starting points for your writing. You need to bring your own interests and insights to any writing assignment. Ask yourself these questions:

- How does the assignment connect with topics that interest me?
- How does it connect with work in my other courses?
- How does it connect with local, state, national, or global issues?

GETTING STARTED

ONE WRITER'S PROCESS

In this and the following five chapters, you will watch student Angela Franco write an essay for her class, Environmental Policies. Start by carefully reading the assignment and discussion below, noting how she thought through the assignment's purpose, audience, form, and assessment method.

Assignment: Explain in a two- to three-page essay how a recent environmental issue is relevant to the world community. Using *The College Writer's Handbook* as your guide, document sources using the APA form, but include no title page or abstract. You may seek revising and editing help from a classmate or the writing center.

Subject

- The subject is a recent environmental issue.

Purpose

- My purpose is to explain how the issue is relevant to all people. That means I must show how this issue affects my audience— both positively and negatively.

Audience

- My audience will be people like me—neighbors, classmates, and community members.
- I'll need to keep in mind what they already know and what they need to know.

Form

- I need to write a two- to three-page essay—that sounds formal.
- I'll need to include a thesis statement as well as references to my sources.

Assessment

- I'll use the guidelines and checklists in the handbook to evaluate and revise my writing.
- I'll get editing feedback from Jeanie and from the writing center.

WAC Link: For each step in the writing process, choose strategies that fit your writing situation, including the assigned form and course. For example, a personal essay in English class might require significant time getting started, whereas a lab report in chemistry class might require little or no preparation.

ETHICS TIP

Reread the assignment and think about the types of sources that Angela may use. Remember the importance of avoiding plagiarism in your writing. (See 50a–50c.)

6b Selecting a Topic

For some assignments, finding a suitable topic takes little effort. For example, if an instructor asks you to summarize an article in a professional journal, your topic is obvious—the assigned article. But suppose the instructor asks you to analyze a feature of popular culture in terms of its effects on society. You won't be sure of a specific writing topic until you explore the possibilities. Keep the following points in mind when you conduct a search. The topic must

- Meet the requirements of the assignment,
- Be limited in scope,
- Seem reasonable (within your means to research), and
- Sincerely interest you.

How can I generate writing ideas?

Finding a writing idea that meets the requirements of the assignment should not be difficult if you know how and where to look. Follow these steps:

1. Check your class notes and handouts for ideas related to the assignment.
2. Search the Internet. Type in a keyword or phrase and see what you can find. Alternatively, follow a subject tree to narrow a subject. (See **49b**.)
3. Consult indexes, guides, and other library references. An electronic database like EBSCOhost, for example, lists articles published on specific topics and explains where to find the articles. (See **49a–49d**.)
4. Discuss the assignment with your instructor or a librarian.
5. Generate ideas with prewriting strategies like those described on the following pages.

USING THE ESSENTIALS OF LIFE LIST

Below is a list of the major categories into which most essential things in our lives are divided. The list provides an endless variety of subject possibilities, from agriculture to science and many topics in between.

The Essentials of Life

agriculture	faith/religion	land/property
art/music	family	laws/government
books	food	love
clothing	freedom/rights	machines
communication	friends	measurements
community	fuel/heat	money/trade
education	goals/purpose	natural resources
energy	health/medicine	occupation
entertainment	housing	plants
environment	identity	recreation
exercise	intelligence	science

GETTING STARTED

How can I select a topic?

Many of your writing assignments might relate to general subject areas that you are currently studying. Your task is then to select a specific topic related to the general area of study—a topic limited enough that you can treat it with some depth in the length specified in the assignment. The following examples show how general subjects are different from limited topics:

- General Subject: Pollution
  Limited Topic: Pollution from coal-fired power plants
- General Subject: Energy sources
  Limited Topic: The cost-effectiveness of wind power

6c Exploring a Topic

You can explore a topic by creating a cluster, freewriting, or listing.

How can I create a cluster?

To begin the clustering process, write in the center of your paper a key word or idea from the assignment. Circle the word, and then cluster ideas around it. Circle each idea as you record it, and draw a line connecting it to the closest related idea. Keep going until you run out of ideas and connections. (See "Angela's Cluster" on the next page.)

How can I freewrite?

Write nonstop for ten minutes or longer to discover possible writing ideas. Start with a key concept related to the assignment. Write whatever comes to your mind—and don't stop to correct typos or other mistakes. Writing ideas will very likely begin to emerge. (See "Angela's Freewriting" on the next page.)

How can I create a list?

List ideas as they come to mind, beginning with a key word or concept in the assignment. For example, if *water* appears in the assignment, write the word; then below it, list related terms like *rivers, drinking water, pollution*, and *wells*.

ESL TIP

Because the point of these activities is to get ideas flowing, feel free to freewrite, list, or cluster in your native language. Later you can translate your ideas into English.

ONE WRITER'S PROCESS

Angela explored her assignment and limited her topic (see **6b**) by clustering and freewriting.

- **Angela's Cluster:** When she considered environmental issues, Angela first thought of water pollution as a possible topic for her essay. After writing the phrase in the center of her page, she drew from her memories, experiences, and readings to list related ideas and details. Notice how she used three colored inks to distinguish the topic (*black*) from ideas (*purple*) from details (*green*).

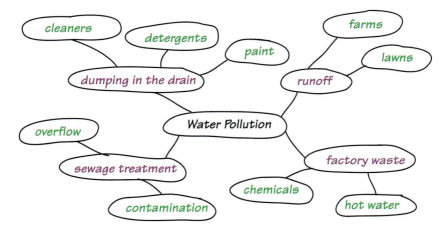

- **Angela's Freewriting:** Angela decided to freewrite about the water pollution caused a few years earlier by improper sewage treatment in a small Canadian town.

  I remember reading an article about pollution problems in a small Canadian town. People actually died. The water they drank was contaminated. This is becoming a problem in developed countries like ours. I thought for a long time this was a problem only in developing countries. So who is responsible for sewage treatment? Who guarantees the safety of our drinking water? How does water get contaminated? Are there solutions for every kind of contamination: mercury, PCBs, sewage?

- **Angela's Narrowed Assignment:** Based on the results of her freewriting, Angela rephrased her assignment to limit her topic.

  Explain in a two- to three-page essay how a recent water pollution problem in a small Canadian town is relevant to the world community.

6d   Collecting Information

Writer and instructor Donald Murray says that writers write with information. If there is no information, there will be no effective writing. How true! To find meaningful sources of information, use the tips below:

1. **Give yourself enough time.** Finding good sources of information can take time. Books and periodicals may be hard to find, your computer service may be down, and so on.

2. **Be aware of the limits of your resources.** Print material may be out-of-date. Online information may be more current, but it may not always be reliable. (See **49a–49d** for help evaluating sources.)

3. **Use your existing resources to find additional sources.** Pay attention to books, articles, and individuals mentioned in reliable sources.

4. **Ask for help.** The specialists in your college library are trained to find information; don't hesitate to ask them for help. (See **48a–48c**.)

5. **Bookmark useful websites.** Include reference works and academic resources related to your major.

6. **Explore different sources of information.** Of course, books and websites are not the only possible sources of information. Primary sources such as interviews, observations, and surveys may lead you to a more thorough, meaningful understanding of a topic. (See **47a–47d**.)

Primary Sources	Secondary Sources
interviews	articles about your topic
observations	reference book entries
participation	books about your topic
surveys	websites

What research methods should I use?

- Use a variety of reliable sources to research your topic.
- Use proper note-taking strategies such as summaries, paraphrases, and direct quotes. (See **46e**.)
- Choose an efficient note-taking method. (See **46a–46c**.)
- Reserve part of a notebook to question, evaluate, and reflect upon your research as it develops.

WAC Link: Early in any course, carefully read through the course syllabus to determine the instructor's requirements regarding the use of research materials, research strategies, and course or departmental style sheets.

ONE WRITER'S PROCESS

Angela first reviewed her narrowed assignment. She then asked and answered the journalistic questions (five W's and H) to further focus her topic.

Narrowed Writing Assignment: Explain in a two- to three-page essay how a recent water pollution problem in a small Canadian town is relevant to the world community.

- **Angela's Topic, Questions, and Answers:**

Topic: Water pollution in a small Canadian town

Who?	- Farm operators, wastewater officials, Walkerton residents
What?	- *E. coli* poisoning
	- Spreads bacteria
	- Causes disease
	- Clean, fresh water is depleted
Where?	- Walkerton, Ontario
When?	- May 2000
Why?	- Improper regulation; human error
How?	- Groundwater from irrigation, untreated sewage, and runoff

- **Angela's Research:** Angela then did additional research to check her information and collect more details for her paper. She recorded all the essential data on each source and then listed the specific details related to her topic. Here's one source:

Nikiforuk, Andrew. "When Water Kills." *Maclean's*. 12 June 2000: 18–21.

- Factory farms hold as many as 25,000 cattle
- Manure contains things like heavy metals (from mineral-rich feed), nutrients, and pathogens (*E. coli*)
- 8,000 hogs can produce as much waste as 240,000 people
- Six rural Ontario counties had high *E. coli* levels in 1990 and 1995

VISUALS TIP

During your research, take time to copy or create appropriate visuals (charts, graphs, or photos) that clarify or enliven details about which you're writing. If you copy an item, be sure to correctly record the source as well. To create your own graphic, gather the data that you want to present, choose the type of graphic (table, pie graph, bar graph) that best displays your point regarding the data, and use Chapter 17, "Designing and Using Visuals," to develop the graphic.

6e Checklist: Getting Started

Use this checklist as a guide to help you plan your writing.

The Assignment: I understand

____ The main action (key words), restrictions, and options for it.

____ Its connection to my personal and course goals.

____ The purpose of the writing—to inform, explain, analyze, or persuade.

____ My audience—who they are, what they know, and what they need to know.

____ The form required (essay, narrative, summary, research paper).

____ The requirements for length, format, and documentation.

____ The criteria that will be used for evaluation.

The Topic: I have

____ Explored possible topics through journal writing, freewriting, listing, clustering, or discussion with others.

____ Chosen a limited topic that fits the assignment and spurs my interest.

____ Recorded what I already know, and what I need to learn.

The Research: I have collected information by

____ Answering the five W's and H (*who, what, when, where, why,* and *how*).

____ Using the types of sources required in the assignment.

____ Carefully taking notes on sources and recording my responses.

LINKS

WAC Link: Whether you're writing a lab report in chemistry, a field report in sociology, or a literary analysis in English, the activities explained in this chapter will help you save time and produce a better paper. Be sure to choose activities that fit the assignment and your angle or focus on the topic.

Service-Learning Link: When getting started on a document that is part of a service-learning project, consider how the strategies explained in this chapter apply to your specific project and to the individual or group whom your project is designed to serve. For example, if you interview an "expert" on your topic, make sure that the group whom you're serving agrees that this person really is an expert.

Workplace Link: In the workplace, you will usually know from the writing situation what topic you must address and what form is required (instructions, proposal, or recommendation). But you must still think about your writing carefully by analyzing your purpose for writing, analyzing your audience, considering how your purpose relates to your other tasks, searching for helpful information, and taking good notes.

Planning

After studying the assignment and choosing your topic, take time to plan your writing. At this point, you have two objectives: (1) to establish a thesis or focus for your writing and (2) to organize the supporting information that you've collected.

What is the thesis statement?

The thesis statement is the most important sentence or two in your writing:

- It identifies the topic that you have selected.
- It pinpoints the special part of the topic that you will focus on.
- It hints at the structure of the rest of the writing.
- It connects to all the material you include.

Because this controlling sentence does so many things, it would be a wise move to spend some time up front creating a solid thesis. This chapter can help. It would also be wise to revisit your thesis statement throughout the writing process—rewriting, revising, tweaking, and perfecting it.

How can I organize my writing?

Once you have a strong thesis statement, you are ready to organize the other details in your work. In this chapter, you will learn how to organize your work using the following:

- A list
- A topic outline
- A sentence outline
- A graphic organizer

What's Ahead

7a Forming a Thesis Statement
7b Using Methods of Development
7c Developing Your Ideas: Outlining and Organizing
7d Using Graphic Organizers
7e Checklist: Planning

PLANNING

7a Forming a Thesis Statement

After you have completed enough research and collected enough information, you should draft a thesis statement that identifies the point you want to make in your writing. The thesis statement usually highlights a special condition or feature of the topic, expresses a specific feeling, or takes a stand.

How can I find a focus?

Start with a general subject area, which is typically built into your writing assignment. Then narrow the writing topic and examine it from a particular angle or perspective. (You will use this focus to form your thesis statement.)

Focusing on a Topic		
General Subject	Limited Topic	Specific Focus
alternative energy sources	wind power	wind power as a viable energy source in the Plains states

How can I write my thesis statement?

You can use the following formula to write a thesis statement for your essay. A thesis statement sets the tone and direction for your writing. Keep in mind that at this point you're writing a working thesis statement—a statement in progress, so to speak. You may change it as your thinking on the topic evolves.

> **A manageable or limited topic** (wind power)
>
> **+ a specific focus** (provides a viable energy source in the Plains states)
> _____
> **= an effective thesis statement:** Wind power provides a viable energy source in the Plains states.

Checklist: Thesis

____ Does the thesis statement reflect a limited topic?

____ Does it clearly state the specific idea you plan to develop?

____ Is the thesis supported by the information that you have gathered?

____ Does the thesis suggest a pattern of organization for your essay?

WRITER'S TIP

Sometimes you will develop a thesis statement early and easily. At other times, the true focus of your writing will emerge only after you've written your first draft.

7b   Using Methods of Development

An organizing pattern for your essay may be built into your assignment. For example, if you were asked to explain a process, you would likely present its steps chronologically. When a pattern is not apparent, one may still evolve during the research process. If this doesn't happen, take a careful look at your thesis statement. An effective thesis will often suggest an organizing pattern.

How does a thesis statement organize writing?

Notice how the thesis statements below provide direction and shape for the writing to follow. For more information on patterns of development, see **12d**.

THESIS FOR A PERSONAL NARRATIVE

What began as a simple prank ended up having serious consequences for all of us.

Discussion: This statement identifies the focus of a personal experience that will be presented chronologically, relaying how a group of high school students plan and execute a prank on their teacher. Writers of personal narratives do not always state a thesis directly, but they will generally have in mind an implied theme or idea that guides their writing.

THESIS FOR A DESCRIPTIVE ESSAY

Sometimes, I want to go back there, back into that photo. I want to step into a time when life seemed safe, and a tiny stream gave us all that we needed.

Discussion: This statement indicates that the writer will describe a place associated with valued childhood memories. This description might be organized spatially, showing scenes along the stream; organized chronologically, describing experiences with the stream; or organized thematically, relaying key experiences and reflecting on their significance. The writer chose the third pattern. (See the essay on **38a**.)

THESIS FOR AN ANALYTICAL ESSAY

But what, exactly, is an adrenaline high, what causes it, what are its effects, and are the effects positive?

Discussion: This thesis (made as a question instead of a statement) indicates that the writer is developing a cause-and-effect essay. Essays following this pattern usually begin with one or more causes followed by an explanation of the effects. In some cases they begin with a primary effect followed by an explanation of the causes. (See the essay on **39b**.)

> **NOTE:** Stating a thesis sentence as a question can be an effective strategy. The writer asks the question and answers it. Some instructors dislike the thesis question, however, because it does not always set out a clear claim and logical pattern for the essay to develop.

PLANNING

THESIS FOR AN ESSAY OF COMPARISON

Why isn't the 9/11 attack considered just a large-scale repeat of the Oklahoma City bombing? Could it be that our grief is more than sorrow, and that our loss is much more than what lies in the rubble?

Discussion: The writer of this thesis compares two historic attacks on the United States. Comparisons like this can be patterned in two ways: Discuss one of the subjects completely and then discuss the other (whole versus whole); or discuss both subjects at the same time (point by point). (See the essay on **39f.**)

THESIS FOR AN ESSAY OF CLASSIFICATION

There are four main perspectives, or approaches, that you can use to converse about literature.

Discussion: The writer uses classification to address his topic. Essays following this pattern identify the main parts or categories of a topic and then examine each one. In this thesis, the writer identifies four ways to discuss literature and then explains and illustrates each one. (See the essay on **39j.**)

THESIS FOR A PROCESS ESSAY

When a cell begins to function abnormally, it can initiate a process that results in cancer.

Discussion: The writer will explain how the behavior of abnormal cells can initiate cancer. Process essays, such as this one, are organized chronologically. Each step is examined to help readers understand the complete process. (See the essay on **39n.**)

THESIS FOR AN ESSAY OF DEFINITION

My memories, like the things I enjoy, can be described in only one way: "eclectic," a word I find endlessly fascinating.

Discussion: This essay provides an interesting personal definition of the word *eclectic*. The writer first explains what the word means and then analyzes her personal interpretation of the term.

THESIS FOR AN ESSAY PROPOSING A SOLUTION

Agroterrorism is a threat that demands our response. Several actions can be taken to discourage agroterrorism as well as to deal with its consequences.

Discussion: The writer of this thesis is developing a problem/solution essay. Essays following this pattern usually begin with a discussion of the problem and its causes and then examine possible solutions. In this essay, the writer first uses a narrative to introduce the problem (agroterrorism), and then he identifies and evaluates possible solutions. (See the essay on **40f.**)

Using Methods of Development

ONE WRITER'S PROCESS

With a thesis selected, Angela thought about the method of development that would best suit her writing.

- ■ **Angela's Review:**
  1. Review your assignment and record your response.

     Assignment: Explain in a two- to three-page essay how a recent environmental issue is relevant to the world community.

     Reflection: *My assignment clearly states that I need to explain my topic, so I have a general idea of how my paper will be organized.*

  2. Study your thesis statement and think about your essay's possible content and organization.

     Thesis Statement: *The pollution incident in Walkerton, Ontario, had a devastating effect that every town should learn from.*

     Reflection: *After reading my thesis statement, it's obvious that I'm going to be writing about a problem and its causes and effects.*

- ■ **Angela's Method of Development:**
  3. Choose an overall method and reflect on its potential effectiveness.

     Reflection: *Looking at the list of methods, I see that I can use cause/ effect or problem/solution. After making two quick lists of my main points using both approaches, I decided to use a problem/solution approach. I will still talk about causes and effects in my essay—they just won't be front and center.*

     With problem/solution, I need to first present the problem clearly so that readers can fully understand it and see why it's important. Then I need to explore solutions to the problem—maybe what they did in Walkerton and what we all need to do to make water safe.

WRITER'S TIP

Many essays you write will be organized according to one basic method or approach. However, within that basic structure, you may want to include other methods.
For example, while developing a comparison essay, you may do some describing or classifying.

PLANNING

7c Developing Your Ideas: Outlining and Organizing

After writing a working thesis (7a) and reviewing the methods of development (7b), you should be ready to organize the information that you have collected. Use a basic list, a topic outline, a sentence outline, or a graphic organizer.

How can I use a basic list?

Create a basic list to jot down main ideas for less-formal assignments. Write short phrases and wording that makes sense to you. (A basic list is rarely turned in with a final paper.)

Four approaches to literary interpretation
—Text centered
—Audience centered
—Author centered
—Ideological

How can I create a topic outline?

In a topic outline, state each main point and essential detail as a word or phrase. (See "Four Ways to Talk About Literature," 39j.) Before you construct your outline, write your working thesis statement at the top of your paper to help you keep focused on the subject. Do not attempt to outline your opening and closing paragraphs unless you are specifically asked to do so.

Thesis: *There are four main perspectives, or approaches, that you can use to converse about literature.*

I. Text-centered approaches
   A. Also called formalist criticism
   B. Emphasis on structure of text and rules of genre
   C. Importance placed on key literary elements
II. Audience-centered approaches
   A. Also called rhetorical or reader-response criticism
   B. Emphasis on interaction between reader and text
III. Author-centered approaches
   A. Emphasis on writer's life
   B. Importance placed on historical perspective
   C. Connections made between texts
IV. Ideological approaches
   A. Psychological analysis of text
   B. Myth or archetype criticism
   C. Moral criticism
   D. Sociological analysis

Developing Your Ideas: Outlining and Organizing

How can I create a sentence outline?

Use complete sentences to explain the main points and essential details that will be covered in the main part of your essay.

Thesis: *There are four main perspectives, or approaches, that you can use to converse about literature.*

    I. The text-centered approach focuses on the literary piece itself.
        A. This approach is often called formalist criticism.
        B. This method examines text structure and the rules of the genre.
        C. A formalist determines how literary elements reinforce meaning.
    II. The audience-centered approach focuses on the "transaction" between text and reader.
        A. This approach is called rhetorical or reader-response criticism.
        B. A rhetorical critic sees the text as an activity that is different for each reader.
    III. The author-centered approach focuses on the origin of a text.
        A. An author-centered critic examines the writer's life.
        B. This method of criticism may include a historical look at a text.
        C. Connections may be made between the text and related works.
    IV. The ideological approach applies ideas outside of literature.
        A. Some critics apply psychological theories to a literary work.
        B. Myth or archetype criticism applies classical studies to a text.
        C. Moral criticism explores the moral dilemmas in literature.
        D. Sociological approaches include feminist and minority criticism.

How can I use graphic organizers?

Use a graphic organizer to map out ideas and illustrate relationships among them. (Other types of organizers are shown on 7d.)

Line Diagram

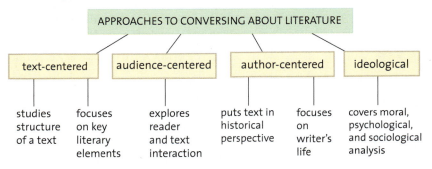

PLANNING

ONE WRITER'S PROCESS

With her working thesis settled, Angela recorded questions that she needed to answer. She then wrote a sentence outline to guide her first draft.

- **Angela's Study of Her Thesis:**

  Thesis Statement: *The water pollution incident in Walkerton, Ontario, had a devastating effect that every town should learn from.*

  Questions That Must Be Answered:
  1. What happened in Walkerton, and why was it a tragedy?
  2. Who was responsible?
  3. What was done about it?
  4. Why do we need to pay attention?

- **Angela's Sentence Outline:**

  I. Walkerton, Ontario, experienced a serious pollution problem.
  - A. The water was contaminated from manure runoff.
  - B. Nothing was done to protect citizens, and many became ill.
  - C. The problem went unnoticed for days.

  II. Several officials shared responsibility.
  - A. Water treatment officials failed to diagnose the problem.
  - B. The government advisory came too late.

  III. The problem required a series of solutions.
  - A. Bottled water was distributed.
  - B. Bleach was made available to homeowners.
  - C. The town's entire system was flushed.

  IV. This event is important to everyone.
  - A. It raises awareness.
  - B. People may now take responsibility for their water.

WRITER'S TIP

You don't need a fully developed outline to start drafting. You could start with a basic outline and then draft part of your essay, pausing now and then to refine the outline as needed.

WAC Link: Some instructors will ask you to write a working thesis, preliminary bibliography, and complete outline—and to discuss all three with them before you begin drafting the paper. They do so to teach key strategies regarding research and writing in their disciplines. Learn from these discussions.

7d Using Graphic Organizers

The line diagram shown at **7c** is one type of graphic organizer; other types are shown below and on the following page. When using a graphic organizer, select the type that most closely matches the methods of development used in your paper (cause/effect, classification, comparison), and then adapt the organizer to fit your specific needs. (See **7b.**)

Cause/Effect

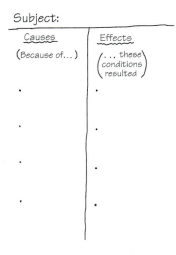

Classification

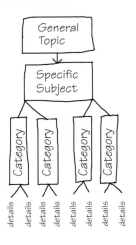

Comparison (Venn Diagram)

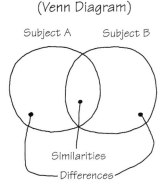

Comparison (Chart)

Qualities	Subject A	Subject B

PLANNING

Process Analysis

Subject:
_____

(Chronological Order)

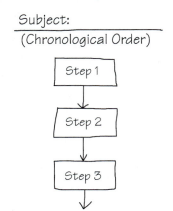

Problem/Solution

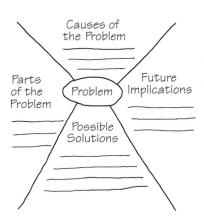

7e   Checklist: Planning

Use this checklist as a guide to help you plan your writing.

Thesis

____ I have reviewed the information that I have collected up to this point.

____ I have selected a specific focus or feature of my limited topic.

____ I have stated my focus in a working thesis statement about the topic.

____ I have tested the thesis to make sure that I can support it.

Development

____ I have chosen an organization pattern appropriate for my thesis and assignment.

____ I have organized my support in a list, an outline, or a graphic organizer.

____ I am prepared to write the first draft.

VISUALS TIP

You can use the seven graphic organizers shown in this chapter as both writing and reading strategies. For example, you could use the problem/solution graphic to organize your ideas when writing. You could also use this graphic to analyze and take notes on a problem/solution essay that you're reading.

Drafting

Just as a sculptor's first image shaped from wet clay is rarely a finished sculpture, so a writer's first draft is rarely a finished document. As their creators complete the shaping and refining processes, the rough image becomes a polished sculpture, and the rough draft becomes a polished essay, memo, report, or story.

What should I focus on as I draft?

Purpose: Remember what your writing must do: explain, persuade, analyze, and so forth. Keep your purpose clearly in mind as you pursue your thesis.

Approach: Keep the following points in mind during drafting:

- Begin when you have found a central focus or promising starting point.
- Use your outline or writing plan as a guide, but don't be limited by it.
- Use tools (pen and paper or computer) that help you write freely.
- Write without being too concerned about neatness and correctness.
- Include as much detail as possible.
- Complete your first draft in one or two sittings.

Ideas: Do three things: (1) stay focused on your purpose and your main point, (2) follow the direction set out in your working thesis and outline, and (3) allow important new ideas to emerge naturally, even if they lead where you hadn't anticipated going. In other words, concentrate on addressing your topic and developing your ideas—not on producing a final copy.

Organization: If the type of writing you've been assigned has a prescribed structure, use it. Otherwise, let the organization develop from your outline, lists, and basic writing moves.

Voice: Use your natural voice so that the writing flows smoothly.

What's Ahead

DRAFTING

8a Opening the Draft

An opening paragraph is one of the most important elements in any composition. It should accomplish three things: (1) engage the reader; (2) establish your direction, tone, and level of language; and (3) introduce your main point.

Advice: The conventional way of approaching the first paragraph is to view it as a kind of "funnel" that draws a reader in and narrows to a main point. Often, the final sentence or paragraph explicitly states the thesis.

Cautions: Don't feel bound by the conventional pattern. If handled well, other patterns can work just fine. Don't let the first paragraph paralyze you. Relax and write; or write the opening paragraph last.

How can I engage my readers?

Your readers will be occupied with other thoughts until you seize, stimulate, and direct their attention. Here are some ways to "hook" readers:

- Mention little-known facts about the topic.
- Pose a challenging question.
- Offer a thought-provoking quotation.
- Tell a brief, illuminating story.
- Forecast intriguing ideas or details addressed later in the writing.
- Show how the topic relates to readers' concerns or aspirations.
- Link the topic to a significant historical problem or current event.

OPENINGS TO AVOID

Whereas lively openings lure readers into essays, dull openings discourage readers from reading further.

Avoid obvious or worn-out expressions:
"Everybody knows that ... "
"As defined in *Webster's Dictionary* ..."

Avoid say-nothing sentences:
"A and B are alike in some ways and different in others."
"Crime is an undesirable element in today's society."

Avoid condescending or deprecating words:
"People your age should know that ..."
"I hope that you're able to understand ..."

 WRITER'S TIP

Writers seldom achieve a polished opening until they've drafted and revised the rest of the document. Changes in the middle and closing may require parallel changes in the opening.

How can I establish my direction?

The direction of your thinking should become clear in your opening. Here are some ways to set the right course:

- **Identify the issue.** Show a problem, a need, or an opportunity.

- **Deepen the issue.** Put the topic into perspective by connecting it to some larger issue; stir the readers' sense of its importance.

- **Acknowledge other views.** Tell what others say or think about the topic.

You may state your main point up front, or you may wait to introduce your thesis until later. Sometimes, as in a personal narrative, your thesis may simply be implied. In any case, the opening should at least lead toward the central issue or thesis of your paper. Here are four ways to get to the point:

- **Narrow your focus.** Show what interests you about the topic.

- **Raise a challenging question.** You can answer the question in the rest of the essay.

- **State your thesis.** If appropriate, include a sentence or two that sets the direction and tone for the writing. You can use the thesis sentence as a "map" for organizing the rest of the essay. (See **7a**.)

- **Follow an organizational pattern.** Choose a pattern that develops your thesis and clarifies your perspective on the topic. (See **7b**.)

SAMPLE OPENING

In the opening below, the writer uses his first paragraph to describe his subject (the cartoon family, the Simpsons), and he uses the second paragraph to raise a question that leads to his thesis (underlined).

> The Simpsons, stars of the TV show by the same name, are a typical American family, or at least a parody of one. Homer, Marge, Bart, Lisa, and Maggie Simpson live in Springfield, U.S.A. Homer, the father, is a boorish, obese oaf who works in a nuclear power plant. Marge is an overprotective, nagging mother with an outrageous blue hairdo. Ten-year-old Bart is an obnoxious, "spiky-haired demon." Lisa is eight and a prodigy on the tenor saxophone and in class. The infant Maggie never speaks but only sucks on her pacifier.
>
> What is the attraction of this yellow-skinned family who star on a show in which all of the characters have pronounced overbites and only four fingers on each hand? I contend that we see a little bit of ourselves in everything they do. <u>The world of Springfield is a parody of our own world, and Americans can't get enough of it.</u>

8b Developing the Middle

The middle of an essay is where you do the "heavy lifting"—constructing the main points that support your thesis statement.

Advice: As you write, you will likely make choices that you didn't foresee when you began. Change your outline or notes as needed to organize these ideas and then write freely to develop them.

Cautions: Writing that lacks effective detail gives only a vague image of the writer's intent. Writing that wanders loses its hold on the essay's overall purpose.

How can I build a coherent structure?

Use each middle paragraph to present main points and details that advance your essay logically and coherently.

- Start a new paragraph whenever a shift or change in the essay takes place. A shift occurs when you introduce a new main point, redirect a point of emphasis, or indicate a change in time or place.
- Arrange middle paragraphs carefully so that each one builds on the preceding paragraphs and leads into the following paragraphs. To achieve this flow, link the first sentence in each new paragraph to the preceding paragraph. Transitional words help you do this. (See **12c**.)
- Shape each paragraph for unity, coherence, and logical organization. For help, see Chapter 12, "Writing Strong Paragraphs."

How can I use different levels of detail?

Try to include three levels of detail in your paragraphs, as seen in these sentences from a paragraph on hypothermia. (See **12d**.)

Level 1: A topic sentence identifies the central idea of the paragraph.
Even a slight drop in the normal human body temperature of 98.6°F causes hypothermia.

Level 2: Clarifying sentences support the main point.
Often produced by accidental or prolonged exposure to cold, the condition forces all bodily functions to slow down. The heart rate and blood pressure decrease. Breathing becomes slower and shallower.

Level 3: A clinching sentence completes the point.
A person can survive in a deep hypothermic state for an hour or longer and be revived without serious complications.

How can I support my main points?

As you write, use an assortment of the following types of details:

- **Facts and statistics** are details that come from research and can be demonstrated to be true. (See "Clean Water is Everyone's Business," **11c**.)
- **Quotations** are the exact words of persons involved in an issue. (See "If We Are What We Wear, What Are We?" **40b**.)
- **Examples and illustrations** are specific instances that concretely demonstrate an idea. (See "Preparing for Agroterror," **40f**.)
- **Background** refers to preliminary information that readers need to understand. (See "Adrenaline Junkies," **39b**.)
- **Anecdotes** are brief stories that illustrate an idea. (See "Wayward Cells," **39n**.)
- **Definitions** are specific explanations of the meaning of terms or ideas. (See "Adrenaline Junkies," **39b**.)
- **Comparisons, analogies, and metaphors** are ways of showing the similarities between things. (See "A Fear Born of Sorrows," **39f**.)
- **Contrasts, distinctions, and negative definitions** are ways of showing the differences between things. (See "Four Ways to Talk About Literature," **39j**.)
- **Descriptions** are detailed explanations of how something looks or works. (See "The Stream in the Ravine," **38a**.)
- **Analyses** are examinations of the parts of something and the ways that the parts relate. (See "Four Ways to Talk About Literature," **39j**.)
- **Arguments** are logical inferences based on evidence and used to prove a claim. (See "Preparing for Agroterror," **40f**.)

How can I test my ideas?

When you write a first draft, test your initial thinking about your topic to determine whether your thesis is valid and whether you have enough compelling information to support it. Here are some ways to test your thinking:

- **Raise questions.** Anticipate—and address—your readers' questions. (See "If We Are What We Wear, What Are We?" **40b**.)
- **Consider alternatives.** Look at your ideas from different angles; weigh different options; reevaluate your thesis. (See "Four Ways to Talk About Literature," **39j**.)
- **Answer objections.** Directly or indirectly deal with possible problems that a skeptical reader would point out. (See "Preparing for Agroterror," **40f**.)
- **Look for logical fallacies.** Review your draft for logical fallacies and revise as needed. (See **4i**.)

DRAFTING

8c Ending the Draft

Closing paragraphs can be important for tying up loose ends, clarifying key points, or shaping a conclusion that mirrors the opening. In a sense, the entire essay is a preparation for an effective ending; the ending helps the reader look back over the essay with new understanding and appreciation.

Advice: Because the ending can be so important, draft a variety of possible endings. Choose the one that best enhances or completes the whole.

Cautions: If your thesis is weak or unclear, you will have a difficult time writing a satisfactory ending. To strengthen the ending, strengthen the thesis. If you need to summarize your ideas, use new words.

How can I sum up my main point?

If the ideas are new or complicated, give readers a brief review or clarification. Show that you are fulfilling the promises you made in the opening.

Remind the readers. Recall what you first set out to do; check off the key points you've covered; or answer any questions left unanswered.

Rephrase the thesis. Restate your thesis in light of the most important support you've given. Deepen and expand your original thesis.

How can I get readers to accept my ideas?

Your readers may still be reluctant to accept your ideas, and the ending is your last chance to gain their acceptance. Here are some possible strategies:

Show the implications. Follow further possibilities raised by your train of thought; be reasonable and convincing.

Look ahead. Suggest other possible connections.

List the benefits. Show readers the benefits of accepting or applying the things you've said.

> **NOTE:** See Chapter 12, "Writing Strong Paragraphs," for help with designing strong paragraphs that
> 1. Are unified, complete, and coherent units of thought.
> 2. Follow these organizational patterns: cause and effect, chronological order, classification, comparison and contrast, and definition.

ETHICS TIP

Do not distort your topic and message by (1) leaving out important information, (2) including nonessential sensitive information, or (3) citing details unsupported by research.

SAMPLE ENDINGS

Below are final paragraphs from three essays in this book. Listen to their tone, watch how they reconsider the essay's ideas, and note how they offer further food for thought.

> Sometimes, I want to go back there, back into that photo. I want to step into a time when life seemed safe, and a tiny stream gave us all that we needed. In that picture, our smiles last, our hearts are calm, and we hear only quiet voices, forest sounds, and my bubbling stream. Bitter words are silenced and tears held back by the click and whir of a camera.
>
> I've been thinking about making the journey again past the hunter's fort, under the stand of cedars, through the muck and mire, and over the rocky rise. But it's been a long summer, and the small seasonal stream running out of the overflow of the pond has probably dried up.

(See **38a** for the full essay.)

> On September 11, 2001, America, along with its Western allies, lost its aura of invincibility. As the whole world watched, the towers fell, and we stumbled in shock and pain. Moreover, as time passes, America may fail to identify its enemy and to understand the attack. If this happens, the oppressed people of the world—to some extent victims of Western culture—will take notice.
>
> It is now one week since the towers fell, and the world still grieves. However, mingled with this grief is the fear that we may be mourning not only for the lives lost, but also for our lost way of life.

(See **39f** for the full essay.)

> Clothing, varied and fun though it can be, is ultimately superficial. What if we dared to reach for more? What if we chose to define ourselves not by what we have, but by what we do? To do more, whether in our own communities or throughout the world, we would have to share more. One way to share our resources is to need less, buy less for ourselves, and give more to others. We can use our resources to help needy people, not only in America, but in other countries as well.

(See **40b** for the full essay.)

VISUALS TIP

Choosing visuals (such as graphs, charts, tables, or drawings) to support your message is part of the drafting process. To identify where visuals are needed, review your writing for passages that seem dense, complex, or dull. Then find or create a visual that delivers the information more clearly or concisely. (Remember, too, that visuals rarely "speak for themselves"; introduce and interpret them properly. For help, see Chapter 17, "Designing and Using Visuals.")

DRAFTING

8d   Angela's First Draft

After composing her opening, middle, and closing paragraphs, Angela put together her first draft. She then added a working title.

Water Woes

> The writer adds a title.

It's a hot day. Several people just finished mowing their lawns. A group of bicyclists—more than 3,000—have been passing through your picturesque town all afternoon. Dozens of Little Leaguers are batting, running, and sweating. What do all these people have in common? They all drink lots of tap water, especially on hot summer days. They also take for granted that the water is clean and safe. But in reality, the water they drink could be contaminated and pose a serious health risk. **That's just what happened in Walkerton, Ontario, where a water pollution incident caused serious problems.**

> She uses a series of images to get the reader's attention.

> The thesis statement (boldfaced) introduces the subject.

What happened in Walkerton, Ontario? Heavy rains fell on May 12. It wasn't untill May 21 that the townspeople were advised to boil their drinking water. The rains washed cattle manure into the town well. The manure contained *E. coli,* a type of bacteria. *E. coli* is harmless to cattle. It can make people sick. Seven days after the heavy rains, people began calling public health officials. The warning came to late. Two people had already died.

> The writer describes the cause of the problem.

Once Walkerton's problem was identified, the solutions were known. The government acted quickly to help the community and to clean the water supply. One Canadian newspaper reported that a $100,000 emergency fund was set up to help families with expenses. Bottled water for drinking and containers of bleach for sanitizing and cleaning were donated by local businesses.

So what messed up Walkerton? Basically, people screwed up! According to one news story, a flaw in the water treatment system allowed the bacteria-infested water to enter the well. The manure washed into the well, but the chlorine should have killed the deadly bacteria. In Walkerton, the PUC group fell asleep at the wheel.

> The writer discusses other causes of the problem.

Angela's First Draft

5   At last, the Provincial Clean Water Agency restored the main water and sewage systems by flushing out all of the town's pipes and wells. The ban on drinking Walkerton's water was finally lifted seven months after the water became contaminated.

> The writer covers the solutions used to resolve the problem.

6   Could any good come from Walkerton's tragedy? Does it have a silver lining? It is possible that more people are aware that water may be contaminated. Today people are beginning to take responsibility for the purity of the water they and their families drink. In the end, more and more people will know about the dangers of contaminated water—without learning it the hard way.

> The concluding paragraph stresses the importance of public awareness.

WORKING BIBLIOGRAPHY

As she researched her topic, Angela kept a working bibliography—a list of resources that she thought might offer helpful information for her essay. During the writing process, she deleted some resources, added others, and finally edited the document that became the references page. (See **11c**.)

Working Bibliography

Wickens, Barbara. "Tragedy in Walkerton." Maclean's. 5 June 2000:
        34–36.

Phone interview with Alex Johnson, Walkerton Police Department,
        23 September 2005.

Blackwell, Thomas. "Walkerton Doctor Defends Response."
        The Edmonton Journal. 9 January 2001.
        <http://www.edmontonjournal.com>.

DRAFTING

8e Checklist: Drafting

Use this checklist as a guide when you develop the first draft of an essay.

Ideas

___ The opening engages readers and identifies the thesis or main point of the essay.

___ The middle advances the thesis by developing main points and offering supporting detail.

___ The ending reasserts the thesis and—if appropriate—encourages readers to act.

Organization

___ The introductory material establishes the direction for the writing.

___ The main points are arranged logically in separate paragraphs.

___ The ending thoughtfully leads up to a final point that engages readers.

Voice

___ The opening is engaging.

___ The middle reveals the writer's interest in the topic.

___ The essay ends in a voice that sincerely connects with readers.

LINKS

WAC Link: Instructors in many disciplines will ask you to keep (and possibly submit) your first drafts. They do this for a variety of reasons, including to track your progress in the writing process, to discuss the process with you, to help you identify and correct weaknesses in your writing, and to teach writing concepts or strategies important in their disciplines. To help your instructors help you, do the following:

• Save and number each draft of your paper.
• Remember that your instructors are knowledgeable in their disciplines and will have insights into how and why writing is done within each field.
• Note how the advice given by each instructor relates to (1) which writing form is assigned (lab report, literary analysis, interview report) and (2) how that form is used within the course and the discipline.

Service-Learning Link: Writing in a service-learning project is often done to help the people you're serving address some need or goal. For example, you may write a job-application letter for an individual or a grant proposal for a group. In any case, carefully confer with your clients both before and after you write the first draft. Aim to shape a message that presents their concerns, in their voices, and for their benefit.

Revising

After finishing a first draft, you might be tempted to run it through the spell checker and then submit the paper. However, professional writers know that only disciplined revision transforms first drafts into quality writing. This chapter details many strategies for improving your writing and producing first-rate papers.

How should I revise?

Set your first draft aside until you can look at it objectively. Then print your paper (double-spaced) and make changes with a pencil or pen. Then focus on the big picture: ideas, organization, and voice.

Ideas: Check your thesis, focus, or theme. Has your thinking on your topic changed? Have you answered readers' questions? Are your main points (or arguments) complete, well reasoned, and supported with clear, convincing details?

Organization: Check your writing to make sure your ideas move smoothly and logically. Does your essay build effectively and shift directions cleanly? Fix structural problems using strategies like these:

- Reorder material to improve the sequence.
- Cut information that doesn't support the thesis.
- Add details where the draft is weak, and rewrite parts that seem unclear.
- Use transitions to improve links between points.

Voice: Does the draft show your genuine interest in the subject and respect for your readers? Does the tone of voice match your purpose (serious, playful, satiric)?

What's Ahead

9a Addressing Whole-Paper Issues

When revising, first look at the big picture. Take it all in. Determine whether the content is interesting, informative, and worth sharing. Note any gaps or soft spots in your line of thinking. Ask yourself how you can improve what you have done so far. The information that follows will help you address whole-paper issues like these.

Have I accomplished my purpose and targeted my audience?

Remember why you are writing—your purpose. Are you sharing information, recalling an experience, explaining a process, or arguing a point? Does your writing achieve that purpose? Also consider your readers. How much do they know about the subject? What else do they need to know?

Is my overall approach solid?

Think of your writing as a whole. Sometimes it's better to start anew if your writing contains stretches of uninspired ideas. Consider making a fresh start if your first draft shows one of these large-scale problems:

- **The topic is worn-out.** An essay titled "Lead Poisoning" may not sound very interesting. Unless you can approach the topic with a new twist ("Get the Lead Out!"), consider cutting your losses and finding a fresh topic.

- **Your voice is predictable or fake.** Avoid the bland "It has come to my attention" or the phony academic "When one studies this significant problem in considerable depth . . ." Be real. Be honest.

- **The draft sounds boring.** If the essay is boring because you pay equal attention to everything and hence stress nothing, try condensing less-important material and expanding crucial points. If the essay is boring because it lacks details, find information that shows the topic's relevance.

- **The essay is formulaic.** That is, it follows the "five-paragraph" format of an opening paragraph, a closing paragraph, and three middle paragraphs, each addressing a main point. This handy framework may limit your thinking, resulting in a predictable treatment of the topic. If your draft is dragged down by a rigid formula, try a more original approach.

WRITER'S TIP

To energize your thinking and writing, try these strategies:
- Freewrite to find a new approach to the topic.
- Review your research notes for additional interesting details.
- List and respond to arguments against your thesis.

9b Revising Your Ideas, Organization, and Voice

You can save time while revising by having specific goals, such as reinforcing your ideas, organization, and voice.

How should I revise for ideas?

As you review your draft for content, make sure that all of the ideas are fully developed and clearly stated. You can strengthen the content by addressing issues like those below. (To test the logic of your ideas, see **4f–4i**.)

CHECK THE THESIS

Make sure that your writing focuses on one main issue or thesis. The original opening below lacks a thesis, while the revision has a clear one.

Original Passage (Lacks a thesis or focus)

Teen magazines are popular with young girls. These magazines contain a lot of how-to articles about self-image, fashion, and boys. Girls read them to get advice on how to act and how to look. Girls who don't really know what they want are the most eager readers.

Revised Version (Includes a clear thesis statement: underlined)

Adolescent girls often see teen magazines as handbooks on how to be teenagers. These magazines influence the way they act and the way they look. For girls who are unsure of themselves, these magazines can exert an enormous amount of influence. <u>Unfortunately, the advice these magazines give about self-image, fashion, and boys may do more harm than good.</u>

CHECK FOR COMPLETE THINKING

How complete is your thinking? Have you answered readers' basic questions? Have you adequately supported the thesis? The original passage below is too general, while the revision is more complete.

Original Passage (Too general)

As soon as you receive a minor cut, the body's healing process begins to work. Blood from tiny vessels fills the wound and begins to clot. In less than twenty-four hours, a scab forms.

Revised Version (More specific)

As soon as you receive a minor cut, the body's healing process begins to work. In a simple wound, the first and second layers of skin are severed, along with tiny blood vessels called capillaries. As these vessels bleed into the wound, minute structures called platelets help stop the bleeding by sticking to the edges of the cut and to one another, forming a clot. The blood clot, with its fiber network, begins to join the edges of the wound together. As the clot dries out, a scab forms, usually in less than twenty-four hours.

REVISING

How should I revise for organization?

Make sure your writing has a structure that leads readers logically from one point to the next. When revising for organization, consider four areas: the overall plan, the opening, the flow of ideas, and the closing.

CHECK THE OVERALL PLAN

Look closely at the sequence of ideas or events. Does that sequence advance your thesis? Do the points build upon one another effectively? Are there gaps in the main or supporting points? Does the thought pattern stray from your writing purpose? Correct the problems with strategies like these:

- Refine the focus or emphasis by moving material within the text.
- Fill in the gaps with new material, using your planning and research notes for help.
- Delete material that wanders from your purpose.
- Use an additional (or different) method of organization. For example, if you are comparing two subjects, add depth to your analysis by contrasting them as well. (See **7b** for more on methods of development.)

WRITER'S TIP

Reviewing your outline and research notes at this stage of your draft may help you locate gaps in the reasoning in your paper. Include any details that will fill these holes and strengthen the support you use for each point.

CHECK THE OPENING

Reread your opening paragraph(s). Is the opening organized effectively? Does it engage readers, establish a direction for your writing, and express your thesis or focus? The original opening below doesn't build to a compelling thesis statement. In contrast, the revised version engages readers and leads to the thesis statement.

Original Opening (Lacks interest and direction)

> The lack of student motivation is a common subject in the news. Educators want to know how to get students to learn. Today's higher standards mean that students will be expected to learn even more. Another problem in urban areas is that large numbers of students are dropping out. How to interest students is a challenge.

Revised Version (Effectively leads readers into the essay)

> How can we motivate students to learn? How can we get them to meet today's rising standards of excellence? How can we, in fact, keep students in school long enough to learn? The answer to these problems is quite simple. Give them money. Pay students to study, to learn, and to stay in school.

Revising Your Ideas, Organization, and Voice

CHECK THE FLOW OF IDEAS

Look closely at the beginning and ending of each paragraph. Have you connected your thoughts clearly? (See **12c** for a list of transition words.) The original opening words of the paragraph sequence below offer no links for readers. The revised versions use strong transitions indicating spatial organization (order by location).

Original First Words in the Four Middle Paragraphs

- There was a huge, steep hill . . .
  Buffalo Creek ran . . .
  A dense "jungle" covering . . .
  Within walking distance from my house . . .

Revised Versions (Words and phrases connect ideas)

- Behind the house, there was a huge, steep hill . . .
  Across the road from the house, Buffalo Creek ran . . .
  On the far side of the creek bank was a dense "jungle" covering . . .
  Up the road, within walking distance from my house . . .

CHECK THE CLOSING

Reread your closing paragraph(s). Do you offer an effective summary, reassert your main point in a fresh way, and leave readers with food for thought? Or is your ending abrupt, repetitive, or directionless? The original ending below adds little to the body of the essay. The revision summarizes the main points and then urges readers to think again about the overall point of the writing.

Original Closing (Sketchy and flat)

Native Son deals with a young man's struggle against racism. It shows the effects of prejudice. Everyone should read this book.

Revised Version (Effectively ends the writing)

Native Son deals with a young man's struggle in a racist society, but the book deals with so much more. It shows how prejudice affects people, how it closes in on them, and what some people will do to find a way out. Anyone who wants to better understand racism in the United States should read this book.

WRITER'S TIP

If you need to collect new ideas for your closing, freewrite answers to questions like these:

- Why is the topic important to me?
- What should my readers have learned?
- What evidence or appeal will help my readers remember my message and act on it?

REVISING

How should I revise for voice?

Generally, readers more fully trust and appreciate writing that speaks in an informed, genuine voice. To develop an informed voice, make sure that your details are correct and complete. To achieve a genuine voice, make sure that your words and sentences sound natural (no pretense).

CHECK FOR COMMITMENT

Check how and to what degree your writing shows that you care about the topic and your readers. Note how the original passage below lacks a personal voice, revealing nothing about the writer's interest in the topic. In contrast, the revision shows that the writer cares about the topic and explains why.

Original Passage (Lacks voice)

Cemeteries can teach us a lot about history. They make history seem more real. There is an old grave of a Revolutionary War veteran in the Union Grove Cemetery.

Revised Version (Personal, sincere voice)

I've always had a special feeling for cemeteries. It's hard to explain any further than that, except to say history never seems quite as real as it does when I walk between rows of old gravestones. One day I discovered the grave of a Revolutionary War veteran in the Union Grove Cemetery.

CHECK THE ENERGY LEVEL

All writing—including academic writing—is enriched by an appropriate level of intensity, or even passion. In the original passage below, the writer's concern for the topic is unclear because the piece sounds neutral: The tone of voice is somewhat flat. In contrast, the revised version exudes energy: The tone conveyed contains an argumentative edge, even anger.

Original Version (Lacks feeling and energy)

Motz blames Barbie dolls for all the problems that women face today. Instead, one should look to romance novels, fashion magazines, and parental training for causes of these societal problems.

Revised Version (Expresses real feelings)

In other words, Motz uses Barbie as a scapegoat for problems that have complex causes. For example, a girl's interest in romance is no more Barbie's fault than the fault of books like *On the Shores of Silver Lake*. Fashion magazines targeted at adolescents are the cause of far more anorexia than is Barbie. And mothers who encourage daughters to find security in men teach female dependency, but Barbie doesn't.

> **NOTE:** Energy is important in writing, but don't overdo it. Academic writing should never shout.

9c Addressing Paragraph Issues

While drafting, you may have constructed paragraphs that are loosely held together, poorly developed, or unclear. When you revise, take a close look at your paragraphs for focus, unity, and coherence. (See 12a–12e.)

How should I revise my paragraphs?

A paragraph should be a concise unit of thinking and writing. Revise each paragraph until it

- Is organized around a controlling idea—often stated in a topic sentence.
- Consists of supporting sentences that develop the controlling idea.
- Concludes with a sentence that addresses the main point and prepares readers for the next paragraph or main point.
- Serves a specific function in a piece of writing—opening, supporting, developing, illustrating, countering, describing, or closing.

SAMPLE PARAGRAPH

> <u>Tumor cells can hurt the body in a number of ways.</u> First, a tumor can grow so big that it takes up space needed by other organs. Second, some cells may detach from the original tumor and spread throughout the body, creating new tumors elsewhere. This happens with lymphatic cancer—a cancer that's hard to control because it spreads so quickly. A third way that tumor cells can hurt the body is by doing work not called for in their DNA. For example, a gland cell's DNA code may tell the cell to produce a necessary hormone in the endocrine system. However, if cancer damages or distorts that code, sick cells may produce more of the hormone than the body can use—or even tolerate (Braun 4). <u>Cancer cells seem to have minds of their own, and this is why cancer is such a serious disease.</u>

Topic sentence

Supporting sentences

Closing sentence

How can I check the purpose of each paragraph?

Use these questions to evaluate the purpose and function of each paragraph:

- What function does the paragraph fulfill? How does it develop the thesis or line of reasoning?
- Would the paragraph be clearer if it were divided in two—or combined with another paragraph?
- Does the paragraph flow smoothly from the previous paragraph, and does it lead effectively into the next one?

REVISING

9d   Angela's First Revision

After finishing her first draft, Angela set it aside. When she was ready to revise it, she looked carefully at global issues—ideas, organization, and voice. She wrote notes to herself to help keep her thoughts together.

Water Woes

> *I need to give my opening more energy.*

      It's ~~a~~ *an unusually* hot ~~day.~~ *Saturday afternoon.* Several people just finished mowing their lawns. A group of bicyclists ~~—more than 3,000—have been~~ *pedal up the street.* ~~passing through your picturesque town all afternoon.~~ Dozens of Little Leaguers are batting, running, and sweating. What do all these people have in common? They all drink lots of tap water, especially on hot summer days. They also take for granted that the water is clean and safe. But in reality, the water they drink could be contaminated and pose a serious health risk. That's just what happened in Walkerton, Ontario, where a water pollution incident caused serious problems.   **1**

> *Does my thesis still fit the paper? — yes.*

> *Using time sequence put this paragraph in better order.*

      What happened in Walkerton, Ontario? Heavy rains fell on May 12. [It wasn't untill May 21 that the townspeople were advised to boil their drinking water.] The rains washed cattle manure into the town well. The manure contained *E. coli*, a type of bacteria. *E. coli* is harmless to cattle. It can make people sick. Seven days after the heavy rains, people began calling public health officials. The warning came to late. Two people had already died.   **2**

> *Move this paragraph. It interrupts the discussion of causes.*

      Once Walkerton's problem was identified, the solutions were known. The government acted quickly to help the community and to clean the water supply. One Canadian newspaper reported that a $100,000 emergency fund was set up to help families with expenses. Bottled water for drinking and containers of bleach for sanitizing and cleaning were donated by local businesses.   **3**

Angela's First Revision

4 So what ~~messed up~~ *went wrong in* Walkerton? ~~Basically, people screwed~~ ~~up!~~ *First,* According to one news story, a flaw in the water treatment system allowed the bacteria-infested water to enter the well. *Even after* The manure washed into the well, ~~but~~ the chlorine should have killed the deadly bacteria. In Walkerton, the ~~PUC group fell~~ ~~asleep at the wheel.~~

Human error was a critical factor.

5 *In addition,* ~~At last,~~ the Provincial Clean Water Agency restored the main water and sewage systems by flushing out all of the town's pipes and wells. The ban on drinking Walkerton's water was finally lifted seven months after the water became contaminated.

6 Could any good come from Walkerton's tragedy? ~~Does it have a silver lining?~~ It is possible that more people are aware that water may be contaminated. Today people are beginning to take responsibility for the purity of the water they and their families drink. In the end, more and more people will know about the dangers of contaminated water—without learning it the hard way.

Public Utilities Commission was responsible for overseeing the testing and treating of the town's water, but it failed to monitor the situation properly. Apparently, shortcuts were taken when tracking the water's chlorine level, and as a result, some of the water samples were mislabeled. There was also a significant delay between the time that the contamination was identified and the time it was reported.

> My voice here is too informal.

> Move paragraph 3 here and combine with paragraph 5.

> Cut the cliché.

9e   Revising Collaboratively

Every writer can benefit from a reader's informed, objective advice. To help you provide and receive such advice, use the tips that follow.

How should I give feedback?

Using a specific approach like the OAQS method will help you give clear, helpful, and complete feedback.

OAQS Method

Respond to a piece of writing by working through these four steps:

1. **Observe:** Notice what the essay is designed to do and comment on its design or purpose. For example, you might say, "Even though you are writing about your boyfriend, it appears that you are trying to get a message across to your parents."

2. **Appreciate:** Praise something that pleases you. For example, you might say, "You make a convincing point" or "With your description, I can actually see his broken tooth."

3. **Question:** Ask whatever you want to know about the essay—background information, a definition, an interpretation, or an explanation. For example, you might ask, "Can you tell us what happened when you got to the emergency room?"

4. **Suggest:** Give helpful advice about possible changes. For example, you might say, "With a little more physical detail—especially more sounds and smells—your third paragraph could be the highlight of the essay."

What type of questions should I ask the writer?

Ask the following types of questions while reviewing a piece of writing.

- **To help writers reflect on their purpose and audience:**
  Why are you writing this?
  Who will read this, and what do they need to know?

- **To help writers focus their thoughts:**
  What message are you trying to get across?
  Do you have more than one main point?
  What are the most important examples?
  Does your writing cover all of the basics (the five W's and H)?

> **NOTE:** The five W's and H are the basic questions: *who, what, where, when, why,* and *how.*

- **To help writers with their opening and closing:**
  What are you trying to say in the opening?
  How else could you start your writing?
  How do you want your readers to feel at the end?

How should I use the writing center?

When you visit your writing center, you can expect the adviser to do certain things. Other things only you can do. For quick reference, refer to the lists below.

Adviser's Job

- Provide time in his or her schedule.
- Discuss your needs.
- Help choose a topic.
- Discuss your purpose and audience.
- Help you generate ideas.
- Help you develop your logic and test your claims.
- Help you understand how to research.
- Read your draft.
- Identify problems in organization, logic, expression, and format.
- Teach ways to correct weaknesses.
- Help with grammar, usage, diction, vocabulary, and mechanics.

Your Job

- Seek help early; use the time offered.
- Be respectful.
- Be ready to work.
- Decide on a topic.
- Know your purpose and audience.
- Embrace the best ideas.
- Consider other points of view; stretch your own perspective.
- Do the research.
- Share your writing.
- Search for alternatives and fix problems.
- Correct all errors.
- Rewrite as soon as possible after, or even during, the advising session.
- Return to the writing center to get a response to your revisions.

ESL TIP

Visit the writing center whenever you need extra help. Take your assignment sheet with you. Read your work aloud, slowly. Listen carefully to all suggestions. Ask questions about anything that you don't understand. Ask for examples or illustrations of important points. Write down all practical suggestions your adviser offers. If necesssary, set up a time when you can return for more help.

REVISING

9f   Angela's Second Revision

Next, Angela asked a peer to review her work. His comments appear in the margin. Angela used them to make additional changes, including writing a whole new opening.

Water Woes

WARNING: City tap water is polluted with animal waste. 1
Using the water for drinking, cooking, or bathing could cause
sickness or death.

According to the Sierra Club, runoff pollutants from farm
cites are steadily seeping into our streams, lakes, reservoirs
and wells. Because much of our drinking water comes from
these resources, warnings like the one above are already posted
in a number of U.S. and Canadian communities, and many more
postings will be needed (Water Sentinels). As the Seirra Club
argues, the pollution and related warnings are serious, and
failure to take them seriously could be deadly. For example, a
few years ago the citizens of Walkerton Ontario, learned that
the water that they believed to be clean was actually poisoned.

The events   *began*
~~What happened~~ in Walkerton, ~~Ontario? Heavy rains fell~~   2
, 2000, when heavy rains
on May 12. ~~The rains~~ washed cattle manure into the town
well. The manure contained *E. coli*, a type of bacteria. *E. coli*
is harmless to cattle. It can make people sick. Seven days after
                to complain of nausea and diarrhea.
the heavy rains, people began calling public health officials. It
wasn't untill May 21 that the townspeople were advised to boil
their drinking water. The warning came to late. Two people
had already died, *, and more than 2,000 were ill (Wickens).*

Several factors contributed to the tragedy in
~~So what went wrong in Walkerton? Human error was a~~   3
Walkerton, including human error.   The Edmonton Journal
~~critical factor.~~ First, according to ~~one news story,~~ a flaw in the
water treatment system allowed the bacteria-infested water to
            (Blackwell)
enter the well. Even after the manure washed into the well, the
chlorine should have killed the deadly bacteria. In Walkerton,
the Public Utilities Commission was responsible for overseeing
the testing and treating of the town's water, but it failed to

---

Margin comments:

Could you make the opening more relevant and urgent?

Could you clarify your focus on the topic?

Add the year.

Add specific details.

Add your sources.

Combine these two sentences.

monitor the situation properly. Apparently, shortcuts were taken when tracking the water's chlorine level, and, as a result, some of the water samples were mislabeled. There was also a significant delay between the time that the contamination was identified and the time it was reported.

4   Once Walkerton's problem was identified, ~~the solutions were known.~~ The government acted quickly to help the community ~~and to clean the water supply.~~ ~~One Canadian newspaper~~ *The Edmonton Journal* reported that a $100,000 emergency fund was set up to help families with expenses. *Local businesses donated* Bottled water for drinking and containers of bleach for basic sanitizing and cleaning ~~were donated by local businesses.~~ In addition, the Provincial Clean Water Agency restored the main water and sewage systems by flushing out all of the town's pipes and wells. The ban on drinking Walkerton's water was finally lifted seven month after the water became contaminated.

> Again, list your sources.

5   *As the Sierra Club warned and the citizens of Walkerton learned, water purity is a life-and-death issue. Fortunately, both the United States and Canada have been addressing the problem. For example, since 2001, more states and provinces have been tightening their clean-water standards, more communities have begun monitoring their water quality, and more individuals have been using water-filtration systems, bottled water, or boiled tap water. However, a tragedy like that in Walkerton could happen again. To avoid such horror, all of us must get involved by demanding clean tap water in our communities and by promoting the policies and procedures needed to achieve that goal.*

> Consider adding details— maybe an entire paragraph— calling readers to action, and stating your thesis clearly.

REVISING

9g   Checklist: Revising the Content

Use this checklist as a guide when you revise your writing.

Ideas

___ My writing has a clear thesis, focus, or theme.

___ I have fully developed and supported that thesis with relevant, accurate details.

Organization

___ My writing follows a clear pattern of organization that advances the main idea.

___ I have cut, reordered, and rewritten material as needed.

___ I have developed points and added details and examples where needed.

___ All of my paragraphs are unified, coherent, and complete.

Voice

___ The voice matches the assignment, the audience, and the purpose.

___ The tone of voice is consistent; any shift in tone is planned and effective.

___ My voice sounds committed and energetic.

WAC Link: Many college assignments will ask that you work with another student to complete a piece of writing, but the nature of that work can vary significantly between courses or between assignments. For example, one assignment might ask that you and a classmate simply respond to each other's writing, while another assignment might ask that you work as a team to co-author a piece. When working with others, follow the guidelines in this book—but stay in accordance with the assignment's guidelines.

ETHICS TIP

In college, students compete for grades; in the workplace, employees compete for promotions and pay raises. However, in both places, competition should not diminish people's efforts to do their work ethically. The peer-response instructions in this chapter are helpful in both settings. The instructions explain how the writer and responder can focus on specific aspects of the writing itself—and not on each other's competing goals.

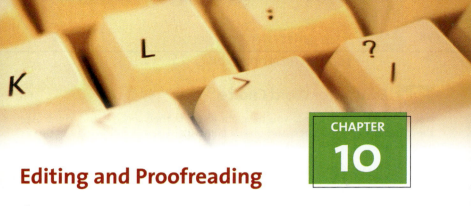

Editing and Proofreading

After you have thoroughly revised your writing, you must edit and proofread it. While editing strengthens your word choice, grammar, and sentence style, proofreading catches errors in punctuation, mechanics, grammar, and spelling.

How should I edit and proofread?

After revising the draft, let it sit for a while and then read it again. If the content seems clear and complete, follow the steps below. (Otherwise, revise again.)

Gather your tools. Use Chapters 19–36 in this book. Also keep a dictionary and thesaurus handy, whether print or electronic. If your instructor wants you to use a style sheet, check it for guidelines related to margin size, typeface, type size, and use of technical terms.

Read your revised writing aloud. Better yet, have a writing peer read it aloud to you. Highlight passages that sound awkward, stiff, or unclear.

Check your writing for these stylistic qualities and edit as needed:

- **Purposeful:** Does your writing sound focused and meaningful?
- **Clear:** Are the ideas conveyed in understandable language?
- **Sincere:** Does the writing sound authentic and honest?

Focus on details. Follow logical steps that address distinct editing and proofreading issues.

1. Edit for effective word choice.
2. Edit sentences for smoothness, variety, and strength.
3. Edit for errors in grammar and usage.
4. Proofread for errors in mechanics, grammar, and spelling.
5. Check the document's format and design.

What's Ahead

EDITING AND PROOFREADING

10a Editing for Word Choice

Carefully check the words you have chosen. Are they specific and vivid? Are they free of jargon, clichés, and biased language? Use the following ten tips as a guide when you edit.

1. Replace general nouns, verbs, and modifiers. General nouns, verbs, and modifiers don't provide the details that readers need to see and appreciate your subject. (See **14a**.)

General: The girl looked at me while she moved on the bench.

Specific: Rosie's dark eyes glared into mine while she slid quietly, but deliberately, to the end of the park bench.

2. Replace clichés with precise words. Clichés are overused words or phrases that present no clear meaning. (See **14b**.)

Cliché: If you've done your research, writing is a *piece of cake;* if you haven't, you're *up a creek without a paddle.*

Precise: If you've done your research, you should be able to complete the assignment well and on time.

3. Replace jargon with clear, simple words. Jargon is language used by people in a particular group or profession. While the words are clear to the group, they may be confusing to others. (See **14d**.)

Jargon: We need to *benchmark our efforts* with *outcome-based criteria* that *assess measurable data.*

Clear: We must measure our efficiency using clear, objective criteria.

4. Replace flowery words with familiar, natural language. Flowery words are unnecessarily long, complex, or unfamiliar terms that sound overwritten and pretentious. (See **14b**.)

Flowery: The bounteous yield of our patch of glowing sunshine should provide us seeds aplenty.

Natural: Our sunflowers have grown well this year, and they contain many seeds.

5. Avoid redundant words. A redundant term merely repeats the first word when they're used together. (See **14c**.)

- repeat again   red in color   refer back
  visible to the eye   join together   final outcome
  basic fundamentals   advance planning   brief moment

6. Correct ineffective repetition. Repetition used effectively adds rhythm and coherence to your writing. Repetition used ineffectively distracts from your message. (See **12c** and **13g**.)

Ineffective: *The man* looked as if he were in his late seventies. *The man* was dressed in an old suit. I soon realized that *the man* was tired and homeless.

Effective: He was a homeless man with gray hair, spectacles, and a worn-out suit. But he was also a dignified man who stood erect, looked at me directly, and nodded politely.

7. Correct errors in usage and grammar. Look for misuse of any **commonly mixed pairs** of words such as *its/it's, there/their/they're, chose/choose,* and *your/you're*. (See **36b**.)

8. Check agreement. Subjects and verbs should agree in number: Singular subjects go with singular verbs, and plural subjects go with plural verbs. Verb tenses should be consistent throughout. (See **20e**.) Review for pronoun/antecedent agreement problems. A pronoun and its antecedent must agree in number. (See **25h**.)

9. Change passive verbs to active verbs. Unless you want to show that the subject (rather than the direct object) received the action of the verb, change **passive verbs** to **active verbs**. (For specific uses of each verb form, see **20f**.)

Passive: The broadleaf weeds *were killed* by the chemical.

Active: The chemical *killed* the broadleaf weeds.

10. Replace biased words. Biased words communicate false, unfair, or disrespectful ideas about others in regard to their ethnicity, age, gender, disability, or occupation. (See **14e**.)

10b Editing for Sentence Weaknesses

Carefully read your sentences, checking for rhythm, fluency, and correctness.

How can I edit for sentence variety?

Use the following strategy to review your writing for sentence variety.

1. In **one column,** list the opening words in each of your sentences. Then edit openings that are ineffectively repeated.

2. In a **second column,** record the number of words in each sentence. Then decide if you need to vary the lengths of some sentences.

3. In a **third column,** list the verbs you use and then replace any you have overused.

EDITING AND PROOFREADING

How can I edit for ineffective constructions?

1. **Short sentences.** Combine or expand any short, choppy sentences. (See **13a**.)
2. **Flat sentences.** Rewrite flat, uninteresting sentences by expanding them with modifying words, phrases, and clauses. (See **13b**.)
3. **Wordy sentences.** Fix rambling sentences by cutting repetitive words, replacing imprecise words, and dividing long sentences into shorter sentences or clauses. (See **13f**.)
4. **Incorrect sentences.** Look carefully for fragments, run-ons, and comma splices and correct them as needed. (See **26b–26c**.)
5. **Unclear sentences.** Edit sentences that contain unclear wording, misplaced modifiers, or incomplete comparisons. (See **26f–26g**.)
6. **Unacceptable sentences.** Change sentences that include double negatives, nonstandard language, or unparallel constructions. (See **26h**.)
7. **Unnatural sentences.** Rewrite sentences that contain jargon, flowery language, or clichés. (See **14b**.)

10c Proofreading Your Writing

How can I review punctuation and mechanics?

1. Check for proper use of commas, semicolons, and dashes for punctuating constructions such as compound sentences, introductory clauses or phrases, and items in a series. (See **28a–29d**.)
2. Look for correct use of apostrophes. (See **29g**.)
3. Examine quotation marks in quoted information, titles, and dialogue. (See **29h**.)
4. Watch for proper use of capital letters. (See **30a–30d**.)

How can I check for spelling errors?

1. Use a dictionary as your primary authority for correct spelling. A spell checker will catch many errors, but it won't catch all of them.
2. Check each spelling that you are unsure of, especially proper names and other special words that your spell checker won't recognize.

How can I check formatting and page design?

1. Make sure your sources are properly documented. (See **52a–58b**.)
2. Check that all visuals, such as tables, pictures, and graphs, are placed effectively on the page and introduced properly in the text. (See **17a–17g**.)
3. Look over the finished copy of your writing. Does it meet the requirements for a final manuscript? (See **16a–16f**.)

10d Angela's Edited Copy

When Angela began editing, she read each sentence aloud to check for clarity and smoothness. **The first page of Angela's edited copy is shown below.**

Water Woes *in Walkerton*

> *Warning: City tap water is polluted with animal waste. Using the water for drinking, cooking, or bathing could cause sickness or death.*

The writer revises the title.

1   According to the Sierra Club, runoff pollutants from farm cites are steadily seeping into our streams, lakes, reservoirs, and wells. Because much of our drinking water comes from these resources, warnings like the one above are already posted in a number of U.S. and Canadian communities, and many more postings ~~will~~ *might* be needed *in the future* (Water Sentinels). As the Seirra Club argues, the pollution and related warnings are serious, and failure to take them seriously could be deadly. For example, a few years ago the citizens of Walkerton Ontario, learned that the water that they believed to be clean was ~~actually~~ *tragically* poisoned.

She qualifies her statement by replacing "will" with "might."

2   The events in Walkerton began on May 12, 2000, when heavy rains washed cattle manure into the town well. The manure contained ~~E. coli,~~ *the* a bacteria, *commonly called* E. coli *While E. coli* is harmless to cattle. It can make people sick. Seven days after the heavy rains, people began calling public health officials to complain of nausea and diarrhea. It wasn't until May 21 that the townspeople were advised to boil their drinking water. The warning came ~~to~~ *too* late. Two people had already died, and more than 2,000 were ill (Wickens).

She rewrites and combines several choppy sentences.

3   Several factors contributed to the tragedy in Walkerton, including human error. First, according to The Edmonton Journal *italic*, a flaw in the water treatment system allowed the bacteria-infested water to enter ~~the~~ *Walkerton's* well (Blackwell). Even after the manure washed into the well, the chlorine should have killed the deadly bacteria. In Walkerton, the Public . . .

She changes a word for clarity.

EDITING AND PROOFREADING

10e   Angela's Proofread Copy

Angela reviewed her edited copy for capitalization, punctuation, spelling, and agreement issues. **The first paragraph of Angela's proofread essay is shown below.**

Water Woes in Walkerton

> *Warning: City tap water is polluted with animal waste. Using the water for drinking, cooking, or bathing could cause sickness or death.*

> The writer corrects an error that the spell checker did not pick up.

> She adds quotation marks and corrects spelling.

> She adds a comma between the city and province.

According to the Sierra Club, runoff pollutants from farm sites are steadily seeping into our streams, lakes, reservoirs, and wells. Because much of our drinking water comes from these resources, warnings like the one above are already posted in a number of U.S. and Canadian communities, and many more postings might be needed in the future ("Water Sentinels"). As the Sierra Club argues, the pollution and related warnings are serious, and failure to take them seriously could be deadly. For example, a few years ago the citizens of Walkerton, Ontario, learned that the water that they believed to be clean was tragically poisoned.

10f   Checklist: Editing and Proofreading

Use this checklist as a guide when you edit and proofread your writing.

Word Choice

___ The writing is free of general words, jargon, and clichés.

___ The language is unbiased and fair.

Sentence Structure

___ Sentences are clear, complete, and correct.

___ They flow smoothly and have varied lengths and beginnings.

Correctness

___ Spelling, punctuation, and mechanics are correct.

___ Verb tenses are correct.

___ Subjects agree with their verbs; pronouns agree with their antecedents.

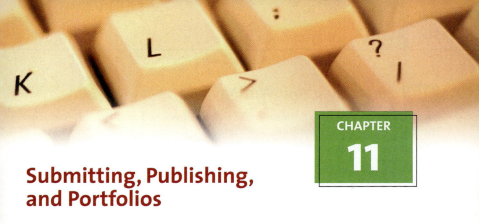

Submitting, Publishing, and Portfolios

After proofreading your draft, you should make a final copy and then "publish" it. While most instructors will ask you to submit your writing to them, some will expect you to publish your writing elsewhere.

What are my publishing goals?

Ask yourself what you are trying to accomplish:

- To complete your assignment, course, or program requirements.
- To improve your writing and presentation skills in your profession.
- To show your skills and qualifications when applying for jobs, scholarships, internships, graduate school, and professional programs.

What publishing method best fits my goals?

Format your work according to your goals.

- Share your writing with classmates or your writing group.
- Submit your work to a local publication or a professional journal.
- Post your writing on an appropriate website, including your own.
- Submit your writing to a college, regional, or national writing contest.
- Revise your writing as a letter to the editor of a newspaper.
- Place the writing in your portfolio. (See **11b**.)

How should I prepare my document for submission?

Submit your writing as a paper document, e-document, or both—depending on the instructor's or publisher's guidelines.

- Print an error-free copy on quality paper using a quality printer.
- Send your writing as an e-mail attachment.

What's Ahead

SUBMITTING, PUBLISHING, AND PORTFOLIOS

11a Formatting Your Writing

The test of a good page design is that it looks polished and uncluttered, fits the writing form and medium, and makes your message clear and easy to understand. Keep the following information in mind when you prepare a final copy of your writing.

How should I format and document my writing?

- Keep the design clear and uncluttered. Aim for a sharp, polished look in all your assigned writing.
- Use white space to focus attention on the prose and graphics and to make reading easy.
- Follow all the requirements for the assigned documentation form: MLA (**51a–53f**), APA (**54a–56e**), CMS (**57a–57b**) or CSE (**58a–58b**).

How should I choose fonts?

- Use an easy-to-read serif font for the main text. **Serif type,** like this, has "tails" at the tops and bottoms of the letters. For most writing situations, use a 10- or 12-point type size. (See **16e**.)
- Consider using a sans serif font for the title and headings. **Sans serif type,** like this, does not have "tails." Use larger, perhaps 18-point, type for your title and 14-point type for any headings. You can also use boldface for headings if they seem to get lost on the page.

VISUALS TIP

While serif fonts are easier to read on the printed page, most people find that sans serif fonts are easier to read on screen. Consider using a sans serif font for the body and a serif font for the titles and headings in any writing that you publish online.

What spacing requirements should I follow?

- Follow all requirements for indents and margins. This usually means indenting the first line of each paragraph by five spaces, maintaining a one-inch margin around each page, and double-spacing.
- Avoid leaving headings, hyphenated words, or single lines of new paragraphs alone at the bottom of a page.

How should I use graphic devices?

- Create bulleted or numbered lists to highlight important points. But be selective: Your writing should not include too many lists.
- Include charts, tables, or other graphics that help develop your message. (See **17a–17g**.)

11b   Preparing Your Portfolio

A writing portfolio is a portable file (electronic, paper, or both) that you use to compile pieces of your writing, develop them, and share them with others. The contents and format of the portfolio depend primarily on whether it is a *working portfolio* or a *showcase portfolio*.

What is a working portfolio?

A **working portfolio** is your personal file used to store, organize, and develop writing for a course, a project, an academic program, or a personal interest. The working portfolio includes your notes, drafts of documents, and finished documents. It helps you to

- Store writing for a course and get help from a tutor or an instructor.
- Find documents that you want to revise and reuse.
- Store material from which you can select items for a showcase portfolio.

What is a showcase portfolio?

A **showcase portfolio** is a file that shows off your best writing. If the file is required by a course or program, your instructor or department will likely specify its contents and organization.

> **NOTE:** If you are using the portfolio to apply for a grant, internship, or job, select only those items that feature the skills or qualities that the evaluators are seeking.

CONTENTS IN A SHOWCASE PORTFOLIO

While the exact contents depend on your writing situation, these items are commonly found in a showcase portfolio:

- A table of contents listing the pieces included in your portfolio
- An opening essay or letter detailing the story behind your portfolio: how you compiled it and how it shows the work, qualities, or skills required by the course, program, or job
- A specified number of your finished pieces (You may be asked to include your planning, drafting, and revising work.)
- Another finished piece illustrating additional qualities or skills
- A cover sheet attached to each piece of writing explaining how you developed it and why you selected it
- Evaluation sheets or checklists charting the basic skills that you have mastered as well as the skills that you still need to polish.

SUBMITTING, PUBLISHING, AND PORTFOLIOS

11c Angela's Finished Essay (with citations)

After proofreading her essay, Angela added a heading, changed the title, and added page numbers. She also added more documentation and a references page. As assigned, she did not include a title page or abstract.

Angela Franco

Professor Van Es

Environmental Policies

20 April 2005

Clean Water Is Everyone's Business

> **Warning**: City tap water is polluted with animal waste. Using the water for drinking, cooking, or bathing could cause sickness or death.

> *Complete details are supplied in the heading.*

> *The title is revised and the warning is in red print.*

> *An appropriate type font and size are used.*

> *Credit is given for a journal and newspaper used as resources.*

According to the Sierra Club, runoff pollutants from farm sites are steadily seeping into our streams, lakes, reservoirs, and wells. Because much of our drinking water comes from these resources, warnings like the one above are already posted in a number of U.S. and Canadian communities, and many more postings might be needed in the future ("Water Sentinels," 2005). As the Sierra Club argues, the pollution and related warnings are serious, and failure to take them seriously could be deadly. For example, a few years ago the citizens of Walkerton, Ontario, learned that the water that they believed to be clean was tragically poisoned.   1

The events in Walkerton began on May 12, 2000, when heavy rains washed cattle manure into the town well. The manure contained the bacteria commonly called *E. coli*. While *E. coli* is harmless to cattle, it can make people sick. Seven days after the heavy rains, people began calling public health officials to complain of nausea and diarrhea. It wasn't until May 21 that the townspeople were advised to boil their drinking water. The warning came too late. Two people had already died, and more than 2,000 were ill (Wickens, 2000).   2

Several factors contributed to the tragedy in Walkerton, including human error. First, according to *The Edmonton*   3

Angela's Finished Essay

Franco 2

Journal, a flaw in the water treatment system allowed the bacteria-infested water to enter Walkerton's well (Blackwell, 2001). Even after the manure washed into the well, the chlorine should have killed the deadly bacteria. In Walkerton, the Public Utilities Commission was responsible for overseeing the testing and treating of the town's water, but it failed to monitor the situation properly ("Walkerton's water-safety," 2000). Apparently, shortcuts were taken when tracking the water's chlorine level, and as a result, some of the water samples were mislabeled. There was also a significant delay between the time that the contamination was identified and the time it was reported.

> The writer's name and page number are used on each page.

> The writer continues to give credit throughout the essay.

4   Once Walkerton's problem was identified, the government acted quickly to help the community. In its December 7, 2000, edition, *The Edmonton Journal* reported that a $100,000 emergency fund was set up to help families with expenses. Local businesses donated bottled water for drinking and containers of bleach for basic sanitizing and cleaning. In addition, the Provincial Clean Water Agency restored the main water and sewage systems by flushing out all of the town's pipes and wells. Seven months after the water became contaminated, the ban on drinking Walkerton's water was finally lifted.

> The final essay is printed on quality paper with a quality printer.

5   As the Sierra Club warns and the citizens of Walkerton learned, water purity is a life-and-death issue. Fortunately, both the United States and Canada have made progress addressing the problem. For example, since 2001, more states and provinces have been tightening their clean-water standards, more communities have begun monitoring their water quality, and more individuals have been using water-filtration systems, bottled water, or boiled tap water. However, a tragedy like that in Walkerton could happen again. To avoid such horror, all of us must get involved by demanding clean tap water in our communities and by promoting the policies and procedures needed to achieve that goal.

> The writer restates her thesis in the last sentence.

Franco 3

References

Blackwell, T. (2001, January 9). Walkerton doctor defends response. *The Edmonton Journal.* Retrieved April 7, 2005, from <http://www.edmontonjournal.com>.

Sierra Club. Water sentinels: Keeping it clean around the U.S.A. Retrieved April 5, 2005, from <http://www.sierraclub .org/watersentinels/>.

Walkerton's water-safety tests falsified regularly, utility official admits. (2000, December 7). *The Edmonton Journal.* Retrieved April 2, 2005, from <http://www .edmontonjournal.com>.

Wickens, B. (2000, June 5). Tragedy in Walkerton. *Maclean's, 113*(23): 34-36.

> Sources are in alphabetical order and in APA style.

11d Checklist: Submitting, Publishing, and Portfolios

Use this checklist to review details regarding submitting, publishing, and portfolios.

___ The publishing method is appropriate for my assignment, program, and career goals.

___ The publishing process and method test and develop my skills as a writer and a scholar.

___ The document's format (paper or electronic; font and typeface; form and documentation; layout and graphics) conforms to all the publisher's guidelines.

___ My portfolio documents address the types of topics and show the level of scholarship expected by my readers.

___ The voice and style of my portfolio documents are appropriate for the kinds of writing done in the program or job for which I am applying.

___ The portfolio includes an engaging essay or cover letter that clearly explains the portfolio's design, purpose, and focus.

Style Issues

Style Issues

CHAPTER

12

Writing Strong Paragraphs

A paragraph is a unit of thought comprising a series of closely related sentences. While the lengths and styles of paragraphs vary greatly, all good paragraphs share these qualities: unity, completeness, and coherence. To understand the qualities of strong paragraphs, read the information below. To develop those qualities in your own writing, study the rest of the chapter.

- **Unity:** A unified paragraph develops one controlling idea that is usually stated in a topic sentence. Supporting sentences develop this main idea by addressing closely related concepts. (See **12a**.)
- **Completeness:** A complete paragraph includes all the details required to support its main or controlling idea. In addition, a complete paragraph includes the transitions needed to link its content to the content of the preceding and following paragraphs.

  The types of details required depend largely on the paragraph's function—whether the paragraph is designed to open a piece of writing, close it, tell a story, describe an object, build an argument, and so on. (See **12b**.)
- **Coherence:** A coherent paragraph holds together as one unit of thought. Transitions enhance coherence by linking words, phrases, and sentences within the paragraph. In addition, organizational strategies (like those listed below) create a smooth, logical flow of ideas. (See **12c**.)

  - Cause and effect
  - Chronological order
  - Classification
  - Climax
  - Comparison and contrast
  - Definition
  - Illustration

What's Ahead

12a Achieving Unity
12b Achieving Completeness
12c Achieving Coherence
12d Arranging Your Details
12e Checklist: Paragraphs

WRITING STRONG PARAGRAPHS

12a   Achieving Unity

A unified paragraph is one in which all details help to develop a single main topic or achieve a single main effect. Test for paragraph unity by following these guidelines.

How can I write a strong topic sentence?

Use a topic sentence to make a paragraph's main idea clear. Either state the idea explicitly in a single topic sentence or state it implicitly through the shared meaning of all sentences. If your paragraph has a topic sentence, check whether it is clear and well focused. Here is a formula for writing good topic sentences:

A topic sentence = **a limited topic +** *a specific feeling or thought about it.*

- **The fear that Americans feel** (limited topic) *comes partly from their insecurity related to the September 11 attacks* (specific thought).

Where should I place the topic sentence?

Although the topic sentence normally appears at the opening of the paragraph, it can appear elsewhere.

Middle placement: Place a topic sentence in the middle of the paragraph when you want to build up to and lead away from the key idea.

> The film *Apocalypse Now* depicts a journey into madness, in which a young American soldier must find an insane special-forces colonel. During the filming, Eleanor Coppola shot a documentary entitled *Hearts of Darkness: A Filmmaker's Apocalypse.* **This documentary shows that, for the cast and crew of *Apocalypse Now,* life came to imitate art.** For example, at one point in the documentary, actor Larry Fishburne shockingly said, "War is fun. . . . Vietnam must have been so much fun." Toward the end of the filming, Martin Sheen suffered a sudden heart attack, and director Francis Ford Coppola exploded, saying, "He's not dead unless I say he's dead." In many ways, the cast descended into moments of madness that paralleled those in the film.

End placement: Place a topic sentence at the end of the paragraph when you want to build to a climax.

> When anglers stop to reflect on why they find fishing so enjoyable, most realize that what they love is the feel of a fish on the end of the line, not necessarily the weight of the fillets in their coolers. Fishing has undergone a slow evolution over the last century. While fishing used to be a way of putting food on the table, most of today's fishermen pursue the sport only for the relaxation that it provides. The barbed hook was invented to increase the quantity of fish a man could land so as to better feed his family. **Because the point of fishing has changed, it's time for the point on fishing hooks to change as well.**

How can I create paragraph unity?

Make sure all sentences in the body of a paragraph support the topic sentence. If any sentences shift the focus away from the topic, revise the paragraph in one of the following ways:

- Delete the material from the paragraph.
- Rewrite the material so that it clearly supports the topic sentence.
- Create a separate paragraph out of the material.
- Revise the topic sentence so that it relates more closely to the supporting sentences.

Examine the following paragraphs about fishing hooks. The original topic sentence focuses on the idea that some anglers prefer smooth hooks instead of barbed hooks. However, the writer doesn't completely develop this idea but rather addresses the cost of new hooks. In his revised version, the writer restores unity by discussing anglers who prefer smooth hooks in the first paragraph and replacement costs in the second paragraph.

ORIGINAL (LACKS UNITY)

According to some anglers who do use smooth hooks, their lures perform better than barbed lures as long as they maintain a constant tension on the line. Smooth hooks can bite deeper than barbed hooks, actually providing a stronger hold on the fish. Some people have argued that replacing all of the barbed hooks in their tackle would be a costly operation.

REVISED VERSION (UNIFIED)

According to some anglers who do use smooth hooks, their lures perform better than barbed lures as long as they maintain a constant tension on the line. Smooth hooks can bite deeper than barbed hooks, actually providing a stronger hold on the fish. These anglers testify that switching from barbed hooks has not noticeably reduced the number of fish that they are able to land. In their experience, and in my own, enjoyment of the sport is actually heightened by adding another challenge to playing the fish (maintaining line tension).

Some people have argued that replacing all of the barbed hooks in their tackle would be a costly operation. While this is certainly a concern, barbed hooks do not necessarily require replacement. With a simple set of pliers, the barbs on most conventional hooks can be bent down, providing a cost-free method of modifying one's existing tackle. . . .

WRITING STRONG PARAGRAPHS

12b   Achieving Completeness

You will need to test each of your paragraphs to determine if it is complete. Add information as needed.

How do I know if my paragraphs are complete?

Begin by checking whether your supporting sentences contain adequate details to develop the paragraph's main idea. If support is incomplete, consider adding details like the following:

- analogies   analyses   anecdotes/comparisons
  definitions   facts   paraphrases/quotations
  statistics   summaries   examples/explanations

Also, be sure to select details that enhance the type of writing you are engaged in.

Describing: Add details that help readers see, smell, taste, touch, or hear the topic.
Narrating: Add details that help readers understand the events and actions.
Explaining: Add details that help readers understand what the topic **means, how it works, or what it does.**
Persuading: Add details that strengthen the logic of your argument.

The original paragraph below does not provide a complete answer to the question posed by the topic sentence. In the revised paragraph, the writer uses an anecdote to answer the question.

ORIGINAL (LACKS COMPLETENESS)

So what is stress? Actually, the physiological characteristics of stress are created by the body's self-defense mechanisms. People experience stress when they are in danger. In fact, stress can be healthy.

REVISED VERSION (FULL DEVELOPMENT)

So what is stress? Actually, the physiological characteristics of stress are created by the body's self-defense mechanisms. Take, for example, a man who is crossing a busy intersection when he spots an oncoming car. Immediately his brain releases a flood of adrenaline into his bloodstream. As a result, his muscles contract, his eyes dilate, his heart pounds faster, his breathing quickens, and his blood clots more readily. Each one of these responses helps the man survive this incident. His muscles contract to give him exceptional strength. His eyes dilate so that he can see more clearly. His heart pumps more blood, and his lungs exchange more air— both to increase his metabolism. If the man were injured, his blood would clot faster, ensuring a smaller amount of blood loss. In this situation and many more like it, stress symptoms are good.

12c Achieving Coherence

When a paragraph is coherent, the parts hold together. A coherent paragraph flows smoothly because each sentence is connected to the others by patterns in the language such as use of repetition and transition words.

How can I use repetition?

To achieve coherence in your paragraphs, consider using repetition—repeating words or synonyms where appropriate to remind readers of what you have already said. You can also use parallelism—repeating phrase or sentence structures to show the relationship between ideas. Both repetition and parallelism can add a unifying rhythm to your writing.

Ineffective: The floor was littered with discarded soda cans, newspapers that were crumpled, and wrinkled clothes.

Coherent: The floor was littered with discarded soda cans, crumpled newspapers, and wrinkled clothes. [Note that the three phrases are now parallel.]

Ineffective: Reading the book was enjoyable; to write the critique was difficult.

Coherent: Reading the book was enjoyable; writing the critique was difficult. [Note that the two clauses are now parallel.]

How can I use transitions?

Transitions and linking words connect ideas by showing the relationship between them. Transitions can show location or time, compare and contrast, emphasize or clarify, and conclude or summarize.

- The paradox of Scotland is that violence had long been the norm in this now-peaceful land. **In fact,** the country was born, bred, and educated in war. [The transition is used to emphasize a point.]

- The production of cement is a complicated process. **First,** the mixture of lime, silica, alumina, and gypsum is ground into very fine particles. [The transition is used to show time order.]

 WRITER'S TIP

Another way to achieve coherence in your paragraphs is to use pronouns effectively. A pronoun links the noun it replaces to the ideas that follow. Be sure that each pronoun's antecedent is clear, and avoid overusing pronouns. (See 19b–19c.)

WRITING STRONG PARAGRAPHS

TRANSITIONS AND LINKING WORDS

The words below can help you link words, phrases, sentences, and paragraphs.

Words used to SHOW LOCATION:

above	behind	down	on top of
across	below	in back of	onto
against	beneath	in front of	outside
along	beside	inside	over
among	between	into	throughout
around	beyond	near	to the right
away from	by	off	under

Words used to SHOW TIME:

about	during	next	till
after	finally	next week	today
afterward	first	second	tomorrow
as soon as	immediately	soon	until
at	later	then	when
before	meanwhile	third	yesterday

Words used to COMPARE THINGS (show similarities):

also	in the same way	likewise
as	like	similarly

Words used to CONTRAST THINGS (show differences):

although	even though	on the other hand	still
but	however	otherwise	yet

Words used to EMPHASIZE A POINT:

again	for this reason	particularly	to repeat
even	in fact	to emphasize	truly

Words used to CONCLUDE or SUMMARIZE:

all in all	finally	in summary	therefore
as a result	in conclusion	last	to sum up

Words used to ADD INFORMATION:

additionally	and	equally important	in addition
again	another	finally	likewise
along with	as well	for example	next
also	besides	for instance	second

Words used to CLARIFY:

for instance	in other words	put another way	that is

ESL TIP

Use transitions to link or expand your ideas, but be careful not to create rambling or run-on sentences. (See 13f and 26c.)

12d Arranging Your Details

Organizing information in a logical pattern within a paragraph strengthens its coherence. The following pages explain and illustrate ten organizational strategies. (See also 7b–7d.)

ANALOGY

An analogy is a comparison a writer uses to explain a complex or unfamiliar phenomenon (how the immune system works) in terms of a familiar one (how mall security works).

> The human body is like a mall, and the immune system is like mall security. Because the mall has hundreds of employees and thousands of customers, security guards must rely on photo IDs, name tags, and uniforms to decide who should be allowed to open cash registers and who should have access to the vault. In the same way, white blood cells and antibodies need to use DNA cues to recognize which cells belong in a body and which do not. Occasionally security guards make mistakes, wrestling Kookie the Klown to the ground while DVD players "walk" out of the service entrance, but these problems amount to allergic reactions or little infections. If security guards become hypervigilant, detaining every customer and employee, the situation is akin to leukemia, in which white blood cells attack healthy cells. If security guards become corrupt, letting some thieves take a "five-finger discount," the situation is akin to AIDS. Both systems—mall security and human immunity—work by correctly differentiating friend from foe.
>
> —Rob Koenig

CAUSE AND EFFECT

Cause and effect organization shows how events are linked to their results. If you start with effects, follow with specific causes; if you begin with causes, follow with specific effects. Below, the writer examines the cause of hypothermia (prolonged exposure to cold) and its many effects on the human body.

> Even a slight drop in the normal human body temperature of 98.6°F causes hypothermia. Often produced by accidental or prolonged exposure to cold, the condition forces all bodily functions to slow down. The heart rate and blood pressure decrease. Breathing becomes slower and shallower. As the body temperature drops, these effects become even more dramatic until somewhere between 86°F and 82°F the person lapses into unconsciousness. When the temperature reaches between 65°F and 59°F, heart action, blood flow, and electrical brain activity stop. Normally such a condition would be fatal. However, as the body cools down, the need for oxygen also slows down. A person can survive in a deep hypothermic state for an hour or longer and be revived without serious complications.
>
> —Laura Black

WRITING STRONG PARAGRAPHS

CHRONOLOGICAL ORDER

Chronological (time) order helps you tell a story or present steps in a process. For example, the following paragraph describes how cement is made. Notice how the writer explains every step and uses transitional words to lead readers through the process.

> The production of cement is a complicated process in itself. The raw materials that go into cement consist of about 60 percent lime, 25 percent silica, and 5 percent alumina. The remaining 10 percent is a varying mixture of gypsum and iron oxide, because the amount of gypsum determines the drying time of the cement. First, this mixture is ground up into very fine particles and fed into a kiln. Cement kilns, the largest pieces of moving machinery used by any industry, are colossal steel cylinders lined with fire-bricks. They can be 25 feet in diameter and up to 750 feet long. The kiln is built at a slant and turns slowly as the cement mix makes its way down from the top end. A flame at the bottom heats the kiln to temperatures of up to 3,000 degrees Fahrenheit. When the melted cement compound emerges from the kiln, it cools into little marble-like balls called clinker. Finally, the clinker is ground to a consistency finer than flour and packaged as cement.
>
> —Kevin Maas

CLASSIFICATION

When classifying a subject, place the subject in its appropriate category, and then show how this subject is different from other subjects in this category. In the following paragraph, a student writer uses classification to describe the theory of temperament.

> Medieval doctors believed that "four temperaments rule mankind wholly." According to this theory, each person has a distinctive temperament or personality (sanguine, phlegmatic, melancholy, or choleric) based on the balance of four elements in the body, a balance peculiar to the individual. The theory was built on Galen's and Hippocrates' notion of "humors," that the body contains blood, phlegm, black bile, and yellow bile—four fluids that maintain the balance within the body. The sanguine person was dominated by blood, associated with fire: Blood was hot and moist, and the person was fat and prone to laughter. The phlegmatic person was dominated by phlegm (associated with earth) and was squarish and slothful—a sleepy type. The melancholy person was dominated by cold, black bile (connected with the element of water) and as a result was pensive, peevish, and solitary. The choleric person was dominated by hot, yellow bile (air) and thus was inclined to anger.
>
> —Jessica Radsma

COMPARISON AND CONTRAST

In the paragraphs below, student writer Kevin Jones both compares and contrasts Lord Tennyson's versions of the literary characters Ulysses and Arthur.

In Alfred, Lord Tennyson's "Ulysses" and *Idylls of the King,* the title heroes, Ulysses and Arthur, are great men plagued with problems that all men face. Both heroes are disappointed in people. In Ithaca, the Greek hero of the Trojan War rules a "savage race" of people who do not know him and do not appreciate him; in Britain, Arthur must engage in battle with knights who once loved him. Furthermore, both Ulysses and Arthur must recognize that their sons do not share their ideals. Telemachus is not a hero; he is "centered in the sphere of common duties." Arthur's illegitimate son, Modred, lacks morals and leads a rebellion against him. Finally, both Ulysses and Arthur face death. The aged Ulysses recognizes that his life is almost over, and in winter, King Arthur is mortally wounded in battle. Clearly, both legendary heroes struggle with universal problems.

Nevertheless, these legendary heroes have distinctly different personalities. Tennyson portrays Ulysses as a self-centered man, while Arthur is a model ruler. Ulysses leaves his subjects in Ithaca before order is fully restored because he finds life too dull there and wants to do some "work of noble note"—possibly to increase his fame. Arthur, on the other hand, loves his people, struggles against evil, and dies trying to restore the glory of the past. In addition, Ulysses draws no emotional response, while Arthur is both hated and loved. Although Ulysses was absent for ten years after the Trojan War, his wife and son are lukewarm toward him and do not beg him to stay at home. Modred, on the other hand, wickedly plots against the virtuous English king. Sir Bedivere weeps as he carries Arthur out of the church, and the three queens receive the dying king with tears. Finally, the gods seem unimportant to Tennyson's Ulysses, while Arthur is religious. Although Ulysses briefly mentions striving with gods in the past, they do not appear to play a role in his daily life. Arthur, however, is a devout Christian who tries to do the will of God and believes in the power of prayer. It seems fair to conclude that, even though Tennyson's Ulysses and Arthur are similar on the surface, a closer look reveals significant differences.

—Kevin Jones

WRITER'S TIP

Use a Venn diagram to structure comparisons and contrasts. List similarities in the shared space (3) and differences in the circles (1 and 2). (See **7d**.)

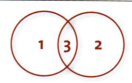

WRITING STRONG PARAGRAPHS

CLIMAX

Climax is a method in which you first present details, and then provide a general climactic statement or conclusion drawn from the details.

> The cockroach is unhonored and unsung. It walks about with downcast eyes. Its head hangs dejectedly between its knees. It lives on modest fare and in humble circumstances. It is drab-colored and inconspicuous. But don't let that Uriah Heep exterior fool you. For there you have Superbug, himself!
>
> —Edwin Way Teale, *The Lost Woods*

DEFINITION

In the paragraph below, the writer begins his definition by posing a question.

> First of all, what is the grotesque—in visual art and in literature? A term originally applied to Roman cave art that distorted the normal, the grotesque presents the body and mind so that they appear abnormal—different from the bodies and minds that we think belong in our world. Both spiritual and physical, bizarre and familiar, ugly and alluring, the grotesque shocks us, and we respond with laughter and fear. We laugh because the grotesque seems bizarre enough to belong only outside our world; we fear because it feels familiar enough to be part of it. Seeing the grotesque version of life as it is portrayed in art stretches our vision of reality. As Bernard McElroy argues, "The grotesque transforms the world from what we 'know' it to be to what we fear it might be. It distorts and exaggerates the surface of reality in order to tell a qualitative truth about it."
>
> —John Van Rys

ILLUSTRATION

An illustration supports a general idea with specific reasons, examples, facts, and details.

> As the years passed, my obsession grew. Every fiber and cell of my body was obsessed with the number on the scale and how much fat I could pinch on my thigh. No matter how thin I was, I thought I could never be thin enough. I fought my sisters for control of the TV and VCR to do my exercise programs and videos. The cupboards were stacked with cans of diet mixes, the refrigerator full of diet drinks. Hidden in my underwear drawer were stacks of diet pills that I popped along with my vitamins. At my worst, I would quietly excuse myself from family activities to turn on the bathroom faucet full blast and vomit into the toilet. Every day I stood in front of the mirror, a ritual not unlike brushing my teeth, and scrutinized my body. My face, arms, stomach, buttocks, hips, and thighs could never be small enough.
>
> —Paula Treick

NARRATION

In the paragraph below, the writer uses narration and chronological order to relate an anecdote—a short, illustrative story.

> When I was six or seven years old, growing up in Pittsburgh, I used to take a precious penny of my own and hide it for someone else to find. It was a curious compulsion; sadly, I've never been seized by it since. For some reason I always "hid" the penny along the same stretch of sidewalk up the street. I would cradle it at the roots of a sycamore, say, or in a hole left by a chipped-off piece of sidewalk. Then I would take a piece of chalk, and, starting at either end of the block, draw huge arrows leading up to the penny from both directions. After I learned to write I labeled the arrows: surprise ahead or money this way. I was greatly excited, during all this arrow-drawing, at the thought of the first lucky passer-by who would receive in this way, regardless of merit, a free gift from the universe. But I never lurked about. I would go straight home and not give the matter another thought, until, some months later, I would be gripped again by the impulse to hide another penny.

—Annie Dillard, *Pilgrim at Tinker Creek*

PROCESS

In the paragraph that follows, a student writer describes the process of entering the "tube" or "green room" while surfing.

> At this point you are slightly ahead of the barreling part of the wave, and you need to "stall," or slow yourself, to get into the tube. There are three methods of stalling used in different situations. If you are slightly ahead of the tube, you can drag your inside hand along the water to stall. If you are a couple of feet in front of the barrel, you can apply all your weight onto your back foot and sink the tail of the board into the water. This is known as a "tail stall" for obvious reasons, and its purpose is to decrease your board speed. If you are moving faster than the wave is breaking, you need to do what is called a "wrap-around." To accomplish this maneuver, lean back away from the wave while applying pressure on the tail. This shifts your forward momentum away from the wave and slows you down. When the wave comes, turn toward the wave and place yourself in the barrel.

—Luke Sunukjian,
"Entering the Green Room"

12e Checklist: Paragraphs

Use the traits to check the quality of your paragraphs and revise as needed.

_____ The **ideas** are engaging. The paragraph focuses on one main or control-ling thought, usually stated in a topic sentence. Supporting sentences address concepts closely related to that thought.

_____ The **organization** is clear with an effective opening, middle, and closing. Organizational patterns (such as cause and effect, compare and contrast) fit the subject and develop the main idea.

_____ The **voice** is informed and engaging, matching the voice of other paragraphs in the piece.

_____ The **words** used include strong verbs, precise nouns, and informative details that complete the paragraph's main idea.

_____ The **sentences** are clear, vary in structure, and read smoothly. Transitions link words, phrases, and sentences, thereby enhancing the paragraph's cohesiveness.

_____ The **copy** includes no errors in spelling, punctuation, mechanics, and grammar.

_____ The **page design** is appropriately formatted (essay, letter, and so on).

WAC Link: While writers in all disciplines use paragraphs to shape their messages in comprehensible units of thought, the manner of constructing paragraphs may vary between disci-plines, or between forms of writing within a discipline. For example, writers in the sciences regularly use topic sentences to introduce paragraphs and concluding sentences to close paragraphs. Writers in the humanities follow the same practice, but not as consistently. In addition, writers in the sciences use more numbered and bulleted lists than their colleagues in the humanities use.

Workplace Link: Like their academic counterparts, writers in the workplace shape their messages into tidy paragraphs. In fact, workplace forms such as position papers and periodic reports commonly contain paragraphs that are as fully developed and traditionally formatted as paragraphs in this book's model essays.

On the other hand, many workplace writers use different paragraphing strategies. For example, journalists regularly write short paragraphs that address specific facets of a topic rather than longer paragraphs that address the entire topic. In addition, most workplace forms regularly include bul-leted lists, numbered paragraphs, and sentences written in an abbreviated, telegraphic style. Workplace writers choose these strategies to make the reading process as quick and easy as possible.

CHAPTER 13

Writing Effective Sentences

Editor Roscoe Born describes a good sentence as a "rifle shot—one missile, precisely aimed—rather than a buckshot load sprayed in the general direction of the target." With this metaphor, Born correctly suggests that effective—or stylistically pleasing—sentences have the following characteristics.

- They are clear, direct, and to the point.
- They have the right sound, balance, and substance.
- They move smoothly from one point to the next.

This chapter will help you write "precisely aimed rifle shots." Specifically, you will learn how to combine, expand, and energize sentences; use parallel structure; divide rambling sentences; and vary sentence kinds and types. Finally, the end-of-chapter checklist will help you assess how well your sentences hit their targets.

For additional help with sentence writing, see the following sections:

- "Agreement Errors" for subject-verb agreement (**25a**); pronoun-antecedent agreement (**25h**); shifts in construction (**26d**); fragments, comma splices, and run-ons (**26a–26c**); misplaced and dangling modifiers (**26f**); ambiguous wording (**26g**)
- "Sentences" for identifying basic sentence parts (**22a–22h**)
- "Punctuation and Mechanics" (**27–32**)
- "Multilingual and ESL Guidelines" for English-language learners (**33–36**)
- The book's CD and website for sentence-writing exercises

What's Ahead

13a Combining Sentences
13b Expanding Sentences
13c Using Active and Passive Voice
13d Using Strong, Effective Constructions
13e Using Parallel Structure
13f Dividing Rambling Sentences
13g Varying Sentence Structure
13h Checklist: Sentences

WRITING EFFECTIVE SENTENCES

13a Combining Sentences

Combine short, choppy sentences to form more complete, sophisticated sentences by using sentence structures that best fit your purpose and readers. For example, read the five short sentences below, and then study the combined sentences that follow. Notice how each of the seven sentences is shaped with a different combining strategy that creates a slightly different emphasis, rhythm, or meaning.

1. The longest and largest construction project in history was the Great Wall of China.

2. The project took 1,700 years to complete.

3. The Great Wall of China is 1,400 miles long.

4. It is between 18 and 30 feet high.

5. It is up to 32 feet thick.

How can I combine sentences?

1. **Use a series** to combine three or more similar ideas.

   The Great Wall of China *is 1,400 miles long, between 18 and 30 feet high, and up to 32 feet thick.*

2. **Use a relative pronoun** (*who, whose, that, which*) to introduce subordinate (less important) ideas.

   The Great Wall of China, *which is 1,400 miles long and between 18 and 30 feet high,* took 1,700 years to complete.

3. **Use an introductory phrase or clause.**

   Having taken 1,700 years to complete, the Great Wall of China was the longest construction project in history.

4. **Use a semicolon (and a conjunctive adverb).**

   The Great Wall took 1,700 years to complete; *however,* it is 1,400 miles long and up to 30 feet high and 32 feet thick!

5. **Repeat a key word or phrase** to emphasize an idea.

   The Great Wall of China was the longest construction project in history, *a project* that took 1,700 years to complete.

6. **Use correlative conjunctions** (*either, or; not only, but also*) to compare or contrast two ideas in a sentence.

   The Great Wall of China is *not only* 30 feet high and 32 feet thick in places, *but also* 1,400 miles long.

7. **Use an appositive** (a phrase that renames) to emphasize an idea.

   The Great Wall of China—*the largest construction project in history*—is 1,400 miles long, and up to 32 feet thick and 30 feet high.

13b **Expanding Sentences**

If a sentence seems weak or incomplete, you can improve the sentence by expanding it with details. Consider the following simple sentence:

- Tony was laughing.

This sentence provides little detail or nuance. It tells *who* (Tony) was doing *what* (laughing), but it does not answer any of the reader's other basic questions, such as *when, where, why,* or *how.* This flat sentence can be expanded by adding details.

How can I use details to expand sentences?

Here are seven ways that you could answer the questions above, expanding the sentence *Tony was laughing:*

1. Add individual modifiers: *halfheartedly*
2. Add prepositional phrases: *with his hands on his face*
3. Add absolute phrases: *his head tilted to one side*
4. Add participial (*-ing* or *-ed*) phrases: *looking puzzled*
5. Add infinitive phrases: *to hide his embarrassment*
6. Add subordinate clauses: *while his friend talked*
7. Add relative clauses: *who usually never laughs*

How can I create a cumulative sentence?

When you add details like these to a simple sentence, you improve it by creating a *cumulative sentence.* Each modifying word, phrase, or clause adds richness to the basic clause.

- With his hands on his face, Tony was laughing, halfheartedly, looking puzzled and embarrassed.

Notice how this sentence presents rich details without rambling. Also notice how each modifier changes the flow or rhythm of the sentence.

- In preparation for her Spanish exam, Martha was studying at the kitchen table, remaining completely focused, memorizing a list of vocabulary words.

Notice how each new modifier adds richness to the basic clause *Martha was studying.* Also notice that each modifying phrase is set off by a comma.

WRITER'S TIP

To expand sentences effectively, you should (1) know your grammar and punctuation rules (especially for commas), (2) practice the tightening, combining, and expanding strategies in this chapter, and (3) look for models of well-constructed sentences whenever you read.

WRITING EFFECTIVE SENTENCES

13c Using Active and Passive Voice

Most verbs can be in either the active or the passive voice. When a verb is active, the sentence's subject performs the action. When the verb is passive, the subject is acted upon.

Active: If you *can't attend* the meeting, *notify* Richard by Thursday.

Passive: If a meeting *can't be attended* by you, Richard *must be notified* by Thursday.

When should I avoid passive voice?

As a rule, avoid the passive voice. It tends to be wordy and sluggish because the verb's action is directed backward, not ahead like a straight road. In addition, passive constructions tend to be impersonal, making the person or thing doing the action disappear.

Passive: The sound system *can* now *be used* to listen in on sessions in the therapy room. Parents *can be helped* by having constructive one-on-one communication methods modeled.

Active: Parents *can* now *use* the sound system to listen in on sessions in the therapy room. Therapists *can help* parents by modeling constructive one-on-one communication methods with children.

When should I use passive voice?

The passive voice has a few important uses: (1) when you need to be tactful (for example, a bad-news letter), (2) if you wish to stress the object or person acted upon, and (3) if the actual actor is understood, unknown, or unimportant.

Active: Our engineers determined that you *bent* the bar at the midpoint.

Passive: Our engineers determined that the bar *had been bent* at the midpoint. (tactful)

Active: Congratulations! We *have approved* your scholarship for $2,500.

Passive: Congratulations! Your scholarship for $2,500 *has been approved*. (emphasis on receiver; actor understood)

ETHICS TIP

Avoid using the passive voice unethically to hide responsibility. This consideration is especially important when phrasing actions, conclusions, and recommendations. For example, if your instructor says, "Your assignments could not be graded because scheduling difficulties occurred," he might be trying to avoid responsibility; "I didn't finish grading your assignments because I ran out of time last night (and wanted to watch *Mystery* on PBS)."

13d Using Strong, Effective Constructions

Avoid constructions (like those below) that weaken your writing.

Why should I avoid nominal constructions?

The nominal construction is both sluggish and wordy. Avoid it by changing the noun form of a verb (*description* or *instructions*) to a verb (*describe* or *instruct*). At the same time, delete the weak verb that preceded the noun.

Nominal Constructions	Strong Verbs
Tim *gave a description* ...	Tim *described* ...
Lydia *provided instructions* ...	Lydia *instructed* ...

Sluggish: John *had a discussion* with the tutors regarding the incident. They *gave* him their *confirmation* that similar developments had occurred before, but that they had not *provided submissions* of their reports.

Energetic: John *discussed* the incident with the tutors. They *confirmed* that similar problems had occurred before, but that they hadn't *submitted* their reports.

Why should I avoid expletives?

Expletives like "it is" and "there is" are fillers that generally serve no purpose in most sentences. While occasional expletives can create emphasis, avoid overusing them.

Sluggish: *It is* likely that Nathan will attend the Journalism Department's Honors Banquet. *There is* a scholarship that he might win.

Energetic: Nathan will likely attend the Journalism Department's Honors Banquet and might win a scholarship.

Why should I avoid negative constructions?

Sentences constructed upon the negatives *no, not,* or *neither/nor* can be wordy and difficult to understand. It's simpler to state what *is* the case.

Negative: During my four years on the newspaper staff, I *have not been* behind in making significant contributions. My editorial skills *have* certainly *not deteriorated,* as I *have never failed* to tackle challenging assignments.

Positive: During my four years on the newspaper staff, I *have made* significant contributions. My editorial skills *have* steadily *developed* as I *have tackled* difficult assignments.

WRITING EFFECTIVE SENTENCES

13e Using Parallel Structure

Common or coordinated sentence elements should be parallel—that is, they should be written in the same grammatical forms. Parallel structures can save words, reduce redundancy, clarify relationships, and present information in the correct sequence. (See **26e**.) Follow these guidelines:

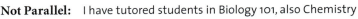

1. **To keep elements consistent** in a series, use parallel words and phrases.

Not Parallel: I have tutored students in Biology 101, also Chemistry 102, not to mention my familiarity with Physics 200.

Parallel: I have tutored students in *Biology 101, Chemistry 102,* and *Physics 200.*

Not Parallel: I have volunteered as a hospital receptionist, have been a hospice volunteer, and as an Emergency Medical Technician.

Parallel: I have done volunteer work *as a hospital receptionist, a hospice counselor,* and *an Emergency Medical Technician.*

2. **To balance a sentence,** use both parts of correlative conjunctions (*either, or; neither, nor; not only, but also; as, so; whether, or; both, and*). (See **26e**.)

Not Parallel: *Not only* did Blake College turn 20 this year, its enrollment grew by 16 percent.

Parallel: *Not only* did Blake College turn 20 this year, *but* its enrollment *also* grew by 16 percent.

3. **To stress a contrast,** place contrasting details in parallel structures (words, phrases, or clauses).

Weak Contrast: The average child watches 24 hours of television a week and reads for 36 minutes.

Strong: Each week, the average child *watches television for 24 hours but reads for only about half an hour.*

WRITER'S TIP

Parallel structure also helps you create a pleasing rhythm in your writing. Even essays and reports should strive for a certain poetry of language. Quality constructions simply convince the reader you know what you are doing.

13f Dividing Rambling Sentences

While choppy sentences dole out information in tidbits, rambling sentences pile up information in long, drawn-out explanations or descriptions.

How do I recognize rambling sentences?

Use the following tests to identify ramblers:

- Scan your writing for sentences longer than twenty words.
- Read sentences aloud, listening for those that leave you confused.
- Check sentences for an overpopulation of coordinating conjunctions (*and, but, or*), subordinating conjunctions (*although, because, since, when*), and/or relative pronouns (*who, whom, which, that*).

How do I fix rambling sentences?

Once you've identified a rambler, consider the following repair strategies and use the one that best addresses your sentence's problem.

1. **Think about your basic point.** Then state that point directly and clearly—without the twists and turns of the rambling original.

2. **Decide what your reader can comfortably comprehend.** Then do the following:
   - Divide your material into comprehensible pieces.
   - Order information by shaping it into lists or numbered steps.
   - Locate and cut say-nothing material from the sentence.

3. **Circle problem words.** Find coordinating conjunctions, subordinating conjunctions, and relative pronouns, and decide how to divide the rambling sentence.

RAMBLING SENTENCE

There's no question that tumor cells can hurt the body in a number of ways, one of which is that a tumor can grow so big that it takes up space needed by other organs, or some cells may detach from the original tumor and spread throughout the body, creating new tumors elsewhere, as does lymphatic cancer, which is so hard to control because it spreads so quickly.

RAMBLING SENTENCE FIXED

Tumor cells can hurt the body in a number of ways. First, a tumor can grow so big that it takes up space needed by other organs. Second, some cells may detach from the original tumor and spread throughout the body, creating new tumors elsewhere. This happens with lymphatic cancer—a cancer that's hard to control because it spreads so quickly.

WRITING EFFECTIVE SENTENCES

13g Varying Sentence Structure

To energize your sentences, vary their structures as shown on this page and the next one.

1. Vary sentence openings. Move a modifying word, phrase, or clause to the front of the sentence to stress that modifier. However, avoid creating dangling or misplaced modifiers. (See **26f**.)

The Norm: We apologize for the inconvenience this may have caused you.

Variation: For the inconvenience this may have caused you, we apologize.

2. Vary sentence lengths. Short sentences (ten words or fewer) are ideal for making points crisply. Medium sentences (ten to twenty words) should carry the bulk of your information. When well crafted, occasional long sentences (more than twenty words) can expand your ideas.

Short: Welcome back to Magnolia Suites!

Medium: Unfortunately, your confirmed room was unavailable last night when you arrived. For the inconvenience this may have caused you, we apologize.

Long: Because several guests did not depart as scheduled, we were forced to provide you with accommodations elsewhere; however, for your trouble, we were happy to cover the cost of last night's lodging.

3. Vary sentence kinds. The most common sentence is declarative—it states a point. For variety, try exclamatory, imperative, interrogative, and conditional sentences.

Exclamatory: Our goal is providing you with outstanding service!

Declarative: To that end, we have upgraded your room at no expense.

Imperative: Please accept, as well, this box of chocolates as a gift to sweeten your stay.

Interrogative: Do you need further assistance?

Conditional: If you do, we are ready to fulfill your requests.

WRITER'S TIP

In creative writing (stories, novels, plays), writers occasionally use fragments to vary the rhythm of their prose, to emphasize a point, or to write dialogue. Avoid fragments in academic or business writing.

4. Vary sentence arrangements. Where do you place the main point of your sentence? You can arrange sentence parts into loose, periodic, balanced, or cumulative patterns to create specific effects.

Loose Sentence: A loose sentence is direct. It states the main point immediately (italics), and then tacks on extra information.

- *The Travel Center offers an attractive flight-reservation plan for students,* one that allows you to collect bonus miles and to receive $150,000 of life insurance per flight.

Periodic Sentence: A periodic sentence postpones the main point (italics) until the end. The sentence builds to the point, creating an indirect, dramatic effect.

- Although this plan requires that you join the Travel Center's Student-Flight Club and pay the $10 admission fee, *you will save money in the long run!*

Balanced Sentence: A balanced sentence equalizes complementary or contrasting points (italics). A conjunctive adverb *(however, instead, nevertheless)* or transitional phrase *(in addition, even so)* will follow the semicolon to clarify the link.

- Joining the club in your freshman year will save you money over your entire college career; *in addition, accruing bonus miles over four years will earn you a free trip to Europe!*

Cumulative Sentence: A cumulative sentence places the main idea (italics) in the middle, surrounding it with modifying words, phrases, and clauses.

- Because the club membership is in your name, *you can retain its benefits as long as you are a student,* even if you transfer to a different college or go on to graduate school.

5. Use positive repetition. Avoid needless repetition; however, you can use repetition to repeat a key word to stress a point.

Repetitive Sentence:

- Each year, over a million young people who read poorly leave high school unable to read well, functionally illiterate.

Emphatic Sentence:

- Each year, over a million young people leave high school functionally illiterate, *so illiterate* that they can't read daily newspapers, job ads, or safety instructions.

WRITING EFFECTIVE SENTENCES

13h Checklist: Sentences

Use this checklist to evaluate and strengthen the sentences in your writing.

___ All my sentences pass the read-aloud test.

___ The sentences are clear, honest, and straightforward—like a straight road.

___ The writing includes no choppy, tired, or rambling sentences.

___ Active and passive voice are used properly.

___ Strong verbs replace nominal constructions.

___ Precise, energetic words and phrases replace expletives.

___ Sentences are positive rather than negative, focusing on *what is* instead of *what is not*.

___ Series of words or phrases within sentences are parallel.

___ Sentences vary in structure, length, and kind.

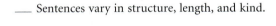

WAC Link: While you can use all of this chapter's sentence-writing strategies in all of your courses, you should apply the strategies in accordance with your document's audience, content, and purpose. For example, your writing in all disciplines should have shorter, simpler sentences if (1) your **audience** is young or struggles with English-language skills, (2) the writing **form** (webpage or lab procedure) requires short or telegraphic sentences, (3) the document's **content** is technical or otherwise dense, or (4) your **purpose** includes publishing the document in a journal whose editors prefer briefer sentences in a journalistic style.

Workplace Link: This chapter's sentence-writing strategies will be helpful in all business-writing situations; however, the manner in which you use each strategy depends on your audience, form, content, and purpose. For example, you should use parallel structure in all documents to make the writing clear, rhythmical, engaging, and grammatically correct. You should use this strategy even more often in resumés, instructions, and web writing than in other business documents that normally require more variety in sentence structure.

Service-Learning Link: If you are tutoring children or adults for a service-learning project, you could use this chapter's instructions as one of your lessons on revising writing.

Strengthening Word Choice

Speaking to budding writers, Kurt Vonnegut advises that "it is the genuine caring [about a subject], and not your games with language, which will be the most compelling and seductive element in your style." When seeking to choose the best words, your aim is *not*, then, to play games with language. Rather, you are seeking to embody ideas that you care about in fresh, clear language.

How can I improve my word choice?

In all your writing, you want to choose words that create verbal sunlight rather than verbal fog, words that connect with readers rather than alienate or confuse them. You want all the right words in all the right places. Develop these word-choice habits in your writing:

- **Be concrete.** Effective writing is specific and vivid. It helps readers see, hear, think, and feel things. Instead of general terms such as *race, administrator,* or *emotion*, strong writing contains specific words like *1500-meter run, Dean of Student Affairs,* or *pent-up anger*. Instead of offering vague generalities and abstractions, good writing uses precise terms.

- **Be energetic.** Energetic language both reflects and embodies energetic thinking. Such writing avoids jargon, clichés, and flowery phrases—all of which function as verbal short circuits that deaden your message.

- **Be appropriate.** Choose language that suits the rhetorical occasion—your readers, your purpose, and the context. Whether you're writing an academic essay, a webpage, or a personal e-mail, choose the best words by considering denotation (literal meaning), connotation (suggested meaning), formality level, and other issues.

What's Ahead

STRENGTHENING WORD CHOICE

14a Selecting Exact Words

For most writing, the best words are the strongest and simplest ones capable of communicating your meaning. These are quality words—precise and clear. By contrast, weak words are vague and imprecise. As novelist Mark Twain puts it, "The difference between the right word and the almost right word is the difference between lightning and the lightning bug."

What is exact language?

While you may sometimes need to use abstract words to convey complex ideas, you should use concrete language to flesh out more precisely what you mean. For example, check the differences between the passages below. Then study the advice on selecting exact nouns, verbs, and modifiers.

Abstract: Conditions were poor, and it was getting late.

Concrete: Six to twelve inches of mud covered the work area (including the ramps into the ditch), the ditch contained water up to the pipe's bottom, a steady rain was falling, and the work crew had only three hours of daylight left.

How do I use specific nouns?

Some nouns are general (*footwear, movement, fruit*) and give readers a vague picture. Other nouns are specific (*flip-flops, Civil Rights, mango*) and give readers a clear, detailed picture. In the example below, note how general nouns are replaced with specific terms.

General: Such equipment can clean up some of the mess, but it doesn't have the strength needed to remove all the dirt from the room, and it uses a lot of water.

Specific: The fire hose works well to wash material from the floor into the drain, but the hose lacks the high pressure needed to remove dried material from walls and equipment, and it uses a high volume of water—600 gallons per cleanup.

NOTE: Check the chart below for examples of the difference between general, specific, and precise nouns.

	PERSON	PLACE	THING	IDEA, CONCEPT
GENERAL	woman	school	book	theory
MORE SPECIFIC	actress	university	novel	scientific theory
PRECISE	Meryl Streep	Notre Dame	*Jane Eyre*	relativity

How can I choose vivid verbs?

Avoid verbs that are too general to create a vivid word picture. Use vivid verbs to make your writing clear. Verbs are the engines that drive your sentences: The stronger and more efficient your verb "engines," the more powerful and economical your sentences.

Use precise rather than general verbs. For example, *brush*, *scrub*, *sanitize*, *dissolve*, and *sweep* are all more precise and vivid than *clean*.

Bland: Clean up with the hose, the soap, and the brush.

Vivid: *Spray* the floor, *pour* soap across it, *scrub* with the brush, and *rinse* away the suds.

Use action instead of linking verbs. When your writing is dominated by linking verbs such as those derived from forms of the verb *to be*, the result is flat, listless writing. For full treatment of this issue, see the discussion of energizing sentences at **13c**.

Bland: The 140-year-old farmhouse *is* in bad shape. Its wiring *is* old, and its plumbing *is* leaky. The boiler in the basement *is* full of asbestos, and the rafters in the attic *are* full of bats.

Vivid: The 140-year-old farmhouse *needs* work. Old wires *snake* through its walls, and old pipes *rust* in its floors. Asbestos *covers* the boiler in the basement, and bats *hang* from the rafters in the attic.

Use verbs in the active voice and the passive voice appropriately. Your choice of verb voice determines the energy level of your sentences. For complete instruction on sentences in active versus passive voice, see **13c**.

How can I choose strong modifiers?

First, use specific adjectives to modify nouns: One strong adjective is better than several weak ones. Second, use adverbs only when needed to clarify the verb's action. Don't use a verb-adverb combination when one vivid verb would be better. Remember that modifiers can be adjectives, adverbs, or phrases or clauses that act as adjectives or adverbs. (See **21a–21c**.)

Weak: A tall, staggering column of rather thick yellow smoke vividly marked the exact spot where the unexpected explosion of the tanker had violently occurred.

Vivid: A column of thick yellow smoke marked the spot where the tanker exploded.

Tired Adjectives: bad, big, certain, cute, fun, funny, good, great, improved, long, neat, new, nice, old, several, short, small, various

Tired Adverbs: absolutely, basically, certainly, essentially, exceptionally, extremely, greatly, highly, hopefully, incredibly, kind of, perfectly, sort of, very

STRENGTHENING WORD CHOICE

14b Selecting Energetic and Positive Language

Tired terms such as flowery phrases, euphemisms, and clichés weaken your writing's clarity and energy. Use more forceful, direct, and energetic language.

What are connotations and denotations?

Words typically have two levels of meaning. First, words have *denotations*—their neutral dictionary definitions. Second, words have *connotations*—personal and cultural associations coloring readers' reactions. Such associations can be positive, negative, or anywhere in between, often depending on the context in which the word is used.

Word: *meek*

- **Denotation:** *easily managed or handled; expressing feelings of humility*
- **Word used in sentences:**
    - Although horses may easily spook and toss their riders, they quickly calm down if well trained—even becoming *meek* after such an episode.
    - The senator offered a *meek* response to the crowd's pressing questions about the environmental impact of the dam.
- **Possible connotations:** Notice that *meek* can have positive and negative connotations, depending on a variety of factors, from the context of the sentence to the readers' beliefs and experiences. With the first sentence, an experienced horse person might find *meek* positive. In the second sentence, a reader's political attitudes toward environmental issues might color his or her interpretation of the word *meek*.
- **Synonyms and their connotations:** Consider how the sentences above might sound different if the words *humble* or *gentle* were substituted. These synonyms, too, have their own connotations that depend on cultural context and individual attitudes.

How can I work with connotations?

1. **Choose words with connotations that fit the situation:** your writing purpose, your audience, the topic, and the form of writing. For example, the words *liberal* and *conservative* might be used with fairly neutral connotations in an academic essay on a political topic, whereas these same words might take on highly charged associations in a newspaper editorial.

2. **Avoid words with negative connotations,** especially words that show insensitivity. For example, words such as *neglect, gullible,* and *foolish* have negative connotations: They are strong but loaded words. When possible, find more neutral substitutions. (See **14e**.)

How can I avoid pretentious language?

Remember that style is not something that you add to your writing—a slick phrase here, a highbrow term there, all designed to sound impressive. Style as it relates to word choice has nothing to do with pretentious and flowery language. Instead, strengthen your style by choosing language that is simple and direct—what's sometimes called plain English.

Pretentious language aims to sound intelligent but comes off sounding phony—as if the writer is trying to sound smarter than he or she actually is. Such language can be so high-blown that meaning is obscured altogether.

> **Pretentious:** Liquid precipitation in the Iberian Peninsula's nation-state of most prominent size experiences altitudinal descent as a matter of course primarily in the region characterized by minimal topographical variation.
>
> **Plain:** The rain in Spain falls mainly on the plain.

Flowery phrases contain language that is overblown and exaggerated. As such, the wording is unnecessarily fancy and often sentimental.

> **Flowery:** The gorgeous beauty of the Great Barrier Reef is fantastically displayed in coral formations of all the colors of the rainbow and in its wondrous variety of delightful tropical fish.
>
> **Fresh:** The beauty of the Great Barrier Reef is displayed in rainbow-colored coral formations and in a wide variety of tropical fish.

Euphemisms are overly polite expressions that avoid stating uncomfortable truths. Choose neutral, tactful phrasing, but avoid euphemisms.

> **Euphemistic:** This environmentally challenged room has the distinct odor of a sanitary landfill.
>
> **Clear:** This dirty room smells like a garbage dump.

Doublespeak is phrasing that deliberately seeks to hide the truth from readers or to understate the situation. Such slippery language is especially tempting when the writer wields authority, power, or privilege in a negative situation (such as a hospital administrator writing a report). Avoid doublespeak; be clear and honest by choosing precise, transparent phrasing.

> **Doublespeak:** The doctor executed a nonfacile manipulation of the instrument.
>
> **Plain Speech:** The doctor dropped the stethoscope.

ETHICS TIP

Words can hide the truth. Whether the writer's motivations for doing so are honorable or dishonorable, plain English is generally preferable.

STRENGTHENING WORD CHOICE

How can I avoid clichés?

A **cliché** or **trite expression** is a phrase that has become tired from overuse. Whereas many clichés were once fresh metaphors or similes, through overuse they have ceased to communicate anything surprising or insightful. For example, the phrase "class clown" seems mundane, not engaging. Writing dominated by clichés conveys a lack of originality and insight, causing readers to tune out.

Clichéd: We need all hands on deck because we have a tough road ahead.

Plain: Everyone will need to work hard on the next project.

Clichéd: There's a beehive of activity under the grass.

Original: The world is a wild wrestle under the grass.   —Annie Dillard

Some Common Clichés:

- like a house on fire
  easy as pie
  as good as dead
  throw your weight around

  stick your neck out
  burn bridges
  work like a dog
  wage a lonely battle

  bitter end
  can of worms
  go for broke
  pay through the nose

WRITER'S TIP

Playing creatively with a cliché may revive its energy. For example, you might use the cliché *disposable income* when discussing the North American culture's wastefulness, including brimming landfills.

How can I use figures of speech effectively?

In any writing, a strong figure of speech can deepen an idea by connecting it to something unexpected or by relating it to something familiar. Notice in the following example how the basic idea comes to life through comparison:

Basic Idea: Our mothers were strong.

Comparison: Our mothers were headragged generals.   —Alice Walker

> **NOTE:** Choose an appropriate figure of speech. Different figures create different effects, so review your options.

Metaphors create direct comparisons between two dissimilar things by establishing an identity or equation between the two. As Gabriele Rico points out, "Metaphors create tension and excitement by producing new connections, and in doing so reveal a truth about the world we had not previously recognized."

- For the soldiers in Tim O'Brien's *The Things They Carried*, the Vietnam War is moral fog.

Similes create indirect or partial comparisons between two dissimilar things by using *like* or *as* to limit the comparison to specific qualities.

- At the beginning of "Sweetheart of the Song Trabong," Mary Anne Bell arrives fresh from America, *like a squeaky clean Barbie doll.*

Analogies clarify unfamiliar ideas or things by likening them to something that readers will find familiar.

- For the average foot soldier, called a grunt, *humping through Vietnam was like wandering aimlessly in a nightmare.*

Personification humanizes ideas, things, processes, or creatures by giving them human qualities (from appearance to emotions to thoughts).

- By the end of the story, Mary Anne Bell has been *seduced by the voice of the jungle.*

Create original comparisons. In other words, avoid clichés—tired metaphors that no longer convey original ideas. (See the previous page.) If you find yourself claiming that a problem *is a fine kettle of fish* that's taking our nation *out of the frying pan and into the fire*, it's time to give your writing *a sound thrashing*.

Make comparisons clear and consistent. Avoid confusing comparisons.

Confusing: In the final debate, Senator Jones dodged each of his opponent's accusations and scored the winning shot.

Consistent: In the final debate, Senator Jones bobbed and weaved away from each of his opponent's accusations before eventually countering with a knockout accusation of his own.

Extend comparisons effectively. Use a solid metaphor or simile to unify a paragraph, a section, or even a whole piece. Extending a comparison in this way helps you expand or clarify an idea.

- The loose ends of his family were reknitted at their July reunion. Whatever feelings had been torn apart over his older brother's divorce, whatever relations had frayed over his grandmother's lingering illness, they were mended in a day of boating, and board games played under the river oaks.

Avoid stretching your comparisons too far. Don't overdo or overuse metaphor to the point where your writing sounds forced.

Forced: He acted as if his new car were a baby, nursing it with the finest gasoline, cradling it in his garage, and constantly fawning over it.

Unforced: He babied his new car and constantly asked, "Isn't it just darling?"

14c Cutting Wordiness

Choosing the best words often means cutting unnecessary words—words that serve no real purpose. The result of such cutting is concise, fat-free writing.

How can I cut deadwood?

Deadwood is filler material—verbal "lumber" that you can remove without harming the sentence. Look for irrelevant information, obvious statements, and awkward phrases.

Deadwood: The company *must undergo a thorough retooling process if it is to be competitive in the fast-paced world of today's* global marketplace.

Concise: The company must change to meet global challenges.

How can I cut redundancy?

Redundancy is unnecessary repetition. Check your sentences for words and phrases that say the same thing.

Redundant: Avoid the construction site, and *be sure to pick a different route* if you want to avoid riding over nails and *risking a flat tire.*

Concise: If you want to avoid a flat tire, don't drive through the construction site.

Check your writing for these common redundancies:

___ Using *together* with verbs such as *combine, join, unite,* and *merge.*

___ Using *new* before *beginner, discovery, fad,* and *innovation.*

___ Using *up* after *connect, divide, eat, lift,* and *mix.*

___ Using *in color* with a color (*green in color*).

___ Using *in shape* with a shape (*round in shape*).

___ Other redundant phrases:

- plan ahead   visible to the eye   small in size
  descend down   resume again   brief in duration
  end result   very unique   repeat again

WRITER'S TIP

Not all repetition is bad. For example, great speeches such as Lincoln's address at Gettysbury and Martin Luther King, Jr.'s, "I Have a Dream" speech made excellent use of repetition. For a look at repetition used for rhythm, balance, and emphasis, check **12c** and **13e**.

How can I cut unnecessary modifiers?

Make sure your modifiers, whether adjectives or adverbs, clarify and specify nouns and verbs. (See **14a** for more on modifiers.) Remove modifiers that make your writing as thick as fudge. Trim back modifiers with these principles:

- Don't use two modifiers when one will do.
- Use precise nouns and verbs to avoid the need for modifiers.
- Generally avoid intensifying adverbs (*very, extremely, intensely, awfully, especially*).
- Delete meaningless modifiers (*kind of, sort of*).

Wordy: To ensure *very healthy, properly growing* trees, whether *deciduous* or *coniferous,* hire a *licensed, professional* tree surgeon.

Concise: To ensure healthy trees, hire a professional tree surgeon.

What phrases and clauses should I edit?

Trim phrases and clauses that pad sentences. (For more discussion on using phrases and clauses, see **23a–24d**.) To get the padding out of your writing, follow these guidelines:

Substitute long phrases and clauses with words. Locate prepositional phrases (*at the beginning of the project*) and relative clauses (*who, which, that* clauses) and replace them whenever possible with simpler words.

Wordy: *At the present time,* we are *proceeding as efficiently as is humanly possible* to modify the boxes, *which are the serial link boxes that you construct for American Linc,* by removing and replacing the *regulators that are faulty.*

Concise: We are currently modifying American Linc's serial link boxes by removing and replacing the faulty regulators.

Avoid wordy phrases with filler nouns such as *case, fact, manner,* and *nature.*

Replace . . .	*With . . .*
in many cases	often
aware of the fact that	aware that
in a rapid manner	rapidly
of a dangerous nature	dangerous

Workplace Link: Concise writing is highly valued in the workplace, especially on the web. Whether it's a simple e-mail message or a 100-page proposal, get to the point without a lot of talky, verbal interference. Develop a concise style that fits with your future profession.

14d Developing an Academic Style

Most college writing requires an academic style. Such a style isn't stuffy; you're not trying to impress your readers with ten-dollar words. Rather, you are using language that facilitates a thoughtful, engaged discussion of the topic. To choose the best words for such a conversation, consider the following issues.

Can I use personal pronouns in academic writing?

In some academic writing, such as reading responses, personal pronouns are acceptable. Generally, however, avoid using *I, we,* and *you* in your academic writing. Instead, focus on the topic itself and let your attitude be revealed indirectly. As E. B. White puts it, "To achieve style, begin by affecting none—that is, begin by placing yourself in the background."

No: I really think that the problem of the homeless in Chicago is serious, given the number of people who are dying, as I know from my experience where I grew up.

Yes: Homelessness in Chicago often leads to death. This fact demands the attention of more than lawmakers and social workers; all citizens must address the problems of their suffering neighbors.

WRITER'S TIP

Use the pronoun *one* carefully in academic prose. When it means "a person," *one* can lead to a stilted style if overused. In addition, the pronoun *their* should not be used with *one*.

What are technical terms and jargon?

Technical terms and jargon—"insider" words—are the specialized vocabulary of a subject, a discipline, a profession, or a social group. As such, jargon can be difficult to read for "outsiders." Follow these guidelines:

- Use technical terms to communicate with people within a profession or discipline, as a kind of shorthand. But be careful that such jargon doesn't devolve into meaningless buzzwords and catchphrases.
- Avoid jargon when writing for readers outside the profession. Use simpler terms and define technical terms that must be used.

Technical: Bin's Douser power washer delivers 2,200 psi p.r., runs off standard a.c. lines, comes with 100 ft. h.d. synthetic-rubber tubing, and features variable pulsation options through 3 adjustable s.s. tips.

Simple: Bin's Douser power washer has a pressure rating of 2,200 psi (pounds per square inch), runs off a common 200-volt electrical circuit, comes with 100 feet of hose, and includes three nozzles.

Developing an Academic Style

What level of formality should I use?

Most academic writing (especially research papers, literary analyses, lab reports, and argumentative essays) should meet the standards of formal English. **Formal English** is characterized by a serious tone; careful attention to word choice; longer, more complex sentences reflecting complex thinking; strict adherence to the traditional conventions of grammar, mechanics, and punctuation; and avoidance of contractions.

- Formal English, modeled in this sentence, is worded correctly and carefully so that it can withstand repeated readings without seeming tiresome, sloppy, or cute.

You may write other papers (personal essays, commentaries, journals, and reviews) in which informal English is appropriate. **Informal English** is characterized by a personal tone, the occasional use of popular expressions, shorter sentences with slightly looser syntax, contractions, and personal references (*I, we, you*), but it still adheres to basic conventions.

- Informal English sounds like one person talking to another person (in a somewhat relaxed setting). It's the type of language you are reading now. It sounds comfortable and real, not too jazzy or breezy.

ESL TIP

In academic writing, generally avoid using **slang**—words considered nonstandard English because they are faddish, familiar to a few people, and sometimes insulting.

What qualifiers should I avoid?

Using qualifiers (such as *mostly, often, likely, tends to*) is an appropriate strategy for developing defendable claims in argumentative writing. (See **4e**.) However, when you "overqualify" your ideas or when you add intensifiers (for example, *really, truly*), the result is insecurity—the impression that you lack confidence in your ideas. The cure? Say what you mean, and mean what you say.

Insecure: I totally and completely agree with the new security measures at sporting events, but that's only my opinion.

Secure: I agree with the new security measures at sporting events.

WAC Link: Each academic discipline has its own vocabulary and its own vocabulary resources. Such resources might be called dictionaries, glossaries, or handbooks. Check your library for the vocabulary resources in your discipline. Then use them regularly to deepen your grasp of that vocabulary.

STRENGTHENING WORD CHOICE

14e Using Fair, Respectful Language

In all your writing, you want to show respect. At heart, respect amounts to being consistently polite, treating others as you would be treated, and seeing yourself as the person about or to whom you are writing. Respect means paying attention to *what* you say, *how* you say it, and what you leave *unsaid*.

How can I show respect for ethnicity and race?

Don't use words that reflect negatively on an ethnic or racial group. Avoid clichés, stereotypes, and extraneous references to cultural characteristics. Your words should show familiarity with and respect for all people and cultures.

1. **Use acceptable general and specific terms.** Follow the practices below to respect racial and ethnic diversity:

   - For citizens of African descent, use *African American* or *black*. The first term is widely accepted, but some people prefer the second.
   - To avoid the notion that *American* by itself means *white*, use *Anglo-American* (for English ancestry) or *European Americans*. More specific terms would be *Irish Americans* or *Ukrainian Americans*.
   - Avoid using the term *Orientals*. Instead, use *Asian*, and when appropriate, *Asian Americans*, and the specific terms *Japanese Americans* and *Chinese Americans*.
   - As a general term, use *Hispanic Americans* or *Hispanics*. For specific terms, use *Mexican Americans*, *Cuban Americans*, and so forth.
   - As a general term, use *Native Indians* or *Native Americans*. Some native peoples prefer to be called by their tribal name: *Cherokee people, Inuit.*

2. **Avoid dated or insulting terms.** Replace negative terms.

Instead of . . .	*Use . . .*
Eurasian or mulatto	person of mixed ancestry
nonwhite	people of color
Caucasian	white

3. **Use the term *American* carefully.** When writing to other U.S. citizens, the terms *America* and *American* are acceptable. However, anyone living in North or South America is an American! Therefore, when communicating with people from outside the United States, use *United States* and *U.S. citizen* in place of *America* and *American*, respectively.

ETHICS TIP

Unless necessary to your discussion, avoid identifying a person's sex, age, race, religion, sexual orientation, ethnicity, or disability. Treat people as individuals, not as representatives of a group.

How can I show respect for disabilities and impairments?

The first rule when writing to or about people with disabilities or impairments is to refer to a condition only if it's relevant to the message. (For example, if you are writing a paper on attention deficit disorder, you can say an interviewee has this learning disorder.) In addition, follow these guidelines:

1. **Put people first.** Avoid referring to people as if they *are* their condition rather than people who simply *have* that condition.

Not Recommended	*Preferred*
the disabled	people with disabilities
dyslexics	students with dyslexia
quadriplegics	people who are quadriplegic

2. **Avoid negative labels.** First, avoid obviously degrading labels such as *crippled*, *deformed,* and *invalid.* Second, avoid using terms with negative connotations that label people as *victims of, suffering from,* or *confined to.*

Not Recommended	*Preferred*
handicapped	disabled
stutter, stammer, lisp	speech impairment
an AIDS victim	a person with AIDS

How can I show respect for age?

Respect people of all ages by using acceptable, neutral terms while avoiding terms with negative connotations.

1. **Use the following terms for general age groups:**

up to age 13 or 14	boys, girls, children
between 13 and 19	youth, young people
late teens and early 20s	young adults, young women, young men
20s to 60s	adults, men, women
65 and older	seniors, senior citizens

2. **Avoid age-related terms that carry negative connotations.** For example, avoid terms such as *kids, juveniles, yuppies, old man,* or *old woman.*

Poor: AARP (American Association of Retired Persons) members are silver-haired citizens interested in old folks' health issues.

Better: AARP (American Association of Retired Persons) members are concerned about the health and financial issues that seniors face.

STRENGTHENING WORD CHOICE

How can I show respect for gender?

Avoid sexist language, which stereotypes both males and females or slants your discussion toward one gender. The guidelines below will help you.

1. **Take care with occupations.** Some words imply that an occupation is restricted to one sex. Use the preferred forms listed below. In addition, avoid using *man, woman, male,* or *female* as adjectives modifying occupations (male nurse, woman doctor, female minister).

Not Recommended	*Preferred*
salesman	sales representative, salesperson
mailman	mail carrier, postal worker, letter carrier
fireman	firefighter
businessman	executive, manager, businessperson
congressman	member of Congress, representative
steward/stewardess	flight attendant
policeman/policewoman	police officer
chairman	chair, chairperson, moderator
clergyman	pastor, minister

2. **Use parallel language for both sexes.** Avoid phrasing that implies inequality. Look especially for subtle differences in the way you treat men and women—attention to appearance, work attitudes, and so on.

   Poor: Percy Bysshe Shelley and his authoress wife, Mary, are one example of a literary couple. Mrs. Shelley drew much of her inspiration for *Frankenstein* from John Milton's *Paradise Lost.*

   Better: Poet Percy Shelley and novelist Mary Shelley are one example of a literary couple. Mary Shelley drew much of her inspiration for *Frankenstein* from John Milton's *Paradise Lost.*

3. **Use neutral terms rather than gendered ones.** When a term implies that only one gender is included, use a more inclusive term.

Not Recommended	*Preferred*
man/men	person/people
mankind	humanity
man-made	synthetic
manpower	human resources, workforce, personnel
craftsman	artisan
housewife	homemaker

ETHICS TIP

Politically-correct writing is more about creating equal opportunity through words than avoiding or muting offensive terms.

4. Avoid masculine-only pronouns when referring to people in general. While this practice was once considered acceptable, such pronoun use now seems restrictive and demeaning. Consider this problem sentence and possible solutions.

- A good **administrator** seeks input from all people affected before **he** implements a change.

5. Make the pronouns and their antecedents plural. Change verbs as needed, and check that pronoun references remain clear.

- Before good **administrators** implement changes, **they** seek input from all people affected.

6. Use _he_ or _she_ with care. Avoid overuse: "When he or she does the laundry, he or she must separate his or her clothes."

- A good administrator seeks input from all people affected before **he** or **she** implements a change.

7. Rewrite the sentence to address the reader directly.

- To be a good administrator, **you** should seek input from all people affected before **you** implement a change.

8. Rewrite the sentence to eliminate pronouns.

- A good administrator seeks input from all people affected before implementing a change.

LINKS

Workplace Link: Using fair, respectful language is crucial in the workplace for practical, ethical, and legal reasons. Negative words may destroy your readers' trust and even lead to legal action. Avoid potentially libelous words— ones like _cheat_ and _liar_—that recklessly attack someone's character or behavior.

Poor: While your past service may have been adequate, this Snorkel Lift fiasco just goes to show that Industrial Aggregate Equipment and project supervisor Nick Luther, in particular, are incompetent, unreliable, and, yes, even dishonest.

Better: In the past, we have appreciated your service and assistance. However, we can only conclude from the problems with the Snorkel Lift rebuild that your level of service has seriously declined.

14f Using Word Tools: Dictionaries and Thesauruses

Dictionary entries, whether from print or electronic resources, offer a wealth of word-related information valuable for your writing. Each entry typically includes its pronunciation, part of speech, and etymology (history), in addition to its meanings.

A **thesaurus** is, in a sense, the opposite of a dictionary. You go to a dictionary when you know the word but need the meaning or related information. You go to a thesaurus when you know the definition of a word but want a similar word (a synonym) or an opposite word (an antonym).

Synonyms are words that are *similar* in meaning but have subtle shades of difference. Therefore, choose the best word by considering these factors:

- Which word seems to fit the best given the context of your sentence?
- What are the connotations (**14b**) of the various words?
- What are the fine distinctions in meaning and emphasis between the words?
- What level of diction is appropriate for your piece of writing?

ESL TIP

Idioms are special or set expressions that cannot be understood simply by reading a separate definition for each word. Rather, the combination of words creates the meaning. Idioms are treated at length on **36a**.

14g Checklist: Word Choice

___ The phrasing is exact and fresh—containing precise nouns, vivid verbs, and strong modifiers.

___ Flowery language, euphemisms, and clichés have been replaced with plain English.

___ Effective comparisons liven the writing—without stretching or confusing the ideas.

___ Phrasing is concise—containing no deadwood, redundancies, multiple modifiers, or phrases and clauses that pad the writing.

___ In academic writing
  - the personal pronouns *I, we,* and *you* are avoided.
  - technical terms and jargon are restricted according to readership.
  - the diction chosen is formal (standard English, no contractions).
  - qualifying words are restricted to keep the tone confident.

___ The wording shows respect for disabilities, race, ethnicity, gender, and age.

___ The wording avoids doublespeak and negative characterizations.

A Glossary of Word Usage

As writers, we sometimes confuse or misuse words—perhaps choosing the wrong one in a pair that sounds similar, or using a colloquial or slang term (something "nonstandard") in an academic, professional, or workplace situation. This chapter addresses such word-usage challenges. Entries are arranged alphabetically, with appropriate cross-referencing.

accept, except The verb *accept* means "to receive or believe"; the preposition *except* means "other than."

> The instructor **accepted** the student's story about being late, but she wondered why no one **except** him had forgotten about the change to daylight saving time.

adapt, adopt, adept *Adapt* means "to adjust or change to fit"; *adopt* means "to choose and treat as your own" (a child, an idea). *Adept* is an adjective meaning "proficient or well trained."

> After much thought and deliberation, we agreed to **adopt** the black Lab from the shelter. Now we have to agree on how to **adapt** our lifestyle to fit our new roommate.

adverse, averse *Adverse* means "hostile, unfavorable, or harmful." *Averse* means "to have a definite feeling of distaste—disinclined."

> Groans and other **adverse** reactions were noted as the new students, **averse** to strenuous exercise, were ushered past the X-5000 pump-and-crunch machine.

advice, advise *Advice* is a noun meaning "information or recommendation"; *advise* is a verb meaning "to recommend."

> Parents will often give you sound **advice**, so I **advise** you to listen.

affect (See *effect*.)

aid, aide As a verb, *aid* means "to help"; as a noun, *aid* means "the help given." An *aide* is a person who acts as an assistant.

all ready, already *Already* is an adverb meaning "before this time" or "by this time." *All ready* is an adjective form meaning "fully prepared." Use *all ready* if you can substitute *ready* alone in the sentence.

> By the time I was a junior in high school, I had **already** taken my SATs.
> That way, I was **all ready** to apply early to college.

A GLOSSARY OF WORD USAGE

all right, alright *Alright* is the incorrect form of *all right*. However, the following are spelled correctly: *always, altogether, already, almost.*

allude, elude *Allude* means "to indirectly refer to or hint at something"; *elude* means "to escape attention or understanding altogether."

> Ravi often **alluded** to wanting a supper invitation. These hints never **eluded** Ma's good heart.

allusion, illusion *Allusion* is an indirect reference to something or someone, especially in literature; *illusion* is a false picture or idea.

> Did you recognize the **allusion** to David in the reading assignment?
> Until I read that part, I was under the **illusion** that the young boy would run away from the bully.

a lot, allot (See **36b**.)

altogether, all together *Altogether* means "entirely." *All together* means "in a group" or "all at once." Use *all together* if you can substitute *together* alone.

> **All together** there are 35,000 job titles to choose from. That's **altogether** too many to even think about.

among, between (See *between*.)

amoral, immoral *Amoral* means "neither moral (right) nor immoral (wrong)"; *immoral* means "wrong, or in conflict with traditional values."

> Carnivores are **amoral** in their hunt; poachers are **immoral** in theirs.

amount, number *Amount* is used for bulk measurement. *Number* is used to count separate units. (See also *fewer.*)

> The can could hold only a certain **amount**, so a **number** of pens lay on the desk.

and/or Generally avoid using *and/or*, except in legal or technical writing, where *and/or* shows that one or both of the terms apply.

> According to their insurance, Jack **and/or** Jill may seek emergency care for injuries sustained while rolling down the hill.

annual, biannual, semiannual, biennial, perennial An *annual* event happens once every year. A *biannual* event happens twice a year (*semiannual* is the same as *biannual*). A *biennial* event happens every two years. A *perennial* event happens throughout the year, every year.

anxious, eager Both words mean "looking forward to," but *anxious* also connotes fear or concern.

> The professor is **eager** to move into the new building, but she's a little **anxious** that students won't be able to find her new office.

anymore, any more *Anymore* means "any longer"; *any more* means "any additional."

> We won't use that textbook **anymore**; please call if you have **any more** questions.

any one (of), anyone; any body, anybody *Any one* means "any one of a number of people, places, or things"; in *any body, any* is an adjective modifying the noun *body. Anyone* and *anybody* are pronouns meaning "any person."

> Choose **any one** of the proposed weekend schedules. **Anyone** wishing to work on Saturday instead of Sunday may do so. **Anybody** may switch shifts—**any** warm **body** will do as a replacement.

anyways, anywheres (See **36b**.)

appraise, apprise *Appraise* means "to determine value." *Apprise* means "to inform."

> Because of the tax assessor's recent **appraisal** of our home, we were **apprised** of an increase in our property tax.

as Don't use *as* in place of *whether* or *if*.

> I don't know **as** I'll accept the offer. [Incorrect]
> I don't know **whether** I'll accept the offer. [Correct]

Don't use *as* when it is unclear whether it means *because* or *when*.

> We rowed toward shore **as** it started raining. [Unclear]
> We rowed toward shore **because** it started raining. [Correct]

assure, ensure, insure (See *insure*.)

awhile, a while As an adverb, *awhile*, meaning "for some time," modifies verbs. *A while* (an article and a noun) typically functions as the object of prepositions such as *for, in,* and *after*.

> "Pull up a chair and sit **awhile**," said Fred. I did, but after **a while**, I excused myself to get back to my nightly blogging session.

backup, back up As a noun or an adjective, *backup* refers to a duplicate available in case an original is lost, damaged, or injured. *Back up* is a verb phrase that means "to go in reverse" or "to make an electronic duplicate."

> As the **backup** quarterback **backed up** his car, the **backup** playbook slipped off the dash and smashed his laptop, which was in the process of **backing up** his GPS data.

bad, badly *Bad* is an adjective, used both before nouns and after linking verbs. *Badly* is an adverb.

> Christina felt **bad** about serving us **bad** food.
> Larisa played **badly** today.

beside, besides *Beside* means "by the side of." *Besides* means "in addition to."

> **Besides** the two suitcases you've already loaded into the trunk, remember the smaller one **beside** the van.

A GLOSSARY OF WORD USAGE

between, among *Between* is used when emphasizing proximity to individuals or a position in the middle of two things; *among* is typically used when emphasizing distribution throughout a body or a group of three or more.

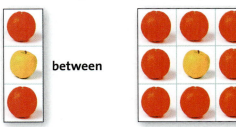

between   among

can, may In formal contexts, *can* is used to mean "being able to"; *may* is used to mean "having permission to."

> **May** I borrow your bicycle to get to the library? Then I **can** start working on our group project.

capital, capitol The noun *capital* refers to a city or to money. The adjective *capital* means "major or important" or "seat of government." *Capitol* refers to a building.

> The **capitol** is in the **capital** city for a **capital** reason. The city government contributed **capital** for the building expense.

censer, censor, censure While a *censer* (noun) is a vessel for burning incense, a *censor* (noun) is a person who reviews and then restricts access to books, movies, and so on. *Censor* (verb) means "to delete objectionable material," whereas *censure* (verb) means "to officially reprimand, criticize, or condemn."

> Fragrant smoke rose from the **censer**.
> Parents may **censor** their children's reading material.
> The city council **censured** the alderman for his unprofessional behavior.

chord, cord *Chord* may mean "an emotion or a feeling," but it also may mean "the combination of three or more tones sounded at the same time," as with a guitar *chord*. A *cord* is a string or a rope.

> The stagehand pulled the **cord** to open the curtain.
> The guitar player strummed the opening **chord**, which struck a responsive **chord** with the audience.

climactic, climatic *Climactic* refers to the climax, or high point, of an event; *climatic* refers to the climate, or weather conditions.

> Because we are using the open-air amphitheater, **climatic** conditions could be an issue by the time we get to the **climactic** third act.

coarse, course *Coarse* means "of inferior quality, rough, or crude"; *course* means "a direction or a path." *Course* also means "a class or a series of studies."

> A basic writing **course** is required of all students. Due to years of woodworking, the instructor's hands are rather **coarse**.

compare with, compare to Things in the same category are *compared with* each other; things in different categories are *compared to* each other.

> **Compare** Christopher Marlowe's plays **with** William Shakespeare's.
> My brother **compared** reading *The Tempest* **to** visiting another country.

complement, compliment *Complement* means "to complete or go well with." *Compliment* means "to offer an expression of admiration or praise."

> We wanted to **compliment** Zach on his decorating efforts;
> the bright yellow walls **complement** the purple carpet.

comprise, compose *Comprise* means "to contain or consist of"; *compose* means "to create or form by bringing parts together."

> Fruitcake **comprises** a variety of nuts, candied fruit, and spice. Fruitcake
> is **composed** of [not *comprised of*] a variety of flavorful ingredients.

conscience, conscious A *conscience* gives one the capacity to know right from wrong. *Conscious* means "awake or alert, not sleeping or comatose."

> Your **conscience** will guide you, but you have to be **conscious** to hear
> what it's "saying."

continual, continuous *Continual* often implies that something is happening often, recurring; *continuous* usually implies that something keeps happening, uninterrupted.

> The **continuous** loud music during the night gave the building manager
> not only a headache, but also **continual** phone calls.

could of, could have (must of, should of, would of) Constructions such as *could of* and *should of* are nonstandard expressions; use *could have* or *should have.*

counsel, counselor, council, councilor When used as a noun, *counsel* means "advice"; when used as a verb, *counsel* means "to advise." A *counselor* is someone who advises (a lawyer, social worker, or psychologist). *Council* refers to a group that advises. A *councilor* is a member of a council.

> The city **council** was asked to **counsel** our student **council** on running an
> efficient meeting. Their **counsel** was very helpful.

desert, dessert The noun *desert* is a barren wilderness. The verb *desert* means "to abandon." *Dessert* is food served at the end of a meal.

differ from, differ with When one thing is unlike another, they *differ from* each other; when one person *differs with* another, they disagree.

> Tony and Charlie **differ from** each other in size and personality. Therefore,
> they frequently differ with **differ with** each other when playing.

different from, different than Use *different from* in formal writing; use either form in informal or colloquial settings.

> Rafael's interpretation was **different from** Andrea's.

A GLOSSARY OF WORD USAGE

discreet, discrete *Discreet* means "showing good judgment, unobtrusive, modest"; *discrete* means "distinct, separate."

> The essay question had three **discrete** parts.
> Her roommate had apparently never heard of **discreet** conversation.

disinterested, uninterested Both words mean "not interested." However, *disinterested* is also used to mean "unbiased or impartial."

> A person chosen as an arbitrator must be a **disinterested** party.
> Ms. Eldridge was **uninterested** in our complaints about the assignment.

effect, affect *Affect* means "to influence"; the noun *effect* means "the result"; and the verb *effect* means "to bring about."

> One blow from an ax **affects** [verb] a log dramatically, splitting it in half. The final **effect** [noun] is a pile of firewood.

elicit, illicit *Elicit* is a verb meaning "to bring out." *Illicit* is an adjective meaning "unlawful."

> It took two quick hand signals from the lookout to **elicit** the **illicit** exchange of cash for drugs.

eminent, imminent *Eminent* means "famous, or prominent"; *imminent* means "ready or threatening to happen."

> With the island's government about to collapse, assassination attempts on several **eminent** officials seemed **imminent**.

ensure (See *insure*.)

eventually, ultimately While *eventually* refers to some time in the future, *ultimately* refers to an end point or a final extent.

> Robin had hoped to change the oil in her AMC Pacer **eventually**.
> Because she never got around to it, she **ultimately** had to junk the car.

except (See *accept*.)

explicit, implicit *Explicit* means "expressed directly or clearly defined"; *implicit* means "implied or unstated."

> The professor **explicitly** asked that the experiment be wrapped up on Monday, **implicitly** demanding that we work through the weekend.

farther, further *Farther* refers to a physical distance; *further* refers to additional time, quantity, or degree.

> **Further** research showed that walking **farther** improves health.

fewer, less *Fewer* refers to separate units; *less* refers to bulk quantity.

> Because of spell checkers, students can produce papers containing **fewer** errors in **less** time.

figuratively, literally • immigrate (to), emigrate (from)

figuratively, literally *Figuratively* means "in an analogous way—describing something by comparing it to something else"; *literally* means "actually."

> The lab was **literally** filled with sulfurous gases—**figuratively** speaking, dragon's breath.

first, firstly Both words are adverbs meaning "before another in time" or "in the first place." However, do not use *firstly*, which is stiff and unnatural.

> **Firstly,** I want to see the manager. [Incorrect]
> **First,** I want to see the manager. [Correct]

fiscal, physical *Fiscal* means "related to financial matters"; *physical* means "related to material things."

> The school's **fiscal** work is handled by its accounting staff.
> The **physical** work is handled by its maintenance staff.

for, fore, four *For* is a conjunction meaning "because" or a preposition used to indicate the object or recipient of something; *fore* means "earlier" or "the front"; *four* is the word for the number 4.

> The crew brought treats **for** the barge's **four** dogs, which always enjoy the breeze at the **fore** of the vessel.

former, latter When two things are being discussed, *former* refers to the first thing, and *latter* to the second.

> Our choices are going to a movie or eating at the Pizza Palace:
> The **former** is too expensive, and the **latter** too fattening.

good, well (See **36b**.)

heal, heel *Heal* means "to mend or restore to health." *Heel* as a noun is the back part of a human foot. *Heel* as a verb means "to walk at the heel."

> The doctor gave me medicine to help **heal** my injured **heel**.
> The dog trainer taught my dog to **heel**.

hopefully As an adverb, *hopefully* means "in a hopeful manner." However, when *hopefully* (often placed at the beginning of a sentence) is used to mean "I hope," this usage is considered nonstandard; use *I hope* instead.

> Ariadne began the exam **hopefully**. "I hope," she said to herself, "that work with my study group will help me ace this test!"

if, whether Use *if* in conditional clauses when no alternatives are involved; use *whether* and *whether or not* when alternatives are offered or implied.

> **If** we move to the country, we'll spend more time commuting to work.
> I guess we'll have to decide **whether** the green fields, the starry nights, and the smell of horse manure are worth it.

illusion, allusion (See *allusion*.)

immigrate (to), emigrate (from) *Immigrate* means "to arrive in a new country." *Emigrate* means "to leave one country to live in another."

A GLOSSARY OF WORD USAGE

imminent, eminent (See *eminent.*)

imply, infer *Imply* means "to suggest without saying"; *infer* means "to draw a conclusion." (A writer or a speaker implies; a reader or a listener infers.)

> Dr. Rufus **implied** I should study more; I **inferred** he meant my grades had to improve or I'd be repeating the class.

ingenious, ingenuous *Ingenious* means "intelligent, clever"; *ingenuous* means "unassuming, natural, showing childlike innocence and candidness."

> Gretchen devised an **ingenious** plan to save time and energy.
> Ramón displays an **ingenuous** quality that attracts others.

insure, ensure, assure *Insure* means "to secure from financial harm or loss"; *ensure* means "to make certain of something"; and *assure* means "to put someone's mind at rest."

> Plenty of studying generally **ensures** academic success.
> Nicole **assured** her father that she had **insured** her new car.

interstate, intrastate *Interstate* means "existing between two or more states"; *intrastate* means "existing within a state."

in, into With *in*, you indicate a location or condition; with *into*, you stress motion or a change.

> As we dragged ourselves **into** the museum to view the Van Gogh exhibit, our art instructor encouraged us to get lost **in** the colors.

its, it's (See **36b**.)

later, latter *Later* means "after a period of time." *Latter* refers to the second of two things mentioned.

> The **latter** of the two restaurants you mentioned sounds good.
> Let's meet there **later**.

lay, lie *Lay* means "to place." *Lay* is a transitive verb. (See **20a**.) Its principal parts are *lay, laid, laid.*

> If you **lay** another book on my table, It will be completely covered.
> Yesterday, you **laid** two books on the table. Over the last few days, you must **have laid** at least twenty books there.

Lie means "to recline." *Lie* is an intransitive verb. (See **20a**.) Its principal parts are *lie, lay, lain.*

> The cat **lies** anywhere it pleases. It **lay** down yesterday on my tax forms.
> It has **lain** many times on the kitchen table.

lead, led *Lead* is both a noun referring to a metal and a verb meaning "to conduct or guide." *Led* is the correct past tense of the verb.

> As Antoinette dauntlessly **led** us into the Mall of America, she proclaimed, "Get the **lead** out. I won't **lead** you astray in our quest for perfect-fitting jeans!"

learn, teach (See **36b**.)

lend, borrow *Lend* means "to give for temporary use"; *borrow* means "to receive for temporary use."

She lends.

He borrows.

> I often **borrow** money from Mom State Bank, and she **lends** it to me without checking my credit rating.

less, fewer (See *fewer.*)

liable, libel *Liable* is an adjective meaning "responsible according to the law" or "exposed to an adverse action"; the noun *libel* is a written defamatory statement about someone, and the verb *libel* means "to publish or make such a statement."

> Supermarket tabloids, **liable** for ruining many a reputation, make a practice of **libeling** the rich and the famous.

liable, likely *Liable* means "responsible according to the law" or "exposed to an adverse action"; *likely* means "in all probability."

> Rain seems **likely** today, but if we cancel the game, we are still **liable** for paying the referees.

like, as *Like* should not be used in place of *as*. *Like* is a preposition, which is followed by a noun, a pronoun, or a noun phrase. *As* is a subordinating conjunction, which introduces a clause. Avoid using *like* in place of *as*.

> You don't know her **like** I do. [Incorrect]
> You don't know her **as** I do. [Correct]
> **Like** the others in my study group, I do my work **as** any serious student would—carefully and thoroughly. [Correct]

literally, figuratively (See *figuratively.*)

loose, lose, loss The adjective *loose* (lüs) means "free, untied, unrestricted"; the verb *lose* (lüz) means "to misplace or fail to find or control"; the noun *loss* means "something that is misplaced and cannot be found or regained."

> Her sadness at the **loss** of her longtime companion caused her to **lose** weight, and her clothes felt uncomfortably **loose**.

may, can (See *can.*)

maybe, may be Use *maybe* as an adverb; use *may be* as a verb phrase.

> She **may be** the computer technician we've been looking for.
> **Maybe** she will upgrade the software and memory.

medium, media, median When *medium* refers to the means by which something is communicated, the correct plural is *media* (not *mediums*). *Mediums* can also refer to people claiming to communicate with the spirits of the dead. *Median* means "in the middle," as in a highway median.

> As Francis ambled across the **median**, he considered what **media** by which to share his amazing story. He chose a blog as the best **medium** for communication.

A GLOSSARY OF WORD USAGE

miner, minor A *miner* digs in the ground for ore. A *minor* is a person who is not legally an adult. The adjective *minor* means "of no great importance."

> The use of **minors** as coal **miners** is no **minor** problem.

moral, morale A *moral* is a lesson drawn from a story; as an adjective, it relates to the principles of right and wrong. *Morale* refers to someone's attitude.

> Ms. Ladue considers it her **moral** obligation to go to church every day.
> The students' **morale** sank after their defeat in the soccer match.

number, amount (See *amount.*)

oral, verbal *Oral* means "uttered with the mouth"; *verbal* means "relating to or consisting of words and the comprehension of words."

> The actor's **oral** abilities were outstanding, but I doubted the play-wright's **verbal** skills after trying to decipher the play's meaning.

passed, past *Passed* is a verb. *Past* can be used as a noun, an adjective, or a preposition.

> That little pickup truck **passed** my 'Vette!
> My stepchildren hold on dearly to the **past**. [noun]
> I'm sorry, but my **past** life is not your business. [adjective]
> The car drove **past** us, not noticing our flat tire. [preposition]

peace, piece *Peace* means "tranquillity or freedom from war." A *piece* is a part or fragment.

> Someone once observed that **peace** is not a condition, but a process—
> a process of building goodwill one **piece** at a time.

people, person Use *people* to refer to human populations, races, or groups; use *person* to refer to an individual or the physical body.

> What the American **people** need is a good insect repellent.
> The forest ranger recommends that we check our **persons**
> for wood ticks when we leave the woods.

percent, percentage *Percent* means "per hundred"; for example, 60 percent of 100 jelly beans would be 60 jelly beans. *Percentage* refers to a portion of the whole. Generally, use the word *percent* after a number. Use *percentage* when no number is used.

> Each person's **percentage** of the reward amounted to $125—25 **percent**
> of the $500 offered by Crime Stoppers.

personal, personnel *Personal* means "private." *Personnel* are people working at a particular job.

> Although choosing a major is a **personal** decision, it can be helpful
> to consult with guidance **personnel**.

perspective, prospective *Perspective* is a person's point of view; *prospective* is an adjective meaning "expected in or related to the future."

> From my immigrant neighbor's **perspective**, any job is a good job.
> **Prospective** employers will find he is a dedicated worker.

pore, pour, poor The noun *pore* is an opening in the skin; the verb *pore* means "to gaze intently." *Pour* means "to move with a continuous flow." *Poor* means "needy or pitiable."

> **Pour** hot water into a bowl, put your face over it, and let the steam open your **pores**. Your **poor** skin will thank you.

precede, proceed *Precede* means "to go or come before," while *proceed* means "to move on after having stopped" or "to go ahead."

> Our biology instructor often **preceded** his lecture with these words: "OK, sponges, **proceed** to soak up more fascinating facts!"

principal, principle As an adjective, *principal* means "primary." As a noun, it can mean "a school administrator" or "a sum of money." A *principle* is an idea.

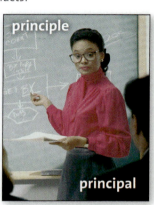

> **Principal** Jones used a flowchart to outline a **principle** of educational economics.
> Her **principal** gripe is lack of freedom. [adjective]

> After twenty years, the amount of interest was higher than the **principal**. [noun]

quiet, quit, quite *Quiet* is the opposite of noisy. *Quit* means "to stop or give up." *Quite* means "completely" or "to a considerable extent."

> The meeting remained **quite quiet** when the boss told us he'd **quit**.

quote, quotation *Quote* is a verb; *quotation* is a noun.

> The **quotation** was from Woody Allen. You may **quote** me on that.

real, very, really Do not use *real* (an adjective) in place of *very* or *really* (adverbs).

> My friend's cake is **very** [not *real*] fresh, but this cake is **really** stale.

ESL TIP

Consider using memory joggers (mnemonics) to remember which word to use. For example, a princi**pal** of a school is a **pal** to students

A GLOSSARY OF WORD USAGE

reason why, reason . . . is because The phrase *reason why* is redundant, so use *reason* by itself. In the construction *reason . . . is because,* *because* should be replaced by *that.*

> The **reason** [not *reason why*] Jane Eyre leaves Lowood School **is that** [not *because*] she feels the need for a change, for, if nothing else, a new servitude.

regardless, irregardless *Irregardless* is an incorrect synonym for *regardless.*

right, write, wright, rite *Right* means "correct or proper"; it also refers to that which a person has a legal claim to, as in *copyright.* *Write* means "to inscribe or record." A *wright* is a person who makes or builds something. A *rite* is a ritual or ceremonial act.

> Did you **write** that it is the **right** of the **shipwright** to perform the **rite** of christening—breaking a bottle of champagne on the bow of the ship?

scene, seen *Scene* refers to the setting or location where something happens; it also may mean "sight or spectacle." *Seen* is the past participle of *see.*

> An exhibitionist likes to be **seen** making a **scene.**

set, sit (See **36b.**)

shall, will In the past, *shall* was used with *I* and *we* to express the future, whereas *will* was used with the other personal pronouns. In contemporary usage, *will* suffices for all personal pronouns, although *shall* may still be used in polite, formal contexts.

sight, cite, site *Sight* means "the act of seeing" or "something that is seen." *Cite* means "to quote" or "to summon to court." *Site* means "a place or location" or "to place on a *site.*"

> After **sighting** the faulty wiring, the inspector **cited** the building contractor for breaking two city codes at a downtown work **site.**

some, sum *Some* refers to an unknown thing, an unspecified number, or a part of something. *Sum* is a certain amount of money or the result of adding numbers together.

> **Some** of the students answered too quickly and came up with the wrong **sum.**

sometime, some time, sometimes As an adverb, *sometime* refers to an indefinite period; *some time* is an adjective plus noun meaning "a space of time." *Sometimes* is an adverb meaning "occasionally, now and then."

> Reviewing Mark's midterm grades, the adviser wryly commented, "**Sometimes,** you just need to take **some time** to study. Make it **sometime** soon."

stationary, stationery *Stationary* means "not movable"; *stationery* refers to the paper and envelopes used to write letters.

> Odina uses **stationery** that she can feed through her portable printer. Then she drops the mail into a **stationary** mail receptacle at the mall.

suppose to, supposed to *Suppose to* is a nonstandard expression; use *supposed to* instead.

take, bring (See **36b**.)

than, then *Than* is used in a comparison; *then* tells when.

>Study more **than** you think you need to. **Then** you will be confident and ready for anything.

that, which (See **19b** and **24c**.)

their, there, they're (See **36b**.)

threw, through *Threw* is the past tense of "throw." *Through* means "from one side of something to the other."

>Sachiko **threw** his cell phone right **through** the window.

to, too, two (See **36b**.)

toward, towards Both *toward* and *towards* work in standard usage; however, *towards* is preferred in Britain, Canada, and elsewhere, whereas *toward* is preferred in the United States.

try to, try and *Try and* is nonstandard; use *try to* instead.

use, usage, use to, utilize As a noun, *use* refers to something's employment or application for a purpose, whereas *usage* refers to the customary or habitual treatment of something. *Use to* is nonstandard; in most contexts, *used to* is preferred. While the verb *use* means "to cause to act or serve for a purpose," the verb *utilize* means "to make use of, to turn to account."

>A good pitcher **utilizes** every type of pitch to outsmart the batter. I **used to** attend baseball's season opener each year, but scandals about steroid **use** have caused me to rethink my love of the game. Perhaps as fans we have too long ignored the ill **usage** of the body among athletes in professional sports.

vary, very *Vary* means "to change"; *very* means "to a high degree."

>To ensure the **very** best employee relations, the workloads should not **vary** greatly from worker to worker.

verbal, oral (See *oral*.)

vial, vile A *vial* is a small container for liquid. *Vile* is an adjective meaning "despicable, repulsive, or foul."

>The **vile** vampire held up a **vial** of blood.

wait, weight *Wait* means "to stay somewhere expecting something." *Weight* refers to heaviness.

>The **weight** of sadness eventually lessens; one must simply **wait**.

A GLOSSARY OF WORD USAGE

wait for, wait on *Wait for* refers to readiness and expectation, whereas *wait on* refers to serving people.

> After **waiting on** the party of ten lawyers, I **waited for** a big tip.

ware, wear, where *Ware* refers to a product that is sold; *wear* means "to have on one's body"; *where* asks the question "In what place?" or "In what situation?"

> The designer boasted, "**Where** can one **wear** my **wares**? Anywhere."

waste, waist The verb *waste* means "to squander" or "to wear away, decay"; the noun *waste* refers to material that is unused or useless. *Waist* is the part of the body just above the hips.

weather, whether *Weather* refers to the condition of the atmosphere. *Whether* refers to a possibility.

> **Weather** affects us, **whether** we are farmers or not.

well, good (See **36b**.)

which, witch *Which* refers to animals or nonliving objects. *Witch* refers to someone believed to have magical powers.

who, which, that *Who* refers to people. *Which* refers to nonliving objects or to animals. (*Which* should never refer to people.) *That* may refer to animals, people, or nonliving objects. (See also **19b**.)

who, whom *Who* is used as the subject of a verb; *whom* is used as the object of a preposition or as a direct object.

> Captain Mather, to **whom** the survivors owe their lives, is the man **who** is being honored today.

who's, whose *Who's* is "who is." *Whose* is a possessive pronoun.

> **Whose** car are we using, and **who's** going to pay for the gas?

your, you're (See **36b**.)

ESL TIP

The mixed pairs that create the most difficulties for ESL students appear in the ESL section. (See **36b**.)

Design Issues

Design Issues

Designing Documents

Whether you are writing a traditional academic paper, developing a brochure, or creating a webpage, you should give special attention to your document's design. Why? Because strong design looks professional, pulls readers into your document, helps them access the content, and promotes their understanding. In other words, appearances count.

How can I create an effective design?

To develop an attractive, easy-to-read-and-use document, start with the three principles below:

- **See readers reading.** Make design choices based on answers to questions like these: Will readers be focused or distracted, motivated or reluctant? Will they be reading a paper or viewing a screen? What language skills do they have? How diverse are they? In a nutshell, *how* will they read and *what* will they bring to their reading?

- **Choose appropriate design features.** Use varied elements, but choose ones that fit the rhetorical context. For example, an academic essay would be appropriately designed with double-spaced text, one-inch margins, and 12-point Times New Roman type. Conversely, a webpage might have a colorful multicolumn format that includes graphics, brief paragraphs, menus, and lists. Whatever your document, however, aim for simplicity. Design should be both functional (easy to navigate) and attractive (inviting to read).

- **Go with the flow.** Readers typically navigate pages from left to right and from top to bottom, so design pages accordingly. Keep pages open and balanced, breaking your message into manageable chunks, and develop consistent visual "cues" that guide readers through the entire document and through each page.

What's Ahead?

DESIGNING DOCUMENTS

16a Planning Your Document's Design

Often, designing a document is as simple as following a template—a standard style and format with well-established rules (such as MLA format for research papers or semiblock format for business letters). However, when you need to plan the design from scratch, consider the issues below.

What design elements should I consider?

FORMAT

- What type of document are you writing (research paper, short story, letter, webpage)?
- Will the document be paper based, electronic, or both?
- What format does your instructor, major, or profession expect you to use?
- Will the pages be bound, and if so, how (staple, binder)?
- How will the document be copied, distributed, and/or posted?

LAYOUT

- What weight, size, and color of paper should you use for standard pages and for special pages?
- What size margins should you use? What line lengths should you set?
- How should lines of text be justified—left only, fully, centered?
- How many columns should you use, what size, and what type?
- What heading system and lists make sense?
- Will you need to integrate text and graphics? How will you do so?

TYPOGRAPHY

- What typefaces (such as Times, Garamond) and sizes should you use for main and special text?
- What type styles should you use for emphasis—uppercase, boldface, italics, underlining, shadow, highlighting?

Workplace Link: Many businesses and organizations have style guides to help employees groom their writing for a professional, reader-friendly appearance. Such businesses understand that employee writing reflects on the company as a whole. The best business designs meet

- Professional standards, such as those for polished company correspondence.
- Industry standards, like those used for newspaper design.
- Government standards, like those regulating signal words such as **WARNING** or **DANGER** in instructions.
- Readers' standards for clear, accessible, attractive documents.

Planning Your Document's Design

How can my design support my goals?

Base design choices on issues related to your document's purpose, audience, and context.

- **Purpose:** What should your document accomplish? Is it informing, persuading, or both? More narrowly, is the document sharing a position, convincing readers to act, or instructing them?
- **Audience:** Who are your readers? How will they find, read, and store the document? What will they expect of it? What will they look for and how will they use the document? What do they value? What are their experiences? How similar or diverse is this audience?
- **Context:** What is the situation behind your document? Is it personal or private? Or is it public and accessible? Is it related to coursework, service learning, a job application? What are the conventions, limitations, and possibilities for this situation?

 GET SMART

Snort. Sniffle. Sneeze. No Antibiotics Please!

Are you aware that colds, flu, and most sore throats and bronchitis are caused by viruses? Did you know that antibiotics do not help fight viruses? It's true. Plus, taking antibiotics when you have a virus may do more harm than good. Taking antibiotics when they are not needed increases your risk of getting an infection later that resists antibiotic treatment.

If You Have a Cold or Flu, Antibiotics Won't Work for You!

- Antibiotics kill bacteria, not viruses such as:
  - Colds or flu;
  - Most coughs and bronchitis;
  - Sore throats not caused by strep; or
  - Runny noses.
- Taking antibiotics for viral infections, such as a cold, cough, the flu, or most bronchitis, will not:
  - Cure the infections;
  - Keep other individuals from catching the illness; or
  - Help you feel better.

 Get Smart   Read The Chart (93kb) to know which common illnesses are usually viral or bacterial and when antibiotics are necessary.

"As a doctor and a dad, I know how sick you or your child can feel with a virus, but antibiotics just won't help. Talk with your doctor or nurse to find out what can help."

Dr. J. Todd Weber, CDC's Director of the Office of Antimicrobial Resistance

What Can I Do to Protect Myself or My Child?

What to Do
- Talk with your healthcare provider about antibiotic resistance.
- When you are prescribed an antibiotic.
  1. Take it exactly as the doctor tells you. Complete the prescribed course even if you are feeling better. If treatment stops too soon, some bacteria may survive and re-infect you.
  2. This goes for children, too. Make sure your children take all the medication prescribed, even if they feel better.
  3. Throw away any leftover medication once you have completed your prescription.

What Not to Do
- Do not take an antibiotic for a viral infection like a cold, a cough, or the flu.
- Do not demand antibiotics when a doctor says they are not needed. They will not help treat your infection.
- When you are prescribed an antibiotic,
  1. Do not skip doses.
  2. Do not save any antibiotics for the next time you get sick.
  3. Do not take antibiotics prescribed for someone else. The antibiotic may not be appropriate for your illness. Taking the wrong medicine may delay correct treatment and allow bacteria to multiply.

November 18, 2004   Page 1 of 2

DEPARTMENT OF HEALTH AND HUMAN SERVICES
CENTERS FOR DISEASE CONTROL AND PREVENTION
SAFER ● HEALTHIER ● PEOPLE

Purpose:
To raise public awareness of antibiotic resistance

Audience:
Busy, concerned parents

Context:
Internet brochure

Design:
Use of color, headings, brief prose, vivid visuals, and lists

DESIGNING DOCUMENTS

16b Considering Color

Good decisions about color are crucial to creating a strong document design. Depending on the situation, black and white is generally more flexible, conservative, and cost-effective—appropriate for the traditional academic essay. However, color—whether in type, background, or graphics—might improve your document by both grabbing your readers' attention and communicating content more clearly.

What is the color wheel?

Design theory as it relates to color is based on the color wheel. Essentially, the wheel pictures the relationship between colors as described below.

- **Primary** colors (red, blue, and yellow) are foundational—not made from blending other colors.

- **Secondary** colors result from the blending of the two primary colors between which they lie. Endless color variations can be created from these building blocks.

USING COMPLEMENTARY COLORS TO CREATE ENERGY

Colors opposite each other on the wheel are complementary. When placed together, these colors "complete" each other, making each appear deeper and richer. Offering a good foundation for your document's color scheme, complementary colors energize your design.

USING RELATED COLORS TO CREATE HARMONY

Colors close together on the color wheel have many similarities and subtle variations in content. When used together, related colors keep things calm and balanced.

WORKING WITH COLOR ASSOCIATIONS

Different colors have different associations for different people. For the purposes of developing an effective document design, you want to take these color associations into account. Consider these factors related to the moods of colors:

- **Color temperature:** Some colors are warm (yellow, orange, red, brown); others are cool (purple, blue, green). This difference refers, in part, to the emotional tone the colors create.

- **Color tone:** Colors have both personal and cultural associations—red with passion, blood, and warnings; blue with sky, water, and stability; green with nature, growth, and cheerfulness.

How can I make the best color choices?

Tie your color scheme to your rhetorical analysis of purpose, audience, and context. Make each color choice an informed choice.

- **Use color to feature material.** Draw readers' attention to key elements and establish patterns that create a visual logic. Focus on headings, bullets, text boxes, tabs, appendices, and so on.
- **Use color consistently.** That is, once you've established a color pattern, use that pattern throughout a document.
- **Use a limited color palette for most documents.** Avoid a confusing look, clashing colors (such as pink and orange), and colors that are hard on the eyes. Consider both color unity and variety.
- **Use color carefully in academic projects.** Conservative colors are suitable for major research reports, poster presentations, and slide shows. Brighter colors may be appropriate for less formal papers.
- **Use color combinations to stress or soften features of the document.** Select colors to create a mood, draw attention to ideas, and develop subtle effects. For example, black, yellow, red, and white pop off the page, whereas blue and ivory create soft, subtle effects.

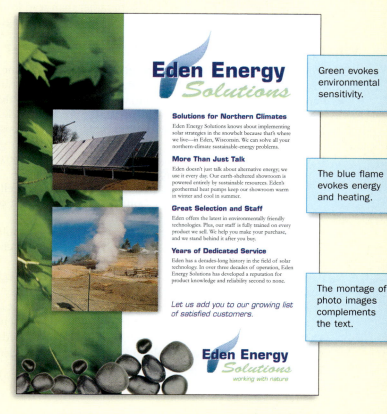

Green evokes environmental sensitivity.

The blue flame evokes energy and heating.

The montage of photo images complements the text.

DESIGNING DOCUMENTS

16c Developing a Document Format

Document format refers to the shape of the whole piece. Sometimes, the format will be specified by your assignment (for example, an essay). Other times, you'll have to develop the format. To do so, consider the issues discussed in the following section.

What delivery method should I use?

Developing a document format begins with choosing a delivery method: paper, electronic, or both. Which medium will best deliver your message, and what document type will best embody that message? Consider these factors:

- **Paper documents** are stable, portable, traditional, and familiar. With word processing, photocopying, and faxing, paper documents can be easily created, copied, distributed, and posted. Readers tend to give paper more in-depth attention.
  Examples: academic essays, field reports, business letters, brochures.

- **Electronic documents** are flexible; are easy to create and modify; may include dynamic multimedia elements; can be quickly posted, distributed, accessed, downloaded, and printed; and allow for rapid response. However, readers tend to skim rather than read in-depth.
  Examples: e-mail messages, jpg files, webpages, blog postings.

What paper types, folds, and bindings should I use?

When you create a print document, consider its immediate, multiple, and long-term uses. Then choose sensible paper, fitting folds, and bindings.

- **Paper type:** Consider size, color, and weight. Choose a size that makes your document easy to send, use, and store. While 8 1/2- × 11-inch paper is standard, other options range from large posters to small cards.
  1. Choose paper colors that fit your document's purpose, structure, and personality. (See **16b** for a discussion of color.)
  2. For most documents, use 20-pound bond. It takes ink well and works in printers and copiers. Consider heavier bond for covers, dividers, posters, and heavily used documents.
- **Paper folds:** While documents such as academic essays should not be folded, other documents—for example, pamphlets and brochures—may be folded in halves, thirds, quarters, and so on.
- **Paper binding:** Multiple pages might be held together through diverse methods.
  1. Paper clips work well when readers need to separate pages.
  2. Staples work well with short- to medium-length documents.
  3. Ring binders allow pages to be removed, added, and reordered.
  4. Saddle binding uses staples along a fold to create a booklet.
  5. Spiral binding lets pages lie flat.

16d Laying Out Pages

Page layout—how you arrange material on a page—determines whether your document is attractive, readable, and accessible. Generally, avoid dense blocks of prose, cluttered pages, or largely empty pages.

What page orientation and column format should I use?

Consider orientation and columns when you plan your format.

- **Orientation:** Standard orientation for most pages is vertical, called *portrait;* such orientation is used for academic essays, business letters, and more. Other documents, such as pamphlets and webpages, follow a horizontal orientation, called *landscape.* Select the orientation that best presents the information.

- **Column types:** With *newspaper columns,* text runs continuously from the bottom of one column over to the top of the next—useful for pamphlets, booklets, and newsletters. With *parallel columns,* the text in each column remains separate—useful for instructions, resumés, itineraries, webpages, and so on. Consider these choices:

BASIC PAGE LAYOUTS

- **One column** is standard for most documents.

- **Two columns (even)** balance the page and allow comparisons and contrasts.

- **Two columns (uneven)** provide a larger column useful for main text and a smaller column for headings, side notes, graphics, and so forth.

- **Three or more columns** break up text into blocks or panels; this is useful for pamphlets, brochures, and newsletters.

DESIGNING DOCUMENTS

How can I create visual cues?

Make sure your page layout distinguishes between main and secondary points, as well as showing how the points are connected. Follow these principles:

- **Stress content connections through design similarities.** Closely related content should be graphically connected through proximity on the page and similar treatment in terms of headings, typography, and color. Repetition of parallel features will create a clear pattern.
- **Stress content contrasts through design differences.** Contrasting ideas can be made graphically distinct through opposing typography, paragraphing, lists, and color.
- **Emphasize primary content with bold design features.** The most important content will jump off the page through prominent headings, boxes, background and text colors, icons, and the like.
- **De-emphasize secondary content with subdued design features.** Less important information might be relegated to smaller print, subsections, footnotes, standard paragraphs, and the like.
- **Supply readers with visual signals.** Generally, create a focal point for each page and design the rest of the page around that focus. Your heading system, indenting practices, paragraphing, lists, icons, visuals, and more—all of these announce the page's information structure and guide readers through the page.

What layout problems should I avoid?

Before printing your document, use your word processor's "print preview" function to check for these design weaknesses:

- **Widows** are single lines of text (such as the last line of a paragraph) that sit alone at the top of a page.
- **Orphans** are first lines of paragraphs left alone at the bottom of a page.
- **Tombstones** are headings or subheadings that sit alone at the bottom of a column or page, detached from the text to which they refer.
- **Split lists** are lists divided between two pages. Especially if the items need to be compared or contrasted, keep the list on one page.

How can I use white space?

To balance dark print, build white space into your page layout. When used well, white space gives readers' eyes a place to rest and highlights key ideas and details.

- **Use generous margins,** at least 1 inch on all sides of a standard 8 1/2- × 11-inch sheet.
- **Adjust margins** to account for the type of page (essay, instructions) and the binding method (spiral, three-ring).
- **Increase line spacing** and add space between paragraphs.
- **Use headings,** bulleted lists, text boxes, and rules.

How can I format lines effectively?

Avoid overly long lines, which make reading difficult, and overly short lines, which suggest a lack of substance. Also, for most text, avoid full justification, which introduces unnatural spaces. Follow these guidelines:

- Set line lengths between fifty and eighty characters (between ten and fifteen words).
- Set body text flush left (ragged right).
- Use centering to emphasize headings.

16e   Making Typographical Choices

Typography refers to the actual print on the page or screen—those marks that in the end communicate your message. With print, your aim is to create a positive impression, make reading easy, and clarify content. To achieve these goals, pay attention to your choices of typeface, type size, and type style.

What typeface should I use?

Typeface refers to the special look shared by the letters and other symbols of a specific type. These typefaces cluster in families—Arial, Courier, and Times Roman, for example. In addition, typefaces are designated as serif or sans serif.

- **Use a serif typeface for main text and a sans serif typeface for headings and other special effects.** Note that you would reverse this practice for documents published online—sans serif for main text, serif for headings—because computer-screen resolution makes sans serif typeface cleaner, crisper, simpler.

Serif typeface, like this, has finishes on the letters that make the type easier to read. _____

A
serifs

Sans serif typeface, like this, has no finishes. The print is clean and modern, but harder to read in extended passages. _____

A
no serifs

Web Link: Certain typefaces such as Verdana and Georgia have been developed specifically for readability on webpages. In general, sans serif faces are easier to read onscreen, and serif faces are easier to read on paper. (See **18a**.)

DESIGNING DOCUMENTS

- **Select a typeface that is readable** given the context of your document. Consider, for example, an e-mail message to a professor. The Tahoma typeface is fitting; the Desdemona typeface isn't.
  - **Tahoma:** Dear Professor Randall, Thank you for your feedback on the first draft of my position paper. . . .
  - **Desdemona:** DEAR PROFESSOR RANDALL, THANK YOU FOR YOUR FEEDBACK ON THE FIRST DRAFT OF MY POSITION PAPER. . . .
- **Select an attractive typeface** that fits the document type. Generally, avoid fancy or unusual typefaces, as well as frequent typeface changes. Focus on readability, but also consider the mood or impression that a typeface makes. Contrast the readability and mood of the following typefaces. Which would be suitable for regular text?

- Times New Roman . . . . conveys tradition, stability, strength
- Lucida Blackletter . . . . . . feels medieval, ornate, even slightly sinister
- Tekton . . . . creates the impression of handwriting
- **Impact** . . . . offers weight and emphasis
- Univers . . . . seems modern, global, tolerant

What should I understand about type size?

Type size is measured in units called points, with 72 points equal to one inch. When readers will sit with the document squarely before them (on paper or on screen), make main text 10–12 points. For titles, headings, and subheadings, increase size by 2–4 points; 12, 14, 16, or 18 points are good choices. Make the jump noticeable but not drastic.

Title (18 points)

ANWR Environmental Impact Report

Heading (16 Points)

History of the Wildlife Refuge

Subheading (14 Points)

Recent Legislation on Oil Drilling

Main Text (12 Points)

Beginning in 1996, legislators in Washington and Alaska . . .

Making Typographical Choices

What type size should I use for special circumstances?

For documents that will be read under difficult conditions, think big. Here are some situations you might encounter.

- **Low light conditions:** If you are preparing instructions to be posted, for example, in a journalism darkroom, try 20-point type.

Use the red light during processing.

- **Dangerous conditions:** If you are preparing warnings, use large type and capital letters.

SAFETY GOGGLES MUST BE WORN.

- **Presentations:** If you are creating slides, overhead transparencies, and multimedia presentations, think of the people in the back row.

Goals for the coming year ...

What type style should I use?

Type style refers to special treatment of type like those shown below. When using different type styles, do so for a reason, not for dazzle. Also, be moderate and avoid combining several techniques.

> UPPERCASE WILL GET THE READER'S ATTENTION BUT IS HARDER TO READ IN EXTENDED PASSAGES.

> Underlining is useful for indicating subheadings, key words, and key sentences, but avoid using it for extended passages.

> Highlighting and similar techniques such as shading and outlining draw attention to key words and statements.

> **Boldface causes print to jump out. It's especially useful for headings, subheadings, warnings, and other key information.**

> *Italics indicates book titles, important words, and key statements. Avoid using it for extended passages because it is difficult to read.*

> Color helps highlight headings, warnings, tips, and other key material. However, make sure that the color is easy to read. (See **16b**.)

DESIGNING DOCUMENTS

16f Checklist: Document Design

As you plan, develop, test, and refine your document, use this checklist to review for effective color, format, page layout, and typography.

___ The overall design is appropriate for the writing situation, type of document, message, and audience.

___ If appropriate, the design follows a standard style guide (MLA, APA).

___ Design elements distinguish the document's topic, main point, and purpose.

___ The layout effectively uses a heading system, lists, margins, columns, and white space to make the message clear and easy to read.

___ The document's format and design make effective use of color; the overall color scheme is both functional and attractive.

___ Accent features such as highlighting, underlining, boldface, italics, and color help call attention to the message and are appropriate for the document's purpose and message.

___ Design elements (such as headings, page numbers, and outlines) clearly identify and organize parts of the message.

___ The document contains all appropriate elements—for example, a title page, table of contents, introduction, outline, visuals, appendices, and index.

___ The color, size, texture, and quality of paper are appropriate for the document's purpose, message, and audience.

___ The typeface and size of fonts are attractive, emphasize information as needed, and fit the document's purpose and audience.

___ The visuals (tables and figures) are well placed to support the message and are well designed (see **17a–17g**).

Web Links: When you design webpages, start with the same principles you use in document design. However, you should also be aware of the following challenges and opportunities offered by the Internet. (See **18a–18c**.)

• **Onscreen readability:** Typefaces and sizes that are readable on print pages may be difficult to make out on the web.

• **Page size:** Webpages that require scrolling are more difficult to read than those that fit on a single screen.

• **Use of graphics:** Photos, drawings, and icons can be very effective, even interactive, on webpages.

• **Page links:** Websites need not be organized sequentially, but instead may use links to connect related material.

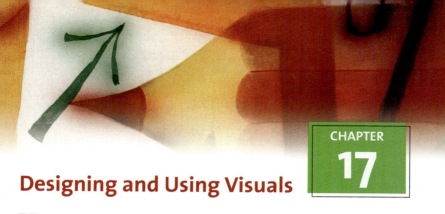

Designing and Using Visuals

Visuals can add a powerful dimension to written ideas by helping to clarify and illustrate information. Using visuals is a smart choice for many (but not all) pieces of writing.

When should I use visuals in my writing?

The points below will help you sort out the relevant issues.

Best uses: Writing benefits from visuals when they are used to

- **Make information readable**—map out relationships between ideas and details.
- **Clarify complex ideas**—"show" in support of your "telling."
- **Focus your analysis**—"picture" what you are carefully observing in your written message (a painting, a film shot, data from an experiment).
- **Dramatize important points**—develop graphic impact for your ideas.
- **Condense information**—let an image save a thousand words.
- **Add persuasive energy**—supplement an argument with graphics.

Cautions: While visuals offer distinct benefits, avoid filling traditional academic writing with flashy, merely decorative visuals. Also, be careful not to assume that visuals speak for themselves. Perhaps most importantly, avoid creating or using visuals that distort and hence falsify ideas.

What's Ahead

DESIGNING AND USING VISUALS

17a Integrating Visuals into Text

Visuals should enhance your document, whether it's an essay, a proposal, or a brochure. Integrate visuals using the tips below and on the facing page.

How can I map my document's visual story?

As you plan your document's visuals, consider how to shape a visual "story":

- What mix of writing and visuals should you use? Will written text support visuals, will visuals support text, or should the two be balanced?
- In what order should the visuals appear? Will later visuals build on earlier ones? For example, should you present a table of numerical data and then break it out into line, bar, or pie graphs?
- Will the visuals be presented in multiple media (print document, webpage, presentation)? If so, how will visuals look photocopied or on a screen? What impact will they have on the audience?

What format should I use for my document?

Consider the amount of text and the number of visuals you plan to use, and select a layout to balance the two. Here are examples:

- **A single column with a large visual (A):** Text and visual create a balanced page; table is placed at bottom after reference in text; table set off by box and shading.
- **Two even columns with a small visual (B):** Even text columns create balance; small visual allows text more weight; visual is properly contained within column margins; visual follows first in-text reference.
- **Two even columns, one with text and one with visuals (C):** Text and visuals have equal weight; visual and textual "stories" run side by side; text refers to visuals on same page.
- **Two uneven columns, one with text and one with visuals (D):** Imbalance gives weight to text; visual and textual stories run side by side.
- **Multiple columns, multiple visuals (E):** Weight given primarily to visual story; text supports and supplements graphics.

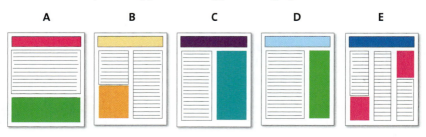

A   B   C   D   E

Integrating Visuals into Text

How can I sketch out my visuals?

Test out your visuals by experimenting on a computer or on paper with titles, shapes, patterns, and colors.

- Work on the title, captions, legends, labels, keys, and notes.
- Use shapes, patterns, and colors that clarify information.
- To prevent confusion, use a limited number of patterns and colors; avoid flashy elements that serve no purpose—elements sometimes referred to as *chartjunk*.
- Use contrasting colors to show differences and shades of a color to emphasize similarities.
- Use bright colors for accents and pale colors for backgrounds.

VISUALS TIP

Shapes, colors, and icons may have different meanings in different cultures. In addition, color visuals may lose sharpness when photo-copied. For more on color, see **16b**.

How should I lay out my visuals?

Consider the size and importance of the visuals when you think about how and where they should be placed on the page.

- Place a small visual on the same page as the reference.
- Place a large visual on a facing page in a double-sided document, or on the page following the reference in a single-sided document.
- Turn a less important or very large visual into an attachment or an appendix item.

Follow these layout principles in particular to integrate visuals. Also turn to **16d** to find more complete instruction on page-layout strategies.

- Position visuals vertically on the page whenever possible.
- Adjust the size and shape of visuals to fit with the written text.
- Place partial-page visuals in boxes at the top or bottom of a page.
- Keep all visuals within the text margins.
- Use white space within and around visuals so they don't appear to be crowded.

Unless the visual is essentially separate from the verbal text (for example, a photograph in a brochure), discuss the visual directly:

- Make points based on key ideas that the visual shows.
- Refer to the visual by noting its number, title, and location.
- Comment on the visual to help readers understand the information.
- Use the same terminology in the written text and the visual.

17b Parts of Visuals

While each type of visual has its own guidelines and features, all visuals share some common elements—a title, a body, and a note or a caption.

How should I title my visuals?

Make sure the title clearly indicates the topic and purpose of the visual. If a document contains more than one visual, each visual should be numbered as well. Organize tables by numbering them sequentially (Table 1, Table 2, and so forth), and organize graphs, charts, and images by numbering them sequentially as figures (Figure 1, Figure 2, and so on).

 WAC Link: Each academic paper style (MLA, APA, CSE, CMS) has specific instructions for titling and numbering visuals. Consult each of the following styles: MLA <www.mla.org>, APA <www.apastyle.org>, CSE <www.councilscienceeditors. org>, and CMS <www.chicagomanualofstyle.org>. If your document does not have to adhere to one of these styles, numbers and titles may be placed above or below the visual. Simply be consistent by using one placement style throughout.

What should I include in the body?

Use the body of the visual to provide the information. Different types of visuals have different components.

- Tables present data using columns and rows; graphs use bars or lines; and charts use shapes, colors, lines, and arrows.
- Maps provide information by using labels, scales, and legends.
- Photos and drawings can also incorporate text to make their points clear. Text information should appear horizontally whenever possible.

How should I create a note or a caption?

Use a note or caption to explain the visual and to connect it to the text around it. The caption should be brief and clear, helping readers understand the significance of the visual. (See **17f** for examples of both notes and captions.)

 ETHICS TIP

To use a visual created by someone else, you may need to obtain permission, particularly if your document has a nonacademic or commercial purpose. Acknowledge the source below the graphic with *Source:*, *Adapted from:*, or *Used with permission of.*

17c Choosing the Right Visuals

The pages that follow show you how to present different types of visuals in your writing. You can quickly review your options by scanning the list below.

ETHICS TIP

Even well-chosen visuals can mislead or misinform readers through inaccuracy or distortion. Be visually responsible by choosing and using visuals to inform and influence, not to distract or manipulate.

TABLES

Arrange data in rows and columns to display information and show the intersection of two factors. (See **17d**.)

Numerical tables: provide amounts, percentages, and so on.

Text tables: use words, not numbers.

FIGURES

Shape information into a visual "story"; interpret data into 2-D images.

Graphs: show relationships between numbers. (See **17e**.)

- Line graphs reveal trends by showing changes in quantity over time.
- Bar graphs compare amounts using a series of bars.
- Pie graphs divide a whole quantity (a circle or "pie") into parts ("pie wedges") to show proportions.

Charts: show relationships between parts or stages (not numbers).

- Organizational charts picture relationships within a group (web).
- Gantt charts provide overview of project tasks and phases (web).
- Flowcharts map out steps in a process.

Images: provide pictures of some portion of reality. (See **17f**.)

- Maps present information oriented according to geography.
- Photographs show detailed reality in a range of formats.
- Line drawings present simplified images of objects.

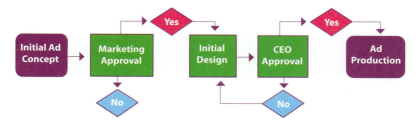

DESIGNING AND USING VISUALS

17d Tables

Tables arrange numbers and words in a grid of rows and columns. Each slot in the grid contains data where two factors intersect (for example, Type of Trip and Length of Trip in the table below). Use tables when you want to

- Categorize data for easy comparison of several factors.
- Provide many exact figures in a compact, readable format.
- Present raw data that are the foundation of later graphs.

DESIGN GUIDELINES

Set up rows and columns in a logical order. Make tables easy to read by using patterns of organization: category, time, place, alphabet, ascending, or descending order.

Label information. Identify columns at the top and rows at the left. Use short, clear headings and set them off with color, screens, or rules (lines).

Present data correctly. In a numerical table, round off numbers to the nearest whole number (if appropriate) and align them at their right edge. Otherwise, align numbers at the decimal point. Indicate a gap in data with a dash or n.a. (not available). With any text in a table, as shown below, use parallel wording.

Types of Weekend Trips in the United States in 2004

Type of Trip	Length of Trip		
	1–2 Nights	**3–5 Nights**	**Total**
Number			
Total trips	252,581	188,804	**441,385**
Business	32,358	33,172	**65,530**
Pleasure	186,219	134,659	**320,878**
Visit friends and relatives	104,438	74,151	**178,589**
Leisure	81,781	60,508	**142,289**
Personal business	34,004	20,970	**54,974**
Percent			
Total trips	100.0	100.0	**100.0**
Business	12.8	17.6	**14.8**
Pleasure	73.7	71.3	**72.7**
Visit friends and relatives	41.3	39.3	**40.5**
Leisure	32.4	32.0	**32.2**
Personal business	13.5	11.1	**12.5**

Web Links: For more advanced instruction on designing tables, try the website at <http://www.ncsu.edu/labwrite/res/gh/gh-tables.html>.

17e   Graphs: Line, Bar, and Pie

Graphs show relationships between numbers—differences, proportions, or trends. When properly designed (without distortion), graphs can clearly portray complex ideas, ranging from patterns in U.S. immigration for the past fifty years to the proportion of the student body in each major at your school this year. Some helpful guidelines follow.

How should I create line graphs?

Use a line graph to show trends at a glance. Usually, such graphs reveal changes in quantity over time—changes in revenue, rates, ratios, and so on. Typically, the horizontal axis measures time (days, months, years), and the vertical axis measures quantities or rates. The quantity for each time period creates a "data point." When joined, these points create the lines that show the trends.

DESIGN GUIDELINES

Start the vertical axis at zero. If it's impractical to show all increments, show a break on the axis and the "trend line."

Avoid distortion. Use all available data points (no skipping). Make sure that vertical and horizontal units match well (roughly equal in scale or ratio).

Identify each axis. Label items clearly (months, percentages), and also use consistent increments. Print all words horizontally, if possible.

Vary line weights. Make data lines heavy, axis lines light, and background graph lines even lighter.

Use patterns or colors. Doing so will help to distinguish multiple lines.

Use a legend. A legend can identify what each line represents.

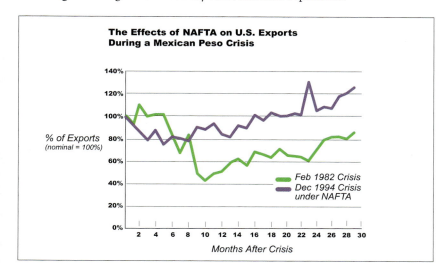

DESIGNING AND USING VISUALS

How should I create bar graphs?

Use a bar graph to compare amounts by using a series of vertical or horizontal bars. The height or length of each bar represents a quantity at a specific time or in a particular place. By comparing bars, readers can quickly see key proportions and patterns. Note, too, that different types of bar graphs accentuate different types of information.

DESIGN GUIDELINES

Develop bars that are accurate and informative.

- Choose a scale that doesn't exaggerate or minimize differences between bars. Keep increments accurate and consistent.
- Maintain a consistent bar width and spacing between bars. Generally, space between bars should be one-half of the bar width.
- Use two-dimensional bars; 3-D bars can blur differences and amounts.
- Present items in a logical order within each group, and add a legend if necessary.

Design bar graphs that are easy to read.

Label bars and axis units clearly.

Whenever possible, print words and numbers horizontally.

Limit to five the number of bars in a group or segments in a bar.

Use patterns or colors to distinguish between bars or segments.

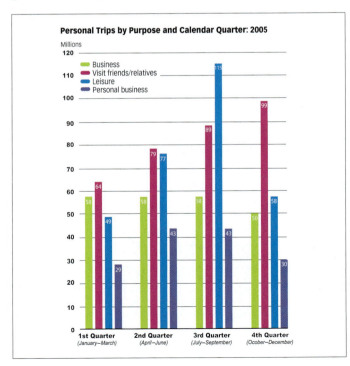

Personal Trips by Purpose and Calendar Quarter: 2005

Millions

Legend:
- Business
- Visit friends/relatives
- Leisure
- Personal business

1st Quarter (January–March): 58, 64, 49, 29
2nd Quarter (April–June): 58, 79, 77, 43
3rd Quarter (July–September): 58, 89, 115, 43
4th Quarter (Ocober–December): 50, 99, 58, 30

Graphs: Line, Bar, and Pie

How should I create pie graphs?

Use pie or circle graphs to represent some whole quantity. Slices of the pie, of different widths, show how parts of the whole stand in proportion to each other and to the whole. A pie graph can make a striking impression on a page, communicating its message at a glance.

DESIGN GUIDELINES

Keep your graph simple. Divide the circle into six or fewer slices. If necessary, combine smaller slices into a "miscellaneous" category, and explain its contents in a note or in the text.

Make your graph clear and realistic. Avoid confusion and distortion.

- Use a moderate-sized circle and avoid 3-D effects.
- Distinguish between slices with shading, patterns, colors, or sharp black/white contrasts.
- Label the whole pie and each slice, horizontally if possible. Try to avoid the need for a legend.

Measure slices (number of degrees) to assure accuracy. Use the following formulas to calculate degrees for each slice:

(amount of part/total amount) x 100 = percentage

percentage x 3.6 = number of degrees

Example: Here are sample calculations and the resulting pie graph:

Paper Supplies:	($775/$1,936) x 100 = 40%	40% x 3.6 = 144.0°
Software Upgrades:	($484/$1,936) x 100 = 25%	25% x 3.6 = 90.0°
Hardware Upgrades:	($415/$1,936) x 100 = 21.4%	21.4% x 3.6 = 77.0°
Hardware Repairs:	($262/$1,936) x 100 = 13.5%	13.5% x 3.6 = 49.0°

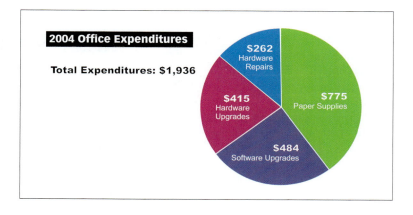

17f   Images: Maps, Photographs, and Line Drawings

Visuals such as maps, photographs, and drawings provide images of places, objects, or people. By stressing certain details, these images help readers understand ideas, visualize concepts, and organize information.

How should I use maps?

Use maps to represent geographic information (related to anything from the Earth's surface to a Civil War battlefield). A map can present a wide range of useful details.

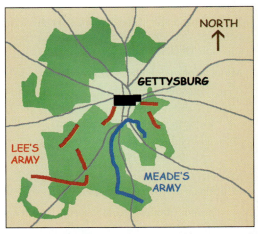

DESIGN GUIDELINES

Make the geographic area clear. Help orient readers by providing a directional arrow (usually north).

Provide useful content. Select details carefully, making sure that features, markings, and symbols are distinct and easy to understand. If necessary, use labels and a legend.

The position of Confederate (red) and Union (blue) troops at the Battle of Gettysburg, July 3, 1863

How should I use photographs?

Use photographs to provide a wealth of vivid, informative details. Infrared pictures, X-rays, 2-D and 3-D computer-generated images, and digital photography offer many ways to augment text.

DESIGN GUIDELINES

Take, develop, and print quality images.

- Use good equipment and seek expert help, if needed.
- Select distances and angles to clarify size and details.
- Enlarge and crop images to focus on key objects.
- Use labels, arrows, size references, and so on to help the reader get an accurate picture.

Images: Maps, Photographs, and Line Drawings

How should I use drawings and other illustrations?

Use line drawings to provide clear, simplified images of objects. Different types of line drawings focus on different ideas, from showing surface appearance to providing humor.

DESIGN GUIDELINES

Use the right tools. Specifically, rely on drawing instruments or a CAD (computer-aided design) program. Get expert help, if necessary.

Select the viewpoint and angle needed to show key details: surface, cutaway, or exploded; front, side, diagonal, back, top, or bottom. Indicate the angle and the perspective in the drawing's title.

Pay attention to scale and proportion to represent the object accurately. Add measurements, if helpful. If the drawing reflects the actual size of the object, indicate this fact.

Include the right level of detail for your specific readers. Avoid clutter, and use colors to highlight and clarify information, not simply for flash.

Use labels, or "callouts," to identify key parts of the object. Whenever possible, write callouts horizontally, and use a line to link the callout to the respective part. Avoid crisscrossing lines; instead, neatly radiate labels and lines around the drawn object.

TYPES OF LINE DRAWINGS

Surface drawings present objects as they appear externally.

Cross-section or cutaway drawings show an object's inside parts.

Illustrations such as cartoons convey ideas, create humor, and evoke varied emotions in viewers.

Exploded drawings "pull apart" an object, showing what the individual parts look like and how they fit together. (See the example below.)

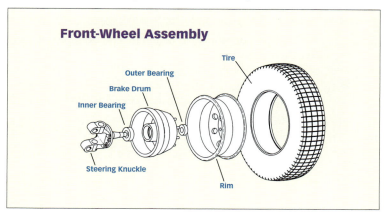

Front-Wheel Assembly

Tire
Outer Bearing
Brake Drum
Inner Bearing
Steering Knuckle
Rim

DESIGNING AND USING VISUALS

17g Checklist: Visuals

Use this checklist to apply the seven traits to the visuals you include with your writing.

____ **Ideas:** Visuals include important information presented clearly, without distortion or deception. Visuals are appropriate for the content, audience, purpose, and document type.

____ **Organization:** Visuals have all needed parts, including labels, legends, notes, and captions. Their placement enhances the message.

____ **Visual Tone:** The combination of words and images is professional, attractive, informative, and helpful. Patterns and colors clarify and enhance the visual's meaning.

____ **Words:** Titles, labels, legends, and notes are precise and consistent with words used in the text.

____ **Sentences:** Visuals include brief phrases or complete sentences as needed, along with clear and smooth captions or notes.

____ **Copy:** Visuals include no errors in grammar, spelling, and punctuation.

____ **Design:** The graphics make information easily accessible by
- Avoiding irrelevant material (chartjunk).
- Using colors, shapes, patterns, and white space to clarify information.
- Using boxes, bullets, screens, or white space to set off or feature information.

Web Links: For more instruction on and examples of visuals, see these websites:
- <http://www.writersatwork.us/>
- <http://www.ncsu.edu/labwrite/res/gh/gh-bargraph.html>
- <http://www.writing.colostate.edu/guides>

Also, check the website of your own college or university to discover if it provides tips or tools for creating your own visuals.

Writing and Designing for the Web

A strong website—whatever its focus—depends on well-written, well-organized, and well-designed content. Developing a strong website requires planning, collaboration, and some understanding of the technical workings—and limitations—of web browsers, pages, sites, and servers. While this chapter does not go into the technical details of HTML or website development, it does address the rhetorical fundamentals of creating a strong website.

What should I know about writing for the web?

When you're writing for the web, remember that web content should be concise, focused, and visually appealing. Consider these web truths:

1. People don't read websites so much as they scan them, so information should be presented in short chunks of text.
2. Webpages should be brief, designed to minimize scrolling and to maximize the use of available screen space. The most important information on each page should be immediately visible.
3. Online, people can be impatient readers, so the writing must clearly address its intended purpose, audience, and topic.
4. Many sites have distinct menus and pages for different audiences (scholars, students, investors), purposes (conducting research, serving customers), and topics (services, organization history).
5. Most websites exist to serve one or more of the following purposes:
   - To present or process information
   - To host online conversations
   - To provide or promote products or services
   - To provide reference material

What's Ahead

18a Webpage Elements
18b Developing a Website and Webpages
18c Checklist: Developing Websites and Webpages

WRITING AND DESIGNING FOR THE WEB

18a Webpage Elements

To design an effective website and develop dynamic webpages, you need to start with a basic understanding of webpage functions and elements. Because webpages use the same elements as printed pages, many of the same design principles apply. However, unlike printed pages, webpages are fluid (flowing their contents to match screen and browser settings), and they can include interactive elements, as shown below and on the facing page.

Sample Webpage and Elements

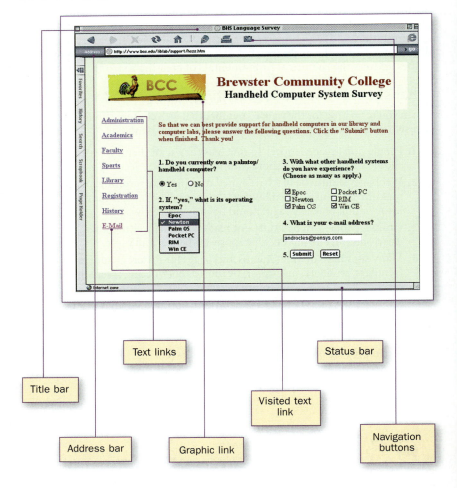

What page elements should I consider?

On the web, page elements are defined primarily by purpose—headings, body text, lists, images, and so on.

1. **Headings** (headers) come in six levels and are used to separate different sections and subsections of web documents. Heading 1 is the largest; heading 6 is the smallest. Default settings are boldface black serif fonts.

2. **Body text** is organized into paragraphs, which are separated by white space. By default, body text is a black sans serif font roughly the same size as a level 4 heading (although not bold).

3. **Lists** can be numbered, bulleted, or neither. Because readers can scan them quickly, lists are an efficient way to present information.

4. **Images** (photographs, clip art, animations) can make a page much slower to display, so use them judiciously. Always be sure you have the legal right to use any images that you include in your pages. (See "Violating Copyright," **50d**.)

5. **Hyperlinks**—*links* for short—are strings of specially formatted text that enable readers to jump to another spot on the web. *Internal links* take you to another section of the same site. *External links* lead to pages on other websites. *Mailto* links allow readers to address e-mail to recipients, such as your professor or a classmate. Most webpages show *visited links* in a lighter color than unvisited links.

6. **Menus** are simple structured lists of links that operate like a website's table of contents. Menus are typically presented in a column or row at the edge of a webpage. Good websites include a site menu on every page.

VISUALS TIP

Because web browsers are designed to flow content to suit each computer screen, changing the default styles can be problematic. It helps to keep the following tips in mind:

- **Simple is best.** Simple pages display the fastest and have the least chance of breaking. The more graphics you add, the longer a page takes to load. The more you change the default font settings, the more complicated the code becomes and the greater the chance of computer error.

- **Different computers display things differently.** Not every computer has the same font styles installed, and colors look different on different monitors. Always check your work on many different systems.

- **The user is king.** No matter what choices of font style and size you make, the reader can change how they display on a computer. Focus on useful content and clear organization instead of struggling to control the graphic design.

18b   Developing a Website and Webpages

Regardless of the purpose, topic, and audience of your website, you can develop it by following the steps outlined here and on the next four pages.

How do I get started?

Create an overview of the project—the purpose, the audience, and the topic. The following questions will help you get focused:

1. **What is the primary purpose of the website?** Are you creating a library of documents that your audience will reference? Are you going to present information and announcements about yourself, your organization? Are you trying to promote a specific product or service?

2. **Who is the site's audience?** Who will seek out this site? Why? What do they need? How often will they visit the site, and how often should it be updated? How comfortable are they using computers and websites? What level of formality is appropriate for the language? What graphics, colors, and design will appeal to them?

3. **What is the site's central topic?** What do you already know about the topic? What do you need to learn, and where can you find the information? What will your audience want to know about the topic? How can you divide the information into brief segments? What visual elements would help present your message? What other websites should you link to?

How can I establish my central message?

After you've made decisions about your purpose, audience, and topic, write out the main idea you want to communicate. You might call this statement the theme or "mission statement" of your website. Begin with the simple statement "The purpose of this website is" and then add a phrase like "to explain," "to provide," "to promote," or "to inform." Finish by inserting your topic, along with the main mission of your website.

- The purpose of this website is to inform my fellow students and the general public about current research into hybrid-vehicle transportation.

> **NOTE:** To help you stay on target, keep this mission statement in plain view. Note, too, that you might modify your purpose as the site develops.

How should I gather and prioritize content?

Brainstorm and research the actual content, with the goal of creating an outline for your site. How many topics will the site address? How wide will your coverage of a topic be? How deep? Your outline may also serve as the website's table of contents, which can be used to create a menu. Based on your research, select the content, features, and functions your site will offer.

How can I map my site?

As you gather content for your site, create a site map. Websites can be as simple as an elementary school bulletin board or as complex as a United States federal government site. Here are four principles to keep in mind:

1. **No one will read your entire site.** People curl up with books, not websites. If your audience is not asking for content, don't provide it.

2. **Your site will have many small audiences**—not one big audience. A site's audience may include anyone with a computer, an Internet connection, and an interest in your site's topic. Keep all potential readers in mind.

3. **Websites are not linear.** While essays proceed paragraph by paragraph from introduction to conclusion, few websites are structured that way. A single "home page" or "splash page" introduces the site, which branches out like tree limbs into pages with varied content. Websites "conclude" whenever the reader quits reading.

4. **You may need to build the site in phases.** You can add pages to a website after it has been published, so be careful that your site's organization does not limit future additions.

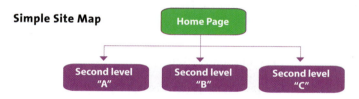

A map for a simple site might include only four items—a home page, page "A," page "B," and page "C"—allowing the site's users to "jump" between any of the secondary-level pages or back to the home page.

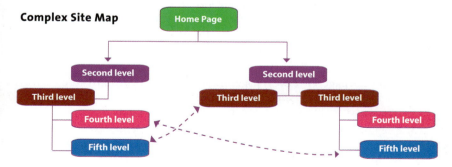

A more complex website typically needs more levels. Likewise, its menu—or menus—will offer more navigation choices. Related pages might be connected with links, as represented by the dotted lines in this example.

How can I learn from similar sites?

Next, check out how similar sites use headings, body text, background color, lists, images, and tables. How do sites use links, menus, and forms? The seven traits (see **5a**) can supply benchmarks for evaluating sites:

1. **Ideas:** Does the site present clear ideas and information?
2. **Organization:** Is the content carefully and clearly structured?
3. **Voice:** Is the tone fitting for the audience?
4. **Words:** Is the language understandable? Is the wording concise?
5. **Sentences:** Are the sentences easy to read and generally short?
6. **Correctness:** Does the site avoid distracting errors?
7. **Design:** Are the pages user-friendly? Is the site easy to navigate?

Web Link: For further analysis of webpages, including non-profit and business sites, go to <www.thecollegewriter.com>. There, you'll also find tutorials on analyzing and evaluating websites.

How should I build my site?

Follow these guidelines as you build your website:

1. **Identify the site.** Working from your mission statement, write an introductory sentence or brief paragraph to appear on your site's home page. Let your visitors immediately know the site's purpose.
2. **Provide clear links.** Create links for your pages, using clear descriptors such as "Original Poetry." (Avoid phrases such as "Click here for poetry.") If necessary, add a descriptive sentence to further identify the link. Let visitors know precisely where each link will take them.
3. **Introduce each page.** Give each page a brief introduction that clearly identifies it. (Search sites may deliver some visitors to a page other than your home page.) Also, link back to your home page.
4. **Title each page.** Give every page on your website a descriptive title. (Check the instructions for your word processor or web-design software.) This title is used by browser bookmarks and search engines.
5. **Keep pages uncluttered.** Use short paragraphs. Dense text is even more difficult to read on screen than on paper. Add headings to identify sections, and include visuals to help break up the text.
6. **Save the page as HTML.** Format pages in Hypertext Markup Language (HTML). Use your word processor's "Save as HTML" or "Save as webpage" option, or use an HTML editing program from the web.

Developing a Website and Webpages

How can I test, refine, and post my site?

Most websites are developed through the combined efforts of writers, graphic designers, and programmers. In such an environment, many content and layout ideas might be considered, rejected, and reformulated to produce and launch the site. Of course, the audience ultimately decides a website's success or failure. For that reason, test and refine your site before posting it.

1. **Check the site yourself.** Open your home page from your web browser. Does the site make sense? Can you navigate it easily?

2. **Get peer review.** Ask classmates—both experienced and inexperienced with the website's topic and with Internet searching—to use your site. Watch them navigate it, and take notes about any confusion.

3. **Check the text.** Reread all the text on your site. Trim wherever possible (the shorter, the better online), and check all spelling and punctuation.

4. **Check the graphics.** Do images load properly? Do they load quickly? Are common elements (such as menus and page headings) in the same place on every page?

5. **Provide a feedback link.** Provide an e-mail address on your site, inviting visitors to contact you with any comments or suggestions after the site goes "live."

6. **Post the site.** Upload the site to your hosting space. (Check your host's instructions for doing so.) Add the posting date to each page, and update it each time you change a page.

7. **Check for universality.** View the site on several different types of computers, using different browsers. Does the layout display well on all of them? Make any needed changes.

8. **Announce the site.** Advertise your site in e-mails. Submit it to search sites. Consider joining a "web ring" of similar sites to draw more traffic. Let professors, classmates, friends, and family know about your site.

9. **Monitor the site.** After a site has been launched, its success may be measured by the amount of traffic it receives, feedback submitted by users, and use of resources or services. (Check with your host for ways to measure traffic.)

10. **Make adjustments and updates.** A website should be a living thing. Update the content when possible to keep it fresh, and make any adjustments needed to adapt to changing technologies.

WRITER'S TIP

Avoid using any features and functions that do not support your overall purpose for writing. If you find yourself distracted by the many bells and whistles of the web, remember that it's better to have a simple website that presents information clearly and effectively than a complex site that does not.

WRITING AND DESIGNING FOR THE WEB

18c Checklist: Developing Websites and Webpages

Use this checklist to review and revise your site and its pages.

____ The purpose of the website is presented—or evident—on the home page and elsewhere on the site.

____ The webpage elements—headlines, body text, preformatted text, background colors, lists, images, and tables—work together and are suited to the page's audience, topic, and purpose.

____ The page functions, including navigation menus, are logically presented and enable readers to find what they need quickly.

____ The content collected for the site (from brochures to reports) and support materials (images, audio, and video) are available, approved, accurate, and in the correct format for presentation or downloading.

____ The site plan allows information to be presented and cross-referenced in logical and efficient pathways.

____ The informational and promotional aspects of the site are proportional to the audience, topic, and purpose.

WAC Link: Study the content, style, and design of websites related to your particular major, field, or discipline. Doing so will help you make appropriate choices related to the webpage elements and functions for any website that you develop as a part of a project in your major. For example, if you are an English Literature major, you could visit academic sites devoted to the study of Shakespeare, Austen, and other authors, as well as sites created by organizations such as the Modern Language Association.

Workplace Link: Businesses rely on websites and web-savvy employees to market their products and services, recruit employees, service customers, share information internally, procure supplies, conduct market research, and plan for the future. Study the websites of businesses, organizations, and professions related to your own career aspirations. Strengthen your web-writing skills now in order to become web-savvy at work.

Grammar

Grammar

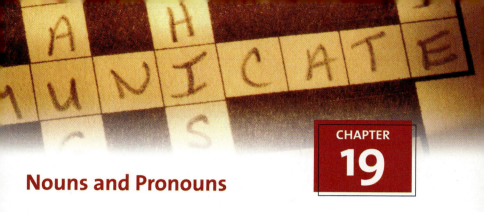

Nouns and Pronouns

Think of a typical sports fan—watching games on television, following the careers of favorite athletes, perhaps even participating in the sport. The fan probably understands most of the rules of the game without ever having read a rule book.

In the same way, you already understand most of the rules of grammar. After all, you've been listening to people speak, reading what they write, and speaking in sentences and paragraphs yourself. As a result, when you read the pages in this chapter, many of the rules will seem familiar.

The rules of grammar begin with the eight parts of speech: noun, pronoun, verb, adjective, adverb, preposition, conjunction, and interjection. (See **19a–21e**.) This chapter focuses on nouns and pronouns.

19a   Nouns

The word *noun* comes from the Latin word for *name*. Nouns name things. All language begins with nouns, from the ancient story of Adam naming the animals to the modern murmurs of a toddler who says "Mama" or "TV." A noun can name a person, a place, a thing, or an idea.

- Clara Barton [a person]   chair [a thing]

  Purdue [a place]   pressure [a thing]

A noun may be introduced with a definite article (*the* pan), an indefinite article (*a* clock, *an* apple), or no article (fear, love). A noun might also be introduced with a demonstrative adjective (*that* girl) or an interrogative adjective (*which* girl).

ESL TIP

Most nouns in English create plurals by adding an *-s* or *-es*, but some show plurals in a different way. These are *noncount nouns*.

homework [singular]

homework assignments [plural—*homework* becomes an adjective]

types of homework [plural—*homework* becomes the object of a preposition]

Note that *homeworks* would be incorrect. For more information about count and noncount nouns, see **34a**.

NOUNS AND PRONOUNS

a closer look

Noun	A **noun** names something: a person, a place, a thing, or an idea.
	Toni Morrison [author] *Lone Star* [film]
	UC-Davis [university] **Renaissance** [era]
	A Congress of Wonders [book]
Pronoun	A **pronoun** is used in place of a noun.
	I my that themselves which
	it ours they everybody you
Verb	A **verb** expresses action or being.
	are break drag fly run
	sit was symbolize catch eat
Adjective	An **adjective** describes or modifies a noun or pronoun. (The articles *a, an,* and *the* are sometimes classified as adjectives.)
	The carbonated drink went down easy on **that hot, dry** day. [*The* and *carbonated* modify *drink; that, hot,* and *dry* modify *day.*]
Adverb	An **adverb** describes or modifies a verb, an adjective, another adverb, or a whole sentence. An adverb generally answers questions such as *how, why, to what degree, when, where, how often,* or *how much.*
	greatly precisely yesterday there consequently
	The car **barely** missed the tree. [The adverb *barely* modifies the verb *missed.*]
Preposition	A **preposition** is a word (or group of words) that shows the relationship between its object (a noun or pronoun that follows the preposition) and another word in the sentence. Prepositions introduce prepositional phrases.
	across for with out to of in spite of
Conjunction	A **conjunction** connects individual words or groups of words.
	Coordinating *Subordinating* *Correlative*
	and **because** **either / or**
	but **until** **not only / but also**
Interjection	An **interjection** is a word that communicates strong emotion or surprise.
	Stop! No! What, am I invisible?

What are the classes of nouns?

All nouns can be classified as either **proper** or **common.** Nouns can also be classified as **individual** or **collective,** and **concrete** or **abstract.**

PROPER NOUNS

A proper noun, which must be capitalized, is the name of a specific person, place, thing, or idea.

- Jan Vermeer [person]   Art Institute [place]
  Big Ben [thing]   Judaism [idea]

Proper: *Big Ben*

Common: *clock*

Concrete: *tower*

Abstract: *time*

COMMON NOUNS

A common noun is a general name for a person, a place, a thing, or an idea. It is not capitalized unless it is the first word of the sentence.

- plumber [person]   clock [thing]
  cafeteria [place]   freedom [idea]

COLLECTIVE NOUNS

A collective noun names a group or a unit.

- team   crowd   class   family   couple

Usually collective nouns are treated as singular and so require a singular verb.

- The **team appreciates** everything that the assistant coach has done.

CONCRETE NOUNS

A concrete noun names a thing that is tangible (can be seen, touched, heard, smelled, or tasted).

- child   singer   Willie Nelson   tower   spinach

ABSTRACT NOUNS

An abstract noun names a thing (idea, condition, or feeling) that is intangible (cannot be seen, touched, heard, smelled, or tasted).

- claustrophobia   fear   love   psychology   time

ESL TIP

Don't confuse the terms *concrete* and *abstract* with the terms *specific* and *general. Singer* and *Willie Nelson* are both concrete, but *Willie Nelson* is more specific. *Fear* and *claustrophobia* are both abstract, but *claustrophobia* is more specific.

NOUNS AND PRONOUNS

What are the forms of nouns?

Nouns are grouped according to their **number, gender,** and **case.**

NUMBER OF NOUNS

Number indicates whether a noun is singular or plural.

A **singular noun** refers to one person, place, thing, or idea.

- rancher   field   (a) sheep   foot

A **plural noun** refers to more than one person, place, thing, or idea.

- ranchers   fields   (many) sheep   feet

ESL TIP

Most nouns in English are made plural by adding *-s* or *-es* to the base word, but some nouns—such as *sheep, deer,* and *fish*—have the same form in both the singular and the plural. Other nouns—such as *mouse/mice, datum/data,* and *focus/foci*—have irregular forms in the plural.

GENDER OF NOUNS

Gender indicates whether a noun is masculine, feminine, neuter, or indefinite.

Masculine
- father   king   brother

Feminine
- mother   queen   sister

Indefinite (masculine or feminine)
- professor   customer   child

Neuter (without gender)
- notebook   monitor   car

CASE OF NOUNS

The case of a noun tells how it is used in a sentence. There are three cases: **nominative** (for subjects), **objective** (for objects), and **possessive** (for showing ownership). Nouns change their form only in the possessive case.

Possessive case is required when a noun is used as a modifier to show possession or ownership.

- Our president's willingness to discuss concerns with students has boosted campus morale. [The singular noun *president* shows possession by adding 's.]

- The deans' meeting has been postponed until next weekend. [The plural noun *deans'* shows possession by adding just an apostrophe.]

19b **Pronouns**

A **pronoun** is a word that is used in place of a noun.

> Roger was the most interesting 10-year-old **I** ever taught. **He** was a good
> thinker and thus a good writer. **I** remember **his** paragraph about the
> cowboy hat **he** received from **his** grandparents. It was "too new looking."
> The brim was not rolled properly. But the hat's imperfections were not
> the main idea in Roger's writing. No, the main idea was about how **he**
> was fixing the hat **himself** by wearing **it** when **he** showered.

What are antecedents?

An antecedent is the noun that the pronoun refers to or replaces. Most pronouns have antecedents, but not all do. Some antecedents are merely implied
(*It* is raining). (See **35c**.) Each pronoun must agree with its antecedent in
number, person, and gender.

- As the wellness **counselor** checked *her* chart, several **students** *who*
  were waiting *their* turns shifted uncomfortably. [*Counselor* is the
  antecedent of *her*; *students* is the antecedent of *who* and *their*.]

In some cases, an antecedent is positioned after the pronoun that refers to it:

- It is not known **when the jury will convene.** [This whole clause is
  the antecedent.]

What are the classes of pronouns?

There are several classes of pronouns: **personal, reflexive, intensive, relative,
indefinite, interrogative, demonstrative,** and **reciprocal.**

PERSONAL PRONOUNS

A personal pronoun refers to a specific person or thing.

- *Marge* started **her** car. **She** drove the antique *convertible* to Monterey,
  where **she** hoped to sell **it** at an auction.

REFLEXIVE PRONOUNS

A reflexive pronoun is formed by adding *-self* or *-selves* to a personal pronoun
(for example, *herself* or *himself*). The pronoun is then used in a sentence
with its antecedent, which becomes the receiver of its own action. A reflexive
pronoun can act as a direct object or an indirect object of a verb, as an object of
a preposition, or as a predicate nominative.

- Charles loves **himself.** [direct object of the verb *loves*]
- Charles gives **himself** A's for fashion sense. [indirect object
  of the verb *gives*]
- Charles smiles at **himself** in store windows. [object of the
  preposition *at*]
- Charles can be **himself** anywhere. [predicate nominative]

NOUNS AND PRONOUNS

Classes of Pronouns	
Personal	
Singular:	I, me, my, mine / you, your, yours / he, him, his, she, her, hers, it, its
Plural:	we, us, our, ours / you, your, yours / they, them, their, theirs
Reflexive and Intensive	
Singular:	myself, yourself, himself, herself, itself
Plural:	ourselves, yourselves, themselves
Relative	who, whose, whom, which, that
Indefinite	all, anything, everyone, neither, one, someone, another, both, everything, nobody, other(s), something, any, each, few, none, several, such, anybody, either, many, no one, some, anyone, everybody, most, nothing, somebody
Interrogative	who, whose, whom, which, what
Demonstrative **Singular:**	this, that
Plural:	these, those
Reciprocal	each other, one another

INTENSIVE PRONOUNS

An intensive pronoun intensifies, or emphasizes, the noun or pronoun to which it refers.

- Leo **himself** taught his children to invest their lives in others.
- The lesson was sometimes painful—but they learned it **themselves**.

RELATIVE PRONOUNS

A relative pronoun "relates" an adjective clause to the noun, pronoun, or clause it modifies. (The noun is italicized in each example below; the relative pronoun is in bold. The whole relative clause is underlined.) Notice that the relative pronoun serves as the subject of the verb in the relative clause. (See **24c**.)

- *Freshmen* **who** believe they have a lot to learn are absolutely right.
- Just navigating this *campus*, **which** is huge, can be challenging.

ESL TIP

Make sure you know when to use the relative pronouns *who* or *whom* and *that* or *which*. (See **15** and **24c**.)

INDEFINITE PRONOUNS

An indefinite pronoun refers to nonspecific or unknown people, places, or things.

- **Everyone** seemed amused when I was searching for my classroom in the student center. [The antecedent of *everyone* is not specified.]
- **Someone** had tampered with the switch. [The antecedent of *someone* is unknown.]

> **NOTE:** The majority of indefinite pronouns are singular; when they are subjects, they should have singular verbs. However, a few indefinite pronouns (*few*, *many*, *others*, *several*, or *both*) are plural and thus require a plural verb, and a few (*all*, *any*, *most*, *none*, or *some*) may be either singular or plural, depending on the items indicated by the noun to which they refer.
>
> - **Some** of the <u>cookie</u> was eaten. [Here *some* is singular because it implies part of a singular cookie.]
> - **Some** of the <u>cookies</u> were eaten. [Here *some* is plural because it implies *more than one* cookie.]

Some was eaten.

Some were eaten.

INTERROGATIVE PRONOUNS

An interrogative pronoun asks a question.

- **Which** of the routes is shorter?
- **What** are we having for dinner?

DEMONSTRATIVE PRONOUNS

A demonstrative pronoun points out people, places, things, or ideas.

- **This** is good advice: Bring along as many maps as you need.
- **Those** are useful tools. **That** is the solution.

"Near" demonstratives—*this*, *these*—point to something near at hand. "Far" demonstratives—*that*, *those*—point to something distant.

> **NOTE:** When the words *this*, *that*, *these*, *those*, *which*, *all*, and *each* modify a noun (instead of replacing it), they become adjectives—*this* teacher, *that* test. (See **21a**.)

RECIPROCAL PRONOUNS

Reciprocal pronouns include words like *one another* or *each other*. These pronouns indicate that an action is performed by two individuals with respect to one another.

- The first-year men painted **each other** blue.

NOUNS AND PRONOUNS

What forms do personal pronouns take?

The form of a personal pronoun indicates its **number** (singular or plural), its **person** (first, second, or third), its **case** (nominative, possessive, or objective), and its **gender** (masculine, feminine, neuter, or indefinite).

NUMBER OF PRONOUNS

A personal pronoun is either singular (*I, you, she, it*) or plural (*we, you, they*).

- **He** should have a budget and stick to **it**. [singular]
- **We** can help new students with **their** budgeting problems. [plural]

PERSON OF PRONOUNS

The person of a pronoun indicates whether the person is speaking (first person), is spoken to (second person), or is spoken about (third person).

First person pronouns name the speaker(s).

- **I** need to handle **my** stress in a healthful way, especially during exam week; **my** usual chips-and-doughnuts binge isn't helping. [singular]
- **We** decided to bike to the tennis court. [plural]

Second person pronouns indicate the person(s) spoken to.

- Maria, **you** grab the rackets, okay? [singular]
- Can **you** find the water bottles near **your** tents? [plural]

Third person pronouns name the person(s) or thing(s) spoken about.

- Today's students are interested in wellness issues. **They** are concerned about **their** health, fitness, and nutrition. [plural]
- Maria practices yoga and feels **she** is calmer for **her** choice. [singular]

CASE OF PRONOUNS

The case of a pronoun tells how it is used in a sentence. There are three cases: **nominative, possessive,** and **objective.**

Nominative case indicates that a pronoun is used as a subject or a subject complement: *I, you, he, she, it, we, they.*

- **He** found an old map in the trunk.   My friend and **I** went biking.
- It was **he** who discovered electricity. [not *him*]

ESL TIP

Be careful not to use an objective-case pronoun in a compound subject. It is incorrect to say "My friend and me went . . ." To check for correctness, simply drop the other element in the compound ("friend"). You would not want to say "Me went . . ."

Possessive-case pronouns show possession or ownership: *my, mine, our, ours, his, her, hers, their, theirs, its, your, yours.*

- This coat is **mine**.   That coat is **hers**.   **Their** coats are lost.

A possessive pronoun may serve as the subject of a sentence, as a subject complement (predicate nominative), as an object of a verb or a preposition, or as an adjective modifying a noun.

- **Mine** was the first to cross the finish line. [*Mine is the subject.*]

  That turtle of **mine** is a winner. [*Mine is an object of the preposition of.*]

- **My** turtle was the first to cross the finish line. [*My is an adjective modifying turtle.*]

Objective case is required when a pronoun is used as a direct or indirect object, or as the object of a preposition: *me, you, him, her, it, us, them.*

- Professor Adler hired **her**. [*Her is the direct object of the verb hired.*]

- He showed Mary and **me** the language lab. [*Me is the indirect object of the verb showed.*]

- He introduced the three of **us**—Mary, Shavonn, and **me**—to the faculty. [*Us is an object of the preposition of. Me is part of an appositive phrase that renames us, so both words must be in the objective case.*]

ESL TIP

Don't use nominative pronouns (*I, he, her*) in compound objects.

- Celia showed her work to Mary and me. [*not Mary and I*]
- This is a secret between you and me. [*not between you and I*]

a closer look

The only other pronouns that show case are the **relative** pronoun *who* and the **interrogative** pronoun *who*. Both types use *who* for the nominative form, *whom* for the objective form, and *whose* for the possessive form (which is used as an adjective).

- The professor **who** wrote the book spoke to our class. [*The relative pronoun who is the subject of the dependent clause who wrote the book.*]

- The student **whom** the driver sideswiped is now in the hospital. [*The relative pronoun whom is the object of the verb sideswiped in the dependent clause.*]

- The contestant **whose** recipe won first prize was ecstatic. [*The relative adjective whose modifies the word recipe.*]

NOUNS AND PRONOUNS

GENDER OF PRONOUNS

The gender of a pronoun indicates whether the pronoun is masculine, feminine, neuter, or indefinite.

Masculine
- he, him, his

Neuter (without gender)
- it, its

Feminine
- she, her, hers

Indefinite (masculine or feminine, plural)
- they, them, their

NUMBER, PERSON, AND CASE OF PERSONAL PRONOUNS	Nominative Case	Possessive Case	Objective Case
First Person Singular	I	my, mine	me
Second Person Singular	you	your, yours	you
Third Person Singular	he, she, it	his, her, hers, its	him, her, it
First Person Plural	we	our, ours	us
Second Person Plural	you	your, yours	you
Third Person Plural	they	their, theirs	them

19c Using Nouns and Pronouns Stylistically

Use the most **specific noun** you can (often a proper noun). Specific nouns make writing clear and exact.

> **General Nouns:** The **class** focused on two **philosophers**.
>
> **Specific Nouns:** **Greek Philosophy 101** focused on **Socrates** and **Plato**.

Use **concrete nouns** to explain and illustrate **abstract nouns.** Concrete nouns help pin down big ideas.

> **Abstract Nouns:** Plato felt a **nation** should be ruled by **wisdom**.
>
> **Concrete Nouns:** He suggested that a **philosopher-king** rule **Greece**.

Most often, make sure your **pronouns** have clear **antecedents.** Unclear antecedents make your meaning murky. (See **19b** and **25h**.)

> **Unclear Antecedent:** Socrates taught Plato, and **he** wrote the *Republic*.
>
> **Clear Antecedent:** Socrates taught Plato, **who** later wrote the *Republic*.

However, when you wish to create suspense in a narrative or story, you can intentionally withhold information by using unclear antecedents.

> As he lay on his deathbed, the hemlock vial clutched in his hand, Socrates looked up and saw her: the one woman he had pursued all through his life but had never caught. She stood before him now, her arms open. With his last breath, he whispered her name, "Sophia"— the name of Wisdom.

Verbs

$\mathbf{F}$or centuries, physicists have grappled with matter and energy—and writers have grappled with nouns and verbs. It's the same struggle, really. After all, nouns describe stuff (matter) and verbs describe motion (energy). When Einstein connected matter and energy, he came up with $E = mc^2$. When Shakespeare connected nouns and verbs, he came up with "There are more things in heaven and earth, Horatio, than are dreamt of in your philosophy." When you understand nouns and verbs, you can create a brilliant new idea.

20a Action Verbs

Verbs are words that show action or being. A noun alone is simply the name of a thing, and a verb alone is simply a word that expresses what is happening. Together, a noun and a verb can create a thought.

Verbs that show action are called **action verbs.**

- throw   shine   think   surround   imply

Action verbs can be transitive or intransitive.

What are transitive and intransitive verbs?

A transitive verb is an action verb that requires a direct object (direct objects indicate *who* or *what* receives the action) to complete its meaning. (See **22d**.)

- The health care industry **employs** more than 7 million workers in the United States. [*Workers* is the direct object of the verb *employs*.]

Intransitive verbs communicate action that is complete in itself, without requiring any object or complement to complete the idea.

- My new roommate **smiles** and **laughs** a lot.

Adverbs may appear either before or after an intransitive verb.

- My roommate typically **smiles** cynically when asked for a favor.

> **NOTE:** Some verbs can be either transitive or intransitive.
>
> - Ms. Hull **teaches** microbiology. [Here the verb *teaches* is transitive because it has a direct object, *microbiology*.]
> - She **teaches** well. [Here the verb is intransitive.]

VERBS

20b Linking Verbs

Verbs that show states of being are called linking verbs. The linking verb is usually part of the *be* verb family.

- I **am** the new student.   **Are** you my tutor?

However, other verbs appealing to the senses or to processes can serve as linking verbs if they do not show actual action. (In other words, the verb *is* can replace them.) Usually an adjective—but sometimes a noun—follows these linking verbs.

- The thunder **sounded** ominous. [adjective]
- Her hair **appeared** a mess. [noun]

Common Linking Verbs							
am	is	are	was	were	be	being	been

Additional Linking Verbs					
appear	become	feel	grow	look	prove
remain	seem	smell	sound	taste	

NOTE: When the additional linking verbs are used as action verbs, an adverb or a direct object may follow them.

- I **looked** carefully at him. [adverb]
- My little brother **grew** corn for a science project. [direct object]

What do linking verbs link?

A linking verb links the subject of a sentence to the **subject complement**—a noun, a pronoun, or an adjective in the predicate. If the subject complement is a noun or noun phrase, the complement is called a **predicate nominative.** If the complement is an adjective or adjectival phrase modifying the subject, the complement is called a **predicate adjective.**

- The streets **are** rivers! [predicate nominative]
- The streets **are** dirty. [predicate adjective]

ESL TIP

Subject complements are not to be confused with **object complements,** which may be either nouns or adjectives completing the sense of a direct object. (See **22d.**)

20c Auxiliary Verbs

Auxiliary verbs (helping verbs) help to form the *tense* (**20e**), *mood* (**20g**), and *voice* (**20f**) of the main verb. In the following example, the auxiliary verbs are in **bold,** and the main verbs are in *italics.*

■ I *believe,* I **have** always *believed,* and I **will** always *believe* in private enterprise as the backbone of economic well-being in America.

—Franklin D. Roosevelt

Common Auxiliary Verbs

am	been	could	does	have	might	should	will
are	being	did	had	is	must	was	would
be	can	do	has	may	shall	were	

ESL TIP

Be auxiliary verbs are always followed by either a verb ending in *-ing* or a past participle.

■ We **are discovering** a few things about auxiliary verbs.

■ We **were invited** to join the Auxiliary Verb Auxiliary.

20d Verb Forms

All English verbs (except *be*) have five forms.

Base Form	Past Tense	Past Participle	Present Participle	-s Form
look	looked	(have) looked	(am) looking	looks
see	saw	(has) seen	(is) seeing	sees

Base Form:	I **water** my plants weekly.
Past Tense:	I **watered** them twice last week.
Past Participle:	I **have watered** them all summer.
Present Participle:	I **am watering** them right now.
-s Form:	My neighbor **waters** them when I'm gone.

A verb's form depends on its **number** (singular, plural), **person** (first, second, third), **tense** (present, past, future), **voice** (active, passive), and **mood** (indicative, imperative, subjunctive).

What are the forms of the verb *be?*

The verb *be* has eight forms because three different *be* verbs are used for forming future, perfect, and progressive tenses: will *be*, has *been*, and are *being.*

■ is   am   are   was   were   be   being   been

VERBS

20e Tense

Tense indicates the *time* in which an action or a state of being occurs. There are three **simple tenses** (present, past, and future).

Present:	I walk.	I bring.	I sing.
Past:	I walked.	I brought.	I sang.
Future:	I will walk.	I will bring.	I will sing.

What is present tense?

Present tense expresses action that is happening at the present time or action that happens continually or regularly.

- In the United States, more than 75 percent of workers **hold** service jobs.
- Seattle **receives** more than triple the annual rainfall of Phoenix.

Present progressive tense also expresses action that is happening at the present time, but this tense stresses the ongoing nature of the action.

- Termites **are chewing** on the foundations even as we speak.

Present perfect tense expresses action that began in the past and has recently been completed or is still occurring at the present time.

- My sister **has taken** four years of swimming lessons.
- John **has collected** bottle caps since he was a child.

Present perfect progressive tense also expresses an action that began in the past, but this tense stresses the continuing nature of the action.

- She **has been taking** swimming lessons since she was six years old.
- The government **has been failing** to provide for its poorest citizens.

What is past tense?

Past tense expresses action that was completed at a particular time in the past.

- A hundred years ago, more than 75 percent of all laborers **worked** in agriculture.

Past progressive tense expresses now-completed action that had occurred over an interval of time in the past.

- A century ago, my great-grandparents **were farming**.

Past perfect tense expresses an action that was completed prior to another past action or prior to a specific past time.

- By dinner time my cousins **had eaten** all the olives.

Past perfect progressive tense expresses a completed past action but stresses the recurring, rather than the completed, nature of the action.

- They **had been eating** the olives long before our arrival.

What is future tense?

Future tense expresses action that will take place in the future.

- Next summer I **will work** as a lifeguard.

Future progressive tense expresses continuous action in the future.

- I **will be working** for the park district at North Beach.

Future perfect tense expresses action that will be completed by a specific time in the future.

- By 10:00 p.m., I **will have completed** my research project.

Future perfect progressive tense expresses future action that will be well under way by a specific time, but (like other progressive tenses) stresses the action's duration or continuous nature rather than its completion.

- I **will have been researching** my project for three weeks by the time it's due.

Verb Conjugation				
	Regular Verb (*Walk*)		***Be* Verbs**	
Present	I walk you walk he/she/it walks	we walk you walk they walk	I am you are he/she/it is	we are you are they are
Past	I walked you walked he/she/it walked	we walked you walked they walked	I was you were he/she/it was	we were you were they were
Future	I will walk you will walk he/she/it will walk	we will walk you will walk they will walk	I will be you will be he/she/it will be	we will be you will be they will be
Present Perfect	I have walked you have walked he/she/it has walked	we have walked you have walked they have walked	I have been you have been he/she/it has been	we have been you have been they have been
Present Progressive	I am walking you are walking he/she/it is walking	we are walking you are walking they are walking	I am being you are being he/she/it is being	we are being you are being they are being

ESL TIP

Speakers of French, German, Russian, and Greek may struggle with progressive forms, since these languages do not include them. Urdu and Hindi speakers should try not to overuse progressive verb forms. (See 34c.)

20f Voice

Voice indicates whether the subject is acting or is being acted upon by someone or something else.

Active voice indicates that the subject of the sentence is performing the action of the verb.

- The ranchers **chase** the horses onto protected lands. [The subject, *ranchers*, is doing the chasing.]

Passive voice indicates that the subject of the verb is being acted upon or is receiving the action. In other words, the action of the verb is performed *not* by the subject, but by another person or thing (who may or may not be mentioned in the sentence). A passive verb is formed by combining a form of the *be* verb with a past participle. (For tips on using passive voice, see **13c**.)

- Wild horses **are chased** onto protected lands. [The subject, *horses*, is receiving the action. The verb's action is performed by someone (ranchers) not mentioned in the sentence.]

ACTIVE AND PASSIVE VOICE

Tense	Active	Passive
Present	I call	I am called
Past	I called	I was called
Future	I will call	I will be called
Present Perfect	I have called	I have been called
Present Progressive	I am calling	I am being called
Present Perfect Progressive	I have been calling	I have been being called
Past Perfect	I had called	I had been called
Past Progressive	I was calling	I was being called
Past Perfect Progressive	I had been calling	I had been being called
Future Perfect	I will have called	I will have been called
Future Progressive	I will be calling	I will be being called
Future Perfect Progressive	I will have been calling	I will have been being called

20g Mood

The mood of a verb indicates the tone or attitude with which a statement is made. Different moods include indicative, imperative, and subjunctive.

Indicative mood, the most common type of mood, is used to state a fact or to ask a question.

- **Can** any theme **capture** the essence of the complex 1960s culture? President John F. Kennedy's directive [stated below] **represents** one ideal that was popular during that decade.

Imperative mood is used to give a command. (The subject of an imperative sentence is *you*, which is usually understood and not stated in the sentence.)

- **Ask** not what your country can do for you—**ask** what you can do for your country.   —John F. Kennedy

Subjunctive mood is gradually falling out of use among many speakers of modern English. In certain situations, however, it is still commonly used in correct speech to express a wish, a possibility, a condition contrary to fact, a formal request, a necessity, or a motion in a formal meeting. The subjunctive mood is often used with *if* or *that*. It is typically formed by using the base form of the verb without altering it to show tense or number.

- We insisted that she **conclude** [not *concluded* or *would conclude*] early.
- The judge suggested that he **be** [not *was*] present at the hearing.
- The English Department requires that every student **pass** a proficiency test.
- I move that the motion **be** passed. [not *is*]

> **NOTE:** In clauses stating wishes, possibilities, or conditions contrary to fact, the subjunctive form of the *be* verb is *were*.

- If she **were** in that car, she might have been killed.
- If I **were** rich, I would travel for the rest of my life.
- **Were** they better trained, they would not have become confused.
- If each of your brain cells **were** one person, there would be enough people to populate twenty-five planets.

ESL TIP

Be careful not to use the subjunctive mood if the condition expressed is true or will probably become true.

- If she **was** [not *were*] an actress, she would know how it feels to perform for an audience. She is likely to travel for the rest of her life if she **becomes** [not *were*] rich.

VERBS

20h Irregular Verbs

Base Form	Past Tense	Past Participle
arise	arose	arisen
awake	awoke	awoken, awaked
be	was, were	been
beat	beat	beaten
become	became	become
begin	began	begun
bite	bit	bitten, bit
blow	blew	blown
break	broke	broken
bring	brought	brought
build	built	built
burn	burned	burned, burnt
buy	bought	bought
catch	caught	caught
choose	chose	chosen
come	came	come
dig	dug	dug
dive	dived, dove	dived
do	did	done
draw	drew	drawn
dream	dreamed	dreamed, dreamt
drink	drank	drunk
drive	drove	driven
eat	ate	eaten
fall	fell	fallen
feel	felt	felt
fight	fought	fought
find	found	found
flee	fled	fled
fly	flew	flown
forget	forgot	forgotten, forgot
freeze	froze	frozen
get	got	got, gotten
give	gave	given
go	went	gone
grow	grew	grown
hang (execute)	hanged	hanged
hang (suspend)	hung	hung
have	had	had
hear	heard	heard
hide	hid	hidden
keep	kept	kept
know	knew	known
lay	laid	laid
lead	led	led
leave	left	left

Base Form	Past Tense	Past Participle
lend	lent	lent
lie (deceive)	lied	lied
lie (recline)	lay	lain
make	made	made
mean	meant	meant
meet	met	met
pay	paid	paid
prove	proved	proved, proven
ride	rode	ridden
ring	rang	rung
rise	rose	risen
run	ran	run
see	saw	seen
shake	shook	shaken
shine (light)	shone	shone
show	showed	shown, showed
shrink	shrank	shrunk
sing	sang	sung
sink	sank	sunk
sit	sat	sat
sleep	slept	slept
speak	spoke	spoken
spend	spent	spent
spring	sprang	sprung
stand	stood	stood
steal	stole	stolen
strike	struck	struck, stricken
strive	strove	striven, strived
swear	swore	sworn
swim	swam	swum
swing	swung	swung
take	took	taken
teach	taught	taught
tear	tore	torn
tell	told	told
think	thought	thought
throw	threw	thrown
wake	woke	woken, waked
wear	wore	worn
weave	wove	woven, weaved
wind	wound	wound, winded
wring	wrung	wrung
write	wrote	written

NOTE: The following verbs are the same in all three principal parts: *burst, cost, cut, hit, let, put, read,* and *set.*

VERBS

20i Verbals

A verbal is a word that is made from a verb but functions as a noun, an adjective, or an adverb. There are three types of verbals: *gerunds, infinitives,* and *participles.* The verbal in combination with objects or modifiers makes up a verbal phrase. The phrase as a whole serves a particular grammatical function—as a *noun,* an *adjective,* or an *adverb.*

What are gerunds?

A gerund is a verbal that functions as a *noun* and ends in *-ing.* A gerund or a gerund phrase may be used in any of the ways a noun is used: as a *subject,* an *indirect object,* a *direct object,* an *object of a preposition,* or a *predicate noun.*

- **Waking** is the first challenge. [gerund as subject]
- **Waking to an alarm each morning** is the first challenge. [gerund phrase as a subject]
- The judges gave her **singing** a thorough evaluation. [gerund as indirect object]
- The judges gave her **singing before an audience** a thorough evaluation. [gerund phrase as an indirect object]
- I start **moving** at about seven o'clock. [gerund as direct object]

What are infinitives?

An infinitive is a base verb preceded by the word *to*—which is the "sign of the infinitive." An infinitive may be used as a *noun,* an *adjective,* or an *adverb.* Like gerunds, infinitives are often accompanied by objects and modifying words.

- **To err** is human, **to forgive** divine. [infinitive as a noun, acting as a subject]
- The general wanted **to attack before dawn**. [infinitive phrase as a noun, acting as a direct object]
- That is the most important thing **to remember**. [infinitive as an adjective modifying *thing*]
- Students are wise **to work hard**. [infinitive phrase as an adverb modifying the predicate adjective *wise*]

ESL TIP

A few verbs—*have, let,* and *make*—call for a noun or pronoun object followed by an infinitive without the normal "to" sign of the infinitive. When you see this "unmarked infinitive," you should still recognize the expression for the infinitive that it is.

- Usually, we **have** the valet *bring* the car around. [not *to bring*]
- The Federal Reserve Chairman **let** inflation *set* in. [not *to set*]

What are participles?

A present participle is a verbal that ends in *-ing* and functions as an *adjective*. A past participle ends in *-ed* (or another past tense form) and also functions as an *adjective*.

- The prospect of **aced** tests and assignments must be **appealing**.
  [*Aced* is a past participle modifying *tests* and *assignments*, and *appealing* is a present participle modifying *prospect*.]

A participial phrase, like each of the other types of verbal phrases, may have a direct object. The object of the participle *reading* below is *handouts*.

- The students **reading** those study-skill handouts look unhappy.
  [*Reading* modifies *students*; the whole participial phrase is underlined.]

Which main verbs take which verbals?

Make sure that you use verbals correctly after main verbs that call for them. After some verbs, such as *begin, continue, hate, like, love, start,* and *try,* you may use either a gerund or an infinitive without altering the intended meaning.

- If Robert **continues** *hitting* his classmate, discipline should follow.
- If Robert **continues** *to hit* his classmate, discipline should follow.

However, after many other verbs—such as *admit, deny, enjoy, imagine, propose, quit,* or *suggest*—only a **gerund** will do.

- Can you **recall** stopping before the march was over? [not *to stop*]

After certain other verbs—such as *claim, expect, hope, manage, offer, plan,* or *want*—an **infinitive** will work fine, but not a gerund.

- Do you **expect** to move that piano by yourself? [not *moving*]

What if a noun or a pronoun follows the verb?

Some active verbs can be followed by an infinitive only if a noun or a pronoun comes first, showing who is supposed to perform the action named in the infinitive. Verbs such as *advise, allow, bid, cause, coax, command, convince, encourage, instruct, order, persuade, press, prevail on, prompt, push, remind, require, tell, urge,* and *warn* work this way.

- The coach **told** the new recruits *to report* to the gym.

Verbs such as *ask, desire, expect, intend, love, need, promise, want,* and *would like* may be followed directly by an infinitive, or they may be followed by a noun or a pronoun followed by an infinitive. However, without the noun or pronoun, the emphasis is on the action the subject will perform. With the noun or pronoun, the emphasis is on the action connected to the object.

- The escaping prisoner **intended** *to run* beyond the border.
- The conductor **expects** the concert *to run* as long as necessary.

20j Using Verbs Stylistically

Verbs are the powerhouses of language. They give writing its spark, its energy, its explosive potential. The right verbs can *show* readers just what you mean, let them *hear* what is happening, and create *metaphors* that let them see ideas in a new way.

How can verbs *show?*

Active verbs show the reader just what is happening, rather than tell them what has happened. Use active verbs rather than linking verbs to make your writing dynamic. (See guidelines for using passive voice, 13c.)

Linking Verb: Josh *was* elated when he won the snowboarding competition.

Active Verbs: Josh *whooped* and *strutted* when he won the snowboarding competition.

How can verbs let readers *hear* what is happening?

Many verbs in English sound like the action they describe. They are **onomatopoetic.** Use onomatopoetic verbs to fill your writing with vivid sounds.

Chomp!

laugh	break	yell	eat
chuckle	crack	holler	gulp
giggle	smash	bellow	gobble
snicker	shatter	blare	chomp
guffaw	crunch	shriek	swallow
cackle	rip	roar	nibble
bray	split	blast	gnaw

How can verbs create metaphors?

Linking verbs create metaphors by equating two dissimilar things.

- The freshman **was** a shy flower. [*Flower* is a predicate noun renaming *freshman*.]
- The senator **became** a bulldozer in Congress. [*Bulldozer* is a predicate noun renaming *senator*.]

In a more sophisticated metaphor, the verb itself expresses the idea.

- The freshman **bloomed** in certain company.
- The senator **bulldozed** his bill through Congress.

Other Parts of Speech

A sentence in English requires, at minimum, a noun and a verb.

- **Henry eats.**

But the richness of the language comes from words that modify the nouns and verbs: adjectives, adverbs, and modifying phrases and clauses.

- My younger brother **Henry eats** by scooping his food with his bare hand and pouring it into his mouth like a backhoe dumping dirt.

This chapter will help you use adjectives, adverbs, prepositions, conjunctions, and interjections effectively.

21a Adjectives

Adjectives are called modifiers because they change the meaning of a noun or pronoun—whether by a little or by a lot. A building is just a building until an adjective makes it *palatial* or *ramshackle*. An adjective modifies a noun or pronoun by answering questions such as *which one*, *what kind*, *how many*, or *how much*.

- *That* solution is *unacceptable* because it has *three* problems.
  [Which?]   [What kind?]   [How many?]

> **NOTE:** Words such as *that, these, many, some,* and *whose* are adjectives when they modify a noun. (Otherwise, they are pronouns.) In the same way, numbers that modify nouns are also adjectives. Even the articles *a, an,* and *the* are technically adjectives.

What other words and phrases act as adjectives?

Participles and participial phrases function as adjectives.

- **Spent**, the climbers reached base camp. [participle as adjective describing *climbers*]
- **Sitting around the campfire**, they waited for shooting stars. [participial phrase as adjective describing *they*]

Prepositional phrases also can function as adjectives.

- The skies **of August** host the Perseid meteor shower.

OTHER PARTS OF SPEECH

What are proper adjectives?

Proper adjectives are created when proper nouns modify nouns. Proper adjectives are capitalized.

- **English** has been influenced by advertising slogans. [proper noun]
- The **English** language is constantly changing. [proper adjective]

What are predicate adjectives?

A predicate adjective follows a form of the *be* verb (or a form of any other linking verb, such as *appear* or *looked*) and describes the subject.

- At its best, advertising is **useful**; at its worst, it is **deceptive**.
  [*Useful* and *deceptive* modify the noun *advertising*.]

What forms can adjectives take?

Adjectives have three forms: *positive*, *comparative*, and *superlative*.

Positive:	fine	good	bad
Comparative:	finer	better	worse
Superlative:	finest	best	worst

good better best

The **positive form** is the adjective in its regular form, which describes a noun or a pronoun without comparing it to anyone or anything else.

- Joysport walking shoes are **strong**.

The **comparative form** (*-er*, *more*, or *less*) compares two things. (The words *more* and *less* are generally used with adjectives of two or more syllables.)

- Mile Eaters are **stronger** than Joysports.

The **superlative form** (*-est*, *most*, or *least*) compares three or more things. (The words *most* and *least* are used with adjectives of two or more syllables.)

- Canvas Wonders are the **strongest** shoes of all.

INCOMPARABLE QUALITIES

Some states of being—such as *pregnant*, *superior*, or *peerless*—are absolute, not matters of degree. Do not use qualifiers, such as *very*, with these words.

- She is pregnant. [not *more pregnant*]
- Edison had a superior intellect. [not *very superior*]

ESL TIP

In standard English, don't use two comparative and superlative words together: *better*, not *more better*; *worst*, not *most worst*.

21b Adverbs

An adverb describes or modifies a verb, an adjective, another adverb, or a whole sentence. An adverb answers questions such as *how, when, where, why, how often, how much,* or *to what degree.*

- The temperature fell **sharply**.
  [*Sharply* modifies the verb *fell*. Fell how?]
- **Yesterday** the temperature was not low.
  [*Yesterday* modifies the whole sentence. When?]
- The temperature dropped **very quickly**.
  [*Very* modifies the adverb *quickly*. How quickly?
  Quickly modifies the verb *dropped*. How did it drop?]
- The temperature **rarely** stays cool.
  [*Rarely* modifies the verb *stays*. How often?]

What types of adverbs are there?

Adverbs can be grouped in four ways: *time, place, manner,* and *degree.*

> **Time:** These adverbs tell *when, how often,* and *how long.*
> - **today, yesterday daily, weekly briefly, eternally**
>
> **Place:** These adverbs tell *where, to where,* and *from where.*
> - **here, there nearby, beyond backward, forward**
>
> **Manner:** These adverbs often end in *-ly* and tell *how* something is done.
> - **precisely regularly regally smoothly well**
>
> **Degree:** These adverbs tell *how much* or *how little.*
> - **substantially greatly entirely partly too**

What else can act as an adverb?

Groups of words serve as adverbs if, taken as a unit, they modify a verb, an adverb, an adjective, or a whole sentence.

- The cat burglar wore his turtleneck **too high to be recognized**.
  [*Too high to be recognized* modifies the verb *wore*.]

In this example, the infinitive phrase *to be recognized* combines with the adverbs *too high* to form an adverb phrase modifying the main verb, *wore.*

- **Because he loved turtlenecks**, he was dubbed "the turtle burglar."
  [*Because he loved turtlenecks* modifies the verb phrase *was dubbed*.]

OTHER PARTS OF SPEECH

What forms do adverbs take?

Adverbs of manner have three forms: *positive*, *comparative*, and *superlative*.

The **positive form** is the adverb in its regular form, often ending in *-ly*. In this form, the adverb describes verbs, adjectives, or other adverbs without comparing them to anyone or anything else.

- With Joysport shoes, you'll walk **quickly**. They support your feet **well**.

The **comparative form** (*-er*, *more*, or *less*) compares two things. (*More* and *less* are generally used with adverbs of two or more syllables.)

- Wear Jockos instead of Joysport, and you'll walk **more quickly**. Jockos' special soles support your feet **better** than the BlisSports' do.

The **superlative form** (*-est*, *most*, or *least*) compares three or more things. (*Most* and *least* are generally used with adverbs of two or more syllables.)

- Really, I walk **most quickly** wearing my old Canvas Wonders. They seem to support my feet, my knees, and my pocketbook **best** of all.

Regular Adverbs

Positive	*Comparative*	*Superlative*
fast	faster	fastest
effectively	more effectively	most effectively

Irregular Adverbs

Positive	*Comparative*	*Superlative*
well	better	best
badly	worse	worst

ESL TIP

Use adverbs to modify action verbs, and use adjectives following linking verbs. Remember that some verbs can act as either action verbs or linking verbs. Verbs such as *appear, taste, smell,* and other words that have to do with physical senses may function either way. Be careful, then, to determine what type of verb you are using—action or linking.

- This chair feels **good**. [In this sentence, *feels* is a linking verb and is followed by the predicate adjective *good*.]
- I can feel its support very **well**. [In this sentence, *feel* is an action verb and is modified by the adverb *well*.]

21c Prepositions

A preposition is a word (or group of words) that shows the relationship between its object (a noun or pronoun following the preposition) and another word in the sentence.

- **Regarding** your request **for** additional time, I can give it **to** you this time. [In this sentence, *request, time,* and *you* are objects of their preceding prepositions *regarding, for,* and *to.*]

How are prepositional phrases formed?

A prepositional phrase is formed from a preposition, the object of the preposition, and any words modifying the object. A prepositional phrase may function as an adjective or an adverb.

- A broader knowledge **of the world** is one benefit **of higher education**. [The two prepositional phrases function as adjectives modifying the nouns *knowledge* and *benefit,* respectively.]
- Exercising your brain may safeguard **against atrophy**. [The phrase functions as an adverb modifying the verb *may safeguard.*]

Common Prepositions

aboard	beneath	in front of	over to
about	beside	in place of	owing to
above	besides	in regard to	past
according to	between	inside	prior to
across	beyond	inside of	regarding
across from	but	in spite of	round
after	by	instead of	save
against	by means of	into	since
along	concerning	like	subsequent to
alongside	considering	near	through
alongside of	despite	near to	throughout
along with	down	notwithstanding	to
amid	down from	of	together with
among	during	off	toward
apart from	except	on	under
around	except for	on account of	underneath
as far as	excepting	on behalf of	until
aside from	for	onto	unto
at	from	on top of	up
away from	from among	opposite	upon
back of	from between	out	up to
because of	from under	out of	with
before	in	outside	within
behind	in addition to	outside of	without
below	in behalf of	over	

OTHER PARTS OF SPEECH

21d Conjunctions

A conjunction connects individual words, phrases, or clauses, showing the logic of their relationship.

Conjunctions		
Coordinating	**Correlative**	**Subordinating**
and for but so or yet nor	both/and either/or neither/nor not only/but also whether/or	after than although, though that, so that as, as if unless because, since until before when, whenever if where, whereas

What are coordinating conjunctions?

Coordinating conjunctions connect a word to a word, a phrase to a phrase, or a clause to a clause. The words, phrases, or clauses joined by a coordinating conjunction are equal in importance and usually are of the same type.

■ Civilization is a race between education **and** catastrophe. [connects two nouns that are objects of the preposition *between*]   —H. G. Wells

■ Civilization begins with order, grows with liberty, **and** dies with chaos. [connects a series of phrases]   —Will Durant

What are correlative conjunctions?

Correlative conjunctions are a type of coordinating conjunction used in pairs to show how two grammatically equal elements are related.

■ There are two inadvisable ways to think: **either** believe everything **or** doubt everything.

■ We must exercise **not only** our bodies **but also** our minds.

What are subordinating conjunctions?

Subordinating conjunctions introduce subordinate (or dependent) clauses, showing how they are related to another element in the sentence.

■ Experience is the worst teacher; it gives the test before it presents the lesson. [The clause *before it presents the lesson* is dependent. It serves as an adverb modifying the verb *gives* in the main clause.]

21e Interjections

An interjection communicates strong emotion or surprise (*oh, ouch, hey,* and so on). A comma or an exclamation point is used to set off an interjection.

■ **Hey! Wait! Well**, so much for catching the bus.

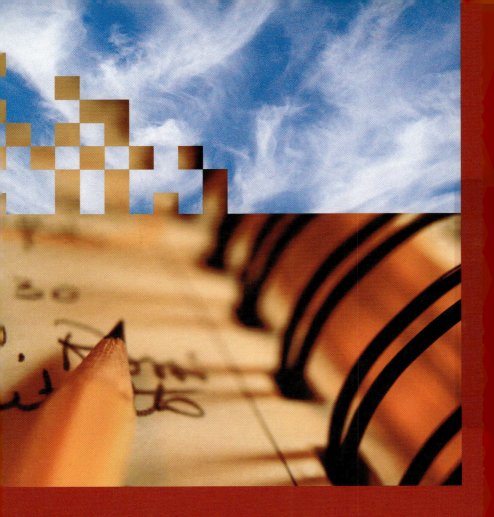

Sentences

Sentences

Sentence Basics

When a noun and a verb team up, magic happens. A noun by itself is just a name, and a verb by itself is just an action, but when you put the two together, you have a whole thought. The sentence is the fundamental unit of thought. Understanding sentences will help you improve your writing and your thinking.

22a Subjects

In a sentence, the subject names the person or thing that the predicate states something about. The subject is most often a noun or a pronoun, but it can also be a gerund or a phrase or clause acting as a noun.

- **Wolves** have clear rankings in their packs.
  [The subject is a noun.]
- The alpha **male** leads the pack.
  [The subject is a noun with modifiers.]
- **It** is often the largest and strongest wolf.
  [The subject is a pronoun.]
- **Howling** allows pack members to communicate across distances.
  [The subject is a gerund, which acts as a noun.]
- **To challenge the alpha male** is dangerous and sometimes deadly.
  [The subject is an infinitive phrase acting as a noun.]

ESL TIP

Some languages allow nouns and pronouns to be doubled up in a subject, but English does not. This is an error called a double subject.

Incorrect:	**Wolves, they** have clear rankings in their packs.
Correct:	**Wolves** have clear rankings in their packs.

Be especially careful to avoid creating a double subject when a phrase or clause comes between the subject and the rest of the sentence.

Incorrect:	**Howling**, which can be heard miles away, **it** allows wolves to communicate.
Correct:	**Howling**, which can be heard miles away, allows wolves to communicate.

What are simple and complete subjects?

The **simple subject** is the noun or pronoun without any words or phrases that modify it. (Hard-core **surfers** flock to Maui.) The **complete subject** is the simple subject plus any words that modify it. (**Hard-core surfers** flock to Maui.)

> **NOTE:** Phrases or clauses functioning as nouns can be simple subjects.
>
> - **To surf Maui's Jaws** may be life-threatening. [infinitive phrase]
> - **Mastering Maui's Jaws** or **surfing in cold water** tests even the world's best surfers. [a combination of gerund phrases]
> - **That Jaws will never be fully conquered** goes without saying. [noun clause]

ESL TIP

To determine the subject of a sentence, ask yourself a question that begins with *who* or *what* and ends with the predicate. The answer to your question is the subject. [What may be life-threatening? *To surf Maui's Jaws*]

What are compound subjects?

A compound subject consists of two or more simple subjects joined by a coordinating or correlative conjunction. The subjects share the predicate.

- **Faculty** and **students** study the currents. [The subjects are joined by the coordinating conjunction *and*; they share the predicate *study*.]
- Neither the **way** we prepare nor the **quality** of our equipment matters. [The subjects are joined by the correlative conjunctions *neither* and *nor*; they share the predicate *matters*.]

> **NOTE:** Do not confuse compound subjects with compound sentences.
>
> **Compound sentences** are made up of two independent clauses joined by a semicolon or a coordinating conjunction preceded by a comma.
>
> Compound subject:
> **Bodyboarding** and **tube riding** are offshoots of surfing. [Do not use a comma between the two parts of a compound subject.]
>
> Compound sentence:
> **Bodyboarding** is an offshoot of surfing, and **tube riding** is considered so as well. [With a coordinating conjunction, a comma is used between the two independent clauses in a compound sentence.]

When should I use commas with compound subjects?

If the compound subject is a series, or if the compound subject contains a nonessential modifying phrase within the compound, use a comma to separate the parts. Study these examples.

Correct: Blue skies, changing leaves, and crisp winds foretell the winter.
[This compound subject needs commas to separate the elements in the series.]

Correct: The equinox, when day and night are equal, and the encroaching darkness give autumn its gentle melancholy.
[This compound subject needs commas to enclose the nonessential appositive clause *when day and night are equal.*]

Incorrect: Closed beaches, and open schools, don't help much, either.
[This compound subject should not be separated by commas.]

What are understood or implied subjects?

Though some languages permit sentences without subjects, English does not. Every sentence in English needs a subject, but it may be an **understood** or **implied subject.**

In imperative sentences, which give commands or make requests, the subject (*you*) is usually understood.

- [You] Watch your breath turn to steam.

In some sentences that discuss weather, time, distance, or other conditions, the pronoun *it* serves as a subject whose general sense is **implied.**

- It was 45 degrees in the sun this afternoon. [*It* = the temperature]
- It was dark when we left class. [*It* = the day]
- It is a long way back to the dorm. [*It* = the distance]

ESL TIP

Some English sentences have a delayed subject, a subject that appears after the verb. These sentences often begin with the expletive *it* or *there.*

- It is an important step. [Not *Is an important step.*]
- There are three apples. [Not *Are three apples.*]

Speakers of Chinese, Japanese, Korean, Thai, Spanish, Portuguese, Italian, German, and Russian should be especially careful not to omit the *it* or *there* when writing these sorts of sentences. Note, however, that overuse of expletives is a stylistic weakness. (See **13d**.)

22b Predicates

The predicate is the part of a clause that states something about the subject. The predicate conveys what the subject does, what the subject is, or what specific characteristic the subject has. At a minimum, the predicate includes a one word verb, but it may also include verbs of more than one word. In addition, a predicate may include complements and modifiers that clarify the sentence's meaning.

What are simple and complete predicates?

A **simple predicate** is the verb or verb phrase (the main verb plus any auxiliary verbs). A **complete predicate** is the verb, its modifiers (adverbs and adverbial phrases or clauses), and any complements (direct objects, indirect objects, object complements, or subject complements).

- Makua Rothman **has won** $66,000 for surfing a 66-foot blue monster at Jaws. [The verb *has won* is the simple predicate.]

- Makua Rothman **has won $66,000 for surfing a 66-foot blue monster at Jaws**. [The verb *has won,* the direct object *$66,000,* and two prepositional phrases make up the complete predicate.]

What are compound predicates?

A compound predicate is composed of two or more simple predicates usually joined by a coordinating or correlative conjunction. The predicates share the same subject.

- Raul **swims** and **skates** for exercise. [The compound predicate is *swims and skates.*]

- The magazine **commissioned** a survey of the water depth and **reported** the results. [In this sentence, *commissioned* is one part of the compound predicate, and *reported* is the other.]

> **NOTE:** As is the case for compound subjects (**22a**), no comma should separate the elements of a compound predicate unless the predicate includes a list or a nonessential phrase or clause.
>
> - The writer **called** the experts, **got** the information, and **wrote** the story. [a list of three phrases in the predicate]
> - The writer called the experts, **who were initially reluctant to reveal the facts**, and wrote the story. [a nonessential clause interrupting two parts of the predicate]

22c   Subject-Predicate Inversions

In most sentences, the subject comes before the verb. However, in some sentences, the subject follows the verb.

Are questions inverted?

The usual subject-verb order is inverted in the phrasing of questions. In many questions, the subject appears between the auxiliary verb and the main verb.

- Was **the film *Casablanca*** shot on location or on a set? [The complete subject *the film* Casablanca *appears between the verbs* was *and* shot.]

In other questions, the subject follows the main verb.

- Who were **the screenwriters?** [The complete subject *the screenwriters* follows the verb *were*.]

What if an adverb starts the sentence?

The subject may follow the verb in a sentence with an adverb in front.

- Rarely were the **scenes** shot as they had first been scripted. [*Rarely* is an adverb modifying *were shot*. The subject *scenes* comes between the verbs.]
- Seldom does so much **chaos** in production make a great film. [*Seldom* modifies *does make*. The subject *chaos* comes between the verbs.]

However, the verb may also follow the subject.

- Surprisingly, the **chaos** provided many opportunities for actors to add their own ideas to the script. [The normal subject-verb order is used.]

What about sentences beginning with *it, here,* and *there*?

The subject follows the verb in sentences beginning with the expletives *it, here,* or *there.* (An **expletive** fills the usual position of the subject.)

- There were two different **scripts** for the ending. [The true subject *scripts* follows the verb *were. There* is an expletive.]
- It was **Humphrey Bogart** and **Ingrid Bergman** who created some of the classic lines. [The compound subject follows *was. It* is an expletive.]

> **NOTE:** Add energy to your writing by replacing expletives with clear subjects and vivid verbs. (See 13d.)

What other sentences are inverted?

Certain rare sentences display inverted subject-verb order for formal literary or rhetorical effect.

- Gone is the **Golden Age** of Hollywood.

22d Complements

A complement is a word, phrase, or clause in the predicate that "completes" the action of the verb. **Transitive verbs** use direct objects, indirect objects, and object complements to complete the action. **Linking verbs** complete the thought by using subject complements: predicate nouns, predicate pronouns, and predicate adjectives. (See **20a** and **20b**.)

What is a direct object?

A direct object completes the meaning of a transitive verb by indicating who or what receives the action stated in the verb.

- ■ The lab **features** [transitive verb] a directional wave **basin** [direct object].

> **NOTE:** To test for the presence of a direct object, do the following: (1) say the subject; (2) say the verb; (3) then ask "What?" or "Who?" The answer will be the direct object. In the sentence above, you would ask, "The lab features what?" A basin.

A direct object may include one or more nouns, pronouns, infinitive phrases, gerund phrases, or noun clauses.

- ■ The lab **features** a large directional wave **basin**, a hydraulic wave **maker**, and a spiral wave **basin**. [compound direct object]
- ■ Simulators **encourage** the **learning** of hydrodynamics. [The gerund *learning* is the direct object. Simulators encourage what? *Learning*]
- ■ Lab simulators **ensure that we understand waves better**. [The direct object is a noun clause. (See **24b**.) Simulators ensure what? *That we understand waves better*]

What is an indirect object?

An indirect object indicates *to whom/to what* or *for whom/for what* something is done. A sentence must have a direct object to have an indirect object.

- ■ The college administration sent **alumni** invitations to the ceremony.

The indirect object may be compound.

- ■ The college administration sent **alumni, faculty, and staff** invitations to the ceremony.

> **NOTE:** To test for the presence of an indirect object, do the following: (1) Say the verb; (2) say the direct object; (3) then ask "To whom/to what?" or "For whom/for what?" In the sentence above , you would ask, "They sent invitations to whom?" Alumni, faculty, and staff

What is a subject complement?

A subject complement is a predicate noun, predicate pronoun, or predicate adjective that follows a linking verb and renames or describes the subject. A predicate noun or a predicate pronoun (also called *predicate nominative*) renames the subject. A predicate adjective describes the subject.

- The wave was a **tsunami**. [predicate noun or predicate nominative]
- That was **it**! [predicate pronoun or predicate nominative]
- The wave was **gigantic**.
  [predicate adjective]

The linking verb used to connect a subject complement to the subject is often a form of "be"—*am, is, are, was, were, will be, will have been*, and so on. The linking verb may also be one of the many verbs that refer to the senses or states of being—*appear, become, look, smell, sound*, and so on.

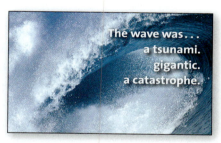

The wave was . . .
a tsunami.
gigantic.
a catastrophe.

- The tsunami **became** an international **catastrophe**.
  [predicate noun]
- The wave **sounded horrible**. [predicate adjective]

What is an object complement?

An object complement is a noun, a pronoun, or an adjective appearing in the predicate after the direct object. The object complement, which renames or describes the direct object, helps to complete the action of the transitive verb and to make a sensible sentence.

- The tsunami **left** the former fishing **village** a smooth mud **plain**.
  [The object complement *plain* is a noun renaming *village*, which is the direct object of the verb *left*.]
- Debris from the flooding **rendered** the drainage **system useless**.
  [The object complement *useless* is an adjective describing *system*. *System* is the direct object of the verb *rendered*.]

> **NOTE:** An adjective placed before the direct object would be a simple modifier, not an object complement.
>
> - Government inspectors examined the **inoperable** system. (In this example, *inoperable* is an adjective, not an object complement.)

SENTENCE BASICS

22e Independent and Dependent Clauses

The combination of a subject with its predicate is called a clause. There are two types of clauses: independent and dependent. Sometimes a complete sentence is referred to as an independent clause—that is, a clause that has all the necessary components to stand by itself as a complete sentence. An independent clause has a complete subject and a complete predicate and expresses a complete thought. A dependent (or subordinate) clause cannot stand alone; it must be attached to an independent clause to form a complete thought. (See **24a–24d**.)

Dependent Clause: When a team of photojournalists finally arrived

Sentence: When a team of photojournalists finally arrived [dependent clause], the warehouse fire had subsided [independent clause].

Notice that both the dependent and independent clauses contain a subject and a predicate (*team + arrived*, and *fire + had subsided*).

22f Fragments

A fragment occurs when a necessary part of the subject or predicate is absent, or when the construction does not express a complete thought.

> **NOTE:** Fragments are often acceptable in poetry, dialogue, and colloquial speech, but not in formal writing.

COMPLETE SENTENCE
- The blaze began when faulty wiring created sparks near gasoline cans. [complete subject + complete predicate = complete thought = complete sentence]

FRAGMENT
- Old cans, some with missing lids. [This group of words is a complete subject but has no predicate and is, therefore, a fragment.]

FRAGMENT
- When the chief of police arrived. [This group of words has both a complete subject and a complete predicate, but it does not express a complete thought. Therefore, the group is a fragment.]

ESL TIP

In some languages, subjects and verbs can be implied, but in most English sentences, subjects and verbs must be stated. Otherwise a fragment results. (See "Imperative Sentences" in **22h**.)

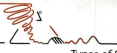

22g Types of Sentences

The four main types of sentence structures are **simple, compound, complex,** and **compound-complex.**

What are simple sentences?

A simple sentence contains one independent clause—a subject and a predicate. Note, however, that the subjects and the predicates may be compound. They may also contain phrases modifying any of the main clause elements.

- **Money talks.** [single subject and predicate]
- **Power** and **money eat** at the same café.
  [compound subject, single predicate]

What are compound sentences?

A compound sentence contains two or more independent clauses joined by a coordinating conjunction (*and, but, or, nor, for, so, yet*).

- We have studied the problem, **and** we know how to fix it.

A semicolon also can join the clauses.

- Nothing has changed; the stars still look down from above.

A semicolon and a conjunctive adverb followed by a comma can join clauses.

- We have studied the problem; **nevertheless,** we're still stumped.

What are complex sentences?

A complex sentence contains one independent clause and one or more dependent clauses. The dependent clauses begin with subordinating conjunctions (in **bold**) or relative pronouns (in *italics*).

- **Since** they had diplomatic immunity, the doctors entered the war-torn area. [one dependent clause with an independent clause]
- A traveler *who* visits a tsunami zone takes a risk, even **if** the risk is slim.
  [two dependent clauses with an independent clause]

What are compound-complex sentences?

A compound-complex sentence contains two or more independent clauses and at least one dependent clause.

- *If* the U.N. had sufficient personnel, the agency would be able to deal with greater crises, and the militaries of large nations would not need to become involved.
  [one dependent clause and two independent clauses]
- *Who* the kidnappers are is still a mystery despite the fact **that** a ransom has been offered; time will tell.
  [two independent clauses and two dependent clauses]

22h Kinds of Sentences

Sentences can make four basic kinds of statements: *declarative, interrogative, imperative,* and *exclamatory.*

Declarative sentences state directly that something is so.

- In 1617, Faust Vrancic used a da Vinci–designed parachute to jump from a tower.

Interrogative sentences ask questions.

- Was Vrancic the first parachutist?

ESL TIP

If the question calls for a "yes" or "no" answer, the auxiliary verb is usually in the front of the sentence.

- **Did** he survive his jump?

Many questions are formed by substituting an interrogative pronoun for the information that is being inquired about.

- **Who** designed the modern parachute?
- **Where** was it tested?
- **When** were parachutes first used in warfare?
- **Why** are some parachutes rectangular?
- **What** is the greatest weight a parachute can bear?

Sometimes sentences that appear to be declarative are meant to be spoken with an inquiring tone. The question mark at the end of the sentence marks it as an interrogative.

- I'm supposed to trust someone else to pack my chute?

Imperative sentences give commands in a direct, even blunt way. They often contain the understood subject *you.* (See **22a**.)

- [You] Jump.
- [You] Don't forget your chute.

Exclamatory sentences communicate strong emotion or surprise.

- Wow, you're bodysurfing in the sky!
- Come on in. The air's fine!

Using Phrases

Although a phrase is more than one word, it functions as a unit and acts as one part of speech. Phrases may be categorized as *nouns, verbs, adjectives*, or *adverbs*, or they may be categorized as a modifier of the whole sentence. A phrase differs from a clause in that a phrase lacks a subject, a predicate, or both and cannot be a complete thought.

23a Types and Functions

Notice the phrases in the following sentence and how each phrase serves a particular function. Remember, a phrase is more than one word, acts as a unit, and functions as one part of speech.

- Beyond the horrific loss of human life, the Indian Ocean tsunami in several minutes had severely damaged Indonesia's coastal environment, causing $675 million in losses to natural habitats.

Noun Phrase: Made up of a noun and its modifiers

- the Indian Ocean **tsunami** [functions as the subject]
- Indonesia's coastal **environment** [functions as the direct object]

Verb Phrase: Made up of a helping verb and main verb

- **had damaged** [functions as the verb]

Prepositional Phrase: Made up of a preposition, its object, and modifiers

- **beyond** the horrific loss [functions as an adverb modifying the verb *had damaged*]
- **of** human life [functions as an adjective modifying the noun *loss*]
- **in** several minutes [functions as an adverb modifying the verb *had damaged*—answering the question "When?"]
- **in** losses [functions as an adjective modifying the noun *$675 million*]
- **to** natural habitats [functions as an adjective modifying the noun *losses*—answering the question "What kind?"]

Participial Phrase: Made up of a participle, its object, and any modifiers

- **causing** $675 million [functions as an adjective modifying *tsunami*]

USING PHRASES

What are the different types of phrases?

There are several types of phrases: *noun, verb, prepositional, verbal, appositive,* and *absolute.* Be careful not to confuse the type of phrase with its grammatical function in the sentence. Some types may serve several different functions.

Type of Phrase	Function of Phrase			
	Verb	Noun	Adverb	Adjective
Noun		◆		
Verb	◆	◆		
Prepositional			◆	◆
Verbal				
Gerund		◆		
Infinitive		◆	◆	◆
Participle				◆
Appositive		◆		
Absolute (modifies whole sentence)			◆	

23b   Noun Phrases

A noun phrase consists of a noun and any words that modify it.

- In 1610, Galileo used **a homemade telescope** to peer at Jupiter.

23c   Verb Phrases

A verb phrase consists of a main verb and any auxiliary verbs.

- He **was observing** four small stars aligned with the planet.

Each verb in a verb phrase helps tell the certainty of an action (mood) and when the action occurs (tense). (See **20g**.)

- Without the telescope, he **could** not **have made** his greatest discovery.
  [*Could* is a modal verb, *have* is a helping verb, and *made* is the main verb. Modal and helping verbs are auxiliary verbs.]

23d   Prepositional Phrases

A prepositional phrase is a phrase that begins with a preposition and ends with an object. The object is a noun or a pronoun. The phrase can also include words that modify the object. Prepositional phrases act as adjectives or adverbs.

- The four "stars" did not move **with other stars**.
  [The phrase acts as an adverb, modifying *move*.]
- Galileo had discovered four **of Jupiter's moons**.
  [The phrase acts as an adjective, modifying *four*.]

Where should I position prepositional phrases?

A prepositional phrase that acts as an adjective typically appears immediately after the noun or pronoun it modifies.

- The Galilean moons **of Jupiter** are Io, Europa, Ganymede, and Callisto. [The phrase acts as an adjective, modifying *moons*.]

A prepositional phrase that acts as an adverb does *not* necessarily come immediately after the word it modifies. The adverbial phrase may appear almost anywhere in a sentence.

- **Over the next four centuries**, astronomers found 59 more moons. [The phrase acts as an adverb, modifying *found*, but it does not immediately follow the verb.]

- Scientists may find more satellites **in coming years**, though none the size of the Galilean moons. [The phrase acts as an adverb, modifying *find*, but it does not immediately follow the verb.]

> **NOTE:** Prepositions can show relations of **space** *(in, over, under, around)*, time *(after, since, during)*, direction *(toward, from)*, belonging *(with, of)*, and so on. Some prepositions, called **phrasal prepositions**, are made of two or more words *(instead of, in addition to)*. See **21c** for a list of prepositions.

23e Verbal Phrases

A verbal phrase is a phrase that begins with one of the three types of verbals: *gerunds, infinitives,* or *participles.* Verbals are verb forms that function as other parts of speech. **Gerunds** function as nouns; **infinitives** function as nouns, adjectives, or adverbs; and **participles** function as adjectives.

A verbal, like a verb, can have a complement (a direct object or a predicate noun). The verbal in combination with its complements and modifiers becomes a *verbal phrase.*

- **Surfing in the morning** thrills me. [*Surfing* is a gerund. In combination with the prepositional phrase, it becomes a gerund phrase. Here it is the subject of the sentence.]

- I intend **to surf today and tomorrow**. [*To surf* is an infinitive. In combination with the adverbs, it becomes an infinitive phrase. Here it is a noun, the direct object of the verb *intend*.]

- That is a **heavily surfed** beach. [*Surfed* is a past participle. In combination with the adverb, it becomes a participial phrase modifying *beach*.]

USING PHRASES

What is a gerund phrase?

A gerund phrase consists of a gerund (a verb form ending in *-ing*) and any of its modifiers or complements. Gerund phrases function as **nouns**—subjects, predicate nominatives, direct objects, indirect objects, objects of prepositions, or objects of another verbal.

- **Becoming a marine biologist** is Keyshaun's dream. [subject of the sentence]
- His favorite hobby is **surfing with friends**. [predicate noun renaming *hobby*]
- Keyshaun gave **surfing at Jaws** his bravest effort. [indirect object of the verb *gave*]
- Keyshaun tried **surfing with the locals**. [direct object of the verb *tried*]
- He was surprised to find **surfing with the locals** scary. [object of the infinitive *to find*]
- He discovered various methods for **surviving dangerous tumbles**. [object of the preposition *for*]

Surfing is a gerund, acting as a noun, as well as a way of life.

What is an infinitive phrase?

An infinitive phrase consists of an infinitive (the word *to* plus the base form of the verb) and its modifiers or complements. The whole phrase functions in the same way as a single **noun**, **adjective**, or **adverb** would.

- **To surf every Pacific beach** is Jana's goal. [noun as subject]
- She plans **to begin in South America**. [noun as direct object]
- The plan **to surf every Pacific beach** could take Jana years. [adjective modifying *plan*]
- She worked two jobs **to finance her travels**. [adverb modifying *worked*]

ESL TIP

Verbs that express wishes and intentions tend to be followed by infinitives. (See 34d.)

- I want **to learn other water sports**. [Not *I want learning other water sports.*]

Verbs that express facts tend to be followed by gerunds.

- I already understand surfing. [Not *I already understand to surf.*]

What is a participial phrase?

A participial phrase consists of a past or present participle along with its modifiers or complements. The participial phrase functions as an **adjective,** modifying a noun or a pronoun.

A **present participle** ends with *-ing.* The **past participle** of regular verbs ends with *-ed.* (See **20h** for the past participles of irregular verbs.)

- **Perched in rocks above the beach**, tide pools host many forms of life.
  [adjective modifying *pools*]

- High tides, **arriving twice a day**, replenish the water in the pools.
  [adjective modifying *tides*]

- Low tides trap some creatures **trying to leave too late**.
  [adjective modifying *creatures*]

- Most animals **remaining in the pool** have chosen it as home.
  [adjective modifying *animals*]

If the participial phrase begins the sentence, it must modify the subject. Otherwise, the sentence is confusing and sometimes comical. (See **26f**.)

Incorrect: Basking in the warm waters, scientists find many anemones and starfish. [The scientists aren't basking.]

Correct: Basking in the warm waters, anemones and starfish make the tide pool their home.

23f   Appositive Phrases

An appositive phrase simply renames a noun or pronoun, following it and adding helpful new information to identify or characterize the noun or pronoun. The phrase acts as a noun.

- Juana Rodriguez, **a marine biologist**, studies tide pools.

- Tide pools, **rocky depressions that catch the high tide**, provide a unique habitat.

> **NOTE:** Many appositive phrases could be easily expanded into adjective clauses (**24c**) beginning with *which/that* or *who:*
>
> - Juana Rodriguez, [who is] a marine biologist, ...
> - Tide pools, [which are] rocky depressions ...
>
> Appositives are essentially relative clauses from which the relative pronoun and the linking verb have been removed, leaving only the predicate nominative. The appositive thus serves as a noun.

23g Absolute Phrases

An absolute phrase usually consists of a noun or a pronoun followed by a participle. The participle's complement, if there is one, and any modifiers may be included. The absolute phrase does not modify any particular word in the sentence; rather, the phrase acts as an adverb that modifies the sentence as a whole (or the independent clause to which it is linked). Notice that absolute phrases are always set off with commas:

- **A blast equaling that of Krakatoa,** the Minoan eruption extinguished all life on Santorini Island in 1643 BCE. [*Equaling is a present-tense participle that follows the noun* blast.]

- **A crater blown out of its center,** the great Minoan city on the island was sunken into the sea. [*Blown is a past participle that follows the noun* crater.]

In each case, the noun before the participle in the absolute phrase acts somewhat like a subject for the participle; however, it does not act as the subject of the main clause.

If an absolute phrase contains the word *being* and a **predicate adjective,** the word *being* is sometimes dropped.

- Some archeologists equate the historical Minoans with the people of mythic Atlantis, **their stories similar**. [The participle *being* has been dropped: "their stories *being* similar."]

WRITER'S TIP

Absolute phrases can add interesting information to a sentence and create a compact and spicy style. However, like spices, absolute phrases can be easily overused. In creating an absolute phrase, be careful not to include a verb with a definite tense. The result will be an ungrammatical comma splice.

Comma Splice:	The ash **had settled** sixty feet deep, parts of the city were buried for 3,000 years.
Correct:	The ash **having settled** sixty feet deep, parts of the city were buried for 3,000 years.

See **26b** and **26c** for more on comma splices and run-on sentences.

NOTE: Phrases can add valuable information to sentences. Even so, some phrases add nothing but "fat" to your writing. For a list of phrases to avoid, see **14c**.

Using Clauses

In the 1935 film *A Night at the Opera*, part of a legal contract confuses Chico Marx. Groucho Marx defends the section as a standard "sanity clause." Chico laughs and says, "You can't fool me! There ain't no Sanity Claus!" Sometimes writers get confused about clauses, too. English is full of them: independent and dependent clauses, noun clauses, adjective clauses, and adverb clauses.

24a Types and Functions

A clause is simply a group of words that has both a subject and a predicate. There are two main types of clauses: **independent clauses** and **dependent clauses.**

What is an independent clause?

An independent clause (also called a *main clause*) expresses a complete thought and can stand alone as a sentence.

- William Faulkner set many novels in a fictional Mississippi county.

  [subject + verb + complete thought = independent clause]

What is a dependent clause?

A dependent clause (also called a *subordinate* or *relative clause*) does not express a complete thought and can't stand alone as a sentence. A dependent clause depends on other words to make the thought complete.

Most dependent clauses start with a subordinating conjunction such as *until* or a relative pronoun such as *which*.

- after the Civil War ended [The word *after* makes this dependent.]
- who inherited a fallen world [The word *who* makes this dependent.]

How does a dependent clause function?

A dependent clause can function as a noun, an adjective, or an adverb. The dependent clause must be attached to an independent clause, modifying it or functioning within it.

- Faulkner wrote about people **who had inherited a fallen world**.

  [The clause functions as an adjective, modifying *people*.]

USING CLAUSES

24b Noun Clauses

A noun clause is a dependent clause that functions as a noun. Noun clauses function as subjects, complements, or objects of prepositions.

- Faulkner explored **how cultural change affects individuals**.
  [noun clause functioning as a direct object]

In addition to *how,* noun clauses often begin with *wh-* words: *what, whatever, when, where, whether, which, whichever, who, whoever, whom, whomever, whose,* and *why.*

ESL TIP

To decide whether a clause is a noun clause, determine its use in the sentence. A quick test is to replace the clause with *something* or *someone*. If the statement still makes sense, it is probably a noun clause.

- Faulkner explored **how cultural change affects individuals**.
- Faulkner explored **something**.
- **Where a person lives** and **when a person lives** determine the individual's character and destiny, according to Faulkner.
- **Something** and **something** determine the individual's character and destiny, according to Faulkner.

What are "that" clauses?

Some noun clauses begin with the word *that* acting as neither a relative pronoun nor a demonstrative pronoun. In such clauses, *that* is a conjunction signaling the beginning of the clause and connecting it to the sentence.

- **That his work was almost forgotten** is amazing.
  [subject]
- An editor decided **that there should be a "portable Faulkner."**
  [direct object of a transitive verb]
- The fact is **that he has had a profound effect on American letters**.
  [predicate nominative after a linking verb]

NOTE: Sometimes it is possible to omit the word *that* before a "that" clause without confusing the reader. Even with *that* removed, this *elliptical clause,* as it is known, remains a dependent clause.

- We are certain [that] Faulkner will continue to be studied.
- Professors realize [that] he had much to say about life in the South.

In **indirect quotations,** a "that" clause substitutes for the words that were actually spoken. Be sure not to use quotation marks or commas to set off indirect quotations. Also be sure to change pronouns and verb forms as necessary.

Correct:	Faulkner advised, "Read. Read. Read. Read everything." [direct quotation]
Incorrect:	Faulkner advised that "Read. Read. Read. Read everything."
Correct:	Faulkner advised writers to read everything. [indirect quotation]

NOTE: A **direct question** states just what a person asked.

- I asked, "Why was Faulkner so long winded?"

An **indirect question** reports a question without stating it outright.

- I asked why Faulkner was so long winded.

Notice that in the direct question, the helping verb *(was)* appears before the noun, but in the indirect question, the usual subject-verb pattern is used. Also, the indirect question does not use quotation marks or a question mark.

What are interrogative clauses?

An interrogative clause is a noun clause introduced by a relative pronoun or a subordinating conjunction that is a question word: *who, whose, whom, which, what, when, where, why,* and *how.* The clause can function as a subject, a direct object, a complement, or an object of the preposition.

- **What Faulkner intended** was to write the way he thought. [subject]
- Understanding **why his style is so dense** helps students appreciate him. [direct object of the gerund *understanding*]
- Faulkner wanted to express "eternal verities," **which are the truths of the human condition**. [appositive]

USING CLAUSES

24c Adjective Clauses

An adjective clause modifies a noun or a pronoun. Usually the clause immediately follows the word it modifies. Adjective clauses begin with either a relative pronoun *(who, whose, whom, which, that, what)* or a subordinating conjunction *(when, where, why)*.

- Urban legends **that often begin "a friend of a friend . . ."** are actually fictional stories. [modifies *legends*]
- The friend of a friend **whom the story refers to** is never available for comment. [modifies *friend*]
- Even so, storytellers point to specific places **where the events supposedly took place**. [modifies *places*]

ESL TIP

Remember to place a relative pronoun first in an adjective clause. That way, the pronoun stays close to the antecedent. (See **35c**.)
- An urban legend **that people have circulated for years** is told as if the event happened yesterday. [*Legend* is the antecedent of *that*, and *that* is the direct object of *circulated*.]

A *subordinating conjunction* does not serve as the subject of an adjective clause but is instead followed by a word that is the subject.

- The time **when the event supposedly took place** is less important than the story itself. [*When* is a subordinating conjunction, and *event* is the subject of the clause.]

What are restrictive and nonrestrictive relative clauses?

The purpose of a *relative clause* is to supply useful information about its *antecedent* (a noun or a pronoun). Sometimes this information is essential to the meaning of the sentence. In that case, the relative clause is called **restrictive**, or **essential**. Do not set off a restrictive clause (or word or phrase) with commas.

- Urban legends **that play on common fears** last the longest.
  [The relative clause is restrictive because it identifies exactly the legends being talked about.]

In other cases, the information supplied in the relative clause is not essential. The details do not specify a particular person or thing but provide only incidental facts that may be interesting or amusing. These clauses are called **nonrestrictive** and are set off by commas.

- Some campfire stories, **which often feature ghost hitchhikers or escaped murderers,** qualify as urban legends. [The relative clause is nonrestrictive because it only adds information. Commas are needed.]

What if the clause ends in a preposition?

Sometimes a clause that ends with a preposition sounds awkward.

- Events **that no one can prepare for** sometimes occur.

The awkward wording can be fixed by moving the preposition to the front of the clause, making the clause into the object of the preposition. (The clause becomes a noun clause.)

- Events for **which no one can prepare** sometimes occur.

NOTE: The relative pronoun *that* can sometimes be deleted from a relative clause (the result is an *elliptical clause*) if the sentence reads clearly without the pronoun.

Don't Omit:

The boats **that landed on the beach** were smashed.

Your Choice:

The boats **that Max had in his shop** could not be repaired.

[In the second example, *that* can be dropped. When analyzing the sentence structure, however, the reader will need to recognize that the pronoun is "understood," not stated.]

WRITER'S TIP

Writers sometimes use the relative pronoun *which* when there is no clear antecedent for it. Make sure you use the word *which* to refer to a noun that has preceded it.

Unacceptable: We robbed our piggy banks, which made us feel guilty. [*Banks* is not the antecedent for the pronoun *which*. In fact, the idea stated in the independent clause is the antecedent for *which*. The sentence should be rewritten.]

Acceptable: Robbing our piggy banks made us feel guilty.

Acceptable: After robbing our piggy banks, we felt guilty.

24d Adverb Clauses

An adverb clause does what a one-word adverb does—it modifies either a verb, an adjective, an adverb, or the whole idea expressed in the main clause.

- **When thermals create friction in a thunderhead**, electrical charges develop. [The adverb clause modifies *develop*.]
- The cloud becomes polarized, **as if it were a giant battery**. [The adverb clause modifies the whole idea of the main clause.]

An adverb clause always begins with a subordinating conjunction, which shows a logical link between the subordinate clause and the word or words it modifies. The clause often answers some question of *time, place, manner, cause, purpose,* or *condition.* (See **21d** for a full list of subordinating conjunctions.)

- **After a charge builds up**, the cloud extends ion trails downward. [Time: When does the cloud extend ion trails?]
- Ion trails reach up from the ground **wherever tall objects stand**. [Place: Where do ion trails reach up?]
- **If a trail extends from your head**, your hair may start to prickle. [Cause: Why does your hair prickle?]
- **If the ion trail from your head meets an ion trail from a cloud**, the pathway for lightning is open. [Condition: On what condition does the pathway open?]
- Stay low and get indoors **so that you don't get struck**! [Purpose: For what reason should you stay low and get indoors?]

Where should I place adverb clauses?

You may move adverb clauses around in a sentence to create special emphasis. However, do not place the clause between a verb and a direct object.

- **As it descends**, lightning can heat air to 10,000 degrees F.
- Lightning, **as it descends**, can heat air to 10,000 degrees F.
- Lightning can heat air to 10,000 degrees F **as the bolt descends**.

WRITER'S TIP

An introductory adverb clause should always be separated from the main clause with a comma. An adverb clause that follows the main clause should *not* be preceded by a comma if the adverb clause is **restrictive** (essential to the meaning of the sentence); use the comma, however, if the adverb clause is **nonrestrictive.**

- Lightning poses little threat **if you take precautions**. [restrictive]
- Lightning is fascinating, **if you want my opinion**. [nonrestrictive]

Agreement Errors

People can agree to disagree, but subjects and predicates don't have that luxury. Neither do pronouns and antecedents. They must "get along."

25a Subject-Predicate Agreement

A predicate must agree with its subject in person: *first, second,* or *third.* In the present tense, most verbs (such as *jump* or *touch*) use the base form with all persons except third person singular. To make a verb agree with a third person singular subject, add *s* or *es* to the verb's base form. (See page **20d.**)

	Singular	(Present)	Plural	(Present)
First Person	I	jump, invite, talk	We	jump, invite, talk
Second Person	You	jump, invite, talk	You	jump, invite, talk
Third Person	He/she/it	jumps, invites, talks	They	jump, invite, talk

The verbs *have* and *be* act a little differently. In the present tense, the third person singular of *have* is *has.* The verb *be* takes on several different forms.

	Singular		Plural	
	(Present)	(Past)	(Present)	(Past)
First Person	I have, am	had, was	We have, are	had, were
Second Person	You have, are	had, were	You have, are	had, were
Third Person	He/she/it has, is	had, was	They have, are	had, were

What is agreement in number?

A verb must agree with its subject in number (singular or plural).

- The **custodian was** available for repair work.
  [The subject *custodian* is singular; the verb *was* is also singular.]

Be sure the verb agrees with its true subject. Don't be thrown off by words that may come between the subject and the verb.

- Power **outages** *with no apparent cause* **happen** often.
  [Mentally block out the phrase *with no apparent cause.*]

AGREEMENT ERRORS

Are all nouns that end in *s* plural?

Not all nouns ending in *s* are plural. Some nouns that end in *s* are actually singular in meaning: *athletics, economics, mathematics, measles, mumps, politics, robotics, statistics,* and so on. These nouns use a singular verb.

- **Economics is** sometimes called "the dismal science."
- The **news is** not very good.

Other nouns that end in *s* are treated as plural even though they refer to single objects: *glasses, jeans, scissors, pliers,* and so on. These nouns use a plural verb.

- The **scissors are** missing again.
- **Are** those **jeans** prewashed?

25b Compound Subjects

A compound subject is two or more subjects connected by a conjunction. The subjects share the same verb. When the subjects are connected by *and*, the compound subject is usually plural and so requires a plural verb.

- **Common sense** and **foresight prevent** most accidents.

What special agreement cases should I watch for?

Watch for subjects joined by *and*. If the subjects joined by *and* refer to a single entity, or if the parts refer to a single person or thing, then the compound subject is considered singular, and the verb form must agree with it.

- **Macaroni and cheese is** popular with students.
  [The compound subject is a single item.]
- My greatest **patron and admirer thinks** I am bound for greatness.
  [The *patron* and the *admirer* are the same person.]
- **Stopping and looking is** a sure way to hold up traffic.
  [*Stopping* and *looking* are thought of as a single action.]

Singular subjects joined by *or, nor, either/or,* or *neither/nor* use a singular verb.

- Neither a **textbook** nor a **notebook is** required for this class.
- A **beaker** or a **test tube lies** shattered on the counter.

When one of the subjects joined by *or, nor, either/or,* or *neither/nor* is singular and one is plural, make the verb agree with the subject nearer the verb.

- Either the concertmaster or the **oboes were** behind by one beat.
  [Because the plural subject *oboes* is nearer the verb, the plural verb form *were* is used.]
- Two tenants or possibly the **owner is** responsible for repairs.
  [Because the singular subject *owner* is nearer the verb, the singular verb form *is* is used.]

25c Collective Nouns as Subjects

Generally, collective nouns (*army, assembly, committee, council, crew, crowd, faculty, pair, species, team,* and so on) take a singular verb unless the individuals in the group are being emphasized.

- The **jury takes** its duty very seriously. [*Jury* refers to the group as a unit; it is a singular subject and needs a singular verb, *takes*.]
- The **jury assume** their opinions will be valued. [In this example, *jury* refers to the individuals within the group; the verb *assume* agrees with the plural subject.]

> **NOTE:** It would be clearer in the second sentence above to use a clearly plural subject, "The jury *members* assume . . ."

25d Numbers and Numerical Terms as Subjects

When numbers or numerical terms function as subjects, determine whether the number refers to a single sum or amount or to many individual pieces or parts. Then use the verb form that agrees with the subject.

- **Three and three is** six. [one math problem]
- **Eighteen is** a large number of pages to read tonight. [a total number]
- **A thousand years is** like a single day in the mind of God. [one period]
- **A thousand years are** needed to grow this many rings in the trunk of a redwood. [many years considered one by one]
- **Forty-two dollars is** a steep price to pay for a video game. [one price]
- **Forty-two dollar bills were left** on the windowsill. [many individual bills]

How should I handle fractions?

With fractions followed by the word *of,* the object of the preposition will indicate whether the number is singular or plural.

- A **fifth** of **them were admitted** on probation.
  [*Them* is plural; therefore, the subject is plural.]
- A **fifth** of **vodka is** one of the ingredients in this sauce.
  [*Vodka* is singular; therefore, the subject is singular.]
- **Three-fourths** of the **enlistees were turned** away. [*Enlistees* is plural.]
- **Three-fourths** of the **pizza was** enough for her. [*Pizza* is singular.]

WRITER'S TIP

Always use words rather than digits to designate a number as the first word in a sentence. If doing so is awkward, rewrite the sentence so the first word is not a number.

AGREEMENT ERRORS

What if the word *number* is in a subject?

If the sentence begins with the words "*The* number of," consider the subject singular and choose the verb form accordingly. Conversely, "*A* number of" is plural.

Singular: **The number** of visits to the counseling center **is** both encouraging and disturbing. [Don't be thrown off by the plural word *visits* in the prepositional phrase that follows the subject.]

Plural: **A number** of complaints concerning air quality **have surfaced**.

25e Delayed Subjects

Most sentences follow a subject-verb pattern. However, some sentences are inverted (verb-subject pattern) and use **delayed** subjects. In inverted sentences, you need to make the verb agree with the true (delayed) subject and not with any noun that might appear in a phrase before the verb.

■ At our university **are** many nontraditional **students**.
[The delayed subject *students* determines the form of the verb, not the singular noun *university*.]

What is the subject of a sentence that starts with *there*?

The expletive *there* signals a delayed subject. (See **22c**.) Therefore, make sure that the verb agrees in number with the delayed subject.

Singular: There **is** a whole **set** of legal documents in that file. [Don't be thrown off by the plural *documents* in the prepositional phrase following the true subject, *set*.]

Plural: There **are**, in even a single pillow, **battalions** of mites. [Don't be thrown off by the singular *pillow* in the prepositional phrase before the true subject, *battalions*.]

What is the subject in a question?

In the structure of many questions (interrogative sentences), the normal subject-verb order is not used. Sometimes the subject is between parts of the verb phrase (verb-subject-verb). In those cases, make sure the first auxiliary verb agrees in number with the delayed subject.

Singular: **Has** the **book** been found?

Plural: **Have** the **books** been found?

WRITER'S TIP

Occasionally using a delayed subject may add flair, variety, or sophistication to your writing. Just remember to make the delayed subject agree with the verb.

25f Relative and Indefinite Pronouns as Subjects

When a relative pronoun *(who, which, that)* is used as the subject of a subordinate clause, the verb in that clause must agree in number with the relative pronoun's antecedent. (Remember: The antecedent is the noun or pronoun to which the pronoun refers.)

- Those singers are **madrigals, who perform** in traditional tights.
  [The antecedent of *who* is the plural noun *madrigals*. The verb *perform* agrees in number with that plural antecedent.]

For clarity, you should try to place the relative pronoun as close as possible to its antecedent. (In fact, it is best if the relative pronoun immediately follows its antecedent.) Sometimes, however, another noun or pronoun may come between them.

WRITER'S TIP

Here are two constructions to watch out for:

- one of the **things that have** [The antecedent of *that* is *things*. The plural verb *have* is correct.]
- the only **one** of the things **that has** [the antecedent of *that* is *one*. The singular verb *has* is correct.]

The difference is the word *only*. It makes the relative clause refer to the (only) *one* instead of the (many) *things*.

- This is the only **one** of our diamonds that **has** a banana shape.
  [Only one diamond has the shape. The verb is singular.]
- This is one of our **diamonds that have** a banana shape.
  [A number of diamonds have the shape. The verb is plural.]

Which indefinite pronouns are singular?

Many indefinite pronouns *(anyone, anybody, anything; each, everyone, everybody, everything; no one, nobody, nothing; someone, somebody, something; either, neither, one)* are treated as singular.

- **Everybody (anybody, nobody) is** welcome to attend the reception.
- **No one was** sent an invitation.

Make sure the verb agrees with the indefinite pronoun in number. Do not be confused by words or phrases that come between the indefinite pronoun and the verb.

- **Each** of the new students **is** encouraged to attend. [not *are*]
- **One** of the tables **has** a large selection of appetizers.

AGREEMENT ERRORS

Which indefinite pronouns are plural?

Some indefinite pronouns *(both, few, many, others,* and *several)* are plural.

- **Many are** offered the opportunity to study abroad.
- **Others take** advantage of internships closer to home.

Some indefinite pronouns *(all, any, most, none,* and *some)* may be either singular or plural, depending on the nouns to which they refer.

- **Some** of the **students were** upset. [*Students, the noun that some refers to, is plural; therefore, the pronoun some is considered plural, and the verb were is used to agree with it.*]
- **Some** of the **cheesecake was** mysteriously missing. [*Cheesecake is singular; therefore, some is singular, and the verb was is used.*]

25g Other Subject-Predicate Errors

Two other common errors involving subjects and verbs involve titles and sentences with predicate nominatives.

Are titles singular or plural?

When the title of a work of art, literature, or music serves as the subject, treat the title as singular, even if it contains a prominent plural noun. The same holds for a word (or a phrase) referred to as the term itself (words used as words) that is used as the subject.

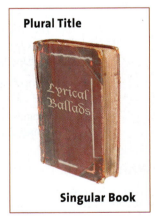

Plural Title

Singular Book

- *Lyrical Ballads* **was published** in 1798 by William Wordsworth and Samuel Taylor Coleridge. [The title is plural in form but names one book.]
- "Over-the-counter drugs" **is** a phrase that means nonprescription medications. [The phrase refers to a specific term.]

What if the subject and predicate nominative don't agree?

When a linking verb connects a subject to a predicate nominative, the verb must agree with the *subject,* not the predicate nominative.

- A huge **problem** for urban dwellers **is** rats. [The verb must agree with *problem,* which is singular, even though *rats* is plural.]
- **Problems** with vision and obesity **are** sometimes a consequence of advanced diabetes. [*Problems* is plural. The verb *are* agrees with it, even though the subject complement *consequence* is singular.]

25h Pronoun-Antecedent Agreement

A pronoun must agree in **number** (singular, plural), **person** (first, second, third), and **gender** (sex) with its *antecedent.* The antecedent is the word to which the pronoun refers. The **case** *(nominative, possessive, or objective)* of a personal pronoun tells how the pronoun is related to the other words within the sentence. (See **19b**.)

- Janice said **she** forgot **her** laptop. [singular, third person, feminine]
- Yoshi and Alice brought **their** laptops, but **they** forgot **their** assignments. [plural, third person, indefinite]
- **We** remembered both **our** laptops and **our** assignments. [plural, first person, indefinite]

What if the antecedent is an indefinite pronoun?

Use a singular pronoun to refer to such antecedents as *another, anybody, anyone, each, either, everybody, everyone, neither, nobody, one,* and *somebody.*

Incorrect: **Each** of the maintenance vehicles has **their** doors locked at night.

Correct: **Each** of the maintenance vehicles has **its** doors locked at night. [The words *each* and *its* are both singular.]

Incorrect: **Somebody** left **their** vehicle unlocked.

Correct: **Somebody** left **his** or **her** vehicle unlocked. [The words *somebody, his,* and *her* are all singular.]

WRITER'S TIP

In order to be inclusive, you might feel tempted to use *they* to refer to an indefinite pronoun. Such a construction is incorrect. One way to fix the problem, but still use inclusive language, is to replace *they* with *he* or *she.*

Incorrect: **Everyone** said **they** enjoyed the party.

Correct: **Everyone** said **he or she** enjoyed the party.

Another solution is to replace the indefinite pronoun.

Correct: **Partygoers** said **they** enjoyed the party.

A third solution is to reword the entire sentence to avoid the pronoun tangle.

Correct: The party was enjoyable for all the guests.

A final solution is to alternate *he* and *she* throughout your work.

- One student may wish to reduce her credit load, and another may wish to add more classes to his schedule.

AGREEMENT ERRORS

What if the antecedent has indefinite gender?

If the gender of a noun is not made obvious by other information in the text, you may be tempted to refer to the noun with a plural pronoun.

Incorrect: **A candidate** must come prepared with **their** resumé.

Avoid making sexist assumptions about the gender implied in the noun.

Incorrect: **A nurse** must come prepared with **her** resumé. [Using *her* is making a sexist assumption. Men are nurses, too.]

To avoid this, try one of these strategies: (1) use *his or her;* (2) make the subject plural; or (3) reword the sentence.

Correct: **A nurse** must come prepared with **his or her** resumé.

Correct: **Nurses** must come prepared with **their** resumé.

Correct: **A nurse** must come prepared with a resumé.

What if there are two or more antecedents?

When two or more antecedents are joined in a compound by *and,* treat the antecedents as plural.

- **Tomas and Jamal** are finishing **their** assignments.

When two or more singular antecedents are joined by *or* or *nor,* treat the antecedents as singular.

- Either **Connie or Shavonn** left **her** headset in the library.

If one of the antecedents is masculine and one is feminine, the pronouns should likewise be masculine and feminine.

- Is either **Ahmad or Phyllis** bringing **his** or **her** laptop computer?

> **NOTE:** You can also rewrite the sentence to avoid awkward wording.
> - Is either Ahmad or Phyllis bringing a laptop computer?

If one of the antecedents joined by *or* or *nor* is singular and one is plural, the pronoun should agree with the nearer antecedent.

- Neither **Ravi nor** his **friends** want to spend **their** time studying.
- Neither the older **Carltons nor** their **daughter** would demonstrate **her** clog dancing.

> **NOTE:** It would sound less awkward to place the plural antecedent closest to the pronoun.
> - Neither **Glenna Carlton nor** her **parents** would demonstrate **their** clog dancing.

25i Ambiguous Antecedents

In sentences where there is more than one possible antecedent for a specific pronoun, the result can be ambiguous, confusing, and in some cases, unintentionally amusing.

- Kathy took Mike for sushi on their first date, which made him sick.

What made Mike sick? Was it the sushi or the date? Did he have some bad fish or an unpleasant time with Kathy? To clear up the ambiguity, the sentence should be rewritten.

- When Kathy took Mike on their first date, he ate some sushi, which made him sick.

How can I correct ambiguous antecedents?

Sometimes, the best way to clear up a problem with antecedents is simply to reword the sentence.

Ambiguous: Tonya thought her new **belt** would match her **blouse**, but **it** was much pinker. [The pronoun *it* could refer to either the belt or the blouse.]

Corrected: The **belt** that Tonya bought turned out to be much pinker than her blouse.

Using indirect quotations may cause ambiguities in pronoun reference.

- **Brianna** told **Julissa** that **she** couldn't dance.
- The **board of trustees** informed the **college** that **it** would no longer hold semiannual meetings.

To clear up any ambiguity, use a direct quotation, if possible. Otherwise, repeat the noun.

- **Brianna** told Julissa, "**I** can't dance." [*Brianna* is the antecedent.]
- Brianna told **Julissa**, "**You** can't dance." [*Julissa* is the antecedent.]
- The **board of trustees** informed the college that **the board** would no longer hold semiannual meetings.

> **NOTE:** When you try to clear up an ambiguous antecedent, make sure not to create tortured sentences. When in doubt, rewrite the sentence.
>
> **Tortured:** Devon had his father complete his (Devon's) application.
> **Rewritten:** Devon's application was completed by his father.

AGREEMENT ERRORS

25j Vague Antecedents

Using pronouns such as *it, that, this,* or *which* in a vague or broad way to connect to a previous idea or sentence can sometimes lead to confusion.

- Often Professor Rubel assigns a long novel on Friday, and **it** has sometimes ruined my weekend. [*It* refers broadly to Professor Rubel's assignment practices, but seems perhaps to refer to *Friday* or *novel.*]
- I skim from the front cover to the back cover, **which** provides little comprehension. [*Which* has no clear antecedent, seeming to refer to *back cover* or *front cover.*]

How can I avoid vague antecedents?

To solve pronoun-antecedent problems like those above, you may rewrite a sentence in one of three ways: (1) add a clear antecedent to the pronoun, (2) use a noun instead of a pronoun, or (3) reword the sentence to avoid the confusion.

- I skim from the front cover to the back cover, **a practice that** provides little comprehension. [The noun *practice* has been added as the antecedent of the pronoun *that.*]
- I skim from the front cover to the back cover, but **skimming** provides little comprehension. [The gerund *skimming* takes the place of the pronoun.]
- I skim from the front cover to the back cover, but I have little comprehension. [The sentence is rewritten to avoid the ambiguity.]

> **NOTE:** Of the three sentences above, the last sentence is the most concise and says in one clause what needs to be said.

WRITER'S TIP

The pronouns *it, they,* and *you* are often used in casual speech without a definite antecedent. In writing, such misuse of pronouns is more noticeable. Correct any sentences that use a vague *it, they,* or *you* by replacing the pronoun with a noun.

Indefinite: On topographical maps, **it** shows fine gradations of elevation.

Revised: On topographical maps, **the contoured lines** show fine gradations of elevation.

Indefinite: At a physician's office, **they** typically want to weigh **you** before an examination.

Revised: At a physician's office, **the charge nurse** typically wants to weigh **patients** before an examination.

Sentence Problems

*S*entence and *sense* come from the same Latin root, a word that means a "feeling or opinion." As a result, a sentence must make sense; it must convey a clear feeling, opinion, or idea. Certain errors can cause a sentence to become confusing, meaningless, or even comical. This chapter will help you correct these problems and write sensible sentences.

26a Sentence Fragments

A fragment is a group of words that is not a complete sentence. A fragment may have a capital letter at the beginning and punctuation at the end, yet the words do not express a complete thought. A fragment may lack a subject, a verb, or another main clause element; or it may be a dependent clause.

- Graffiti removal ground to a halt. [sentence]
- Not for lack of funds. [fragment]

How can I fix a fragment?

To fix a fragment, you must attach it to another sentence or add the necessary elements to make the fragment stand on its own as a sentence.

- Even with sufficient funds, graffiti removal ground to a halt. [The fragment is turned into a modifying phrase.]
- Graffiti removal ground to a halt, although the reason was not a lack of funds. [The fragment is made into a subordinate clause.]
- Graffiti removal ground to a halt. Lack of funds, however, was not the reason. [Elements are added to make the fragment a sentence.]

WRITER'S TIP

When you join a fragment to an independent clause, examine the ideas in both to see which group of words deserves the emphasis. Then put those ideas in the main clause.

- **Graffiti removal ground to a halt** although cleanup funds were available. [Emphasis is on the *graffiti removal.*]
- Although graffiti removal ground to a halt, **cleanup funds were available**. [Emphasis is on the *cleanup funds.*]

SENTENCE PROBLEMS

26b Comma Splices

A comma splice occurs when a mere comma is used to connect (or "splice") two independent clauses. A comma is not strong enough for the job.

- Some politicians treat all casualties of war as noble sacrifices, letters from soldiers tell a different story. [The words before the comma are one independent clause; the words after the comma are another.]

How can I fix a comma splice?

Here are six strategies for fixing a comma splice.

1. **Treat the two clauses as separate sentences.**

   - Some politicians treat all casualties of war as noble sacrifices. Letters from soldiers tell a different story. [This method stresses the independence and equal weight of the two separate thoughts.]

2. **Use a semicolon instead of a comma.**

   - Some politicians treat all casualties of war as noble sacrifices; letters from soldiers tell a different story. [The semicolon implies a logical relationship between the ideas.]

3. **Use a semicolon followed by a conjunctive adverb and a comma.**

   - Some politicians treat all casualties of war as noble sacrifices; however, letters from soldiers tell a different story. [The conjunctive adverb makes the relationship between the clauses explicit and formal. Other conjunctive adverbs are *nevertheless*, *indeed*, *therefore*, and *accordingly*.]

4. **Use a comma and a coordinating conjunction *(and, but, or, nor, for, so, yet)*.**

   - Some politicians treat all casualties of war as noble sacrifices, but letters from soldiers tell a different story. [The comma and coordinating conjunction create a compound sentence. The relationship of the ideas is indicated by the conjunction.]

5. **Turn one of the independent clauses into a subordinate clause.**

   - Although some politicians treat all casualties of war as noble sacrifices, letters from soldiers tell a different story. [This method softens the impact of the subordinated statement.]

6. **Rewrite the two independent clauses as one independent clause.**

   - The speeches of politicians and the letters of soldiers disagree as to whether war is a noble sacrifice. [This method offers nearly countless options. You may have to add or subtract ideas to make your rewritten sentence work.]

26c Fused or Run-On Sentences

The term *fused* or *run-on sentence* refers to the joining of two sentences without proper punctuation or a connecting word.

■ The Alamo holds a special place in American history this fort was the site of an important battle between the United States and Mexico.

How can I fix a run-on sentence?

There are six ways to correct run-on sentences.

1. **Treat the two clauses as two separate sentences.**

   ■ The Alamo holds a special place in American history. This fort was the site of an important battle between the United States and Mexico.

2. **Use a semicolon.**

   ■ The Alamo holds a special place in American history; this fort was the site of an important battle between the United States and Mexico.

3. **Use a semicolon followed by a conjunctive adverb and a comma.**

   ■ The Alamo holds a special place in American history; **indeed,** this fort was the site of an important battle between the United States and Mexico.

4. **Use a comma and a coordinating conjunction** *(and, but, or, nor, for, so, yet).*

   ■ The Alamo holds a special place in American history, **for** this fort was the site of an important battle between the United States and Mexico.

5. **Turn one of the independent clauses into a subordinate clause.**

   ■ The Alamo holds a special place in American history **because** this fort was the site of an important battle between the United States and Mexico. [Notice that the subordinate clause beginning with *because* is restrictive and therefore is not preceded by a comma. See **24c** for more information on restrictive clauses.]

6. **Rewrite the two independent clauses as a single independent clause.**

   ■ An important battle between the United States and Mexico earned the Alamo its important place in American history.

SENTENCE PROBLEMS

26d Shifts in Sentence Construction

Some writers work verbal magic by using clever shifts in writing. For example, Oscar Wilde uses a brilliant shift in tone in this quotation: "Arguments are to be avoided; they are always vulgar and often convincing." He starts out with a cautious tone and ends up with a witty remark. But shifts in sentence construction, as in tone, can cause problems when they happen by accident.

What are mixed sentence patterns?

A mixed sentence pattern occurs when a writer starts with one sentence pattern and switches to another. The result is a mismatch. To repair a mixed construction, rewrite the sentence so that it follows only one sentence pattern.

Mixed:	By moving from a cold climate to a warmer one would make me happy. [The prepositional phrase at the beginning of the sentence cannot be the subject.]
Corrected:	Moving from a cold climate to a warmer one would make me happy. [Dropping the preposition turns the phrase into a gerund, which can be the subject of a sentence.]
Mixed:	Jamaica's climate **is where** anyone would be comfortable. [The adverb clause following the linking verb cannot be a predicate adjective.]
Corrected:	Jamaica's climate **is one** where anyone would be comfortable. [Now a predicate noun follows the linking verb.]

What are shifts in person or in number?

A shift in **person** means changing the point of view in your writing. For example, a shift occurs when a writer moves from first person *(I or we)* to second person *(you)* to third person *(he/she/it* or *one* or *they)*, and so on.

Shift:	**One** may get spring fever unless **you** live in the Sun Belt. [The third person pronoun *one* shifts to the second person *you.*]
Corrected:	**One** may get spring fever unless **he or she** lives in the Sun Belt. [*One* and *he or she* are singular third person pronouns.]

A shift in **number** means illogically slipping from singular into plural (or vice versa).

Shift:	**One** may get spring fever unless **they** live in the Sun Belt. [The singular pronoun *one* shifts to the plural pronoun *they.*]
Corrected:	**People** may get spring fever unless **they** live in the Sun Belt. [*People* and *they* are both plural.]

What are shifts in tense?

A shift in tense occurs when past, present, and future verbs are used in combination. Unintentional shifts in tense confuse the logic of time relationships.

Tense Shift: Sheila *looked* at nine apartments in one weekend before she *has chosen* one. [Verb tense shifts from past to present perfect for no good reason.]

Corrected: Sheila *had looked* at nine apartments in one weekend before she finally *chose* one. [The past perfect and past tenses show that both actions happened in the past, but one happened before the other.]

WRITER'S TIP

Shifts in verb tense are sometimes necessary to show that the action named in one verb occurs at a different time than the action named in another. Such "tense sequences" follow certain rules.

(1) Use **past perfect tense** to show action completed *before* the time implied by a **simple past tense** verb.

  ■ We **discarded** the mayonnaise that **had sat** unrefrigerated.

(2) Use **present perfect** to show an action completed *after* the time implied by a **simple past tense** verb.

  ■ I **have contacted** the agency as you **requested**.

What are shifts in mood?

Shifts in mood occur when a writer moves from one mood to another. Verbs may appear in any of three moods: indicative, imperative, or subjunctive. The **indicative** mood is used for statements of fact, for opinions, or for questions. **Imperative** is used for giving orders or advice. **Subjunctive** is used for stating wishes, possibilities, or conditions contrary to fact. A writer should choose an appropriate mood and stick with it.

Mood Shift: The thumb **should slide** under the fret board, and **place** the fingers on the strings. [The mood shifts from indicative to imperative.]

Corrected: **Slide** the thumb under the fret board and **place** the fingers on the strings. [Both verbs are now in the imperative mood.]

Mood Shift: Senator Zacagna suggested that we **be patient** and that we **should express** our dissatisfaction in the form of a letter. [The mood shifts from subjunctive to indicative.]

Corrected: Senator Zacagna suggested that we **be patient** and that we **express** our dissatisfaction in the form of a letter. [Both verbs are now in the subjunctive mood.]

SENTENCE PROBLEMS

ESL TIP

An indirect quotation can require the verb to shift in mood. For example, in an indirect quotation, the verb *will* should be replaced by the verb *would*.

Incorrect:	The judge **said** that she **will be** here by six.
Corrected:	The judge **said** that she **would be** here by six. [Substitute *would* for *will*.]
Corrected:	The judge **said**, "I **will be** there at six." [Quote directly.]

What are shifts in voice?

A shift in voice occurs when a writer indiscriminately changes from passive to active. Needless voice shifts within a sentence cloud the picture of who is doing what. Usually, a sentence beginning in active voice should remain so to the end of the sentence.

Voice Shift:	Professor Sturgis **canceled** [active] the class, and the teaching assistant **was** never **informed** [passive].
Corrected:	Professor Sturgis **canceled** the class but never **informed** his teaching assistant. [Both verbs are now in active voice.]

What are shifts from direct to indirect quotations or questions?

Sometimes writers suddenly shift from direct constructions to indirect constructions (or vice versa). To avoid confusion, stick with either direct or indirect constructions, and be careful to use the correct punctuation, pronouns, and verbs for each.

Shift:	The janitor said please turn out the lights and that we should lock the door when we leave.
Corrected:	The janitor said that we should turn out the lights and lock the door when we leave. [The entire quotation is now indirect.]
Corrected:	The janitor said, "Turn out the lights and lock the door when you leave." [The entire quotation is now direct.]
Shift:	Can I look at your lab notes, and I wonder if I could use them tonight.
Corrected:	Can I look at your lab notes and use them tonight? [The entire sentence now presents a direct question.]
Corrected:	I wonder if I could look at your lab notes and use them tonight. [The entire sentence now poses an indirect question.]

26e Faulty Parallelism

Careful writers use parallel structures to show the connection between closely related ideas. For example, if the first item in a series is a gerund *(swimming)*, the other items should be gerunds as well *(hiking, rowing,* and *rock-climbing).* Use a parallel structure when you list items, compare and contrast, or link items with *or, but,* or *and.* Also, use parallel structures with pairs of conjunctions, such as *if/then, either/or,* or *both/and.*

Faulty: The road sign in Australia's outback warned of **wandering camels, wombats that scuttle, and leaping kangaroos on the highway**.

Corrected: The road sign in Australia's outback warned of **wandering camels, scuttling wombats, and leaping kangaroos on the highway**. [The three items in the series are now parallel; they are all nouns preceded by an adjective.]

Faulty: Polo is both **a gracious sport**, and **it is a physically demanding one**.

Corrected: Polo is both **a gracious sport** and **a physically demanding one**. [The words after each of the correlative conjunctions are now parallel; both sets of words start with an article and end with a noun.]

Faulty: We were neither **aware** nor **excited about** the fund-raising plan.

Corrected: We were neither **aware of** nor **excited about** the fund-raising plan. [The words after each of the correlative conjunctions are now parallel; each predicate adjective, *aware* and *excited*, is followed by the appropriate preposition.]

WRITER'S TIP

When the two parts of a parallel structure have identical wording, it is permissible—in some cases, even elegant—to omit some of the words in the second half of the construction. These "elliptical structures" are still regarded as parallel in form.

Elliptical Structure:

- Before the game, his mood was grim; afterward, elated. [In this example, some of the words are understood, or not expressed: Before the game, his mood was grim; afterward, *his mood was* elated.]

SENTENCE PROBLEMS

26f Misplaced and Dangling Modifiers

Modifying words, phrases, and clauses can create confusion when they are placed in the wrong part of the sentence (misplaced modifiers) or when they do not modify anything in the sentence (dangling modifiers). Sentences with **misplaced** or **dangling modifiers** can result in confusing, ambiguous, or comical statements.

What is a misplaced modifier?

A misplaced modifier is a word, phrase, or clause that does not clearly connect to the word it modifies. Modifiers can be misplaced in one of several ways.

- The modifier is detached from the word it modifies.

  Misplaced: I have several very old dresses from my grandmother **in great condition**.

  Corrected: I have several very old dresses **in great condition** from my grandmother.

- The modifier is placed where it disrupts the flow of an idea.

  Misplaced: Dixon became a, **perhaps because of his bad luck**, pessimist.

  Corrected: **Perhaps because of his bad luck**, Dixon became a pessimist.

- The modifier "squints" ambiguously at both the word before it and the word after it.

  Misplaced: Simon's complaining **strongly** hints at his insecurity.

  Corrected: Simon's complaining hints **strongly** at his insecurity.

- A "limiting" modifier—*almost, barely, even, just, merely, only,* or *really*—limits the wrong word.

  Misplaced: The provost **almost** cut half the food budget.

  Corrected: The provost cut **almost** half the food budget.

What is a dangling modifier?

A dangling modifier is a word, phrase, or clause that has no logical word within the sentence to modify. That is why a dangling modifier is said to "dangle." Sometimes the modifier implies someone or something is performing an action, but the actor is not named in the sentence. Another word—often one that makes a ridiculous connection to the dangling modifier—takes on the role of "actor."

- **Cycling down the block**, the dog followed her. [The modifier, *cycling down the block*, should logically connect to the subject of the sentence, *dog*. However, since there really is no word for the phrase to connect to, the modifier dangles.]

- **Racing to the blaze**, the prairie fire was extinguished. [The participial phrase doesn't describe the *fire*; what does it modify?]

Misplaced and Dangling Modifiers

How can I correct a dangling modifier?

You cannot simply move a dangling modifier to another spot in the sentence and expect to correct the sentence error. To fix a dangling modifier, you may use one of two methods:

Reword the main clause.

- Cycling down the block, **the girl was followed by a dog**.
  [The modifier, *cycling down the block*, now logically connects to the subject, *girl*.]

Rewrite the modifier as a subordinate clause and insert the actor in it.

- **As the girl cycled down the block**, the dog followed. [The modifier is now a subordinate clause with the actor, *girl*, named.]

- **As the firefighters raced to the blaze**, the prairie fire extinguished itself. [The actor, *firefighters*, is named in the new subordinate clause.]

a closer look

Here are some of the most common types of dangling modifiers.

PARTICIPIAL PHRASE

Incorrect:	**Singing karaoke**, the police interrupted the loud party.
Corrected:	Singing karaoke, the party **guests** were interrupted by the police.

PREPOSITION WITH GERUND PHRASE AS OBJECT

Incorrect:	**After swimming the Channel**, the church bells rang.
Corrected:	**After Albert swam the Channel**, the church bells rang.

INFINITIVE PHRASE

Incorrect:	**To reach ground safely**, proper parachute packing is necessary.
Corrected:	**To reach ground safely**, jumpers must properly pack their parachutes.

SUBORDINATE CLAUSE WITH IMPLIED SUBJECT

Incorrect:	**When confronted with the prank**, his reputation was his only concern.
Corrected:	**When Shay was confronted with the prank**, his reputation was his only concern.

SENTENCE PROBLEMS

26g Ambiguous Wording

Ambiguous wording robs a sentence of its meaning. The sentence could mean more than one thing or mean nothing at all. Conscientious writers correct ambiguities such as incomplete comparisons or confusing logic.

What are incomplete comparisons?

A comparison is complete only if it includes both items being compared and the basis for the comparison. To remedy an incomplete comparison, supply the needed information, repeating words if necessary to make the comparison clear.

Incomplete: Today, **more** doctors recommend Fibrex for your diet.

Complete: Today, **more** doctors **than** nutritionists recommend Fibrex for your diet. [compare like items: *doctors/nutritionists*]

Today **more than** ever, doctors recommend Fibrex for your diet. [compare like items: *today/ever*]

What is confusing logic?

Confusing logic occurs when a writer does not supply all the words needed to make a sentence clear. Writers should be especially careful to avoid indefinite references.

Unclear: Our 32-ounce bottle contains 33 percent more! [It contains 33 percent more than what?]

Corrected: Our 32-ounce bottle contains 33 percent more than our 24-ounce bottle. [This clear comparison demonstrates that the ad isn't saying much.]

Unclear: Joe intended to go to the writing center when he finished his rough draft, but he never did. [It is unclear which thing he *never did*—finish his rough draft or go to the writing center.]

Corrected: Joe intended to go to the writing center when he finished his rough draft, but he never did **go to the writing center**.

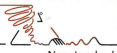

26h   Nonstandard Language

Nonstandard language is language that does not conform to the standards set by schools, the media, and public institutions. Nonstandard language is often acceptable in everyday conversation and in some literature, but it is seldom acceptable in formal speech or edited forms of writing.

What is colloquial language?

Colloquial language is language often used in informal conversation. It is unacceptable in formal writing.

Colloquial: Shoot, we've been jacked around one too many times.

Standard: Others have taken advantage of us one too many times.

What are double prepositions?

Colloquial language uses certain double prepositions, such as *off of* or *from off.* These constructions are unacceptable in formal writing.

Double Preposition: Pick up the dirty clothes **from off** the floor.

Standard: Pick up the dirty clothes **from** the floor.

What word substitutions should I avoid?

Avoid substituting *and* for *to.*

Substitution: Try **and** get to class on time.

Standard: Try **to** get to class on time.

Avoid substituting *of* for *have* when used with *could, would, should,* or *might.*

Substitution: I **should of** studied for that exam.

Standard: I **should have** studied for that exam.

ESL TIP

A double negative is a sentence that contains two negative words used to express a single negative idea. Double negatives are unacceptable in academic writing.

Double Negative: After paying for gas, I **haven't got no** money left.

Standard: After paying for gas, **I have no** money left.

Can I use slang?

Avoid the use of slang or any "in" words in academic writing.

Slang: The way Hemingway wrote was **way cool**.

Standard: The way Hemingway wrote was **amazing**.

26i Checklist: Avoiding Sentence Problems

Use the checklist below to address agreement errors and sentence problems.

Does every subject agree with its verb? (See 25a–25f.)

____ in person and number?

____ when a word or phrase comes between the subject and verb?

____ when the subject is delayed?

____ when the subject is a title?

____ when a compound subject is connected with *and*?

____ when a compound subject is connected with *or*?

____ when the subject is a collective noun (*faculty, team, crowd*)?

____ when the subject is a relative pronoun (*who, which, that*)?

____ when the subject is an indefinite pronoun (*everyone, anybody, many*)?

Does every pronoun agree with its antecedent? (See 25h.)

____ in number, person, and gender?

____ when the antecedent is a singular indefinite pronoun (*each, either, another*)?

____ when two or more antecedents are joined with *and*?

____ when two or more antecedents are joined with *or*?

Have I avoided or corrected all sentence problems? (See 26a–26c.)

____ sentence fragments?

____ comma splices?

____ run-ons?

Did I catch and correct inappropriate shifts? (See 26d.)

____ in number?

____ in person?

____ in tense?

____ from active to passive voice?

Did I correct any faulty parallelism? (See 26e.)

Did I correct any misplaced modifiers or ambiguous wording? (See 26f–26g.)

Did I delete any nonstandard language? (See 26h.)

WRITER'S TIP

The best sentence is a clear sentence. Although you may feel pressure to create complicated, collegiate-sounding prose, your sentences should never be more complex than they need to be.

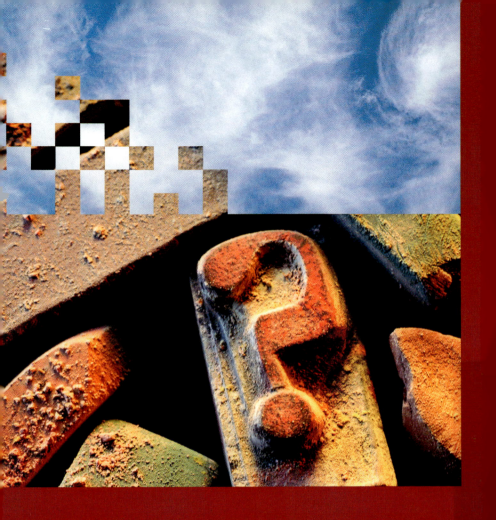

Punctuation and Mechanics

Punctuation and Mechanics

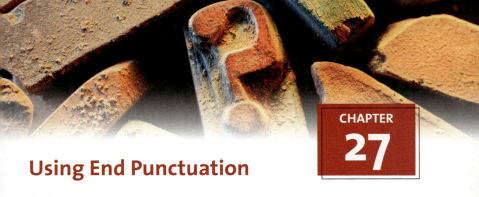

Using End Punctuation

When someone speaks, the words carry all sorts of information: pitch, rhythm, tempo, intonation, inflection. Spoken language has its own music. Written language can be musical, too, but must rely on words, sentences, and punctuation to convey that same rich sound.

To understand punctuation, the best place to start is at the end—the end of the sentence. Those tiny little dots and curves tell us just what sort of sentence we have. To see the power of end punctuation, read the following out loud: Does your voice rise right before a question mark?

27a Periods

A period at the end of a sentence indicates finality. In fact, outside of the United States and Canada, it is often called a *full stop*. Sometimes we even speak the period, indicating that the discussion is over: "Leonardo da Vinci was the greatest genius of the Italian Renaissance Period, period."

Which sentences should end with a period?

Use a period to end any sentence except for a direct question or an exclamation. Sentences that make a statement, request something, report a question indirectly, give a mild command, or make a mild exclamation use periods.

Statement:	Lightning caused the computer malfunction.
Request:	Please read the instructions carefully.
Indirect question:	Frank asked if the ball game would be a doubleheader.
Mild command:	If your topic sentence isn't clear, rewrite it.
Mild exclamation:	Barb finally got a job with the Rockettes.

> **NOTE:** It is *not* necessary to place a period after a statement that has parentheses around it if the parenthetical sentence is within another sentence.
> - Think about joining a club (the student affairs office has a list of organizations) for fun and leadership experience.

USING END PUNCTUATION

When should I use a period within a sentence?

Use a period after an initial and in some abbreviations. (See **32b–32c**.)

- A. A. Milne   Mr.   Jr.   M.A.   Dr.
  Booker T. Washington Mrs.   Sr.   Ph.D.   D.D.S.
  Sen. Russ Feingold   Ms.   B.A.   a.m.   p.m.

> **NOTE:** When an abbreviation with a period is at the end of a sentence, do not use a second period to finish the sentence.
>
> - Mikhail had a six-week internship in Washington, D.C.

When should I *not* use a period?

Don't use periods with the following shortened forms of words:

Initialisms or acronyms (See **32c**.)

- **ASAP**—as soon as possible
- **HIV**—human immunodeficiency virus
- **WYSIWYG**—What You See Is What You Get

Names of well-known organizations

- **NYU**—New York University
- **NAACP**—National Association for the Advancement of Colored People
- **NATO**—North Atlantic Treaty Organization
- **FBI**—Federal Bureau of Investigation
- Standard Postal Service abbreviations of state or province names—
  AZ, NM, MA, CA, WY, ON, QC (See **32c**.)

27b Question Marks

Some scholars believe the question mark came from the Latin abbreviation for *question*—*Qo*. Over time, the capital *Q* was written above the lowercase *o*. Others suggest that the mark began as a musical notation, telling the speaker to raise the pitch at the end of the sentence. The true origins remain in question.

Which sentences should end with a question mark?

Use a question mark at the end of a direct question.

- Can you get here by 6:30 p.m.?

Direct questions include both *rhetorical questions* (questions asked with no answer expected) and *elliptical* (*abbreviated*) *questions*.

Rhetorical question:

- Since when do you have to agree with people to defend them from injustice?
  —Lillian Hellman

Question Marks

Elliptical question:

- How did the army expect to be greeted**?** With flowers**?** With hugs**?** [The phrases represent the complete questions "Did they expect to be greeted with flowers?" and "Did they expect to be greeted with hugs?"]

When should I *not* use a question mark?

Do *not* use a question mark after an **indirect question,** which restates a question. An indirect question often takes the form of a subordinate clause beginning with an interrogative word (*who, what, when, where, how,* and so on).

- After listening to Kareem sing, Ms. Cannelloni asked him what formal voice training he had had. [The direct question would be "What formal voice training have you had?"]

> **NOTE:** Single words such as *where, when,* or *why* may at times be integrated into the flow of a sentence so that capitalization and special punctuation are not required. However, be sure to put the words in italics if you are referring to the words as words.
>
> - The issues we must tackle at the team-building weekend include *whether, where, when,* and *why.*

How do question marks work with other punctuation?

A question within parentheses or quotation marks—or a question set off by dashes—is punctuated with a question mark unless the sentence ends with a question mark.

- You must consult your handbook (what choice do you have**?**) when you need to know a punctuation rule. [The question mark belongs to the parenthetical sentence.]

- Should I use your charge card (you have one, don't you) or pay cash**?** [The question mark belongs to both questions, so it appears at the end.]

- Rita has red hair—doesn't she**?**—and an infectious smile.

- "Will he—can he—build the house in time**?**" asked José.

WRITER'S TIP

Do not use several question marks to make a question seem more urgent. Multiple question marks have an immature appearance on the page. One question mark is sufficient.

USING END PUNCTUATION

27c Exclamation Points

When people in ancient Rome felt joy, they shouted, "Io!" Some scholars suggest that the capital *I* eventually slid over the lowercase *o*, creating the exclamation point. Two thousand years later, people still use the mark to exclaim ("Yee-haw!"), to command ("Halt!"), and to express strong emotion ("You're here!").

When should I use an exclamation point?

Use an exclamation point to express especially strong excitement or emphasis. The exclamation point may be placed at the end of a sentence (or an elliptical expression that stands for a sentence).

- "That's not the point," said Wangero. "These are all pieces of dresses Grandma used to wear. She did all this stitching by hand. Imagine!"
  —Alice Walker, "Everyday Use"

- Su-su-something's crawling up the back of my neck!
  —Mark Twain, *Roughing It*

- She was on tiptoe, stretching for an orange, when they heard, "HEY YOU!"
  —Beverley Naidoo, *Journey to Jo'burg*

When should I *not* use an exclamation point?

When in doubt, leave it out. Use a period or comma instead. Unless you are writing dialogue for a comic book, you need very few exclamation points.

- Cut out all those exclamation marks. An exclamation mark is like laughing at your own joke.   —F. Scott Fitzgerald

Here are specific warnings about exclamation points:

Do not use exclamation points for mild assertions.

- I wish the car hadn't broken down.
  [no exclamation]
- The car is rolling into the lake!
  [exclamation]

Do not use exclamation points with question marks.

- Didn't you set the brake? [not *brake?!*]

Do not use multiple exclamation points.

- There goes the car!
  [not *car!!!*]

Commas

The comma may seem lowly, but it is the workhorse of the English language. It has about as many uses as all other punctuation marks combined. A comma is a sign not to stop but to pause briefly. Without it, misreadings are possible.

Confusing:	While I lecture David will take notes.
Clear:	While I lecture**,** David will take notes.
Confusing:	As I was driving a bus slammed on its brakes in front of me.
Clear:	As I was driving**,** a bus slammed on its brakes in front of me.

The addition of commas (after *lecture* and *driving*) makes it clear that I am not *lecturing David* or *driving a bus*. Learn comma rules—but learn the gentle art of commas, too.

28a Commas in Compound Sentences

When two independent clauses are linked together with a coordinating conjunction (*and, but, or, nor, for, so, yet*) to make a compound sentence, place a comma between the two clauses just before the conjunction.

- The $10 million makeup budget was the most ever for a film**, but** it became a box-office hit and more than paid for itself. [The independent clauses are linked with a comma and the word *but*.]

What is a comma splice?

A comma splice is an error that occurs when a comma is left standing by itself between two independent clauses. (See **26b**.)

| **Comma Splice:** | The hype preceding the concert was extraordinary, the performance exceeded expectations. |
| **Corrected:** | The hype preceding the concert was extraordinary**, yet** the performance exceeded expectations. [A coordinating conjunction now connects the two clauses.] |

COMMAS

What other comma errors should I avoid?

Do not use a comma **after** a coordinating conjunction.

Incorrect: Almost no one attended the art opening so, the gallery closed.

Correct: Almost no one attended the art opening**,** so the gallery closed.

Do not use a comma between compound subjects, predicates, direct objects, or prepositional phrases.

- Anyone who is interested in the marketing campaign **and** wants a preview of the video should come to room 244.
  [No comma is used when *and* links two predicates.]

- Young people should show courtesy **and** respect to their elders.
  [No comma is used when *and* links two direct objects.]

- The easels are located behind the door **but** within easy reach.
  [No comma is used when *but* links two prepositional phrases.]

28b Commas in a Series

If a series has three or more items in it, separate the items with commas. The items may be words, phrases, or clauses.

Words in a series

- The rock climber was strong, agile, and determined.

Phrases in a series

- The rock climber was covered with sweat, aching from exertion, and determined not to fail.

Clauses in a series

- The rock climber was covered with sweat, he was aching from exertion, and he was determined not to fail.

> **NOTE:** Use a comma before the final item in the series. This comma is called the "serial" comma and is needed to prevent ambiguity or confusion.

How do I use commas with compounds?

If the last item in a series is a compound, remember to include a comma and a conjunction before the compound.

Confusing: For my lunch, pack cheese, bread, spaghetti and meatballs.

Clear: For my lunch**,** pack cheese**,** bread**, and** spaghetti and meatballs.

When should I *not* use commas in a series?

Do not use commas

- When all the items in a series are connected with *or, nor,* or *and.*

  Incorrect: Should I study, or do laundry, or go out?

  Correct: Should I study or do laundry or go out?

- Before or after a series.

  Incorrect: They carried, water, energy bars, and trail mix in their packs.

  Incorrect: They carried water, energy bars, and trail mix, in their packs.

  Correct: They carried water**,** energy bars**,** and trail mix in their packs.

- Use semicolons between subgroups that already include commas. (See **29a**.)

  Incorrect: The lunch included a hamburger, a hot dog, or a veggie sub, baked potatoes, French fries, or chips, and a house salad or a cup of soup.

  Correct: The lunch included a hamburger**,** a hot dog**,** or a veggie sub**;** baked potatoes**,** French fries**,** or chips**;** and a house salad or a cup of soup.

28c Commas with Adjectives

Use commas to separate adjectives that modify the same noun equally.

- You should exercise regularly and follow a sensible**,** healthful diet.

a closer look

Use the two tests below to check for equal adjectives.

- Matt was tired of working in the hot**,** crowded lab and decided to take a short coffee break.

1. Reverse the order of the adjectives; if the sentence is clear, the adjectives are coordinated. (Coordinated adjectives such as **hot** and **crowded** can be reversed, and the sentence is still clear. **Short** and **coffee** are not coordinated and cannot be reversed.)

2. Insert *and* between the adjectives; if the sentence reads well, use a comma when *and* is omitted. (The word **and** can be inserted between **hot** and **crowded**, but not between **short** and **coffee**.)

When should I *not* use commas with modifiers?

Do not use a comma between an adjective and a noun, between an adverb and an adjective it modifies, or between cumulative adjectives.

- Jan is a **brilliant student**. She is an **exceptionally committed** scholar and a **helpful math-teaching** assistant.

COMMAS

28d Commas with Introductory Words

When a sentence begins with introductory words, use a comma to set off the material. (The sentence you just read is an example of this rule.)

How do I recognize introductory words?

Introductory words are phrases or clauses that modify the subject, the verb, or the sentence as a whole.

- **On the first day,** Regina arrived late. [prepositional phrase]
- **Peering over his reading glasses,** Professor Chapman paused in his lecture. [participial phrase]
- **Though Regina gave an excuse,** he noted her tardiness. [subordinate clause]
- "**To arrive on time,** you must leave on time," he said. [infinitive phrase]

A single participle or conjunctive adjective also should be set off with a comma.

- **Blushing,** Regina took her seat. [participle]
- **Consequently,** she decided to leave earlier next time. [conjunctive adverb]

> **NOTE:** For short prepositional phrases, the comma is optional.

What common mistakes should I avoid?

If a word, phrase, or clause functions as the subject of the sentence, don't place a comma after it.

- **Blushing** is one of Regina's weaknesses. [*Blushing* is the subject.]
- **Arriving late for class** is another one. [*Arriving late for class* is the subject.]
- **To become punctual** is her goal. [*To become punctual* is the subject.]

28e Commas with Explanatory Words

Use a comma to separate words, phrases, or clauses that provide extra (non-essential) information. These are called **nonrestrictive modifiers.**

- Historians believe there was a real Arthur**, ruler of Britain**.
- Arthur would have been a *dux bellorum***, Latin for "duke."**
- He lived in a lawless time**, when Rome had abandoned England to brigands**.

Do not use a comma to separate **restrictive modifiers** at the end of the sentence.

- Arthur fought the Germanic tribes **that invaded in the east and south.**

What if the explanation interrupts the sentence?

When words, phrases, or clauses interrupt the usual flow of thought, set them apart using commas. These, too, are nonrestrictive modifiers.

- The new library, down the street from the old one, was paid for by alumni.
- The library stacks, where many students once roamed, have largely been replaced by computer holdings.

Do I use commas with restrictive modifiers?

Don't set off interrupting words that are necessary to the meaning of the sentence. Such words are restrictive modifiers.

- Hemingway's novel **A Farewell to Arms** reflects his experiences as a medic. [Because Hemingway wrote many novels, the name of the novel is essential information.]

WRITER'S TIP

You can identify a nonrestrictive modifier by mentally removing it from the sentence. If the sentence still makes sense and is clear, the modifier is nonrestrictive—not essential to the meaning of the sentence. Set the modifier off with commas.

28f Commas with Dialogue

Use commas to set off the directly quoted words of the speaker from the rest of the sentence. If the quotation appears before the attribution (such as *he said*), place a comma inside the quotation marks at the end of the quotation.

- "Acting is happy agony," Sir Alec Guinness once said.

When the quotation ends with either an exclamation point or a question mark, do not place a comma after it.

- "Cap'n, we're breaking up!" Scotty shouted almost once every episode.

If the attribution appears before the quotation, place a comma after the lead-in phrase.

- Dr. Melba Colgrove has said, "Joy is the feeling of grinning on the inside."

Sometimes the attribution appears in the middle of a quoted sentence. After the first part of the quotation, place one comma inside the quotation marks. Place another comma after the attribution.

- "Delay always breeds danger," said Miguel de Cervantes, author of *Don Quixote*, "and to protract a great design is often to ruin it."

COMMAS

Do I use commas with indirect quotations?

The rules for using commas with direct quotations do not apply to indirect quotations. Indirect quotations are paraphrases of the original, often introduced by the word *that*. Incorporate the indirect quotation into your sentence without using a comma or quotation marks.

- The Water Board stated **that there was no danger of a drought this season**.

Do I use commas when speaking directly to someone?

A comma is needed in direct address. When a word or phrase suspends the sentence for a moment, mark the suspension with a comma or commas that set off or enclose it.

- **Curtis,** would you close the blinds so that we can watch the movie?

  Have you**, ladies and gentlemen of the jury,** reached your verdict?

28g Commas with Interjections and Tags

Use commas to set off mild interjections from the rest of the sentence.

- "**Prithee,** do not turn me about; my stomach is not constant."

Use a comma before tags, which are short additions or questions that come at the ends of sentences.

- That's Shakespeare**, isn't it**?
- I like Shakespeare**, just not when I'm eating**.

28h Commas with Titles and Initials

Use commas to enclose titles, initials, or given names that follow a surname.

- Until Martin**,** Sr.**,** was 15, he never had more than three months of schooling in any one year.
  —Ed Clayton,
  Martin Luther King: The Peaceful Warrior

- The genealogical files included the names Sanders**,** L. H.**,** and Sanders**,** Lucy Hale.

NOTE: It is now quite common to see Sr. and Jr. used without commas.

28i   Commas with Addresses, Dates, and Numbers

Use commas to set off items in an address and the year in a date.

- Send your letter to 1600 Pennsylvania Avenue, Washington, DC 20006, before January 1, 2006, or send e-mail to <president@whitehouse.gov>.

> **NOTE:** No comma is placed between the state and ZIP Code. Also, no comma separates the items if only the month and year are given (January 2006) or if date and month are reversed, military or European style (13 January 2006).

Use commas to separate the digits in long numbers into groups of three, marking hundreds, thousands, millions, and so on.

- Do you know how to write the amount $2,025 on a check?

  25,000   973,240   18,620,194

> **NOTE:** No comma is necessary in years, in street addresses, or in ZIP Codes.

A GOOGOL

One followed by 100 zeroes (and quite a few commas)

10,000,000,000,000,000,
000,000,000,000,000,000,
000,000,000,000,000,000,
000,000,000,000,000,000,
000,000,000,000,000,000,
000,000,000,000

28j   Commas to Prevent Confusion

Use commas to separate contrasted elements within a sentence.

- **Deeds, rather than words,** are what we need now.
- We work **to become, not to acquire**.

—Eugene Delacroix

Use a comma to mark a place where repeated words have been intentionally left out (elided).

- To err is human; to **forgive, divine**.

—Alexander Pope

Use a comma for clarity or for emphasis. Sometimes none of the traditional rules call for a comma, but a comma is needed to prevent confusion or awkwardness in repeated words or phrases, or to emphasize an important idea.

- What she **does, does** matter to us. [clarity in repetition]
- It may be those who **do most, dream most**. [emphasis]

—Stephen Leacock

28k Common Comma Errors

Do not use a comma

- Between a subject and its verb.

  Incorrect: The circus tigers, paced in their cages.

  Correct: The circus tigers paced in their cages.

- Between a verb and its object.

  Incorrect: The ringmaster introduced, the famed acrobats.

  Correct: The ringmaster introduced the famed acrobats.

- After *such as* or *like*.

  Incorrect: We saw other acts such as, performing elephants and a magic show.

  Correct: We saw other acts such as performing elephants and a magic show.

- Between a comparative and *than*.

  Incorrect: Those lion tamers are braver, than I will ever be!

  Correct: Those lion tamers are braver than I will ever be!

- Before a parenthesis.

  Incorrect: A funambulist, (a rope walker) carries a long balancing rod.

  Correct: A funambulist (a rope walker) carries a long balancing rod.

ESL TIP

Remember these five places to use commas.

1. Before *and, but,* or *or* in a compound sentence
   - I'll study comma use, **and** it will eventually get easier.

2. After each item in a series (except the last)
   - Then I'll focus on **semicolons, colons,** and dashes.

3. After introductory phrases and clauses
   - **With a little work,** I'll perfect my punctuation.

4. Around the name of a person being spoken to
   - If you want, **Raul,** I'll help you study.

5. Around words that interrupt a sentence
   - The rules of punctuation, **at least on this side of the Atlantic,** are very complex.

Other Punctuation

When you consider the complete array of punctuation in English—commas, semicolons, colons, hyphens, dashes, parentheses, brackets, and so on—you might wish for a simpler language. Remember, though, that many ancient texts were written with no punctuation and often no spaces at all.

Punctuation in English is not meant to make your writing more difficult, but rather to make it clearer and easier to understand.

29a   Semicolons

The semicolon (;) sometimes acts as a comma, creating greater separation among items in a series. At other times, the semicolon acts as a period, creating a closer connection between two sentences.

How can I use a semicolon in a series?

Use a semicolon to separate items in a series that already contains commas.

- My favorite foods are pizza with pepperoni, onions, and olives**;** peanut butter and banana sandwiches**;** and liver with bacon, peppers, and onions.

How can I use a semicolon to connect sentences?

Use a semicolon to join two or more closely related independent clauses that are not connected with a coordinating conjunction.

- I was thrown out of college for cheating on the metaphysics exam**;** I looked into the soul of the boy next to me.   —Woody Allen

Place a semicolon before a conjunctive adverb or transitional phrase used in a compound sentence. (A comma often follows these conjunctive adverbs or transitional phrases; see list on the following page.)

- Many college freshmen are on their own for the first time**;** *however,* others are already independent and even have families.
- Pablo was born in the Andes**;** *as a result,* he loves mountains.

OTHER PUNCTUATION

> **Common Conjunctive Adverbs**
> also, besides, however, instead, meanwhile, then, therefore
>
> **Common Transitional Phrases**
> after all, in addition, at the same time, as a matter of fact, even so, in conclusion, on the contrary, as a result, for example, in fact, on the other hand, at any rate, for instance, in other words, in the first place

Use a semicolon to join independent clauses that contain internal commas, even when they are connected by a coordinating conjunction. This helps to clarify the two separate ideas.

- Make sure your CD player, computer, bike, and other valuables are covered by a homeowner's insurance policy**;** and be sure to use the locks on your door, bike, and storage area.

29b Colons

The colon (:) shows a special relationship between two pieces of information. A colon can connect a title and a subtitle, a chapter and a verse, an hour and a minute, or a category and its subcategories. Think of the material before the colon as the "big idea," and the material that follows after it as the particular details.

How do I use a colon with lists and quotations?

You can introduce a list or quotation with a colon. However, make sure the colon follows a complete sentence.

- Successful college students have three resources**:** basic skills, creativity, and determination. [not *Successful college students have: basic skills . . .*]
- John Locke is credited with this prescription for a good life**:** "A sound mind in a sound body." [not *John Locke is credited with: "A sound mind . . .*]

A colon may also be used to introduce a block quotation.

- King's feminist beliefs frequently surface in *Le Morte d'Avalon***:**

   There she stands, tied to the great stake. [. . .] There stands Guinevere, caught as all women are caught on the claims of father and brother and husband. Of course Arthur sentenced her to death. She stole his most prized possession, her own body, and gave it to another man. It is an old, old crime. There are a hundred names for women who commit it, but only one sentence: Death.

How do I use a colon for emphasis?

Use a colon to emphasize a word, a phrase, or a clause that explains or adds impact to the main clause. Make sure the colon follows a complete sentence.

- I have one goal for myself: to become the first person in my family to graduate from college.

How do I use colons in business letters?

Use a colon in the following parts of a business letter (see **42a**):

- **Following a salutation:** Dear Professor Higgins:
- **Between the writer's and typist's initials:** DW: am
- **Between "Encl." and the item:** Encl.: report
- **After "c" (copies):** c: Lee Erickson

How do I use a colon with time or ratios?

Use a colon between hours, minutes, and seconds.

- 8:30 p.m.   9:45 a.m.   10:24:55

Use a colon between two numbers in a ratio.

- The ratio of computers to students is 1:20.

How do I use colons with publication parts?

Use a colon between title and subtitle, volume and page, and chapter and verse.

- *Ron Brown: An Uncommon Life*   Britannica 4: 211   Psalm 23:1–6

29c Hyphens

The hyphen (-) is a short mark that connects words and separates syllables. It should not be confused with the dash (—), which is longer.

Use a hyphen to make some compound words.

- great-great-grandfather [noun]   starry-eyed [adjective]
- mother-in-law [noun]   three-year-old [noun or adjective]

> **NOTE:** Some compound words (*living room*) do not use a hyphen and are written separately. Some are written solid (*bedroom*). Some do not use a hyphen when the word is a noun (*ice cream*) but do when it is a verb or an adjective (*ice-cream sundae*). Consult a dictionary.

Writers will sometimes use hyphens to combine words in unexpected ways.

- And they pried pieces of baked-too-fast sunshine cake from the roofs of their mouths and looked once more into the boy's eyes.

—Toni Morrison, *Song of Solomon*

OTHER PUNCTUATION

How can I use hyphens to form adjectives?

Use a hyphen to join two or more words that serve as a single-thought adjective before a noun.

- In real life I am a large, **big-boned** woman with rough, **man-working** hands. —Alice Walker, "Everyday Use"

> **NOTE:** Most single-thought adjectives are not hyphenated after the noun.
> - In real life, I am large and **big boned**.

When the first of these words is an adverb ending in *-ly*, do *not* use a hyphen. Also, do not use a hyphen when a number or a letter is the final element in a single-thought adjective.

- freshly painted barn   grade A milk [letter is the final element]

How can I use hyphens to create new words?

Use a hyphen to form new words beginning with the prefixes *self-*, *ex-*, *all-*, and *half-* or ending with the suffixes *-elect* or *-free*. Also use a hyphen to join any prefix to a proper noun, a proper adjective, or the official name of an office.

- post-Depression   mid-May   ex-mayor   governor-elect   scent-free

Use a hyphen to join a letter (capital or lowercase) to a noun or a participle.

- T-shirt   U-turn   V-shaped   x-axis

How do I use hyphens with numbers?

Use a hyphen to join the words in compound numbers from *twenty-one* to *ninety-nine* when it is necessary to write them out. (See 32a.)

- Forty-two people found seats in the cramped classroom.

Use a hyphen between the numerator and denominator of a fraction, but not when one or both of these elements are already hyphenated.

- four-tenths   five-sixteenths   seven thirty-seconds [7/32]

Use a hyphen to join numbers indicating a range, a score, or a vote.

- Students study 30-40 hours per week.
- The final score was 84-82.

What special uses do hyphens have?

Use a hyphen when two or more words have a common element that is omitted in all but the last term.

- We have cedar posts in four-, six-, and eight-inch widths.

Use a hyphen with prefixes or suffixes to avoid confusion.

- re-cover [not *recover*] the sofa   shell-like [not *shelllike*] shape

How should I divide syllables?

Use a hyphen to divide a word between syllables at the end of a line of print.

> **Guidelines for Word Division**
>
> 1. Leave enough of the word at the end of the line to identify the word.
> 2. Never divide a one-syllable word: **rained**, **skills**, **through**.
> 3. Avoid dividing a word of five or fewer letters: **paper**, **study**, **July**.
> 4. Never divide a one-letter syllable from the rest of the word: **omit-ted**, not **o-mitted**.
> 5. Always divide a compound word between its basic units: **sister-in-law**, not **sis-ter-in-law**.
> 6. Never divide abbreviations or contractions: **shouldn't**, not **should-n't**.
> 7. When a vowel is a syllable by itself, divide the word after the vowel: **epi-sode**, not **ep-isode**.
> 8. Avoid dividing a numeral: **1,000,000**, not **1,000,-000**.
> 9. Avoid dividing the last word in a paragraph.
> 10. Never divide the last word in more than two lines in a row.

29d Dashes

The dash can be a dramatic punctuation mark, giving words special emphasis, showing sudden shifts in thought, and even indicating missing or interrupted words. Given its penchant for drama, the dash should not be overused.

Most word processors automatically create a dash out of two hyphens. In typewriter-generated material, create a dash by using two hyphens (--) with no space before or after them. Do not use a single hyphen in place of a dash.

How can I use dashes in sentences?

Use a dash to set off any nonessential elements—explanations, examples, or definitions—you want to emphasize.

- Near the semester's end—and this is not always due to poor planning—some students may find themselves in academic trouble.
- The term *caveat emptor*—let the buyer beware—is especially appropriate to Internet shopping.

Use a dash to set off an introductory series from the main clause.

- Cereal, coffee, and a newspaper—without these, I just can't wake up.

Use a dash to introduce or to emphasize a word, a series, a phrase, or a clause.

- Jogging—that's what he lives for.
- This is how the world moves—not like an arrow, but a boomerang.

—Ralph Ellison

OTHER PUNCTUATION

How can I show missing text or interrupted speech?

Use a dash to show that words or letters are missing.

- ■ Mr. — won't let us marry. —Alice Walker, *The Color Purple*

Use a dash (or ellipsis) to show interrupted or faltering speech in dialogue.

- ■ Well, I—ah—had this terrible case of the flu, and—then—ah—the library closed, and—well—the high humidity jammed my printer.
- ■ "You told me to tell her about the—"
  "Oh, just stop."
  —Joyce Carol Oates, "Why Don't You Come Live with Me It's Time"

29e Parentheses

The word *parenthesis* comes from a Greek verb meaning "to insert" or "to place within." Parentheses indicate an idea inserted within a larger flow of ideas. Milder insertions can be set off with commas or dashes.

How should I use parentheses with words?

When using a full "sentence" within another sentence, do not capitalize the inserted sentence or use a period inside the parentheses.

- ■ Your friend doesn't have the assignment (he was just thinking about calling you), so you'll have to make a couple more calls.

> **NOTE:** When the parenthetical sentence comes after the end punctuation of the main sentence, capitalize and punctuate it the same way you would any other complete sentence.

How should I use parentheses with words?

Use parentheses to enclose explanatory or other material that interrupts the normal sentence structure.

- ■ The resident assistant (RA) became my best friend.

How should I use parentheses with numbers?

Use parentheses to set off numbers used with a series of words or phrases.

- ■ Dr. Beck told us to (1) plan ahead, (2) stay flexible, and (3) follow through.

Use parentheses to set off references to authors, titles, pages, and years.

- ■ The statistics are alarming (see page 9) and demand action.

(Greek for "insert")
Parentheses let you add an idea.
∧

29f Brackets

Brackets are simply squared-off parentheses, and they are used only in special circumstances. For example, if a parenthetical idea must be inserted in another parenthetical idea, use brackets.

- The cats (all 24 of them [see photo, top left] residing on the premises) were taken to the animal shelter.

Otherwise, the main use of brackets is to indicate editorial additions.

How can brackets show editorial additions?

Use brackets before and after words that are added to a quotation.

- "They'd [the sweat bees] get into your mouth, ears, eyes, nose. You'd feel them all over you."

  —Marilyn Johnson and Sasha Nyary, "Roosevelts in the Amazon"

> **NOTE:** The brackets indicate that the words *the sweat bees* are not part of the original quotation but were added for clarification.

Place brackets around comments that have been added by someone other than the author or speaker.

- "In conclusion, *docendo discimus*. Let the school year begin!" [Huh?]

Brackets should be placed around the word *sic* (Latin for "so" or "thus") in quoted material; the word indicates that an error appearing in the quoted material was made by the original speaker or writer.

- "There is a higher principal [*sic*] at stake here: Is the school board aware of the situation?"

Place brackets around an editorial explanation or clarification.

- Professional skier Scott McKenzie relates, "Extreme skiing is exhilarating—but also whacked [dangerous] for anyone inexperienced with these moves or these conditions."

> **NOTE:** The brackets in the sentence above indicate that an editor has explained the speaker's original word, *whacked*, using the word *dangerous*.

OTHER PUNCTUATION

29g Apostrophes

The word *apostrophe* comes from the Greek word for "turn away" (*apo*—away, *strophe*—turn). In that way, the mild-mannered apostrophe is related to the word *catastrophe* (to turn over).

How do apostrophes form contractions?

Use an apostrophe to show that one or more letters have been left out.

- don't [*o* is left out]　　she'd [*woul* is left out]　　it's [*i* is left out]

An apostrophe is also used to show that one or more numerals or letters have been left out of numbers or words.

- class of '02 [20 is left out]　　good **mornin'** [*g* is left out]

ESL TIP

Remember that the apostrophe stands for the missing letters in a contraction.

- it's [contraction of *it is* or *it has*]　　its [possessive of *it*]
- who's [contraction of *who is* or *who has*]
  whose [possessive of *who*]

How do apostrophes form possessives?

For most singular nouns, add an apostrophe and an *s*.

- **Spock's** ears　　my **computer's** memory

Some singular nouns end in an *s* or *z* sound. If the noun is only one syllable, add *'s* to form the plural.

- I used my **boss's** tickets to go to **Kiss's** last concert. [one-syllable word]

If the noun has two or more syllables, you can use only the apostrophe.

- **Dallas'** sports teams (or) **Dallas's** sports teams [two-syllable word]

The possessive form of plural nouns ending in *s* is made by adding just an apostrophe.

- **boys'** toys　　the **Joneses'** great-grandfather　　**bosses'** offices

For plural nouns not ending in *s*, add an apostrophe and *s*.

- **women's** health issues　　**children's** program

WRITER'S TIP

You will punctuate possessives correctly if you remember that the word that comes immediately before the apostrophe is the owner.

- **girl's** guitar [*girl* is the owner] **girls'** guitar [*girls* are the owners]
- **boss's** office [*boss* is the owner] **bosses'** offices [*bosses* are the owners]

Do possessive pronouns have apostrophes?

Possessive pronouns (*hers, whose, its*) **do not** use apostrophes. Do not confuse these with contractions such as *who's* or *it's*.

However, the possessive form of an indefinite pronoun is made by adding an apostrophe and an *s* to the pronoun. (See **19b**.)

- **everybody's** grades   **no one's** mistake   **one's** choice

In expressions using *else*, add the apostrophe and *s* after the last word.

- anyone **else's**   somebody **else's**

How can I show shared possession?

When possession is shared by more than one noun, use the possessive form for the last noun in the series.

- Jason, Kamil, and **Elana's** sound system [All three own the same system.]
- **Jason's**, **Kamil's**, and **Elana's** sound systems [Each owns a separate system.]

How can I show possession with compound nouns?

The possessive of a compound noun is formed by placing the possessive ending after the last word.

- his **mother-in-law's** name [singular]
- the **secretary of state's** career [singular]
- their **mothers-in-law's** names [plural]
- the **secretaries of state's** careers [plural]

When should I use apostrophes to form plurals?

Use an apostrophe and an *s* to form the plural of a letter, a number, a sign, or a word discussed as a word.

- A – **A's**   8 – **8's**   + – **+'s**   and – **and's**
- You use too many **and's** in your writing.

> **NOTE:** If two apostrophes are called for in the same word, omit the second apostrophe.
> - Follow closely the **do's** and **don'ts** [not *don't's*] on the checklist.

Can apostrophes show time or amount?

In expressions indicating time or amount, use an apostrophe and an *s*.

- **yesterday's** news
- a **day's** work
- a **month's** wages

OTHER PUNCTUATION

29h   Quotation Marks

Quotation marks (" ") indicate the exact words of someone, identify some titles, and designate special words. These little marks are so valuable that we even sometimes use our fingers to form them as we speak—punctuating our own spoken messages.

How should I punctuate direct quotations?

Use quotation marks before and after a direct quotation—a person's exact words.

- I remember Jana saying, "Don't go to the party with him."

Do not use quotation marks for indirect quotations.

- I remember Jana saying that I should not date him.

How do quotation marks work with other punctuation?

Always place periods and commas after a quotation inside the quotation marks.

- "Dr. Slaughter wants you to have liquids, Will," Mama said anxiously. "He said not to give you any solid food tonight."

  —Olive Ann Burns, *Cold Sassy Tree*

Place an exclamation point or a question mark inside quotation marks when it punctuates both the main sentence and the quotation *or* just the quotation; place it outside when it punctuates only the main sentence.

- Did you ever ask yourself, "What is my potential?"
- Did he really say, "Finish this by tomorrow"?

Notice what happens when an exclamation point is used in a quotation within a question. (The exclamation point applies to the quotation, and the question mark applies to the whole sentence.)

- How can a parent compel a child to go to school when the child screams, "I will not go!"?

Always place semicolons or colons outside quotation marks.

- I just read "Computers and Creativity"; I now have some different ideas about the role of computers in the arts.

How should I quote passages?

Use quotation marks before and after a quoted passage. Any word that is not part of the original quotation must be placed inside brackets.

Original: First, it must accept responsibility for providing shelter for the homeless.

Quotation: "First, it [the federal government] must accept responsibility for providing shelter for the homeless."

How should I punctuate long quotations?

If more than one paragraph is quoted, quotation marks are placed before each paragraph and at the end of the last paragraph (**Example A**).

Quotations that are five or more lines or forty words or more are usually set off from the text by indenting ten spaces from the left margin (a style called "block form"). Do not use quotation marks before or after a block-form quotation (**Example B**), except in cases where quotation marks appear in the original passage.

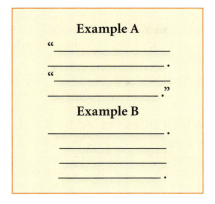

What if a quotation contains another quotation?

Use single quotation marks to punctuate titles enclosed in quotation marks or quoted material within a quotation.

- "I was lucky," said Jane. "The proctor announced, 'Put your pencils down,' just as I was filling in the last answer."

How should I punctuate titles?

Use quotation marks to punctuate titles of most shorter works. (See **29i**.)

- "Two Friends" [short story]
- "New Car Designs" [newspaper article]
- "Desperado" [song]
- "Annabel Lee" [short poem]
- "The Goal Gate" [one-act play]
- "Multiculturalism and the Language Battle" [lecture title]
- "The New Admissions Game" [magazine article]
- "Reflections on Advertising" [chapter in a book]
- "Force of Nature" [television episode from *Star Trek: The Next Generation*]

How should I punctuate special words?

Use quotation marks (1) to indicate that a word is slang, (2) to point out that a word is being used in a humorous or ironic way, or (3) to define a word.

- I drank a Dixie and ate bar peanuts and asked the bartender where I could hear "chanky-chank," as Cajuns call their music.

  —William Least Heat-Moon, *Blue Highways*

- In an effort to be popular, he works very hard at being "natural."

OTHER PUNCTUATION

29i Italics

Italics is a style of type that is slightly slanted. In this sentence, the word *happiness* is printed in italics. In material that is handwritten or typed on a machine that cannot print in italics, underline each word or letter that should be in italics.

■ In <u>The Road to Memphis</u>, racism is a contagious disease. [handwritten]

Mildred Taylor's *The Road to Memphis* exposes racism. [printed]

Which titles should be italicized?

Use italics to indicate the titles of most longer or larger works: magazines, newspapers, books, pamphlets, full-length plays, films, videos, radio and television programs, book-length poems, ballets, operas, lengthy musical compositions, cassettes, CDs, paintings and sculptures, legal cases, websites, and names of ships and aircraft. (Also see **29h**.)

■ *Newsweek* [magazine]   *The Nutcracker* [ballet]
  New York Times [newspaper]   *Babe* [film]
  Sister Carrie [book]   *The Thinker* [sculpture]
  Othello [full-length play]   *Nightline* [television program]
  Enola Gay [airplane]   *GeoCities* [website]
  The Joshua Tree [CD]   *College Loans* [pamphlet]
  ACLU v. the State of Ohio [legal case]

When one title appears within another title, punctuate as follows:

■ "*The Fresh Prince of Bel-Air* Rings True" is an article I read.
  [title of TV program in an article title]
■ He wants to watch *Inside the "New York Times"* on PBS tonight.
  [title of newspaper in title of TV program]

Which words should be italicized?

Italics are often used for a key term in a discussion or for a technical term, especially when it is accompanied by its definition. Italicize the term the first time it is used. Thereafter, put the term in roman type.

■ This flower has a *zygomorphic* (bilaterally symmetric) structure.

Also use italics to show that a word is being discussed as a word.

■ A commentary on the times is that the word *honesty* is now preceded by *old-fashioned*.
                                                        —Larry Wolters
■ I always wanted to write a book that ended with the word *mayonnaise*.
                                                        —Richard Brautigan

When should foreign words and scientific names be italicized?

Use italics for scientific names and foreign words that have not been adopted into the English language; check a dictionary when in doubt.

- Say *arrivederci* to your fears and try new activities. [foreign word]
- The voyageurs discovered the shy *Castor canadensis*, or North American beaver. [scientific name]

29j Ellipses

The word *ellipsis* literally means "omission." These three periods—with a space between each and a space on either end—indicate an intentional omission.

How can I use an ellipsis to show an omission?

Place the ellipsis where the omitted words would have been.

Preamble, U.S. Constitution

Original: We the people of the United States, in order to form a more perfect Union, establish justice, insure domestic tranquility, provide for the common defense, promote the general welfare, and secure the blessings of liberty to ourselves and our posterity, do ordain and establish this Constitution for the United States of America.

Quotation: "We the people . . . in order to form a more perfect Union . . . establish this Constitution for the United States of America."

> **NOTE:** Omit internal punctuation (a comma, a semicolon, a colon, or a dash) on either side of the ellipsis unless it is needed for clarity.

If words from a quotation are omitted at the end of a sentence, place the ellipsis after the period or other end punctuation.

Quotation: "Five score years ago, a great American, in whose symbolic shadow we stand, signed the Emancipation Proclamation. . . . But one hundred years later, we must face the tragic fact that the Negro is still not free."

—Martin Luther King, Jr., "I Have a Dream"

The first word of a sentence following a period and an ellipsis may be capitalized, even though it was not capitalized in the original.

Quotation: "Five score years ago, a great American . . . signed the Emancipation Proclamation. . . . But one hundred years later . . . the Negro is still not free."

—Martin Luther King, Jr., "I Have a Dream"

OTHER PUNCTUATION

What if the quoted material is a complete sentence?

If the quoted material is a complete sentence (even if it was not in the original), use a period, then an ellipsis.

Original: I am tired; my heart is sick and sad. From where the sun now stands I will fight no more forever.

—Chief Joseph of the Nez Percé

Quotation: "I am tired. **. . .** I will fight no more forever."

—Chief Joseph of the Nez Percé

What other use does an ellipsis have?

Use an ellipsis to indicate a pause or to show unfinished thoughts.

- Listen **. . .** did you hear that?
- I can't figure out **. . .** this number doesn't **. . .** how do I apply the equation?

29k   Diagonals/Slashes/Virgules

Ironically, the heading above not only shows three names for the slash, but also demonstrates one of the uses of the slash: to show options. Any of these three names is an acceptable option.

When quoting poetry, use a slash (with one space before and after) to show where each line ends in the actual poem.

- A dryness is upon the house **/** My father loves and tended **/** Beyond his firm and sculptured door **/** His light and lease have ended.

—Gwendolyn Brooks,
"In Honor of David Anderson Brooks, My Father"

A slash is also used to show fractions.

- My running shoe size is 11 1**/**2; my dress shoes are 10 1**/**2.

Capitalization

When Johannes Gutenberg invented movable type, he stored the type in two separate cases. He put the capital letters in a case on the top of a rack (the upper case) and the small letters in a case on the bottom (the lower case). When he wanted an uppercase letter, he had to shift his whole arm, but you just need to shift your pinky finger (if you are typing). This chapter will help you know when, and why, to capitalize.

`30a` First Words

Capitalize the first word of a sentence and the first word of a direct quotation.

- **Attending** the orientation for new students is a good idea.
- Max suggested, "**Let's** tour the campus."

However, do not capitalize the second part of a quoted sentence that is split by words such as *he said*.

- "I think, considering the size of the hailstones," he said sadly, "**that** I'll stay in today."

The first word of a line of traditional poetry should be capitalized.

- **Some** say the world will end in fire,
  Some say in ice.

What about first words in lists?

The first words of items in vertical lists are normally capitalized.

- The United States government is divided into three branches:
  1. Executive
  2. Legislative
  3. Judicial

NOTE: Do not capitalize the first words in numbered lists **within** a sentence.

- The United States government consists of the (1) executive, (2) legislative, and (3) judicial branches.

Capitalization at a Glance

	PROPER NOUNS	COMMON NOUNS
Days of the week	**Sunday, Monday, Tuesday**	a day last week
Months	**June, July, August**	last month
Holidays, holy days	**Thanksgiving, Easter, Hanukkah**	a holiday
Periods, events in history	**the Great Depression**	the crash of 1929
Special events	**Tate Memorial Dedication Ceremony**	the ceremony
Political parties	**Republican Party, Socialist Party**	a political party
Official documents	**the Declaration of Independence**	a document
Trade names	**Levi's, Coca-Cola, Kleenex**	jeans, cola, tissue
Formal epithets	**Alexander the Great**	the leader
Official titles	**Senator Feinstein**	the senator
Educational institutions	**University of Notre Dame**	the university
Departments	**Communications Department**	a department
Other institutions	**Aldi Foods, Labtec**	that company
Governmental bodies,	**the United States Congress**	the legislative body
agencies, and	**the Central Intelligence Agency**	the agency
departments	**the Department of Education**	a department
Electronic sources	**World Wide Web, Internet**	a webpage

Geographical Names

Planets, heavenly bodies	**Earth, Jupiter, the Milky Way**	a planet, a galaxy
Continents	**Australia, South America**	a continent
Countries	**Ireland, Grenada, the Philippines**	a country
States, provinces	**Ohio, Utah, Nova Scotia**	a state, a province
Cities, towns, villages	**El Paso, Dover, Wonewoc**	a city, a town, a village
Streets, roads, highways	**Fifth Street, Interstate 94**	a street, a highway
Nicknames of places	**the Badger State, the Windy City**	a city that's windy

Adjective Use

Place names	a **Florida** vacation	a beach vacation
Countries	**Mexican** and **Thai** food	ethnic food
Cities/states	a **Chicagoan**, a **Californian**	a city or state resident
Oceans	the **Arctic** icebergs	ocean icebergs
Personal names	**Jungian** ideals	psychological concepts

What about sentences in parentheses or after a colon?

Capitalize the first word in a sentence within parentheses unless the parenthetical sentence is inserted within another sentence.

- The bookstore has the software. (**Now** all I need is the computer.)
- Smith refers to Einstein's work (**see** page 263).

Capitalize a complete sentence that follows a colon.

- Sydney Harris had this to say about computers: "**The** real danger is not that computers will begin to think like people, but that people will begin to think like computers."

> **NOTE:** If words following a colon cannot stand alone as a sentence, do not capitalize the first word unless it is a proper noun, a proper adjective, or the pronoun *I*.
>
> - I have decided when I will call you: **when** pigs fly. [dependent clause]
> - There are two dominant Indian tribes in Montana: **Arapahoe** and Shoshone. [proper nouns]

30b Special Forms

The long-established traditions of scholarship and business require certain parts of outlines and business letters to be capitalized.

What should I capitalize in an outline?

Capitalize the first word in each outline heading.

- I. Theater architecture
  - A. Stages
    - 1. Proscenium
    - 2. Arena
    - 3. Thrust
  - B. Wings

What should I capitalize in a business letter?

In the salutation, capitalize the first word, any names, and courtesy titles.

- Dear Personnel Director: To whom it may concern:

In the complimentary closing, capitalize only the first word.

- Sincerely yours,   Take care,

Capitalize the writer's initials but not the typist's initials.

- DK: bm   AR: ft

30c Proper Nouns

Once upon a time, all English nouns were automatically capitalized. (This is still the case in German.) Modern English, however, capitalizes only proper nouns—the names of specific people, places, things, and ideas.

What are some examples of proper nouns?

Capitalize the name of an organization or a team and its members.

- American Indian Movement   Republican Party
  Tampa Bay Buccaneers   Tucson Drama Club

Capitalize languages, ethnic groups, and nationalities.

- Spanish   African American   Latino   French

> **NOTE:** Although most proper adjectives are capitalized, a proper adjective is often lowercased when a term has been adopted into common usage.
>
> - french fry   arabic numbers   roman numerals

Capitalize religions and religious followers.

- Islam [the religion]   Muslim [a follower of Islam]
- Christianity [the religion]   Christian [a follower of Christianity]

Nouns that refer to the Supreme Being and holy books are also capitalized.

- God   Allah   Jehovah   the Koran   Exodus   the Bible

How should I capitalize titles?

In a title (or a subtitle), capitalize the first word, the last word, and every word in between except for articles (*a, an, the*), short prepositions, and coordinating conjunctions. Also capitalize any important word following a hyphen in a compound term. Follow this rule for titles of books and chapters, newspapers, magazines, poems, plays, songs, articles, films, works of art, online documents, and stories.

- *Going to Meet the Man* [book]   *Chicago Tribune* [newspaper]
  "Research and Writing" [chapter]   "Nothing Gold Can Stay" [poem]
  "Jobs in the Cyber Arena" [article]   *Romeo and Juliet* [play]
  The Passion of the Christ [movie]

WAC Link: When citing titles in a bibliography, check the style manual you've been asked to follow. MLA uses the style above. APA's style is to capitalize only the first word of a title or subtitle (as well as any proper nouns).

Should I capitalize words used as names?

Capitalize words like *father, mother, uncle, senator,* and *professor* when they are parts of titles that include a personal name or when they are substituted for proper nouns (especially in direct address).

- Hello, **Senator Feingold**. [*Senator* is part of the name.]
- I think we've met before, **Senator**, at a town hall meeting. [The title is used in place of a personal name, so it is capitalized.]
- Our **senator** is an environmentalist.

WRITER'S TIP

To test whether a word is being substituted for a proper noun, simply read the sentence with a proper noun in place of the word. If the proper noun fits in the sentence, the word being tested should be capitalized. Usually the word is not capitalized if it follows a possessive such as *my, his, our,* or *your.*

What about courses, lectures, and academic degrees?

Words such as *technology, history,* and *science* are proper nouns when they are included in the titles of specific courses; they are common nouns when they name a field of study. Language names, such as *French,* are always capitalized.

- Who teaches **Art History 202**? [title of a specific course]
- Professor Bunker loves teaching **history**. [field of study]
- I enjoy **Latin**. [language name]

Capitalize the names of lecture series and individual lectures (the latter are usually enclosed in quotation marks).

- The **Modern Women Writers Lecture Series** was a huge success.
- The third session, "**Second-Class No More**," had to be repeated.

Capitalize an academic degree used after someone's name, but do not capitalize it when used as a general term.

- Walter Ziffer, **Doctor** of **Philosophy**
- Walter Ziffer, **Ph.D.**
- a **doctor of philosophy degree**

When should I capitalize *north, south, east,* and *west*?

Words that indicate sections of the country are proper nouns and should be capitalized. Words that simply indicate direction are not proper nouns.

- Many businesses move to the **South**. [section of the country]
  They move **south** to cut fuel costs and other expenses. [direction]

CAPITALIZATION

30d Other Capitalization Rules

English has special capitalization rules for abbreviations and Internet terms.

How should I capitalize abbreviations?

Capitalize abbreviations of academic degrees, of social and professional titles, of organizations, and of certain terms for a period of time. (Some other abbreviations are also capitalized; see **32c**.)

- **M.D.** [Doctor of Medicine]   **Ph.D.** [Doctor of Philosophy]
- **Sen.** David Myer [civil title]   **Capt.** Marion Smythe [military title]
- **NALA** [National Association of Legal Assistants]
- **CE** or **C.E.** [Common Era]
- **BCE** or **B.C.E.** [before the Common Era]

> **NOTE:** If a civil or military title precedes a surname alone, spell it out (for example, Captain Smythe).

When should I capitalize individual letters?

Capitalize letters used to indicate a form or shape.

- **U**-turn   **I**-beam   **S**-curve   **V**-shaped

Which Internet terms are capitalized?

The words *Internet* and *World Wide Web* are always capitalized because they are considered proper nouns. When your writing includes a web address (URL), capitalize any letters that the site's owner does.

- When doing research on the **Internet**, be sure to record **web** addresses.

Which words should I *not* capitalize?

Do not capitalize any of the following: a prefix attached to a proper noun; seasons of the year; words used to indicate direction or position; and common nouns and titles that appear near, but are not part of, a proper noun.

Capitalize	Do Not Capitalize
American	**un**-American
January, February	**winter, spring**
The **South** is quite hospitable.	Turn **south** at the stop sign.
Duluth City College	a Duluth **college**
Chancellor John Bohm	John Bohm, our **chancellor**
Earth (the planet)	**earthmover**

31

Spelling and Plurals

In 1783, Noah Webster published *A Grammatical Institute of the English Language,* a book meant to simplify and standardize spelling in English in the United States. Simplify? Standardize? Students of modern English might wonder if Mr. Webster failed mightily. Even so, we have Webster to thank that the rules of English spelling make as much sense as they do.

The following pages provide a few simple rules for general spelling and a few rules for creating plurals.

ESL TIP

Some common words spelled differently in American and British (or Canadian) English are listed below. Check a dictionary for others.

American	British
aging	ageing
analyze	analyse
argument	arguement
bank	banque
catalog	catalogue
center	centre
checker	chequer
color	colour
criticize	criticise
draft	draught
dreamed	dreamt
enrollment	enrolment
favorite	favourite
fulfill	fulfil
honor	honour
leaped	leapt
license	licence
maneuver	manoeuvre
meter	metre
plow	plough
program	programme

SPELLING AND PLURALS

31a Spelling Rules

The problem spots in English spelling center on a few culprits: *i* and *e*, consonant endings, silent *e*, and words ending in *y*.

Which comes first, *i* or *e*?

Write *i* before *e*—except after *c* or when sounded like *a*, as in *neighbor* and *weigh*.

- believe   relief   receive   eight

> **NOTE:** This sentence contains eight exceptions:
> - Neither sheik dared leisurely seize either weird species of financiers.

When should I double a final consonant?

When a one-syllable word (*bat*) ends in a consonant (*t*) preceded by one vowel (*a*), double the final consonant before adding a suffix that begins with a vowel (*batting*).

- sum—**summary**   god—**goddess**

When a multisyllabic word (*control*) ends in a consonant (*l*) preceded by one vowel (*o*), the accent is on the last syllable (*con-tról*), and the suffix begins with a vowel (*-ing*)—the same rule holds true: double the final consonant (*controlling*).

- prefer—**preferred**   begin—**beginning**
- forget—**forgettable**   admit—**admittance**

When should I drop a final silent *e*?

If a word ends with a silent *e*, drop the *e* before adding a suffix that begins with a vowel. Do not drop the *e* when the suffix begins with a consonant.

- state—**stating**—**statement**   like—**liking**—**likeness**
- use—**using**—**useful**   nine—**ninety**—**nineteen**

> **NOTE:** Exceptions are *judgment, truly, argument,* and *ninth.*

What should I do with a final *y*?

When *y* is the last letter in a word and the *y* is preceded by a consonant, change the *y* to *i* before adding any suffix except those beginning with *i*.

- hurry—**hurried**—**hurrying**   fry—**fries**—**frying**
- lady—**ladies**   ply—**pliable**

When the *y* is preceded by a vowel, just add the suffix.

- gray—**grayness**   employ—**employment**   monkey—**monkeys**

31b   Forming Plurals

English also has specific rules for creating the plural forms of its nouns.

How do I form the plurals of most nouns?

A few nouns remain unchanged when used as plurals (*species, moose, halibut,* and so on), but the plurals of most nouns are formed by adding an *s* to the singular form.

■ dorm—**dorms**   credit—**credits**   midterm—**midterms**

To make the plurals of nouns ending in *sh, ch, x, s,* and *z,* add *es.*

■ wish—**wishes**   lunch—**lunches**   class—**classes**

What if the noun ends in *y?*

The plurals of common nouns that end in a *consonant + y* are formed by changing the *y* to *i* and adding *es.*

■ dormitory—**dormitories**   duty—**duties**

Make the plurals of common nouns that end in a *vowel + y* by adding an *s.*

■ attorney—**attorneys**   monkey—**monkeys**   toy—**toys**

The plurals of all *proper nouns* ending in *y* (whether preceded by a consonant or a vowel) are formed by adding an *s.*

■ the three **Kathys**   area **Piggly Wigglys**

What about nouns ending in *o?*

The plurals of words that end in a *vowel + o* are formed by adding an *s.*

■ radio—**radios**   cameo—**cameos**   studio—**studios**

Make the plurals of most nouns that end in a *consonant + o* by adding *es.*

■ echo—**echoes**   hero—**heroes**   tomato—**tomatoes**

Form the plural of Spanish words and musical terms by adding just an *s.*

■ burrito—**burritos**   banjo—**banjos**   solo—**solos**   piano—**pianos**

What about nouns ending in *f* or *fe?*

The plurals of nouns that end in *f* or *fe* are formed in one of two ways: If the final *f* sound is still heard in the plural form of the word, simply add *s;* however, if the final sound is a *v* sound, change the *f* to *ve* and add an *s.*

Plural ends with *f* sound: roof—**roofs**   chief—**chiefs**
Plural ends with *v* sound: wife—**wives**   loaf—**loaves**

> **NOTE:** The plurals of some nouns ending in *f* or *fe* can be formed either way.
> ■ hoof—hoofs, hooves

SPELLING AND PLURALS

Which plurals have irregular spellings?

Often words that come from other languages form plurals as in the original language. Others are now also acceptable with the commonly used *s* or *es* ending. Take time to check a dictionary.

- alumnus, alumna—**alumni, alumnae** [Latin origin]
- château—**châteaus, châteaux** [French origin]
- syllabus—**syllabi, syllabuses** [Latin/Greek origin]
- radius—**radii, radiuses** [Latin origin]
- datum—**data** [Latin origin]

Several words of English origin have an irregular spelling of the plural form.

- child—**children**   man—**men**   woman—**women**
  tooth—**teeth**   goose—**geese**   mouse—**mice**

What if the noun ends in *-ful*?

If a noun ends in *-ful*, form the plural by adding an *s* at the end.

- three **teaspoonfuls**   two **tankfuls**   four **bagfuls**

How can I make plurals of compound nouns?

The plurals of compound nouns are usually formed by adding an *s* or an *es* to the important word in the compound.

- **brothers**-in-law   **maids** of honor   **secretaries** of state

What other plural rules should I know?

The plurals of numbers, abbreviations, symbols, letters, and words discussed as words are formed either by adding an apostrophe and an *s* or by adding just the *s* (omit the apostrophe). Either use is correct as long as it is consistent.

- **1990's** or **1990s** [numbers]   **®'s** or **®s** [symbols]
- **YMCA's** or **YMCAs**   **CD's** or **CDs** [abbreviations]
- When did the addition of so many *likes* (or *like's*) to everyday language become so commonplace? [words discussed as words]
- Many colleges have now added **A/B's** as standard grades. —or—
  Many colleges have now added **A/Bs** as standard grades. [letters]

> **NOTE:** To avoid confusion, the plural of lowercase letters is formed by adding an apostrophe before the *s*.
>
> - He spells his last name with two **t's**.

Form the plural of an abbreviation with two or more interior periods by adding the *s* with the apostrophe.

- **M.A.'s** and **Ph.D.'s**

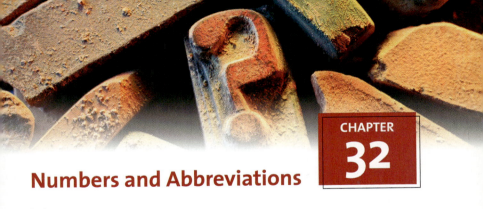

Numbers and Abbreviations

The following pages will guide you through correct use of numbers, abbreviations, acronyms, and initialisms.

32a Numbers

All numbers can be written as words, though, of course, not all words can be written as numbers.

Should I write numerals or spell them out?

Numbers from one to one hundred are usually written as words; numbers 101 and greater are usually written as numerals. Hyphenate numbers written as two words if the numbers are less than one hundred.

- two   seven   ten   twenty-five   106   1,079

The same rule applies to the use of ordinal numbers.

- second   tenth   twenty-fifth   ninety-eighth   106th   333rd

If numbers greater than 101 are used infrequently in a piece of writing, you may spell out those that can be written in one or two words.

- two hundred   fifty thousand   six billion

You may use a combination of numerals and words for very large numbers.

- 1.5 million   3 billion to 3.2 billion   6 trillion

Numbers being compared or contrasted should be kept in the same style.

- 8 to 11 years old   eight to eleven years old

Particular decades may be spelled out or written as numerals, but should remain consistent throughout a document.

- the '80s and '90s   the eighties and nineties

ESL TIP

Some numbers show a place in a series or a part of a whole: the **fifth** game of the World Series. These are called *ordinal numbers*. They can be written as numerals or words.

- 1st   first | 21st   twenty-first
  2nd   second | 22nd   twenty-second
  3rd   third | 23rd   twenty-third
  4th   fourth | 24th   twenty-fourth

NUMBERS AND ABBREVIATIONS

What about numbers with time and money?

If time is expressed with an abbreviation, use numerals; if it is expressed in words, spell out the number.

- **4:00** a.m.   **four** o'clock (not 4 o'clock)
- the **5:15** p.m. train   a **seven** o'clock wake-up call

If money is expressed with a symbol, use numerals; otherwise, spell it out.

- **$20**   **twenty** dollars (not 20 dollars)

Which forms always use numerals?

Generally, use numerals for decimals, percentages, parts of a book or a play, addresses, dates, telephone numbers, identification numbers, and statistics.

Decimals	26.2
Percentages	8 percent
Parts of a book	volume 3, chapter 7, page 189
Parts of a play	act III, scene iii; or act 3, scene 3
Dates	May 8, 2005
Telephone numbers	(212) 555-1234
Identification numbers	serial number 10988675
Statistics	a vote of 23 to 4
Addresses	77 Latches Lane, 519 West 142nd Street

Which forms always use words?

Use words to express numbers that begin a sentence, or rewrite the sentence.

- **Fourteen** students "forgot" their assignments.
- **Three hundred** contest entries were received.
- The contest received **300** entries.

Use words for numbers before a compound modifier with a numeral.

- She sold **twenty** 35-millimeter cameras in one day.

If the compound modifier has a number, use a numeral.

- The chef prepared **24** eight-ounce filets.

Use words for the names of numbered streets of one hundred or less.

- **Ninth** Avenue   123 **Forty-fourth** Street

Use words for the names of buildings if that name is also its address.

- **One Thousand** State Street   **Two Fifty** Park Avenue

Use words for references to particular centuries.

- the **twenty-first** century   the **fourth** century B.C.E.

How do numbers work with abbreviations and symbols?

Abbreviations and symbols are typically used in charts, graphs, footnotes, and so forth, as well as in scientific, mathematical, statistical, and technical texts. Always use numerals with abbreviations and symbols.

- **5'4"** **8%** **10 in.** **3 tbsp.** **6 lb.** **$35** **90°F** **No. 12** (or **no. 12**)
- Between **20%** and **23%** of the cultures yielded positive results.
- Your model requires **220 V** electricity.
- Sophocles (**495-406 B.C.E.**) was arguably the greatest of all tragedians.

Use numerals after the name of local branches of labor unions.

- the Office and Professional Employees International Union, **Local 8**

When are numbers hyphenated?

Numbers from twenty-one to ninety-nine are hyphenated when spelled out.

- thirty-two   eighty-eight   ninety-three

Hyphens are used to form compound modifiers indicating measurement. They are also used for inclusive numbers and written-out fractions.

- the **2001-2005** presidential term   a **13-foot** clearance
  a **2,500-mile** road trip   **one-sixth** of the pie

> **NOTE:** Whole numbers with fractions may be spelled out but are often better expressed in numerals (8 11/16).

32b Abbreviations

An abbreviation is the shortened form of a word or a phrase. The following abbreviations are always acceptable in both formal and informal writing.

- Mr.   Mrs.   Ms.   Dr.   Rev.   Prof. (preceding a full name)
  Jr.   Sr.   Ph.D.   M.D.   M.A.   LL.D.   D.D.S.
  a.m. (A.M.)   p.m. (P.M.)   CE   BCE   AD   BC

> **NOTE:** If you use commas around Jr. and Sr., use them both before and after the abbreviation, and use them consistently. Do not use commas to set off II, III, and so on, when following a name.

Eras are designated in one of two ways: either CE and BCE (of the Common Era; before the Common Era), or AD and BC (*anno Domini,* "in the year of our Lord"; before Christ). While AD precedes the year number, the other forms follow the year number.

- 200 BCE   1964 CE   AD 1964

NUMBERS AND ABBREVIATIONS

When should I *not* use abbreviations?

In formal writing, do not abbreviate the names of people, states (except for D.C.), countries, days, months, holidays, units of measurement, divisions of written works, or courses of study. *Exception:* Once "United States" is spelled out in a document, it is acceptable to use the abbreviation *U.S.* as an adjective or *U.S.A.* as a noun.

Do not use signs or symbols (%, &, #, @) in place of words. (The dollar sign, however, is appropriate when numerals are used to express an amount of money.) Do not abbreviate the words *Street, Avenue, Incorporated,* and similar words when they are part of a proper name. (However, in company names, use abbreviated forms such as *Co., Inc.,* and *&* if they are part of the official name.)

When should I use postal abbreviations?

The two-letter, no-period postal abbreviation for a state should always be used when followed by a ZIP code. Additionally, they may be used in other contexts where abbreviations are appropriate. See the chart on the following page.

32c Acronyms and Initialisms

Use acronyms and initialisms only after you have explained them. The first mention should always include the full name followed by the abbreviation in parentheses. If you are not sure whether to use periods with these abbreviations, consult a dictionary or a publication by the agency in question.

What are acronyms?

An acronym is a word formed from the first (or first few) letters of words in a set phrase. Acronyms usually appear in full capitals and without periods.

- **CARE**   Cooperative for Assistance and Relief Everywhere
- **NASA**   National Aeronautics and Space Administration
- **VISTA**   Volunteers in Service to America
- **FICA**   Federal Insurance Contributions Act
- **radar**   radio detecting and ranging

What are initialisms?

An initialism is similar to an acronym (all caps, no periods) except that the initials used to form this abbreviation are pronounced individually.

- **CIA**   Central Intelligence Agency
- **FBI**   Federal Bureau of Investigation

Acronyms and Initialisms

States/Territories	Standard	Postal	States/Territories	Standard	Postal
Alabama	Ala.	AL	North Dakota	N.Dak.	ND
Alaska	Alaska	AK	Ohio	Ohio	OH
Arizona	Ariz.	AZ	Oklahoma	Okla.	OK
Arkansas	Ark.	AR	Oregon	Ore.	OR
California	Cal.	CA	Pennsylvania	Pa.	PA
Colorado	Colo.	CO	Puerto Rico	P.R.	PR
Connecticut	Conn.	CT	Rhode Island	R.I.	RI
Delaware	Del.	DE	South Carolina	S.C.	SC
District of Columbia	D.C.	DC	South Dakota	S.Dak.	SD
Florida	Fla.	FL	Tennessee	Tenn.	TN
Georgia	Ga.	GA	Texas	Tex.	TX
Guam	Guam	GU	Utah	Utah	UT
Hawaii	Hawaii	HI	Vermont	Vt.	VT
Idaho	Idaho	ID	Virginia	Va.	VA
Illinois	Ill.	IL	Virgin Islands	V.I.	VI
Indiana	Ind.	IN	Washington	Wash.	WA
Iowa	Ia.	IA	West Virginia	W.Va.	WV
Kansas	Kans.	KS	Wisconsin	Wis.	WI
Kentucky	Ky.	KY	Wyoming	Wyo.	WY
Louisiana	La.	LA			
Maine	Maine	ME			
Maryland	Md.	MD	**Canadian Provinces**	**Standard**	**Postal**
Massachusetts	Mass.	MA	Alberta	Alta.	AB
Michigan	Mich.	MI	British Columbia	B.C.	BC
Minnesota	Minn.	MN	Labrador	Lab.	NL
Mississippi	Miss.	MS	Manitoba	Man.	MB
Missouri	Mo.	MO	New Brunswick	N.B.	NB
Montana	Mont.	MT	Newfoundland	N.F.	NL
Nebraska	Neb.	NE	Northwest Territories	N.W.T.	NT
Nevada	Nev.	NV	Nova Scotia	N.S.	NS
New Hampshire	N.H.	NH	Nunavut	Nunavut	NU
New Jersey	N.J.	NJ	Ontario	Ont.	ON
New Mexico	N.Mex.	NM	Prince Edward Island	P.E.I.	PE
New York	N.Y.	NY	Quebec	Que.	QC
North Carolina	N.C.	NC	Saskatchewan	Sask.	SK
			Yukon Territory	Y.T.	YT

Address Abbreviations					
Apartment	Apt.	APT	Parkway	Pky.	PKY
Avenue	Ave.	AVE	Place	Pl.	PL
Boulevard	Blvd.	BLVD	Plaza	Plaza	PLZ
Circle	Cir.	CIR	Ridge	Rdg.	RDG
Court	Ct.	CT	River	R.	RV
Drive	Dr.	DR	Road	Rd.	RD
Expressway	Expy.	EXPY	Room	Rm.	RM
Freeway	Frwy.	FWY	Rural Route	R.R.	RR
Heights	Hts.	HTS	Shore	Sh.	SH
Highway	Hwy.	HWY	Square	Sq.	SQ
Junction	Junc.	JCT	Station	Sta.	STA
Lake	L.	LK	Street	St.	ST
Lakes	Ls.	LKS	Suite	Ste.	STE
Lane	Ln.	LN	Terrace	Ter.	TER
Meadows	Mdws.	MDWS	Turnpike	Tpke.	TPKE
Palms	Palms	PLMS	Union	Un.	UN
Park	Pk.	PK	View	View	VW
			Village	Vil.	VLG

NUMBERS AND ABBREVIATIONS

Common Abbreviations, Acronyms, and Initialisms

A.M., a.m. before noon (*ante meridiem*)
AC, ac alternating current, air-conditioned
APR annual percentage rate
ASAP as soon as possible
avg., av. average
B.A. bachelor of arts degree
BCE, B.C.E. before Common Era
B.S. bachelor of science degree
bio. biography
C 1. Celsius 2. centigrade 3. coulomb
c. 1. circa (about) 2. cup(s)
CE, C.E. Common Era
c/o care of
cc 1. cubic centimeter 2. carbon copy
chap. chapter(s)
cm centimeter(s)
cu 1. cubic 2. cumulative
D.A. district attorney
DC, dc direct current
dept. department
e.g. for example (Latin *exempli gratia*)
ed. edition, editor
etc. and so forth (Latin *et cetera*)
F Fahrenheit, Friday
FM frequency modulation
FYI for your information
g 1. gravity 2. gram(s)
gal. gallon(s)
GNP gross national product
GPA grade point average
hp horsepower
i.e. that is (Latin *id est*)
ibid. in the same place (Latin *ibidem*)
id. the same (Latin *idem*)
inc. incorporated
IQ, I.Q. intelligence quotient
IRS Internal Revenue Service
ISBN International Standard Book Number
K Kelvin (temperature scale)
kc kilocycle(s)
kg kilogram(s)
km kilometer(s)
kW kilowatt(s)
l, L liter(s)
l.c. lowercase
lat. latitude
log logarithm, logic
long. longitude
Ltd., ltd. limited
m meter(s)
M.A. master of arts degree

M.D. doctor of medicine (Latin *medicinae doctor*)
M.S. master of science degree
MC master of ceremonies
Mc, mc megacycle
mfg. manufacture, manufacturing
mg milligram(s)
mi. 1. mile(s) 2. mill(s) (monetary unit)
misc. miscellaneous
ml, mL milliliter(s)
mm millimeter(s)
mpg, m.p.g. miles per gallon
mph, m.p.h. miles per hour
MS 1. manuscript 2. multiple sclerosis
N.S.F., n.s.f. not sufficient funds
neg. negative
oz, oz. ounce(s)
P.M., p.m. after noon (*post meridiem*)
PAC political action committee
pd. paid
pg., p. page
Ph.D. doctor of philosophy
PIN personal identification number
POP point of purchase
POW, P.O.W. prisoner of war
pp. pages
PR, P.R. public relations
PSA public service announcement
psi, p.s.i. pounds per square inch
R.A. residence assistant
R.P.M., rpm revolutions per minute
R.S.V.P., r.s.v.p. please reply (French *répondez s'il vous plaît*)
SAT Scholastic Aptitude Test
SOS international distress signal
Sr. 1. senior 2. sister (religious)
std. standard
SUV sport utility vehicle
syn. synonymous, synonym
T.A. teaching assistant
tbs., tbsp. tablespoon(s)
v 1. physics: velocity 2. volume
V electricity: volt
VA Veterans Administration
VIP informal: very important person
vol. 1. volume 2. volunteer
vs. versus, verse
W 1. watt(s) 2. work 3. west
w/o without
WHO World Health Organization
wt. weight

Multilingual and ESL Guidelines

Multilingual and ESL Guidelines

33 Surviving College

34 Understanding Words

35 Understanding Sentences

36 Understanding Idioms and Mixed Pairs

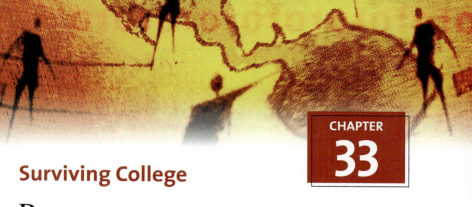

Surviving College

Do you sometimes struggle with English? It's not surprising when you consider how many different "Englishes" there are. The English that you hear in movies and on television is different from the English that you hear in college classrooms. The English that you read in a science text is different from the English that you read in Shakespeare. For that matter, the English that you learned anywhere else in the world is different from the English that is used in the United States and Canada.

Don't worry. This brief survival guide will answer your basic questions about understanding and using English in North American colleges and universities.

33a Understanding the Basics

This chapter gives general guidelines for succeeding in North American colleges and universities. The next chapters provide specific help with problem areas of language use.

Where can I get support?

Investigate the resources offered by your college or university.

- **Get to know your school's ESL support services.** They often offer help with time management, study habits, and cultural adjustment.

- **Check out your school's writing lab.** Writing labs provide guidance, reviews, critiques, and help in revising and editing student writing.

- **Consider online writing labs (OWLs).** Many schools have OWLs that you can access.

- **Attend help sessions.** Some professors or teaching assistants offer sessions to help students who need a little support.

- **Check out tutoring options.** A tutoring program might be school-wide, department-wide, or the work of one professor or student. The right tutor can make a big difference.

- **Make friends.** The best way to learn any language is to use it all the time. By making friends with other English-speaking students, you will learn faster than any other way—and you might get help with assignments.

SURVIVING COLLEGE

How can I improve my writing?

Here is a brief list of the steps to follow to succeed at formal assignments.

- **Understand the assignment.** Know the paper's purpose—to explain a concept, to defend a position, to show research, and so forth. Also, make sure you understand the specific form of writing—research paper, position paper, or literary analysis. (See **6a**.)

- **Schedule time to work.** Find out when the paper is due, and set a number of due dates for yourself. For example, here is a quick schedule for a paper due in ten days:

Wed	Thur	Fri	Sat	Sun	Mon	Tues	Wed	Thur	Fri
Pick topic	Research	Research	Day off	Day off	Write draft	Go to writing lab	Revise	Edit and proof	Turn in

- **Use the writing process.** Give yourself time to plan, research, organize, write, revise, and edit your work. (See **7a–10e**.) Rarely is a one-night paper a success when graded.

- **Understand the function of each part:** the beginning, the middle, and the ending. (See **8a–8c**.)

- **Provide different kinds of support.** Include supporting details such as facts, statistics, examples, quotations, and anecdotes. (See **8b**.)

- **Connect your ideas.** Use transition words and phrases and logical connections to make your ideas flow smoothly. (See **12c**.)

- **Use an appropriate writing voice.** Make sure the sound of your writing is appropriate to your topic, your purpose, and your readers (the professor and other students).

- **Get help.** Take your work to a writing lab, tutor, or classmate for help with revising and editing.

- **Document your sources.** Follow your professor's instructions about direct quotations, text citations, and documentation. (See **46e** and **50g**.)

- **Carefully check for errors.** Make sure your punctuation, spelling, capitalization, and grammar are correct according to U.S. English conventions. (See **27a–31b**.)

VISUALS TIP

Design your document well. Leave at least a one-inch margin on each page, number your pages, use an easy-to-read typeface, use bulleted lists and numbered lists where appropriate, and include visuals that support your thesis. (See **17a–17g**.)

33b Frequently Asked Questions (FAQs)

The following FAQs explain college culture in North America.

Why do professors want me to cite sources?

In many cultures, the traditions of scholarship allow students to adopt and present the ideas and sometimes the words of another writer. The traditions of scholarship in North America do not allow this practice, however, considering it *plagiarism.* By citing sources, you can avoid plagiarism. (See **50a–50c**.)

Why are students and professors so direct?

Some cultures prefer a formal style in classroom situations, but at most North American colleges and universities, the classroom environment is more informal. Students and professors prefer using direct, clear language in speaking and writing, and as a result they may sometimes seem impolite or blunt. Most often, this is not the intention.

Why do students speak up in class?

In many societies, the ancient roles of teachers and students are clearly defined: Professors have authority and students do not. In North America, professors and students participate together in the process of establishing authority. Students are expected to present their own well-considered opinions, to argue points, to grapple with ideas, and to ask questions.

How can I learn English idioms?

Turn to the list on **36a**. It provides idioms such as "You have your head in the sand" and defines them: "You ignore serious problems." Also, by making English-speaking friends, you can learn idioms and practice using them (but avoid idioms in formal writing).

33c Targeting Trouble Spots

Every language has different rules for words and sentences. For example, Thai, Japanese, and Chinese do not use articles (*a*, *an*, and *the*), so for speakers of these languages, articles in English can pose a real challenge. The following lists give advice for speakers from specific language groups.

What should speakers of Middle Eastern languages do?

SURVIVING COLLEGE

What should speakers of Latin American languages do?

What should speakers of East Asian languages do?

What should speakers of African and Caribbean languages do?

What should speakers of European languages do?

Understanding Words

In every language, sentences are made up of nouns, verbs, and words that modify them. These are the *parts of speech*. Each language also has its own rules for the use of the parts of speech, and the rules that govern nouns and verbs in Spanish or Japanese often differ from the rules of English. This chapter will guide you through the features of the parts of speech as they are used in English sentences.

34a Nouns

No language would get far without nouns. **Nouns** tell *who* or *what* is being talked about, and they identify people, places, things, and ideas. English uses both **count nouns** and **noncount nouns.**

ESL TIP

The following material is especially helpful for speakers of Spanish and Japanese, which have different rules for count and noncount nouns. It is also helpful for any student who is learning about articles *(a, an, the)* in English.

What are count nouns?

Count nouns refer to things that can be counted. They can have *a, an, the,* or a number in front of them. (One or more adjectives can come between the number, *a, an,* or *the* and the noun: *a big apple.*) Count nouns can also follow possessive nouns or pronouns (*Tim's apple*), demonstrative pronouns (*this apple*), and indefinite pronouns (*many apples*).

- ■ **an** apple, **one** orange, **her red** plum
  plums, apples, oranges (no *a* or *an*)
  I used **the** apples to make a pie.
  These plums are so juicy!

WRITER'S TIP

When count nouns are plural, they never have *a* or *an* in front of them. Also, there are different ways to create the plural forms of nouns. For more information, see **19a**.

UNDERSTANDING WORDS

What are noncount nouns?

Noncount nouns refer to things that cannot be counted. Do not use *a*, *an*, or a number in front of them. Noncount nouns take a singular verb.

- furniture, rain, thunder, advice

Some noncount nouns end in *s*. They are still singular.

- mathematics, news, aeronautics

Abstract nouns name conditions or ideas rather than people, places, or objects. Many abstract nouns are noncount nouns.

- The students had **fun** at the party. Good **health** is a wonderful gift.

Collective nouns name a category or group and are often noncount nouns.

- homework, money, faculty, committee, flock

NOTE: A group or category named by a noncount noun (*furniture*) may contain parts or components that are named by count nouns (*chair, lamp,* and *couch*).

Lamp

Chair

(Count Nouns)

Couch

Furniture (Noncount Noun)

What are two-way nouns?

Some nouns can be used as either count or noncount nouns.

- I would like a **glass** of water. [count noun]
- **Glass** is used to make windows. [noncount noun]

34b Articles and Other Noun Markers

English uses little words called *articles* before many nouns. Articles help tell whether a noun refers to a general thing (**a** car) or a specific thing (**the** car).

- I received **an** assignment today.
  [Use *an* before a general noun that starts with a vowel.]
- I also got **a** headache.
  [Use *a* before a general noun that starts with a consonant.]
- **The** class is Freshman Composition. [Use *the* before a specific noun, but not before most proper nouns: not *the Freshman Composition*.]

ESL TIP

Many East Asian languages contain no articles, and many European and African languages have different rules for article use. If you speak one of these languages, study the use of articles in English.

How should I use articles?

These guidelines will help you know when to use articles.

> **Using Articles**
>
> Use *a* or *an* with singular count nouns that don't refer to a specific item.
>
> - **A zebra** has black and white stripes. **An apple** is good for you.
>
> Do not use *a* or *an* with plural count nouns.
>
> - **Zebras** have black and white stripes. **Apples** are good for you.
>
> Do not use *a* or *an* with noncount nouns.
>
> - **Homework** needs to be done promptly.
>
> Use *the* with singular or plural count nouns that refer to specific items.
>
> - **The apple** you gave me was delicious.
> - **The zebras** at Brookfield Zoo were healthy.
>
> Use *the* to refer to specific noncount nouns.
>
> - **The money** from my uncle is a gift.
>
> Use *the* with plural proper nouns.
>
> - **the Joneses** (both Mr. and Mrs. Jones), **the United States**
>
> Do not use *the* with most singular proper nouns.
>
> - **Mother Teresa** loved the poor and downcast.

How can I show ownership?

Use special forms of nouns and pronouns to show ownership. Singular possessive nouns usually end in *'s*, and plural possessive nouns usually end in *s'*.

- **Tanya's** car has a flat tire. [singular noun ending in *'s*]
- Luckily, the **Joneses'** other car is in fine shape. [plural noun ending in *s'*]

Possessive pronouns such as *her* or *hers* do not contain apostrophes. Use one form before the noun (How do you like **her** shoes?) and the other after a linking verb (Those shoes are **hers**.).

> **NOTE:** Possessive pronouns before the noun are also referred to as adjectives.

Before the Noun	After a Linking Verb
my/our	mine/ours
your	yours
his/her	his/hers
its/their	its/theirs

UNDERSTANDING WORDS

How can I demonstrate an exact thing?

English includes words that let you point to something. These words are called *demonstrative adjectives* because they demonstrate the exact noun you mean. Use *this, that, these,* and *those* to point to count nouns.

■ **Those** chairs are lovely. **These** cushions match them nicely.

Use *this* or *that* to point to noncount nouns.

■ **This** furniture is the color of **that** grass. [Not *those furniture* or *these grass.*]

How can I show quantities of nouns?

In English, you can correctly say, "I have six assignments," but not "I have six homeworks." The difference is simply that *assignments* is a count noun, and *homework* is a noncount noun.

The following expressions of quantity can be used with count nouns: *each, every, both, a couple of, a few, several, many, a number of.*

■ We enjoyed **both** concerts we attended. **A couple of** songs performed were familiar to us.

Use a number to indicate a specific quantity of a group.

■ I saw **fifteen** cardinals in the park.

ESL TIP

Here is one way to show quantities of noncount nouns:

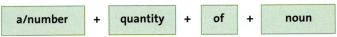

a/number + **quantity** + **of** + **noun**

■ a herd of deer
■ two pieces of music

You also can turn the noncount noun into an adjective.

■ a deer herd
■ two musical pieces

The following expressions can be used with noncount nouns: *a little, much, a great deal of.*

■ We had **much** wind and **a little** rain as the storm passed through yesterday.

The following expressions of quantity can be used with both count and noncount nouns: *no/not any, some, a lot of, lots of, plenty of, most, all, this, that.*

■ I would like **some** apples [count noun] and **some** rice [noncount noun], please.

34c Verbs

Just as nouns tell *who* or *what* is being talked about, verbs show what nouns are *doing* or *being*. In English, verbs express action (*hop, giggle, soar, stagger*) and states of being (*is, am, are, was, were*). A verb teams up with a noun to create a complete sentence.

How does English show ongoing action?

Some verbs in English are called *progressive* verbs, because they show that an action is continuing. Progressive forms show present, past, and future tenses.

ESL TIP

Russian, German, French, and Greek have no progressive forms. Speakers of Hindi and Urdu must be careful not to overuse progressive forms: "I am liking this idea" is more natural in English as "I like this idea."

To form the **present progressive** tense, use the auxiliary verb *am, is,* or *are* with the *-ing* form of the main verb.

■ He **is washing** the car right now.

■ Kent and Chen **are painting** the bedroom.

To form the **past progressive** tense, use the auxiliary verb *was* or *were* with the *-ing* form of the main verb.

■ Yesterday he **was working** in the garden all day.

■ Kent and Chen **were painting** the bedroom.

To form the **future progressive** tense, use *will,* the auxiliary verb *be,* and the *-ing* form of the main verb.

■ Next week they **will be painting** the kitchen.

Some verbs are generally not used in the progressive tenses, such as verbs that express thoughts, attitudes, and desires: *know, understand, want, prefer.*

■ Kala **knows** how to ride a motorcycle.

[Not *Kala is knowing how to ride a motorcycle.*]

were painting   *are painting*   *will be painting*

PAST PROGRESSIVE   **PRESENT PROGRESSIVE**   **FUTURE PROGRESSIVE**

UNDERSTANDING WORDS

34d Verb Complements

In English, linking verbs such as *is, am,* and *are* can be followed by words, phrases, and clauses that rename or describe the subject. These words are called *complements.*

- I am **Rob**. [a proper noun, renaming *I*]
- I am **a writer**. [a noun phrase renaming *I*]
- I am **somewhat successful**. [an adjective phrase describing *I*]
- I am **certain that someday I will be famous**.
  [an adjective followed by a clause that describes the adjective]

However, some action verbs must be followed by specific types of phrases. For example, the word *hope* must be followed by a phrase starting with *to* (an infinitive), but the word *imagine* must be followed by a phrase starting with an *-ing* word (a gerund).

ESL TIP

Chinese, Vietnamese, French, Greek, Portuguese, Spanish, and Arabic do not differentiate between infinitives and gerunds. Speakers of these languages should pay close attention to the rules that follow.

Which verbs are followed by infinitives?

Infinitives follow verbs that express intention, hopes, and desires: *agree, appear, attempt, consent, decide, demand, deserve, endeavor, fail, hesitate, hope, intend, need, offer, plan, prepare, promise, refuse, seem, tend, volunteer, wish.* (See **20i**.)

- He promised **to bring** some samples.

The following verbs are among those that can be followed by a noun or pronoun plus the infinitive: *ask, beg, choose, expect, intend, need, prepare, promise, want.*

- I expect you **to be** there on time.

Except in the passive voice (see **20f**), the following verbs must have a noun or pronoun before the infinitive: *advise, allow, appoint, authorize, cause, challenge, command, convince, encourage, forbid, force, hire, instruct, invite, order, permit, remind, require, select, teach, tell, tempt, trust.*

- I will authorize Emily **to use** my credit card.

Which verbs are followed by gerunds?

Gerunds can follow verbs that express facts: *admit, avoid, consider, deny, discuss, dislike, enjoy, finish, imagine, miss, quit, recall, recommend, regret.* (Also see **20i**.)

- I recommended **hiring** Jamir for the job.

Which verbs are followed by infinitives or gerunds?

Either gerunds or infinitives can follow these verbs: *begin, continue, hate, like, love, prefer, remember, start, stop, try.*

- I hate **having** cold feet.   I hate **to have** cold feet.

Sometimes the meaning of a sentence will change depending on whether you use a gerund or an infinitive.

- I stopped **to smoke**. [I paused to smoke a cigarette.]
- I stopped **smoking**. [I no longer smoke.]

34e Modal Verbs

English also includes a number of verbs that express wishes, hopes, and conditions that aren't true. Words such as *could, would, should, will,* and *might* are called modal verbs. They work with a main verb to express specific meaning.

How should I use modal verbs?

Use modal verbs as helping verbs, and leave the main verb in the present tense.

- I **would like** a class schedule. [not *would liked*]

Also, make sure not to use the *-ing* form of the verb.

- I **might take** anthropology. [not *might taking*]

Finally, make sure not to use *to* with the verb.

- I **could become** an anthropologist. [not *could to become*]

Modal	Expresses	Sample Sentence
could	ability	I could baby-sit Tuesday.
	possibility	He could be sick.
might	possibility	I might be early.
may, might	possibility	I may sleep late Saturday.
	request	May I be excused?
must	strong need	I must study more.
have to	strong need	I have to (have got to) exercise.
ought to	feeling of duty	I ought to (should) help Dad.
should	advisability	She should retire.
	expectation	I should have caught that train.
shall, will	intent	Shall I stay longer?
would	intent	I would like to see you.
	repeated action	He would walk in the meadow.
would + you	polite request	Would you help me?
could + you	polite request	Could you type this letter?
will + you	polite request	Will you give me a ride?

UNDERSTANDING WORDS

34f Two-Word Verbs

Some English verbs include two words, such as *break down* or *call off*. They might look like a verb and a preposition, but these two words actually function as a single unit. Nevertheless, other words can sometimes be inserted between them: *break it down* or *call the party off.*

What are the most common two-word verbs?

Refer to this chart for common two-word verbs.

Verb	Definition
break down	to take apart or fall apart
call off	cancel
call up	make a phone call
cross out	draw a line through
do over	repeat
figure out	find a solution
fill in/out	complete a form or an application
fill up	fill a container or a tank
find out	discover
get in	enter a vehicle or a building
get out of	leave a car, a house, or a situation
get over	recover from a sickness or a problem
give in/up	surrender or quit
hand in	give homework to a teacher
hand out	give someone something
hang up	put down a phone receiver
leave out	omit or don't use
let in/out	allow someone or something to enter or go out
look up	search for
mix up	confuse
pick out	choose
point out	call attention to
put away	return something to its proper place
put off	delay doing something
shut off	turn off a machine or a light
talk over	discuss
think over	consider carefully
try on	put on clothing to see if it fits
turn down	lower the volume
write down	write on a piece of paper

34g ## Verb Tenses

The oldest verbs in English show past tenses by changing form: *swim, swam, swum.* The things you can imagine a peasant doing one thousand years ago (when English was still forming) are irregular verbs: *arise, begin, burn, dig, fall, go, lend, prove,* and *sing.* These are **irregular verbs.** (See **20h.**)

Other verbs in English form tenses by adding endings such as *-ed, -ing, -es,* and *-s.* These are **regular verbs.**

ESL TIP

Verb tenses are especially challenging for speakers of East Asian and Middle Eastern languages. If you speak one of these languages, pay close attention to tenses in English.

How do I use *-ed* to make a past tense?

- **Add *-ed:***

    When a verb ends with two consonants:
    touch—**touched**, ask—**asked**, pass—**passed**

    When a verb ends with a consonant preceded by two vowels:
    heal—**healed**, gain—**gained**

    When a verb ends in *y* preceded by a vowel:
    annoy—**annoyed**, flay—**flayed**

    When the last syllable in a multisyllabic verb is not stressed:
    budget—**budgeted**, enter—**entered**, interpret—**interpreted**

- **Change *y* to *i* and add *-ed:***

    When a verb ends in a consonant followed by *y*:
    liquefy—**liquefied**, worry—**worried**

- **Double the final consonant and add *-ed:***

    When a verb has one syllable and ends with a consonant preceded by a vowel:
    wrap—**wrapped**, drop—**dropped**

    When a multisyllabic verb's last syllable (ending in a consonant preceded by a vowel) is stressed:
    admit—**admitted**, confer—**conferred**

UNDERSTANDING WORDS

How do I use -*d* to make a past tense?

- **Add -*d*:**

  When a verb ends with *e*: chime—**chimed**, tape—**taped**

  When a verb ends with *ie*: tie—**tied**, die—**died**, lie—**lied**

How do I use -*s* or -*es* in the present tense?

- **Add -*es*:**

  When a verb ends in *ch*, *sh*, *s*, *x*, or *z*: watch—**watches**, fix—**fixes**

  To *do* and *go*:   do—**does**, go—**goes**

- **Change *y* to *i* and add -*es*:**

  When the verb ends in a consonant followed by *y*:

  liquefy—**liquefies**, quantify—**quantifies**

- **Add -*s*:**

  To most other verbs, including those already ending in *e* and those that end in a vowel followed by *y*: write—**writes**, buy—**buys**

How do I use -*ing* in the present tense?

- **Drop the *e* and add -*ing*:**

  When the verb ends in *e*: drive—**driving**, rise—**rising**

- **Double the final consonant and add -*ing*:**

  When a verb has one syllable and ends with a consonant preceded by a vowel: wrap—**wrapping**, sit—**sitting**

  When a multisyllabic verb's last syllable (ending in a consonant preceded by a vowel) is stressed:

  forget—**forgetting**, begin—**beginning**, abut—**abutting**

- **Change *ie* to *y* and add -*ing*:**

  When a verb ends with *ie*: tie—**tying**, die—**dying**, lie—**lying**

- **Add -*ing*:**

  When a verb ends with two consonants:

  touch—**touching**, ask—**asking**, pass—**passing**

  When a verb ends with a consonant preceded by two vowels:

  heal—**healing**, gain—**gaining**

  When a verb ends in *y*: buy—**buying**, study—**studying**, cry—**crying**

  When the last syllable of a multisyllabic verb is not stressed:

  budget—**budgeting**, enter—**entering**, interpret—**interpreting**

34h Adjectives

Adjectives modify nouns and pronouns by answering a simple question: *which? what kind? how many?* and *how much?* For example, an adjective can tell you whether a college course is *exciting* or *boring, science* or *business.*

ESL TIP

In Chinese and Japanese, adjectives and nouns have the same form. In English, the forms are often different.

- She is an *intelligent* professor. [not an *intelligence* professor]

In Spanish, adjectives show plurals, but they do not in English.

- We are *compatible* roommates. [not *compatibles* roommates]

Where should I place adjectives?

You probably know that an adjective often comes before the noun it modifies. When more than one adjective is used in a row to modify a single noun, it is important to arrange the adjectives in a well-established sequence.

First, place	
1. articles	a, an, the
demonstrative adjectives	that, those
possessives	my, her, Misha's

Then, place words that	
2. indicate time	first, next, final
3. tell how many	one, few, some
4. evaluate	beautiful, dignified, graceful
5. tell what size	big, small, short, tall
6. tell what shape	round, square
7. describe a condition	messy, clean, dark
8. tell what age	old, young, new, antique
9. tell what color	blue, red, yellow
10. tell what nationality	English, Chinese, Mexican
11. tell what religion	Islamic, Jewish, Protestant
12. tell what material	satin, velvet, wooden

Finally, place	
13. nouns used as adjectives	computer [monitor], spice [rack]

Example	
gorgeous young white swans (evaluation, age, color, noun)	

UNDERSTANDING WORDS

Can present and past participles function as adjectives?

Both the present participle, which always ends in -*ing,* and the past participle can be used as adjectives. A participle acting as an adjective can come either before a noun or after a linking verb.

A present participle used as an adjective should describe a person or a thing.

- Her **annoying** phone call made us angry.

A past participle should describe a person or a thing that experiences a feeling or a situation.

- We were **annoyed** because she made us wait so long.

Annoyed
Annoying

NOTE: Within each of the following pairs, the present participle (-*ing* form) and past participle (-*ed* form) have different meanings. Be careful when choosing whether to use the present or the past participle. (See 20i.)

annoying/annoyed	depressing/depressed	exciting/excited
fascinating/fascinated	boring/bored	exhausting/exhausted
surprising/surprised	confusing/confused	

Can nouns function as adjectives?

Nouns sometimes function as adjectives by modifying another noun. When a noun is used as an adjective, the noun is always singular.

- Many European cities have **rose** gardens.
- Marta recently joined a **book** club.

WRITER'S TIP

Try to avoid using more than two nouns as adjectives for another noun. These "noun compounds" can get confusing:

- Omar is **a second-shift restaurant kitchen crew** member.

Prepositional phrases may get the meaning across better than long noun compounds.

- Omar works **in** a restaurant kitchen **as** a crew member **during** the second shift.

34i Adverbs

Adverbs modify verbs, adjectives, and other adverbs. An adverb answers a basic question (*how? when? where? why? to what degree?* and *how often?*) about the word it modifies. Adverbs clarify the quality of an action or a state of being.

Where should I place adverbs?

Refer to the following guidelines for placing adverbs correctly. See **21b** for more information about adverbs.

- Place adverbs that tell how often (*frequently, seldom, never, always, sometimes*) after an auxiliary verb and before the main verb. In a sentence without an auxiliary verb, adverbs that tell how often are placed before an action verb but after a *be* verb.

  The sales clerk will **usually** help me.

- Place adverbs that tell when (*yesterday, now*) at the end of a sentence.

  Auntie El came home **yesterday**.

- Adverbs that tell where (*nearby, around, downstairs*) usually follow the verb they modify. Many prepositional phrases (*at the beach, under the stairs, below the water*) are used as adverbs that tell where.

  We waited **on the porch**.

- Adverbs that tell how (*quickly, slowly, loudly*) can be placed either at the beginning, in the middle, or at the end of a sentence—but not between a verb and its direct object.

  Softly he called my name.
  He **softly** called my name.
  He called my name **softly**.

- Place adverbs that modify adjectives directly before the adjective.

  That is a **most** unusual dress.

- Adverbs that modify clauses are most often placed in front of the clause, but they can also go inside or at the end of the clause.

  Fortunately, we were not involved in the accident.
  We were not involved, **fortunately**, in the accident.
  We were not involved in the accident, **fortunately**.

ESL TIP

Adverb placement can be especially challenging to speakers of French, which allows adverbs to be positioned before verbs or between verbs and objects. English does not.

- I will complete the assignment **tomorrow**. [not *will tomorrow complete*, **or** *will complete tomorrow the assignment*]

UNDERSTANDING WORDS

34j Prepositions

A preposition combines with a noun or a pronoun to form a prepositional phrase, which usually acts as an adverb or adjective. See **21c** for a list of common prepositions and for more information about prepositions.

How should I use *in, on, at,* and *by?*

In, on, at, and *by* are four common prepositions that refer to time and place. Here are some examples of how these prepositions are used in each case.

- **To show time**

  on a specific day or date: *on* June 7, *on* Wednesday

  in a period of time: completed *in* an hour, *in* 2003, *in* April, *in* the afternoon

  by a specific time or date: *by* noon, *by* the fifth of May

  at a specific time of day or night: *at* 3:30 this afternoon

- **To show place**

  at a place or location: *at* school, *at* the park, *at* the intersection

  on a surface: left *on* the floor

  on an electronic medium: *on* the Internet, *on* television

  in an enclosed space: *in* the box, *in* the room

  in a geographic location: *in* New York City, *in* Germany

  in a print medium: *in* a journal

  by a specific location: *by* the fountain

WRITER'S TIP

Do not insert a preposition between a transitive verb and its direct object. (See **20a**.) Intransitive verbs, however, are often followed by a prepositional phrase (a phrase that begins with a preposition):

- I **cooked** hot dogs on the grill. [transitive verb]

  I **ate** in the park. [intransitive verb]

What are phrasal prepositions?

Some prepositional phrases begin with more than one preposition. These phrasal prepositions are commonly used in both written and spoken communication. A list of common phrasal prepositions follows:

- according to   because of   in case of   on the side of

  across from   by way of   in spite of   up to

  along with   except for   instead of   with respect to

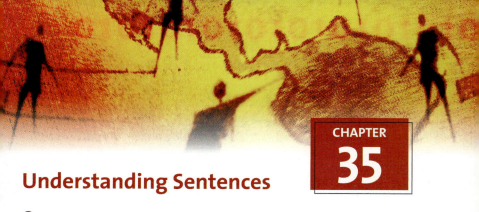

Understanding Sentences

Sentences in English can be very simple. For example, think of the short sentence spoken by a bride or groom: "I do." Those two little words (just three little letters!) can change a person's life forever.

Sentences in English can also be very complex. Consider the first sentence in "The Star-Spangled Banner": "Oh say, can you see by the dawn's early light, what so proudly we hailed at the twilight's last gleaming, whose broad stripes and bright stars through the perilous fight, o'er the ramparts we watched were so gallantly streaming?"

Whether simple or complex, all sentences in English follow a few basic rules. This chapter will help you sort them out.

35a Sentence Patterns

Simple sentences in the English language follow five basic patterns:

Subject + Verb

    ┌─S─┐┌─V─┐
    Naomi winked.

Some verbs, like *winked,* are intransitive. Intransitive verbs do not need a direct object to express a complete thought. (See **20a**.)

Subject + Verb + Direct Object

    ┌─S─┐┌─V─┐   ┌─DO─┐
    Harris grinds his teeth.

Some verbs, like *grinds,* are transitive. Transitive verbs do need a direct object to express a complete thought. (See **20a**.)

Subject + Verb + Indirect Object + Direct Object

    ┌─S─┐┌─V─┐   ┌─IO─┐   ┌─DO─┐
    Elena offered her friend an anchovy.

The direct object names *who* or *what* receives the action; the indirect object names *to whom* or *for whom* the action was done.

UNDERSTANDING SENTENCES

Subject + Verb + Direct Object + Object Complement

S —— V — DO   — OC —
The chancellor named Ravi the outstanding student of 2006.

The object complement renames or describes the direct object.

Subject + Linking Verb + Predicate Noun (or Predicate Adjective)

S ⌐ LV   — PN —
Paula is a computer programmer.

S ⌐ LV   — PA —
Paula is very intelligent.

A linking verb connects the subject to the predicate noun or predicate adjective. The predicate noun renames the subject; the predicate adjective describes the subject.

What is inverted order?

In the five basic sentence patterns, the subject comes before the verb. In a few types of sentences, such as those below, the subject can come after the verb. This is called *inverted order.*

Linking Verb + Subject + Predicate Noun

LV ⌐ S ⌐ ⌐ PN ⌐
Is Larisa a poet? [a question]

***There* + Linking Verb + Subject**

LV   ⌐ S ⌐
There was a meeting. [a sentence beginning with *there*]

ESL TIP

Diagramming sentences may help you understand the basic sentence patterns in the English language. Sentence diagramming shows you the function of each word in a sentence. See <www.thecollegewriter.com> for more information on diagramming.

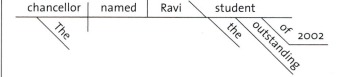

35b Sentence Problems

This section looks at potential trouble spots and sentence problems. For more information about English sentences, their parts, and ways to construct them, see Chapters 22 through 26.

What are double negatives?

A double negative is an error that results from using two negatives (*not, never, rarely, hardly, seldom,* and so on) in a sentence, instead of one. (See **26h**.)

- We **never** know what Professor Smith will do. [not *hardly never*]

What is subject-verb agreement?

Subjects and their verbs must agree in person and number.

- The **student was** rewarded for her hard work. [third-person singular]
- The **students were** rewarded for their hard work. [third-person plural]
- The **instructor**, as well as the students, **attends** the orientation.
- The **students**, as well as the instructor, **attend** the orientation.

What is a double subject?

A double subject results from repeating the subject of a sentence or clause.

- The doctor prescribed an antibiotic.

  [not *The doctor she prescribed an antibiotic.*]
- Jack forgot his girlfriend's flowers.

  [not *Jack he forgot his girlfriend's flowers.*]

What are run-on sentences and comma splices?

Run-on sentences and comma splices result when two sentences are improperly joined. (See **26b–26c**.) A compound sentence requires **both** a comma and a coordinating conjunction (*and, but, or, nor, for, so,* or *yet*). A **run-on sentence** results when neither is used.

> **Run-on:** Astronomy is amazing we get to use the university telescope.
>
> **Corrected:** Astronomy is amazing, and we get to use the university telescope.

A **comma splice** results when only a comma is used.

> **Comma splice:** The labs involve a lot of math, they are tough.
> **Corrected:** The labs involve a lot of math, so they are tough.

> **NOTE:** A semicolon also can join two independent clauses.
>
> - The labs involve a lot of math; they are tough.

UNDERSTANDING SENTENCES

What are conditional sentences?

Conditional sentences are complex sentences that express possibilities. The dependent clause states a condition that must be met for the independent clause to be true. Selecting the correct verb tense for use in the two clauses of a conditional sentence can be problematic.

1. **Factual conditional sentences:** Usually the dependent clause begins with *if, when, whenever,* or a similar expression. The verbs in the dependent clause and the independent clause should be in the same tense.

   - **Whenever** we **had** time, we **took** a break and **went** for a swim.
   - **If** work **demanded**, we **slaved** all day.

2. **Predictive conditional sentences:** These sentences express future conditions and possible results. The dependent clause begins with *if* or *unless* and has a present tense verb. The independent clause uses a modal verb (*will, can, should, may, might*).

   - **Unless** we **find** a better deal, we **will buy** this sound system.
   - **If** we **host** a rock concert, we **may need** a bigger system.

3. **Speculative conditional sentences:** These sentences describe a situation that is unlikely to happen or that is contrary to fact. The dependent clause uses a past or past perfect tense verb. The independent clause uses a verb formed from *would, could,* or *might* plus the past participle.

   - **If** we **had started** out earlier, we **would have arrived** on time.
   - **If** we **bought** groceries once a week, we **would** not **have** to go to the store so often.

How do I create direct and indirect quotations?

Direct quotations are the exact words from a source other than the author. These words are enclosed in quotation marks. Reported speech, or **indirect quotations,** report nearly exact words without quotation marks. (See **29h** for a review of the use of quotation marks.)

Direct quotation: Felicia said, "Don't worry about tomorrow."

Indirect quotation: Felicia said that you don't have to worry about tomorrow.

In the case of a question, when a direct quotation is changed to an indirect quotation, the question mark is not needed and pronouns often change.

Direct quotation: Ahmad asked, "Will you give me a hand?"

Indirect quotation: Ahmad asked if I would give him a hand.

35c   Tricky Constructions

Every language has its own rules for building sentences. These two pages contain answers to common questions about building sentences in English.

Do I always have to include a subject?

Yes. Every English sentence has a subject, and even a dependent clause has to have a subject. The only time that English allows a subject to be implied is in a command or request, when the implied subject is "you."

- [You] Take a gift when you go to the party.

  [The first *You* can be implied, but not the second—not *when go to the party*.]
- [You] Make sure to thank the host even if others do not.

  [Not *even if do not*]

English sometimes uses the placeholder words *there* or *it* (expletives) when the subject is delayed.

- **There** is no excuse for rude behavior.

  [The subject is *excuse*. This statement can't be written *Rude behavior is no excuse* or *Is no excuse for rude behavior*.]
- **It** will reflect well on you to be polite.

  [The subject is *to be polite*, but do not omit the *it*.]

In these constructions, you must include the *there* or *it*.

Do I always have to include the *be* verb?

Again, the answer is yes. Many languages allow a *be* verb to be inferred, but English does not. Whenever a *be* verb is needed, include it explicitly.

- Polite behavior **is** a ticket to more parties.

  [Not *Polite behavior a ticket to more parties*.]

Do I always have to include objects with transitive verbs?

Most often, the answer is yes. Though other languages allow objects and object complements to be implied, English requires them to be stated.

- You should give the **gift** of good manners.

  [Not *You should give of good manners*.]
- A polite guest is always **welcome**.

  [Not *A polite guest is*.]

> **NOTE:** Sometimes, a relative pronoun is omitted but understood.
> - I forgot the flowers I intended to give to my hosts.
>   [The relative pronoun *that* is omitted after the word *flowers*.]

UNDERSTANDING SENTENCES

Why are noun clauses so tricky?

Noun clauses are tricky because they function as *part of* a longer sentence.

- I know **that a noun clause can be a direct object**.
  [The clause is the direct object of *know*.]

When a noun clause functions as the subject, the independent clause is not complete without it. However, long noun clauses can make the sentence sound top heavy.

- **That noun clauses work in this way** confuses me.

As a result, English often delays the subject, using the word *it* (an expletive).

- It confuses me **that noun clauses work in this way**.
  [The noun clause still functions as the subject.]

Why are adjective clauses so tricky?

In most Asian and Middle Eastern languages, adjective clauses are constructed like parenthetical statements.

- The sociology class **(I took it last semester)** taught me so much.

In English, the adjective clause is written without the object (in this case, *it*). Leaving the object in place would be an error in English.

- The sociology class **I took last semester** taught me so much.

Speakers of European languages might have trouble with another kind of adjective clause:

- The sociology class **(I enrolled in it last semester)** taught me so much.
- The sociology class **I enrolled in last semester** taught me so much.

This second sentence might seem wrong because the preposition *in* is stranded without the object of the preposition *it*. However, this sentence is correct in English, and leaving *it* in place would be incorrect. One other way to write this clause would be as follows:

- The sociology class **in which I enrolled last semester** taught me so much.

Why are adverb clauses so tricky?

An adverb clause begins with a subordinating conjunction (such as *before, when, although, provided that,* or *unless*). These conjunctions turn the whole clause into an adverb. As a result, these clauses do not need another conjunction to connect them to the sentence.

- **Although** some languages use two conjunctions, English uses one.
  [not *Although some languages use two conjunctions, but English uses one.*]

Do not use both a subordinating and a coordinating conjunction with adverb clauses.

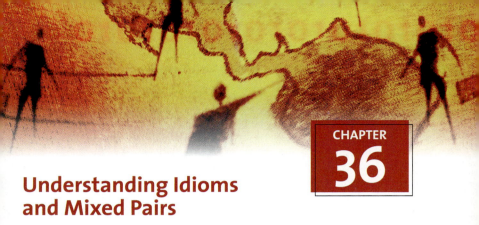

Understanding Idioms and Mixed Pairs

One of the most frustrating aspects of learning any language is learning idioms—phrases used in a special way. For example, in English, the idiom *bury the hatchet* means "settle an argument," even though the individual words mean something different.

But idioms (and mixed pairs) don't have to be troublesome. Once you understand them, they can be fun. This chapter lists some of the most common idioms and mixed pairs in English.

36a Idioms A–Z

an axe to grind
Mom has **an axe to grind** with the dog that dug up her flower garden.
[a problem to settle]

as the crow flies
She lives only two miles from here **as the crow flies**. [in a straight line]

bad apple
One troublemaker on a team may be called a **bad apple**. [bad influence]

beat around the bush
Dad said, "Where were you? Don't **beat around the bush**."
[avoid getting to the point]

benefit of the doubt
Ms. Hy gave Henri the **benefit of the doubt** when he explained why he fell asleep in class. [another chance]

blew my top
When my money got stolen, I **blew my top**. [showed great anger]

bone to pick
Nick had a **bone to pick** with Adrian when he learned they both liked the same girl. [a problem to settle]

UNDERSTANDING IDIOMS AND MIXED PAIRS

break the ice
Shanta was the first to **break the ice** in the room full of new students.
[start a conversation]

burn the midnight oil
Carmen had to **burn the midnight oil** the day before the big test.
[work late into the night]

chomping at the bit
Dwayne was **chomping at the bit** when it was his turn to bat.
[eager, excited]

cry wolf
If you **cry wolf** too often, no one will come when you really need help.
[say you are in trouble when you aren't]

drop in the bucket
My donation was a **drop in the bucket**. [comparatively small amount]

face the music
José had to **face the music** when he got caught cheating on the test.
[deal with the consequences]

flew off the handle
Tramayne **flew off the handle** when he saw his little brother playing with
matches. [became very angry]

floating on air
Carl was **floating on air** when he read the
report. [feeling very happy]

food for thought
The coach gave us **food for thought** when
she said that winning isn't everything.
[something to think about]

get down to business
You need to **get down to business** on this
assignment. [start working]

get the upper hand
The other team will **get the upper hand** if we don't play better in the
second half. [gain control]

give the cold shoulder
Alicia always **gives me the cold shoulder** after we argue. [ignores me]

go overboard
The teacher told us not to **go overboard** with fancy lettering on our
posters. [do too much]

have your head in the sand
You **have your head in the sand**. [ignore serious problems]

hit the hay
Patrice **hit the hay** early because she was tired. [went to bed]

in a nutshell
In a nutshell, Coach Roby told us to play our best. [to summarize]

in the nick of time
Zong grabbed his little brother's hand **in the nick of time**, before he touched the hot pan. [just in time]

in the same boat
My friend and I are **in the same boat** when it comes to doing Saturday chores. [having the same problem]

iron out
Jamil and his brother were told to **iron out** their differences about cleaning their room. [solve, work out]

keep your nose to the grindstone
If I **keep my nose to the grindstone**, I will finish my presentation in one hour. [work hard]

knuckle down
Grandpa told me to **knuckle down** at college. [work hard]

learn the ropes
Being new in school, I knew it would take some time to **learn the ropes**.
[get to know how things are done]

let's face it
"**Let's face it**!" said Mr. Sills. "You're a better long-distance runner than a sprinter." [let's admit it]

let the cat out of the bag
Tia **let the cat out of the bag** and got her sister in trouble.
[told a secret]

on cloud nine
Walking home from the party, I was **on cloud nine**.
[feeling very happy]

on pins and needles
I was **on pins and needles** as I waited to see the doctor.
[feeling nervous]

UNDERSTANDING IDIOMS AND MIXED PAIRS

put his foot in his mouth
Chivas **put his foot in his mouth** when he called his teacher by the wrong name. [said something embarrassing]

put your best foot forward
Grandpa said that whenever you do something, you should **put your best foot forward**. [do the best that you can do]

rock the boat
The coach said, "Don't **rock the boat**." [cause trouble]

rude awakening
I had a **rude awakening** when I saw the letter *F* at the top of my Spanish quiz. [sudden, unpleasant surprise]

see eye to eye
My sister and I finally **see eye to eye** about who gets to use the phone first after school. [are in agreement]

take it with a grain of salt
If my sister tells you she has no homework, **take it with a grain of salt**. [think critically about what you learn and read]

take the bull by the horns
This team needs to **take the bull by the horns** to win the game. [take control]

through thick and thin
Max and I will be friends **through thick and thin**. [in good times and in bad times]

time flies
When you're having fun, **time flies**. [time passes quickly]

time to kill
We had **time to kill** before the ballpark gates would open. [extra time]

under the weather
I was feeling **under the weather**, so I didn't go to school. [sick]

word of mouth
We found out who the new teacher was by **word of mouth**. [talking to other people]

36b Commonly Mixed Pairs A–Z

Mixed pairs are simply words that are easily confused. *Too* often, *two* or more words are difficult *to* tell apart. The words *too, two,* and *to* in this sentence sound the same, but each has a different meaning and use. The following list of mixed pairs will help you select just the right word.

a, an Use *a* as the article before words that begin with consonant sounds and before words that begin with the long vowel sound *u* (yü). Use *an* before words that begin with other vowel sounds.

> **An** older student showed Kris **an** easier way to buy food. **A** union debit card is **a** quick way to access **a** student account.

a lot, alot, lots, many, allot *Alot* is not a word; *a lot* (two words) and *lots* are vague descriptive terms that should be used sparingly, especially in formal writing. Normally, *many* is the preferred term. *Allot* means to give someone a share.

> Prof. Dubi **allots** each of us five spelling errors per semester, and he thinks that's **a lot**. **Many** [not *lots of*] students use up their five errors in their first paper.

anyways, anywheres Both *anyways* and *anywheres* (plural) are nonstandard. Use the singular *anyway* and *anywhere* instead.

bring, take *Bring* suggests the action is directed toward the speaker; *take* suggests the action is directed away from the speaker.

> If you're not going to **bring** the video to class, **take** it to the resource center.

cent, sent, scent *Cent* is a coin; *sent* is the past tense of the verb *send; scent* is an odor or a smell.

> For thirty-seven **cents**, I **sent** my friend a love poem in a perfumed envelope. She adored the **scent** but hated the poem.

chose, choose *Chose* (chōz) is the past tense of the verb *choose* (chüz).

> For generations, people **chose** their careers based on their parents' careers; now people **choose** their careers based on the job market.

good, well *Good* is an adjective; *well* is nearly always an adverb. (When used to indicate state of health, *well* is an adjective.)

> Ricardo approaches, kicks **well**, makes a **good** shot, and scores!

I, me *I* is a subject pronoun; *me* is used as an object of a preposition, a direct object, or an indirect object.

> My roommate and **I** went to the library last night.
>
> Rasheed gave the concert tickets to Erick and **me**.

Good shot!

He kicks well.

UNDERSTANDING IDIOMS AND MIXED PAIRS

it's, its *It's* is the contraction of "it is." *Its* is the possessive form of "it."
> **It's** not hard to see why my husband feeds that alley cat; **its** pitiful limp and mournful mewing would melt any heart.

learn, teach *Learn* means "to acquire information"; *teach* means "to give information."
> Computers help teachers **teach** and students **learn**.

off, off of *Off of* is nonstandard; use *off* by itself.

OK, okay This expression, spelled either way, is appropriate in informal writing; however, avoid using it in papers, reports, or formal correspondence of any kind.
> Your proposal is satisfactory [not *okay*] on most levels.

set, sit *Set* means "to place." *Sit* means "to put the body in a seated position." *Set* is a transitive verb; *sit* is an intransitive verb.
> While my friends **sit** expectantly, I **set** down the tray of cupcakes.

their, there, they're *Their* is a possessive personal pronoun. *There* is a pronoun used as a function word to introduce a clause or an adverb used to point out location. *They're* is the contraction for "they are."
> **There** is a comfortable place for students to study for **their** exams, so **they're** more likely to do a good job.

to, too, two *To* is a preposition that can mean "in the direction of." *To* is also used to form an infinitive. *Too* means "also" or "very." *Two* is the number 2.
> **Two** causes of eye problems among students are lights that fail **to** illuminate properly and computer screens with **too** much glare.

your, you're *Your* is a possessive pronoun. *You're* is "you are."
> If **you're** like most Americans, you will have held eight jobs by **your** fortieth birthday.

NOTE: For more help with additional mixed pairs and usage errors, see Chapter 15: "A Glossary of Word Usage."

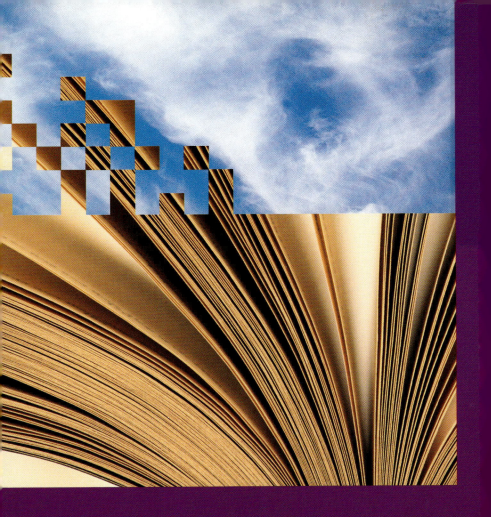

Writing Across
the Curriculum

Writing Across the Curriculum

Forms of College Writing: An Overview

In college, professors in nearly all departments assign writing. Why? Because they know that writing helps you in two ways: (1) to learn course content and (2) to learn how to carry on a written dialogue with others in your field. In other words, writing helps you learn course material today, but it also helps you use that information in subsequent college courses and in the workplace.

The purpose of this chapter is to show you three things about writing across the curriculum:

- How a college curriculum and faculty are organized
- What kinds of writing you can expect to do in all of your courses
- How writing and thinking skills required in one class are linked to writing and thinking skills required in another class

To accomplish these tasks, the chapter begins by showing the big picture: the three divisions into which most college curricula are divided, and the academic departments that constitute each division. The chapter then presents more specific information about academic departments, including the topics that they study, the forms of writing that they assign, and the traits of those forms.

Use this chapter to learn what writing across the curriculum entails and what kinds of writing assignments you can expect in your major. Then when you receive an assignment, use one of the chapters in this section of the handbook to find specific guidelines, models, and checklists that will help you complete your work.

What's Ahead

37a Three Curricular Divisions
37b Types of Writing in Each Division
37c Traits of Writing Across the Curriculum

FORMS OF COLLEGE WRITING: AN OVERVIEW

37a Three Curricular Divisions

Based on each department's area of study and focus, the college curriculum is generally divided into three groups: Humanities, Social Sciences, and Natural and Applied Sciences. These groups are then subdivided into specific departments, such as Biology, Chemistry, and Physics. Below you will find an explanation of each division, along with its more common departments.

What are the humanities?

The humanities focus on human culture, both past and present. Humanities scholars examine topics such as the history of civilization, cultural trends and institutions, religious beliefs and practices, languages and their use, and artwork and performance skills. Some departments within this division include the following:

- Archeology
  Asian Studies
  Dance
  English

  Ethnic Studies
  Film Studies
  Graphic Design
  History

  Modern Languages
  Music
  Philosophy
  Religion

  Theater Arts
  Theology
  Visual Arts
  Women's Studies

What are the social sciences?

The social sciences focus on human behavior and societies, using research strategies adapted from the natural sciences. For example, a researcher may develop a hypothesis regarding a topic or phenomenon, and then devise an experiment to test that hypothesis. Students study topics such as economic systems, correctional programs, and personality disorders. Departments in this division include the following:

- Anthropology
  Business
  Communication
  Criminology

  Economics
  Education
  Genetics
  Geography

  Geophysics
  Government
  Health & Phys. Ed.
  Political Science

  Psychology
  Social Work
  Sociology
  Urban Planning

What are the natural and applied sciences?

The natural sciences (such as biology, zoology, and chemistry) focus on specific aspects of nature such as animal life, plant life, and molecular structures. In contrast, the applied sciences (such as mathematics, computer science, and engineering) consider how to use scientifically based information and practices to understand concepts and develop artifacts. Here are some of the departments in this division:

- Agriculture
  Agronomy
  Anatomy
  Architecture
  Astronomy

  Biology
  Botany
  Chemistry
  Computer Science
  Engineering

  Environment
  Forestry
  Mathematics
  Nutrition
  Oceanography

  Physics
  Physiology
  Public Health
  Space Science
  Zoology

37b   Types of Writing in Each Division

Listed below are the types of writing commonly assigned in the three academic divisions. Often instructors in different divisions will assign the same type of writing—but with a different purpose or focus. When an assigned form differs from the one shown in the book, adapt the guidelines in the book to the form stated in the assignment.

What types of writing are done in the humanities?

Application Writing (**42d**)

Arguing a Point (**40a**)

Cause and Effect (**39a**)

Classification (**39i**)

Comparison and Contrast (**39e**)

Definition (**5b**)

Essay Test (**44b**)

Explaining a Process (**39m**)

Interview Report (**47c**)

Literary Analysis (**41a**)

Oral Presentations (**43a**)

Personal Essay (**38a**)

Proposing a Solution (**40e**)

Research Paper (**51e** and **54c**)

Web Writing (**18b**)

What types of writing are done in the social sciences?

Abstracts/Summaries (**54c**)

Application Writing (**42d**)

Arguing a Point (**40a**)

Cause and Effect (**39a**)

Classification (**39i**)

Comparison and Contrast (**39e**)

Definition (**5b**)

Essay Test (**44b**)

Experiment Report (**54c**)

Explaining a Process (**39m**)

Interview Report (**47c**)

Literary Analysis (**41a**)

Oral Presentations (**43a**)

Personal Essay (**38a**)

Proposing a Solution (**40e**)

Research Report (**51e** and **54c**)

Web Writing (**18b**)

What types of writing are done in the natural and applied sciences?

Abstracts/Summaries (**54c**)

Application Writing (**42d**)

Arguing a Point (**40a**)

Cause and Effect (**39a**)

Classification (**39i**)

Comparison and Contrast (**39e**)

Definition (**5b**)

Describing a Process (**39m**)

Field Report (**47a**)

Interview Report (**47c**)

Personal Essay (**38a**)

Proposing a Solution (**40e**)

Research Paper (**51e** and **54c**)

Web Writing (**18b**)

FORMS OF COLLEGE WRITING: AN OVERVIEW

37c Traits of Writing Across the Curriculum

Below are listed the more common writing tasks in each of the three divisions, along with seven traits that distinguish good writing for each task.

What type of writing is done in the humanities?

Idea:	**Personal writing:** Explores and expresses the writer's ideas, experiences, and feelings
Organization:	Narratives—usually chronological
Voice:	Narratives—engaging, fits the story; others—honest, direct
Word Choice:	Words are precise and fit the writer's topic, purpose, audience, and characters.
Sentences:	Narratives—appropriate for dialogue and description; others use varied forms
Correctness:	Documentation follows MLA or CMS style.
Design:	Designed as an essay with proper formatting and typeface

Idea:	**Analyze a work of art:** Describes the work and analyzes its parts and how they function
Organization:	Appropriate for the work and the writer's focus
Voice:	Objective appraisal and analysis, supported by evidence
Sentences:	Varied in length and structure, with clear transitions
Word Choice:	Appropriate for the art form; technical terms explained
Correctness:	Documentation follows MLA or CMS style.
Design:	Designed as an essay with proper formatting and typeface

Idea:	**Argue a point:** Persuades the reader regarding the point's meaning, importance, and truth
Organization:	Order fits the topic and purpose: cause/effect, comparison/contrast, and so on
Voice:	Informed, impartial, inviting
Word Choice:	Precise, with scholarly terms used in the discipline
Sentences:	Tend to be longer; complexity fits the topic and audience
Correctness:	Documentation follows MLA or CMS style.
Design:	Designed as an essay with proper formatting and typeface

Idea:	**Analyze a phenomenon:** Explains its meaning in relation to its historical, social, and/or natural context (Marxism)
Organization:	Often combines cause/effect, comparison/contrast, and examples
Voice:	Scholarly, fair, informed, balanced
Word Choice:	Precise, often including scholarly terms used in the discipline
Sentences:	Tend to be longer; complexity fits the topic and audience
Correctness:	Documentation follows MLA or CMS style.
Design:	Designed as an essay with proper formatting and typeface

Traits of Writing Across the Curriculum

What type of writing is done in the social sciences?

Idea: **Case study:** Describes and analyzes the topic, identifies the methodology, gives results

Organization: Gives overview, presents steps chronologically, analyzes outcome

Voice: Impartial reporting; respectful, thoughtful analysis

Word Choice: Precise statistics and discipline-related terms

Sentences: Medium-length sentences with clear transitions

Correctness: Documentation follows APA or CMS style.

Design: Formatted as a report for easy reading and in accordance with the discipline's or department's style guide

---

Idea: **Literature review:** Summarizes and evaluates journal articles (usually research-based) on a topic

Organization: Each article is discussed separately followed by conclusions.

Voice: Unbiased reporting, formal tone, logical analysis

Word Choice: Includes precise technical terms and statistics

Sentences: Shorter sentences and paragraphs with clear transitions

Correctness: Documentation follows APA or CMS style.

Design: Formatted as a report for easy reading and in accordance with the discipline's or department's style guide

---

Idea: **Analyze a policy or project:** Analyzes the topic, its history, and its effects

Organization: Analysis often uses cause/effect, classification, and comparison/contrast

Voice: Impartial, informed, concerned, thoughtful

Word Choice: Includes precise technical terms and statistics

Sentences: Sentences are varied in length and structure, with clear transitions.

Correctness: Documentation follows APA or CMS style.

Design: Formatted as a report for easy reading and in accordance with the discipline's or department's style guide

---

Idea: **Describe a process:** Describes materials, steps in the process, and its importance

Organization: Usually states topic and outcome, gives steps chronologically

Voice: Objective, yet concerned about effectiveness and safety

Word Choice: Precise, often including technical terms

Sentences: Sentences tend to be short, direct.

Correctness: Documentation follows APA or CMS rules.

Design: Formatted as a report for easy reading and in accordance with the discipline's style guide; or as workplace instructions including numbered steps and graphics

FORMS OF COLLEGE WRITING: AN OVERVIEW

What type of writing is done in the natural and applied sciences?

Idea: **Lab or experiment report:** Includes clear data, logical analysis, unbiased reporting

Organization: States issues and hypothesis, methods with procedure, results with data; and discusses results

Word Choice: Precise, often including scientific and technical terms

Sentences: Medium length, logical, passive voice only when needed

Voice: Interested, curious, impartial, logical, meticulous

Correctness: Documentation follows CSE or APA style.

Design: Formatted as a report in accordance with the discipline's style guide; graphics (such as tables, charts) are clear

---

Idea: **Field report:** Includes clear data and unbiased reporting

Organization: States focus and issues, methods with procedure, results with data; and discusses results

Voice: Interested, curious, logical, meticulous

Word Choice: Precise, often including scientific and technical terms

Sentences: Medium length, logical, passive voice only when needed

Correctness: Documentation follows CSE or APA style.

Design: Formatted as a report in accordance with the discipline's style guide; graphics (such as tables, photos) are strong

---

Idea: **Literature review:** Summarizes and compares journal articles (usually research-based)

Organization: Each article is discussed separately, followed by conclusions.

Correctness: Documentation follows CSE or APA style.

Design: Formatted as a report with proper spacing and typeface

---

Idea: **Describe a process:** Describes each step in a process

Organization: Usually states topic, gives steps chronologically, closes

Voice: Impartial, concerned about effectiveness and safety

Word Choice: Precise, often including scientific and technical terms

Sentences: Description of a process—sentences vary in form; instructions—short, direct

Correctness: Follows CSE or APA style

Design: Formatted as an essay or workplace instructions

LINKS

Web Links:

MLA Modern Language Association <**www.mla.org**>
APA American Psychological Association <**www.apa.org**>
CMS Chicago Manual of Style <**www.press.uchicago.edu**>
CSE Council of Science Editors <**www.councilscienceeditors.org**>

Personal Essays

In a **personal essay,** you describe a person, place, or thing (*event, object, idea*) that is important to you, and you explain why it's important.

What is my goal?

Your goal is to help readers experience your topic: to sense the topic's nature, to recognize its qualities, and to understand how it has affected your life.

What are the keys to my success?

Recall precise details. To understand and appreciate your topic, you must show readers those key details (sights, smells, sounds, textures, tastes) that make the experience memorable to you—and worth reflecting on.

Probe the topic. The treasure-search aspect of writing this essay happens while asking *so–why* questions: So why does this picture still make me smile? Why does his comment still hurt? Why did I do that when I knew better? Did I know better?

Tell what you find. Your readers need to see the treasures you discover, so don't hide what's embarrassing, painful, or still unclear. Show them the details clearly, explain your insights honestly, and then trust readers to respond with sensitivity, appreciation, and respect.

What topics should I consider?

The most promising topics are those that gave you insight into yourself, and possibly into others as well. Often such an experience will have led you or others to change patterns of thought, feelings, or behavior.

- Times when you felt secure, hopeful, distraught, appreciated, confident, frightened, exploited, misunderstood, or challenged
- Times when you made a decision about friendships, lifestyles, careers, education, fashion, politics, religion, or leaving home

What's Ahead
38a Student Essay: Description of a Place
38b Guidelines: Personal Essay
38c Checklist: Personal Essay

PERSONAL ESSAYS

38a Student Essay: Description of a Place

Nicole Suurdt, a student from Ontario, Canada, describes a time and place that she loved as a child and yearns for as an adult.

The Stream in the Ravine

> The writer introduces the topic and then gives background information.

Behind my childhood home is a small ravine, and through it runs the seasonal overflow of a little pond deep within the woods. It's a noisy stream, just narrow enough for an eight-year-old to take one stretching step across and reach the other side with dry shoes. And when I was eight, this stream was everything to me.

You see, for most of my childhood, I lived on a small hobby farm in Ontario, Canada, where rolling pasture and croplands surrounded my home. The pasture fenced in Scottish Highland cattle with terrifying horns, unbroken horses with skittish hooves, and one half-blind, unpredictable donkey. These creatures separated me from the woods just beyond the pasture. But when I was little, it wasn't simply my fear of these fitful animals that penned me in on my side of the fence—it was a fear of what lay beyond the shadowy barrier of maples and pines.

> Description of the visits builds tension.

It's not that I'd never been to the woods before. I had—twice. The first time, my brother took me in search of the tallest tree in the forest and got us lost for a couple of hours. My second visit was a dark winter journey. Dad dragged the family into the woods late one night in search of a missing cow. We found her half-devoured body lying in bloodstained snow, packed down by wolves' paws.

> A transition signals a shift in the action.

But eventually, curiosity overpowered my fears. One spring day when I was eight, armed with a staff, I skirted the pasture and headed for the forest. I approached the fence that my dad had put up to ward off the woods. Quickly I scaled the fence, but then stood some time holding on to its boards, figuring that if a wolf came along, I could scramble back to the other side. However, after five minutes passed and no wolf appeared, I calmed down, let go of the fence, and stepped into the forest—lured on by the sound of chipmunks, birds, wind through trees, and snapping twigs.

Drawn forward, I discovered rocky burrows of unknown creatures. I chased chipmunks. I sang. I passed a hunter's fort perched high in a pine, deserted after last fall's deer-hunting season. I passed under an archway of tall cedars. I waded through the muck and mire surrounding a small swamp and

1

2

3

4

5

Student Essay: Description of a Place

plodded my mud-caked shoes up a small rise, thick with the faded, crumbled leaves of last year's fall. One particular sound kept pulling me forward—the gurgle of running water.

6   Standing at the peak of the rise, with brown leaves stuck to my muddy sneakers, I found the source. Below me, within its shallow bed, ran a tiny stream—little more than a trickle, really. But to me it was a beautiful, rushing brook, my own source of clear, cold water protected by oak, maple, and pine sentries. That day I spent hours scooping decaying leaves out of my stream's bed and sitting by her side to watch the water spill over the rocks and roots. She was my own discovery, my own territory, my own secret place. From that day on, the little stream past the hunter's fort, under the cedar archway, through the muck and the mire, and over the rocky rise became my quiet, private place.

> The writer describes the stream and reflects on its importance.

7   But I never could keep a secret for long. During dinner one Sunday, I told my parents about my stream. I figured that it needed a bridge, something only Dad could help me build. And so, that afternoon, I led Mom and Dad over the fence, into the woods, and up to my secret stream. Together, we built a bridge using the fallen branches lying about. Mom took a picture of Dad and me sitting on our homemade, lopsided bridge, the water washing over the toes of the big rubber boots that she had insisted we wear.

> The writer focuses on the image in the photo.

8   My parents separated eight years after that picture was taken, and I haven't gone back to my stream since, though I think of it often. Somewhere, tucked away in Mom's photo albums, is the picture of a little girl in her dreamland, her dad beside her, his big feet hanging near her small ones. Her mom stands in the water just a few feet away behind the camera lens.

9   Sometimes, I want to go back there, back into that photo. I want to step into a time when life seemed safe, and a tiny stream gave us all that we needed. In that picture, our smiles last, our hearts are calm, and we hear only quiet voices, forest sounds, and my bubbling stream. Bitter words are silenced and tears held back by the click and whir of a camera.

> The closing deepens and unifies the reflection.

10   I've been thinking about making the journey again past the hunter's fort, under the stand of cedars, through the muck and mire, and over the rocky rise. But it's been a long summer, and the small, seasonal stream running out of the overflow of the pond has probably dried up.

PERSONAL ESSAYS

38b Guidelines: Personal Essay

1. **Select a topic.** Choose a person, a place, an event, or an experience that influenced you in some key way—either confirming what you thought or planned at that time or changing those thoughts or plans. (Also see "What topics should I consider?" in the introduction to this chapter.)

WRITER'S TIP

Try listing topics related to the following statement: Reflect on times when you discovered that the world was one of the following —*strange, wonderful, frightening, boring, small, uncaring, like you,* or *unlike you.* Who or what shaped the experiences? How did these experiences affect who you are today?

2. **Get the big picture.** Once you have chosen an appropriate topic, gather your thoughts by reflecting on the questions below.

   ■ What are the key moments—the pivotal points—in your experience?
   ■ What led to these key moments? Why? What resulted from them?
   ■ What was going on from your perspective?
   ■ What did others do, and how did they affect you?
   ■ What did you learn and why?
   ■ Did this experience end as you had hoped? Why or why not?
   ■ What themes, conflicts, lessons, and insights arise from this experience?
   ■ How do your feelings now differ from your feelings then?

3. **Get organized.**

   ■ Review your brainstorming or freewriting, and highlight key details, quotations, or events.
   ■ Draft a brief outline that shows where details and ideas fit into the big picture.
   ■ List the main events in chronological order or use a cluster to gather details related to your experience, people, and places.

4. **Deepen the description.**

   ■ Generate sensory details by listing colors, sounds, sights, tastes, and textures.
   ■ Develop comparisons by describing your topic with similes, metaphors, and analogies.
   ■ Draft anecdotes (including quotations) that illustrate or characterize your topic.

Guidelines: Personal Essay

5. **Write the first draft.** Review your outline and then develop the first draft in one sitting. Test your reflection for its significance. Does it answer these questions: What happened? How did the experience affect you? How do you feel about it now?

6. **Review and revise.** After drafting the essay, take a break. Then read your document again for accuracy and completeness. Look first at the entire piece. Does it say what you wanted to say? Does it include any gaps or weak spots? Check your outline to make sure all key details are covered and in the right sequence.

> **NOTE:** You can use the checklist at **38c** for more guidelines on how best to review and revise your writing.

7. **Test your reflection.** Review what you say about the experience.
   - Does the tone—whether sarcastic, humorous, regretful, or meditative—fit the content of the essay?
   - Have you established a viewpoint, and does the essay explore this point of view? (For more on point of view, see <www.thecollegewriter.com>.)
   - Will the readers appreciate your treatment of the subject?

8. **Get feedback.** Ask a classmate or someone in the writing center to read your paper, looking for the following:
   - An opening that pulls the reader into the reflection
   - Experiences that are portrayed vividly through sharp details, enlightening anecdotes, and helpful comparisons
   - An explanation of how or why the experience is important to you
   - Transitions that connect paragraphs effectively
   - A conclusion that clearly and succinctly refocuses on the point of the reflection

9. **Edit and proofread the essay.** Once you have revised the content, organization, and voice, polish the essay. Carefully check your choice of words, the clarity of your sentences, and your grammar, usage, and mechanics.

10. **Publish your writing by doing one of the following:**
    - Submit a copy to your instructor.
    - Share your essay with friends and family.
    - Publish it in a journal, in a blog, or on a website.
    - Place a copy in your professional portfolio.
    - Read the paper to a college or community writer's club.

PERSONAL ESSAYS

38c Checklist: Personal Essay

Use the seven traits to check the quality of your writing and revise as needed.

____ The **ideas** give insight into the identity, complexity, and significance of the topic. The dominant impression is clear and captivating.

____ The **organization** includes an engaging opening that leads smoothly into the description of the topic. Paragraphs follow a clear and logical order signaled by smooth transitions. The closing completes and unifies the essay.

____ The **voice** is informed, inviting, reflective, and lively.

____ The **words** include strong verbs and precise nouns. Adverbs and adjectives are used sparingly to refine the meaning.

____ The **sentences** are clear, vary in structure, and read smoothly. Transitions between sentences help unify paragraphs.

____ The final draft includes **no errors** in spelling, punctuation, mechanics, or grammar.

____ The **page design** is formatted appropriately for the reader and situation. Visuals such as photos or drawings clearly support the message.

WAC Link: Writers in all disciplines use narration, description, and reflection—three elements common in personal writing. For example, in the humanities, writers use all three when retelling and critiquing an artwork's "story," or when presenting and analyzing a historical event. In the social sciences, writers use narration and description to distinguish people and events in a case study or report. In the sciences, writers use narration and description to tell what they did or found in a lab report or field study.

Workplace Link: Many workplace forms, such as incident reports, project proposals, recommendations, and instructions, include narrative and descriptive writing. In most cases, the narration provides a context and framework for the message, and the description presents details that the reader needs to understand and appreciate the ideas.

VISUALS TIP

Visuals such as photos, drawings, and graphics can help tell your "story." However, just as you must choose words carefully, you must also select visuals judiciously to avoid distracting the reader from your message.

Analytical Essays

In an **analytical essay**, you think through what your topic is, how it functions, or what it means. This chapter explains how to write using these analytical patterns: cause/effect, comparison/contrast, classification, and process.

39a Cause and Effect: The Basics

The cause and effect essay has a challenging two-part structure. It might explain one cause and its single effect, many causes and their single effect, a single cause and its many effects, or many causes and effects.

What is my goal?

Your goal is to analyze and explain the causes, the effects, or both the causes and the effects of some phenomenon (fact, occurrence, or circumstance).

What are the keys to my success?

Know your readers. Consider what your readers know and think about your topic. Are they aware of the cause/effect connection associated with it? If they deny the existence or relevance of the connection, what arguments support their position?

Think logically. Linking cause to effect, or vice versa, requires clear and logical thinking supported by strong evidence. To practice this reasoning, (1) research the topic for evidence connecting a specific cause and/or effect to a specific phenomenon, (2) draft a working thesis stating that connection, and (3) explain the connection clearly.

What topics should I consider?

If you are not assigned a topic, choose one that you care about and want to dig into. Begin by listing topics related to the following broad categories: campus life, politics, society, environment, health careers, and entertainment.

What's Ahead

ANALYTICAL ESSAYS

39b **Student Essay: Cause and Effect**

Sarah Hanley is a college student living on a U.S. military base in Germany. In the essay below, she uses both research and her military experience to identify the causes and effects of adrenaline highs.

Adrenaline Junkies

What do you picture when you hear the phrase "adrenaline junkie"? Evel Knievel soaring through the air on a motorcycle? Tom Cruise rappelling down the side of a mountain? An excited retiree stuffing quarters in a slot machine? Actually, all three qualify as adrenaline junkies if they do the activities to get their adrenaline highs. But what, exactly, is an adrenaline high, what causes it, what are its effects, and are those effects positive?

Adrenaline (also called epinephrine) is a hormone linked to the two adrenal glands located on top of the kidneys. Each gland has two parts: the outer portion called the cortex, and the inner portion called the medulla. When a person experiences an unusual exertion or a crisis situation, his or her brain triggers the medullas, which release little packets of adrenaline into the bloodstream (Nathan). The rush of adrenaline in the blood leads to increased blood pressure, heart rate, sugar metabolism, oxygen intake, and muscle strength. All these phenomena cause an adrenaline high: feeling highly alert and very energetic (Scheuller 2).

However, while all healthy people experience adrenaline highs, different people need different levels of stimulus to trigger the highs. The level of stimulus that a person needs depends on the amount of protein in his or her medullas. In other words, the medullas release adrenaline through channels containing a certain protein. If the channels contain a large amount of the protein, they release adrenaline more easily than channels containing less protein. Therefore, a person with a higher level of protein in the channels of his or her medullas experiences an adrenaline release more easily than someone with a lower level of the protein (Scheuller 4).

To illustrate this difference, we'll call the people with a higher level of protein (and a more easily stimulated output of adrenaline) Type N, for nervous; the others we'll call Type C, for calm. Because Type N people release adrenaline more easily than Type C people do, Type N's require a lesser stimulus to trigger an adrenaline release. For example, a Type N person

The writer introduces the topic and then gives background information.

She describes the causes and effects of an adrenaline high.

The writer uses first-person pronouns to engage the reader, and she uses an illustration to clarify a point.

1

2

3

4

Student Essay: Cause and Effect

may get an adrenaline high from finishing his research paper on time, whereas a Type C person will get a similar buzz when she parachutes from a plane at 10,000 feet!

5   While different people get their adrenaline highs differently, any person's highs can be channeled for healthy or harmful effects. For example, the Type N person who gets a rush from finishing the research project could do good work as a junkie research technician in a science lab. As long as he avoids becoming a workaholic, seeking the highs won't threaten his health, and the work may contribute to the overall welfare of society. Similarly, the Type C person who gets her highs by jumping out of airplanes could do good work as a junkie firefighter or a junkie brain surgeon. As long as she gets periodic relief from the tension, the highs won't hurt her health, and the work could help her community.

6   On the other hand, pursuing the wrong type of adrenaline high, or seeking too many highs, can be destructive. Examples of this kind of behavior include compulsive gambling, drug use, careless risk taking in sports, and win-at-all-costs business practices. Destructive pursuits have many high-cost results, including bankruptcy, broken relationships, physical injury, drug addiction, and death (Lyons 3).

An introductory phrase signals a shift in focus.

7   Because adrenaline highs can lead to positive results, maybe we waste time worrying about becoming adrenaline junkies. Instead, we should ask ourselves how to pursue those highs positively. In other words, the proteins, hormones, and chemical processes that produce adrenaline highs are, themselves, very good—and they can be used for good. In fact, someday we may figure out how to bottle the stuff and put it on the market!

The writer concludes by reviewing her main points.

NOTE: The Works Cited page is not shown for this essay. For sample pages, see MLA (51e), APA (54c), CSE (58b), and CMS (57b).

39c Guidelines: Cause and Effect Essay

1. **Select a topic.** Look again at the list of topics that you generated in response to "What topics should I consider?" in **39a**. Expand the list by jotting down additional items for each category, or listing new categories, along with related items. From this finished list, choose a topic and prove its causes, its effects, or both.

2. **Narrow and research the topic.** Write down or type your topic. Below it, brainstorm a list of related causes and effects in two columns. Next, do preliminary research to expand the list and distinguish primary causes and effects from secondary ones. Revise your topic as needed to focus on primary causes and/or effects.

Cause/Effect

Topic (state topic) _____

Causes (because of . . .)   *Effects (. . . these conditions resulted)*

1.   1.
2.   2.
3.   3.

---

3. **Draft and test your thesis.** Based on your preliminary research, draft a working thesis (you may revise it later) that introduces the topic, along with the causes and/or effects that you intend to discuss. Limit your argument to only those points that you can prove.

4. **Gather and analyze information.** Research your topic for clear evidence that links specific causes to specific effects. Avoid arguments mistaking a coincidence for a cause/effect relationship.

> **NOTE:** Use the list of logical fallacies (**4i**) to weed out common errors in logic. For example, finding chemical pollutants in a stream running beside a chemical plant does not "prove" they came from the plant.

5. **Get organized.** Develop an outline that lays out your thesis and argument in a clear pattern. Under each main point asserting a cause/effect connection, list details from your research that support the connection.

Thesis: _____

Point 1   **Point 2**   **Point 3**
- Supporting details   - Supporting details   - Supporting details
- Supporting details   - Supporting details   - Supporting details

Guidelines: Cause and Effect Essay

6. Use your outline to draft the essay. Try to rough out the overall message before you attempt to revise it. As you write, show how each specific cause led to each specific effect, citing examples as needed. To indicate those cause/effect relationships, use transitional words like the following:

- accordingly   for this purpose   since   therefore
  as a result   for this reason   so   thus
  because   hence   such as   to illustrate
  consequently   just as   thereby   whereas

7. Revise the essay. Whether your essay presents causes, effects, or both, use the checklist below to trace and refine your argument.

___ The thesis statement and introduction clearly identify the causes and/or effects.

___ All major causes and/or effects are addressed.

___ Statements regarding causes and/or effects are sufficiently limited and focused.

___ Supporting details are researched, relevant, and strong.

___ Links between causes and effects are clear and logical.

___ The conclusion restates the argument and unifies the essay.

8. Get feedback. Ask a peer reviewer or someone from the college's writing center to read your essay for the following:

- An engaging opening
- A clear and logical thesis
- Clear reasoning linking specific causes to specific effects
- A closing that wraps up the essay, leaving no loose ends

9. Edit the essay for clarity and correctness. Check carefully for the following:

- Precise, appropriate word choice
- Complete, smooth sentences
- Clear transitions between paragraphs
- Correct names, dates, and supporting details
- Correct citation of sources
- Correct mechanics, usage, and grammar

10. Publish the essay. Share your writing with others as follows:

- Submit it to your instructor or post it on the class's website.
- Submit the essay for presentation at an appropriate conference.
- Send it as a service to relevant nonprofit agencies.
- Submit it to a professional magazine or journal.

ANALYTICAL ESSAYS

39d Checklist: Cause and Effect Essay

Use the seven traits to check the quality of your writing and revise as needed.

___ The **ideas** explain the causes and/or effects of the topic in a clear, well-reasoned argument supported with credible information.

___ The **organization** helps the reader understand the cause/effect relationship. The links between main points and supporting points are clear.

___ The **voice** is informed, polite, and professional.

___ The **words** are precise and clear. Technical or scientific terms are defined. Causes are linked to effects with transitional words and phrases such as *therefore, as a result,* and *for this reason.*

___ The **sentences** are clear, varied in structure, and smooth.

___ The final draft has **no errors** in spelling, usage, punctuation, mechanics, or grammar.

___ The **page design** is appropriate for the audience and situation; visuals are clear and relevant; white space, typeface, and fonts fit the document's purpose and situation.

WAC Link: Writers in the humanities often use cause/effect reasoning to analyze topics such as historical phenomena or artworks. However, writers in the sciences use the approach more frequently, perhaps because the scientific method of reasoning requires analysis of phenomena in terms of their causes and effects. Examples of such writing include field reports, lab reports, proposals, and position statements.

Service-Learning Link: Analyzing the causes and effects of an individual's or community's problem can be an effective strategy for solving the problem and empowering the individual or group.

Workplace Link: Writers in the workplace use cause/effect reasoning in documents as diverse as recommendations, collection letters, claim letters, fund-raising messages, incident reports, investigative reports, and project proposals. Analyzing phenomena in terms of their causes and/or effects helps writers objectively explain the nature of problems and present convincing solutions.

VISUALS TIP

To analyze or evaluate cause/effect relationships, writers often support their word pictures with visuals such as tables, graphs, line drawings, or photographs. These visuals help the writers show and prove their assertions. (For help using these visuals, see Chapter 17.)

39e   Comparison and Contrast: The Basics

Comparing and contrasting is a writing-and-thinking strategy that helps you study two or more objects together in an effort to see each one more clearly.

What is my goal?

Your goal is to write an essay that (1) sets two or more subjects side by side, (2) shows how they are similar or different, and (3) draws conclusions or makes a clear point based on what you have shown in your essay.

What are the keys to my success?

Think about your readers. What do they know about the subject? What should they know? Why should they care? Answering these questions will help you understand both your readers and your purpose for writing.

Know your purpose. Decide what you want your essay to do: Inform? Explain? Persuade? Some combination of these? Knowing your purpose will help you decide what to include in the essay and how to organize the contents.

Be logical. Comparing and contrasting is a logical process that helps you understand your subjects more fully and explain them more clearly. Begin by determining the basis of your comparison: How are the subjects related? Then decide whether to compare, to contrast, or to do both.

When comparing subjects, show how they are similar. When contrasting them, show how they are different. When comparing and contrasting subjects, show how they are similar and different. To choose which of the three patterns to follow, think about your purpose. Which pattern will help your essay do what you want it to do?

What topics should I consider?

Choose subjects that are related in some important way. To get started, think about pairs of objects, events, places, processes, people, ideas, beliefs, and so on. For inspiration, read the model in this chapter as well as "Four Ways to Talk About Literature" in 39j. Both of these essays use comparison and contrast strategies. Then list topics similar to those in the models.

What's Ahead

39f Student Essay: Comparison and Contrast
39g Guidelines: Comparison and Contrast Essay
39h Checklist: Comparison and Contrast Essay

ANALYTICAL ESSAYS

39f **Student Essay: Comparison and Contrast**

One week after the September 11, 2001, attack on the World Trade Center, when the causes and consequences were still unclear, Canadian student Anita Brinkman wrote this editorial. To make her point, she compares the attack to other significant tragedies.

A Fear Born of Sorrow

> **The writer cites statistics that introduce her topic.**

More than 100 people were killed in the tragic bombing of the Oklahoma City Federal Building in 1995. About 6,000 die in Africa each day of AIDS. Between 8,000 and 10,000 people worldwide die of starvation daily. Tragedies occur all around us, and we accept them out of necessity as a part of life. But sometimes the horror of a tragedy affects us in a new way: It overwhelms a nation and stuns the international community. This is what happened last week when two hijacked passenger planes hit the twin towers of the World Trade Center, and their resulting collapse killed thousands of people from several countries. News of the tragedy flashed around the globe. Everywhere, it seemed, people in uncomprehending horror listened to reports on their radios or watched endless replays on their televisions. Several countries declared days of mourning and scheduled services of remembrance. Now, one week after the attack, tokens of grief and letters of condolence still flood U.S. embassies and government offices worldwide. But why is the outpouring of grief so much deeper for this tragedy than for others? Why isn't the attack considered just a large-scale repeat of the Oklahoma City bombing? Could it be that our grief is more than sorrow, and that our loss is much more than what lies in the rubble?

> **She states her thesis as a question.**

> **The writer compares and contrasts the September 11 attack with the Oklahoma City bombing.**

The Oklahoma City bombing was grievous and alarming, but localized. The bomber was soon arrested, his motives deduced, and justice served. While lives were changed and a nation was shaken, the world community remained composed. However, the September 11 attack unsettled us more, in part because the World Trade Center stood for so much more than the Oklahoma City Federal Building did. The twin towers symbolized American domination of world finances: They were a major center for the Internet, a hub for international business, and an emblem of American life. The fall of the towers struck violently at the nation's psyche, and the manner in which they were destroyed—with America's own airplanes filled with passengers—has raised questions about America's

1

2

security and future. Threatened to their core, Americans have demanded retaliation—but against whom? The terrorists' identity is not clear, and evidence seems elusive. In a sense, an unknown offender has injured Americans, and they beat the air in the dark. In such a case, terrorism is aptly named, for America's outcry expresses more than sorrow—it also expresses fear.

3 The fear that Americans feel comes partly from the uncertainty related to this attack. The attackers demonstrated technical and planning skills that have surprised Americans, making them question their safety and fear future attacks. Air travel, long considered safe, now includes security measures like armed guards, luggage searches, and bomb-sniffing dogs— all strategies to achieve safety. As Americans struggle to find answers in the shattered peace, nations are forming alliances, war seems imminent, and the whole world waits anxiously to see where it all will lead.

> The word *fear* links this paragraph with the next one.

4 Fear and uncertainty are new to Americans living today because America has not been attacked in this way since Britain ruled her as a colony. While the bombing of Pearl Harbor awoke many to the fact that America could be targeted, the Japanese bombers hit Hawaii—then a U.S. territory, not a state, and not the mainland. Following World War II, many in the world community again thought of America as the invulnerable Land of Opportunity. However, this belief is now shattered, and many citizens of the global village fear that what was lost last week includes more than what lies in the rubble.

> The writer contrasts the September 11 and Pearl Harbor attacks.

> She shows how the events differ.

5 On September 11, 2001, America, along with its Western allies, lost its aura of invincibility. As the whole world watched, the towers fell, and we stumbled in shock and pain. Moreover, as time passes, America may fail to identify its enemy and to understand the attack. If this happens, the oppressed people of the world—to some extent victims of Western culture— will take notice.

6 It is now one week since the towers fell, and the world still grieves. However, mingled with this grief is the fear that we may be mourning not only for the lives lost, but also for our lost way of life.

> She restates her thesis.

ANALYTICAL ESSAYS

39g Guidelines: Comparison and Contrast Essay

1. **Select a topic.** List subjects that are similar and/or different in ways that you find interesting, perplexing, disgusting, infuriating, charming, or informing. Then choose two subjects whose comparison and/or contrast gives the reader some insight into who or what they are. For example, you could explain how two chemicals that appear to be similar are actually different—and how that difference makes one more explosive, poisonous, or edible.

2. **Get the big picture.** Using a computer or a paper and pen, create three columns as shown below. Brainstorm a list of traits under each heading. (Also see the Venn diagram in section **7d**.)

Traits of Subject 1	Shared Traits	Traits of Subject 2

3. **Gather information.** Review your list of traits, highlighting those that could provide insight into one or both subjects. Research the subjects, using hands-on analysis when possible. Consider writing your research notes in the three-column format shown above.

4. **Draft a working thesis.** Review your expanded list of traits and eliminate those that now seem unimportant. Write a sentence stating the core of what you learned about the subjects and whether you are comparing, contrasting, or both. If you're stuck, try completing the sentence below. (Reverse the terms *different* and *similar* if you wish to stress similarities.)

   While _____ and _____ seem similar, they are different in several ways, and the differences are important because _____.

5. **Get organized.** Decide how to organize your essay. Generally, subject by subject works better for short, simple comparisons. Trait by trait works better for longer, more complex comparisons.

Subject by Subject	Trait by Trait
Introduction	**Introduction**
Subject 1	**Trait A**
• Trait A	• Subject 1
• Trait B	• Subject 2
• Trait C	**Trait B**
Subject 2	• Subject 1
• Trait A	• Subject 2
• Trait B	**Trait C**
• Trait C	• Subject 1
	• Subject 2

Guidelines: Comparison and Contrast Essay

6. Draft the essay. Review your outline and then write your first draft in one sitting if possible. Check your outline for details.

Subject-by-subject pattern

Opening: Get the readers' attention and introduce the two subjects and thesis.

Middle: Describe one "package" of traits representing the first subject and a parallel set of traits representing the second subject.

Closing: Point out similarities and/or differences, note their significance, and restate your main point.

Trait-by-trait pattern

Opening: Get the readers' attention and introduce the thesis.

Middle: Compare and/or contrast the two subjects trait by trait (include transitions that help readers look back and forth between the two subjects).

Closing: Summarize the key relationships, note their significance, and restate your main point.

7. Revise the essay. Check the essay for the following:

- Balanced comparisons and contrasts of comparable traits
- Complete and thoughtful treatment of each subject
- Genuine and objective voice
- Title and introduction that spark interest
- Thoughtful, unifying conclusion

8. Get feedback. Ask a classmate or someone in the writing center to read your paper, looking for the following:

- An engaging introduction
- A clear, interesting thesis
- A middle that compares and/or contrasts significant, parallel traits
- Ideas that offer insight into the subject
- A conclusion that restates the main point and unifies the essay

9. Edit and proofread the essay. Look for the following:

- Transitions that signal comparisons and link paragraphs: *on the other hand, in contrast, similarly, also, both, even though, in the same way*
- Correct quotations, documentation, and conventions

10. Publish the essay. Share your writing with others:

- Submit it to a journal; present it at a conference.
- Share it with other students or publish it on a website.

39h Checklist: Comparison and Contrast Essay

Use the seven traits to check the quality of your writing and revise as needed.

____ The **ideas** (points made or conclusions drawn from comparing and contrasting) provide insight into who or what both subjects are and why they are important. The basis for comparison is clear.

____ The **organizational pattern** (subject by subject, trait by trait) helps the reader grasp the similarities and/or differences between subjects.

____ The **voice** is informed, polite, and genuine.

____ The **words** are precise and clear. Technical or scientific terms are defined. Links between subjects are communicated with transitions:

again	but	in contrast	on the other hand
although	either one	in the same way	similarly
as a result	for this reason	likewise	therefore
both	however	neither	unlike

____ The **sentences** are clear, well reasoned, varied in structure, and smooth.

____ The copy has **no errors** in punctuation, spelling, usage, grammar, or mechanics.

____ The **page design** follows a format (for example, essay, report) that fits the writing situation and uses appropriate design elements such as typeface, fonts, and white space. Visuals are clear, relevant, and accessible.

WAC Link: In his plays, Shakespeare often juxtaposed families (the Montagues and Capulets, for example), characters, or subplots. As a result, we see each element more clearly by comparing and contrasting it with its counterpart.

In the humanities, writers use comparison/contrast strategies not only to write plays but also to critique artwork, to analyze historical situations, or to distinguish philosophical ideas. In the sciences, writers use comparison and contrast often, particularly in field reports, case studies, and literature reviews.

Workplace Link: In the workplace, writers use comparison and contrast to do a wide range of tasks: to feature skills in a resumé, to advertise products, to propose solutions, or to recommend applicants for jobs.

VISUALS TIP

In both academics and the workplace, writers regularly support their written messages by using tables, graphs, charts, or photos to compare and/or contrast related information. The visuals can accent details expressed in words alone.

39i   Classification: The Basics

Classification is an organizational strategy that helps a writer make sense of a complex set of things by (1) breaking it into clearly distinguishable subgroups, (2) looking at subgroups individually, and/or (3) comparing and contrasting them.

What is my goal?

Your goal is to divide a group of people, places, things, or concepts into subgroups, and then to write an essay that helps readers understand each of the components, the subgroups, and the topic as a whole.

What are the keys to my success?

Choose classification criteria that fit the topic. Use classification criteria to distinguish one subgroup from another. For example, to help students understand literary criticism, Professor John Van Rys groups common approaches to criticism into four subgroups, and he distinguishes each subgroup according to its philosophical perspective. Traits of each perspective are the criteria used to distinguish subgroups (see **39j**).

Illustrate distinctions among subgroups. To help students see how literary critics' philosophical perspectives affect their assessment of literature, Van Rys shows how four subgroups of critics could interpret the same piece of literature very differently based on their particular perspectives.

Follow classification principles. Sort items into subgroups according to these principles:

- **Consistency:** Use the same criteria in the same way when deciding which individual items to place in which subgroups. For example, Van Rys classifies all critics based on their philosophical perspectives.
- **Exclusivity:** Establish distinct subgroups. For example, no common approach to criticism fits in more than one of Van Rys's subgroups.
- **Completeness:** Every component of the group must fit in a subgroup with no component left over. For example, all common approaches to literary criticism fit in one of Van Rys's four subgroups.

What topics should I consider?

For ideas, see "Select a topic" in **39k**.

What's Ahead

ANALYTICAL ESSAYS

39j Sample Essay: Classification

In this essay, college professor John Van Rys classifies four basic approaches to literary criticism.

Four Ways to Talk About Literature

The writer introduces the topic and criterion for creating four subgroups.

Have you ever been in a conversation where you suddenly felt lost—out of the loop? Perhaps you feel that way in your literature class. You may think a poem or short story means one thing, and then your instructor suddenly pulls out the "hidden meaning." Joining the conversation about literature—in class or in an essay—may indeed seem daunting, but you can do it if you know what to look for, and what to talk about. There are four main perspectives, or approaches, that you can use to converse about literature.

He describes the first subgroup and gives an example.

Text-centered approaches focus on the literary piece itself. Often called formalist criticism, such approaches claim that the structure of a work and the rules of its genre are crucial to its meaning. The formalist critic determines how various elements (plot, character, language, and so on) reinforce the meaning and unify the work. For example, the formalist may ask the following questions concerning Robert Browning's poem "My Last Duchess": How do the main elements in the poem—irony, symbolism, and verse form—help develop the main theme (deception)? How does Browning use the dramatic monologue genre in this poem?

He describes the second subgroup and gives an example.

Audience-centered approaches focus on the "transaction" between text and reader—the dynamic way the reader inter-acts with the text. Often called rhetorical or reader-response criticism, these approaches see the text not as an object to be analyzed, but as an activity that is different for each reader. A reader-response critic might ask these questions of "My Last Duchess": How does the reader become aware of the duke's true nature? Do men and women read the poem differently?

He describes the third subgroup and gives examples.

Author-centered approaches focus on the origins of a text (the writer and the historical background). For example, an author-centered study examines the writer's life—showing connections, contrasts, and conflicts between his or her life and the writing. Broader historical studies explore social and intellectual currents, showing links between an author's work and the ideas, events, and institutions of that period. Finally, the literary historian might make connections between the text in question and earlier and later literary works. The author-

1

2

3

4

centered critic might ask these questions of "My Last Duchess": What were Browning's views of marriage, men and women, art, class, and wealth? As an institution, what was marriage like in Victorian England (Browning's era) or Renaissance Italy (the duke's era)? Who was the historical Duke of Ferrara?

5   The fourth approach to criticism applies ideas outside of literature to literary works. Because literature mirrors life, argue these critics, disciplines that explore human life can help us understand literature. Some critics, for example, apply psychological theories to literary works by exploring dreams, symbolic meanings, and motivation. Myth or archetype criticism uses insights from psychology, cultural anthropology, and classical studies to explore a text's universal appeal. Moral criticism, rooted in religious studies and ethics, explores the moral dilemmas literary works raise. Marxist, feminist, and minority criticism are, broadly speaking, sociological approaches to interpretation. While the Marxist examines the themes of class struggle, economic power, and social justice in texts, the feminist critic explores the just and unjust treatment of women as well as the effect of gender on language, reading, and the literary canon. The critic interested in race and ethnic identity explores similar issues.

He describes the fourth approach and gives examples of each subgroup in it.

6   Such ideological criticism might ask a wide variety of questions about "My Last Duchess": What does the poem reveal about the duke's psychological state and his personality? How does the reference to Neptune deepen the poem? What does the poem suggest about the nature of evil and injustice? In what ways are the duke's motives class-based and economic? What is the status of women in this society?

He cites sample questions.

7   If you look at the variety of questions critics might ask about "My Last Duchess," you see both the diversity of critical approaches and the common ground between them. In fact, interpretive methods actually share important characteristics: (1) a close attention to literary elements such as character, plot, symbolism, and metaphor; (2) a desire not to distort the work; and (3) a sincere concern for increasing interest and understanding in a text. In actual practice, critics may develop a hybrid approach to criticism, one that matches their individual questions and concerns about a text. Now that you're familiar with some of the questions defining literary criticism, exercise your own curiosity (and join the ongoing literary dialogue) by discussing a text that genuinely interests you.

The closing presents qualities shared by all four approaches.

ANALYTICAL ESSAYS

39k Guidelines: Classification Essay

1. **Select a topic.** To choose a topic, start by writing a half-dozen headings like the academic headings below. Then list two or three related topics, and pick one that can best be explained by breaking it into subgroups.

Engineering	Biology	Social Work	Education
Bridges	Fruits	Adoption Services	ESL Theories
Buildings	Genes	Agency Policies	Learning Styles
Cars	Whales	Child Welfare	Testing Methods

2. **Get the big picture.** Do preliminary research to get an overview of your topic. Review your purpose (to explain, persuade, inform, and so on), and consider what classification criteria will help you divide the subject into distinct, understandable subgroups.

3. **Choose and test your criterion.** Choose a criterion for creating subgroups. Make sure it produces subgroups that are *consistent* (all members fit the criterion), *exclusive* (subgroups are distinct—no member of the group fits into more than one subgroup), and *complete* (each member fits into a subgroup with no member left over).

VISUALS TIP

To better visualize how you are dividing your topic and classifying its members, take a few minutes to fill out a graphic organizer like the one shown below. (Also see the graphic organizer in section **7d**.)

4. **Gather and organize information.** Gather information from a wide variety of sources, including interviews. To take notes and organize your information, consider using a grid like the one below. List the classification criteria down the left column and list the subgroups in the top row of the columns. Then fill in the grid with appropriate traits or details.

	Subgroup 1	Subgroup 2	Subgroup 3	Subgroup 4
Classification Criteria	*Text-centered approach*	*Audience-centered approach*	*Author-centered approach*	*Ideas outside literature*
Focus of the critical approach	• Trait 1 • Trait 2 • Trait 3	• Trait 1 • Trait 2 • Trait 3	• Trait 1 • Trait 2 • Trait 3	• Trait 1 • Trait 2 • Trait 3

5. **Draft a thesis.** Draft a working thesis that states your topic and main point and introduces your criteria for classifying the subgroups.

6. Draft the essay. Write your first draft, using either the organizational pattern in the classification grid or an outline.

Opening: Get the readers' attention, introduce the subject and thesis, and give your criteria for dividing the subject into subgroups.

Middle: Develop the thesis by discussing each subgroup, explaining its traits, and showing how it is distinct from the other subgroups. For example, in the model at **39j** the writer first shows the unique focus of each of the four approaches to literary criticism, and then illustrates each approach by applying it to the same poem.

Closing: While the opening and middle of the essay separate the subjects into components and subgroups, the closing brings the components and subgroups back together. For example, in "Four Ways to Talk About Literature," the writer closes by identifying three characteristics that the four subgroups share. (See **39j.**)

7. Get feedback. Ask a classmate or someone from the writing center to read your essay looking for the following:

- An engaging opening that introduces the subject, thesis, and criteria for classifying
- A well-organized middle that distinguishes subgroups, shows why each subgroup is unique, and includes adequate details
- A clear closing that reaches some sort of conclusion

8. Revise the essay. Check the essay for the following:

- Subgroups that are consistent, exclusive, and complete
- Appropriate examples that clarify the nature and function of each subgroup
- A unifying conclusion

9. Edit and proofread the essay. Check for the following:

- An informed, reader-friendly voice
- Clear, complete sentences
- Unified paragraphs linked with appropriate transitions
- Formatting is appropriate for the purpose, audience, and situation. Check that each visual (table, graph, map) is clearly introduced and integrated into the text.

10. Publish the essay. Share your writing by doing the following:

- Place a copy in your professional portfolio.
- Submit the piece to a news organization as an editorial or a report.

ANALYTICAL ESSAYS

39I Checklist: Classification Essay

Use the seven traits to check the quality of your writing and revise as needed.

____ The **ideas** in the classification criteria are logical and clear. The criteria result in subgroups that are consistent, exclusive, and complete.

____ The **organization** of the essay helps the reader understand the components, the subgroups, and the subject as a whole.

____ The **voice** is informed, courteous, and professional.

____ The **words** are precise, descriptive, and appropriate for the subject. Terms used to classify components are used in the same way throughout the essay.

____ The **sentences** are complete, varied, and easy to read. Appropriate transitions link sentences and paragraphs.

____ The final draft includes **no errors** in spelling, punctuation, mechanics, or grammar.

____ The **page design** is balanced, attractive, and readable. The typeface, fonts, white space, and graphics fit the document's contents and the writing situation.

LINKS

WAC Link: In the humanities, writers often use classification to distinguish concepts such as philosophical or theological perspectives, national or historical worldviews, types of plays or music, architectural styles, types of languages, or distinctions in ethnicity.

Service-Learning Link: Helping individuals or members of a community classify their strengths and weaknesses can enhance their understanding of and control over issues.

Workplace Link: Writers in the workplace regularly use classification. For example, in instructions, writers distinguish these groups: tools, materials, and steps needed to complete the task. In proposals, writers commonly distinguish these groups: steps taken to assess a problem, steps in the solution that will address the problem, and steps needed to implement the plan. In trip reports, writers might create these groups: actions taken to analyze a problem, actions taken to resolve the problem, and follow-up actions required to avert future problems.

VISUALS TIP

Visuals such as tables and graphs help writers sort and display large amounts of data into clearly distinguishable subgroups. Use these visuals to support or clarify points that are not easily communicated in words; avoid visuals that merely repeat clearly stated points.

39m Process: The Basics

Process writing answers *how* questions like "How does cancer spread?", "How does blood clot?", or "How do you load digital photos on a computer?"

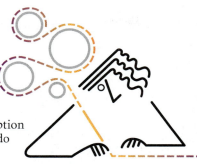

What is my goal?

Your goal is to analyze a process, break it into specific stages or steps, and write about it using one of these forms: a description of a process, or instructions on how to do the process.

What are the keys to my success?

Think logically. To write either form, you must study the process, understand it, and write clearly about it. In other words, you must know and show how each step leads logically to the next, and how all the steps together make up the whole process.

Know your purpose and audience. Decide what your writing should do and choose the form that best fits your purpose and audience:

- To inform a broad audience how something happens, describe the process in an essay that tells how the process unfolds (see **39n**).
- To help readers who wish to do the process themselves, provide how-to information in the form of clear instructions (see **39o** and **39p**).

Consider all of your readers. Regardless of the form that you choose, make your writing accessible to all of your readers by addressing the reader who knows the least about your topic. Include all the information that this person needs, and use language that everyone can understand.

What topics should I consider?

- Course-related process
  Process that keeps you healthy
  Process for success in college

  Process in the news
  Process that helps you get a job
  Process that helps you keep a job

What's Ahead

ANALYTICAL ESSAYS

39n **Student Essay: Describing a Process**

Student writer Kerry Mertz writes this essay (a description of a process) to show how cancer cells multiply and affect the body.

Wayward Cells

> The writer uses the title and an analogy to introduce the topic.

Imagine a room containing a large group of people, all working hard toward the same goal. Each person knows his or her job, does it carefully, and cooperates with other group members. Together, they function efficiently and smoothly—like a well-oiled machine.

Then something goes wrong. One guy suddenly drops his task, steps into another person's workstation, grabs the material that she's working with, and begins something very different—he uses the material to make little reproductions of himself, thousands of them. These look-alikes imitate him—grabbing material and making reproductions of themselves. Soon the bunch gets so big that they spill into other people's workstations, getting in their way, and interrupting their work. As the number of look-alikes grows, the work group's activity slows, stutters, and finally stops.

> She uses a simile to explain the analogy.

A human body is like this room, and the body's cells are like these workers. If the body is healthy, each cell has a necessary job and does it correctly. For example, right now red blood cells are running throughout your body carrying oxygen to each body part. Other cells are digesting your lunch, and others are patching up that cut on your left hand. Each cell knows what to do because its genetic code—or DNA—tells it what to do. When a cell begins to function abnormally, it can initiate a process that results in cancer.

> She describes the first step in the process and cites a potential cause.

The problem starts when one cell "forgets" what it should do. Scientists call this "undifferentiating"—meaning that the cell loses its identity within the body (Pierce 75). Just like the guy in the group who decided to do his own thing, the cell forgets its job. Why this happens is somewhat unclear. The problem could be caused by a defect in the cell's DNA code or by something in the environment, such as cigarette smoke or asbestos (German 21). Causes from inside the body are called genetic, whereas causes from outside the body are called carcinogens, meaning "any substance that causes cancer" (Neufeldt and Sparks 90). In either case, an undifferentiated cell can disrupt the function of healthy cells in two ways: by not doing its job as specified in its DNA and by not reproducing at the rate noted in its DNA.

1

2

3

4

5   Most healthy cells reproduce rather quickly, but their reproduction rate is controlled. For example, your blood cells completely die off and replace themselves within a matter of weeks, but existing cells make only as many new cells as the body needs. The DNA codes in healthy cells tell them how many new cells to produce. However, cancer cells don't have this control, so they reproduce quickly with no stopping point, a characteristic called "autonomy" (Braun 3). What's more, all their "offspring" have the same qualities, and the resulting overpopulation produces growths called tumors.

> She describes the next step and its result.

6   Tumor cells can hurt the body in a number of ways. First, a tumor can grow so big that it takes up space needed by other organs. Second, some cells may detach from the original tumor and spread throughout the body, creating new tumors elsewhere. This happens with lymphatic cancer—a cancer that's hard to control because it spreads so quickly. A third way that tumor cells can hurt the body is by doing work not called for in their DNA. For example, a gland cell's DNA code may tell the cell to produce a necessary hormone in the endocrine system. However, if cancer damages or distorts that code, sick cells might produce more of the hormone than the body can use—or even tolerate (Braun 4).

> She describes the third step—how tumors damage the body.

7   Fortunately, there is hope. Scientific research is already helping doctors do amazing things for people suffering with cancer. One treatment that has been used for some time is chemotherapy, or the use of chemicals to kill off all fast-growing cells, including cancer cells. Another common treatment is radiation, or the use of light rays to kill cancer cells. One of the newest and most promising treatments is gene therapy—an effort to identify and treat chromosomes that carry a "wrong code" in their DNA. A treatment like gene therapy is promising because it treats the cause of cancer, not just the effect. Year by year, research is helping doctors better understand what cancer is and how to treat it.

> A transition signals a shift in focus from the illness to the treatments.

8   Much of life involves dealing with problems like wayward workers, broken machines, or dysfunctional organizations. Dealing with wayward cells is just another problem. While the problem is painful and deadly, there is hope. Medical specialists and other scientists are making progress, and someday they will help us win our battle against wayward cells.

NOTE: The Works Cited page is not shown. For sample pages, see MLA (51e), APA (54c), CSE (58b), and CMS (57b).

390 **Instructions Containing Photographs**

**Downloading Photographs
from the MC-150 Digital Camera**

Note: MC-150 software must be loaded on your computer to download photographs from the camera.

1. Turn your computer on.

2. Plug the camera's USB cable into your computer.

3. Turn the camera's mode dial to the **data transfer setting** (Figure 1).

Figure 1: Data Transfer Setting

4. Open the camera's flashcard door and plug the other end of the USB cable into the **camera port** (Figure 2).

5. Select USB transfer from the camera screen menu. The MC-150 software will then launch onto your computer.

Figure 2: Camera Port

6. Follow the instructions on the computer screen to download all of your photos or specific photos.

7. When your download is complete, turn the camera off and unplug the USB cable from the camera and the computer.

Note: If the MC-150 software doesn't launch, disconnect the camera (step 7), restart the computer, and continue on from step 2.

39p   Instructions with Drawings

**Instructions for Replacing
Auger Bearing on Bale-Press 64-D**

Use the instructions below to replace the right, rear auger bearing on the Bale-Press 64-D.

Parts Needed

Item No.	Qty.	Part No.	Description
1	1	RRAB20024	right, rear auger bearing
2	1	RRASP20007	right, rear auger-support post
3	2	BLT5/8X3.5HX	5/8" × 3 1/2" hex bolt
4	2	NUT5/8HX	5/8" hex nut
5	2	CP1/8X2	1/8" × 2" cotter pin

WARNING: SHUT OFF ENGINE AND REMOVE KEY!

Steps

1. Take out the existing bearing by removing the two 1/8" cotter pins, two 5/8" hex nuts, and two 5/8" hex bolts. (See Figure 1.)

2. Insert the new bearing (item 1) into the 4 3/8" hole on the post (item 2).

3. Fasten the bearing to the post with two 5/8" hex bolts (item 3), two 5/8" hex nuts (item 4), and two 1/8" cotter pins (item 5).

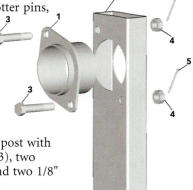

Figure 1

Note: For ease of installation, insert both bolts before tightening the nuts.

Caution: For safer installation, fasten the replacement bearing with the new bolts, nuts, and cotter pins included with the replacement kit.

Opening

Identify topic. List the parts needed in a table format. If helpful, add illustrations.

Middle

Indicate danger with a **WARNING** message in capital letters and in boldface print.

Give steps in chronological order.

Use the same terms in the steps as were used in the parts list.

Place the illustration next to the steps.

Closing

Use **Cautions** (boldface without capital letters) to warn of damage.

ANALYTICAL ESSAYS

39q Guidelines: Process Essay

1. **Select a topic.** Choose a topic from the list "What topics should I consider?" in **39m**. If you're stuck, review your notes and textbooks to generate more course-related topics.

2. **Review the process.** Use your present knowledge of the topic to fill out an organizer like the one on the right. List the subject at the top, each of the steps in chronological order, and the outcome at the bottom. Review the organizer to identify issues that you need to research.

> **Process Analysis**
> **Subject**:
> • Step 1
> • Step 2
> • Step 3
> **Outcome:**

3. **Research as needed.** Find information that spells out the process: what it is, what steps are required, what order the steps should follow, how to do the steps, what outcome the process should produce, and what safety precautions are needed. If possible, observe the process in action or perform it yourself. Carefully record correct names, materials, tools, and safety or legal issues.

4. **Get organized.** After conducting your research, revise the organizer by adding or reordering steps as needed. Then develop an outline, including steps listed in the organizer as well as supporting details from your research.

5. **Draft the document.** Write the essay or instructions using the guidelines below.

Describing a Process	Writing Instructions
Opening: Introduce the topic, stating its importance and giving an overview of the steps. **Middle:** Describe each step clearly (usually in separate paragraphs), and link steps with transitions such as *first, second, next, finally,* and *while.* Describe the outcome and its importance. **Closing:** Describe the process as a whole and restate key points.	**Opening:** Name the process in the title; then summarize the process and list any materials and tools needed. **Middle:** Present each step in a separate—usually one- or two-sentence— paragraph. Number the steps and state each clearly, using commands directed to the reader. **Closing:** In a short paragraph, explain any follow-up action.

Guidelines: Process Essay

6. Revise the writing. Check for the following and revise as needed:

- A clear opening that identifies the process
- Steps that are stated clearly and in the correct order
- ***For instructions:***
  - Clear details explaining how to perform each step
  - A closing that includes necessary follow-up activity
  - Correct safety cautions including signal words like **DANGER, WARNING,** and **Caution.**

7. Test the writing. Read the writing for organization and completeness. For explanations and instructions, perform the process yourself using the writing as a guide. For each step, do only what you are told to do and how you are told to do it. Note where the writing is incomplete, out of order, or lacking adequate safety precautions. Revise as needed.

8. Get feedback. Ask a classmate who is unfamiliar with the process to read the writing for clarity, completeness, and correctness. For instructions, have the person use the writing as a guide to perform the process, noting where details are incomplete or unclear, and noting where word choice is either imprecise or too technical. Use the feedback to guide further revision.

9. Edit the writing by looking for the following:

- Word choice appropriate for your least-informed reader
- Clear transitions between steps
- Consistent verb tense in all steps
- For instructions—verbs that give clear commands
- Correct, consistent terminology
- Informed, respectful voice
- Proper format and adequate white space

10. Publish the writing.

- Offer it to instructors or students working with the process.
- Offer to write explanations and instructions for people on campus or at nonprofit agencies who can use the writing to do their work.
- Post the writing on a suitable website.

WRITER'S TIP

When writing your instructions, present all safety-related details (including signal words and symbols) in strict accordance with guidelines set by professional organizations such as the American National Standards Institute (ANSI).

ANALYTICAL ESSAYS

39r Checklist: Process Essay

Use the seven traits to check the quality of your writing and revise as needed.

___ The **ideas** describe or explain the process clearly and completely.

___ The **organization** helps clarify the process. In instructions, the organization is chronological and helps the reader work through the process.

___ The **voice** matches the writer's purpose. Cautions regarding safety or legal issues sound serious, but are not alarming.

___ The **words** are precise and technical terms are defined.

___ The **sentences** are smooth, varied in structure, and engaging. In instructions, sentences are shaped as clear, brief, no-nonsense commands.

___ The final draft includes **no errors** in mechanics, usage, or grammar.

___ The **page design** is formatted properly as an essay or as instructions. Visuals are used effectively to help readers identify items and picture the process.

LINKS

WAC Link: Writers in all three curricular divisions write essays to explain processes. For example, a person in music or theater might explain the collaborative writing process used by Richard Rodgers and Oscar Hammerstein. A biologist might explain how a plant transmits nutrients from the soil to the leaves. A sociologist might explain how a business can develop a supportive work climate for its employees.

People in the sciences also write instructions, particularly when they must explain how to use a piece of equipment, conduct an experiment, or complete a procedure.

Workplace Link: In the workplace, people write formal procedures and instructions—both to help employees do their jobs and to help customers use the products or services that an organization produces.

VISUALS TIP

Process writing, in both essays and instructions, regularly includes drawings and photos to help readers understand a process or to successfully and safely complete a task. When writing instructions for tasks that could cause property damage or personal injury, include signal words (like **DANGER, WARNING,** or **Caution**), along with the correct signs and symbols. For guidelines, check with professional organizations such as the American National Standards Institute (ANSI) or the International Organization for Standardization (ISO).

CHAPTER 40

Persuasive Essays

In a **persuasive essay,** you present a point of view and support it in an effort to have the reader agree with you. This chapter explains two types of persuasive writing: arguing a point and proposing a solution.

40a Arguing a Point: The Basics

What do you imagine when you hear the word *argument*—an unfriendly squabble, a family feud, or a heated shouting match? Too often, the word *argument* has these negative connotations.

In college, written arguments are meant to be positive and productive. They are opportunities to debate controversial issues, to reach logical conclusions, and perhaps even to achieve agreement. Sometimes, however, you must focus on disagreement. That is the purpose of an essay that argues against a point. You take issue with a currently held view and make your case against the position. In the end, you may argue for an alternative or a compromise.

What is my goal?

Your goal is to build a strong argument based on logical reasoning and reliable evidence versus mere opinion or clichéd thought.

What are the keys to my success?

Understand the elements of persuasion. These elements include a claim about an issue, a persuader and an audience, a clear message with strong appeals, and an outcome. (See **4a** for details.)

Shape an engaging argument. Use appropriate appeals such as appeals to reason, character, or emotion. (See **4b–4d** for details.)

Build a logical argument. Develop and refine your claim, supporting it with solid reasoning. (See **4e–4h** for details.)

Practice clear, ethical thinking. Avoid fuzzy or dishonest thinking based on logical fallacies. (See **4i** for details.)

What's Ahead

40b Student Essay: Arguing a Point
40c Guidelines: Arguing a Point
40d Checklist: Arguing a Point

PERSUASIVE ESSAYS

40b Student Essay: Arguing a Point

In the essay below, student writer Allison Young describes America's spending practices, arguing that they are "ultimately superficial."

If We Are What We Wear, What Are We?

The writer starts with a personal story with which readers may identify.

I've always loved new clothes. When I was younger, I loved going to the mall each fall to buy school clothes: new shirts and jeans and shoes. Now I have a job and buy my own clothing; when I want something new, I go shopping with friends to find those clearance jeans or funky shoes.

In fact, most of us have closets full of clothes: jeans, sweaters, khakis, T-shirts, and shoes for every occasion. We love having a variety of clothes that look good on us and express our personalities. To keep up with the trends, we buy and buy—usually long before our old clothes wear out.

The problem is introduced and explored with thoughtful quotes and questions.

In his article "Trapped in the Cult of the Next Thing," Mark Buchanan argues that our urge to consume the latest and best traps us in this mind set: "Crave and spend, for the Kingdom of Stuff is here." As a result, we're driven to possess as much new, fashionable stuff as possible—including clothing. It's part of the American dream, this feeling that we need to have more and more. But what does this craving really cost?

Statistics help the writer make a comparison/contrast point.

To have more, we need to spend more. According to the U.S. Census Bureau, in 1995 Americans spent more than $323 billion on clothing and accessories. That same source lists the 1995 gross national product (GNP) of sixty-six countries: fifty-four of those countries had a GNP of less than $323 billion, and thirty-two had a GNP of less than $100 billion.

I have contributed my share to that $323 billion. In my closet I have twelve T-shirts, twenty-three short-sleeved shirts, and twenty-six long-sleeved shirts. I have six pairs of jeans (only four of which I wear), two pairs of khakis, five pairs of shorts, three pairs of pajama pants, and a pair of tear-away pants. I have twelve pairs of shoes, nine skirts, and four dresses. And I know I'm not the only "poor college kid" to have a ton of clothing. I have so much—and I like having so much.

The writer digs deeper into opposing perspectives.

The American excuse for owning multiples is that clothing styles change so rapidly. At the end of the 1980s, trends in high fashion changed every two and one-half months (Durning 95). Even for those of us who don't keep up with high fashion, styles change often enough that our clothing itself lasts much longer than the current trend. Perhaps this is one of the reasons the average American spent $997 on clothing in 1996 (U.S. Department of Commerce).

1

2

3

4

5

6

7   While Americans are spending $1,000 or more a year on clothing, people in Ethiopia make an average of only $96 a year, those in Bangladesh make $280, and the average Filipino worker makes $1,052 annually (United Nations Statistics Division). I, on the other hand, made more than $5,000 last year, and that job was only part-time. When an American college student can earn more money at her part-time job than three billion people each make for a living, it's time to question our culture and ask, as Alan Durning did, "How much is enough?"

8   "Enough is never enough," claims Dolores Curran in "There Is a Lot to Be Said for Less." Soon, she adds, we become "possessed by our possessions." But what does our passion for having more of "the latest" reveal about our culture? Are we so accustomed to this way of life, to having closets full of fashionable clothes, that we don't see the flaws in our lifestyle? And even if we become aware of the problems, how should we respond?

9   One solution is to take G. K. Chesterton's advice: "There are two ways to get enough. One is to accumulate more. The other is to need less" (qtd. in Buchanan). But too often Americans accumulate more to please—or to impress—those around them. As Dolores Curran explains, "What we once considered luxuries we come to regard as necessities, and eventually we become dependent upon the things we acquire." Instead of choosing a generic-brand sweater, we pay three times more for a Tommy Hilfiger label because we think that we are what we wear.

10   If that's true, then what are we? If our identity is so intertwined with what we wear, then what do our appetites for clothing make us? A name-brand label? A trend? A style decided by others? If so, are we saying that we're willing to be what others want us to be? Have we become imitation human beings, superficial replicas of other people?

11   Clothing, varied and fun though it can be, is ultimately superficial. What if we dared to reach for more? What if we chose to define ourselves not by what we have, but by what we do? To do more, whether in our own communities or throughout the world, we would have to share more. One way to share our resources is to need less, buy less for ourselves, and give more to others. We can use our resources to help needy people, not only in America, but in other countries as well.

The writer cites data that support her argument.

Possible responses and changes are introduced and explored.

In closing, the writer presses readers to change their thinking and behavior.

NOTE: The Works Cited page is not shown. For sample pages, see MLA (51e), APA (54c), CSE (58b), and CMS (57b).

PERSUASIVE ESSAYS

40c Guidelines: Arguing a Point

1. **Select a topic.** Choose a clearly debatable topic—a topic about which thoughtful people can disagree. Avoid "straw man" arguments that anyone can knock down.

 - **Current affairs:** Explore recent trends and controversies in the news, professional journals, and online discussion groups.
 - **Burning issues:** What issues related to work, education, or politics do you care about enough to confront? Choose one and then dig into it for a compelling angle and convincing details.
 - **Dividing lines:** What dividing lines characterize communities to which you belong? In other words, what issues can set people against one another? Religion, gender, money, class? Consider one of these.
 - **Fresh fare:** Choose a topic that interests you and your readers. Avoid tired issues, such as abortion or capital punishment, unless you can address them with a fresh perspective.

2. **Take stock.** Before you dig into your topic, assess your starting point.

 - What is your current position on the topic? Why? What evidence do you have?
 - What does your audience know about the topic? What positions could they take? Why?

3. **Get inside the issue.** Study the issue carefully using the following strategies to measure and develop what you know:

 - Investigate all possible positions on the issue. Through brainstorming and research, think through all arguments.

 > **NOTE:** With some topics, doing firsthand research will help you speak with authority and passion.

 - Write your main argument at the top of a page. Below it, set up "Pro" and "Con" columns and list arguments in each column.
 - Develop a line of reasoning supporting your position. Then test that reasoning for two things:
 First, no logical fallacies, such as broad generalization, either-or thinking, oversimplification (See **4i.**)
 Second, an effective range of support: statistics, observations, expert testimony, comparisons, and analysis (See **4f.**)

4. **Refine your position.** Before you organize and draft your essay, clarify your position. If it helps, use this formula:

 I believe this to be true about _____ :

 _____ .

5. Organize your development and support. Before drafting, review these organizational options:

- **Traditional pattern:** Introduce the issue, state your position, support it, refute the opposition, and restate your position.
- **Delayed gratification:** In the first part of your essay, explore the various positions available on the topic; compare and contrast them, and then defend your position.
- **Changed mind:** If your research changed your mind on the topic, consider building that shift into the essay itself.
- **Winning over:** If your readers may strongly oppose your position, then focus on that opposition. Defend your position by anticipating and answering each question or concern they may have.

6. Write the first draft. If you find it helpful, set aside your notes and get your argument and support down on paper. If you prefer, you can work closely from your outline. Here are some possible strategies:

Opening: Raise readers' concern for the issue with a dramatic story, a pointed example, a thought-provoking question, or a personal confession. Supply background information to help readers understand the issue.

Development: Deepen, clarify, and support your argument, using solid logic and reliable support. A clear, well-reasoned defense will help readers accept your position.

Closing: End on a lively, thoughtful note that stresses your commitment to the issue. If appropriate, ask readers to adopt your position.

7. Share your position. Get feedback on your position from a peer or a tutor in the writing center.

8. Revise the writing. Consider your reviewer's comments. Cut, change, and add material with the following questions in mind:

- Is the argument stated clearly? Is it effectively qualified?
- Have you shown how your stand affects yourself and others?
- Are the reasoning and support sound and complete?
- Does the essay show awareness of concerns and other positions?
- Do the ideas flow smoothly?
- Is the tone confident and sincere, not bullying or apologetic?

9. Edit and proofread. See 10a–10c for guidelines, but check for slogans, clichés, platitudes, insults, and jargon. Make needed changes.

10. Prepare and publish the final essay. In addition to submitting your paper to your instructor, share it with friends or online readers.

PERSUASIVE ESSAYS

40d Checklist: Arguing a Point

Use the seven traits to check the quality of your writing and revise as needed.

____ The **ideas** establish and defend a stand on a debatable issue. The essay provides sound reasoning and support that help the reader understand and appreciate the position.

____ The **organization** includes an engaging opening that raises the issue, a carefully sequenced argument, and a reflective closing.

____ The **voice** is thoughtful, measured, committed, convincing, and knowledgeable. The feelings addressed are appropriately strong.

____ The **words** are precise, concrete, lively, and polite. Jargon, clichés, platitudes, and demeaning language are avoided.

____ The **sentences** flow smoothly and their lengths are varied. Short sentences make snappy points, while longer sentences convey more complex thoughts.

____ The final draft includes **no errors** in spelling, punctuation, documentation, or grammar.

____ The page **design** is properly formatted as an essay. Typeface, fonts, white space, and other design elements focus attention on the argument and make reading easy.

WAC Link: Scholars in any discipline find countless issues worthy of debate. As a result, position papers are written across the curriculum. In fact, taking logical, well-researched positions on relevant topics must be part of academic life if colleges are to be places where students and faculty think carefully for the benefit of their communities and the world.

Service-Learning Link: Helping individuals state their needs in convincing letters or proposals can build their self-confidence and achieve change.

Workplace Link: While people in the workplace rarely write formal essays to argue a point, they do take stands on difficult issues nearly every day. Claims letters, collection letters, recommendations, policies, proposals, and incident reports are just a few examples of such writing.

VISUALS TIP

Visuals should be included whenever they can strengthen a document's argument. For example, tables, graphs, or drawings that present complex data quickly and objectively are always appropriate.

40e Proposing a Solution: The Basics

A proposal is a remedy in writing, a clear prescription for change. A strong proposal helps readers understand a problem and embrace the solution.

What is my goal?

Your goal is to convince readers to accept and contribute to a positive change. To accomplish this goal, you need to describe a problem, thoroughly analyze its causes and effects, and show that the solution you are proposing is both feasible and desirable.

What are the keys to my success?

Show passion for change. Proposal writing requires (1) a willingness to challenge the status quo and (2) a mind that is open to creative possibilities. Dare to ask, "What is really wrong here, and how can we fix it?"

Avoid Band-Aid solutions. Base your solution on a clear understanding of the problem and a bold analysis of possible solutions. Choose the best solution by weighing each option carefully. Consider especially how each solution attacks root causes, creates real benefits, and proves workable.

Know your readers. Who can bring about the change that you envision? What are their allegiances and alliances? How can you speak convincingly to them, build a spirit of teamwork, and persuade them to change?

Conduct quality research. Your proposal will stand or fall on the quality of your reasoning and its support. (See "Developing Your Line of Reasoning," **4f**.)

What problems should I consider?

College problems: List the top ten problems faced by college students, plus the top ten problems addressed by experts in your major.

Social problems: What problems does your community, state, or country face? Where do you see suffering, injustice, waste, or harm?

Workplace problems: What key on-the-job problems will you have to solve during your career?

What's Ahead

PERSUASIVE ESSAYS

40f   Student Essay: Proposing a Solution

In this essay, student writer Brian Ley defines agroterrorism, predicts that it could become a serious problem, and proposes a solution.

Preparing for Agroterror

The writer opens by illustrating the problem.

An Al Qaeda terrorist in Africa obtains a sample of fluid from a cow infected with foot-and-mouth disease, and he sends the fluid to an accomplice in a small, rural American town. This terrorist takes the sample and rides around the country, stopping at several points to place small amounts of the fluid on objects that animals are likely to touch. When he is finished, he calmly drives to the nearest airport and leaves the country unnoticed.

1

Cows, pigs, and sheep then come into contact with this highly contagious disease. Over the next few days, farmers see blisters on the feet and mouths of their animals. Thinking that the animals have a bacterial infection, the farmers administer antibiotics and wait for improvement. However, because antibiotics cannot kill a virus, the animals get sicker. Meanwhile, the virus is spreading by means of wind and the movement of animals and humans. Within a few weeks, the virus rages out of control.

2

While the story above is hypothetical, it is also very possible. People used to think of terrorists as men in ski masks blowing up embassies and taking hostages. But after the events of September 11, 2001, and the subsequent anthrax scares, we realize that more kinds of terrorism are possible.

3

He defines the problem and presents expert testimony.

One type that we rarely consider is agroterrorism, which involves using diseases as weapons to attack a country's agriculture industry as a way to attack the country itself. The agroterrorist's weapons of choice are those diseases that affect plants, animals, and even humans. Professor Peter Chalk of the RAND Corporation, an expert on transnational terrorism, believes that agroterrorism should be a huge concern for Americans because it has many advantages from a terrorist's point of view.

4

He analyzes why the problem could become serious.

First, an attack on the agricultural sector of the United States would be quite easy. The diseases needed to kill large populations of animals can be obtained with little difficulty; the most devastating ones are ready for use in their natural form. These samples pose little risk to the terrorist because many of the diseases are harmless to humans.

5

In addition, doing agroterrorism is less risky in terms of getting caught and getting punished. Agroterrorism is hard

6

to trace, especially because Americans have assumed that all animal epidemics are natural in origin and that American livestock contract such diseases only by accident. Consequences for those caught inflicting a disease on animals are also less severe than for terrorists who harm humans. In fact, because agroterrorism first affects the health of plants and animals rather than humans, terrorists using this strategy can even escape some guilt for their actions.

7   However, while agroterrorist diseases would have little direct effect on people's health, they would be devastating to the agricultural economy, in part because of the many different diseases that could be used in an attack. One of the most devastating is foot-and-mouth disease. This illness hurts all infected animals by impeding their weight gain, and it hurts dairy cows by decreasing their milk production. Because the disease is highly contagious, all infected animals, along with any cloven-hoofed animals within about fifty miles of the infection site, must be killed.

8   While foot-and-mouth disease is not dangerous to humans, other animal diseases are. One of these is bovine spongiform encephalopathy, better known as mad-cow disease. This illness is not easily spread, but a few cases in the United States would send people into a panic. Meat consumption would drop sharply, and the agricultural economy would be deeply shaken.

9   Another disease that could be used as a weapon is West Nile encephalitis. This virus can be spread by insects and can even cross species, affecting horses, birds, pigs, and humans. In many cases, the illness is fatal. These diseases plus more could be used in an attack.

10   The agricultural community is particularly susceptible to a terrorist attack. Unlike "typical" terrorist targets in metropolitan areas, farms do not have sophisticated security systems to protect against intruders. The average farmer's security system includes a mean dog and a shotgun: the dog for humans and the gun for animal pests. If terrorists wanted to infect a dairy, swine operation, or even a large-scale cattle-finishing operation, they would encounter few obstacles. To start an epidemic, the terrorists merely have to place a piece of infected food in an area with livestock.

11   Agroterrorism is a threat that demands our response. Several actions can be taken to discourage terrorism as well as to deal with its consequences. One of the first steps is convincing all citizens—farmers and nonfarmers alike—that agroterrorism could happen, and that it could cause horrific consequences. Farmers must realize that they are susceptible to

> Using specific details, he outlines the problem's potential effects.

> The writer proposes a multifaceted solution.

PERSUASIVE ESSAYS

an attack even though they may live far from large metropolitan areas. Nonfarmers must realize how an attack could affect them. If nonfarmers know that an attack could create panic, drive up food prices, and possibly eliminate food sources, they will look out for suspicious activity and report it.

> The writer builds paragraphs by using topic sentences, examples, and other supporting details.

Preventive action on farms is needed to ensure the safety 12 of our food supply. For example, the South Dakota Animal Industry Board recently published a newsletter outlining several precautions that farmers can take. Farms should have better security, especially in areas where animals are kept. These security measures include allowing only authorized persons to have access to farm buildings and animals, and keeping all key farm buildings locked.

Farmers also need training to detect the diseases that 13 terrorists might use, and to know what actions can contain and decontaminate an infected area. For example, if a farmer discovers that cows have blisters on their tongues and noses and are behaving abnormally, the owner should immediately call a veterinarian to assess the situation. Because the cause might be foot-and-mouth disease, no cattle should leave the farm until a diagnosis has been made.

In addition, public authorities need a plan for responding 14 to an identified agroterrorism attack. For example, thousands of animals may have to be killed and disposed of—an action that raises significant environmental concerns. Moreover, public money should be used for continued research of the diseases that may be spread by agroterrorists. Vaccines and treatments may be produced that would stop diseases or limit them from becoming epidemic.

> The closing stresses the problem's seriousness and calls for action.

Agroterrorism has not yet been used on a large scale 15 anywhere on the globe. However, its use seems inevitable. The United States is a prime target for terrorism of this sort because we have the largest, most efficiently raised food supply in the world. Destroying part of this supply would affect not only our own country but also all those countries with which we trade. Because we are prime targets, we must act now to develop our defenses against agroterrorism. If we wait until an attack happens, people may become ill, our overall economy could be damaged, and our agricultural economy might never recover.

NOTE: The Works Cited page is not shown. For sample pages, see MLA (**51e**), APA (**54c**), CSE (**58b**), and CMS (**57b**).

40g Operational Improvement Proposal

An operational improvement proposal is a workplace document written to persuade readers to improve workplace practices or conditions. In the piece below, the writer proposes scheduling communication workshops.

Date: January 6, 2006

To: Maria Estavez
           Training Supervisor

From: Jamie Tobias
           Director of Marketing

Subject: Concept Proposal for Speaking/Listening Training

Maria, I'm writing to propose a workshop for our sales and marketing staff that could sharpen their skills in speaking and listening to clients.

The Need: Connecting with and Keeping Clients

Clients must feel that their needs are being heard and acted upon. Through recent client feedback, I've learned about some problems, including our staff's poor responses to questions and complaints. This behavior hurts our relationships with customers and strains relationships between staff.

Possible Solutions: Training in Speaking and Listening

I suggest that we hire a trainer who can lead communication workshops with our sales and marketing staff. This training would address issues such as communicating with respect, interviewing clients to discover their needs, observing telephone etiquette, and making persuasive presentations. If well done, the training will help staff (1) present our products more effectively, (2) strengthen our relationships with clients, and (3) improve internal communication.

One possible trainer is Verne Meyer, co-author of *Write for Business*. I know that he has done successful communication workshops at two other companies in our community.

Please let me know when you're able to discuss this matter.

Opening
State the subject positively.

Middle
Explain the problem objectively, stressing its impact on the reader and/or company.
Offer your solution, focusing on its benefits.

Closing
State the next step, offer help, and/or invite feedback.

PERSUASIVE ESSAYS

40h Guidelines: Proposing a Solution

1. **Select and narrow a topic.** Choose a problem from "What problems should I consider?" in **40e**, or search for one in periodicals, on news programs, or on the Internet. Then test your topic:
   - Is the problem real, serious, and fairly complex?
   - Do you care about this problem and believe it must be solved?
   - Can you offer a workable solution? Should you narrow the focus to part of the problem or a local angle?

2. **Identify and analyze your readers.** Potentially, you could have three audiences: decision makers with the power to deliver change, people affected by the problem, and a public that needs to learn about the problem. Once you've determined your audience, study them:
   - What do they know about the problem? What are their attitudes toward it, their likely questions, and their potential concerns?
   - Why might they accept or resist change?
   - Does the problem affect them directly or indirectly? What can and can't they do about the problem?
   - What arguments and evidence would convince them to admit the problem exists, care about it, and take action?

3. **Probe the problem.** If helpful, use the graphic organizer at **7d**.
   - **Define the problem.** What is it exactly? What are its parts?
   - **Determine the problem's seriousness.** Why should it be fixed? What are its immediate, long-term, and potential effects?
   - **Analyze causes.** What are its root causes and contributing factors?
   - **Explore context.** What are the problem's background and connection to other problems? What solutions have been tried? Who, if anyone, benefits from the problem's existence?
   - **Think creatively.** Look at the problem from other perspectives—other states and countries, both genders, different races, and so on.

4. **Brainstorm possible solutions.** List all imaginable solutions—both modest and radical fixes. Then evaluate the alternatives:
   - List criteria that any solution should meet.
   - Compare and contrast alternatives by examining strengths, weaknesses, and workability.

5. **Choose the best solution and map out support.** In a sentence, state the solution that best solves the problem. Try this pattern: Given [the problem—its seriousness, effects, or causes], we must [the solution]." Next, identify support for your solution. Compared with alternatives, why is it preferable? Is it more thorough, beneficial, and practical?

Guidelines: Proposing a Solution

6. Outline your proposal and complete a first draft. A proposal's structure is quite simple: describe the problem, offer a solution, and defend the solution. Within each section of your proposal, choose strategies that fit your purpose and audience.

- **The problem:** Consider whether readers understand the problem and accept its seriousness. Inform them about the problem by using appropriate background information, cause/effect analysis, examples, parallel cases, visuals, and expert testimony.
- **The solution:** If necessary, first argue against alternative solutions. Then present your solution. State clearly what should happen, who should be involved, and why. For a complex solution, lay out the different stages.
- **The support:** Show how the solution solves the problem. Use facts and analysis to argue that your solution is feasible and to address objections. You may choose to accept the validity of some objections while refuting others.

7. Get feedback and revise the draft. Share your draft with a peer or a tutor in the writing center, asking these questions:

- Is the problem defined and explained clearly?
- Have you shown convincingly that the problem is serious and must be solved?
- Is the organization logical, and is the transition between problem and solution smooth?
- Does the solution fit the problem? Is the proposal precise, realistic, and complete? Does it address all possible objections?
- Is the evidence clear, credible, and compelling?
- Is the voice serious and tactful?
- Is the opening engaging? Is the closing thoughtful and clear?

8. Edit and proofread the essay. Check for accurate word choice; smooth, energetic sentences; and correct grammar, spelling, and format.

9. Prepare and share the final essay. Submit your proposal to the appropriate readers.

- If you are writing an essay, submit the document to your instructor, a website, or a professional journal.
- If you are writing a workplace document, send copies to the addressed readers as well as to others affected by the problem.

VISUALS TIP

Review your draft and look for ways to clarify or otherwise strengthen your writing with visuals such as tables, graphs, or photos. Make sure that your visuals are suitable for your proposal's audience as well.

40i Checklist: Proposing a Solution

Use the seven traits to check the quality of your writing and revise as needed.

____ The **ideas** show a thorough understanding of the problem and present a workable solution. The proposal uses strong reasoning and well-researched evidence.

____ The **organization** convincingly moves from problem to solution to support. Strategies such as cause/effect, comparison/contrast, or process are used well to clarify the message.

____ The **voice** is positive, confident, objective, and sensitive to opposing viewpoints. The tone fits the seriousness of the problem.

____ The **words** are precise and effectively defined.

____ The **sentences** read smoothly, with effective variations and logical transitions.

____ The final draft includes **no errors** in spelling, mechanics, usage, or grammar.

____ The page **design** is attractive, follows proper formatting for an essay or a workplace proposal, and uses appropriate design elements.

WAC Link: To do their work, all academics must research problems related to their disciplines, analyze possible solutions, choose the best option, and engage others in implementing the solution. As a result, proposals are written across the curriculum and in a variety of forms. For example, writers wanting to encourage academic dialogue may compose a proposal in essay form. Writers calling for quick action may draft the proposal as a memo or an e-mail.

Service-Learning Link: Teaching people how to write effective proposals helps them get the aid they need—in their communities and in the workplace.

Workplace Link: Like academics, people in the workplace write proposals often. For a smaller problem, they may write a proposal as a memo, as an e-mail, or as one segment of a lengthy report. For a significant problem, they may shape the proposal into a complete document, such as a troubleshooting proposal, justification proposal, or major bid.

VISUALS TIP

Visuals such as charts, graphs, and tables are effective tools for (1) showing data distinguishing a problem and (2) showing data illustrating the strength of a solution. Other visuals such as drawings help communicate information more clearly.

CHAPTER 41

Literary Analysis

Analyzing a piece of literature is a rewarding activity during which you think through what you have read as well as how and why the piece is effective.

What is my goal?

Your goal is to read the literature carefully, understand its elements, and then explain what the piece is about and how it communicates its message. If your task includes evaluation, then you also explain why the reading experience did or did not satisfy you.

What are the keys to my success?

Know your subject. Read the piece multiple times, first for enjoyment only, and then to assess the writer's specific choices and their effects.

Analyze the work's key elements. In works of fiction, for example, consider issues such as point of view, setting, plot, character, and theme.

Compare it. If the work reminds you of some other piece, review the second work and note similarities and differences between the two.

What topics should I consider?

Choose a piece of literature that you find interesting and meaningful.

- **Poems and short stories:** You could choose one of thousands of great poems or short stories from literature anthologies.
- **Plays:** Plays considered by critics to be outstanding are collected in anthologies. Individual scripts of other plays can be found in libraries, theater departments, or literary magazines. (Note: You could also review a live performance.)
- **Novels:** You can find novels in libraries and bookstores. Consider great novelists of the past (Austen, Dickens, Melville) or award-winning contemporary authors (Kingsolver, Atwood, Walker).

What's Ahead
41a Student Essay: Analysis of a Short Story
41b Guidelines: Literary Analysis
41c Checklist: Literary Analysis

LITERARY ANALYSIS

41a **Student Essay: Analysis of a Short Story**

In the essay below, student writer Anya Terekhina analyzes the characters and ideas in Flannery O'Connor's short story "Good Country People."

"Good Country People":

Broken Body, Broken Soul

> The writer provides background for understanding the characters in O'Connor's stories.

Flannery O'Connor's short stories are filled with characters who are bizarre, freakish, devious, and sometimes even murderous. Every short story, according to O'Connor in <u>Mystery and Manners: Occasional Prose</u>, should be "long in depth" and meaning (94). To achieve this, O'Connor develops characters with heavily symbolic attributes and flaws, and "it is clearly evident that boldly outlined inner compulsions are reinforced dramatically by a mutilated exterior self" (Muller 22). In "Good Country People," Joy-Hulga is a typical O'Connor character—grotesque yet real. Her realness comes from her many flaws and, ironically, her flaws are a self-constructed set of illusions. Throughout the story, O'Connor carefully links Joy-Hulga's physical impairments with deeper handicaps of the soul; then, at the closing, she strips Hulga of these physical flaws while helping her realize that her corresponding beliefs are flawed as well.

> The writer begins listing the protagonist's physical disabilities and explains how each one symbolizes a deeper problem in her soul.

O'Connor first introduces her character as Joy Hopewell, a name of optimism. However, we soon understand that her chosen name *Hulga* is more fitting. The new name distresses her mother, Mrs. Hopewell, who is "certain that she [Joy] had thought and thought until she had hit upon the ugliest name in any language" (O'Connor 1943). Hulga has connotations of "hull = hulk = huge = ugly" (Grimshaw 51), and all of these are accurate descriptions of her. Far from having a sweet temperament, Hulga stomps and sulks around the farm, "constant outrage . . . [purging] every expression from her face" (1942).

Although Hulga's demeanor could be blamed on her physical impairments, she devises her own rationalizations for behaving as she does. Ironically, each rationale is symbolized by one of her physical disabilities, yet she doesn't recognize the handicaps for what they imply.

One of Hulga's many ailments is her weak heart, which will likely limit her lifespan. Hulga blames this affliction for keeping her on the Hopewell farm, making "it plain that if it had not been for this condition, she would be far from these red hills and good country people" (1944). Having a Ph.D. in

1

2

3

4

philosophy, Hulga claims to want work as a university professor, lecturing to people at her intellectual level. Hulga's weak heart functions as more than a dream-crusher; it "symbolizes her emotional detachment—and inability to love anyone or anything" (Oliver 233). She exhibits no compassion or love for anything, not even "dogs or cats or birds or flowers or nature or nice young men" (1944–45).

5   Hulga also suffers from poor vision. Without her eyeglasses, she is helpless. Strangely though, her icy blue eyes have a "look of someone who has achieved blindness by an act of will and means to keep it" (1942). Her self-induced blindness symbolizes her blindness to reality. She is indeed intelligent, but she has packed her brain full of ideas and thoughts that only obscure common sense, let alone truth. Because of Hulga's extensive education and her focus on philosophical reasoning, she considers herself superior to everyone around her. For example, she yells at her mother, "Woman! . . . Do you ever look inside and see what you are not? God!" (1944).

6   Hulga's last and most noticeable physical impairment is her missing leg, which was "literally blasted off" (1944) in a hunting accident when she was ten years old. In <u>Mystery and Manners</u>, O'Connor stresses that the wooden leg operates interdependently at a literal and a symbolic level, which means "the wooden leg continues to accumulate meaning" throughout the story (99). Hulga's biggest physical handicap symbolizes her deepest affliction: her belief in nothing.

> She points out the root of the protagonist's problems: her lack of belief in anything.

7   Hulga's philosophical studies did focus on the study of nothing, particularly on the arguments of the French philosopher Nicolas Malebranche. O'Connor describes Hulga as believing "in nothing but her own belief in nothing" (<u>Mystery</u> 99). Over time, Hulga's belief in nothing develops into more than just academic study. Her nihilism becomes her religion—suitable for a woman who considers herself superior and despises platitudes. As she explains to Manley Pointer, "We are all damned . . . but some of us have taken off our blindfolds and see that there's nothing to see. It's a kind of salvation" (1952). Hulga's religious terms suggest that she uses faith in nothingness to find the meaning that she can't find elsewhere.

8   Hulga's nihilism is symbolized by her wooden leg, which is the only thing she tends to with care: "She took care of it as someone else would his soul, in private and almost with her own eyes turned away" (1953). This limb is wooden and corresponds to Hulga's wooden soul. Whereas she believes she

LITERARY ANALYSIS

worships Nothing, what she actually worships is an "artificial leg and an artificial belief" (Oliver 235).

Not realizing that her false leg and false religion cripple her both physically and spiritually, Hulga considers seducing Manley Pointer, the Bible salesman. She delightfully imagines that she will have to help him deal with his subsequent remorse, and then she will instruct him into a "deeper understanding of life" (1950). Of course, her intellectual blindness keeps her from realizing that her superiority is only an illusion. Instead, she views Manley as "a vulnerable innocent, a naïve Fundamentalist, and she wishes to seduce him to prove that her sophisticated textbook nihilism is superior to his simpleminded faith" (Di Renzo 76). 9

In classic O'Connor fashion, the characters and situation reverse dramatically at the end of the story. Hulga and Manley are alone in a hayloft and begin embracing. At first, Hulga is pleased with her reaction to kissing as it aligns well with Malebranche's teachings: "it was an unexceptional experience and all a matter of the mind's control" (1951). Soon, however, she realizes that she is enjoying the first human connection of her life. At this point, the *innocent* Bible salesman has already stripped Hulga of her first physical impairment: her weak heart. 10

Hulga hardly notices when Manley takes advantage of her next impairment: "when her glasses got in his way, he took them off of her and slipped them into his pocket" (1952). With her heart opened and her intellectual perspective fuzzy, Hulga swiftly descends into what she despises—platitudes. Hulga and Manley exchange mumbled clichés of love, and this leads Manley to ask if he can remove her artificial leg. After brief hesitation, Hulga agrees because she feels he has touched and understood a central truth inside her. She considers it a complete surrender, "like losing her own life and finding it again, miraculously, in his" (1953). 11

As soon as the artificial leg is off, Manley whips out one of his Bibles, which is hollow. Inside are whiskey, obscene playing cards, and contraceptives. In only moments, Hulga loses control: as each of her physical handicaps is exploited, pieces of her worldview crumble, leaving her confused and weak. 12

In an ironic reversal, Hulga becomes the naïf and Manley becomes the cynic. Hulga pleads in disbelief, "'Aren't you . . . just good country people?'" (1954). She knows that she has reverted to her mother's platitudes: "If the language is more sophisticated than any at Mrs. Hopewell's command, it is no 13

The writer demonstrates how the protagonist's flaws lead her to make distorted judgments.

She revisits the protagonist's physical disabilities, showing how the Bible salesman exploits each one.

less trite, and the smug self-deception underlying it . . . is, if anything, greater" (Asals 105). Manley assumes a startling, haughty air, exclaiming, "'I hope you don't think . . . that I believe in that crap! I may sell Bibles but I know which end is up and I wasn't born yesterday and I know where I'm going!'" (1954). Although they exchange roles, both characters use clichés to express their immature, yet authentic, worldviews.

The writer reflects on the change in both characters.

14   Manley runs off with Hulga's wooden leg, leaving her vulnerable and dependent, two things she previously despised. But "Hulga's artificial self—her mental fantasy of her own perfection—has gone out the door with her artificial limb. She is stuck in the hayloft with her actual self, her body, her physical and emotional incompleteness" (Di Renzo 79).

15   In one brief morning of delusional seduction, Hulga learns more about herself and her world than she learned in all her years of university. Forced to acknowledge her physical, emotional, and spiritual disabilities, Hulga begins to realize what she is not—neither a wise intellectual for whom there *is hope*, nor "good country people" who merely *hope well*.

The closing explains how Hulga finally acknowledges the truth about herself.

Works Cited

Asals, Frederick. <u>Flannery O'Connor: The Imagination of Extremity</u>. Athens: U of Georgia P, 1982.

Di Renzo, Anthony. <u>American Gargoyles: Flannery O'Connor and the Medieval Grotesque</u>. Carbondale: Southern Illinois UP, 1995.

Grimshaw, James A. <u>The Flannery O'Connor Companion</u>. Westport: Greenwood, 1981.

Muller, Gilbert H. <u>Nightmares and Visions: Flannery O'Connor and the Catholic Grotesque</u>. Athens: U of Georgia P, 1972.

O'Connor, Flannery. "Good Country People." <u>Anthology of American Literature: Realism to the Present</u>. Vol. 2. 6th ed. Ed. George McMichael. Upper Saddle River: Simon & Schuster, 1993. 1941–54.

- - -. <u>Mystery and Manners: Occasional Prose</u>. New York: Farrar, 1969.

Oliver, Kate. "O'Connor's GOOD COUNTRY PEOPLE." <u>Explicator</u> 62.4 (2004): 233–36. <u>Academic Search Elite</u>. EBSCOhost. Dordt College John and Louise Hulst Library. 29 June 2005 <http://search.epnet.com>.

41b Guidelines: Literary Analysis

1. **Select a topic.** Choose a literary work that interests you. For ideas, review "What topics should I consider?" at the start of this chapter.

2. **Understand the work.** Read it thoughtfully several times, looking carefully at its content, form, and overall effect.

   - For plays, examine the plot, setting, characters, dialogue, lighting, costumes, sound effects, music, acting, and directing.
   - For novels and short stories, focus on point of view, plot, setting, characters, style, symbolism, and theme.
   - For poems, examine diction, simile, tone, sound, figures of speech, irony, form, theme, and symbolism.
   - For songs, (1) use the poetry terms to examine the lyrics and (2) use music terms to evaluate the score: harmonic and rhythmic qualities, dynamics, and melodic lines.

3. **Gather information.** Take notes on what you experienced, using the list above to guide your thoughts. Seek to understand the work as a whole before you analyze the parts. Consider freewriting briefly on one or more aspects of the work to dig more deeply into the work.

4. **Get organized.** Review the notes that you took as you analyzed the work. What key insight about the work has your analysis led you to see? Turn that insight or judgment into your thesis, and then order supporting points logically in an outline.

5. **Write the first draft.**

   Opening: Use ideas like the following to gain your readers' attention, identify your topic, narrow the focus, and state your thesis:

   - Summarize your subject briefly. Include the title, the author, and the literary form or performance.

     Example: "The Darkling Thrush," a poem written at the end of the nineteenth century, expresses Thomas Hardy's gloomy outlook.

   - Start with a quotation from the literary work and then comment on its importance.
   - Explain the writer's purpose and describe how well he or she achieves it.
   - Open with a general statement about life that relates to the focus of your analysis.

     Example: "Hardy compares the world to the dying day and winter."

   - Begin with a general statement about the literary work.
   - Assert your thesis. State the key insight about the work that your analysis has revealed.

Middle: Develop and support your thesis by following this pattern:

- State the main points, relating them to the thesis of your essay.
- Support each main point with specific details or quotations.
- Explain how these details prove your point.

Closing: Tie key points together to focus your analysis. Assert your thesis or evaluation in a fresh way, leaving readers with a sense of the larger significance of your analysis.

6. **Review and revise.** Once you have a first draft written, relax for a time, and then reread your essay for its logic and completeness. Check whether you have supported each of your observations with evidence from the literary work. Test your analysis with questions like these:

- Did you explore the ironies, if present, or any important images, vocal nuances, dramatic actions, shifts in setting, or symbolism?
- Did you bring your analysis to a clear conclusion?

7. **Get feedback.** Ask a knowledgeable classmate, friend, or tutor to read your essay, looking for the following:

- An analytical thesis statement supported by evidence
- Key insights into both content or meaning on the one hand and form or style on the other hand
- Supporting details that clarify what you experienced and how you responded
- Clear transitions between sentences and paragraphs
- A tone that is respectful, honest, objective, and informed

8. **Edit and proofread the essay.** Once you have revised your writing, clarified your transitions, and checked your evidence, polish the phrasing and diction. Make certain your paper is free of awkward syntax or errors in usage, punctuation, spelling, or grammar.

LINKS

Web Link: Check that you have used literary terms accurately in your essay. For help, review the literary terms found in *The College Writer's Handbook* website at <www.thecollegewriter.com>.

9. **Publish the essay.**

- Share your essay with friends and family.
- Publish it in a journal or on a website.
- Place a copy in your personal or professional portfolio.
- If you wrote about a short story, poem, or song, consider sharing both the artwork and your review with a high school English class.

LITERARY ANALYSIS

41c Checklist: Literary Analysis

Use the seven traits to check the quality of your writing and revise as needed.

____ The **ideas** offer insight regarding what the literature is about and how it communicates its message.

____ The **organization** of the essay flows logically and provides an easy-to-follow pattern.

____ The **voice** is positive, confident, and objective. The tone fits the work discussed.

____ The **words** are precise and effectively defined; passages from the literature are quoted correctly and introduced objectively.

____ The **sentences** read smoothly, with effective variations and logical transitions.

____ The final draft includes **no errors** in spelling, mechanics, usage, or grammar; documentation follows MLA style.

____ The **page design** is properly formatted as an essay; any visuals from the literature are shown clearly.

LINKS

WAC Link: Scholars in all disciplines write literature reviews to report on or critique the research and writing within their disciplines. For example, a person in educational psychology might report on current studies of dyslexia (a learning disability) before asserting her own theory of dyslexia. However, these literature reviews should not be confused with literary analyses written about the content, style, and form of the arts such as poetry, drama, or novels.

Service-Learning Link: Teaching children how to analyze and write about literature can strengthen their reading, writing, and thinking skills. A service-learning project could include reading to students and discussing the literature with them. Alternatively, a project could show students how to share their writing with one another and respond to it.

Workplace Link: People who work in the media or arts-related fields often write or read literary reviews of current films, novels, plays, or concerts. In addition, educators often write and read literary reviews to make decisions regarding their book purchases and teaching.

VISUALS TIP

When reviewing literature that includes drawings or illustrations, you might show examples of the visuals to help your readers grasp what the piece of literature is and how it communicates its message.

Business and Application Writing

In business, good writing practices can land you a job, promote your ideas, and ensure efficiency.

What is my goal?

Your goal when writing business documents is to deliver a clear, succinct message that convinces the reader to help you accomplish your writing purpose. For example, you want an application letter or resumé to convince the reader to offer you whatever you have applied for—or at least offer you an interview.

What are the keys to my success?

Know your reader. If you are writing to request a recommendation, review what that person knows about you and your qualifications, and consider how you could politely remind her or him of key details. If you are writing an application letter, an application essay, or a resumé, ask the following questions: What does the reader know, or need to know, to do what I want done?

Know the organization. Where is the organization located, and what are its products or services? What type of work does it do, how many employees does it have, and how do the employees rate their organization?

Focus on your purpose. In a polite and confident voice, deliver your message clearly. In application letters, thank-you letters, and job-acceptance letters, state your point early. In job-rejection letters, express your appreciation for the job offer; then politely decline the offer.

Do necessary research. To answer questions like those listed above, study the organization's website, brochures, flyers, newsletters, and annual reports.

What's Ahead

BUSINESS AND APPLICATION WRITING

42a Formatting the Business Letter

All letters should include a clear message and information about the writer and reader. Details for both are listed below and modeled on the facing page.

What are the parts of a business letter?

Heading: The heading gives the writer's complete address, either in the letterhead (company stationery) or typed out. Spell out words such as *Road, Street,* and *West.* Don't abbreviate the month or use a number rather than the word.

Inside address: The inside address gives the reader's name and address.

- If you're not sure which person to address or how to spell someone's name, you could call the company for the information.
- If the person's title is a single word, place it after the name and a comma (Su Ling, President). A longer title goes on a separate line.

Salutation: The salutation begins with *Dear* and ends with a colon.

- Use *Mr.* or *Ms.* plus the person's last name, unless you are well acquainted. Do not guess at *Miss* or *Mrs.*
- If you cannot get the person's name, replace the salutation with *Dear* or *Attention* followed by the title of an appropriate reader.

Body: The body contains the message stated in single-spaced paragraphs with double spacing between paragraphs. It is usually organized into three parts:

- An opening that states why you are writing
- A middle that gives needed details
- A closing that focuses on what should happen next

> **NOTE:** If the body goes to a second page, put the reader's name at the top left, the number 2 in the center, and the date at the right margin.

Complimentary closing: For the complimentary closing, use *Sincerely, Yours sincerely,* or *Yours truly* followed by a comma.

Signature: Includes both the writer's handwritten and typed names.

Initials: When someone types the letter for the writer, the person's initials appear (in lowercase) after the writer's initials (in capitals) and a colon.

Enclosure: If a document (brochure, form, copy, or other form) is enclosed with the letter, the word *Enclosure* or *Encl.,* followed by a colon, appears below the initials.

Copies: If a copy of the letter is sent elsewhere, type the letter *c:* beneath the enclosure line, followed by the person's or department's name.

Box 143
Balliole College
Eugene, OR 97440-5125
August 27, 2005

Four to Seven Spaces

Ms. Ada Overlie
Ogg Hall, Room 222
Balliole College
Eugene, OR 97440-0222

Double Space

Dear Ms. Overlie:

Double Space

As the president of the Earth Care Club, I welcome you to
Balliole Community College. I hope the year will be a great
learning experience.

Double Space

That learning experience is the reason I'm writing—to
encourage you to join the Earth Care Club. As a member, you
could participate in the action-oriented mission of the club.
The club has most recently been involved in the following:

- Organizing a recycle program on campus
- Promoting cloth rather than plastic bag use
- Advising the college administration on landscaping,
  renovating, and building for energy efficiency
- Putting together the annual Earth Day celebration

Double Space

What are your environmental concerns? Bring them with
you to the Earth Care Club at our next meeting in AG 203
at 7:00 p.m., September 3.

Double Space

Yours sincerely,

Four Spaces

Dave Wetland

Dave Wetland
President

Double Space

DW:kr
Encl.: membership form
c: Anne Turek, membership committee

BUSINESS AND APPLICATION WRITING

42b Writing Memos

A memorandum is a written message sent to readers who are usually within the same organization. A memo can vary in length from one sentence to a five-page report and can be delivered in person or sent via mail or e-mail.

How can I write effective memos?

Memos are most often written to create a flow of information within an organization—answering questions, describing procedures, and reminding people about appointments. Here are some guidelines:

- Write memos only to people who need them.
- Distribute them via appropriate media—mail, fax, bulletin board, kiosk, or e-mail.
- Make your subject line precise so that the topic is clear and the memo is easy to file.
- Get to the point: (1) state the subject, (2) give necessary details, and (3) state the response you want.

MEMORANDUM

Date:	September 27, 2005
To:	All Users of the Bascom Hill Writing Lab
From:	Kerri Kelley, Coordinator
Subject:	New Hours/New Equipment

The subject line clarifies the memo's purpose.

Beginning October 15, the Bascom Hill Writing Lab will expand its weekend hours as follows: Fridays, 7:00 a.m.–11:00 p.m.; Saturdays, 8:00 a.m.–11:00 p.m.

The main point is stated immediately.

Also, six additional computers will be installed next week, making it easier to get computer time. We hope these changes will help meet the increased demand for time and assistance we've experienced this fall.

Readers are asked to note a few final facts.

Finally, long-range planners, mark your calendars. The lab will be closed on Thanksgiving Day morning, but open from 1:00 p.m. to 11:00 p.m. We will also be closed on Christmas and New Year's Day. We will post our semester-break hours sometime next month.

42c Writing E-Mail

With e-mail, you can do the following:

- Send, forward, and receive many messages quickly and efficiently.
- Send the same message to several people at the same time.
- Organize messages in "folders" for later reference.

E-MAIL TIPS

Revise and edit messages. Check your e-mails for correctness and clarity before sending them. Confusing sentences, grammatical errors, and typos on paper or on a computer screen distract from your message and reflect poorly on you.

Use e-mail maturely. Sooner or later you will send e-mail to the wrong person. Avoid problems by never writing anything that would embarrass you if the wrong party received it.

Make messages easy to read and understand. (1) Provide a clear subject line so readers can scan it and decide whether to read the message. (2) Type short paragraphs, with line lengths of no more than sixty-five characters.

Respect your readers and other writers. Send messages only to readers who need them, and do not forward a message without the writer's permission.

BUSINESS AND APPLICATION WRITING

42d Writing Application Correspondence

When you apply for most jobs, you will have to write a letter of application, request letters of recommendation, and develop or update a resumé and an application essay. To write these documents, use the instructions and models that follow.

How can I create an effective application letter?

Your letter of application (or cover letter) introduces you to an employer and often highlights information on an accompanying resumé. Your goal is to convince the employer to invite you for an interview.

Ogg Hall, Room 222
Balliole College
Eugene, OR 97440-0222
April 17, 2006

Address a specific person, if possible.

Professor Edward Mahaffy
Greenhouse Coordinator
Balliole College
Eugene, OR 97440-0316

Dear Professor Mahaffy:

State the desired position and your chief qualification.

I recently talked with Ms. Sierra Arbor in the Financial Aid Office about work-study jobs for 2006–2007. She told me about the Greenhouse Assistant position and gave me a job description. I'm writing to apply for this position. I believe that my experience qualifies me for the job.

Focus on how your skills meet the reader's needs.

As you can see on my resumé, I spent two summers working in a raspberry operation, doing basic plant care and carrying out quality-control lab tests on the fruit. Also, as I was growing up, I learned a great deal by helping with a large farm garden. In high school and college, I studied botany. Because of my interest in this field, I'm enrolled in the Environmental Studies program at Balliole.

Request an interview and thank the reader.

I am available for an interview. You may phone me any time at 341-3611 or e-mail me at dvrl@balliole.edu. Thank you for considering my application.

Yours sincerely,

Ada Overlie

Ada Overlie

Encl. resumé

How should I write a recommendation-request letter?

When you apply for a job or program, you may need to ask people familiar with your work (instructors and employers) to write recommendation letters explaining your fitness for the position. You can do so in person, by phone, or in a clear letter or e-mail message.

2456 Charles Street
Lexington, KY 40588-8321
March 21, 2006

Dr. Rosa Perez
271 University Boulevard
University of Kentucky
Lexington, KY 40506-1440

Dear Dr. Perez:

As we discussed on the phone, I would appreciate your writing a recommendation letter for me. You know the quality of my academic work, my qualities as a person, and my potential for working in the medical field.

As my professor for Biology 201 and 202, you are familiar with my grades and work habits. As my adviser, you know my career plans and can assess whether I have the qualities needed to succeed in the medical profession. I am asking for your recommendation because I am applying for summer employment with the Lexington Ambulance Service. I recently received my Emergency Medical Technician (Basic) license to prepare for such work.

By April 8, please send your letter to Rick Falk, EMT Coordinator, at the University Placement Office. Let me know if you need any other information (phone 231-6700; e-mail jnwllms@ukentucky.edu). Thank you for your help.

Yours sincerely,

Jon Williams

Jon Williams

Situation
Remind the reader of your relationship to him or her; then ask the person to write a recommendation or to serve as a reference.

Explanation
Describe the work you did and the type of job, position, or program for which you are applying.

Action
Explain what form the recommendation should take, to whom it should be addressed, and where and when it needs to be sent.

BUSINESS AND APPLICATION WRITING

42e Guidelines: Application Essay

For some applications, you will be asked to submit an essay or a personal statement. Whatever the situation, your goal is to address the assigned topic specifically, telling who you are, how you think, and why you are drawn to the position, program, or profession.

1. **Prewrite.** Consider your purpose, your audience, and the context.
   - Who will read your essay? What skills or insights are they looking for?
   - How does the topic relate to the organization and job?
   - Prepare to draft. Study the assigned question or topic.
     - Read the instructions carefully, noting the topic and what you are asked to do: analyze, explain, describe, or evaluate. Also note the requested form and length.
     - Use prewriting activities such as clustering, listing, freewriting, and outlining to generate and organize your ideas.
     - Draft a sentence stating your main point or thesis regarding the topic.

2. **Draft.** Organize your writing into three parts.

   Opening: Introduce the topic in an engaging way, provide a context, and state your thesis politely but with confidence.

   Middle: Develop your thesis clearly and concisely using details consistent with the instructions and fitting for the position and readers. Use each paragraph to advance the thesis. Avoid vague or unrealistic claims.

   Closing: Stress an appropriate, positive point and look forward to participating in the program or organization.

3. **Revise.** Review your draft for ideas, organization, and voice.
   - Is your main idea logical, clear, fully developed, and well supported?
   - Are your ideas effectively shaped into coherent paragraphs?
   - Is the tone positive, but also objective, reasonable, and thoughtful?

4. **Refine.** Check your writing line by line for the following:
   - ___ Clear, concise, professional wording
   - ___ Readable sentences and helpful transitions
   - ___ Correct grammar, punctuation, and spelling
   - ___ Effective format (spacing, margins, fonts, type size)

APPLICATION ESSAY

The document below was written by a job applicant who was asked to explain her interest in and qualifications for a social-work position.

Heart, Knowledge, Skills, and Opportunity

During my early years, Bunde, Minnesota, was home. Now no more than a church and a few houses, then it was a cohesive village of about fifty-five people who looked after one another. For example, when Leo Folken lost his arm in a corn-picking accident, the community harvested his crop. When Jean O'Malley returned from Kansas City bruised and pregnant, the community adopted both mother and child. In other words, Bunde residents taught me that helping those in need is not one person's choice—it is everyone's responsibility.

When I left for Clark College in Kansas, my experiences in little Bunde prompted me to choose social work as my major. During the next four years, I studied psychology and sociology, as well as the history and practice of social work. In addition, I volunteered for three semesters in Clark's Social-Outreach Program. The courses helped me understand the needs of those living without adequate housing, health care, or career skills; the volunteer work helped me practice addressing those needs.

The following three years at the University of Nebraska provided further study of key topics related to social work, such as economics and state and federal social programs. In addition, my yearlong internship at Hope Services enabled me to work with a professional team in an urban setting. Earning my M.S.W. provided both the certification and the knowledge needed for a career in social work.

While I am certainly prepared to join the staff at Regis Community Services, I am also eager to do so for a number of reasons. First, Regis's fine facilities and convenient location enable it to serve clients throughout downtown Tulsa. Second, Regis's strong financial base supports the organization's excellent services. But most importantly, Regis's staff have both the skills and the passion required to deliver those services.

In summary, Bunde gave me the heart to become a social worker. Clark College and the University of Nebraska provided the knowledge and skills. But it is Regis Community Services that can offer the opportunity.

Opening

Get the reader's attention and introduce the main idea.

Middle

Develop that idea with details fitting the topic and position.

Write unified paragraphs linked with clear transitions. Use a thoughtful tone.

Closing

Summarize and look ahead.

BUSINESS AND APPLICATION WRITING

42f Guidelines: Resumé

When writing a resumé, your goal is to show that your skills, knowledge, and experience match the requirements for a specific job. Each style of resumé presents that information differently. A *chronological* resumé features your work history (from most current to least current); a *functional* resumé features your skills; and a *combination* resumé does some of both. In addition, each type can be formatted as a paper document or as an electronic document.

1. Review your goals.

- Show that your skills and experience match the job description.
- Choose the style of resumé (chronological, functional, or combination) that best highlights your qualifications.
- Choose the format (paper or electronic) that the employer prefers.

2. Gather detail about the following:

- Your career objective, worded to match the job description
- Your educational experiences (schools, degrees, certification)
- Your work experiences (employers and dates; responsibilities, skills, and titles; special projects, leadership roles, and awards)
- Activities and interests directly or indirectly related to the job
- Responsible people who are willing to recommend you

3. Organize the resumé into three parts.

Opening: List your contact information and job objective.

Middle: Write appropriate headings, and list educational and work experiences in parallel phrases or clauses. Refer to your training and skills with key words that match the job description.

Closing: List names, job titles, and contact information for references (or state that references are available upon request).

4. Review your resumé for ideas, organization, and voice.

- Check for skills and key words listed in the job description.
- Check for organization, details, and a professional tone.

5. Check your resumé line by line for the following:

___ Strong verbs, precise nouns, and parallel phrases

___ Formatting for a paper document or an e-mail attachment: can include columns, bullets, underlining, and boldface

___ Formatting for e-mail and scanners: one column, asterisks as bullets, sans serif typeface, flush left margin, ASCII or RTF text (for scanners), and no italics, boldface, or underlining

CHRONOLOGICAL RESUMÉ:
FORMATTED AS A PAPER DOCUMENT OR AN E-MAIL ATTACHMENT

LLOYD A. CLARK
1913 Linden Street
Charlotte, NC 28205-5611
(704) 555-2422
lloydac@earthlink.net

Opening
List contact
details and
state your
employment
objective.

EMPLOYMENT OBJECTIVE
Law enforcement position that calls for technical skills, military experience,
self-discipline, reliability, and people skills

WORK EXPERIENCE
Positions held in the United States Marine Corps:
- Guard Supervisor—Sasebo Naval Base, Japan, 1999–2005
  Scheduled and supervised 24 guards
- Marksmanship Instructor—Sasebo Naval Base, Japan, 1997–1999
  Trained personnel in small-arms marksmanship techniques
- Company Clerk—Okinawa, Japan, 1996–1997

SKILLS AND QUALIFICATIONS
- In-depth knowledge of laws and regulations concerning apprehension,
  search and seizure, rules of evidence, and use of deadly force
- Knowledge of security-management principles, training methods, and
  countermeasures
- Experience in physical-training management, marksmanship, and
  weaponry
- Computer word-processing and database skills on an IBM-compatible
  system
- Excellent one-on-one skills and communication abilities

Middle
List
experiences,
skills, and
training
(most recent
first).
Keep all
phrases
and clauses
parallel.
Formatting
includes
boldface and
bullets.

EDUCATION
- Arrest, Apprehension, and Riot Control Course, Sasebo, Japan, 1998
- Marksmanship Instructor Course, Okinawa, Japan, 1997
- Sexual-Harassment Sensitivity Training, Camp LeJeune, NC, 1996
- School of Infantry, Camp Pendleton, CA, 1996

AWARDS AND HONORS
- Promoted meritoriously from Private (E-1) to Lance Corporal (E-3):
  promoted meritoriously to final rank of Corporal (E-4) in less than
  two years
- Achieved "Expert" rating for pistol at annual marksmanship qualification
  (three years)
- Represented Marine Barracks, Japan, in division shooting matches
  (placed in top half)

List awards
and honors
in order of
importance.

References available upon request

Closing
Offer
references.

BUSINESS AND APPLICATION WRITING

COMBINATION RESUMÉ:
FORMATTED AS A PAPER DOCUMENT OR AN E-MAIL ATTACHMENT

Opening
Present contact information and your employment objective.

MICHELLE MOORE
3448 Skyway Drive
Missoula, MT 59801-2883
(406) 555-2166
E-mail: mimoore@earthlink.net

EMPLOYMENT OBJECTIVE
Electrical Engineer—designing or developing digital and/or microprocessor systems

QUALIFICATIONS AND SKILLS

Design
- Wrote two "C" programs to increase production-lab efficiency
- Built prototypes in digital and analog circuit design
- Designed and worked with CMOS components
- Wrote code for specific set of requirements
- Helped implement circuitry and hardware for a "bed-of-nails" test

Middle
Feature skills by referring to work and educational experiences. Put the most important skills first.
Format for paper or e-mail attachment:
- boldface
- underlining
- bulleted lists
- two columns

Troubleshooting and Repair
- Repaired circuit boards of peripheral computer products
- Helped maintain equipment using circuit-board testing
- Improved product quality by correcting recurring problems
- Debugged IBM-XT/Fox Kit Microprocessor Trainer (Z80)

Management
- Trained and supervised production technicians
- Facilitated smooth operation of production lab
- Assisted Microprocessors and Digital-Circuits instruction

EDUCATION
Montana State University, Bozeman, MT
- Bachelor of Science in Engineering, 2002
- Major: Electrical Engineering
- Independent Study: C programming, DOS and BIOS interrupts

EXPERIENCE
June 2002 to present	Production Engineer (full-time) Big Sky Computer Products, Inc., Missoula, MT
September 2001 to May 2002	Engineering Assistant Montana State University, Bozeman, MT
May 2000 to September 2001	Engineering Intern Montana State University, Bozeman, MT

Closing
Offer references.

References available upon request

Guidelines: Resumé

CHRONOLOGICAL RESUMÉ:
FORMATTED FOR SCANNERS, E-MAIL, AND WEBSITES

Jonathan L. Greenlind
806 5th Avenue
Waterloo, IA 50701-9351
Phone: 319.555.6955
E-mail: grnind@aol.com

OBJECTIVE
Position as hydraulics supervisor that calls for hydraulics expertise,
technical skills, mechanical knowledge, reliability, and enthusiasm

SKILLS
Operation and repair specialist in main and auxiliary power systems,
subsystems, landing gears, brakes and pneumatic systems, hydraulic
motors, reservoirs, actuators, pumps, and cylinders from six types of
hydraulic systems. Dependable, resourceful, strong leader, team worker.

EXPERIENCE
Aviation Hydraulics Technician
United States Navy (1990–present)
* Repair, test, and maintain basic hydraulics, distribution systems, and
  aircraft structural hydraulics systems
* Manufacture low-, medium-, and high-pressure rubber and Teflon
  hydraulic hoses
* Perform preflight, postflight, and other periodic aircraft inspections
* Supervise personnel

Aircraft Mechanic
Sioux Falls International Airport (1988–1990)
Sioux Falls, South Dakota
* Performed fueling, engine overhauls, minor repairs, and tire and oil
  changes of various aircraft

EDUCATION
United States Navy (1990–2004)
Certificate in Hydraulic Technical School; GPA 3.8/4.0
Certificate in Hydraulic, Pneumatic Test Stand School; GPA 3.9/4.0
Courses in Corrosion Control, Hydraulic Tube Bender, Aviation Structural
Mechanics
Equivalent of ten semester hours in Hydraulic Systems Maintenance and
Structural Repair

References available upon request

Opening
Present contact information and employment objective.

Middle
List skills, experiences, and education using key words that the employer's scanner will identify. Format as follows:
· One column
· Asterisks as bullets
· Simple sans serif typeface
· Flush left margin
· No italics, boldface, or underlining
· ASCII or RTF text (readable by all computers)

Closing
Offer references.

BUSINESS AND APPLICATION WRITING

42g Checklist: Application Documents

Use the seven traits to check your documents and then revise as needed.

Letters and Essays

____ The **ideas** show that I understand the job, want the job, and am qualified to do the job.

____ The **organization** in the letter is direct. The essay's organization is set by the opening, topic sentences, and closing.

____ The **voice** is informed, thoughtful, polite, and sincere.

____ The **words** include precise nouns, strong verbs, and few modifiers; job-related terms are clear; and all names and titles are correct.

____ The **sentences** are complete, energetic, varied in structure, and clear. The essay includes a clear main idea or theme.

____ The final draft includes **no errors** in grammar, spelling, or mechanics.

____ The **page design** for letters includes correct formatting; the essay's design includes appropriate margins and white space.

Resumés

____ The **ideas** show that I understand the job and have the required training, skills, and experiences.

____ The **organization** is correct for a chronological, a functional, or a combination resumé; the headings clearly foreshadow the details that follow.

____ The **voice** is confident and knowledgeable, but not arrogant.

____ The **words** include strong verbs, key terms from the job description, and accurate terms for academic degrees, professional certifications, and job titles.

____ The **sentences** are complete only when needed to make a point; they provide information in parallel lists, phrases, and clauses.

____ The final draft uses periods after clauses and includes **no errors** in grammar or mechanics.

____ The **page design** is correct:

Paper only—bulleted lists, boldface, underlining, business typeface, two columns

Electronic—ASCII or RTF text, sans serif typeface, single-column format, and asterisks as bullets, but no boldface or underlining

ETHICS TIP

State details correctly in your resumé. You want the employer's background check to find you qualified and honest.

Oral Presentations

Throughout your career (including your college years), you will give many oral presentations—from brief introductions to lengthy reports. In each situation, following these basic steps will help you deliver a strong message.

What are my goals?

Your goal is to develop a presentation that is engaging, purposeful, and clear.

What are the keys to my success?

State your purpose.

- Am I going to explain something?
- Am I trying to persuade or inspire my audience to do something?
- Am I hoping to teach my audience about something?

Identify your audience.

- How many people are in the audience, and what are their ages, backgrounds, and interests?
- What will people already know about the topic, and what will they want or need to know?
- What will their attitude be toward the topic and toward me?

Select and research your topic.

- What topics will fulfill my assignment, help me achieve my purpose, and appeal to my audience?
- Which of these topics do I find interesting and challenging?
- What do I need to learn about the topic, and where can I find the information?
- What support materials (displays, computer projections, handouts) would help me present my message?

What's Ahead

43a Organizing the Presentation

Next, you must organize and develop an introduction, body, and conclusion.

How should I develop my introduction?

Develop an introduction that does the following:

- Greets the audience and grabs their attention
- Communicates your interest in the audience
- Introduces your topic and main idea
- Shows that you have something worthwhile to say
- Establishes an appropriate tone

WRITER'S TIP

You could open with one of these attention-grabbing strategies:

- A little-known fact
  A series of questions
  A humorous anecdote
  An appropriate quotation
  A description of a problem

  A cartoon or picture
  A short demonstration
  The topic's importance
  An eye-catching prop
  A video or an audio clip

How should I organize the body?

Before you outline the body, take a moment to review what you want your presentation to do: Explain a problem? Promote an idea? Teach a process? Be sure the organizational pattern will help you achieve that goal.

- Chronological order
- Order of importance
- Comparison/contrast

- Cause/effect
- Order of location
- Problem/solution

After deciding how to organize your message, write it out in either outline or manuscript form. For help, see the tips below and the model shown at **43b**.

How should I develop my conclusion?

In your conclusion, restate your main idea, reinforce the tone, and refocus the audience on what it should think about or do. Here are some strategies for concluding a presentation:

- Review your main idea and key points.
- Issue a personal challenge.
- Return to your opening point.
- Recommend a plan of action.
- Suggest additional sources of information.
- Thank the audience and ask for questions.

43b Writing the Presentation

How much of your presentation you actually write out depends on your topic, audience, purpose, and—of course—personal style. The most commonly used written forms to make a presentation are a list, an outline, and a manuscript.

List: Use a basic list for making a short, informal speech such as an after-dinner introduction. Think about your purpose and then list the following:

- Your opening sentence (or two)
- A summary phrase for each of your main points
- Your closing sentence

1. Opening sentence or two
2. Phrase 1
   Phrase 2
   Phrase 3
3. Closing sentence

Outline: Use an outline for a more complex or formal topic. You can organize your material in greater detail without tying yourself to a word-for-word presentation. Here's one way you can do it:

- Opening (complete sentences)
- All main points (sentences)
- Supporting points (phrases)
- Quotations (written out)
- All supporting technical details, statistics, and sources (listed)
- Closing (complete sentences)
- Notes on visual aids (in capital letters or boldface)

Manuscript: Use the guidelines below if you plan to write out your presentation word for word:

- Double-space pages (or cards).
- Number pages (or cards).
- Use complete sentences on a page (do not run sentences from one page to another).
- Mark difficult words for pronunciation.
- Mark the script for interpretation using symbols such as boldface or italics to signal emphasis or vocal color.

I.   Opening statement
   A. Point with support
   B. Point (purpose or goal) [VISUAL 1]
II. Body (with three to five main points)
   A. Main point
      1. Supporting details
      2. Supporting details
   B. Main point
      1. Supporting details
      2. Supporting details
   C. Main point
      1. Supporting details
      2. Supporting details
III. Closing statement
   A. Point, including restatement of purpose
   B. Point, possibly a call to action [VISUAL 2]

ORAL PRESENTATIONS

43c Student Manuscript for a Formal Presentation

In her presentation below, student Burnette Sawyer argues that college students must begin a retirement savings plan today. Notice that she uses italics to mark words needing vocal color and boldface to mark words needing emphasis. She places all visual aid cues in color.

Save Now or Pay Later

Imagine that you've finished school, gotten a job, worked hard all week, and this dollar bill represents your whole paycheck. [hold up dollar bill] As your employer, I'm about to hand you the check when I stop, tear off about 20 percent like this, give it to Uncle Sam, and say, "Here's my employee's income tax." Then I tear off another 30 percent like this, give that to Uncle Sam too, and say, "And here's her Medicare and Social Security tax." 1

Finally, I give you this half and say, "Here, hard worker, this is what's left of your *whole paycheck.*" 2

Does that sound like science fiction? 3

Senator Alan Simpson doesn't think so. In the magazine *Modern Maturity,* he says that unless legislation changes the Social Security system, *our generation* will have to pay 20 percent [SLIDE 1] of our paychecks as income tax, and about 30 percent [SLIDE 2] as Social Security tax. That means we can keep just **50 percent** [SLIDE 3] of what we earn. 4

But the news gets **worse.** Remember this 30 percent that we paid to Social Security? [hold up piece of dollar bill] Well, that won't be enough money for retired people to live on in the year 2043. Remember that year, 2043—we'll come back to it soon. 5

What's the problem? The Social Security system can't ensure our savings for retirement. 6

What's the solution? We have to start our own savings plans, and the *earlier,* the *better.* 7

Ever since the Social Security system started back in 1935 [SLIDE 4], it has never been *secure.* While the system has been "fixed" a number of times, these fix-it jobs haven't solved the problem. For example, writer Keith Carlson points out that in 1983 [SLIDE 5] Congress raised payroll taxes, extended the retirement age, and said that the system would be in good financial shape until 2056. 8

Sidebar annotations:

The speaker begins with an anecdote.

She tears the dollar for emphasis.

The speaker asks questions to involve the audience.

9   But then, says Carlson, *just nine years later*, a report came out saying that Congress had been **wrong**. The report [SLIDE 6] said in 1992 that Social Security money wouldn't even last that long—it would run out by 2043. *Remember that year, 2043?* That's before many of us are supposed *to retire at age 67!*

10   Do you think this news is bad? The AARP Bulletin reported on the Bipartisan Commission on Entitlement and Tax Reform. This commission warned that entitlement programs like Social Security [SLIDE 7] are growing so fast they could "bankrupt the country" by the year 2029—long before we retire!

> Throughout the speech, she uses eleven slides to give her listeners a clear understanding of the main points.

11   So what should we do? This fall many of us will vote in a presidential election for the first time. Both Democrats and Republicans say they have a plan to fix Social Security. What if we all vote for the presidential candidate with the best plan? Will that save our retirement funds? **Don't count on it!** As the track record for Social Security shows, one more fix-it job won't fix the system. We have to start *our own* retirement plans—and do it early in our careers.

12   In fact, in his book *Retirement 101*, Willard Enteman says that we should start a personal savings plan the day we get our first paychecks. In sociology class last week, Mr. Christians made the same point. He gave us this bar graph [SLIDE 8] showing that if our goal is to save $500,000 by age 67, we had better *start early* before saving gets too expensive.

13   As you can see from the graph, if we start saving when we're 25, we can reach $500,000 by saving just $121 a month. [SLIDE 9] If we wait until we're 35, we'll have to save $282 a month. [SLIDE 10] If we wait until we're 45, we'll have to put away $698 a month. [SLIDE 11] And if we wait until we're 55, we'll need $2,079 a month.

> The closing paragraphs help readers reflect on the subject.

14   **Look at the difference.** To reach $500,000 by age 67 would cost $121 a month if we start at 25, and $2,079 a month if we start at 55.

15   What's my point? The Social Security system *can't promise us* financial security when we retire in 2050.

16   What's the solution? We have to start our own savings plans; and the *earlier* we start, the *easier* it will be to reach our goals.

NOTE: Sample graphics for this presentation are found in "How can I use visual aids?" on the following page.

ORAL PRESENTATIONS

How can I use visual aids?

While constructing your presentation, create or select visual aids that will grab the audience's attention and help them understand the message. For example, during her presentation, Ms. Sawyer used the computer-generated graphics below.

Sample Graphics

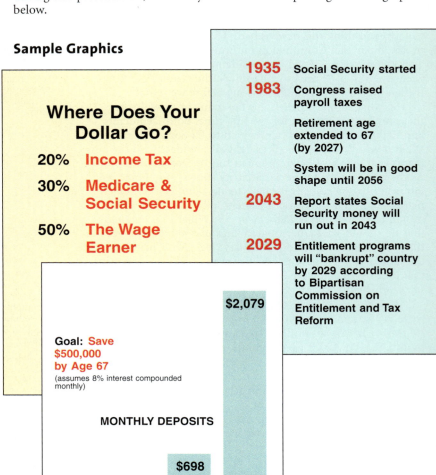

Where Does Your Dollar Go?

20% **Income Tax**

30% **Medicare & Social Security**

50% **The Wage Earner**

1935 **Social Security started**

1983 **Congress raised payroll taxes**

Retirement age extended to 67 (by 2027)

System will be in good shape until 2056

2043 **Report states Social Security money will run out in 2043**

2029 **Entitlement programs will "bankrupt" country by 2029 according to Bipartisan Commission on Entitlement and Tax Reform**

Goal: Save $500,000 by Age 67
(assumes 8% interest compounded monthly)

MONTHLY DEPOSITS

$2,079

$698

$282

$121

Age 25   Age 35   Age 45   Age 55

43d Guidelines: Developing Computer Presentations

To help you use presentation software effectively, follow the guidelines below.

1. **Develop a design.** Be sure your graphic design fits your topic and your audience—polished for a serious topic or casual for an informal topic.

2. **Create pages.** If a main idea has several parts, present each one on its own page. Each click of the mouse button (or computer key) should reveal a new detail.

3. **Use transitions.** Dissolves, fades, wipes, and other transitional visual effects refine a computer presentation and keep the audience's attention (as long as the devices don't detract from the message).

 VISUALS TIP

Text can be animated to appear from off screen at just the right moment. Graphics can be made to appear one element at a time, and illustrations can change before the viewer's eyes. Remember to use special effects—especially animation—wisely.

4. **Add sound.** Just as graphics and animation can enhance a presentation, so, too, can sound. Music can serve as an introduction or a backdrop, and sound effects can add emphasis. Voice recording can add authority and help drive home key points.

5. **Fine-tune your presentation.** Practice delivering your presentation while clicking through your pages. Try out your delivery with an audience of fellow students, if possible, and ask for their input.

6. **Check for word choice and style.** Make sure that the words on the screen are key words. Use these words as talking points—don't try to cover any point word for word. Also, check that transitions, animations, and sounds are smooth and not disruptive.

7. **Edit the final version.** Check your spelling, punctuation, usage, and other mechanics. On-screen errors are glaringly obvious to everyone.

8. **Rehearse.** Practice running the equipment until you can use it with confidence. (Have a backup plan in case the equipment malfunctions.)

9. **Make a backup copy.** Protect all the effort you invested in creating your presentation.

ORAL PRESENTATIONS

43e Checklist: Overcoming Stage Fright

While it's okay to feel a little nervous before a presentation (the emotion keeps you alert), overwhelming stage fright can limit your ability to communicate. The remedy for stage fright is confidence—confidence in what to say and how to say it. To develop that confidence, do the following:

Personal Preparation

___ Know your subject well.

___ Rehearse the presentation thoroughly, including the use of visuals.

___ Schedule your time carefully, making sure to arrive early.

SPEAKER'S TIP

Try to relax before the presentation by stretching or doing a deep-breathing exercise, remembering that your presentation can be successful without being perfect.

The Room and Equipment

___ Confirm that the room is clean, comfortable, and well lit.

___ Make sure that tables and chairs are set up and arranged correctly.

___ Check that AV equipment is in place and working.

___ Test microphone volume.

___ Position the screen and displays for good visibility.

Personal Details

___ Check your clothing and hair.

___ Arrange for drinking water to be available.

___ Put your script and handouts in place.

Speaking Strategies

___ Be confident, positive, and energetic.

___ Maintain eye contact when speaking or listening.

___ Use gestures naturally—don't force them.

___ Provide for audience participation; survey the audience: "How many of you . . . ?"

___ Maintain a comfortable, erect posture.

___ Speak up and speak clearly—don't rush.

___ Reword and clarify when necessary.

___ After the presentation, ask for questions and answer them clearly.

___ Thank the audience.

CHAPTER 44

Objective and Essay Tests

When taking tests, you want to show that you understand the assigned material and can discuss it intelligently. This chapter helps you do that.

What is my goal?

Your goal is to improve your test-taking skills for objective and essay tests.

How can I succeed in tests?

The following tips can help you prepare both mentally and physically for any test you may encounter.

- **Study wisely.** Use a variety of study and memory techniques to help you see your coursework from several different angles.
- **Review with others.** Join a study group and prepare with them. Also, ask a classmate or family member to quiz you on key points.
- **Prepare yourself physically.** Get a good night's sleep, exercise, and eat a healthful, light meal before the test.
- **Get to class early** . . . but not too early! Hurrying increases anxiety, but so does waiting.
- **Relax.** Take a deep breath, close your eyes, and think positive thoughts. Relaxation enhances recall and clear thinking.
- **Glance through the entire test.** Read all directions carefully. Then plan your time, spending most of it on test questions that count most.
- **Fill in all the answers you know.** This process relieves anxiety and triggers you to remember answers to other questions.
- **Don't panic.** If other people start handing in their papers long before you are finished, don't worry.
- **Use your time well.** After you have finished writing, use the remaining time to revise and proofread.

What's Ahead

OBJECTIVE AND ESSAY TESTS

44a Taking an Objective Test

Even though objective tests are generally straightforward and clear, these tips can help you avoid making foolish mistakes.

What strategies should I use on true/false tests?

- Read the entire question. Often the first half of a statement will be true or false, while the second half is just the opposite. For an answer to be true, the entire statement must be true.
- Read each word and number. Pay special attention to names, dates, and numbers that are similar and could easily be confused.
- Beware of true/false statements that contain words such as *all, every, always,* and *never.* Very often these statements will be false.
- Watch for statements that contain more than one negative word. **Remember:** Two negatives make a positive: It is *unlikely* ice *will not* melt when the temperature rises above 32 degrees Fahrenheit.

What strategies should I use on matching tests?

- Read through both lists quickly before you begin answering. Note any descriptions that are similar and pay special attention to the differences.
- When matching a word to a word, determine the part of speech of each word. If the word is a verb, for example, match it with another verb.
- When matching a word to a phrase, read the phrase first and look for the word it describes.
- Cross out each answer as you find it—unless you are told that the answer can be used more than once.
- Use capital letters rather than lowercase letters because they are less likely to be misread by the person correcting the test.

What strategies should I use on multiple-choice tests?

- Read the directions to determine whether you are looking for the *correct* answer or the *best* answer. Also, check whether some questions can have two (or more) correct answers.
- Read the first part of the question, looking for negative words such as *not, never, except,* and *unless.*
- Try to answer the question in your mind before looking at the choices.
- Read all the choices before selecting your answer. This step is especially important for tests in which you must select the best answer, or for tests in which one of your choices is a combination of two or more answers:
  - d) Both a and b
  - e) All of the above
  - f) None of the above.

44b   Taking an Essay Test

If you're like most college students, taking essay tests is a frequent (though possibly unpleasant) affair. To make the experience more pleasant— and more successful—practice the advice below.

Following is a list of key terms, along with a definition and an example of how each is used. Studying these terms carefully is the first step in writing thoughtful answers to essay questions.

Analyze   To analyze is to break down a problem, a situation, an object, or a phenomenon into separate parts and to show their relationships.

> Analyze the major difficulties found at urban housing projects.

Classify   To classify is to place persons or things (especially animals and plants) together in a group because they share similar characteristics. Science uses a special classification or group order: *phylum, class, order, family, genus, species,* and *variety.*

> Classify three kinds of trees found in the rainforests of Costa Rica.

Compare   To compare is to explain how things are similar in one or more important ways.

> Compare the vegetation in the rainforests of Puerto Rico with the vegetation in the rainforests of Costa Rica.

Contrast   To contrast is to explain how things are different in one or more important ways.

> Contrast the views of George Washington and Harry S. Truman regarding the involvement of the United States in world affairs.

Compare and contrast   To compare and contrast is to use examples that show the major similarities and differences between two things (or people, events, ideas, and so forth). Comparing and contrasting things distinguishes the nature or meaning of each.

> Compare and contrast people-centered leadership with task-centered leadership.

Define   To define is to give the literal meaning for a term. Generally, it involves identifying the class to which a term belongs and telling how it differs from other things in that class.

> Define the term *emotional intelligence* as it pertains to humans.

Describe   To describe is to give a detailed sketch or impression of a topic.

> Describe how the Euro tunnel (the Chunnel) was built.

OBJECTIVE AND ESSAY TESTS

Diagram To diagram is to explain with lines or pictures—a flowchart, a map, or another graphic device. Generally, a diagram will label all of the important points or parts.

Diagram the parts of a DNA molecule.

Discuss To discuss is to review an issue from all sides. A discussion answer must be carefully organized to stay on track.

Discuss the ethics of protecting the anonymity of news sources.

Evaluate To evaluate is to make a value judgment by giving the pluses and minuses along with supporting evidence.

Evaluate the efforts of midsize cities to improve public transportation services.

Explain To explain is to bring out into the open, to make clear, and to analyze. This term is similar to *discuss* but places more emphasis on cause/effect relationships or step-by-step sequences.

Explain the hazards of household pollutants to the public health.

Outline To outline is to organize a set of facts or ideas by listing main points and subpoints. A good outline shows at a glance how topics or ideas fit together or relate to one another.

Outline the events that caused the United States to enter World War II.

Prove To prove is to bring out the truth by giving evidence to back up a point.

Prove that there is or is not a "lawsuit industry" in the United States.

Review To review is to reexamine or to summarize the key characteristics or major points of the topic. Generally speaking, a review presents material in the order in which it happened or in decreasing order of importance.

Review the events since 1976 that have led to the current hip-hop culture.

State To state is to present concisely a position, fact, or point of view.

State the factors that determine whether or not a new business will survive its first year.

Summarize To summarize is to present the main points of an issue in a shortened form. Details, illustrations, and examples are usually omitted.

Summarize the primary responsibilities of a college in a democracy.

Trace To trace is to present—in a step-by-step sequence—a series of facts that are somehow related. Usually the facts are presented in chronological order.

Trace the events that led to the fall of the Union of Soviet Socialist Republics.

44c Planning and Writing an Essay-Test Answer

When answering an essay question, follow these steps.

1. **Reread the question several times.** Pay special attention to any key words used in the question. (See **44b**.)

2. **Rephrase the question into a topic sentence/thesis statement** with a clear point.

    Question: Explain why public housing was built in Chicago in the 1960s.

    Thesis statement: Public housing was built in Chicago because of the Great Migration, the name given to the movement of African Americans from the South to the North.

3. **Outline the main points you plan to cover in your answer.**

4. **Write your essay (or paragraph).** Begin with your thesis statement (or topic sentence). Add needed background information and then follow your outline.

How should I write a one-paragraph answer?

If you must write one paragraph to answer the question, use the main points of your outline as supporting details for your topic sentence.

Question: Explain why public housing was built in Chicago in the 1960s.

> **Public housing was built in Chicago because of the Great Migration, the name given to the movement of African Americans from the South to the North.** The mechanical cotton picker, introduced in the 1920s, replaced field hands in the cotton fields of the South. At that time Chicago's factories and stockyards were hiring workers. In addition, Jim Crow laws caused hardships and provided reasons for African Americans to move north. Finally, some African Americans had family and relatives in Chicago who had migrated earlier and who, it was thought, could provide a home base for the new migrants until they could get work and housing. According to the U.S. Census Reports, there were 109,000 African Americans in Chicago in 1920. By 1960, there were more than 800,000. This increase in population could have been absorbed, except that the public wanted to keep the African Americans in the Black Belt, an area in South Chicago. Reluctant lending agencies and Realtors made it possible for speculators to operate. Speculators increased the cost of houses by 75 percent. All of these factors led to a housing shortage for African Americans, which public housing filled.

Topic sentence

Supporting details

Conclusion

OBJECTIVE AND ESSAY TESTS

How should I write a multiparagraph answer?

If you are required to write a complete essay, your opening paragraph should include your thesis statement and any essential background information. Begin your second paragraph by rephrasing one of the main points from your outline into a suitable topic sentence. Support this topic sentence with examples, reasons, or other appropriate details. Handle additional paragraphs in the same manner. If time permits, add a summary or concluding paragraph to bring all of your thoughts to a logical close.

Question: Explain the advantages and disadvantages of wind energy.

Thesis: The advantages of wind energy seem to outweigh the disadvantages.

OUTLINE
I. ADVANTAGES OF WIND ENERGY
   A. RENEWABLE
   B. ECONOMICAL
   C. NONPOLLUTING
II. POTENTIAL DISADVANTAGES OF WIND ENERGY
   A. INTERMITTENT
   B. UNSIGHTLY
   C. A DANGER TO SOME WILDLIFE

The introductory paragraph sets up the essay's organization.

1   Wind energy has both advantages and disadvantages. It is renewable, economical, and nonpolluting; but it is also intermittent, unsightly, and dangerous to the bird population.

2   Wind energy is renewable. No matter how much wind energy is used today, there will still be a supply tomorrow. As evidence indicates that wind energy was used to propel boats along the Nile River about 5000 B.C.E., it can be said that wind is an eternal, renewable resource.

Each paragraph follows a point in the outline.

3   Wind energy is economical. The fuel (wind) is free, but the initial cost for wind turbines is higher than for fossil-fueled generators. However, wind energy costs do not include fuel purchases and feature only minimal operating expenses. Wind power could potentially reduce the amount of foreign oil the United States imports and reduce health and environmental costs caused by pollution. Is it possible to sell excess power? The Public Utilities Regulatory Policy Act of 1978 (PURPA) states that a local electric company must buy any excess power produced by a qualifying individual. This act encourages the use of wind power.

4   Wind energy does not pollute. Whether one wind turbine is used by an individual or a wind farm supplies energy to many people, no air pollutants or greenhouse gases are emitted. California reports that 2.5 billion pounds of carbon dioxide and 15 million pounds of other pollutants have not entered the air thanks to wind energy.

> Specific details explain the main point.

5   How unfortunate is it that wind energy is intermittent? If the wind does not blow, there is little or no electrical power. One way to resolve this dilemma is to store the energy that wind produces in batteries. The word *intermittent* also refers to the fact that wind power is not always available at the places where it is needed most. Often the sites that offer the strongest, steadiest winds are located in remote locations far from the cities that demand great electrical power.

6   Are wind turbines unsightly? A home-sized wind machine rises about 30 feet and has rotors between 8 and 25 feet in diameter. The largest machine in Hawaii stands about 20 stories high and has rotors a little longer than the length of a football field. It supplies electricity to 1,400 homes. Does a single wind turbine upset the aesthetics of a community as much as a wind farm? The old adage "Beauty is in the eye of the beholder" holds up wherever wind turbines rotate. If ongoing electrical costs are almost nil, that wind turbine may look beautiful.

> Questions help the reader understand the issue.

7   How serious is the issue of bird safety? The main questions are these: (1) Why do birds come near wind turbines? (2) What, if any, are the effects of wind development on bird populations? (3) If wind turbines do negatively affect bird populations, what can be done to lessen the problem? If even one bird of a protected species is killed, the Endangered Species Act has been violated. If wind turbines kill migratory birds, the Migratory Bird Treaty Act has been violated. As a result of these concerns, many countries and agencies are studying the problem carefully.

8   The advantages of wind energy seem to outweigh the disadvantages. The wind energy industry has been growing steadily in the United States and around the world. The new wind turbines are reliable and efficient. People's attitudes toward wind energy are mostly positive. Many manufacturers and government agencies are now cooperating to expand wind energy, making it the fastest-growing source of electricity in the world.

> The ending makes a final conclusion.

44d Checklist: Taking the Essay Test

____ Make sure you are ready for the test both mentally and physically.

____ Listen to or carefully read the instructions.

- How much time do you have to complete the test?
- Do all the essay questions count equally?
- Can you use any aids, such as a dictionary or handbook?
- Are there any corrections, changes, or additions to the test?

____ Begin the test immediately and watch the time. Don't spend so much time answering one question that you run out of time before answering the others.

____ Read all essay questions carefully, paying special attention to the key words. (See **44b**.)

____ Ask the instructor for clarification if you don't understand something.

____ Rephrase each question into a controlling idea for your essay answer. (This idea becomes your thesis statement.)

____ Think before you write. Jot down the important information and work it into a brief outline. Do this on the back of the test sheet, on a piece of scrap paper, or in the margin of your answer sheet.

____ Use a logical pattern of organization and a strong topic sentence for each paragraph. Tie your points together with clear, logical transitions.

____ Write concisely. Don't, however, use abbreviations or nonstandard language.

____ Be efficient. First write about those facets of the subject about which you are most certain; then work on other areas as time permits.

____ Keep your test paper neat and use reasonable margins. Neatness is always important, and readability is a must, especially on an essay exam.

____ Revise and proofread. Read through your essay as carefully and completely as time permits.

VISUALS TIP

Often it can be helpful to draw a graphic (a map, Venn diagram, cluster, and so on) to quickly record and organize your thoughts about the essay topic before you begin writing.

Research Writing

Research Writing

Planning Your Research Project

In a sense, all writing is rooted in research. Informal writing depends on memories or undocumented sources, whereas formal writing requires highly varied, documented sources. Fundamentally, all research is about asking questions and finding answers.

How should I begin a research project?

As with any form of writing, understanding a research project begins with understanding the purpose, form, audience, and voice.

- **Purpose:** Because an assignment usually relates to a course concept, consider what your instructor wants you to learn. While the project aims to teach you to do research and share results, your main goal is to discover the complex truth about a topic.
- **Form:** The traditional research paper is an essay complete with thesis, support, and documentation. However, some research projects result in different outcomes such as a proposal or a multimedia presentation.
- **Audience:** Normally, the research paper addresses "the academic community"—curious, educated readers like your professor and classmates. Sometimes, however, your audience may be more specific (for example, fellow nursing majors).
- **Voice:** The tone usually is semiformal, but check your instructor's expectations. In any research paper, strive to sound confident and thoughtful, not pedantic.

What's Ahead

45a Following the Research Process
45b Getting Focused: Topics, Questions, and Theses
45c Developing a Research Plan
45d Using Primary and Secondary Sources
45e Exploring Possible Information Resources and Sites
45f Researching for Different Forms of Writing
45g Checklist: Research Planning

PLANNING YOUR RESEARCH PROJECT

45a Following the Research Process

The research process includes four phases: **getting started, planning your research, conducting research,** and **organizing and drafting.** This process is flexible enough to be adapted to any research project. In fact, real research is typically dynamic: You might think that you've nailed down your topic only to discover a surprising topical detour. Be prepared to tailor the process to each specific project.

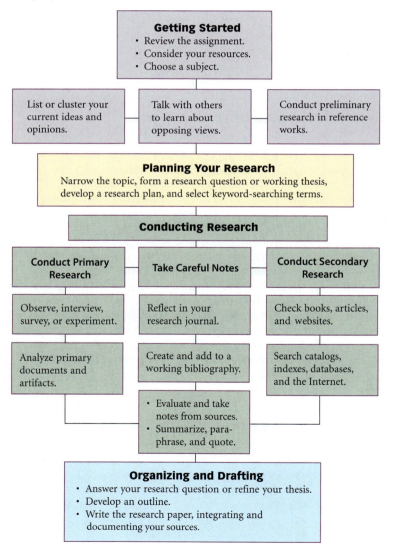

Getting Started
- Review the assignment.
- Consider your resources.
- Choose a subject.

List or cluster your current ideas and opinions.

Talk with others to learn about opposing views.

Conduct preliminary research in reference works.

Planning Your Research
Narrow the topic, form a research question or working thesis, develop a research plan, and select keyword-searching terms.

Conducting Research

Conduct Primary Research

Take Careful Notes

Conduct Secondary Research

Observe, interview, survey, or experiment.

Reflect in your research journal.

Check books, articles, and websites.

Analyze primary documents and artifacts.

Create and add to a working bibliography.

Search catalogs, indexes, databases, and the Internet.

- Evaluate and take notes from sources.
- Summarize, para-phrase, and quote.

Organizing and Drafting
- Answer your research question or refine your thesis.
- Develop an outline.
- Write the research paper, integrating and documenting your sources.

45b Getting Focused: Topics, Questions, and Theses

Early in your project, get focused by narrowing your topic, brainstorming research questions, and developing a working thesis. For help understanding assignments and selecting topics, see **6a–6c**.

How can I find a manageable focus?

Once you have a broad topic, you need to narrow your focus to a specific feature or angle that allows for in-depth research.

Broad Topic	Manageable Focus
Homelessness	Homeless Families in Los Angeles
Bacteria and Viruses	Bacterial Resistance to Antibiotics
Alternative Energy Sources	Development of Hybrid-Electric Vehicles

How can I gather good research questions?

Here are some suggestions for gathering good research questions:

- **List both simple and substantial questions.** Basic questions aim for facts; substantial questions get at analysis, synthesis, and evaluation.

  Question of Fact: What are the government's figures on homelessness?

  Question of Interpretation: When did homelessness become a problem?

- **List main and secondary questions.** Ask a primary question about your topic—the main issue that you want to get at. Then answer the five W's and H about the topic.

  Main Question: Should consumers embrace hybrid cars?

  Sample Secondary Question: How does hybrid technology work?

How can I develop a working thesis?

Develop a working thesis that seems debatable or that requires some explanation. Try this formula:

FORMULA

>   Limited topic
> + Tentative claim, statement, or hypothesis
> = Working thesis

Example

> *Hybrid cars* are a positive step forward from the average internal-combustion car, but they don't go far enough toward cleaner air.

PLANNING YOUR RESEARCH PROJECT

45c Developing a Research Plan

With your limited topic, main research question, and working thesis in front of you, plan out your project more fully.

Which research methods should I use?

Consider these questions: What do I already know about the topic? What do I need to know? What resources will help me answer my research question? What resources does the assignment require? Then map out a research method.

- **Background Research:** Conduct a preliminary search of the library catalog, journal databases, and the Internet. Use specialized reference works to find background information, definitions, facts, and statistics. (See **48b**.)
- **Primary Research:** Use interviews, conduct surveys, make observations, and analyze key documents or artifacts related to your topic. (See **47**.)
- **Library Research:** Use scholarly books, news sources, magazines, scholarly journals, trade journals, and other library resources, such as documentaries, pamphlets, marketing studies, or government publications. (See **48**.)
- **Internet Research:** Use search engines and subject guides to find reputable websites. (See **49**.) Test all resources for quality and reliability. (See **46d**.)

How can I organize my research project?

Here's how you can get yourself organized.

Establish a schedule. Generally you should spend about half your time on research and half on writing. Sketch out a preliminary schedule with tentative deadlines for completing each phase of your work.

Develop a research proposal. For some research projects, you may have to formalize your plan by writing a research proposal. Such a proposal aims to show that the research is both valid (makes good scholarly sense) and valuable (will lead to significant knowledge). A proposal should also communicate your enthusiasm for the project, show that your plan is workable within the constraints of the assignment, and gain your instructor's feedback and approval. Such a proposal typically includes a project description, plan, timetable, and list of expected outcomes.

Web Link: A sample research schedule and sample proposal, along with guidelines and instructions, are available at <www.thecollegewriter.com>.

45d Using Primary and Secondary Sources

Depending on your assignment, you may be expected to use primary, secondary, or both kinds of sources.

What are primary sources?

A primary source is an original source, such as a log, a person, or an event, that gives firsthand information on a topic. Common forms are observations, interviews, surveys, experiments, and analyses of documents and artifacts. Here are sample primary sources for a research project on hybrid-car technology:

- E-mail interview with an automotive engineer
- Documents detailing fuel-efficiency legislation
- Test drive of a hybrid car at a Honda dealership

Upside: Primary sources produce information precisely tailored to your research needs and give you direct, hands-on access to your topic.

Downside: Obtaining primary sources can take much time and many resources. It can also require specialized skills for designing surveys and analyzing statistics.

What are secondary sources?

Secondhand information has been compiled, summarized, interpreted, and evaluated by someone studying primary sources. Journal articles, encyclopedia entries, and documentaries are typical examples. Secondary sources for a report about hybrid-car technology might include the following:

- Journal article discussing the development of hybrid-car technology
- Newspaper editorial on fossil fuels
- TV news magazine roundtable discussion of hybrid-car advantages and disadvantages
- Manufacturer's promotional literature for a specific hybrid car
- Published statistics about hybrid-car sales

Upside: Secondary sources can save research time and provide extensive data while offering expert analysis of the topic.

Downside: Secondhand information can require digging to find relevant data, and the original research may be faulty.

> **NOTE:** Whether a source is primary or secondary depends on what you are studying. For example, if you were studying U.S. attitudes toward hybrid cars (and not hybrid-car technology itself), the newspaper editorial and TV roundtable would be primary sources.

45e Exploring Possible Information Resources and Sites

To conduct thorough, creative, but efficient research, you need a sense of what types of resources are available for your project and where to find them. Check the tables that follow.

Which resources should I use?

Examine the range of resources available and decide which ones will give you the best information for your project. A well-rounded research paper relies on a range of quality resources and avoids insubstantial web information.

Type of Resource	Examples
Personal, direct resources	Memories, diaries, journals, logs Experiments, tests, observations Interviews, surveys
Reference works (print and electronic)	Dictionaries, thesauruses Encyclopedias, almanacs, atlases Directories, guides, handbooks Indexes, abstracts, catalogs, bibliographies
Books (print and electronic)	Nonfiction, how-to, biographies Fiction, trade books, scholarly and scientific studies
Periodicals and news sources	Print newspapers, magazines, and journals Broadcast news and news magazines Online magazines, news sources, and discussion groups

Audiovisual, digital, and
multimedia resources
	Graphics (tables, graphs, charts,
	  maps, drawings, photos)
	Audiotapes, CDs, videos, DVDs
	Webpages, online databases, computer
	  files and programs, CD-ROMs

Government publications	Guides, programs, forms Legislation, regulations Reports, records, statistics
Business and nonprofit publications	Reports, pamphlets, brochures, ads Instructions, handbooks, manuals Policies and procedures Displays, presentations, demonstrations Catalogs, newsletters, news releases

Which information "sites" should I go to?

An information site is a place you can go to—or a person you can consult—to find information for your project. Consider the sites listed below, remembering that many resources may be available in different forms in different locations.

Information Location	Examples
People	Experts (knowledge area, skill, occupation) Population segments or individuals (with representative or unusual experiences)
Libraries	General: public, college, online Specialized: legal, medical, government, business
Computer resources	Computers: software, disks, CD-ROMs Networks: Internet and other online services (e-mail, limited-access databases, discussion groups, MUDs, chat rooms, websites); intranets
Mass media	Radio (AM and FM) Television (network, public, cable, satellite) Print (newspapers, magazines, journals)
Testing, training, meeting, and observation sites	Plants, facilities, field sites, laboratories, research centers, universities, think tanks Conventions, conferences, seminars Museums, galleries, historical sites
Municipal, state, and federal government offices	Elected officials, representatives Offices and agencies Government Printing Office (GPO) website <www.gpoaccess.gov>
Workplace	Computer databases, company files Desktop reference materials Bulletin boards (physical and electronic) Company and department websites Departments and offices (customer service, public relations, and so on) Associations, professional organizations Consulting, training, and business information services

PLANNING YOUR RESEARCH PROJECT

45f Researching for Different Forms of Writing

Different forms of college writing generally rely on specific research strategies. Here's an overview; use this table to plan research for your next assignment.

Forms of Writing	Recommended Research Strategies

Personal Essays (38)
Personal narrative
Personal reflection
Description of
  a person, place,
  or event
	Focus on primary research.
	Search your memories; reflect on your experiences.
	Study artifacts such as photographs, diaries, old
	  newspapers, and videos.
	Observe locations and events.
	Interview participants.
	Use secondary research to clarify facts, background,
	  definitions, and other details.

Analytical Essays (39)
Cause/effect
Comparison/
  contrast
Classification
Process
Definition
	Generally, start with primary research.
	Study texts, documents, maps, events, and videos.
	Conduct observations, experiments, and tests.
	Use secondary research to support primary research:
	  Go to specialized reference works, journal articles,
	  books, and online sources to support and clarify
	  details of analysis.

Persuasive Essays (40)
Arguing a point
Problem/solution
	Generally, rely on secondary research.
	Review the literature on your topic.
	Find trustworthy information in reference works,
	  journal articles, and substantial websites.
	Use primary research in a supporting role:
	■ Conduct interviews and surveys to get
	    others' opinions on your topic.
	■ Observe to "see for yourself."
	■ Study primary texts and artifacts to get
	    unbiased, objective information.

Reports (on website) Interview Experiment or lab Field report	**For reports, perform primary research but consider background research.** Use reference works and literature reviews of secondary sources to prepare for primary research.

45g Checklist: Research Planning

___ I have clarified my assignment: the purpose, readers, and resources.

___ I have selected an appropriate topic, conducted preliminary research, narrowed my focus, and developed a working thesis.

___ I have chosen research methods and am organized to do my research.

___ I have considered possible primary and secondary resources.

Note-Taking Strategies

The quality of your note taking can make or break your research project. Research requires careful management of material—especially with so much information and powerful technology at your fingertips. Therefore, learn to select reliable sources and take strong notes.

ETHICS TIP

Avoiding Unintentional Plagiarism
Careful note taking can help prevent unintentional plagiarism. Plagiarism—using source material without giving credit—is treated more fully elsewhere in this book (**50a**). Essentially, however, *unintentional* plagiarism happens when you *accidentally* use a source's ideas, phrases, or information without documenting that material. To prevent this problem, practice these strategies:

- Maintain an accurate working bibliography (**46c**).
- When taking notes, clearly distinguish between source material and your own thinking by using quotation marks, codes, and/or separate columns or note cards.
- If you copy and paste digital material, always track the origins with codes, abbreviations, or separate columns.
- Treat web sources like print sources.
- When you draft your paper, transfer source material carefully by coding material that you integrate into your discussion, using quotation marks, and double-checking your typing.

What's Ahead

NOTE-TAKING STRATEGIES

46a Developing a Note-Taking System

Accurate, thoughtful notes create a solid foundation for your research writing. In fact, putting quality time into note taking will help you efficiently draft a quality paper. The trick is to choose an efficient note-taking system.

What are you trying to do when you take notes on sources? What you are *not* doing is (1) collecting quotations to plunk in your project, (2) piling data into a growing stack of disconnected facts, or (3) taking notes on every source you find.

How can I choose a note-taking strategy?

Be selective. Guided by your research questions and working thesis, focus on sources that are central to your project. From these sources, record information on your limited topic, but also take notes on what surprises or puzzles you. Be selective, avoiding notes that are either too thin or too extensive. Suppose, for example, that you are writing a paper on the engineering problems facing NASA's space shuttle. You might take careful notes on material describing the shuttle's technical details, but not on the experiences of astronauts in space.

Develop accurate, complete records. Your notes should
- Accurately summarize, paraphrase, and quote from sources (**46e**).
- Clearly show where you got your information.
- Cover all the research you've done—primary research, books, periodicals, and online sources.

Engage your sources. Constantly evaluate what you are reading and develop your own responses and ideas. (See **46d**.) For example, with an article about NASA's space shuttle, you might test the author's biases, credentials, and logic; and you might respond with knowledge you have gained about other space programs in other countries.

VISUALS TIP

Take good notes on graphics in sources—tables, line graphs, flow-charts, photographs, maps, and so on. Such graphics are typically packed with information and powerfully convey ideas. (See "Critical Thinking Through Visual Images," **3a–3d**.) For example, a photograph or line drawing could communicate clearly many of the complex technical details of how the booster rockets work on the shuttle.

Which note-taking system should I use?

Use one of the note-taking systems outlined on the pages that follow. Choose the system that works best for your project, or combine elements to develop your own system. A good note-taking system should do the following:

- Avoid unintentional plagiarism by keeping accurate records and separating source material from your own ideas
- Work flexibly with a wide range of resources—primary and secondary, print and electronic, verbal and visual
- Be accurate and complete so that you don't need to reread sources
- Efficiently develop your paper's outline and first draft

SYSTEM 1: PAPER OR ELECTRONIC NOTE CARDS

Using paper note cards is the traditional method of note taking; however, note-taking software is now available. Here's how a note-card system works:

1. Establish one set of cards for your working bibliography (**46c**).
2. On a second set of cards, take notes on sources:

   - Record one point from one source per card.
   - Clarify the source: List the author's last name, a shortened title, or a code from the matching bibliography card. Include a page number.
   - Write a heading to help you categorize and organize information.
   - Label the note as a summary, a paraphrase, or a quotation of the original.
   - Distinguish between the source's information and your own thoughts, perhaps by recording your ideas on separate cards.

Upside: Note cards are highly systematic, helping you categorize material and organize it for an outline and first draft.

Downside: This method can be initially tedious and time-consuming.

SYSTEM 2: THE DOUBLE-ENTRY NOTEBOOK

The double-entry notebook involves parallel note taking—notes from sources are placed beside your personal reactions. Using a double-entry notebook (or the columns feature of your word-processing program), do the following:

1. Divide notebook pages in half vertically.
2. In the left column, record bibliographic information and take notes on your sources.
3. In the right column, write your responses. Think about what the source is saying, why the point is important, and how it relates to your topic.

Upside: The double-entry method helps you create accurate source records while encouraging thoughtful responses; also, it can be done on a computer.

Downside: Organizing material for drafting may be a challenge.

NOTE-TAKING STRATEGIES

SYSTEM 3: COPY AND ANNOTATE

The copy-and-annotate method involves working with photocopies, print versions, or digital texts of sources. (For a sample of annotation in action, see 1b.) Here's how to do it:

1. Selectively photocopy, print, or copy the text of important sources. (Copy carefully, making sure that you have page numbers.)

2. As needed, add identifying information on the copy—author, publication details, and date. Each page should be easy to identify and trace.

3. As you read, mark up the copy and highlight key statements. In the margins or digital file, record your ideas:

   - Ask questions. Insert a "?" in the margin, or write out the question.
   - Make connections. Draw arrows to link ideas, or make notes like "see page 36."
   - Add asides. Record what you think and feel while reading.
   - Define terms. Note important words that you need to understand.
   - Create a marginal index. Write key words to identify themes and main parts.

Upside: The copy-and-annotate method helps you record sources accurately; annotating encourages careful reading and thinking.

Downside: Organizing material for drafting is inconvenient. When done poorly, annotating and highlighting involve skimming, not critical thinking.

SYSTEM 4: THE COMPUTER NOTEBOOK OR RESEARCH LOG

The computer-notebook or research-log method involves note taking on a computer or on sheets of paper. Here's how it works:

1. Establish a central location for your notes—a notebook, file folder, binder, or electronic folder.

2. Take notes one source at a time, making sure to identify the source fully. Number your note pages.

3. Using your initials or some other symbol, distinguish your own thoughts from source material.

4. Use codes in your notes to identify which information in the notes relates to which topic in your outline. Then under each topic in the outline, write the page number in your notes where that information is recorded. With an electronic notebook or log, you may be able to rearrange your notes into an outline by using copy-and-paste—but don't lose source information in the process!

Upside: Taking notes feels natural without being overly systematic.

Downside: Outlining and drafting may require a good deal of time-consuming paper shuffling.

46b Conducting Effective Keyword Searches

Keyword searching is a vital research skill. With a whole range of research tools, what you find and how fast you find it often depend on which keywords you select.

Which keywords should I use?

Brainstorm a list of possible keywords. Based on your research questions, working thesis, and background reading, brainstorm topics, titles, and names to use in searches. If you were studying illegal immigration, for example, you might come up with these terms:

- illegal immigration
- migrant workers
- Immigration and Naturalization Service
- border patrols

Consult the Library of Congress subject headings. These books list keywords that librarians use to classify materials. This information (1) shows the basic structure of your subject, (2) tells you the best keywords to use in searches, and (3) helps you narrow or broaden your project's focus.

Get to know databases. Whether you use EBSCOhost, LexisNexis, JSTOR, or ERIC, look for an instructions page, help file, tutorial, or FAQ area that answers these questions:

- What material does the database contain, and what time frames are included?
- What are the search rules? What limiters can you use to narrow the search? What expanders can you use to broaden it?
- What details will you get in search results—authors, titles, call numbers, a list of subject terms, abstracts, full-text material?

Use a shotgun approach. Start with the most likely keyword. If you get no "hits," choose a related term. Once you get some hits, check the citations carefully for clues about keywords to use as you continue searching.

Use Boolean operators *(and, or, not)* **to refine searches.** Often, combining keywords by using Boolean logic leads to better research results. When you combine keywords with Boolean operators, the search string reads from left to right.

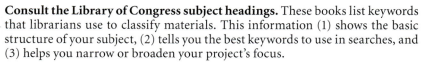

WRITER'S TIP

To get the best results, avoid these problems: misspelling keywords; using vague or broad keywords *(education, business)*; incorrectly combining operators; and shortening words too much.

46c Developing a Working Bibliography

A working bibliography lists sources that you intend to use. It helps you track your research, develop your final bibliography, and avoid plagiarism.

How should I prepare my bibliography?

Select an efficient approach for your project:

Paper Note Cards: Use 3″ × 5″ cards, and record one source per card.

Paper Notebook: Use a small, spiral-bound book to record sources.

Computer Program: Record source information by capturing citation details from online searches or by entering them manually.

What information should I include for each source?

Start by giving each source a code number or letter. Then include specific details for each kind of source listed below.

Books: author, title, publication details (place, publisher, date)

Periodicals: author, article title, journal name, publication information (volume, number, date), page numbers

Online Sources: author (if available), document title, site sponsor, database name, publication or posting date, access date, other publication information

Primary or Field Research: date conducted; name and descriptive title of interviewee, place observed, survey conducted, document analyzed

WAC Link: Consider recording bibliographic details in the format of the documentation system you are using—MLA, APA, CSE, or CMS. Doing so now will save time later. In addition, some research software allows you to automatically format bibliographic information in any of the systems.

What locating information should I include?

Because you may need to retrace your research footsteps, include details about your research path:

Articles: Note where and how you accessed them.

Webpages: Carefully record the complete URL, not just the site address.

Field Research: Include a telephone number or e-mail address.

46d   Engaging and Evaluating Your Sources

Engage and evaluate all sources before you rely on them in your writing. After all, credible sources help your own credibility.

How can I engage my sources?

Test each source to see if it's worth reading. When reviewing source citations and generating a working bibliography, consider the length and publication date and ask these questions:

- How closely related to my topic is this source?
- Is this source too basic, overly complex, or just right?
- What could this source add to my overall balance of sources?

Skim sources before reading them in-depth. Consider marking key pages or passages with sticky tabs or a digital bookmark.

- Review the author biography, preface, and/or introduction to discover the perspective, approach, scope, and research methods.
- Using your keywords, review any outline, abstract, table of contents, index, or home page to get a sense of coverage.

Read with an open (but not empty) mind. Carry on a dialogue with the source, asking questions like "Why?" and "So what?"

- Note the source's purpose and audience. Was it written to inform or to persuade? Is it aimed at the public, supporters, or opponents?
- Relate the source to your research question: How does the source affect my ideas? Synthesize what you read with what you know.
- Record your reactions to the material.
- Consider how you might use this source—for background, key facts, important ideas, opposing perspectives, or examples.
- Check footnotes, references, and links for further research leads.

How can I evaluate my sources?

You should judge each source on its own merit. Generally, however, types of sources can be rated for depth and reliability, as shown in the table on the next page, based on their authorship, length, topic treatment, documentation, publication method, review process, distance from primary sources, allegiances, stability, and so on. Use the table to

- Target sources that fit your project's goals.
- Assess the approximate quality of the sources you're gathering.
- Build a strong bibliography that readers will respect.

NOTE-TAKING STRATEGIES

Deep

Scholarly Books and Articles: Largely based on careful research; written by experts for experts; address topics in depth; involve peer review and careful editing; offer stable discussion of topic

Trade Books and Journal Articles: Largely based on careful research; written by experts for educated general audience. Sample periodicals: *Atlantic Monthly, Scientific American, Nature, Orion*

Reliable

Government Resources: Books, reports, webpages, guides, statistics developed by experts at government agencies; provided as a service to citizens; relatively objective. Sample resource: *Statistical Abstract of the United States*

Credible

Reviewed, Official Online Documents: Internet resources posted by legitimate institutions—colleges and universities, research institutes, service organizations; although offering a particular perspective, sources tend to be balanced

Reference Works and Textbooks: Provide general and specialized information; carefully researched, reviewed, and edited; lack depth for focused research (such as a general encyclopedia entry)

News and Topical Stories from Quality Sources: Provide current affairs coverage (print and online), introduction-level articles of interest to general public; may lack depth and length. Sample sources: the *Washington Post,* the *New York Times; Time, Psychology Today;* NPR's *All Things Considered*

Shallow

Popular Magazine Stories: Short, introductory articles often distant from primary sources and without documentation; heavy advertising. Sample sources: *Glamour, Seventeen, Reader's Digest*

Business and Nonprofit Publications: Pamphlets, reports, news releases, brochures, manuals; range from informative to sales-focused

Unreliable

List Server Discussions, Usenet Postings, Blog Articles, Talk Radio Discussions: Highly open, fluid, undocumented, untested exchanges and publications; unstable resource

Incredible

Unregulated Web Material: Personal sites, joke sites, chat rooms, special-interest sites, advertising and junk e-mail (spam); no review process, little accountability, bias present

Tabloid Articles (Print and Web): Contain exaggerated and untrue stories written to titillate and exploit. Sample source: the *National Enquirer*

Engaging and Evaluating Your Sources

How should I evaluate print and online sources?

As you work with a source, you need to test its reliability. The benchmarks that follow apply to both print and online sources.

Credible Author: Is the author an expert *on this topic?* What are his or her credentials, and can you confirm these?

- **Web Test:** Is an author indicated? If so, are the author's credentials noted and contact information provided?

Reliable Publication: Has the source been published by a scholarly press, a quality trade book publisher, or a trusted news source?

- **Web Test:** Which individual or group posted this page? Is the site rated by a subject directory or library organization? How stable is the site—has it been around for a while? Check the site's home page, looking for evidence of the organization's perspective, history, and trustworthiness.

Unbiased Discussion: While all sources come from a specific perspective, a *biased* source may be pushing an agenda in an unfair, unbalanced, or incomplete manner. Watch for bias toward a certain region, political party, gender, race, or religion.

- **Web Test:** Is the online document one-sided? Is it pushing a cause, product, or belief? How do advertising or special interests affect the site?

Current Information: A five-year-old book on computers may be outdated, but a forty-year-old book on Abraham Lincoln could still be the best source. Given what you need, is this source's discussion up-to-date?

- **Web Test:** When was the material originally posted and last updated? Are links current?

Accurate Information: Check the source for factual errors, statistical flaws, and conclusions that don't add up.

- **Web Test:** Is the site filled with helpful, factual materials? Can you trace and confirm sources by following links or conducting your own search?

Full, Logical Support: Is the discussion of the topic reasonable, balanced, and complete? Are claims backed up with quality evidence? Does the source avoid twisted statistical analysis and logical fallacies?

- **Web Test:** Does the site offer links to other reputable sites?

Quality Writing and Design: Is the source well written? Is it free of derogatory terms, clichés, mindless slogans, and spelling errors?

- **Web Test:** Are words neutral or emotionally charged? Are pages well designed and easy to navigate? Is text well written, and are graphics well done?

46e Summarizing, Paraphrasing, and Quoting Sources

As you work with sources, you must decide what to put in your notes and how to record it—as a summary, paraphrase, or quotation. The passage below comes from an article on GM's development of fuel-cell technology. Review the passage; study how the researcher summarizes, paraphrases, and quotes from the source; and then practice these same strategies in your work with sources.

When Karl Benz rolled his Patent Motorcar out of the barn in 1886, he literally set the wheels of change in motion. The advent of the automobile led to dramatic alterations in people's way of life as well as the global economy—transformations that no one expected at the time. The ever increasing availability of economical personal transportation remade the world into a more accessible place while spawning a complex industrial infrastructure that shaped modern society.

Now another revolution could be sparked by automotive technology: one fueled by hydrogen rather than petroleum. Fuel cells—which cleave hydrogen atoms into protons and electrons that drive electric motors while emitting nothing worse than water vapor—could make the automobile much more environmentally friendly. Not only could cars become cleaner, but they could also become safer, more comfortable, more personalized—and even perhaps less expensive. Further, these fuel-cell vehicles could be instrumental in motivating a shift toward a "greener" energy economy based on hydrogen. As that occurs, energy use and production could change significantly. Thus, hydrogen fuel-cell cars and trucks could help ensure a future in which personal mobility—the freedom to travel independently—could be sustained indefinitely, without compromising the environment or depleting the Earth's natural resources.

A confluence of factors makes the big change seem increasingly likely. For one, the petroleum-fueled internal-combustion engine (ICE), as highly refined, reliable, and economical as it is, is finally reaching its limits. Despite steady improvements, today's ICE vehicles are only 20 to 25 percent efficient in converting the energy content of fuels into drive-wheel power. And although the U.S. auto industry has cut exhaust emissions substantially since the unregulated 1960s—hydrocarbons dropped by 99 percent, carbon monoxide by 96 percent, and nitrogen oxides by 95 percent—the continued production of carbon dioxide causes concern because of its potential to change the planet's climate.

From "Vehicle of Change," by Lawrence D. Burns, J. Byron-McCormick, and Christopher E. Borroni-Bird. Copyright ©2002 by Scientific American, Inc. All rights reserved.

Summarizing, Paraphrasing, and Quoting Sources

When should I summarize passages?

Summarize when the source provides relevant ideas and information on your topic. When you summarize, you condense in your own words the main points in a passage. Follow these steps:

1. Reread the passage, jotting down a few key words.
2. State the main point in your own words. Add key supporting points, leaving out examples, details, and long explanations. Be objective: Don't mix your reactions with the summary.
3. Check your summary against the original, making sure that you used quotation marks around any exact phrases you borrowed.

Sample Summary

> While the introduction of the car in the late nineteenth century has led to dramatic changes in society and world economics, another dramatic change is now taking place in the shift from gas engines to hydrogen technologies. Fuel cells may make the car "greener," and perhaps even more safe, comfortable, and cheap. These automotive changes will affect the energy industry by making it more environmentally friendly; as a result, people will continue to enjoy mobility while transportation moves to renewable energy. One factor leading to this technological shift is that the internal-combustion engine has reached the limits of its efficiency, potential, and development—while remaining problematic with respect to emissions, climate change, and health.

Web Link: For help with writing summaries (also called abstracts) of whole research papers, go to *The College Writer's Handbook* website at <www.thecollegewriter.com>.

When should I paraphrase passages?

Paraphrase passages that present important points but lack memorable or straightforward wording. Follow these steps:

1. Go through the passage carefully, sentence by sentence.
2. State the ideas in your own words, defining words as needed.
3. If you borrow phrases directly, put them in quotation marks.
4. Check your paraphrase against the original for accuracy.

NOTE-TAKING STRATEGIES

SAMPLE PARAPHRASE OF THE SECOND PARAGRAPH IN THE PASSAGE

Automobile technology may lead to another radical economic and social change through the shift from gasoline to hydrogen fuel. By breaking hydrogen into protons and electrons so that the electrons run an electric motor with only the by-product of water vapor, fuel cells could make the car a "green" machine. But this technology could also increase the automobile's safety, comfort, personal tailoring, and affordability. Moreover, this shift to fuel-cell engines in automobiles could lead to drastic, environmentally friendly changes in the broader energy industry, one that will now be tied to hydrogen rather than fossil fuels. The result of this shift will be radical changes in the way we use and produce energy. In other words, the shift to hydrogen-powered vehicles could maintain our society's valued mobility, even as the clean technology would preserve the environment and its natural resources.

When should I quote phrases, sentences, and passages?

Quote a source word-for-word when it states an idea using exact and memorable language. If you omit words, note that omission with an ellipsis (. . .). If you change words for grammatical reasons, put your changes in brackets. (See **29f**.)

SAMPLE QUOTATIONS

- "[H]ydrogen fuel-cell cars and trucks could help ensure a future in which personal mobility [. . .] could be sustained indefinitely, without compromising the environment or depleting the Earth's natural resources."

- "[T]he petroleum-fueled internal-combustion engine (ICE), as highly refined, reliable, and economical as it is, is finally reaching its limits."

46f   Checklist: Note Taking

____ I have taken notes carefully to prevent unintentional plagiarism.

____ I have established and used a note-taking system that effectively keeps track of research resources, helps me gather key ideas and information from these sources, and encourages me to build my own thinking.

____ I have carefully engaged and evaluated all my sources.

____ I have sensibly summarized, paraphrased, and quoted sources in my notes.

Doing Primary Research

Primary research offers fresh information. Such information hasn't been interpreted or analyzed by someone else and presented in prepackaged form. When you engage in primary research, you gather information firsthand by observing locations, interviewing people, and analyzing documents.

What types of primary research should I do?

Check the options below and select the forms that will be most useful for your project. Then review the guidelines on the appropriate pages.

- **Observations, inspections, and field research** involve systematically examining and analyzing places, spaces, scenes, equipment, work, or events. (See **47a**.)
  Value: Such research provides a range of information— from personal impressions to precise data.

- **Analyses of texts, documents, records, and artifacts** involve studying original correspondence, reports, legislation, literary works, tools, and so on. (See **47b**.)
  Value: Such research often provides direct evidence, key facts, and in-depth insights into the topic.

- **Interviews** involve consulting people who are experts on your topic, or people whose experiences with the topic can supply useful information. (See **47c**.)
  Value: Such firsthand research can add authority and perspective to your writing.

- **Surveys, forms, and inquiry letters** gather information as written responses you can review, tabulate, and analyze. (See <www.thecollegewriter.com>.)
  Value: Such research provides varied information (from simple facts to personal opinions) for statistical analysis.

What's Ahead

DOING PRIMARY RESEARCH

47a   Making Observations

Observation is a common form of research. Such research, which involves watching, listening, recording, and analyzing, is useful for gathering a range of information.

What should I do before an observation?

1. **Know what you want to accomplish.** Do you need to understand a process? Solve a problem? Answer a question?

2. **Consider your vantage point.** Should you observe the site passively or interact with it? Should you remain objective as you record data, or should you include analysis and impressions?

3. **Plan your observation.** Good preparation involves the following:
   - Creating a list of specific things to look for
   - Asking permission if the site isn't public
   - Scheduling a visit
   - Gathering observation tools (pen, paper, camera, recorder)

What should I do during an observation?

1. **Be flexible.** Follow your plan, but remain open to surprises.

2. **Identify your position.** What is your personal and cultural stance (gender, socioeconomic background, nationality, age, and so on)?

3. **Take notes on impressions.** Focus on your five senses:
   - *Sights*—record colors, shapes, and appearance
   - *Sounds*—listen for loud and subtle sounds
   - *Smells*—check out both pleasant and unpleasant odors
   - *Textures*—note temperature, smoothness, and roughness
   - *Tastes*—if your site permits, test for sweet, sour, bitter, and so on

4. **Gather other forms of evidence.** Take measurements, use recording technology, gather samples, interview people, and collect brochures.

What should I do after an observation?

1. **Look over your notes.** Watch for patterns and themes.

2. **List your conclusions.** Record your insights from your observations.

3. **Relate your observations to your other research.** Explore how your observations confirm, contradict, or complement other sources.

47b Analyzing Texts, Documents, Records, and Artifacts

An original document or record is one that directly relates to the event, issue, object, or phenomenon that you are researching. Examining original documents and artifacts can involve studying letters, e-mail exchanges, literary texts, legislation, and works of art. You examine such documents to understand a topic, arrive at a coherent conclusion about it, and support that judgment.

LINKS

Web Link: Many government, university, and scholarly websites provide access to original documents. Whereas once researchers had to travel to county courthouses or to specialty libraries to pour through microfiche files, now many of those public documents are available online. For example, Biblical scholars can find excerpts from the *Codex Sinaiticus*, and physicists can find Einstein's original notes on General Relativity.

Which documents should I choose?

Begin by considering the documents and artifacts directly connected to your topic. The closer to the topic, the more primary the source. Select materials that address your research questions or working thesis.

Imagine you are researching English labor riots of the 1830s.

- To understand what rioters were demanding, study copies of speeches given at demonstrations.
- To know who the rioters were, gather names from police reports or union-membership lists.
- To learn the political response to the riots, read political speeches or legislation.
- To better understand the attitudes of people from that time, review newspaper reports, art works, or novels from that period.

How can I get the most out of each source?

To make sense of the text, document, record, or artifact, list the secondary questions that you want to answer.

To study the legislative background behind the development of cleaner cars, such as the hybrid-fuel vehicle, you could access the Clean Air Act of 1990. As you study this legislation, you could frame your reading with these questions:

- What are the requirements of the Clean Air Act?
- How do those requirements affect automotive technology?
- Are schedules for change or specific deadlines written into the act?

How can I put the source in context?

First think about how the source fits in with its time and place in history. This is called the **external context.** Often, questions based on the five W's and H can help you understand the external context:

Who was Mary Wollstonecraft?

When and **where** did she write *A Vindication of the Rights of Woman*?

What type of document is it?

Why did she write it?

How did its publication affect the political climate of the time?

Next think about the source itself—how it is put together, how its different parts relate to one another, and how it uses language. These factors are the **internal context.** Analytical questions that begin with *what* can help you understand the whole source and its parts.

What is Wollstonecraft's central argument?

What evidence does she use to support her views?

What is the strongest part of her position?

What is the weakest part?

How can I apply the source's ideas to my research?

Apply the ideas by asking the question "how." For example, if you were writing a research paper about hybrid cars, you could apply the ideas in the Clean Air Act of 1990 by asking the following questions:

How has the Clean Air Act affected hybrid-car technology?

How has the Clean Air Act affected air quality?

How has hybrid-car technology helped achieve the goals of the act?

How has the technology failed to achieve the goals?

WAC Link: Studying primary documents and artifacts is central to many disciplines: history, literature, theology, philosophy, political studies, and archaeology, for example. Good analysis depends on asking research questions appropriate for the discipline. Using the English labor riots of the 1830s again as an example, here's what two disciplines might ask:

Political Science: What role did political theories, structures, and processes play in the riots—both in causing them and in responding to them?

Art: How were the concerns of the rioters embodied in the new "realist" style of the mid-1800s? Did artists sympathize with and address an alienated working-class audience? How did art comment on the social

47c Conducting Interviews

In an interview, you talk with someone who has expert knowledge about your topic or important experiences that would provide new insights and perspectives.

What should I do before an interview?

1. **Think about the topic.** Consider what you already know. Be informed so that you can build on that knowledge throughout the interview.

2. **Consider the person.** Think about what the person's expertise and experiences are and how you can learn from him or her.

3. **Arrange the interview.** Honor the interviewee's preferred time, place, and medium (in person, telephone, e-mail). Explain who you are, what your purpose is, and which topics you would like to cover. If you want to record the interview, ask for permission to do so.

4. **Brainstorm questions.** With your research goal in mind, develop your questions *(who, what, when, where, why,* and *how)*. Use open questions, which require more than a "yes" or "no" answer.

   - Start with a simple question that will establish rapport.
   - Arrange your questions logically.
   - Leave room for quotations, information, and impressions.
   - Highlight target questions—ones that you must ask.

What should I do during the interview?

1. **Be natural, sincere, and professional.** Arrive on time, introduce yourself, and remind the interviewee why you've come. Thank the person for the interview and provide necessary background information.

2. **Create a record of the interview.** Write down key facts, quotations, and impressions. If the person has given permission, tape the interview.

3. **Listen actively.** Use body language (nods, smiles, and eye contact). Pay attention not only to what the person says but also to how he or she says it—tone, context, and body language. Listen more than you talk.

4. **Be tactful and flexible.** If the person looks puzzled by a question, rephrase it or ask another one. If the discussion gets off track, gently redirect it. Ask pertinent follow-up questions.

> **NOTE:** When you end the interview, ask if the person wants to add, clarify, or emphasize anything.

DOING PRIMARY RESEARCH

What should I do after an interview?

1. **Study your notes and records.** As soon as possible, review all your notes and fill in responses you remember but couldn't record at the time. If you recorded the interview, replay or review it, looking carefully for key ideas and information.

2. **Analyze the results.** Study the information, insights, and quotations you gathered. What do they reveal about the topic? How does the interview confirm, complement, or contradict other sources on the topic?

3. **If appropriate, contact the interviewee.** By note, e-mail, or phone, do the following:

   - Thank the person for his or her time and help.
   - Ask the interviewee to confirm statements and details (if necessary).
   - Offer to let the person see the interview's outcome—the research paper, for example.

LINKS

WAC Link: Interviewing is foundational research in many disciplines, particularly in the social sciences where people are the focus. For example, for a sociology class, you might interview local taxicab or truck drivers about their work. For a botany project, you might discuss the pluses and minuses of forest fires with a Department of Natural Resources scientist. Consider possibilities that make sense given the subject matter of your major.

Workplace Link: Interviewing is a common practice in many professions. Human resources workers interview potential hires; police officers and lawyers interview witnesses; product-development and marketing staff set up focus groups; social workers meet with parents interested in adoption. Research the interview practices of professionals in your field.

47d Checklist: Primary Research

____ I have chosen methods of primary research that fit the assignment.

____ I have effectively prepared to do the research.

____ I have systematically and carefully gathered primary information.

____ I have followed up in fitting ways to make sense of the research results.

____ I have conducted the primary research according to ethical standards.

Doing Library Research

A good library is your doorway to print and digital information, providing a wide range of resources for your research.

Familiarity with your college's library system dramatically improves your ability to succeed in research projects. Join tours or attend orientation sessions. Then check out the many research resources your library provides.

Which library resources can help my research?

Collections provide a variety of research materials:

- Books, videotapes, CD-ROMs, CDs, and DVDs
- Periodicals—journals, magazines, and newspapers
- Reference materials—handbooks, encyclopedias, and almanacs
- Special collections—government publications, historical documents, artifacts, and archived material

Research tools can direct you to specific materials:

- The online catalog allows you to search the library's holdings.
- Subscription databases (such as EBSCOhost) and print indexes point you to periodical articles.
- Internet access connects you with other library catalogs, online reference help, and other web resources.
- Tutorials and guides support your research.

Special services may also help you complete research projects:

- Interlibrary loans let you get materials from other libraries.
- Photocopiers, CD burners, scanners, word-processing software, and presentation software help you complete and share your research.

What's Ahead

DOING LIBRARY RESEARCH

48a Searching the Library's Electronic Catalog

Library materials are catalogued so that they are easy to find. In most college libraries, books, videos, and other holdings are catalogued in an electronic database, often web-based, organized by the Library of Congress classification system. Other libraries, especially public libraries, may use the Dewey Decimal system.

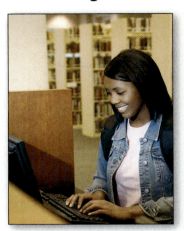

To find material in your library, learn to do basic and advanced searches of the online catalog. (Often, your library will offer orientation sessions and online tutorials to help.) As you search, practice keyword-searching strategies (**46b**) to improve your efficiency and overall results.

How can I use full citations?

When you check the full citation for a book or other resource, some or all of the information shown below will be provided. Use that information

- To determine whether the resource is worth exploring further.
- To locate the resource in the library.
- To discover other research pathways.

For example, through the links provided in the citation, you may be able to find other works written by the same author or track down related resources through the *subject terms* offered. In addition, you may be able to retain citation information through a print, save, or e-mail function, which allows you to conveniently build your working bibliography (**46c**).

AUTHOR OR EDITOR'S NAME	Motavalli, Jim
TITLE AND SUBTITLE	Forward drive: the race to build "clean" cars for the future
PUBLICATION INFORMATION	San Francisco: Sierra Club Books, ©2001.
PHYSICAL DESCRIPTION	xxiv, 280 p.; 21 cm.
SUBJECT TERM	Hybrid-electric cars. Fuel cells. Automobiles—Electric. Automobiles—Environmental aspects. Automobiles—Fuel systems.
CALL NUMBER	TL221.15.M68
LOCATION	On shelf

How can I locate resources using call numbers?

Use the call number as the resource's code. Here is a sample call number for *Forward Drive: The Race to Build "Clean" Cars for the Future:*

TL221.15.M68 2001

This Library of Congress call number combines letters and numbers to specify a resource's broad subject area, topic, and authorship or title. Therefore, finding an item involves combining alphabetical and numerical order.

subject area (**TL**) topic number (**221**) subtopic number (**15**)
cutter number (**M68**) publication date (**2001**)

To find this resource in the library, first look for any tab, such as VIDEO or REF. Though not part of the call number, this locator indicates a resource format and sends you to a specific location. Once there, follow the call number elements one at a time:

1. Find the section on motor vehicles, aeronautics, and astronautics, the **TL** designation, and follow the numbers until you reach **221**.
2. Within the **221** items, find those with the subtopic **15**.
3. Use the cutter **M68** to locate the resource alphabetically with **M** and numerically with **68**.
4. Use the publication date (**2001**) if necessary.

> **NOTE:** In the Library of Congress system, pay careful attention to subject-area letters, topic numbers, and subtopic numbers: **T416** comes before **TL221**; **TL221** before **TL1784**; **TL221.M98** before **TL221.15.M68**. While the Library of Congress classification system combines letters and numbers, the Dewey Decimal system uses numbers only.

Both the Library of Congress and the Dewey Decimal systems organize non-fiction first by general topic. The benefit of this approach is that once you find the shelf that holds a specific book on your topic, you will find many other books on the topic as well. Make sure to consider them.

WAC Link: To become a more efficient researcher, explore those areas of the classification system that are directly related to your major. Learn how the subject breaks down into topics and subtopics, and note the range of call numbers. Such familiarity with the system will make your quest to find materials more efficient.

48b Using Reference Resources

In general, reference works can be divided into two categories: (1) research tools and (2) information sources. These works can be general or specific and may take the form of books, CD-ROMs, subscription databases, or websites. These resources can be general or specialized. While reference works may not end up on your works-cited page, they are crucial to your research because they can

- Provide an overview of your topic.
- Supply basic facts—definitions, statistics, dates, and names.
- Indicate what's common knowledge.
- Offer ideas for furthering your research.

Which research tools should I use?

1. **Indexes** point you to useful resources. Some indexes are general, such as the *Readers' Guide to Periodical Literature*, while others pertain to a specific topic, such as the *Environment Index* and *Index to Legal Periodicals.* Note, however, that print indexes are often available electronically through subscription databases. See **48c.**

2. **Bibliographies** list resources on a specific topic or by a specific author. A good, current bibliography saves you a lot of the work that goes into compiling your own bibliography on a topic.
   - *The Basic Business Library: Core Resources*

3. **Abstracts,** like indexes, direct you to articles on a topic. But abstracts also summarize those materials so you know whether a resource is relevant before you invest time in locating and reading it. Abstracts are usually organized into subject areas.
   - *Computer Abstracts   Environmental Abstracts   Social Work Abstracts*

> **NOTE:** Abstracts are often integrated into online database citations.

4. **Guides and handbooks** can help you explore a knowledge area or work in a discipline.
   - **Guides to Fields or Disciplines:** *Standard Handbook for Electrical Engineers; Treasurer's and Controller's Desk Book* (e-book)
   - **Topical Guides:** *Peterson's Graduate and Professional Programs; The Global Etiquette Guide to Mexico and Latin America*

Which information sources should I use?

1. **Almanacs, yearbooks, and statistical resources,** which are normally published annually, contain diverse facts.
   - *The World Almanac and Book of Facts* presents information on business, history, religion, education, sports, and so on.
   - The *Statistical Abstract of the United States* provides data on population, social trends, politics, and employment.

2. **Encyclopedias** supply information and overviews for topics arranged alphabetically. General encyclopedias cover many fields of knowledge.
   - *Encyclopedia Britannica*   *Collier's Encyclopedia*

   Specialized encyclopedias focus on a single area of knowledge.
   - *McGraw-Hill Encyclopedia of Science and Technology*
   - *Encyclopedia of American Film Comedy*

3. **Vocabulary resources** supply information on languages. General dictionaries, such as the *American Heritage College Dictionary,* supply definitions, pronunciations, and histories for a range of words. Specialized dictionaries define words common to a field, topic, or group of people.
   - *The New Harvard Dictionary of Music*
   - *Dictionary of Environment and Sustainable Development*

 ESL TIP

When necessary, you can use a bilingual dictionary to translate words from one language to another.

4. **Biographical resources** supply information about people. General biographies cover a range of people. Other biographies focus on people from a specific group (an industry, vocation, race, and so on).

5. **Atlases** contain maps, charts, and diagrams that present data on geography, climate, and human activities. Generally, they present two types of map information. First, they can portray physical boundaries (land, water, rivers, mountains) and political boundaries (nations, states, counties). Second, atlases can offer thematic maps that represent topics such as natural resources, climate, and population density.
   - *The New Rand McNally College World Atlas* provides global information useful in a variety of disciplines.

6. **Directories** supply contact information for people and organizations.
   - *USPS Zip Code Lookup*
   - *Address Information* (online); *Official Congressional Directory*

48c Finding Periodical Articles

Periodicals are publications or broadcasts produced at regular intervals (daily, weekly, monthly, quarterly). Although some are broad in their subject matter and audience appeal, generally periodicals focus on a narrow range of topics for a particular audience.

- **Daily newspapers and newscasts** provide current information on events, opinions, and trends—from politics to natural disasters (*The Wall Street Journal, The NewsHour*).

- **Weekly and monthly magazines** provide more in-depth information on a wide range of topics (*Time, Consumer Reports, Scientific American, 60 Minutes*).

- **Journals** provide specialized, scholarly information for a narrowly focused audience (*Journal of Labor Economics, Energy Policy*).

Begin researching by learning (1) which search tools your library offers, (2) which periodicals it has available in which forms, and (3) how to gain access to those periodicals.

How can I search online databases?

If your library subscribes to EBSCOhost, LexisNexis, or another database service, use keyword searching (**46b**) to find citations on your topic. Even with a basic search, using limiters, expanders, and other advanced features will help you find the highest-quality materials. A more focused research strategy would involve turning to specialized databases, which are available for virtually every discipline. For a list of these databases, see **48d**.

> **NOTE:** If you need articles published before 1985, you may need to refer to the *Readers' Guide to Periodical Literature* or another print index.

How can I generate a citation list?

Perform a database search to generate lists of citations, brief descriptions of articles that were flagged through keywords in titles, subject terms, abstracts, and so on. At this point, study the results and do the following:

- Refine the search by narrowing or expanding.
- Mark specific citations for "capture" or further study.
- Re-sort the results.
- Follow links in a specific citation to further information.

How should I study citations?

Study citations, especially abstracts, to determine three things:

- Is this article relevant to my research?
- Is an electronic full-text version available?
- If not, does the library have this periodical?

To develop your working bibliography (**46c**), you should also "capture" the article's identifying details by using the save, print, or e-mail function. Otherwise, you can manually record the periodical's title, the issue and date, and the article's title and page numbers. These functions are shown in the EBSCOhost citation below.

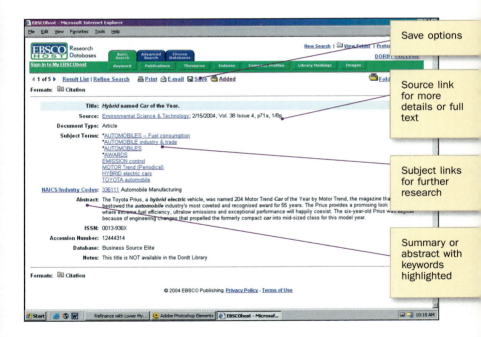

How can I retrieve articles?

When citations indicate that you have promising articles, access those articles efficiently, preferably through a direct link in the citation to an electronic copy. If the article is not available electronically, track down a print version.

- Check the online citation to see if your library has the article.
  If necessary, check your library's inventory of periodicals held,
  a list available online or in print.
- To get the article, follow your library's procedure. If the article
  is unavailable online or in your library, use an interlibrary loan.

48d Databases for Disciplines

Most libraries offer access to databases from a wide range of disciplines. Check your library's website for access to databases like these:

Agricola offers more than three million bibliographic citations from the National Agricultural Library group.

ARTbibliographies Modern abstracts articles and books on modern and contemporary art.

CAIRSS for Music offers bibliographic citations for articles on music-related topics, from music education to music therapy.

Engineering E-journal Search Engine offers free, full-text access to more than 150 online engineering journals.

ERIC offers citations, abstracts, and digests for more than 980 journals in the education field.

GPO, the Government Printing Office, offers access to more than 450,000 U.S. government documents.

Health Source offers access to almost 600 medical journals and material on health-related topics, from nutrition to sports medicine.

Ingenta offers citations for more than 25,000 journals, particularly in the sciences.

JSTOR offers full-text access to articles in a full range of disciplines, articles once available only in print.

Math Database offers access to article citations for international mathematics research.

Medline offers access to journals in medicine and medicine-related disciplines.

National Environmental Publications Internet Site (NEPIS) offers access to more than 6,000 EPA documents (full text, online).

PsycINFO, from the American Psychological Association, offers access to materials in psychology and psychology-related fields.

Scirus indexes science resources by offering citations with article titles and authors.

Vocation and Career Collection offers full-text access to more than 400 career-related periodicals.

Worldwide Political Science Abstracts offers citations in politics-related fields, from public policy to international law.

48e Checklist: Library Research

____ I have become familiar with my library's resources and services.

____ Using solid keyword-searching strategies, I have effectively searched the library's holdings for items relevant to my topic.

____ Using my library's access to other libraries, I have located and requested items on my topic.

____ I have tapped my library's print and electronic reference works for information.

____ I have scoured my library's print and electronic periodical search tools and holdings for relevant articles on my topic.

Doing Internet Research

If you're young enough, it's probably hard for you to imagine a pre-web world. Those of us old enough to remember life BI (Before the Internet) can testify that the digital revolution has radically transformed research—for good and for ill. To benefit from the Internet, researchers both young and old must develop positive e-search skills and strategies.

How should I use the Internet?

The Internet can be a great resource or a great waste of time. To use it well, consider its benefits, drawbacks, best uses, and abuses:

- **Benefits:** The Internet contains a wealth of current information in text, sound, and visual formats. Because the information is digital, it can be searched quickly and conveniently, and it can be copied, saved, and sent. Moreover, the Internet is always open.

- **Drawbacks:** The Internet lacks quality control: Virtually anyone can post anything. As a result, every source must be carefully evaluated. Also, the Net changes rapidly—what's here today may be gone or changed tomorrow.

- **Best Uses:** Use Internet information from sites sponsored by legitimate, recognizable organizations: government agencies, nonprofit groups, and educational institutions. To find quality resources, use your library's website, the Librarians' Internet Index subject directory, and WorldCat's Internet limiter.

- **Abuses:** Never use the Internet to plagiarize—downloading a paper or pasting chunks of an online resource into your paper. In addition, for most research projects, avoid relying solely on websites.

What's Ahead

49a Locating Reliable Information on the Net
49b Using Helpful Links and Subject Trees
49c Using Search Engines
49d Checklist: Internet Research

DOING INTERNET RESEARCH

49a   Locating Reliable Information on the Net

Because the Internet contains so much information of varying reliability, you must be familiar with search tools that locate trustworthy information.

ETHICS TIP

Adhere to your assignment's restrictions on using websites. Some instructors may not allow web resources for specific projects. When you are allowed to use web resources, check the reliability of online information by using the benchmarks outlined at 46d.

How can my library help me find information?

At its website, your library may provide access to quality Internet resources that the librarians themselves have reviewed. Look for the following:

- Tutorials on using the Internet
- Links to online document collections (Project Gutenberg, E-text Archives, New Bartleby Digital Library)
- Connections to virtual libraries, subscription databases, engines, directories, government documents, and online periodicals

> **NOTE:** Your library may give you access to WorldCat. If you click on the "Internet" limiter, you'll be able to search specifically for websites and other Internet information recommended by librarians.

How should I use URLs?

Finding useful Internet resources can be as easy as typing in a URL (Universal Resource Locator):

- If you know the address of the website that you want to visit, type or copy-and-paste it into the location field of your web browser. Reproduce the URL exactly: Include every letter and punctuation mark.

- If you don't have the exact URL, sometimes you can guess it, especially for an organization (company, government agency, or nonprofit group). Try the organization's name or a logical abbreviation to get the home page. If that doesn't work, enter the company's name into a search engine.

  Formula: <www.organization-name.domain-name>
  Examples: www.nasa.gov   www.habitat.org   www.ucla.edu

- If you find yourself diving deep in a website and want to surface at the site's home page, backspace part by part on the URL in the address bar, or click on the "home" icon.

49b **Using Helpful Links and Subject Trees**

Locating information on the Net can involve "surfing" leads:

- If you come across a helpful link (often highlighted in blue), click on the link to go to that new page. Note that the link may be internal to the site or external.
- Your browser keeps a record of the pages that you visit during a search session. Click the back arrow on your browser's toolbar to go back one page or the forward arrow to move ahead again. Right-clicking the mouse button on these arrows shows a list of recently visited pages.
- If you get lost while on the Net, click on the "home" symbol to return your browser to its starting place.

WRITER'S TIP

Sponsored links listed at a website are essentially a form of advertising. Although they may contain useful information, their purpose is commercial.

What is a subject tree?

A *subject tree,* sometimes called a *subject guide* or *directory,* lists websites organized into categories by experts who have reviewed those sites. Use subject trees or directories to narrow a broad topic, find evaluated sites, or search for quality instead of quantity.

Essentially, a subject tree allows you to select from a broad range of subjects or "branches." With each topic choice, you narrow your selection through subtopics until you arrive at a list of websites. In addition, a subject tree may allow you to search selected websites by keyword. For example, your library may subscribe to a service such as NetFirst, a database in which subject experts have catalogued Internet resources by topic. Here are some other subject directories that you can likely access at your library:

- **WWW Virtual Library:**
  http://vlib.org

- **Open Directory Project:**
  http://dmoz.org

- **Librarians' Internet Index:**
  http://www.lii.org

- **Google Directory:**
  http://www.google.com/dirhp

- **LookSmart:**
  http://search.looksmart.com

DOING INTERNET RESEARCH

Sample Subject Tree

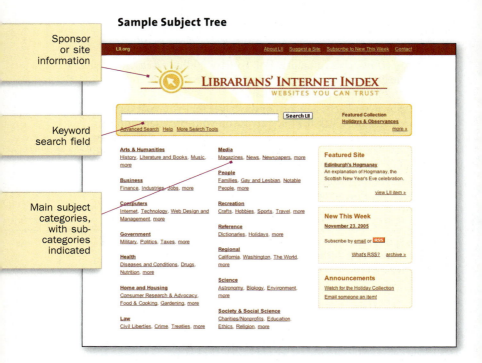

Sponsor or site information

Keyword search field

Main subject categories, with sub-categories indicated

How should I use a subject tree?

You can use a subject tree by following these three steps:

Step 1: Study the subject tree above provided by the Librarians' Internet Index (Lii). To find reviewed websites containing information on hybrid-electric cars, you could select a range of categories, depending on the angle that you want to explore. Another option would be to use the keyword search feature shown.

Step 2: Choose one category, such as *Science.* Then you can do the following: (1) select *Environment,* or (2) do a keyword search of this now more limited grouping of websites. You may benefit by trying all these options.

Step 3: As you work down through narrower branches of the tree, you will arrive at a listing of relevant websites. All of these sites have been reviewed in terms of quality, although you still need to evaluate what you find. Study the site title, the description of information available, the site sponsorship, and the web address (particularly the domain name). Use that information to determine the site's relevance to your research.

49c Using Search Engines

Unlike a subject directory, which is constructed with human input, a search engine is a program that automatically scours a large amount of Internet material for keywords that you submit.

When should I use a search engine?

Use a search engine when

- You have a very narrow topic in mind.
- You have a specific word or phrase to use in your search.
- You want a large number of results.
- You are looking for a specific type of Internet file.
- You have the time to sort the material for reliability.

How should I choose a search engine?

Choose a search engine that covers a large portion of the Internet, has quality indexing, and has high-powered search capabilities. Essentially, it's best to become familiar with a few search engines—which areas of the Internet they search, whether they are full-text, what rules you must follow to ensure successful searches, and how they order or prioritize results.

- **Basic Search Engines:** Search millions of webpages gathered automatically. *Example:* Google <http://www.google.com>.
- **Metasearch Tools:** Search several basic search engines at once, saving you the time and effort of checking more than one search engine. *Example:* Ask Jeeves <http://www.ask.com>.
- **"Deep Web" Tools:** Check Internet databases and other sources not accessible to basic search engines. *Example:* Complete Planet <http://aip.completeplanet.com>.

If you were interested in information specifically on the Toyota hybrid-electric vehicles (a fairly narrow search term), you could conduct a search using the metasearch engine Ask Jeeves. Using the keyword-searching strategies at **46b** might lead to the results shown on the next page. You could then refine your initial search by

- Following links to related topics.
- Searching "sponsored web results"—essentially advertising sites, such as Toyota's own website for the Prius.
- Searching "web results"—sites that generally go beyond advertising into more in-depth information.
- Exploring a related search of other topics and Internet resources.

> **NOTE:** Not all search engines are the same. Some search just citations of Internet materials, whereas others conduct full-text searches.

DOING INTERNET RESEARCH

Sample Search Engine

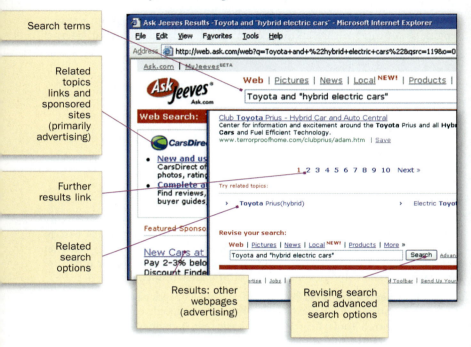

Search terms

Related topics links and sponsored sites (primarily advertising)

Further results link

Related search options

Results: other webpages (advertising)

Revising search and advanced search options

Example: You might choose to check Toyota's pages on the Prius, to view Toyota's North American Environmental Report at its website, or to examine the "Honda Insight / Toyota Prius" comparison, which comes from an educational site (.edu). The key is to use sound judgment when assessing where the information comes from, which sites provide the most reliable information, how the information relates to your research question, and what web graphics offer as potential resources for your research writing.

49d Checklist: Internet Research

____ I have used Internet search tools intelligently—from URL addresses to subject trees to search engines—to find quality, reliable information on my topic.

____ I have carefully saved Internet information through bookmarking, printing, saving, or e-mailing.

____ I have carefully evaluated each Internet source for credible authorship, reliable sponsorship, lack of bias, accuracy, logical support, and quality design (see **46d** for more details on evaluating web resources).

Drafting Papers with Documented Research

As you draft your research paper, you must also strive to present compelling ideas, provide support from credible sources, and document your sources. That's a lot to accomplish. If you're staring blankly at this page, your forehead beading with sweat, you aren't alone. You've just been "caught in the draft."

But drafting doesn't have to be so frightening. If you keep a few simple concepts in mind as you write your first draft, you'll do just fine.

How should I write my first draft?

- **Present your own ideas clearly and honestly.** While considering others' research, let *your thinking*—not your sources—drive the paper forward.
- **Be selective.** Don't try to cram everything you've found into your draft. If you've done good research, you may have four or five times more material than you could use. Select what's most relevant.
- **Respect your sources.** As you draft, track borrowed information and ideas by using codes, abbreviations, and quotation marks. Also, avoid overusing one source and overdoing direct quotations.
- **Imagine yourself addressing your readers.** What do they already know? What do they need to know? What do they need first, second, and third, so that they understand your points and accept your arguments? Let the answers guide what you say, in what order.

What's Ahead

50a Recognizing Plagiarism

Plagiarism refers to borrowing someone's words, ideas, or images (what's called intellectual property) and using the material so it appears to be your own. When you plagiarize, you use source material—whether published in print or online—without acknowledging the source. Plagiarism refers to a range of thefts:

- Submitting a paper you didn't write yourself
- Passing off large chunks of a source as your own work
- Using summaries, paraphrases, or quotations without documenting the origins
- Using the exact phrasing of a source without quotation marks
- Failing to distinguish source material from your own ideas
- Using images, tables, graphs, maps, or music without giving credit

ETHICS TIP

The road to plagiarism may be paved with the best intentions—or the worst. Either way, the result is a serious academic offense. As you write your research paper, do everything you can to stay off that road! Start by reviewing your school's student handbook and your instructor's guidelines for stated policies on plagiarism and other academic offenses. Then study the following pages.

What exactly does plagiarism look like?

Read the passage below, which comes from an article about the United Nations economic sanctions against Iraq in the 1990s (pages 748–749 of "Are Sanctions Just? The Problematic Case of Iraq," by David Cortright and George Lopez, published in the *Journal of International Affairs* [Spring 1999, Volume 52:2]: 735–755). Then review the five types of plagiarism that follow, noting how each misuses the source.

ORIGINAL ARTICLE

> As noted earlier, sanctions can help to encourage a process of dialogue and negotiation, but they cannot by themselves remove a targeted regime or force a drastic change in policy. Sanctions should not be used in a purely punitive manner to starve an opponent into submission. Sanctions work best in combination with incentives and other forms of external influence as part of a carrot-and-stick diplomacy designed to resolve a conflict through negotiation.

TYPES OF PLAGIARISM

Using Copy-and-Paste. Avoid splicing chunks of material from a source into your paper without acknowledgment.

- For sanctions to work, we need to understand their value and their limits. **Sanctions can help to encourage a process of dialogue and negotiation, but they cannot by themselves remove a targeted regime or force a drastic change in policy.**

  [The writer pastes in the passage and changes a few words, but does not use quotation marks or a citation.]

Failing to Cite a Source. Borrowed material must be documented. Even if you use information accurately and fairly, neglecting to cite the source is plagiarism.

- Sanctions alone do not force unjust governments to change. Instead, sanctions should be combined with other negotiation tactics.

  [The writer correctly summarizes the passage's idea but offers no citation.]

Neglecting Necessary Quotation Marks. Whether it's a paragraph or a phrase, if you use a source's exact wording, that material must be in quotation marks.

- Sanctions fail when they are used in a **purely punitive manner** (Cortright and Lopez 749).

  [The writer cites the source but doesn't use quotation marks around a borrowed phrase (boldfaced).]

Confusing Borrowed Material with Your Own Ideas. Through carelessness (often in note taking), you may confuse source material with your own thinking.

- Sanctions work best "to encourage a process of dialogue and negotiation" (Cortright and Lopez 748). By themselves, they fail to get results and should not be used as a club to force a government to comply.

  [The writer indicates that he borrowed material in the first sentence but fails to indicate that he also borrowed the idea in the next.]

Submitting Another Writer's Paper. The most blatant plagiarism is taking an entire paper and claiming it as your own work. Here are some examples:

- Downloading, reformatting, and submitting an article as your own work
- Buying a paper or taking a "free" paper off the Internet
- Turning in another student's work as your own

WRITER'S TIP

Just as it's easy to plagiarize using the Internet, it's easy for your professors to recognize and track down plagiarism using Internet tools.

50b Understanding Why Plagiarism Is Serious

Perhaps the answer is obvious. But some people believe that material on the Internet (whether text, visual, or sound) is "free" and therefore fair game for research writing. After all, a lot of information on the web doesn't even list an author of any kind, so what's the harm?

Why is plagiarism so bad?

Plagiarism is cheating—stealing another's intellectual property and passing it off as one's own work. It is often punished in one or more ways:

- A failing grade for the assignment
- A failing grade for the course

Workplace Link: In some instances, plagiarism can result in expulsion from college or in a note on your academic transcript (often seen by potential employers) that failure resulted from academic dishonesty.

How does plagiarism hurt anyone?

The research paper represents your dialogue with other members of the academic community. When you plagiarize, you short-circuit the dialogue:

- You gain an unfair advantage over your classmates, those who follow the rules and earn their grades.
- You disrespect other writers, researchers, and scholars.
- You disrespect your readers by passing off others' ideas as your own.
- You insult your instructor, a person whose respect you need.
- You harm your college by risking its reputation and integrity.

Most of all, plagiarism hurts you. It robs you of the chance to learn course-related concepts, it prevents you from gaining research skills, and it undercuts your personal integrity.

Web Link: The Internet may have made plagiarism more tempting, but it also has made it easier for professors to discover and punish. The website <www.plagiarism.org> features just two of the many commercial programs available for detecting plagiarism. A time is coming when plagiarism protection will be as common as virus protection.

50c Avoiding Plagiarism

Preventing plagiarism begins the moment you get an assignment. Essentially, prevention requires your commitment and diligence throughout the project.

How can I avoid plagiarism?

Resist temptation. With the Internet, plagiarism is just a few mouse clicks away. Avoid last-minute all-nighters by starting research projects early. If you do get stuck, it's better to ask for an extension or accept a penalty for lateness than to plagiarize.

Play by the rules. Become familiar with your college's definition, guidelines, and policies regarding plagiarism so that you don't unknowingly violate them. When in doubt, ask your instructor for clarification.

Take orderly, accurate notes. Carefully keep track of source material and distinguish it from your own thinking. Specifically, do the following:

- Maintain an accurate working bibliography (**46c**).
- Adopt an effective note-taking system (**46a**).
- Accurately summarize, paraphrase, and quote sources in your notes (**46e**).

Document borrowed material. Give credit for all information that you have summarized, paraphrased, or quoted from any source, including facts, statistics, graphics, phrases, or ideas. Readers can then see what's borrowed and what's yours, and do their own follow-up research.

WRITER'S TIP

Common Knowledge Exception: Common knowledge is information —a basic fact, for instance—that is generally known to readers or easily found in several sources, particularly reference works. Because it's common, such knowledge need *not* be cited. However, when you go beyond common knowledge into research findings—theories, interpretations of the facts, explanations, claims, arguments, and graphics—you *must* document the source.

Example: The fact that automakers are developing hybrid-electric cars is common knowledge, whereas the precise details of GM's AUTOnomy project are not.

Work carefully with source material in your paper. See **50f** and **50g** for more information on integrating and documenting sources, but here briefly are your essential responsibilities:

- Distinguish borrowed material from your own thinking by signaling where source material begins and ends.
- Indicate the source's origin with an attributive phrase and a citation.
- Provide full source information in a works-cited or references page.

50d Avoiding Other Source Abuses

Plagiarism, while the most serious offense, is not the only source abuse to avoid when writing a paper with documented research.

How important is accuracy?

Accuracy is crucial. When you get a quotation wrong, botch a summary, paraphrase poorly, or misstate a statistic, you misrepresent the original.

- According to Cortright and Lopez, "sanctions should be used in a purely punitive fashion to bully an opponent into submission" (749).

  [The writer carelessly drops the important word "not" and replaces "starve" with "bully."]

Does the author's original intent matter?

Absolutely. By ripping a statement out of its context and forcing it into yours, you can make a source seem to say something that it didn't really say.

- The example of Iraq proves the failure of "carrot-and-stick diplomacy designed to resolve a conflict through negotiation" (Cortright and Lopez 749).

  [The writer uses part of a statement to say the opposite of the original.]

Should I give a citation for every sentence in my work?

No. Much of your paper should show your own thinking. When your paper reads like a string of references, especially quotations, your own thinking begins to disappear.

- It is important to understand that "sanctions can help to encourage a process of dialogue and negotiation, but they cannot by themselves remove a targeted regime or force a drastic change in policy." Moreover, "Sanctions should not be used in a purely punitive manner to starve an opponent into submission." Instead, say the authors, "Sanctions work best in combination with incentives ..." (Cortright and Lopez 748–749).

  [The writer takes the source passage, chops it up, and splices it together.]

What is "plunking"?

You "plunk" quotations into your paper by failing to prepare for them and follow them up. The discussion then becomes choppy and disconnected.

- In Iraq, the UN sanctions failed to bring results. "As noted earlier, sanctions can help to encourage a process of dialogue and negotiation" (Cortright and Lopez 748).

  [The writer interrupts the flow of ideas with a quotation "out of the blue." The quotation also hangs at the end of a paragraph with no follow-up or transition.]

Avoiding Other Source Abuses

How clear do my citations need to be?

Very clear. Your reader shouldn't have to guess where borrowed material begins and ends. For example, if you place a parenthetical citation at the end of a paragraph, does that citation cover the whole paragraph or just the final sentence?

Also, all in-text citations must clearly refer to accurate entries in the works-cited, references, or endnotes page. You should never use an in-text citation that refers to a source that is not listed in the bibliography.

What other offenses should I avoid?

Beyond plagiarism and related source abuses, avoid these academic offenses:

Double-Dipping. When you submit one paper in two different classes without first obtaining permission from both instructors, you take double credit for one project.

Falstaffing. This practice refers to a particular type of plagiarism where one student submits another student's work. Know that you are guilty of Falstaffing if you let another student submit your paper.

Relying on One Source. If your writing is dominated by one source, readers may doubt the depth and integrity of your research.

Violating Copyright. When you copy, distribute, or post in whole or in part any intellectual property without permission from or payment to the copyright holder, you commit a copyright infringement. To avoid copyright violations in your research projects, do the following:

- Observe *fair-use guidelines:* Quote small portions of a document for limited purposes, such as education or research. Avoid copying large portions for your own gain.

- Understand what's in the ***public domain:*** You need not obtain permission to copy and use public domain materials—primarily documents created by the government.

- Observe ***intellectual property*** and ***copyright laws:*** First, know your college's policies on copying documents. Second, realize that copyright protects the expression of ideas in a range of materials— writings, videos, songs, photographs, drawings, computer software, and so on.

VISUALS TIP

Avoid changing a source (including a photo or other graphic) without the permission of the creator or copyright holder.

50e Drafting the Paper

As you write your paper, your goals are to develop and support your ideas, integrate sources naturally, and provide correct documentation.

Which drafting method should I use?

Choose a method that makes sense for your project and your writing style. Consider these two options or something in between:

WRITING SYSTEMATICALLY

- Develop a detailed outline, including supporting evidence.
- Arrange your notes in precise order.
- Write methodically, following your thesis, outline, and notes.
- Cite your sources as you write.

WRITING FREELY

- Review your working thesis and notes. Then set them aside.
- If you need to, jot down a brief outline.
- Write away—get all your research-based thinking down on paper.
- Going back to your research notes, integrate citations.

Which parts should I include in the first draft?

To successfully complete your paper's first draft, develop the following parts. Note that you can draft the parts in any order. For more on drafting, see **8**.

1. **Draft an introduction.** The introduction to your paper should offer something engaging about your subject and build toward your thesis or key research question. Consider these strategies: Tell a revealing story, quote an authority, give important background, or ask thought-provoking questions.

2. **Draft the body.** Expand and support your thesis with explanations and/or arguments shaped by compelling evidence. Present each main point and develop it through discussion. Support each with facts or examples and provide documentation.

3. **Draft a conclusion.** Tie together important points and reassert your thesis. Expand the paper's scope by connecting the topic with readers' experiences or another aspect of life.

4. **Create a working title.** Try to capture your paper's primary focus.

WRITER'S TIP

In the past, research writers avoided *I* and *you* to show objective distance. Unfortunately, the result was often an awkward use of *one* and the passive voice. Today, your instructor may allow *I* and *you*, but keep focused on your topic. See **14d** for more on academic style.

50f   Integrating Your Sources

From your first word to your last, readers should be able to recognize what material is yours and what comes from other sources. Moreover, those sources should be integrated smoothly into your discussion.

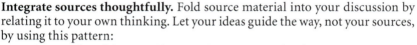

How should I integrate sources?

Use sources for the right reasons. Focus on what you want to say, not all the source material you've collected. Use sources to do the following:

- Support your point with facts, statistics, and details.
- Give credibility to your point by presenting an expert's support.
- Bring your point to life with an example, observation, or illustration.
- Address alternatives, opposition, and counterarguments.

Integrate sources thoughtfully. Fold source material into your discussion by relating it to your own thinking. Let your ideas guide the way, not your sources, by using this pattern:

- State and explain your idea, creating a context for the source.
- Identify the source and link it to your discussion.
- Summarize, paraphrase, or quote the source, providing a citation in an appropriate spot.
- Use the source by explaining, expanding, or refuting it.

Use quotations sparingly. In most research documents, restrict your quoting to key statements by authorities:

- Use well-phrased claims and conclusions (such as a powerful conclusion by an ethicist about the problem with the media's coverage of cloning debates and developments).
- Use passages where a careful word-by-word analysis and interpretation are important for your argument (such as an excerpt from a speech made by a politician about the future of NASA's space shuttle program).

> **NOTE:** Quotations, especially long ones, must pull their weight, so generally paraphrase or summarize source material instead.

WRITER'S TIP

When a primary text or document (such as a novel, a piece of legislation, or a speech) is a key piece of evidence or the actual focus of your project, more extensive use of quotations is required. (See **47b** for more.)

DRAFTING PAPERS WITH DOCUMENTED RESEARCH

What do integrated sources look like?

Writer's ideas	The motivation and urgency to create and improve hybrid-electric technology comes from a range of complex forces. Some of these forces are economic, others environmental, and still others social. In "Societal lifestyle costs of cars with alternative fuels/engines," Joan Ogden, Robert Williams, and Eric Larson argue that "[c]ontinued reliance on current transportation fuels and technologies poses serious oil supply insecurity, climate change, and urban air pollution risks" (7). Because of the nonrenewable nature of fossil fuels as well as their negative side effects, the transportation industry is confronted with making the most radical changes since the introduction of the internal-combustion automobile more than 100 years ago. Hybrid-electric vehicles are one response to this pressure.

Writer's ideas — Attributive phrase — Paraphrase, quotation, or summary — Citation — Commentary — Conclusion

How should I smoothly integrate quotations?

Use enough of the quotation to make your point without changing the meaning of the original. Enclose exact wording in quotation marks.

- Ogden, Williams, and Larson also conclude that the hydrogen fuel-cell vehicle is "a strong candidate for becoming the Car of the Future," given the trend toward "tighter environmental constraints" and the "intense efforts" by automakers to develop commercially viable versions of such vehicles (25).

If a quotation is longer than four typed lines, set it off from the main text. Introduce the quotation with a complete sentence and a colon. Indent the whole quotation one inch (ten spaces) and double-space it, but don't put quotation marks around it. Put the parenthetical citation outside the final punctuation mark.

- Toward the end of the study, Ogden, Williams, and Larson argue that changes to the fuel delivery and filling system must be factored into planning:

     In charting a course to the Car of the Future, societal LCC comparisons should be complemented by considerations of fuel infrastructure requirements. Because fuel infrastructure changes are costly, the number of major changes made over time should be minimized. The bifurcated strategy advanced here—of focusing on the H_2 FCV for the long term and advanced liquid hydrocarbon-fueled ICEVs and ICE/HEVs for the near term—would reduce the number of such infrastructure changes to one (an eventual shift to H_2). (25)

Integrating Your Sources

How should I integrate poetry?

When quoting poetry, use a diagonal (/) to indicate breaks between lines. Inset quotations longer than three lines of the poem, maintaining the integrity of the lines and indenting each line one inch (ten spaces).

- In the last stanza of the poem, Frost's speaker laments that "The woods are lovely, dark and deep, / But I have promises to keep, / And miles to go before I sleep" (lines 13–15).

  In his poem "Diamond Days," J. Robert King likens the human experience to the wear and tear on an old phonograph needle:

  > I am such a stylus
  > set in such a groove,
  > and as I run my course
  > through the valley where I am placed,
  > every ecstatic ridge and rill
  > that resonates through me
  > also eats me away. (lines 11–17)

When should I use ellipses or brackets?

Normally, maintain the wording, capitalization, and punctuation of the original. However, you may shorten or change a quotation so that it fits more smoothly into your sentence—but don't alter the original meaning.

Use an ellipsis within brackets to indicate that you have omitted words from the original. An ellipsis is three periods with a space before and after each.

- In their projections of where fuel-cell vehicles are heading, Ogden, Williams, and Larson discuss GM's AUTOnomy vehicle, with its "radical redesign of the entire car. [. . .] In these cars, steering, braking, and other vehicle systems are controlled electronically" (24).

Use brackets to indicate a clarification, to change a pronoun or verb tense, to indicate your use of an ellipsis, or to switch around uppercase and lowercase.

- As Ogden, Williams, and Larson explain, "[e]ven if such barriers [the high cost of fuel cells and the lack of an H_2 fuel infrastructure] can be overcome, decades would be required before this embryonic technology could make major contributions in reducing the major externalities that characterize today's cars" (25).

WRITER'S TIP

> If you find yourself using quite a few brackets or ellipses, reconsider using the quotation. The reason for providing a direct quotation is that the original source material uses succinct and memorable wording. If the quotation must be chopped up and explained to make it usable, you should consider paraphrasing or summarizing it instead.

DRAFTING PAPERS WITH DOCUMENTED RESEARCH

50g Documenting Your Sources

When you document sources, make sure to signal the start and end of the material you are borrowing, and provide clear references.

How should I refer to the source the first time?

Use an attributive statement that indicates some of the following information: the author's name and credentials, the title of the source, the nature of the study or research, and helpful background.

- *Joan Ogden, Robert Williams, and Eric Larson, members of the Princeton Environmental Institute, explain* that modest improvements in emissions reductions will not be enough over the next century (7).

How should I refer to the source later?

Use a simplified attributive phrase for later references to your source, such as the author's last name or a shortened version of the title.

- *Ogden, Williams, and Larson go on to argue* that "[e]ffectively addressing environmental and oil supply concerns will probably require radical changes in automotive engine/fuel technologies" (7).

Do I need an attributive phrase every time?

If the parenthetical citation supplies sufficient attribution, you can simply skip the attributive phrase.

- Various types of transportation are by far the main consumers of oil (three-fourths of world oil imports); moreover, these same technologies are responsible for one-fourth of all greenhouse gas sources (Ogden, Williams, and Larson 7).

The verb you use to introduce source material is a key part of the attribution. Use fitting verbs, such as those in the table on the next page. Normally, use attributive verbs in the present tense. Use the past tense only when you need to emphasize a source's "pastness."

- In their 2004 study, "Societal Lifecycle Costs of Cars with Alternative Fuels/Engines," Ogden, Williams, and Larson *present* a method for . . . In an earlier study, these authors *had made* preliminary steps toward this analysis. . . .

WRITER'S TIP

The attributive phrase and the parenthetical citation work as a team, surrounding the material from another source. If the start of the borrowed material is obvious, use just a parenthetical citation.

Example Attributive Verbs: Synonyms for "Says"			
accepts	contradicts	hypothesizes	replies
acknowledges	contrasts	identifies	responds
adds	criticizes	insists	shares
affirms	declares	interprets	shows
argues	defends	lists	speculates
asserts	denies	maintains	states
believes	describes	outlines	stresses
cautions	disagrees	points out	suggests
claims	discusses	praises	summarizes
compares	emphasizes	proposes	supports
concludes	enumerates	proves	urges
confirms	explains	refutes	verifies
considers	highlights	rejects	warns

How do I show where source material ends?

You show the end of a source quotation by using closing quotation marks and a citation. With summaries and paraphrases, the situation is more challenging. Generally, place the citation immediately after a quotation, paraphrase, or summary. However, you may instead place the citation at the end if it is too obtrusive otherwise. When you discuss several facts or quotations from a page in a source, use an attributive phrase at the beginning of your discussion and then a single citation at the end.

50h Revising Your Draft

When you have completed a first draft of your research paper, breathe a sigh of relief and pat yourself on the back (at the same time). After all, a research paper is one of your toughest college assignments. But don't settle for turning in that first draft! Let it sit. Then go back to it. Better yet, share it with a class-mate, a writing-center tutor, or someone who represents your intended reader. Let fresh eyes (yours or someone else's) check for these issues:

- A clear thesis and strong support
- An organization creating a logical chain of ideas—no repetition, gaps, or imbalance
- Convincing, fair use of source material and no accidental plagiarism
- Well-developed paragraphs with sources introduced and discussed
- A length and format that meet the assignment requirements

WRITER'S TIP

Cut, add, clarify, and reorder material, as needed. Then when you're ready to edit your paper, use the checklist on the next page.

50i Checklist: Documented Paper

Use the seven-traits checklist below to review any paper that contains documented research.

Ideas

___ The thesis is clear, sharp, and thoughtful.

___ The support is strong and balanced.

___ Researched data are accurate and complete.

___ Interpretations and conclusions follow logically from the information.

___ All ideas and information are properly credited.

Organization

___ Information is delivered in a logical, structured format.

___ The paper includes a clear opening that presents the purpose and scope of the research, a middle that provides complete data and discussion, and a closing that focuses on conclusions and next steps.

___ Paragraphs are well-developed "packages" that build on one another.

Voice

___ The tone is confident but also sincere, measured, and objective. Where uncertainty exists, that is noted objectively.

___ Personal pronouns *I* and *you* are used or avoided, as directed by the instructor.

Words

___ Precise, clear phrasing is used throughout the paper—language that readers will understand, not obscure jargon.

___ Terms are defined as needed.

Sentences

___ Constructions flow smoothly, with a good blend of sentence lengths (short and punchy, long and thoughtful) and patterns (loose, balanced, periodic).

___ Source material is carefully integrated.

Copy

___ Grammar, punctuation, mechanics, usage, and spelling are correct—especially punctuation used with source material.

___ Documentation of research is complete and correct, following an appropriate style (MLA, APA, CSE, CMS).

Design

___ The document's font, format, and page layout are all reader-friendly.

___ Data are effectively presented in discussion, lists, tables, charts, graphs, and so on.

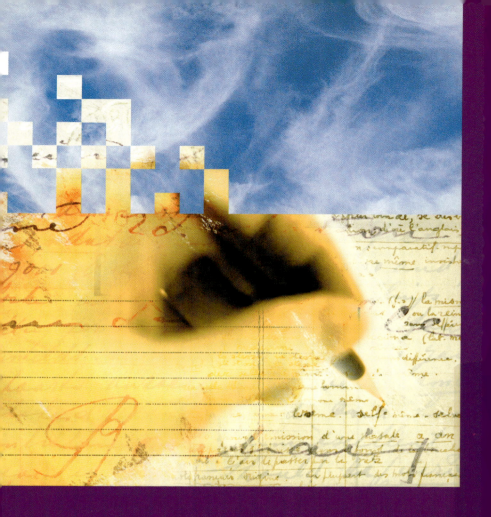

MLA

MLA

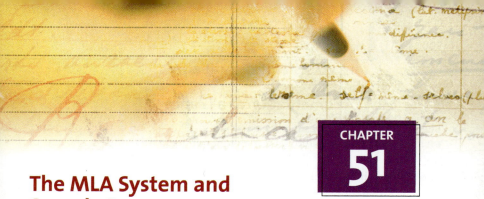

The MLA System and Sample Paper

If you've been told to submit an assigned paper in MLA format, you're looking for answers to questions like these: How do I format my paper in MLA? How do I document my research? For answers, read on.

What is the MLA?

MLA stands for the Modern Language Association of America—a professional organization to which many English and other humanities professors belong.

What is MLA style?

MLA style refers to a method of documenting research and formatting a research paper—a method and format used in English and other humanities disciplines. In a nutshell, MLA style offers guidelines for the following:

- **In-text citation**—the use of author and page-number references within parentheses.
- **Works cited**—a list of resources referred to in your paper.
- **Paper format**—margins, heading, pagination, indenting, and so on.
- **Punctuation and mechanics rules**—matters such as quotation marks, end punctuation, underlining, and brackets.

Where can I find more information about MLA style?

This section of your handbook gives you most of the information that you need to know—drawn from these official MLA resources, which you can consult further:

- Joseph Gibaldi's *MLA Handbook for Writers of Research Papers* (6th ed.).
- The MLA website <www.mla.org>: Check especially the FAQ pages.

What's Ahead

THE MLA SYSTEM AND SAMPLE PAPER

51a MLA Documentation at a Glance

The MLA system involves two parts: (1) an in-text citation within your paper when you use a source and (2) a matching bibliographic entry at the end of your paper. Note these features of the MLA system:

- **It's minimalist.** In your paper, you provide the least amount of information needed for your reader to identify the source in the works-cited list.

- **It uses signal phrases and parenthetical references** to set off source material from your own thinking and discussion. A signal phrase names the author and places the material in context (for example, "As Margaret Atwood argues in Survival").

- **It's smooth, unobtrusive, and orderly.** MLA in-text citations identify borrowed material while keeping the paper readable. Moreover, alphabetized entries in the works-cited list at the end of the paper make locating source details easy.

What does MLA documentation look like?

You can see these features at work in the example below.

IN-TEXT CITATION IN BODY OF PAPER

Linda Bren of FDA Consumer explains that doctors often inappropriately prescribe antibiotics for viral infections because of uncertainty about the type of infection present, limits on time for further testing, and pressure from patients demanding prescriptions (30).

"Linda Bren" and "(30)" tell the reader the following things:

- The borrowed material came from a source written by Linda Bren.
- The specific material can be found on page 30 of the source.
- Full source details are in the works-cited list under the author's last name.

MATCHING WORKS-CITED ENTRY AT END OF PAPER

Bren, Linda. "Battle of the Bugs: Fighting Antibiotic Resistance." FDA Consumer July/Aug. 2002: 28-34.

How do I make MLA in-text citations?

Refer to the author (plus the work's title, if helpful) and a page number by using one of these methods:

Last name and page number in parentheses:

- Intestinal bacteria have a vital nutritional function, producing several B vitamins and vitamin K (Levinson and Jawetz 22).

Name cited in sentence, page number in parentheses:

- As Levinson and Jawetz point out, intestinal bacteria have a vital nutritional function, producing several B vitamins and vitamin K (22).

How should I punctuate citations?

Present and punctuate citations according to these rules:

- Place the parenthetical reference after the source material.
- Within the parentheses, normally give the author's last name only.
- Do not put a comma between the author's last name and the page reference.
- Cite the page number as a numeral, not a word.
- Don't use the abbreviations *p., pp.,* or *page(s)* before page number(s).
- Place any sentence punctuation after the closed parenthesis.

> **NOTE:** For many of these rules, exceptions exist. For example, classic literary texts could be cited by chapters, books, acts, scenes, or lines. Moreover, many electronic sources have no stated authors and/or no pagination. See **52a–52b** for complete coverage of in-text citation practices.

How do I create MLA works-cited entries?

Complete coverage of MLA works-cited issues (examples included) is offered in **53a–53f**, rules for formatting the works-cited page are at **51b**, and a sample works-cited page is shown at **51e**. But here are some templates for common entries:

TEMPLATE FOR PRINT BOOK

Author's Last Name, First Name. <u>Title of Book</u>. Publication City: Publisher, year of publication. (Other publication details are integrated as needed.)

> Levy, Stuart B. <u>The Antibiotic Paradox: How the Misuse of Antibiotics Destroys Their Curative Power</u>. Cambridge, MA: Perseus, 2002.

TEMPLATE FOR PRINT PERIODICAL ARTICLE

Author's Last Name, First Name. "Title of Article." <u>Journal Title</u> volume, issue, and/or date details: page numbers. (Other publication details are integrated as needed.)

> Bren, Linda. "Battle of the Bugs: Fighting Antibiotic Resistance." <u>FDA Consumer</u> July/Aug. 2002: 28-34.

TEMPLATE FOR A WEBPAGE

Author's or Editor's Last Name, First Name (if available). "Title of Page, Posting, or Document." <u>Title of the Site</u> or description such as Home Page. Date of electronic publication, last update, or posting. If available, number of pages, paragraphs, sections (if numbered). Access date <URL>.

> "Fact Sheet: The Problem of Antibiotic Resistance." <u>National Institute of Allergy and Infectious Diseases</u>. Apr. 2004. 31 Mar. 2005 <http://www.niaid.nih.gov/factsheets/antimicro.htm>.

51b MLA Format Guidelines

First-Page Format

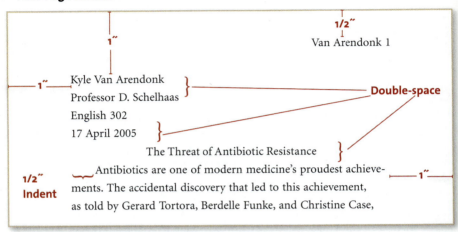

Format of Pages Within the Paper

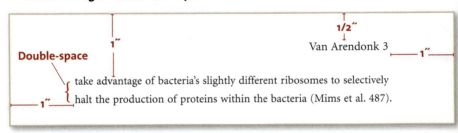

Format for the Works-Cited List

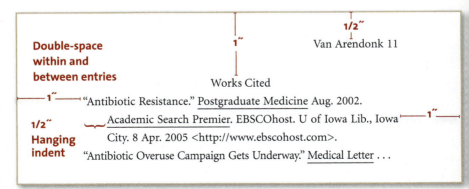

How should I format my MLA paper?

RUNNING HEAD AND PAGINATION

- Number pages consecutively in the upper-right corner, one-half inch from the top and flush with the right margin (one inch).
- Use numerals only—without *p.*, *page*, *#*, or any other symbol.
- Include your last name on each page typed one space before the page number. (Your name identifies the page if it's misplaced.)

HEADING ON FIRST PAGE

Include the following flush left and double-spaced, one inch from the top:

- Your name, both first and last in regular order.
- Your professor's or instructor's name (presented as he or she prefers).
- The course name and number, plus the section number if it is appropriate (History 100-05). Follow your instructor's directions.
- The date that you are submitting the paper: Use the international format (11 November 2005).

PAPER TITLE

- Double-spaced below the heading, center your paper's title.
- Do not italicize, underline, or boldface the title; do not put it in quotation marks or all capital letters.
- Follow standard capitalization practices for titles. (See **30c**.)

WORKS-CITED LIST

Format your works-cited list according to these guidelines:

- Start the list on a new page immediately after your paper's conclusion or, if applicable, after the "Notes" page. (See **51c**.)
- Continue the running head and pagination.
- Center the heading "Works Cited" one inch from the top of the page; don't use underlining, boldface, or any other typographical markers.
- Begin your list two spaces below the heading. Arrange all entries alphabetically by the authors' last names; for sources without identified authors, alphabetize using the work's title.
- If you are listing two or more works by the same author, alphabetize them by the titles of the works. Use the author's name for the first entry; in later entries, replace the name with three hyphens.
- Start each entry flush left; indent second and subsequent lines for specific entries one-half inch or five spaces. Use your word-processing program's hanging indent feature.
- Do not repeat the heading if your list runs longer than one page.

> **NOTE:** Double-space within and between all entries and follow standard rules for capitalization, underlining, quotation marks, and punctuation.

THE MLA SYSTEM AND SAMPLE PAPER

Which typographical issues should I consider?

Typeface Choose a standard serif typeface like Times New Roman.

Type Size Use a readable type size, preferably 12 points, throughout.

Type Styles (underlining, italics, bold) For ease of reading, use underlining rather than italics for titles of resources and individual words requiring this feature. Avoid using boldface, yellow highlighting, all capital letters, and so on.

WRITER'S TIP

You can set up many of these formatting features quickly and easily using your word-processing software. Try creating a template for all of your academic papers.

How should I handle tables and illustrations?

Position tables, illustrations, and other visuals near your discussion of them—ideally, immediately after your first reference to the graphic. Observe these rules:

Tables Identify all tables using "Table," an arabic numeral, and a caption or title. Both numbers and captions should be flush left, appropriately capitalized. Provide source information and explanatory notes below the table. Identify notes with superscript lowercase letters, not numerals. Double-space throughout the table.

Illustrations Number and label other visuals (graphs, charts, drawings, photos, maps) using "Figure" or "Fig.," an arabic numeral (followed by a period), and a title or caption one space after the period—all flush left below the illustration, along with source information and notes.

> **NOTE:** If your instructor accepts or encourages electronic submission, follow his or her guidelines concerning these issues:
>
> **Mode of Submission** E-mail the document as an attachment, place it on a server, or submit it on disk.
>
> **Pagination/Reference Markers** If your document will not have stable page numbers, number the paragraphs. Place the paragraph number in brackets, follow with a space, and then begin the paragraph.
>
> **Internet Addresses** If appropriate, reverse the MLA print practice of putting URLs in angle brackets; instead, format the URLs so that they become live links.

Which page layout issues should I consider?

Margins Set the margins at one inch on the top, bottom, left, and right, with the exception of the running head (one-half inch from the top).

Line Spacing Double-space the entire paper—including the heading and works-cited entries, as well as tables, captions, and inset quotations.

Line Justification Use left justification throughout, except for the running head (right justification) and the title and works-cited heading (both centered).

Spacing After Punctuation Use one space after most forms of punctuation, including end punctuation—but not before or after a dash or a hyphen.

Paragraph Indenting Indent all paragraphs five spaces (one-half inch).

Longer (Inset) Quotations (See **50f.**) Indent ten spaces (one inch) all verse quotations longer than three lines and all prose quotations longer than four typed lines. Use no quotation marks, and place the parenthetical citation after the closing punctuation.

- With a verse quotation, set each line of the poem or play as a new line; do not run the lines together. Follow the indenting and spacing in the verse itself.

- To quote two or more paragraphs, indent the first line of each paragraph three spaces (one-quarter inch) in addition to the ten spaces (one inch) for the whole passage. However, if the first sentence quoted does not begin a paragraph in the source, do not include the additional indent.

Verse	Prose	Long Prose

Paper Size Print on standard 8.5- × 11-inch paper.

Paper Weight and Quality Use quality 20-pound bond white paper.

Print Quality Use a laser or inkjet printer to create a crisp, clean copy. Avoid submitting a paper with handwritten corrections; however, if you must make a change, insert a caret symbol (^), put a single clean line through words that must be dropped, and write additions above the line.

Binding As a first choice, use a paperclip. A single staple in the upper-left corner may be acceptable to your instructor, but avoid covers or bindings.

Single-Sided Printing Print your essay single-sided.

51c Footnotes and Endnotes in MLA Documentation

Generally, MLA in-text citation rules make footnotes and endnotes unnecessary. Nevertheless, in advanced research papers, consider using two kinds of notes.

How should I use content notes?

Develop a note to share information indirectly related to your discussion—material that would otherwise interrupt the flow of your paper.

Sentence in Paper

- Once bacteria have gained antibiotic-resistant abilities through genetic mutations, they often pass the mutations on to other cells.[1]

Footnote or Endnote

- [1] This transfer of mutated genetic material from antibiotic-resistant bacteria occurs by any of three bacterial mechanisms of conjugation, transduction, and transformation.

How should I use bibliographic notes?

Use a note that supplies extra information about sources in two situations: (1) to offer an evaluative comment about a source and (2) to supply additional references without interrupting the flow of your argument.

Sentence in Paper

- Programs like the CDC's National Campaign for Appropriate Antibiotic Use are trying to raise awareness of antibiotic resistance and its threat to health care.[2]

Footnote or Endnote

- [2] For additional information about this program, visit <http://www.cdc.gov/drugresistance/community/#campaign>.

How should I format endnotes?

The best way to format endnotes is to use the footnote/endnote feature on your word processor. (MLA style recommends endnotes over footnotes.) A note in the text is signaled by a superscript arabic numeral placed outside the end punctuation. The notes themselves appear in numerical order on a separate page before the works-cited page. Follow these guidelines for laying out your notes page:

- Include your running head in the upper right.
- Center the word "Notes" one inch from the top of the page. Do not use underlining, bold, italics, all capital letters, or quotation marks.
- Arrange your notes sequentially (not alphabetically).
- Double-space within and between all notes.
- For each note, indent five spaces or one-half inch, type the number slightly raised (as a superscript), leave one space, and then start your note. Keep second and subsequent lines flush left (not indented).

51d In-Text Abbreviations in MLA Format

Recognizable abbreviations offer writers and readers convenient shorthand for communicating information. However, in the body of your paper, restrict your use of abbreviations by following the guideline and using the forms below.

> **NOTE:** Works-cited entries use specialized abbreviations, such as n. pag. (no pagination given) and UP (University Press). For guidelines on using abbreviations in works-cited entries, see **53f**.

When can I use abbreviations in text?

Use standard abbreviations in your citations, tables, illustrations, footnotes, endnotes, and works-cited list. The abbreviations below may be acceptable in the text of your research paper, report, or other document. To be sure, check your instructor's requirements.

Signal Abbreviations

- e.g.   for example; *exempli gratia* [followed by a comma]
- i.e.   that is; *id est* [preceded and followed by commas]
- *sic*   thus in the source [used within brackets to indicate that an error in a quotation is from the original source]
- vs. (v.)   versus [v. preferred in legal-case titles]

Abbreviations for Time

- A.D.   after the birth of Christ; *anno Domini* [placed before numerals but after century references]
- C.E.   Common Era [after numerals and century references]
- B.C.   before Christ [after numerals and century references]
- B.C.E.   before the Common Era [after numerals and century references]
- a.m.   before noon; *ante meridiem*
- p.m.   after noon; *post meridiem*
- c.   approximately [for date]; *circa*

WRITER'S TIP

Time abbreviations can be incorporated smoothly in the regular flow of your writing. Signal abbreviations, however, tend to interrupt the flow, so they are better used within parentheses or brackets.

51e Sample MLA Paper

Student writer Kyle Van Arendonk wrote the following research paper on the problem of antibiotic resistance. Use this model paper in three ways:

- To study how a well-written research paper builds a discussion
- To examine how sources are integrated into research writing
- To see the format and documentation practices of MLA style

How should I set up the outline for my paper?

If your instructor requires an outline, format it like the one below.

The Threat of Antibiotic Resistance

Introduction—Alexander Fleming discovered the first antibiotic by accident.

I. <u>Antibiotic</u> means "against life"—meaning "against bacterial life."

   A. Antibiotics are chemicals that kill microorganisms.

   B. Antibiotics stemmed the tide of tuberculosis, pneumonia, and gastrointestinal infections.

II. Bactericidal antibiotics kill bacteria, while bacteriostatic antibiotics inhibit their growth.

   A. Antibiotics target the differences between bacterial and human cells.

   B. Bacteria have different ribosomes, nucleic acids, and cell membranes, and also have a cell wall.

III. Antibiotic-resistant bacteria can avoid inhibitory effects.

   A. Bacterial mutations create plugs, enzymes, and blockers.

   B. Mutated bacterial DNA is transferred through conjugation, transduction, and transformation.

IV. Antibiotic resistance is a huge threat to the health care system.

   A. The Centers for Disease Control and Prevention estimates 90,000 people die each year from infections contracted in hospitals, and 70 percent of those infections are caused by resistant bacteria.

   B. Resistance makes common diseases harder to treat.

V. Health care workers and the public should use antibiotics wisely.

   A. Antibiotics should not be used against viruses.

   B. Antibiotics should be targeted against specific bacteria.

   C. Antibiotic soaps and agricultural fertilizers should be limited.

Conclusion—The CDC is working to reduce antibiotic abuse and slow the spread of resistant bacteria, but it needs everyone's help.

Sidebar annotations:

Center the title one inch from the top of the page.

Double-space throughout.

Use phrases or complete sentences consistently, as required.

Set off the introduction and the conclusion.

How should I set up my first page?

Normally, an MLA research paper begins with a page like the one below—with the header (last name and page number), the heading, and the title as key identifying information. As you review the paper, notice the margin notes with page references: These references will take you to more complete discussions of the issues involved.

Van Arendonk 1

Kyle Van Arendonk

Professor D. Schelhaas

English 302

17 April 2005

The Threat of Antibiotic Resistance

Antibiotics are one of modern medicine's proudest achievements. The accidental discovery that led to this achievement, as told by Gerard Tortora, Berdell Funke, and Christine Case, occurred in 1928. A scientist named Alexander Fleming noticed an unusual occurrence on a Petri plate of growing bacteria. The Petri plate had been contaminated by a small amount of mold, and the bacteria in the region around this mold were not growing normally. Fleming saw a clearly defined area around the mold in which the bacteria were inhibited. He determined that the mold was a species of Penicillium and found a way to extract the organism's chemical that inhibited the bacteria's growth. He named the chemical penicillin, the first antibiotic, and doctors were soon using it to treat a wide variety of bacterial infections (13).

Since Fleming's great discovery, scientists have discovered many other antibiotics. The word antibiotic, at first glance, may seem like a misnomer, considering its use in the medical field. According to Stedman's Medical Dictionary, the Greek word from which antibiotic is derived actually translates as "against (anti) life (bios)" (Pugh and Werner, 96). However, while antibiotics work for the lives of human patients, they work against the lives of the microorganisms that cause infections.

According to Tortora, Funke, and Case, antibiotics can be broadly defined as any microorganism-produced substances that can inhibit the growth of other microorganisms (549). Most antibiotics, like erythromycin and bacitracin, now come from certain strains of bacteria, but antibiotics

---

Margin notes:

The heading supplies identifying details (**51b**).

The title indicates the topic and the theme (**51b**).

The opening uses an anecdote to create context and background.

Authors' names, titles of works, and page references create clear, accurate citations for borrowed material (**52a**).

The writer offers basic definitions and explanations.

How should I set up the body of my paper?

Van Arendonk 2

Facts and statistics are carefully documented.

can also be found in fungi like the Penicillium mold and made synthetically (549-550). Antibiotics have greatly enhanced the treatment of many human sicknesses caused by bacterial infections. Strep throat, sinus infection, urinary tract infection, and ear infection are all less serious now than in the past because antibiotic therapies are available. For example, while tuberculosis, pneumonia, and gastrointestinal infections, all caused by bacteria, were the three major causes of death near the beginning of the twentieth century, respiratory tract infections were the only bacterial infection remaining in the top ten causes of death by the end of the twentieth century (Wenzel and Edmond 1961). The availability and use of antibiotics were responsible in most part for this impressive change. However, after all of this success with antibiotic use, a phenomenon called antibiotic resistance is now seriously threatening the effectiveness of antibiotic use in medicine.

The writer states his thesis (7a).

"Mims et al." refers to a source with more than three authors (52b-6).

To understand antibiotic resistance, one first needs to understand how antibiotics work. Although the distinction is not always clear, antibiotics can be divided into two groups: agents that kill bacteria (bactericidal) and agents that only inhibit the growth of bacteria (bacteriostatic) while giving the body's immune system the time it needs to fight off the invader on its own (Mims et al. 487). Antibiotics typically achieve their restraining effects in one of several ways. The key to these methods lies in selective toxicity, defined by Medical Microbiology and Immunology as "selective inhibition of the growth of the microorganism [a bacterium] without damage to the host [the human patient]" (Levinson and Jawetz 48). To accomplish this discriminatory damage, antibiotics exploit one of the main differences between human cells and bacterial cells. Bacteria differ from human cells in certain steps of their metabolic pathways; in the structure of their ribosomes, nucleic acids, and cell membrane; and in the presence of a cell wall, which human cells lack (48-49). By using these differences, antibiotics are able to selectively inhibit bacterial growth. For example, aminoglycoside antibiotics like gentamicin and streptomycin

The writer uses a quotation from an authoritative source to provide a precise definition (46e); brackets indicate changes and clarifications made by the writer (29f, 50f).

Van Arendonk 3

take advantage of bacteria's slightly different ribosomes to selectively halt the production of proteins within the bacteria (Mims et al. 487).

Antibiotic resistance, then, refers to the ability of some microorganisms to avoid these inhibitory effects of antibiotics. Antibiotics become ineffective against such organisms through two natural processes: first, genetic mutation; and second, the subsequent transfer of this mutated genetic material to other organisms, which appears to be the main way that bacteria attain a state of resistance (Davies par. 5).

First, the genetic material of bacteria, DNA, can spontaneously mutate. Sometimes, albeit very rarely, these mutations can be advantageous to the bacteria, specifically when the mutation allows the bacteria to survive the presence of antibiotics.

In an article in <u>Review of Optometry</u>, David Kairys, an optometrist and instructor at Pennsylvania State University, explains that three main types of genetic mutations can provide bacteria with a means of antibiotic resistance. First, mutations can produce "plugs" that block an antibiotic from entering the bacterial cell. Second, mutations can enable the production of new enzymes that break down the antibiotic after it has entered the bacteria. Third, genetic mutations can offer bacteria the ability to make proteins that effectively block the antibiotic from attaching to its target site—often the bacteria's ribosomes, where proteins are produced (42–44). From these mutations, bacteria find a way to survive the presence of normally lethal antibiotics. Bacteria without these mutations are inhibited normally, and in a type of natural selection, antibiotic-resistant bacteria become prevalent as the others die out.

Once bacteria have gained antibiotic-resistant abilities through genetic mutations, they often pass the mutations on to other cells. This occurrence is the second process involved in developing antibiotic resistance. The transfer of mutated genetic material from antibiotic-resistant bacteria to normal bacteria occurs by any of the three bacterial mechanisms of conjugation, transduction, and transformation (Kairys 44). Regardless of the specific transfer mechanism, bacteria normally sensitive to an antibiotic are transformed into the resistant form unaffected by the antibiotic. This

For a source without pagination, the writer uses paragraph numbers to indicate the location of the information (52a and 52b-13).

Indicating the author and his credentials, the writer effectively summarizes the source (46e).

Strong topic sentences offer transitions between paragraphs and move the discussion forward (12a–12c).

THE MLA SYSTEM AND SAMPLE PAPER

Van Arendonk 4

process is pictured in more detail in Figure 1 below, in which antibiotic-resistant genes are shown creating efflux "pumps" that get rid of antibiotics (a), creating enzymes that break down antibiotics (b), or changing the antibiotic chemically to make it ineffective (c). As a result of this process, these exchanges of genetic mutations between bacteria, along with spontaneous mutations, rapidly increase the proportion of bacteria that are resistant to an antibiotic. While the normal bacteria decrease in number as the antibiotic inhibits their growth, the resistant forms of the bacteria thrive and reproduce to quickly increase in number.

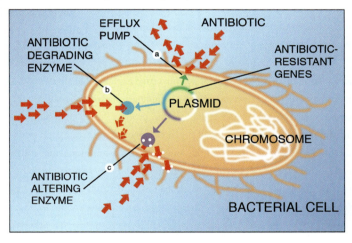

Figure 1. Strategies of Antibiotic-Resistant Genes. Illustration by Sol Ivanski in S. S. Davidson, "Perils of Antibiotic Overuse," Genetic Frontiers July 2005.

Clearly, the development of antibiotic-resistant organisms poses a huge threat to the present system of health care, a system that relies heavily on antibiotic therapies. Antibiotics normally used to treat bacterial infections are becoming increasingly ineffective as the number of antibiotic-resistant organisms increases. According to Linda Bren, a staff writer for FDA Consumer, the threat is large and is getting worse:

> For some of us, bacterial resistance could mean more visits to the doctor, a lengthier illness, and possibly more toxic drugs.

Van Arendonk 5

> For others, it could mean death. The Centers for Disease Control
> and Prevention (CDC) estimates that each year, nearly 2 million
> people in the United States acquire an infection while in a
> hospital, resulting in 90,000 deaths. More than 70 percent of
> the bacteria that cause these infections are resistant to at least
> one of the antibiotics commonly used to treat them. (28)

The results of antibiotic resistance can range from minor inconveniences to higher health care costs and even to death. This widespread resistance to antibiotics affects doctors' abilities to treat many human infections. The National Institute of Allergy and Infectious Diseases reports that antibiotic resistance has caused common diseases like tuberculosis, gonorrhea, pneumonia, and ear and urinary tract infections to become increasingly difficult to treat ("Fact Sheet").

To maintain the efficacy of antibiotics for the future, health care workers and the general public must cooperate to limit any further increase in antibiotic-resistant organisms. While a certain level of antibiotic resistance develops naturally, several controllable factors have greatly accelerated the increase in antibiotic-resistant organisms. First, the widespread overuse and misuse of antibiotics within the medical field has greatly contributed to this problem. The Medical Letter on the CDC and FDA suggests that the unnecessary use of antibiotics, the use of the wrong antibiotic, and patients' failure to finish an antibiotic prescription are all causing an increase in the level of antibiotic resistance ("Antibiotic Overuse," 25).

Antibiotics are effective only against infections caused by bacteria and should never be used against infections caused by viruses. Using an antibiotic against a viral infection is like throwing water on a grease fire—water may normally put out fires but will only worsen the situation for a grease fire. In the same way, antibiotics fight infections, but they only cause the body harm when used to fight infections that are caused by viruses. Viruses cause the common cold, the flu, and most sore throats, sinus infections, coughs, and bronchitis. Yet antibiotics are commonly prescribed for these viral infections. The New England Journal of Medicine reports

A quotation longer than four lines is introduced with a complete sentence and a colon, and is indented ten spaces.

A source without an author is referenced by sponsoring agency; the citation uses a shortened version of the title (52b-8).

A source's authority is emphasized through its links to government agencies.

An analogy clarifies a concept.

THE MLA SYSTEM AND SAMPLE PAPER

Van Arendonk 6

that 22.7 million kilograms (25,000 tons) of antibiotics are prescribed each year in the United States alone (Wenzel and Edmond 1962). Meanwhile, the CDC reports that approximately 50 percent of those prescriptions are completely unnecessary ("Antibiotic Overuse" 25). "Every year, tens of millions of prescriptions for antibiotics are written to treat viral illnesses for which these antibiotics offer no benefits," says the CDC's antimicrobial resistance director David Bell, M.D. (qtd. in Bren 30).

A lack of knowledge is certainly one cause of this misuse. According to the Medical Letter on the CDC and FDA, a study by the Council for Affordable and Quality Health Care (an alliance of health care providers) found that one out of three U.S. citizens thinks that antibiotics are effective against the viruses that cause colds and flu and uses them in those situations ("Antibiotic Overuse" 25). Poor decision making by physicians also causes antibiotic misuse. Linda Bren of FDA Consumer explains that doctors often inappropriately prescribe antibiotics for viral infections because of uncertainty about the type of infection present, limits on time for further testing, and pressure from patients demanding prescriptions (30). The problem is worsened by the fact that in many underdeveloped countries, antibiotics are available without any prescription (Tortora, Funke, and Case 569). Without extensive medical education, the lay people of these countries use antibiotics in hopes of treating many sicknesses that are not caused by bacteria—even common ailments like headaches (569).

Similarly, even when antibiotics are properly prescribed for bacterial infections, the wrong antibiotic is often used. To save money, people often use a friend's or family member's leftover antibiotic prescription. But antibiotics are tailored to inhibit the growth of specific bacteria, so a friend's prescription is not guaranteed to attack the bacteria actually causing an infection. Patients' failure to complete antibiotic prescriptions causes further misuse of antibiotics. One survey even found that 59 percent of patients in a general-practice setting did not finish the prescribed course of antibiotic treatment (Davies par. 7). When symptoms go away, people are tempted to discontinue the antibiotic prescription for an infection.

Van Arendonk 7

But premature termination of an antibiotic therapy encourages the survival of some bacteria, specifically those with antibiotic resistance.

All of this misuse and overuse of antibiotics creates unnecessary problems. The antibiotics kill off susceptible bacteria, while antibiotic-resistant bacteria, the "fittest" organisms, survive and multiply to increase the population of resistant organisms and decrease the antibiotic's future usefulness. In addition, unnecessary antibiotics can destroy the valuable bacteria that live in the human body. These bacteria are helpful and necessary for the body's proper functioning. For example, intestinal bacteria have a vital nutritional function, producing several B vitamins and vitamin K (Levinson and Jawetz 22). The removal of these bacteria not only is dangerous to a patient's health but also allows antibiotic-resistant bacteria to thrive. In the absence of these useful, nonpathogenic bacteria, the antibiotic-resistant organisms are no longer held in check by the competition for nutrients and the inhibition provided by the bacteria normally residing in the body.

Several other situations have also contributed to the problem of antibiotic resistance. The use of antibacterial soaps, detergents, lotions, and other household items is becoming increasingly common. Stuart Levy, M.D., president of the Alliance for the Prudent Use of Antibiotics, says that "there has never been evidence that they [antibacterial products] have a public health benefit. Good soap and water is sufficient in most cases" (qtd. in Bren 31). People buy into the idea that antibacterial products are of great benefit to public health, that these products are dutifully protecting them from pathogens lurking all around them. Usually, however, these products just kill off harmless bacteria on the surface of the skin while encouraging the development of resistant strains of bacteria.

Finally, the extensive use of antibiotics in agriculture also contributes to this problem. Of the 160 million prescriptions written for antibiotics each year in the United States, approximately 50 percent of those antibiotics are used in animals, agriculture, and aquaculture (Wenzel and Edmond 1962). Plants used for food are often sprayed with antibiotic fertilizers, and food-producing animals are often given antibiotics in their food. These

The writer summarizes his discussion and deepens it with a related point backed up with a documented example.

Summaries and paraphrases from sources are used to explain concepts (46e).

To strengthen a quotation's credibility, the writer gives the source's credentials in an attributive phrase (50f).

The writer includes an unusual twist to the topic near the end of his discussion.

THE MLA SYSTEM AND SAMPLE PAPER

Van Arendonk 8

measures help to control diseases and improve growth rates, but they also increase the unnecessary exposure of bacteria to antibiotics (Tortora, Funke, and Case 562). This exposure encourages the growth of antibiotic-resistant bacteria, and these bacteria can then be passed to humans where their infections can no longer be treated with past antibiotic therapies.

The conclusion restates the seriousness of the problem and focuses on potential solutions (8c).

As antibiotic resistance reaches a threatening level, several organizations have started educational campaigns that seek to teach health care workers and the public about the proper use of antibiotics. Programs like the CDC's National Campaign for Appropriate Antibiotic Use are trying to raise awareness of antibiotic resistance and its threat to health care. Many more educational efforts are needed to limit the overuse and misuse of antibiotics that are causing the threatening rise of antibiotic resistance. In addition to these efforts, researchers are working to develop new antibiotics that can target the organisms that have grown resistant to the present arsenal of antibiotics. Until these new antibiotics are found, however, we must do everything possible to extend the effectiveness of the antibiotics that we already have. The proper use of antibiotics can limit the development of antibiotic resistance and prolong our ability to use the current antibiotics to successfully treat diseases. As we face the challenge of antibiotic resistance, we must not allow indiscriminate use to destroy the great medical benefits of antibiotic therapies.

The final sentence offers a collective challenge to readers.

How should I set up my works-cited list?

- Begin the list of works cited on a separate page and include the title, header, and page number.
- List sources in alphabetical order by author (or by title if no author is given).
- Underline titles. Do not italicize them or place them in quotation marks (29h–29i).
- Double space items throughout. Indent second and subsequent lines (a hanging indent).
- Use correct abbreviations throughout (53f).

Van Arendonk 9

Works Cited

"Antibiotic Overuse Campaign Gets Underway." <u>Medical Letter on the CDC and FDA</u> 23 Feb. 2003: 24-25. <u>Academic Search Premier</u>. EBSCOhost. U of Iowa Lib., Iowa City. 4 Apr. 2005 <http://www.ebscohost.com>.

Bren, Linda. "Battle of the Bugs: Fighting Antibiotic Resistance." <u>FDA Consumer</u> July/Aug. 2002: 28–34. <u>Academic Search Premier</u>. EBSCOhost. U of Iowa Lib., Iowa City. 8 Apr. 2005 <http://www .ebscohost.com>.

Davies, Peter D. "Does Increased Use of Antibiotics Result in Increased Antibiotic Resistance?" <u>Clinical Infectious Diseases</u> 39.1 (2004). <u>PubMed</u>. U of Iowa Lib., Iowa City. 3 Apr. 2005 <http://www.ncbi .nlm.nih.gov/entrez/query.fcgi>.

"Fact Sheet: The Problem of Antibiotic Resistance." <u>National Institute of Allergy and Infectious Diseases</u>. Apr. 2004. 31 Mar. 2005 <http://www. niaid.nih.gov/factsheets/antimicro.htm>.

Kairys, David J. "The Science Behind Antibiotic Resistance." <u>Review of Optometry</u> 15 Oct. 2002: 39-44. <u>Academic Search Premier</u>. EBSCOhost. U of Iowa Lib., Iowa City. 5 Apr. 2005 <http://www.ebscohost.com>.

Levinson, Warren, and Ernest Jawetz. <u>Medical Microbiology and Immunology</u>. Stamford, CT: Appleton and Lange, 1996.

Mims, Cedric, Hazel M. Dockrell, Richard V. Goering, Ivan Roitt, Derek Wakelin, and Mark Zuckerman. <u>Medical Microbiology</u>. Edinburgh: Mosby, 2004.

Pugh, Maureen B., and Barbara Werner, eds. "Antibiotic." <u>Stedman's Medical Dictionary</u>. 27th ed. Philadelphia: Lippincott Williams & Wilkins, 2000.

"Survey: One-Third of Americans Use Antibiotics Inappropriately." <u>Medical Letter on the CDC and FDA</u> 19 Jan. 2003: 9-10. <u>Academic Search Premier</u>. EBSCOhost. U of Iowa Lib., Iowa City. 8 Apr. 2005 <http:// www.ebscohost.com>.

Tortora, Gerard J., Berdell R. Funke, and Christine L. Case. <u>Microbiology: An Introduction</u>. San Francisco: Benjamin Cummings, 2002.

Wenzel, Richard P., and Michael B. Edmond. "Managing Antibiotic Resistance." <u>New England Journal of Medicine</u> 343.26 (2000): 1961-63.

Entries have hanging indents.

Periods separate most items in individual entries but are never underlined.

Internet addresses are placed between angle brackets.

THE MLA SYSTEM AND SAMPLE PAPER

ETHICS TIP

For research papers, it's commonly said, "You are commanded to borrow but forbidden to steal." MLA documentation helps you avoid plagiarism (50a) and allows readers to evaluate and build on your research. In other words, MLA offers you rules for participating in an academic dialogue.

51f Checklist: MLA System

___ All borrowed material is acknowledged with an attributive phrase and/or in-text citation indicating author and page number, as appropriate.

___ All in-text citations effectively point readers to resources in the works-cited list.

___ The works-cited list includes entries for all works referred to in the body of the paper. No sources are missing from the list; no extra sources are listed that have no reference within the paper.

___ The entire works-cited list is properly alphabetized by authors' last names (or by the first main word in the title for anonymous works).

___ Each works-cited entry (whether for a book, an article, a webpage, or other source) contains the maximum amount of identifying and publication information, in the proper order, using the expected abbreviations.

___ The entire paper is properly formatted, from the first page heading and title to the final works-cited page entry.

___ Placement, spacing, and margins are correct for the paper's header (writer's last name and page number), the heading, the title, and works cited.

___ Pagination is correct and consistent.

___ First lines of paragraphs and inset quotations are properly indented; works-cited entries are properly formatted with a hanging indent.

___ The paper is cleanly printed single-sided on quality paper in a professional-looking typeface and in 12-point type size (without fancy type style features).

___ The paper is properly bound with a paperclip or clasp in the upper-left corner.

MLA In-Text Citations

In-text citations allow you to get credit for all the research you have done—and to give credit to your sources. A citation refers to the author or title of a source and to the page number that the information came from (VanderMey 525). The citation then points to a complete entry on the works-cited page:

> VanderMey, Randy, et al. <u>The College Writer's Handbook</u>. Boston: Houghton Mifflin, 2006.

It's as simple as that. This chapter provides instructions and examples for creating in-text citations for different types of sources.

Directory to In-Text Citations

What's Ahead

52a Guidelines for In-Text Citations
52b Sample In-Text Citations

52a Guidelines for In-Text Citations

The *MLA Handbook for Writers of Research Papers* suggests giving credit for your sources of information in the body of your research paper. The simplest way to do so is to insert the appropriate information (usually the author and page number) in parentheses after the words or ideas taken from the source.

Sometimes a citation can appear within a sentence before internal punctuation such as a comma or semicolon. These in-text citations (sometimes called "parenthetical references") refer to sources listed on the "Works Cited" page at the end of your paper. (See **53a–53f**.)

How should I cite works in text?

As you integrate citations into your paper, follow the guidelines below, referring to the sample citation as needed.

SAMPLE IN-TEXT CITATION

Linda Bren of <u>FDA Consumer</u> explains that doctors often inappropriately prescribe antibiotics for viral infections because of uncertainty about the type of infection present, limits on time for further testing, and pressure from patients demanding prescriptions (30).

- Make sure each in-text citation clearly points to an entry in your list of works cited. The identifying information provided (usually the author's last name) must be the word or words by which the entry is alphabetized in that list.

- When paraphrasing or summarizing rather than quoting, make it clear where your borrowing begins and ends. Use stylistic cues to distinguish the source's thoughts ("Kalmbach points out . . . ," "Some critics argue . . .") from your own ("I believe . . . ," "It seems obvious," "however").

- When using a shortened title of a work, begin with the word by which the work is alphabetized in your list of works cited ("Antibiotic Overuse," not "Overuse Campaign," for "Antibiotic Overuse Campaign Gets Underway").

- For inclusive page numbers larger than ninety-nine, give only the two digits of the second number (113-14, not 113-114).

- When including a parenthetical citation at the end of a sentence, place it before the end punctuation. (Citations for long, indented quotations are an exception. See **50f**.)

 WRITER'S TIP

Keep citations as brief as possible, and integrate them smoothly into your writing. To avoid disrupting your writing, place citations where a pause would naturally occur, usually at the end of a sentence.

What should I do if there is no author or page number?

Today, several sources, especially electronic ones, have no stated authors and/or no pagination. For such sources, use these in-text citation strategies.

SOURCE WITHOUT A STATED AUTHOR

In a signal phrase or in the parenthetical reference, identify the source as precisely as possible by indicating the sponsoring agency, the type of document, or the title (shortened in the parenthetical reference). (See 52b-8.)

- **The National Institute of Allergy and Infectious Diseases** reports that antibiotic resistance has caused common diseases to become increasingly difficult to treat **("Fact Sheet").**

SOURCE WITH NO PAGINATION

If no pagination exists within the document, reference any stable, internal divisions available—paragraph numbers, chapter titles, headings, and so forth. (See 52b-13.)

- Antibiotics become ineffective against such organisms through two natural processes: first, genetic mutation; and second, the subsequent transfer of this mutated genetic material to other organisms (Davies **par. 5**).

Also follow these guidelines when referring to sources without pagination:

- If you refer to document divisions other than page numbers, use abbreviations: par. (paragraph), ch. (chapter), sec. (section), introd. (introduction).

- When you have no parenthetical reference to mark the end of borrowed material, signal a shift back to your own discussion with a source-reflective statement indicating your thinking about the source.

  - . . . the main effects of antibiotic resistance. Bren's description of these effects helps us understand the seriousness of the problem.

Web Link: Stable pagination for many electronic resources is available when you use the "PDF" rather than the "HTML" version of the source.

52b Sample In-Text Citations

The following entries illustrate the most common sorts of in-text citations.

1. One Author: A Complete Work

You do not need an in-text citation if you identify the author in your text. (See the first entry below.) However, you must give the author's last name in an in-text citation if it is not mentioned in the text. (See the second entry.) When a source is listed in your works-cited page with an editor, a translator, a speaker, or an artist instead of the author, then use that person's name in your citation.

> **WITH AUTHOR IN TEXT (the preferred way of citing a complete work)**
>
> In <u>No Need for Hunger</u>, Robert Spitzer recommends that the U.S. government develop a new foreign policy to help Third World countries overcome poverty and hunger.
>
> **WITHOUT AUTHOR IN TEXT**
>
> <u>No Need for Hunger</u> recommends that the U.S. government develop a new foreign policy to help Third World countries overcome poverty and hunger (Spitzer).

Do not offer page numbers when citing complete works, articles in alphabetized encyclopedias, one-page articles, or unpaginated sources.

2. One Author: Part of a Work

List the necessary page numbers in parentheses if you borrow words or ideas from a particular source. Leave a space between the author's last name and the page reference. No abbreviation or punctuation is needed.

> **WITH AUTHOR IN TEXT**
>
> Bullough writes that genetic engineering was dubbed "eugenics" by a cousin of Darwin's, Sir Francis Galton, in 1885 (5).
>
> **WITHOUT AUTHOR IN TEXT**
>
> Genetic engineering was dubbed "eugenics" by a cousin of Darwin's, Sir Francis Galton, in 1885 (Bullough 5).

3. Two or More Works by the Same Author(s)

In addition to the author's last name(s) and page number(s), include a short version of the title of the work when you are citing two or more works by the same author(s). In parentheses, authors and titles are separated by a comma, as in the second example.

> **WITH AUTHOR IN TEXT**
>
> Wallerstein and Blakeslee claim that divorce creates an enduring identity for children of the marriage (<u>Unexpected Legacy</u> 62).
>
> **WITHOUT AUTHOR IN TEXT**
>
> They are intensely lonely despite active social lives (Wallerstein and Blakeslee, <u>Second Chances</u> 51).

4. Works by Authors with the Same Last Name

When citing different sources by authors with the same last name, it is best to use the authors' full names in the text so as to avoid confusion. However, if circumstances call for parenthetical references, add each author's first initial. If first initials are the same, use each author's full name.

> Some critics think *Titus Andronicus* too abysmally melodramatic to be a work of Shakespeare (A. Parker 73). Others suggest that Shakespeare meant it as black comedy (D. Parker 486).

5. A Work by Two or Three Authors

Give the last names of every author in the same order that they appear in the works-cited section. (The correct order of the authors' names can be found on the title page of the book.)

> Students learned more than a full year's Spanish in ten days using the complete supermemory method (Ostrander and Schroeder 51).

6. A Work by Four or More Authors

Give the first author's last name as it appears in the works-cited section followed by *et al.* (meaning "and others").

> Communication on the job is more than talking; it is "inseparable from your total behavior" (Culligan et al. 111).

7. A Work Authored by an Organization

If a book or other work was written by an organization such as an agency, a committee, or a task force, it is said to have a corporate author. (See also **52a**.) If the corporate name is long, include it in the text (rather than in parentheses) to avoid disrupting the flow of your writing. After the full name has been used at least once, use a shortened form of the name (common abbreviations are acceptable) in subsequent references. For example, *Task Force* may be used for *Task Force on Education for Economic Growth*.

> The Task Force on Education for Economic Growth details a strong connection between education and the depth and breadth of the workforce (105).

> The thesis of the report is that economic success depends on our ability to improve large-scale education and training as quickly as possible (Task Force 113-14).

8. An Anonymous Work

When there is no author listed, give the title or a shortened version of the title as it appears in the works-cited section. (See also **52a**.)

> Statistics indicate that drinking tap water can account for up to 20 percent of a person's total exposure to lead (Information 572).

9. Two or More Works Included in One Citation

To cite multiple works within a single parenthetical reference, separate the references with a semicolon.

> In Medieval Europe, Latin translations of the works of Rhazes, a Persian scholar, were a primary source of medical knowledge (Albe 22; Lewis 266).

10. A Series of Citations from a Single Work

If no confusion is possible, it is not necessary to name a source repeatedly when making multiple parenthetical references to that source in a single paragraph. If all references are to the same page, identify that page in a parenthetical note after the last reference. If the references are to different pages within the same work, you need identify the work only once, and then use a parenthetical note with page number alone for the subsequent references.

> Domesticating science meant not only spreading scientific knowledge, but also promoting it as a topic of public conversation (Heilbron 2). One way to enhance its charm was by depicting cherubic *putti* as "angelic research assistants" in book illustrations (5).

11. A Work Referred to in Another Work

If you must cite an indirect source—that is, information from a source that is quoted from another source—use the abbreviation *qtd. in* (quoted in) before the indirect source in your reference.

> Paton improved the conditions in Diepkloof (a prison) by "removing all the more obvious aids to detention. The dormitories [were] open at night: the great barred gate [was] gone" (qtd. in Callan xviii).

12. A One-Page Work

Cite a one-page work just as you would a complete work. (See 52b-1.)

> As S. Adams argues in her editorial, it is time for NASA "to fully reevaluate the Space Shuttle's long-term viability for sending humans into space."

13. A Work Without Page Numbers

If a work has no page numbers or other reference numbers, treat it as you would a complete work. (See 52b-1.) This is commonly the case with electronic resources, for example. Do not count pages to create reference numbers of your own; however, if possible, refer to stable divisions within the document, such as sections or paragraphs. (See 52b-2.)

> Antibiotics become ineffective against such organisms through two natural processes: first, genetic mutation; and second, the subsequent transfer of this mutated genetic material to other organisms, which appears to be the main way that bacteria attain a state of resistance (Davies par. 5).

14. A Work in an Anthology or a Collection

When citing the entirety of a work that is part of an anthology or a collection, if it is identified by author in your list of works cited, treat the citation as you would for any other complete work. (See **52b-1**.)

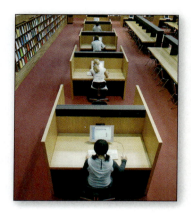

> In "The Canadian Postmodern," Linda Hutcheon offers a clear analysis of the self-reflexive nature of contemporary Canadian fiction.

Similarly, if you are citing particular pages of such a work, follow the directions for citing part of a work. (See **52b-2**.)

> According to Hutcheon, "postmodernism seems to designate cultural practices that are fundamentally self-reflexive, in other words, art that is self-consciously artifice" (18).

15. An Item from a Reference Work

An entry from a reference work such as an encyclopedia or a dictionary should be cited similarly to a work from an anthology or a collection (**52b-14**). For a dictionary definition, include the abbreviation *def.* followed by the particular entry designation.

> This message of moral superiority becomes a juggernaut in the truest sense, a belief that "elicits blind devotion or sacrifice" ("Juggernaut," def. 1).

While many such entries are identified only by title (as above), some reference works include an author's name for each entry (as below). Others may identify the author by initials, with a list of full names elsewhere in the work.

> The decisions of the International Court of Justice are "based on principles of international law and cannot be appealed" (Pranger).

16. A Part of a Multivolume Work

When citing only one volume of a multivolume work, if you identify the volume number in the works-cited list, there is no need to include it in your in-text citation. However, if you cite more than one volume of a work, then each in-text reference must identify the appropriate volume. Give the volume number followed by page number, separated by a colon and a space.

> "A human being asleep," says Spengler, ". . . is leading only a plantlike existence" (2: 4).

When citing a whole volume, however, either identify the volume number in parentheses with the abbreviation *vol.* (using a comma to separate it from the author's name) or use the full word *volume* in your text.

> The land of Wisconsin has shaped its many inhabitants more significantly than they ever shaped that land (Stephens, vol. 1).

MLA IN-TEXT CITATIONS

17. A Sacred Text or Famous Literary Work

Because sacred texts and famous literary works are published in many editions, include sections, parts, or chapters. If using page numbers, list them first, followed by an abbreviation for the type of division and the division number.

> The more important a person's role in society—the more apparent power an individual has—the more that person is a slave to the forces of history (Tolstoy 690; bk. 9, ch. 1).

Books of the Bible and well-known works may be abbreviated.

> "A generation goes, and a generation comes, but the earth remains forever" (The New Oxford Annotated Bible, Eccles. 1:4)

> Hamlet observes, "One may smile [. . .] and be a villain" (Ham. 1.5.104).

18. Quoting Verse

Cite classic verse plays and poems by division (act, scene, canto, book, part) and line, using arabic numerals for the various divisions unless your instructor prefers roman numerals. Use periods to separate the various numbers.

> In the first act of the play, Hamlet comments, "How weary, stale, flat and unprofitable, / Seem to me all the uses of this world" (1.2.133-134).

> **NOTE:** A slash, with a space on each side, shows where each new line of verse begins. If you are citing lines only, use the word *line* or *lines* in your first reference and numbers only in additional references.

> In book five of Homer's Iliad, the Trojans' fear is evident: "The Trojans were scared when they saw the two sons of Dares, one of them in fright and the other lying dead by his chariot" (lines 22-24).

19. Quoting Prose

To cite prose from fiction, list more than the page number if the work is available in several editions. Give the page reference first, and then add a chapter or section, if appropriate, in abbreviated form after a semicolon.

> In The House of the Spirits, Isabel describes Marcos, "dressed in mechanic's overalls, with huge racer's goggles and an explorer's helmet" (13; ch. 1).

When you are quoting any sort of prose that takes more than four typed lines, indent each line of the quotation one inch (ten spaces) and double-space it; do not add quotation marks. In this case, you put the parenthetical citation (the pages and chapter numbers) outside the end punctuation mark.

> Allende describes the flying machine that Marcos has assembled:

>> The contraption lay with its stomach on terra firma, heavy and sluggish, looking more like a wounded duck than like one of those newfangled airplanes they were starting to produce in the United States. There was nothing in its appearance to suggest that it could move, much less take flight. (12; ch. 1)

MLA Works Cited

The first part of the MLA documentation system involves in-text citations within your paper when you use a source. The second part of the system is the works-cited list—an alphabetized list of bibliographic entries for all the resources that you referred to in your paper. This chapter offers instruction on setting up that list and on creating different types of entries.

53a Guidelines for MLA Works Cited

The works-cited section lists all of the sources you have cited (referred to) in your text. Begin your list of works cited on a new page (after the text), and number each page, continuing from the number of the last page of the text.

How should I set up my works-cited page?

Follow these general guidelines when formatting your works-cited page:

- Type the page number in the upper-right corner, one-half inch from the top of the page, with your last name before it.
- Center the title *Works Cited* (not in italics or underlined) one inch from the top; then double-space before the first entry.
- Begin each entry flush with the left margin. If the entry runs more than one line, indent additional lines one-half inch (five spaces) or use the hanging indent function on your computer.
- Use a single space after all punctuation in a works-cited entry.
- Double-space lines within each entry and between entries.
- List each entry alphabetically by the author's last name. If there is no author, use the first word of the title (disregard *A, An,* and *The*).

What's Ahead

MLA WORKS CITED

Directory to MLA Works-Cited Entries

53b Works-Cited Entries: Books and Other Documents

The entries that follow illustrate the information needed to cite books, sections of a book,
pamphlets, and government publications.
The possible components of these entries are
listed in order below:

- Author's name
- Title of a part of the book (an article in
  the book or a foreword)
- Title of the book
- Name of editor or translator
- Edition
- Number of volume
- Name of series
- Place of publication, publisher, year
  of publication
- Page numbers, if citation is to only a part (For page spans, use a hyphen.
  If clarity is maintained, you may also drop a digit from the second
  number: 141-43, but 201-334.)

> **NOTE:** In general, if any of these components do not apply, they are not
> included in the works-cited entry. However, in the rare instance that a book
> does not state publication information, use the following abbreviations in
> place of information you cannot supply:
>
> - n.p.   No place of publication given
> - n.p.   No publisher given
> - n.d.   No date of publication given
> - n. pag.   No pagination given

How should I list cities and publisher names?

List only the city for the place of publication if the city is in the United States.
For cities outside the United States, add an abbreviation for the country if
necessary for clarity. If several cities are listed, give only the first.

WRITER'S TIP

Publishers' names should be shortened by omitting articles
(*a, an, the*), business abbreviations *(Co., Inc.)*, and descriptive words
(Books, Press). Abbreviate University Press as *UP*. Also use standard
abbreviations whenever possible. See **53f** for more details.

MLA WORKS CITED

1. A Book by One Author

Baghwati, Jagdish. In Defense of Globalization. New York: Oxford UP, 2004.

2. Two or More Books by the Same Author

List the books alphabetically according to title. After the first entry, substitute three hyphens for the author's name.

Dershowitz, Alan M. Rights from Wrongs. New York: Basic Books, 2005.

- - - .Supreme Injustice: How the High Court Hijacked Election 2000.
Oxford: Oxford UP, 2001.

3. A Work by Two or Three Authors

Bystydzienski, Jill M., and Estelle P. Resnik. Women in Cross-Cultural Transitions. Bloomington, IN: Phi Delta Kappa Educational Foundation, 1994.

> **NOTE:** List the authors in the same order as they appear on the title page. Reverse only the name of the first author.

4. A Work by Four or More Authors

Schulte-Peevers, Andrea, et al. Germany. Victoria, Austral.: Lonely Planet, 2000.

> **NOTE:** You may also choose to give all names in full in the order used on the title page.

5. A Work Authored by an Agency, a Committee, or Other Organization

Exxon Mobil Corporation. Great Plains 2000. Lincolnwood, IL: Publications Intl., 2001.

6. An Anonymous Book

Chase's Calendar of Events 2002. Chicago: Contemporary, 2002.

7. A Single Work from an Anthology

Mitchell, Joseph. "The Bottom of the Harbor." American Sea Writing. Ed. Peter Neill. New York: Library of America, 2000. 584-608.

8. A Complete Anthology

If you cite a complete anthology, begin the entry with the editor(s).

Neill, Peter, ed. American Sea Writing. New York: Library of America, 2000.

Smith, Rochelle, and Sharon L. Jones, eds. The Prentice Hall Anthology of African American Literature. Upper Saddle River, NJ: Prentice Hall, 2000.

9. Two or More Works from the Same Anthology or Collection

To avoid unnecessary repetition when citing two or more entries from a larger collection, you may cite the collection once with complete publication information (see *Forbes* below). The individual entries (see *Joseph* and *MacNeice* below) can then be cross-referenced by listing the author, title of the piece, editor of the collection, and page numbers.

Forbes, Peter, ed. <u>Scanning the Century</u>. London: Penguin, 2000.

Joseph, Jenny. "Warning." Forbes 335-36.

MacNeice, Louis. "Star-Gazer." Forbes 504.

10. One Volume of a Multivolume Work

Cooke, Jacob Ernest, and Milton M. Klein, eds. <u>North America in Colonial Times</u>. Vol. 2. New York: Scribner's, 1998.

> **NOTE:** If you cite two or more volumes in a multivolume work, give the total number of volumes after each title. Offer specific references to volume and page numbers in the parenthetical reference in your text, like this: (8: 112–114). (See **52b-16**.)
>
> Salzman, Jack, David Lionel Smith, and Cornel West. <u>Encyclopedia of African-American Culture and History</u>. 5 vols. New York: Simon, 1996.

11. An Introduction, a Preface, a Foreword, or an Afterword

To cite the introduction, preface, foreword, or afterword of a book, list the author of the part first. Then identify the part by type, with no quotation marks or underlining, followed by the title of the book. Next, identify the author of the work, using the word "By." (However, if the book author and the part's author are the same person, give just the last name after "By.") For a book that gives cover credit to an editor instead of an author, identify the editor as usual. Finally, list any page numbers for the part being cited.

Barry, Anne. Afterword. <u>Making Room for Students</u>. By Celia Oyler. New York: Teachers College, 1996.

Lefebvre, Mark. Foreword. <u>The Journey Home</u>. Vol. 1. Ed. Jim Stephens. Madison: North Country, 1989. ix.

12. A Republished Book (Reprint)

Give the original publication date after the title.

Atwood, Margaret. <u>Surfacing</u>. 1972. New York: Doubleday, 1998.

> **NOTE:** New material added to the reprint, such as an introduction, should be cited after the original publication facts: Introd. C. Becker.

MLA WORKS CITED

13. A Book with Multiple Publishers

When a book lists more than one publisher (not just different offices of the same publisher), include all of them in the order given on the book's title page, separated by a semicolon.

> Wells, H. G. The Complete Short Stories of H. G. Wells. New York: St. Martin's; London: A. & C. Black, 1987.

14. Second and Subsequent Editions

An edition refers to the particular publication you are citing.

> Joss, M. Looking Good in Presentations. 3rd ed. Scottsdale: Coriolis, 1999.

15. An Edition with an Author and an Editor

The term *edition* also refers to the work of one person that is prepared by another person, an editor.

> Shakespeare, William. A Midsummer Night's Dream. Ed. Jane Bachman. Lincolnwood, IL: NTC, 1994.

16. A Translation

> Lebert, Stephan, and Norbert Lebert. My Father's Keeper. Trans. Julian Evans. Boston: Little, 2001.

17. An Article in a Familiar Reference Book

It is not necessary to give full publication information for familiar reference works (encyclopedias and dictionaries). For these titles, list only the edition (if available) and the publication year. If an article is initialed, check the index of authors (in the opening section of each volume) for the author's full name.

> "Technical Education." Encyclopedia Americana. 2001 ed.

> Lum, P. Andrea. "Computed Tomography." World Book. 2000 ed.

When citing a single definition of several listed, add the abbreviation *Def.* and the particular number or letter for that definition.

> "Deaf." Def. 2b. The American Heritage College Dictionary. 4th ed. 2002.

18. An Article in an Unfamiliar Reference Book

Give full publication information as for any other sort of book.

> "S Corporation." The Portable MBA Desk Reference. Ed. Paul A. Argenti. New York: Wiley, 1994.

19. A Government Publication

State the name of the government (country, state, and so on) followed by the name of the agency. Most U.S. federal publications are published by the Government Printing Office (GPO).

> United States. Dept. of Labor. Bureau of Labor Statistics. Occupational Outlook Handbook 2004-2005. Washington: GPO, 2004.

When citing the *Congressional Record*, list only the date and page numbers.

> Cong. Rec. 5 Feb. 2002: S311-15.

20. A Book in a Series

Give the series name and number (if any) before the publication information.

> Paradis, Adrian A. <u>Opportunities in Military Careers</u>. VGM Opportunities
> Series. Lincolnwood, IL: VGM Career Horizons, 1999.

21. A Book with a Title Within Its Title

If the title contains a title normally in quotation marks, keep the quotation marks and underline the entire title.

> Stuckey-French, Elizabeth. <u>"The First Paper Girl in Red Oak, Iowa" and Other
> Stories</u>. New York: Doubleday, 2000.

If the title contains a title that is normally underlined, do not underline that title in your entry:

> Beckwith, Charles E. <u>Twentieth Century Interpretations of </u>A Tale of Two
> Cities<u>: A Collection of Critical Essays</u>. Upper Saddle River, NJ: Prentice
> Hall, 1972.

22. A Sacred Text

The Bible and other such sacred texts are treated as anonymous books. Documentation should read exactly as it is printed on the title page.

> <u>The Jerusalem Bible</u>. Garden City: Doubleday, 1966.

23. The Published Proceedings of a Conference

The published proceedings of a conference are treated like a book. However, if the title of the publication does not identify the conference by title, date, and location, add the appropriate information immediately after the title.

> McIlwaine, Ia C., ed. <u>Advances in Knowledge Organization</u>. Vol. 9. Proc.
> of Eighth Intl. ISKO Conf., 13-16 July 2004, London. Wurzburg:
> Ergon-Verlag, 2004.

24. A Published Dissertation

An entry for a published dissertation contains the same information as a book entry, with a few added details. Add the abbreviation *Diss.* and the degree-granting institution before the publication facts.

> Jansen, James Richard. <u>Images of Dostoevsky in German Literary
> Expressionism</u>. Diss. U of Utah, 2003. Ann Arbor: UMI, 2003.

25. A Pamphlet, Brochure, Manual, or Other Workplace Document

Treat any such publication as you would a book.

> Grayson, George W. <u>The North American Free Trade Agreement</u>. New York:
> Foreign Policy Assn., 1993.

If publication information is missing, list the country of publication [in brackets] if known. Use the abbreviation *n.p.* (no place) if the country or the publisher is unknown and the abbreviation *n.d.* if the date is unknown.

> <u>Pedestrian Safety</u>. [United States]: n.p., n.d.

53c Works-Cited Entries: Periodicals

The possible components of these entries are listed in order below:

- Author's name, last name first
- Title of article, in quotation marks and headline style
- Name of periodical, underlined
- Series number or name, if relevant (not preceded by a period or comma)
- Volume number (for a journal)
- Issue number, separated from volume with a period but no space
- Date of publication (abbreviate all months except May, June, and July)
- Page numbers, preceded by a colon, without *p.* or *pp.*

NOTE: If any of the components listed above do not apply, they are not listed. The entries that follow illustrate the information needed to cite periodicals.

26. An Article in a Weekly or Biweekly Magazine

List the author (if identified), article title (in quotation marks), publication title (underlined), full date of publication, and page numbers for the article. Do not include volume and issue numbers.

> Goodell, Jeff. "The Uneasy Assimilation." Rolling Stone 6-13 Dec. 2001: 63-66.

27. An Article in a Monthly or Bimonthly Magazine

As for a weekly or biweekly magazine, list the author (if identified), article title (in quotation marks), and publication title (underlined). Then identify the month(s) and year of the issue, followed by page numbers for the article. Do not give volume and issue numbers.

> "Patent Pamphleteer." Scientific American Dec. 2001: 33.

28. An Article in a Scholarly Journal Paginated by Issue

Rather than month or full date of publication, scholarly journals are identified by volume number. If each issue is numbered from page 1, your works-cited entry should identify the issue number as well. List the volume number immediately after the journal title, followed by a period and the issue number, and then the year of publication (in parentheses). End with the page numbers of the article, as usual.

> Chu, Wujin. "Costs and Benefits of Hard-Sell." Journal of Marketing Research 32.2 (1995): 97-102.

29. An Article in a Scholarly Journal with Continuous Pagination

For scholarly journals that continue pagination from issue to issue, no issue number is needed in the works-cited entry.

> Tebble, Nicola J., David W. Thomas, and Patricia Price. "Anxiety and Self-Consciousness in Patients with Minor Facial Lacerations." Journal of Advanced Nursing 47 (2004): 417-26.

30. A Printed Interview

Begin with the name of the person interviewed when that's whom you are quoting.

> Cantwell, Maria. "The New Technocrat." By Erika Rasmusson. Working Woman Apr. 2001: 20-21.

If the interview is untitled, the word *Interview* (no italics) and a period follow the interviewee's name.

31. A Newspaper Article

A signed newspaper article follows the form below:

> Bleakley, Fred R. "Companies' Profits Grew 48% Despite Economy." Wall Street Journal 1 May 1995, Midwest ed.: 1.

> **NOTE:** Cite the edition of a major daily newspaper (if given) after the date (1 May 1995, Midwest ed.: 1). If a local paper's name does not include the city of publication, add it in brackets (not underlined) after the name.
>
> To cite an article in a lettered section of the newspaper, list the section and the page number. (For example, A4 would refer to page 4 in section A of the newspaper.) If the sections are numbered, however, use a comma after the year (or the edition); then indicate sec. 1, 2, 3, and so on, followed by a colon and the page number (sec. 1: 20).

An unsigned newspaper article follows the same format:

> "Bombs—Real and Threatened—Keep Northern Ireland Edgy." Chicago Tribune 6 Dec. 2001, sec. 1: 20.

32. A Newspaper Editorial

Put *Editorial* (no italics) and a period after the title.

> "Hospital Power." Editorial. Bangor Daily News 14 Sept. 2004: A6.

33. A Letter to the Editor

Put *Letter* (no italics) and a period after the author's name.

> Sory, Forrest. Letter. Discover July 2001: 10.

MLA WORKS CITED

34. A Review

Begin with the author (if identified) and title of the review. Use the notation *Rev. of* (no italics) between the title of the review and that of the original work. Identify the author of the original work with the word *by* (no italics). Then follow with publication data for the review.

> Olsen, Jack. "Brains and Industry." Rev. of <u>Land of Opportunity</u>, by Sarah
> Marr. <u>New York Times</u> 23 Apr. 1995, sec. 3: 28.

35. An Abstract

To cite an abstract, first give the publication information for the original work (if any); then list the publication information for the abstract itself. Add the term *Abstract* and a period between them if the journal title does not include that word. If the journal identifies abstracts by item number, include the word *item* followed by the number. (Add the section identifier [A, B, or C] for those volumes that have one.) If no item number exists, list the page number(s).

> Faber, A. J. "Examining Remarried Couples Through a Bowenian Family
> System Lens." <u>Journal of Divorce and Remarriage</u> 40.3/4 (2004):
> 121–133. <u>Social Work Abstracts</u> 40 (2004): item 1298.

36. An Unsigned Article in a Periodical

If no author is identified for an article, list the entry alphabetically by title among your works cited (ignoring any initial *A, An,* or *The*).

> "Feeding the Hungry." <u>Economist</u>. 371.8374 (2004): 74.

37. An Article with a Title or Quotation Within Its Title

Use single quotation marks around the shorter title if it is normally punctuated with quotation marks.

> Morgenstern, Joe. "Sleeper of the Year: 'In the Bedroom' Is Rich Tale of
> Tragic Love." <u>Wall Street Journal</u> 23 Nov. 2001: W1.

38. An Article Reprinted in a Loose-Leaf Collection

The entry begins with original publication information and ends with the name of the loose-leaf volume (<u>Youth</u>), editor, volume number, publication information including name of the information service (SIRS), and the article number. (In the example below, the plus sign indicates continuing but nonconsecutive pages—see **53c-39**.)

> O'Connell, Loraine. "Busy Teens Feel the Beep." <u>Orlando Sentinel</u> 7 Jan.
> 1993: E1+. <u>Youth</u>. Ed. Eleanor Goldstein. Vol. 4. Boca Raton: SIRS, 1993.
> Art. 41.

39. An Article with Pagination That Is Not Continuous

For articles that are continued on a nonconsecutive page, whatever the publication type, add a plus sign (+) after the first page number.

> Garrett, Robyne. "Negotiating a Physical Identity: Girls, Bodies and Physical
> Education." <u>Sport, Education & Society</u> 9 (2004): 223+.

53d Works-Cited Entries: Online Sources

Citations for online sources follow the strategies used for print sources, with a few additions
to reflect the changeable nature of the Internet.
After the author's name and the title of the
document, include any print publication information, then the electronic publication details
and access information.

- Author's name
- Title of article or webpage
- Print publication information
- Title of Internet site
- Site editor's name
- Version (volume or issue) number
- Date of electronic publication
- Name of subscription service (or website)
- Name of list or forum
- Number range or total number of pages (or other sections)
- Site sponsor's name
- Date of access
- URL in angle brackets
  (For guidelines on long URLs, see **53d-44**.)

If any of these components do not apply, they are not listed. For documents
with no listed date of electronic publication, use the site's posting date, date of
update, or copyright date if available. MLA asks for page, paragraph, or section
numbers if the document includes them. Date of access means the most recent
date on which you viewed the document online. URLs are enclosed in angle
brackets and should identify the complete address, including the access-mode
identifier (http, ftp, telnet, and so on).

40. A Personal Site

After the author's name, list the site title (underlined) or the words *Home page*
(without italics), whichever is appropriate, followed by a period. Add the date of
publication or most recent update, your date of visit, and the URL.

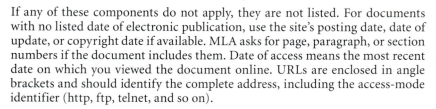

> Mehuron, Kate. Home page. 30 Sept. 2004 <http://www.emich.edu/public/
> history/faculty/mehuron.html>.

41. A Professional Site

Generally, no author is identified for a professional site, so the entry begins
with the site title. Use the copyright date if no date of update is given, followed
by the site sponsor, your date of access, and the URL for the home page.

> Latimes.com. 1 Oct. 2004. Los Angeles Times. 1 Oct. 2004 <http://www
> .latimes.com/>.

MLA WORKS CITED

42. A Site for a Department of a College or University

Begin with the name of the department, followed by a description such as *Dept. home page* (without italics), followed by a period. Then list the name of the institution, your date of access, and the URL. No date of publication or latest update is necessary.

> Department of Foreign Languages and Literatures. Dept. home page.
> Marquette U College of Arts & Sciences. 6 Nov. 2004 <http://
> www.marquette.edu/fola/>.

43. A Site for a Study Course

Start with the instructor's name, reversed as for an author. Then give the course title, without quotation marks, underlining, or italics. Follow with the phrase *Course home page* (without italics), then a period, the course dates, and the department and institution. End with your date of access and the URL.

> Strickland, Ron. Shakespeare on Stage. Course home page. 14 June 2004–4
> Aug. 2004. Dept. of English. Illinois State U. 4 Oct. 2004 <http://
> www.english.ilstu.edu/strickland/378/>.

44. A Site with a Long URL

If you must include a line break in a URL, do so only after a slash (see above) or a period, and do not add a hyphen to indicate the break. For a URL that is long and complicated enough to invite errors in transcription, give the URL of the site's search page instead.

> MacLeod, Donald. "Shake-Up for Academic Publishing." Education Guardian
> .co.uk. 10 Nov. 2004 <http://www.guardian.co.uk/Archive/>.

If no search page is available, give the home page URL and path of links to the document.

> "Frederica: An 18th-Century Community." National Register of Historic
> Places. National Parks Service. 27 Feb. 2004 <http://www.cr.nps.gov/
> nr/>. Path: Education; Hispanic Heritage Month; Frederica.

45. An Online Book

In general, follow the format for printed books. Include publication information for original print version if available. Follow the date of publication with the access date and web address.

> Simon, Julian L. The Ultimate Resource II: People, Materials, and
> Environment. College Park: U of Maryland, 1996. 9 Apr. 2001
> <http://www.juliansimon.org/Ultimate_Resource/>.

When citing part of an online book, the title (or name of the part, such as *Foreword*) follows the author's name; the title of the book (underlined) is followed by its author's name if different from the first name listed.

> Untermeyer, Louis. "Author's Apology." The Donkey of God. 1999.
> iUniverse. 7 Mar. 2003 <http://books.iuniverse.com/>.

Works-Cited Entries: Online Sources

46. An Article in an Online Periodical

Begin with the author's name; the article title in quotation marks; and the underlined name of the periodical, its volume or issue number, and date of publication. Include page numbers (or other sections) if numbered. Close with the date of access and URL.

> Dickerson, John. "Nailing Jello." Time.com 5 Nov. 2001. 9 Dec. 2001
> <http://www.time.com/time/columnist/dickerson/>.

47. An Article in an Online Reference Work

Unless the author of the entry is identified, begin with the entry name in quotation marks. Follow with the usual online publication information.

> "Eakins, Thomas." Britannica Concise Encyclopaedia 2004. Encyclopaedia
> Britannica. 26 Sept. 2004 <http://concise.britannica.com/
> ebcarticle?tocId=9363299>.

48. An Article in an Online Service

When you use a library to access a subscription service, add the name of the database if known (underlined), the service, and the library. Then give the date of access, followed by the Internet address for the home page of the service (if known). If no Internet address is given for an entry, add a keyword or path statement in its place, if appropriate.

> Davis, Jerome. "Massacre in Kiev." Washington Post 29 Nov. 1999, final ed.:
> C12. National Newspapers. ProQuest. Gateway Technical College Elkhorn
> Campus Library. 30 Nov. 1999 <http://proquest.umi.com/pqdweb>.

49. A Scholarly Project or Information Database

The title of the site is listed first, then the name of the editor (if given). Follow this information with the version number (if relevant), date of publication or update, name of the sponsor, date of access, and URL.

> Wired Style: Principles of English Usage in the Digital Age. 1994. Wired
> Digital Inc. 5 Nov. 2001 <http://hotwired.lycos.com/hardwired/
> wiredstyle/>.

If you are citing a book that is part of an online scholarly project, first list information about the printed book, followed by publication information for the project. End with the URL of the book and a period.

> Astell, Mary. Reflections on Marriage. London: Wilkin, 1706. Women Writers
> Project. Providence: Brown UP, 1999. 7 Feb. 2002 <http://www.wwp
> .brown.edu/texts/astell/marriage.html>.

50. An Online Government Publication

As with a government publication in print, begin with the name of the government (country, state, and so on), followed by the name of the agency. After the publication title, add the electronic publication information. (When citing the *Congressional Record*, the date and page numbers are all that are required.)

> United States. Dept. of Labor. Women's Bureau. WB—An Overview. 12 Aug. 2005
> <http://www.dol.gov/wb/factsheets/Qf-nursing.htm>.

MLA WORKS CITED

51. An Online Posting in a List Server

Begin a citation for a posting distributed by a list server as you would any other e-mail message, with author name and document title (from the subject line). Follow this with the description *Online posting* (without italics) and a period, the date of posting, the name of the group, your date of access, and the URL of the list's Internet site (if any) or the e-mail address of the list's moderator. Whenever possible, cite an archived version of the posting so that your readers can find the source for themselves.

> Moody, Ellen. "Alternate Persuasions." Online posting. 25 Apr. 1998. The Austen-L Mailing List. 12 Jan. 2005 <http://lists.mcgill.ca/scripts/wa .exe?A2+ind9804D&L=austen-1&P=%5882>.

52. An Online Posting in a Web Forum

List the author's name and the title of the posting (in quotation marks), followed by *Online posting* (without italics) and a period. Then give the posting date, the forum name, your date of access, and the URL of the posting.

> Cubby, J. "Re: Connecting Playwrights & Theatre Companies." Online posting. 27 May 2004. AACT Online Forums: Playwriting & Playwrights. 12 Jan. 2005 <http://www.aact.org/cgi-bin/yabb/ YaBB.cgi?board=playwright;action=display;num=1085448764>.

53. An Online Posting in a Newsgroup

Start a newsgroup message as you would a posting to a list server or web forum, with the author's name, the posting title, the description *Online posting* (without italics), and a period. Then give the date of posting and your date of access, followed by the name of the group in brackets, with the prefix *news:* (no italics).

> Silverman, Neal. "Re: Perimeter of a Triangle." Online posting. 1 Oct. 2004. 12 Dec. 2004 <news:geometry.college>.

54. An Online Posting in a Real-Time (Synchronous) Communication Forum

If you are citing a particular speaker, identify that person. Follow with the event description, the date of the event, the communication forum, the date of access, and the Telnet URL.

> Del Rey, Juan Roberto. Online defense of dissertation "Chaos, Cadence, Tonality, Dissonance, and Meaning in the Music of Leonard Bernstein." 18 July 2005. Connections. 18 July 2005 <telnet://connections.moo .mud.org:3333>.

> **NOTE:** If possible, give readers a link to an archived version of the posting.
>
> Del Rey, Juan Roberto. Online defense of dissertation "Chaos, Cadence, Tonality, Dissonance, and Meaning in the Music of Leonard Bernstein." 18 July 2005. Connections. 3 Aug. 2005 <http://web.nwe.ufl.edu/ ~tari/connections/archives/delrey_phd_defense.txt>.

Works-Cited Entries: Online Sources

55. An Online Poem

List the poet's name, the title of the poem, and print publication information before the electronic publication details.

> Nemerov, Howard. "Found Poem." <u>War Stories</u>. By Nemerov. U of Chicago
> Press: 1987. Poets.org. 5 Oct. 2004 <http://www.poets.org/>.

56. An Online Multimedia Resource

After the usual information for the type of work (painting, photograph, musical composition, film) being cited, add electronic publication information.

> Goya, Francisco de. <u>Saturn Devouring His Children</u>. 1819-1823. Museo del
> Prado, Madrid. 13 Dec. 2003 <http://www.usc.edu/schools/annenberg/
> asc/projects/comm544/library/>.

57. An Online Transcript of a Broadcast

Give the original publication information for the broadcast. (See **53e-64**.) Then add the description *Transcript* (without italics), followed by a period, and the electronic publication information for that document.

> Lehrer, Jim. "Character Above All." <u>The NewsHour with Jim Lehrer</u> 29 May
> 1996. Transcript. 23 Apr. 2004 <http://www.pbs.org/newshour/
> character/transcript/trans1.html>.

58. A Publication in More Than One Medium

For a work that consists of more than one type of medium, either list all the media that make up the work or cite only the medium that contains the specific material cited in your paper.

> <u>CultureGrams</u>. Book, CD-ROM. Lindon, UT: Axiom, 2002.

59. A Document Accessed by FTP

Cite a document accessed by FTP with the protocol *ftp://* in the URL.

> Lewis, Winfred. "Three Translations of Rainer Rilke's 'Along the Sun-Drenched
> Roadside, from the Great.'" 19 Feb. 2005 <ftp://english.saku.edu/
> writingprograms/documents/rilke_trans.rtf>.

60. An E-Mail Communication

Identify the author of the e-mail, then list the "Subject" line of the e-mail as a title, in quotation marks. Next, include a description of the entry, including the recipient—usually *E-mail to the author* (no italics), meaning you, the author of the paper. Finally, give the date of the message.

> Barzinji, Atman. "Re: Frog Populations in Wisconsin Wetlands." E-mail
> to the author. 1 Jan. 2005.

61. An Online Posting

Follow the author's name and title with *Online posting*. The posting date is next, followed by the name of the forum, if known; date of access; and address.

> Wilcox, G. "White Gold Finch." Online posting. 7 Nov. 2001. IN-Bird. 9 Nov.
> 2001 <http://www.virtualbirder.com/bmail/inbird/latest.html#1>.

53e Other Sources: Primary, Personal, and Multimedia

62. A Periodically Published Database on CD-ROM, Diskette, or Magnetic Tape

Citations for materials published on CD-ROM, diskette, or magnetic tape are similar to those for print sources, with these added considerations: (1) The contents of a work may vary from one medium to another; therefore, the citation should always identify the medium. (2) The publisher and vendor of the publication may be different, in which case both must be identified. (3) Multiple versions of the same database may exist, which calls for citation of both the date of the document cited and the date of the database itself.

> Ackley, Patricia. "Jobs of the Twenty-First Century." New Rochelle Informer 15 Apr. 1994: A4. New Rochelle Informer Ondisc. CD-ROM. Info-Line. Oct. 1994.

63. Computer Software

If you use a reference book recorded on CD-ROM, use the form below. If available, include publication information for the printed source.

> The American Heritage Dictionary of the English Language. 3rd ed. Boston: Houghton-Mifflin, 1992. CD-ROM. Cambridge, MA: Softkey Intl., 1994.

64. A Television or Radio Program

> "The Ultimate Road Trip: Traveling in Cyberspace." 48 Hours. CBS. WBBM, Chicago. 13 Apr. 1995.

65. A Film

The director, distributor, and year of release follow the title. Other information may be included if pertinent.

> Eternal Sunshine of the Spotless Mind. Dir. Michel Gondry. Perf. Jim Carey, Kate Winslet. Focus Features, 2004.

66. A Video Recording

Cite a filmstrip, slide program, videocassette, or DVD like a film, but include the medium before the name of the distributor.

> Monet: Shadow & Light. Videocassette. Devine Productions, 1999.

67. An Audio Recording

If you are not citing a CD, indicate *LP, Audiocassette,* or *Audiotape* (without italics), followed by a period. If you are citing a specific song on a musical recording, place its title in quotation marks before the title of the recording.

> Ackroyd, Peter. Shakespeare. Audiocassette. Random House Audio, 2005.

Other Sources: Primary, Personal, and Multimedia

68. A Performance

Treat this similarly to a film, adding the location and date of the performance.

> Chanticleer. Young Auditorium, Whitewater, Wisconsin. 23 Feb. 2003.

69. An Artwork on Display

> Titian. The Entombment. The Louvre, Paris.

70. A Letter or Memo Received by the Author (You)

> Thomas, Bob. Letter to the author. 10 Jan. 2005.

71. An Interview by the Author (You)

> Brooks, Sarah. Personal interview. 15 Oct. 2004.

72. A Cartoon or Comic Strip (in Print)

> Luckovich, Mike. "The Drawing Board." Cartoon. Time 17 Sept. 2001: 18.

73. An Advertisement (in Print)

List the subject of the advertisement (product, company, organization, or such), followed by *Advertisement* (without italics) and a period. Then give the usual publication information.

> Vaio Professional notebooks. Advertisement. Campus Technology Oct.
> 2004: 45.

74. A Lecture, a Speech, an Address, or a Reading

If there is a title, use it instead of the descriptive label (for example, *Lecture*).

> Annan, Kofi. Lecture. Acceptance of Nobel Peace Prize. Oslo City Hall,
> Oslo, Norway. 10 Dec. 2001.

75. A Legal or Historical Document

Familiar historical documents such as the U.S. Constitution are typically not included in a works-cited list because they can so easily be abbreviated in a parenthetical note within the text of your paper: "(US Const., art. 4, sec. 1)," for example. (Note that such documents are not underlined.)

To list a legislative act in your works cited, begin with its name, then give its public law number, its date of enactment, and its Statutes at Large number.

> Do-Not-Call Implementation Act. Pub. L. 108-010. 11 Mar. 2003. Stat.
> 117-557.

Abbreviate the names of law cases (spelling out the first important word of each party's name). Do not underline the name in your works cited (although it should be underlined within the body of your paper). Follow with the case number, the name of the court, and the date of decision.

> Missouri v. Seibert. No. 02-1371. Supreme Ct. of the US. 28 June 2004.

76. A Map or Chart

Follow the format for an anonymous book, adding the word *Map* or *Chart* (without italics), followed by a period.

> Wisconsin Territory. Map. Madison: Wisconsin Trails, 1988.

MLA WORKS CITED

53f Abbreviations for Works-Cited Entries

In your works-cited entries, you may be able to use a range of abbreviations. Consider these guidelines and the abbreviations listed below:

1. Use two-letter, capitalized state and province abbreviations after the city of publication when the city alone may not be clear enough for readers.

2. Use standard month abbreviations in dates for journals, websites, and so on. Exceptions are May, June, and July, which are always spelled out in full.

    Jan.   Feb.   Mar.   Apr.   Aug.   Sept.   Oct.   Nov.   Dec.

3. In your works-cited entries, MLA style encourages you to shorten publishers' names by doing the following:

    ■ Cut any articles (*a, an, the*), business terms (*Co., Inc., Ltd.*), and descriptive terms (*House, Press*). *Exception:* university presses.

    ■ For publishing houses named after one or more people, abbreviate the name to the first person's last name.

    ■ For publishers whose name is recognizable by initials, use the initialism (MLA, NCTE, ALA).

    ■ For a university press, use *U* for University and *P* for Press.

anon.	anonymous	**no.**	number(s)
bk.	book(s)	**n.p.**	no place of publication, no publisher given
chap., ch.	chapter(s)	**n. pag.**	no pagination
comp.	compiler, compiled, compiled by	**op. cit.**	in the work cited; *opere citato*
ed.	editor(s), edition(s), edited by	**p., pp.**	page(s), if needed for clarity
et al.	and others; *et alii, et aliae*	**+**	plus the pages that follow
ex.	example	**pub. (publ.)**	published by, publication(s), reviewed by
fig.	figure(s)		
ibid.	in the same place; *ibidem*	**qtd.**	quoted
illus.	illustration, illustrated by	**rev.**	revised by, revision, review, reviewed by
introd.	introduction, introduced by	**rpt.**	reprinted by, reprint
lib.	library	**sc.**	scene
loc. cit.	in the place cited; *loco citato*	**sec. (sect.)**	section(s)
ms., mss.	manuscript(s)	**trans. (tr.)**	translator, translation
narr.	narrated by, narrator(s)	**viz.**	namely; *videlicet*
n.d.	no date given	**vol.**	volume(s): capitalize if used with roman numerals

APA, Chicago, and CSE

APA, Chicago, and CSE

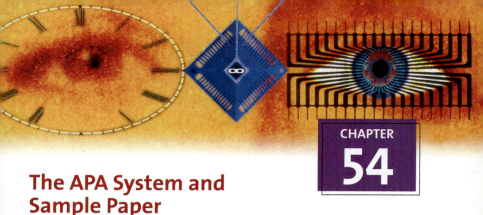

The APA System and Sample Paper

Because you're looking at this page, you've probably been told to submit an assigned paper in APA format. You're looking for answers to questions like these: How do I format my paper in APA style? How do I document my research? For answers, read on.

What is the APA?

APA stands for the American Psychological Association—the professional organization to which psychology teachers and practicing psychologists belong.

What is APA style?

APA style refers to a method of documenting research and formatting a research paper—a method and format used in psychology and social science disciplines. In a nutshell, APA style offers guidelines for the following:

- **In-text citation**—the use of author/publication date/page-number references within parentheses.
- **References**—a list of resources that you used in your paper.
- **Paper format**—title page, abstract, margins, visuals, and so on.
- **Punctuation and mechanics rules**—from capitalization practices for titles to use of ampersands.

Where can I find information about APA style?

This section of your handbook gives you most of what you need to know— drawn from these official APA resources, which you can consult further:

- *Publication Manual of the American Psychological Association* (fifth edition): Check your library's reference section.
- The APA website, <www.apastyle.org>.

What's Ahead

54a APA Documentation at a Glance

The APA system involves two parts: (1) an in-text citation within your paper when you use a source and (2) a matching bibliographic entry at the end of your paper. Note these features of the APA author-date system:

- **It uses signal phrases and parenthetical references** to set off source material from your own thinking and discussion.

  Note: A signal phrase names the author and places the material in context (for example, "As Jung describes it, the collective unconscious . . .").

- **It's date-sensitive.** Because the publication dates of resources are especially important in social science research, the publication year is included in the parenthetical reference and after the authors' names in the reference entry.

- **It's smooth, unobtrusive, and orderly.** APA in-text citations identify borrowed material while keeping the paper readable. Moreover, alphabetized reference entries at the end of the paper make locating source details easy.

What does APA documentation look like?

You can see these features at work in the example below.

IN-TEXT CITATION IN BODY OF PAPER

> According to some researchers, most of the results so far indicate that cognitive function is not affected significantly by short-term fasting (Green et al., 1996, p. 246).

The parenthetical material "(Green et al., 1996, p. 246)" tells the reader the following things:

- The borrowed material came from a source coauthored by Green and others.
- The source was published in 1996.
- The specific material can be found on page 246 of the source.
- Full source details are in the references list under "Green."

MATCHING REFERENCES ENTRY AT END OF PAPER

> Green, M. W., Elliman, N. A., & Rogers, P. J. (1996). Lack of effect of short-term fasting on cognitive function. *Journal of Psychiatric Research, 29,* 245-253.

> **NOTE:** The title of the article uses a capital letter for only the first word (and any proper nouns).

How do I make APA in-text citations?

See 55a–55b for complete details on in-text citation. Generally, however, refer to the author(s) and date of publication by using one of these methods:

Last name[s] and publication date [plus page number] in parentheses:

> The glucostatic theory seemed logical because glucose is the brain's primary fuel (Pinel, 2000).

Name[s] cited in text, publication date [plus page number] in parentheses:

> Research by Green, Elliman, and Rogers (1995, 1997) has found that food deprivation ranging from missing a single meal to twenty-four hours without eating does not significantly impair cognition.

Present and punctuate citations according to these rules:

- Keep authors and publication dates as close together as possible in the sentence.
- Separate the author's last name, the date, and any locating detail with commas.
- If referencing part of a source, use an appropriate abbreviation: p. (page), chap. (chapter), para. (paragraph).

How do I create APA reference entries?

TEMPLATE FOR PRINT BOOK

> Author's Last Name, First and Middle Initials. (Publication Year). *Title of book*. Publication City: Publisher. [Other publication details are integrated as needed.]

> Meyer, V., Sebranek, P., & Van Rys, J. (2006). *Effective e-mail made e-z*. Burlington, WI: UpWrite Press.

TEMPLATE FOR PRINT PERIODICAL ARTICLE

> Author's Last Name, First and Middle Initials. (Publication Year). Title of article. *Journal Title, volume*, page numbers. [Other publication details are integrated as needed. For an online periodical article, add the retrieval date and source.]

> Eisenberger, R., & Leonard, J. M. (1980). Effects of conceptual task difficulty on generalized persistence. *American Journal of Psychology, 93*, 285-298.

TEMPLATE FOR ONLINE DOCUMENT

> Author's Last Name, First and Middle Initials. (Publication Year). Title of work. Retrieval date and source.

> American Psychological Association. (2000, January). Successful aging: The second 50. *APA Monitor*. Retrieved May 6, 2005, from http://www.apa.org/monitor/jan00/cs.html

54b APA Format: Whole-Paper Guidelines

To submit a polished academic paper using the APA system, follow the rules below and refer to the sample APA paper that follows.

TITLE PAGE

On the first page, include the paper's title, your name, and your institution's name on three separate lines. The instructor's name and the course title are not listed. Double-space and center the lines beginning approximately one-third of the way down from the top of the page. (See also "Page Numbers" below.)

ABSTRACT

On the second page, include an abstract—a 100- to 150-word paragraph summarizing your paper. Place the title *Abstract* approximately one inch from the top of the page and center it.

BODY

Format the body (which begins on the third page) of your paper as follows:

Margins Leave a one-inch margin on all four sides of each page. A justified right margin and end-of-line hyphens are acceptable.

Line Spacing Double-space your entire paper, unless your instructor allows single spacing for tables, titles, captions, and so on, for the sake of readability.

Page Numbers Place your short title (the first two or three words) and the page number at the upper-right margin of all pages, including the title page.

Headings Like an outline, headings show the organization of your paper and the importance of each topic. All topics of equal importance should have headings of the same level, or style. Below are the various levels of headings used in APA papers. (In most research papers, only levels 1, 3, and 4 are used.)

Level 1: Centered Uppercase and Lowercase Heading

Running on Empty: The Effects of Food Deprivation on
Concentration and Perseverance

Level 2: Centered, Italicized Uppercase and Lowercase Heading

History of Research into Food Deprivation

Level 3: Flush Left, Italicized Uppercase and Lowercase Side Heading

The Global Challenge of Food Deprivation

Level 4: Indented, Italicized Lowercase Paragraph Heading with Period

The case of Somalia.

> **NOTE:** If your instructor requires it, place your charts, tables, and graphs in an appendix. Otherwise, include them within the body of your paper.

54c Sample APA Research Paper

Student writers Thomas Delancy and Adam Solberg wrote the following research paper based on an experiment that they conducted in a psychology course. You can use this model paper in three ways:

- To study how a well-written research paper based in experimentation structures and builds a discussion from start to finish
- To examine how sources are used in social-science research writing— a full-length example of the strategies addressed in 50a–50i
- To see in detail the format and documentation practices of APA style

How should I set up my title page?

> Place manuscript page headers one-half inch from the top. Put five spaces between the page header and the page number.

> Center the full title, authors, and school name on the page. Do not list the instructor's name or course title.

Running on Empty   1

Running on Empty:
The Effects of Food Deprivation on
Concentration and Perseverance
Thomas Delancy and Adam Solberg
Dordt College

How should I set up my abstract?

Running on Empty   2

Abstract

This study examined the effects of short-term food deprivation on two cognitive abilities—concentration and perseverance. Undergraduate students ($N = 51$) were tested on both a concentration task and a perseverance task after one of three levels of food deprivation: none, 12 hours, or 24 hours. We predicted that food deprivation would impair both concentration scores and perseverance time. Food deprivation had no significant effect on concentration scores, which is consistent with recent research on the effects of food deprivation (Green, Elliman, & Rogers, 1995, 1997). However, participants in the 12-hour deprivation group spent significantly less time on the perseverance task than those in both the control and 24-hour deprivation groups, suggesting that short-term deprivation may affect some aspects of cognition and not others.

> In the abstract, summarize the problem, participants, hypotheses, methods used, results, and conclusions.

How should I set up the body of my paper?

Running on Empty: The Effects of Food Deprivation
on Concentration and Perseverance

Many things interrupt people's ability to focus on a task. To some
extent, people can control the environmental factors that make it difficult
to focus. However, what about internal factors, such as an empty stomach?
Can people increase their ability to focus simply by eating regularly?

One theory that prompted research on how food intake affects the
average person was the glucostatic theory, which suggested that the brain
regulates food intake (and hunger) in an effort to maintain a blood-
glucose set point. This theory seemed logical because glucose is the brain's
primary fuel (Pinel, 2000; Martinez, 2004). The earliest investigation of
this theory found that long-term food deprivation (36 hours or more) was
associated with sluggishness, depression, irritability, reduced heart rate,
and inability to concentrate (Keys, Brozek, Henschel, Mickelsen, & Taylor,
1950). Since then, research has focused mainly on how nutrition affects
cognition. However, as Green, Elliman, and Rogers (1995) point out, the
effects of food deprivation on cognition have received comparatively less
attention in recent years, leaving room for further research.

According to some researchers, most of the results so far indicate that
cognitive function is not affected significantly by short-term fasting (Green
et al., 1995, p. 246). However, this conclusion seems premature: No study
has tested perseverance, despite its importance in cognitive functioning.
Perseverance may be a better indicator than achievement tests in assessing
growth in learning and thinking abilities, as it helps in solving complex
problems (Costa, 1984). Testing as many aspects of cognition as possible is
key because the nature of the task is important when interpreting the link
between deprivation and cognitive performance (Smith & Kendrick, 1992).

Therefore, the current study helps us understand how short-term
food deprivation affects concentration on and perseverance with a difficult
task. Specifically, participants deprived of food for 24 hours were expected
to perform worse on a concentration test and a perseverance task than

The title is centered one inch from the top. The text is double-spaced throughout.

The introduction states the topic and the main questions to be explored.

The researchers supply background information by discussing past research on the topic.

Clear transitions guide readers through the researchers' reasoning.

The researchers support their decision to focus on concentration and perseverance.

Sample APA Research Paper

those deprived for 12 hours, who in turn were predicted to perform worse than those who were not deprived of food.

The researchers state their initial hypotheses.

Method

Participants

Participants included 51 undergraduate student volunteers. The mean college grade point average (GPA) was 3.19. Potential participants were excluded if they were dieting, menstruating, or taking special medication. Those who had ever struggled with an eating disorder were excluded, as were potential participants who were addicted to nicotine or caffeine.

Headings and subheadings show the paper's organization.

Materials

Concentration, speed, and accuracy were measured using a numbers-matching test that consisted of 26 lines of 25 numbers each. Scores were calculated as the percentage of correctly identified pairs out of a possible 120. Perseverance was measured with a puzzle that contained five octagons, which were to be placed on top of each other in a specific way to make the silhouette of a rabbit. However, three of the shapes were slightly altered so that the task was impossible. Perseverance scores were calculated as the number of minutes that a participant spent on the puzzle task before giving up.

The experiment's method is described, using the terms and acronyms of the discipline.

Procedure

At an initial meeting, participants gave informed consent and supplied their GPAs. Students were informed that they would be notified about their assignment to one of the three groups and were given instructions.

Participants were then randomly assigned to one of the experimental conditions using a design based on the GPAs (to control individual differences in cognitive ability). Next, participants were informed of their group assignment and reminded of their instructions. Participants from the control group were tested at 7:30 p.m. on the day the deprivation started. Those in the 12-hour group were tested at 10 p.m. on that same day. Those in the 24-hour group were tested at 10:40 a.m. on the following day.

Passive voice is used to emphasize the experiment, not the researchers; otherwise, active voice is used.

At their assigned time, participants arrived at a computer lab for testing. After all participants had completed the concentration test and their

The experiment is laid out step by step, with time transitions like "then" and "next."

Running on Empty   5

scores were recorded, participants were each given the silhouette puzzle. They were told that (1) they would have an unlimited amount of time to complete the task, and (2) they were not to tell any other participant whether they had completed the puzzle or simply given up. This procedure prevented group influence. Any participant still working on the puzzle after 40 minutes was stopped.

Results

Perseverance data from one control-group participant were eliminated, and concentration data from another control-group participant were dropped. The average concentration score was 77.78 ($SD = 14.21$), which was very good considering that anything over 50 percent is labeled "good" or "above average." The average time spent on the puzzle was 24.00 minutes ($SD = 10.16$).

We predicted that participants in the 24-hour deprivation group would perform worse on the concentration test and the perseverance task than those in the 12-hour group, who in turn would perform worse than those in the control group. A one-way analysis of variance (ANOVA) showed no significant effect of deprivation condition on concentration, $F(2,46) = 1.06$, $p = .36$ (see Figure 1). Another one-way ANOVA indicated a significant effect of deprivation condition on perseverance time, $F(2,47) = 7.41$, $p < .05$. Post-hoc Tukey tests indicated that the 12-hour deprivation group ($M = 17.79$, $SD = 7.84$) spent significantly less time

Figure 1.

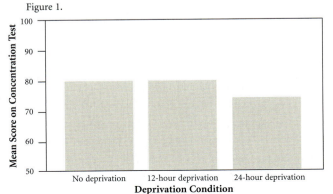

Margin notes:

Attention is shown to the control features.

The writers summarize their findings.

"See Figure 1" sends readers to a figure (graph, photograph, chart, or drawing) contained in the paper.

Figure 2.

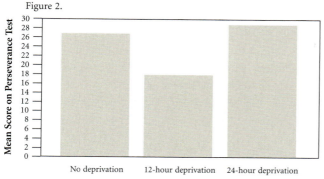

All figures are numbered in the order that they are first mentioned in the paper.

on the perseverance task than either the control group ($M = 26.80$, $SD = 6.20$) or the 24-hour group ($M = 28.75$, $SD = 12.11$), with no significant difference between the latter two groups (see Figure 2). Unexpectedly, food deprivation had no significant effect on concentration scores. Overall, we found support for our hypothesis that 12 hours of food deprivation would significantly impair perseverance when compared to no deprivation. Unexpectedly, 24 hours of food deprivation did not significantly affect perseverance relative to the control group.

Discussion

The purpose of this study was to test how different levels of food deprivation affect concentration on and perseverance with difficult tasks. We predicted that the longer people had been deprived of food, the lower they would score on the concentration task, and the less time they would spend on the perseverance task. In this study, those deprived of food did give up more quickly on the puzzle, but only in the 12-hour group. Thus, the hypothesis was partially supported for the perseverance task. However, concentration was found to be unaffected by food deprivation, and thus the hypothesis was not supported for that task.

In terms of concentration, the findings of this study are consistent with those of Green et al. (1995), where short-term food deprivation did not affect some aspects of cognition, including attentional focus. The

The researchers restate their hypotheses and the results, and go on to interpret those results.

findings on perseverance, however, are not as easily explained. We surmise that the participants in the 12-hour group gave up more quickly on the perseverance task because of their hunger. But those in the 24-hour group failed to yield the same effect. We postulate that this result can be explained by the concept of "learned industriousness," wherein participants who perform one difficult task do better on a subsequent task than participants who never did the initial task (Eisenberger & Leonard, 1980; Hickman, Stromme, & Lippman, 1998). Another possible explanation is that the motivational state of a participant may be a significant determinant of behavior under testing (Saugstad, 1967; Yang & Hamilton, 2002).

Research on food deprivation and cognition could continue in several directions. First, other aspects of cognition may be affected by short-term food deprivation, such as reading comprehension or motivation. Perhaps, then, the motivation level of food-deprived participants could be effectively tested. Second, longer-term food deprivation periods, such as those experienced by people fasting for religious reasons, could be explored. It is possible that cognitive function fluctuates over the duration of deprivation. Third, and perhaps most fascinating, studies could explore how food deprivation affects learned industriousness.

In conclusion, the results of this study provide some fascinating insights into the cognitive and physiological effects of skipping meals. Contrary to what we predicted, a person may indeed be very capable of concentrating after not eating for many hours. On the other hand, when performing a tedious task that requires perseverance, one may be hindered by not eating for a short time, as shown by the 12-hour group's performance on the perseverance task. Many people have to deal with short-term food deprivation, either intentional or unintentional. This research and other research to follow will contribute to knowledge of the disadvantages—and possible advantages—of skipping meals. The mixed results of this study suggest that we have much more to learn about short-term food deprivation.

The writers speculate on possible explanations for the unexpected results.

The conclusion summarizes the outcomes, stresses the experiment's value, and anticipates further advances on the topic.

References

Costa, A. L. (1984). Thinking: How do we know students are getting better at it? *Roeper Review, 6,* 197-199.

Eisenberger, R., & Leonard, J. M. (1980). Effects of conceptual task difficulty on generalized persistence. *American Journal of Psychology, 93,* 285-298.

Green, M. W., Elliman, N. A., & Rogers, P. J. (1995). Lack of effect of short-term fasting on cognitive function. *Journal of Psychiatric Research, 29,* 245-253.

Hickman, K. L., Stromme, C., & Lippman, L. G. (1998). Learned industriousness: Replication in principle. *Journal of General Psychology, 125,* 213-217.

Keys, A., Brozek, J., Henschel, A., Mickelsen, O., & Taylor, H. L. (1950). *The biology of human starvation* (Vol. 2). Minneapolis: University of Minnesota Press.

Martinez, R. J. (2004). Repeated fasting/refeeding elevate glucose levels. *Behavior Research, 62,* 459-464. Retrieved September 29, 2005, from http://www.behaviorresearch.com/041204.html

Pinel, J. P. (2000). *Biopsychology* (4th ed.). Boston: Allyn & Bacon.

Saugstad, P. (1967). Effect of food deprivation on perception-cognition: A comment [Comment on the article by David L. Wolitzky]. *Psychological Bulletin, 68,* 345-346.

Smith, A. P., & Kendrick, A. M. (1992). Meals and performance. In A. P. Smith & D. M. Jones (Eds.), *Handbook of human performance: Vol. 2, Health and performance* (pp. 1-23). San Diego: Academic Press.

Yang, W. & Hamilton, J. B. (2002). Effect of food deprivation on motivation. *Psychology Research Today, 38,* 15-32. Retrieved October 11, 2005, from http://www.psychrt.com/journals/yang38425.html

54d Checklist: APA System

____ All borrowed material is acknowledged with an attributive phrase and/or in-text citation indicating author(s), publication date, and page number, as appropriate.

____ All in-text citations effectively point readers to resources in the references list (or to personal communication not listed).

____ The references list includes entries for all works referred to in the body of the paper. No sources are missing from the list; no extra sources are listed that have no reference within the paper. *Exception:* Personal communications are identified in in-text citations but not in the reference list.

____ The entire references list is properly alphabetized by authors' last names (or by the first main word in the title for anonymous works).

____ Each references entry (whether for an article, a book, an online document, or other source) contains the maximum amount of identifying and publication information, in the proper order, using the expected abbreviations.

____ The entire paper is properly formatted, from the title page to any appendix.

- Placement, spacing, and margins are correct for the title page, abstract, report, and references list.

- Pagination is correct and consistent, as is the paper's header.

- First lines of paragraphs, including paragraphs under headings, and inset quotations are properly indented; references entries are properly formatted with hanging indent.

- The paper is cleanly printed single-sided on quality paper in a professional-looking typeface and in 12-point type size (without fancy type style features).

- Rules for capitalization, lowercase, quotation marks, and italics are observed throughout the text, especially with names and titles.

WRITER'S TIP

Along with its distinctive format, APA style also has distinctive guidelines for using the passive voice of verbs in research writing. For a discussion of active and passive voice, see **13c**.

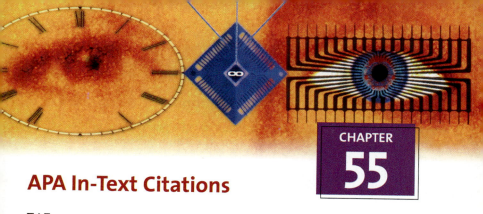

APA In-Text Citations

When you write a research paper, you join an ongoing discussion about your topic. The discussion began long before you started writing, and it will continue long after you stop. Documenting sources shows that you have listened to and credited the thoughts of those who came before you. Documentation also allows those who come after you to credit your thoughts.

With the APA system, giving credit involves two steps: (1) placing a citation in the text and (2) providing a list of references (56a–56e). This chapter contains detailed strategies for citing works in text.

Directory to In-Text Citations

What's Ahead

55a Guidelines for In-Text Citations

In APA style, as in the MLA system, you must cite your source in the text (in parentheses) each time you borrow from it. Each of these parenthetical citations, except for those referencing personal communications (such as letters, e-mail, or phone conversations) must be matched to an entry in a list at the end of your paper called "References." Each item in the "References" list should, in turn, be cited in the text.

What form does an APA citation take?

The APA documentation style is sometimes called the "author-date" system because both the author and the date of the publication must be mentioned in the text when citing a source. Both might appear in the flow of the sentence, like this:

- Only South Africa has more people infected with AIDS than India, according to a 2001 article by Mike Specter.

If either the name or the date does not appear in the text, it must be mentioned in parentheses at the most convenient place, like this:

- According to an article by Mike Specter (2001), only South Africa . . .
- According to a recent article (Specter, 2001), only South Africa . . .

What points should I remember about APA citations?

You need to remember that APA citations must be clearly attributed and titles shortened appropriately. Follow the guidelines below.

- When paraphrasing rather than quoting, make it clear where your borrowing begins and ends. Use cues to distinguish the source's thoughts ("Kalmbach points out . . . ," "Some critics argue . . .") from your own ("I believe . . . ," "It seems obvious, however . . .").

- When using a shortened title of a work, begin with the word by which the work is alphabetized in your references list (for example, for "Measurement of Stress in Fasting Man," use "Measurement of Stress" not "Fasting Man").

- When including a parenthetical citation at the end of a sentence, place it before the end punctuation.

WRITER'S TIP

The most important rule for making in-text citations is that they must clearly point to the correct entries in the references list. The second most important rule is that citations must indicate borrowed material without derailing the flow of thought in the text.

55b Sample In-Text Citations

1. One Author: A Complete Work

The correct form for a parenthetical reference to a single source by a single author is parenthesis, last name, comma, space, publication year, parenthesis. Also note that final punctuation should be placed outside the parentheses.

> The great majority of Venezuelans live near the Caribbean coast (Anderson, 2001).

2. One Author: Part of a Work

When you cite a specific part of a source, give the page number, chapter, or section, using the appropriate abbreviations (p. or pp., chap., or sec.). Always give the page number for a direct quotation.

> Bush's 2002 budget, passed by Congress, was based on revenue estimates that "now appear to have been far too optimistic" (Lemann, 2003, p. 48).

3. One Author: More Than One Publication in the Same Year

If the same author has published two or more articles in the same year, avoid confusion by placing a small letter *a* after the first work listed in the references list, *b* after the next one, and so on. The order of such works is determined alphabetically by title.

Parenthetical Citation

> Coral reefs harbor life forms heretofore unknown (Milius, 2001a, 2001b).

References

> Milius, D. (2001a). Another world hides inside coral reefs. *Science News,* *160* (16), 244.
>
> Milius, D. (2001b). Unknown squids—with elbows—tease science. *Science News, 160* (24), 390.

4. Works by Authors with the Same Last Name

When citing different sources by authors with the same last name, it is best to add the authors' initials to avoid confusion, even if the publication dates are different.

> While J. D. Wallace (2005) argued that privatizing Social Security would benefit only the wealthiest citizens, others such as E. S. Wallace (2006) supported the movement toward greater control for individuals.

WRITER'S TIP

When possible, mention the author's name in text the first time material is used. Afterward, including the name in parentheses is appropriate.

5. Two to Five Authors

In APA style, all authors—up to as many as five—must be mentioned in the first text citation, like this:

> Love changes not just who we are, but who we can become, as well (Lewis, Amini, & Lannon, 2000).

> **NOTE:** The last two authors' names are always separated by a comma and an ampersand (&) when enclosed in parentheses.

After the first mention, use only the name of the first author followed by "et al." (the Latin abbreviation for *et alii*, meaning "and others"), like this:

> These discoveries lead to the hypothesis that love actually alters the brain's structure (Lewis et al., 2000).

6. Six or More Authors

If your source has six or more authors, refer to the work by the first author's name followed by "et al.," for both the first reference in the text and all references after that. However, in your references list, be sure to list the first six authors; any additional authors can be shortened to "et al."

> According to a recent study, post-traumatic stress disorder (PTSD) continues to dominate the lives of Vietnam veterans, though in modified forms (Trembley et al., 2005).

7. A Work Authored by a Committee or Other Organization

Treat the name of the group as if it were the last name of the author. If the name is long and easily abbreviated, provide the abbreviation in square brackets. Use the abbreviation without brackets in subsequent references, as follows:

First Text Citation

> A continuing problem for many veterans is heightened sensitivity to noise (National Institute of Mental Health [NIMH], 2005).

Subsequent Citations

> In addition, veterans suffering from PTSD continue to have difficulty discussing their experiences and sharing suicidal thoughts with family members or mental health professionals (NIMH, 2005).

8. A Work with No Author Indicated

If your source lists no author, treat the first two or three words of the title as you would an author's last name. A title of an article or a chapter belongs in quotation marks, whereas the titles of books or reports should be italicized:

> One key to avoiding serious back injuries and long-term back pain is adopting low-stress postures especially in the workplace ("Diagnosing Back," 2001).

Sample In-Text Citations

9. A Work Referred to in Another Work

If you need to cite a source that you have found referred to in another source, mention the original source in your text. Then, in your parenthetical citation, cite the secondary source, using the words "as cited in," like this:

> A key development in the research on bipolarity was the theorem given by Richards (as cited in McDonald, 1998).

> **NOTE:** In your references list at the end of the paper, you would write out a full citation for McDonald, not Richards.

10. A Work in an Anthology

When citing an article or a chapter in an anthology or a collection, use the authors' names for the specific article, not the names of the anthology's editors. (The article should also be listed by its authors' names in the references section.)

> Phonological changes can be understood from a variationist perspective (Guy, 2005).

11. An Electronic or Other Internet Source

As with print sources, cite an electronic source by the author (or by a shortened title if the author is unknown) and the publication date (not the date that you accessed the source). If citing a specific part of the source, use an appropriate abbreviation: p. (page), chap. (chapter), or para. (paragraph).

> One study compared and contrasted the use of Web and touch screen transaction log files in a hospital setting (Nicholas, Huntington, & Williams, 2001).

12. An Entire Website

Whenever possible, cite a website by its author and posting date. In addition, refer to a specific page or document rather than to a home page or a menu page. However, if you are referring to a specific part of a webpage that does not have page numbers, direct your reader, if possible, with a section heading and a paragraph number.

> According to the National Multiple Sclerosis Society (2003, "Complexities" section, para. 2), understanding of MS could not start to take shape until the 1920s, when scientists began to research nerve transmission.

13. Two or More Works in a Parenthetical Reference

Sometimes it is necessary to provide several citations in one parenthetical reference. In that case, cite the sources as you usually would, separating the citations with semicolons. Place the citations in alphabetical order, just as they would be ordered in the references list:

> These near-death experiences are reported with conviction (Rommer, 2000; Sabom, 1998).

APA IN-TEXT CITATIONS

14. A Sacred Text or Famous Literary Work

Sacred texts and famous literary works are published in many different editions. For that reason, the original date of publication may be unavailable or not pertinent. In these cases, use your edition's year of translation (trans. 2003) or indicate your edition's year of publication (2003 version). When you are referring to specific sections of the work, it is best to identify parts, chapters, or other divisions instead of your version's page numbers.

> An interesting literary case of such dysfunctional family behavior can be found in Franz Kafka's *The Metamorphosis,* where it becomes the commandment of family duty for Gregor's parents and sister to swallow their disgust and endure him, endure him and nothing more (trans. 1972, part 3).

Books of the Bible and other well-known literary works may be abbreviated, if no confusion is possible.

> "Generations come and generations go, but the earth remains forever" (*The New International Version Study Bible,* 1985 version, Eccles. 1.4).

15. A Personal Communication

If you do the kind of personal research recommended elsewhere in *The College Writer's Handbook*, you may have to cite personal communications that have provided you with some of your knowledge. Personal communications may include personal letters, phone calls, memos, e-mail messages, and so forth. Because they are not published in a permanent form, APA style does not place them among the citations in your references list. Instead, cite them only in the text of your paper in parentheses, like this:

> The manifestation of such kleptomania late in life can be explained by the disintegration of certain inhibitions, according to M. T. Cann (personal communication, April 1, 2005).

> However, such criminal trespasses are minor compared with the more serious breakdown of mental processes through dementia (M. T. Cann, personal communication, April 1, 2005).

Web Link: For more information about APA style, check out <www.apastyle.org>. There you can find a list of answers to frequently asked questions, the most recent details for citing electronic sources, and advice for avoiding bias about gender, race, sexuality, and disabilities in your writing.

APA References

The first part of the APA documentation system, as shown in **55a–55b**, involves citations within your paper. The second part is the references list—at the end of your paper, an alphabetized list of resources you referred to in your paper.

56a Guidelines for APA References

The references section of an APA research paper lists all the sources you have cited in your text. Begin your references list on a new page and number each references page, continuing the numbering from the text.

How should I set up my references page?

Format your references list by following the guidelines below:

1. Type the short title of the paper and page number in the upper-right corner, approximately one-half inch from the top of the page.

2. Center the title, *References,* approximately one inch from the top; then double-space before the first entry.

3. Begin each entry flush with the left margin. If the entry runs more than one line, indent additional lines approximately one-half inch.

4. Adhere to the following conventions on your references pages:
   - Double-space between all lines on the references pages.
   - Use one space following each word and each punctuation mark.
   - With book and article titles, capitalize only the first letter of the title (and subtitle) and proper nouns.
   - Use italics for titles of books and periodicals, not underlining. Do not use quotation marks for any titles.

5. List each entry alphabetically by the last name of the author, or, if no author is given, by the title (disregarding *A, An,* or *The*).

What's Ahead

56b Reference Entries: Books and Other Documents
56c Reference Entries: Periodicals
56d Reference Entries: Online Sources
56e Reference Entries: Other Sources

APA REFERENCES

Directory to APA References Entries

56b Reference Entries: Books and Other Documents

The general form for a book or brochure entry is this:

Author, A. (year). *Title.* **Location: Publisher.**

- Author's last name and initial(s) followed by a period
- Year of publication in parentheses followed by a period
- Title lowercased in italics, with only the first word and any proper nouns capitalized, followed by a period
- Publication city (and state, province, or country if the city is not well known for publishing) followed by a colon
- Publisher name followed by a period

1. A Book by One Author

> Guttman, J. (1999). *The gift wrapped in sorrow: A mother's quest for healing.* Palm Springs, CA: JMJ Publishing.

2. A Book by Two or More Authors

Follow the first author name (or names) with a comma; then join the last and next-to-last names with an ampersand (&) rather than with the word *and*. List up to six authors; abbreviate subsequent authors as "et al."

> Lynn, J., & Harrold, J. (1999). *Handbook for mortals: Guidance for people facing serious illness.* New York: Oxford University Press.

3. An Anonymous Book

If an author is listed as "Anonymous," treat it as the author's name. Otherwise, follow this format:

> American Psychological Association. (2001). *The publication manual of the American Psychological Association* (5th ed.). Washington, DC: Author.

> **NOTE:** In this title, the words *American Psychological Association* are capitalized because they are a proper name. The words *publication manual* are not capitalized.

4. A Chapter from a Book

List the chapter title after the date of publication, followed by a period or appropriate end punctuation. Use the word *In* before the book title, and follow the book title with the inclusive page numbers of the chapter.

> Tattersall, I. (2002). How did we achieve humanity? In *The monkey in the mirror* (pp. 138-168). New York: Harcourt.

APA REFERENCES

5. A Single Work from an Anthology

Start with information about the individual work, followed by details about the collection in which it appears, including the page span. When editors' names come in the middle of an entry, follow the usual order: initial first, surname last. Note the placement of the word *Eds.* in parentheses.

> Guy, G. R. (2005). Variationist approaches to phonological change. In B. D. Joseph & R. D. Janda (Eds.), *The handbook of historical linguistics* (pp. 369-400). Malden, MA: Blackwell.

6. One Volume of a Multivolume Edited Work

Indicate the volume in parentheses after the work's title.

> Salzman, J., Smith, D. L., & West, C. (Eds.). (1996). *Encyclopedia of African-American culture and history* (Vol. 4). New York: Simon & Schuster.

7. A Separately Titled Volume in a Multivolume Work

When a work is part of a larger series or collection, as with this example, make a two-part title of the series and the particular volume you are citing.

> The Associated Press. (1995). *Twentieth-century America: Vol. 8. The crisis of national confidence: 1974-1980.* Danbury, CT: Grolier Educational Corp.

8. An Edited Work, One in a Series

Start the entry with the work's author, publication date, and title. Then follow with publication details about the series.

> Marshall, P. G. (2002). The impact of the Cold War on Asia. In T. O'Neill (Ed.), *World history by era: Vol. 9. The nuclear age* (pp. 162-166). San Diego: Greenhaven Press.

9. A Group Author as Publisher

When the author is also the publisher, simply put the word *Author* in the spot where you would list the publisher's name.

> Amnesty International. (2000). *Hidden scandal, secret shame: Torture and ill-treatment of children.* New York: Author.

10. An Edition Other Than the First

Indicate a second or subsequent edition with that edition's publication date (not the first edition's), plus the edition number in parentheses after the title.

> Trimmer, J. (2001). *Writing with a purpose* (13th ed.). Boston: Houghton Mifflin.

WRITER'S TIP

Writers accustomed to MLA citations must remember that APA references capitalize only the first word and any proper nouns in a title.

11. Two or More Books by the Same Author

When you are listing multiple works by the same author, arrange them by the year of publication, earliest first.

Dershowitz, A. (2000). *The Genesis of justice: Ten stories of biblical injustice that led to the Ten Commandments and modern law.* New York: Warner Books.

Dershowitz, A. (2002). *Shouting fire: Civil liberties—past, present, and future.* Boston: Little, Brown.

12. An English Translation

Setha, R. (1998). *Unarmed* (R. Narasimhan, Trans.). Chennai, India: Macmillan. (Original work published 1995)

> **NOTE:** If you use the original work, cite the original version; the non-English title is followed by its English translation, not italicized, in square brackets.

13. An Article in a Reference Book

Start the entry with the author of the article, if identified. If no author is listed, begin the entry with the title of the article.

Lewer, N. (1999). Non-lethal weapons. In *World encyclopedia of peace* (pp. 279-280). Oxford: Pergamon Press.

14. A Reprint, Different Form

Albanov, V. (2000). *In the land of white death: An epic story of survival in the Siberian Arctic.* New York: Modern Library. (Original work published 1917)

> **NOTE:** This work was originally published in Russia in 1917; the 2000 reprint is the first English version. If you are citing a reprint from another source, the parentheses would contain "Reprinted from Title, pp. xx-xx, by A. Author, year, Location: Publisher."

15. A Technical or Research Report

Taylor, B. G., Fitzgerald, N., Hunt, D., Reardon, J. A., & Brownstein, H. H. (2001). *ADAM preliminary 2000 findings on drug use and drug markets: Adult male arrestees.* Washington, DC: National Institute of Justice.

16. A Government Publication

Generally, refer to the government agency as the author. When possible, provide an identification number for the document after the title in parentheses.

National Institute on Drug Abuse. (2000). *Inhalant abuse* (NIH Publication No. 00-3818). Rockville, MD: National Clearinghouse on Alcohol and Drug Information.

56c   Reference Entries: Periodicals

The general form for a periodical entry is this:

> **Author, A. (year). Article title.** *Periodical Title, Volume Number,* **page numbers.**

- Last name and initial(s) as for a book reference
- Year of publication in parentheses and followed by a period
- Title of article in lowercase, except for the first word and any proper nouns (not italicized or in quotations) followed by a period
- Title and volume number of periodical italicized and capitalized, each followed by a comma
- Inclusive page numbers, with all digits repeated, separated by a dash

Include some other designation with the year (such as a month or season, spelled out in full) if a periodical does not use volume numbers. The entries that follow illustrate the information and arrangement needed to cite periodicals.

17. An Article in a Scholarly Journal, Consecutively Paginated

Pay attention to the features of this basic reference to a scholarly journal:

> Epstein, R., & Hundert, E. (2002). Defining and assessing professional competence. *JAMA, 287,* 226-235.

18. An Abstract of a Scholarly Article (from a Secondary Source)

When referencing an abstract published separately from an article, provide publication details of the article followed by information about where the abstract was published.

> Shlipak, M. G., Simon, J. A., Grady, O., Lin, F., Wenger, N. K., & Furberg, C. D. (2001, September). Renal insufficiency and cardiovascular events in postmenopausal women with coronary heart disease. *Journal of the American College of Cardiology, 38,* 705-711. Abstract obtained from *Geriatrics,* 2001, *56*(12), Abstract No. 5645351.

WRITER'S TIP

When the dates of the article and the secondary-source abstract differ, the reference in your text would cite both dates, the original first, separated by a slash (2001/2002). When the abstract is obtained from the original source, the word *Abstract* is placed in brackets following the title (but before the period).

19. A Journal Article, Paginated by Issue

Lewer, N. (1999, summer). Nonlethal weapons. *Forum, 14*(2), 39-45.

> **NOTE:** When the page numbering of the issue starts with page 1, the issue number (not italicized) is placed in parentheses after the volume number.

20. A Journal Article, More Than Six Authors

Wang, X., Zuckerman, B., Pearson, C., Kaufman, G., Chen, C., Wang, G., et al. (2002, January 9). Maternal cigarette smoking, metabolic gene polymorphism, and infant birth weight. *JAMA, 287*, 195-202.

21. A Review

To reference a book review or a review of another medium (film, exhibit, and so on), indicate the review and the medium in brackets, along with the title of the work being reviewed by the author listed.

Updike, J. (2001, December 24). Survivor/believer [Review of the book *New and Collected Poems 1931–2001*]. *The New Yorker,* 118-122.

22. A Magazine Article

Silberman, S. (2001, December). The geek syndrome. *Wired, 9*(12), 174-183.

> **NOTE:** If the article is unsigned, begin the entry with the title of the article: Tomatoes target toughest cancer. (2002, February). *Prevention, 54*(2), 53.

23. A Newspaper Article

For newspaper articles, include the full publication date, year first followed by a comma, the month (spelled out), and the day. Identify the article's location in the newspaper using page numbers and section letters, as appropriate. If the article is a letter to the editor, identify it as such in brackets following the title. For newspapers, use "p." or "pp." before the page numbers; if the article is not on continuous pages, give all the page numbers, separated by commas.

Stolberg, S. C. (2002, January 4). Breakthrough in pig cloning could aid organ transplants. *The New York Times,* pp. 1A, 17A.

AOL to take up to $60 billion charge. (2002, January 8). *Chicago Tribune,* sec. 3, p. 3.

24. A Newsletter Article

Newsletter article entries are very similar to newspaper article entries; only a volume number is added, in italics.

Teaching mainstreamed special education students. (2002, February). *The Council Chronicle, 11,* 6-8.

56d   Reference Entries: Online Sources

APA style prefers a reference to the print form of a source, even if the source is available online. If you have read only the electronic form of an article's print version, add the words *Electronic version* in brackets after the title of the article. (The electronic address [URL] is not required if a print version exists.)

If an online article has been changed from the print version or has additional information, follow the same general format for the author, date, and title elements of print sources, but follow it with a "retrieved from" statement, citing the date of retrieval and the URL.

25. A Periodical, Identical to Print Version

Author, A., & Author, B. (year, Month day). Title of article, chapter, or webpage [Electronic version]. *Title of Periodical, volume number* or other designation, inclusive page numbers (if available).

Ashley, S. (2001, May). Warp drive underwater [Electronic version]. *Scientific American* (2001, May).

26. A Periodical, Different from Print Version or Online Only

Author, A., & Author, B. (year, Month day). Title of article, chapter, or webpage. *Title of Periodical, volume number,* inclusive page numbers (if available). Retrieved Month day, year, from electronic address

Nicholas, D., Huntington, P., & Williams, P. (2001, May 23). Comparing web and touch screen transaction log files. *Journal of Medical Internet Research, 3.* Retrieved November 15, 2001, from http://www.jmir.org/2001/2/e18/index.htm

> **NOTE:** Include an issue number in parentheses following the volume number if each issue of a journal begins on page 1. Use the abbreviation *pp.* (page numbers) in newspapers. Page numbers are often not relevant for online sources. End the citation with a period unless it ends with the electronic address.

27. A Multipage Document Created by a Private Organization

National Multiple Sclerosis Society. (n.d.) *About MS: For the newly diagnosed.* Retrieved May 20, 2002, from http://www.nationalmssociety.org

> **NOTE:** Use "n.d." (no date) if a date is unavailable. Provide the URL of the home page for an Internet document when its pages have different URLs.

28. A Document from an Online Database

Author, A., & Author, B. (year). Title of article or webpage. *Title of Periodical, volume number,* inclusive page numbers. Retrieved Month day, year, from name of database.

Belsie, L. (1999). Progress or peril? *Christian Science Monitor, 91*(85), 15. Retrieved September 15, 1999, from DIALOG online database (#97, IAC Business A.R.T.S., Item 07254533).

> **NOTE:** If the document cited is an abstract, include "Abstract" before the "retrieved from" statement. The item or accession numbers are optional.

29. Other Nonperiodical Online Document

Author, A., & Author, B. (year, Month day). *Title of work.* Retrieved Month day, year, from electronic address

Boyles, S. (2001, November 14). *World Diabetes Day has people pondering their risk.* Retrieved November 16, 2001, from http://my.webmd.com/content/article/1667.51328

> **NOTE:** To cite only a chapter or section of an online document, follow the title of the chapter with "In *Title of document* (chap. number)." If the author is not identified, begin with the title of the document. If a date is not identified, put "n.d." in parentheses following the title.

Catholic Near East Welfare Association. (2002). Threats to personal security. In *Report on Christian emigration: Palestine* (sect. 5). Retrieved May 20, 2002, from http://www.cnewa.org/news-christemigrat-part1.htm

30. A Document or an Abstract Available on a University Website

Author, A., & Author, B. (year). *Title of work.* Retrieved Month day, year, from name of host: electronic address

Magill, G. (2001). *Ethics of stem cell research.* Retrieved November 23, 2001, from St. Louis University, Center for Health Care Ethics website: http://www.slu.edu/centers/chce/drummond/magill.html

> **NOTE:** Name the university or government agency (and the department or division, if it is named), followed by a colon and the URL.

APA REFERENCES

31. A Report from a University, Available on a Private Organization Website

List the university and the institute as authors, followed by the publication date, the report's title, and retrieval information.

> **University, Institute. (year, Month).** *Title of work.* **Retrieved Month day, year, from electronic address**

> University of Wisconsin, Sonderegger Research Center and Kaiser Family Foundation. (2000, July). *Prescription drug trends—a chartbook.* Retrieved November 19, 2001, from http://www.kff.org/content/2000/3019/

> **NOTE:** If the private organization is not listed as an author, identify it in the "retrieved from" statement.

32. A U.S. Government Report Available on a Government Agency Website

> **Name of government agency. (year, Month day).** *Title of report.* **Retrieved Month day, year, from electronic address**

> United States Department of Commerce, Office of the Inspector General. (2001, March). *Internal controls over bankcard program need improvement.* Retrieved July 23, 2001, from http://www.oig.doc.gov/elibrary/reports/ recent/recent.html

> **NOTE:** If no publication date is indicated, use "n.d." in parentheses following the agency name.

33. A Paper Presented at a Symposium or Other Event, Abstract Retrieved from a University Website

> **Author, A. (year, Month day).** *Title of paper.* **Paper presented at name of event. Abstract retrieved Month day, year, from electronic address**

> Smale, S. (2001, November 7). *Learning and the evolution of language.* Paper presented at Brains and Machines Seminar Series. Abstract retrieved November 23, 2001, from http://www.ai.mit.edu/events/talks/ brainsMachines/abstracts/F2001/200111071700_StephenSmale.shtml

> **NOTE:** To cite a virtual conference, do not use "Abstract" before the "retrieved from" statement.

34. An E-Mail Message

E-mail is cited only in the text of the paper, not in the references list. See "A Personal Communication" at **55b-15**.

56e Reference Entries: Other Sources

The following citation entries are examples of audiovisual media sources and other sources available electronically.

35. Specialized Computer Software with Limited Distribution

Standard, nonspecialized computer software does not require a reference entry. Treat software as an unauthored work unless an individual has property rights to it. Indicate the software version in parentheses after the title, and note the medium in brackets.

> Carreau, S. (2001). Champfoot (Version 3.3) [Computer software]. Saint Mandé, France: Author.

36. An Electronic Abstract of a Journal Article Retrieved from a Database

The following format applies whether the database is on CD, on a website, or a university server. The item or accession number is not required, but may be included in parentheses at the end of the retrieval statement.

> Seyler, T. (1994). College-level studies: New memory techniques. *New Century Learners, 30*, 814-822. Abstract retrieved February 1, 1995, from Platinum File: EduPLUS database (40-18421).

37. A Television or Radio Broadcast

List a broadcast by the show's producer or executive producer, and identify the type of broadcast in brackets after the show's title.

> Crystal, L. (Executive Producer). (2005, February 11). *The NewsHour with Jim Lehrer* [Television broadcast]. New York and Washington, DC: Public Broadcasting Service.

38. A Television or Radio Program (Episode in a Series)

When identifying a specific episode in a television or radio series, identify the episode by its writers, if possible. Then follow with the airing date, the episode title, the type of series in brackets, and details about the series itself.

> Berger, C. (Writer). (2001, December 19). Feederwatch [Radio series program]. In D. Byrd & J. Block (Producers), *Earth & Sky*. Austin, TX: The Production Block.

39. An Audio Recording

Begin the entry with the speaker's or writer's name, not the producer's. Indicate the type of recording in brackets.

> Kim, E. (Author, speaker). (2000). *Ten thousand sorrows* [CD]. New York: Random House.

APA REFERENCES

40. A Music Recording

Give the name and function of the originators or primary contributors. Indicate the recording medium (CD, record, cassette, and so on) in brackets, immediately following the title.

ARS Femina Ensemble (Performers). (1998). *Musica de la puebla de Los Angeles: Music by women of baroque Mexico, Cuba, & Europe* [CD]. Louisville, KY: Nannerl Recordings.

41. A Motion Picture

Give the name and function of the director, producer, or both. If its circulation was limited, provide the distributor's name and complete address in parentheses.

Jackson, P. (Director). (2001). *The lord of the rings: The fellowship of the ring* [Motion picture]. United States: New Line Productions, Inc.

42. A Published Interview, Titled, Single Author

Start the entry with the interviewer's name, followed by the date and the title. Place the interviewee's name in brackets before other publication details.

Fussman, C. (2002, January). What I've learned [Interview with Robert McNamara]. *Esquire, 137*(1), 85.

43. An Unpublished Paper Presented at a Meeting

Indicate when the paper was presented, at what meeting, in what location.

Lycan, W. (2002, June). *The plurality of consciousness.* Paper presented at the meeting of the Society for Philosophy and Psychology, New York, NY.

NOTE: Use the abbreviations below in all APA reference entries:

- With author's names, shorten first and middle names to initials, leaving a space after the period. For a work with more than one author, use an ampersand (&) before the last author's name.
- For publisher locations, use the full city name plus the two-letter U.S. Postal Service abbreviation for the state. For international publishers, include a province and country name; for well-known publishing cities such as Boston, you may offer the city only.
- Spell out "Press" in full, but for other publishing information, use the abbreviations below.

p. (pp.)	Page (pages)	chap.	Chapter	ed.	Edition
Rev. ed.	Revised edition	2nd ed.	Second edition	Ed. (Eds.)	Editor (editors)
Trans.	Translator(s)	n.d.	No date	Vol.	Volume
vols.	Volumes	No.	Number	Pt.	Part

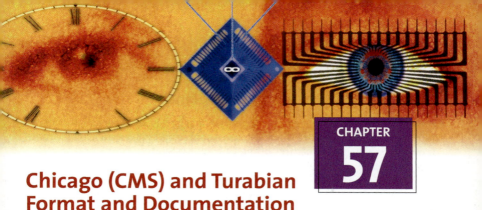

Chicago (CMS) and Turabian Format and Documentation

Because you're looking at this page, you've probably been told to submit an assigned paper in Chicago (CMS) or Turabian format. You're looking for answers to questions like these: How do I format my paper? How do I document my research? For answers, read on.

What is the CMS, and who is Turabian?

The Chicago Manual of Style is published by the University of Chicago Press, a leading academic publisher. Kate Turabian has published a Chicago manual especially for students writing college-level papers.

What is the Chicago/Turabian style?

Chicago/Turabian style refers to a method of documenting and formatting a research paper. The Chicago system is best known as a note-based system with in-text citations that use superscript numbers indicating source material. The footnotes or endnotes supply complete information when a source is first used, plus shortened information for subsequent references.

Where can I find more information about Chicago style?

This chapter offers a very brief introduction to CMS/Turabian. For further information, consult the following resources:

- *The Chicago Manual of Style* (fifteenth edition) and its website, <www.press.uchicago.edu/Misc/Chicago.cmosfaq/>

- Kate Turabian, *A Manual for Writers of Term Papers, Theses, and Dissertations* (sixth edition)

- This book's website, <www.thecollegewriter.com>

What's Ahead?

57a CMS Documentation at a Glance
57b CMS Format

57a CMS Documentation at a Glance

The Chicago (CMS) system involves two parts: (1) a superscript (raised) number within your paper when you use a source and (2) a matching footnote or endnote. Note these features of the Chicago system:

- It uses signal phrases and superscript numbers to set off source material from your own thinking and discussion. A signal phrase names the author and places the material in context (for example, "As Paul Ricoeur argues in *The Symbolism of Evil* . . .").
- The Chicago system is flexible and unobtrusive. Bibliographic notes corresponding to the superscript numbers can be placed at the bottom of the page (footnotes) or collected on a "Notes" page at the end of the paper (endnotes). As a result, the paper's flow is relatively uninterrupted by references.

How do CMS notes work?

You can see CMS features at work in the examples below. The reference to Loyal Jones and the superscript number "1" tell the reader the following things:

- The borrowed material came from a source authored by Jones.
- Bibliographic information can be found under note "1" on the endnotes page.

In-Text Citation

As Loyal Jones points out, much of country music's influences came from immigrants originating in countries such as Germany, England, France, Ireland, and Scotland.[1]

Matching Endnote

1. Loyal Jones, "Singing Cowboys and Musical Mountaineers: Southern Culture and the Roots of Country Music," *The Journal of Southern History* 60, no. 4 (1994): 849-850. http://www.jstor.org/ (accessed 26 March 2005).

How should I place CMS in-text citations?

The placement of an in-text citation follows these simple rules:

- **Signal the beginning of source material.** Typically, you can use a reference to the author or the work's title.

    Louise Pound, author of *The "Uniformity" of the Ballad Style,* explains ballads by looking at the origins . . .

- **Insert a superscript number after the source material.** Your word-processing program allows you to create superscripts and the accompanying footnote or endnote automatically. Except when used with dashes, place superscript numbers after punctuation marks (periods, commas, quotation marks).
- **Number notes consecutively.** As your paper proceeds, number each source reference with a new number.

How should I set up endnotes?

Here are some templates for the most common CMS entries. For a complete listing of entries, consult *The Chicago Manual of Style* (fifteenth edition) in your library.

TEMPLATE FOR PRINT PERIODICAL ARTICLE

Number. Author's First and Last Name, "Title of Article," *Journal Title* volume, number (year): page numbers. [Other publication details are integrated as needed. For an online periodical article, add the Internet address followed by the access date in parentheses.]

12. Charlie Seemann, "The Cowboys Poetry Gathering," *The Journal of American Folklore* 104, no. 414 (1991): 505.

TEMPLATE FOR ONLINE DOCUMENT

Number. Author's First and Last Name [if available], "Document Title," *Journal or Site Title,* publication information [volume, posting date], Internet address (access date).

7. Len Green, "Trail of Tears," *The Choctaw Nation of Oklahoma,* Home Page, July 1, 2002, http://www.choctawnation.com/trailoftears.htm (accessed May 17, 2005).

Web Link: With the advent of Project Gutenberg and the Google Book Search Library Project, more and more scholarly texts will be available online. To keep current with the CMS citation styles for the texts, go to <www.thecollegewriter.com>.

TEMPLATE FOR PRINT BOOK

Number. Author's First and Last Name, *Full Title of Book* (Publication City: Publisher, publication year). [Other publication details are integrated as needed.]

4. Garry Wills, *Lincoln at Gettysburg: The Words That Remade America* (New York: Simon & Schuster, 1992).

SECOND AND SUBSEQUENT NOTES FOR SOURCES

When you refer to a source after the initial note and it is separated in sequence from the previous reference, provide the author's last name, a shortened title, and a page number.

16. Wills, *Lincoln at Gettysburg,* 43.

For a reference to the same work as the reference that came before it, use the Latin abbreviation *Ibid.*

17. Ibid., 43.

CHICAGO (CMS) FORMAT AND DOCUMENTATION

57b CMS Format

The Chicago Manual of Style offers format guidelines for page layout, spacing, and typography—from the first page of your paper to the "Notes" and bibliography pages. The sample pages that follow offer a CMS-formatted version of the MLA model on **51e**. The full CMS version of the paper is available at this book's website, <www.thecollegewriter.com>.

How should I set up my first page?

Place your last name and the page number flush right.

Place your name, the professor's name, the course, and the date flush left.

Center the title below the heading and double-space.

Van Arendonk   1

Kyle Van Arendonk

Professor David Schelhaas

English 302

April 17, 2005

The Threat of Antibiotic Resistance

Antibiotics are one of modern medicine's proudest achievements. The accidental discovery that led to this achievement, as told by Gerard Tortora, Berdell Funke, and Christine Case, occurred in 1928. . . . He named the chemical penicillin, the first antibiotic, and doctors were soon using it to treat a wide variety of bacterial infections.[1]

Since Fleming's great discovery, scientists have . . .

How should I set up my endnotes page?

Number each entry and indent the first line.

For later entries, use a shortened form or *Ibid.*

Van Arendonk   8

Notes

1. Gerard Tortora, Berdell Funke, and Christine Case, *Microbiology: An Introduction* (San Francisco: Benjamin Cummings, 2002), 13.

2. Maureen Pugh and Barbara Werner, eds., "Antibiotic," in *Stedman's Medical Dictionary,* 27th ed. (Philadelphia: Lippincott Williams & Wilkins, 2000), 96.

3. Tortora, Funke, and Case, *Microbiology,* 549.

4. Ibid., 549–50.

5. Richard Wenzel and Michael Edmond, "Managing Antibiotic Resistance," *New England Journal of Medicine* 343, no. 26 (2000): 1961-63.

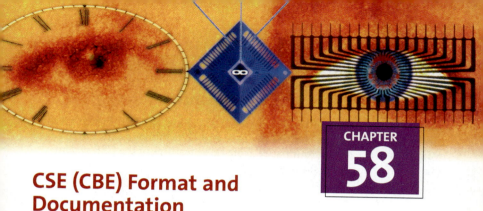

CSE (CBE) Format and Documentation

Because you're looking at this page, you've probably been told to submit an assigned paper in CSE (or CBE) format. You're looking for answers to questions like these: How do I format my paper in CSE? How do I document my research? For answers, read on.

What is the CSE?

CSE stands for the Council of Science Editors, a professional organization of authors, editors, and publishers in the natural and applied sciences. (Note that this organization used to be the CBE—the Council of Biology Editors.)

What is CSE style?

CSE style refers to a method of documenting research and formatting research writing in biology and other natural and applied-science disciplines. CSE style offers two choices: the name-year system and the citation-sequence system. Because the name-year system is similar to the APA system (**54a–56e**), this chapter focuses on the citation-sequence option.

- **In-text citation**—the use of a superscript number or a number in parentheses corresponding to a numbered entry in a references list
- **References**—a list of numbered resources sequenced according to the first reference to the source in the paper (not alphabetically)

Where can I find more information about CSE style?

This chapter offers a brief introduction to CSE style. For further information, consult the following resources:

- *Scientific Style and Format: The CBE Manual for Authors, Editors, and Publishers* (sixth edition, 1994).
- The CSE website, <www.councilscienceeditors.org>.
- This book's website, <www.thecollegewriter.com>.

What's Ahead
58a CSE Documentation at a Glance
58b CSE Format

CSE (CBE) FORMAT AND DOCUMENTATION

58a **CSE Documentation at a Glance**

The CSE citation system involves two parts: (1) a numbered in-text citation within your paper when you use a source and (2) a bibliographic entry keyed by number at the end of your paper. Note these features of the CSE system:

- **It refers to entire sources using numbers.** Each number is assigned sequentially as sources are used within the text. When the source is referred to again in the paper, the assigned number is reused.
- **It lists sources by number, not by alphabet.** Unlike other systems that arrange references in the end-of-paper list alphabetically by authors' last names, CSE lists sources in the order that they first appear in the text.

What does CSE documentation look like?

You can see these features at work in the example below. The reference to David Kairys and the superscript number "1" tell the reader the following things:

- The borrowed material came from a source authored by Kairys.
- Publication information for the source is listed under note "1" on the references page.
- The superscript is followed by information on the source.

In-Text Citation in Body of Paper

In an article in <u>Review of Optometry</u>, David **Kairys**[1], an optometrist and instructor at Pennsylvania State University, explains three main types of genetic mutations that can provide bacteria with a means of . . .

Matching References Entry at End of Paper

1. **Kairys DJ.** The science behind antibiotic resistance. Rev of Optometry 2002 Oct 15: 39-44.

How do I make CSE in-text citations?

Follow these rules when using the citation-sequence approach:

- Place the number immediately after the words to which they refer. Whether you are referencing a specific author or a topic, place the superscript (raised) number immediately after the word, not at the end of a sentence or passage.
- Use either a superscript number or a number in parentheses. Both methods are acceptable, although the superscript approach is preferred. To insert a superscript number, check the "insert" function on your word-processing program.
- Number sources in the order they initially appear in your writing. For second references to a source, use the originally assigned number.
- For references to multiple sources, use hyphens and commas. When referring, for example, to sources 3, 4, and 5, use "3-5"; when referring to sources 3 and 5, use "3,5."

How do I make CSE references?

Use the templates below and refer to the references page at the end of this chapter. Note that each entry is double-spaced and that second and subsequent lines line up under the first letter of the first word, not the number. Also note the lack of italics and quotation marks.

TEMPLATE FOR PRINT PERIODICAL ARTICLE

Source Number. Author's Last Name First Initials. Title of article. Journal Title abbreviated year; volume (issue): page numbers.

> 3. Wenzel RP, Edmond MB. Managing antibiotic resistance. New Engl J Med 2000; 343: 1961-3.

TEMPLATE FOR PRINT BOOK

Source Number. Author's Last Name Initials. Title of book. Publication City: Publisher; publication year. Number of pages.

> 1. Tortora GJ, Funke BR, Case CL. Microbiology: an introduction. San Francisco: Benjamin Cummings; 2002. 832 p.

TEMPLATE FOR ONLINE DOCUMENT

Source Number. Author's Last Name Initials. Title of work. [Medium]. Place of publication or [place unknown]: Publisher (person or organization) or [publisher unknown]. Date of publication [date last updated or modified; date cited, accessed, or retrieved]; page, document, volume, and issue numbers. Approximate length [pages, paragraphs, screens]. Available from: address.

> 6. Davies PD. Does increased use of antibiotics result in increased antibiotic resistance? Clinical Infectious Diseases [database on the Internet]. 2004 [cited 2005 Apr 3]; 39(1). Available from: http://www.ncbi.nlm.nih.gov/ entrez/query.fcgi.

58b CSE Format

Because the research paper format in the natural sciences is determined by the form (lab report, field report), the CSE does not advocate a strict format. However, science papers and reports should share general characteristics of format, layout, and typography. The sample pages that follow offer a CSE-formatted version of a paper submitted in a biology class.

Web Link: The full CSE version of the paper is available at this book's website, <www.thecollegewriter.com>, as are a variety of science reports.

CSE (CBE) FORMAT AND DOCUMENTATION

How should I set up my first page?

1

The Threat of Antibiotic Resistance

Kyle Van Arendonk

April 17, 2005

Introduction

Antibiotics are one of modern medicine's proudest achievements. The accidental discovery that led to this achievement, as told by Gerard Tortora, Berdell Funke, and Christine Case[1], occurred in 1928. A scientist named Alexander Fleming noticed an unusual occurrence on a Petri plate of growing bacteria. The Petri plate had been contaminated by a small amount of mold, and the bacteria in the region around this mold were not growing normally. Fleming saw a clearly defined area around the mold in which the bacteria were inhibited. He determined that the mold was a species of Penicillium[1] and found a way to extract the organism's chemical that inhibited the bacteria's growth. He named the chemical penicillin, the first antibiotic, and doctors were soon using it to treat a wide variety of bacterial infections.

Since Fleming's great discovery, scientists have discovered many other antibiotics. The word antibiotic, at first glance, may seem like a misnomer considering its use in the medical field. According to Stedman's Medical Dictionary[2], the Greek word from which antibiotic is derived actually translates as "against (anti) life (bios)" (96). However, while antibiotics work for the lives of human patients, they work against the lives of the microorganisms that cause infections.

According to Tortora, Funke, and Case[1], antibiotics can be broadly defined as any microorganism-produced substances that can inhibit the growth of other microorganisms. Most antibiotics, like . . .

Margin notes:

Place page numbers in the upper-right corner. Center the report's title, your name, and the date.

Use headings for sections of your paper: for example, "Introduction," "Results," and "Discussion."

Indent paragraphs and double-space throughout the text.

Indicate source references with superscript citations numbered by the order in which sources are used in the paper.

How should I set up my references page?

10

References

1. Tortora GJ, Funke BR, Case CL. Microbiology: an introduction. San Francisco: Benjamin Cummings; 2002. 832 p.

2. Pugh MB, Werner B. Antibiotic. Stedman's medical dictionary. 27th ed. Philadelphia: Lippincott Williams & Wilkins; 2000. 2098 p.

3. Wenzel RP, Edmond MB. Managing antibiotic resistance. New Engl J Med 2000; 343: 1961-3.

4. Mims C, Dockrell HM, Goering RV, Roitt I, Wakelin D, Zuckerman M. Medical microbiology. Edinburgh: Mosby; 2004. 660 p.

5. Levinson W, Jawetz E. Medical microbiology and immunology. Stamford CT: Appleton and Lange; 1996. 523 p.

6. Davies PD. Does increased use of antibiotics result in increased antibiotic resistance? Clinical Infectious Diseases [database on the Internet]. 2004 [cited 2005 Apr 3]; 39(1). Available from: http://www.ncbi.nlm.nih.gov/entrez/query.fcgi.

7. Kairys DJ. The science behind antibiotic resistance. Rev of Optometry [database on the Internet]. 2002 15 Oct [cited 2005 Apr 5]: 39-44. Available from: http://www.ebscohost.com.

8. Bren L. Battle of the bugs: fighting antibiotic resistance. FDA Consumer [database on the Internet]. 2002 July/Aug [cited 2005 Apr 8]: 28-34. Available from: http://www.ebscohost.com.

9. Fact sheet: the problem of antibiotic resistance. National Institute of Allergy and Infectious Diseases [Internet]. 2004 Apr [cited 2005 Mar 31]. Available from: http://www.niaid.nih.gov/factsheets/antimicro.htm.

Start on a new page after the text. Number consecutively.

Center the title "References."

List all sources summarized, paraphrased, or quoted in your paper.

Number and sequence sources in the order that you first referred to them.

Use double-spacing between and within all entries.

Use initials and abbreviations as shown.

Credits

P. 13 "The Media and the Ethics of Cloning," by Leigh Turner, as appeared in *The Chronicle of Higher Education*, September 26, 1997. Reprinted by permission of Dr. Leigh Turner.

P. 442 From, "Vehicle of Change," by Lawrence D. Burns, J. Byron-McCormick, and Christopher E. Borroni-Bird. Copyright © 2002 by Scientific American, Inc. All rights reserved.

Cover Images: © 2006 Jack Hollingsworth/Getty Images; © 2006 Digital Vision/Getty Images

Tab Images: [Tab 1] © 2006 Photodisc Collection/Getty Images; [Tab 2] © 2006 Corbis; [Tab 3] © 2006 Jupiter Images/Nola Lopez (Graphistock); [Tab 4] © 2006 Corbis; [Tab 5] © Dan Farrall/Getty Images; [Tab 6] © Lucia Zeccarra/Getty Images; [Tab 7] © 2006 Don Farrall/Getty Images; [Tab 8] © Photodisc Collection/Getty Images; [Tab 9] © 2006 Robert Stahl/Getty Images; [Tab 10] © 2006 Corbis; [Tab 11] © 2006 Don Farrall/Getty Images; [Tab 12] © 2006 A T Willett/Getty Images.

Tips & Links Images: [E-Mail Tip] © 2006 Comstock/Fotosearch; [ESL Tip] © 2006 Maciej Frolow/Getty Images; [Ethics Tip] © 2006 Lawrence Lawry/Getty Images; [Links] © 2006 Photodisc Collection/Getty Images; [Visuals Tip] © 2006 ImageState/Fotosearch; [What's Ahead] © 2006 Brand X Pictures/Fotosearch; [Writer's Tip] © 2006 Flying Colours Ltd/Getty Images.

Screen shots: p. 475 Reprinted by permission of EBSCO; p. 480 © 2005 LII.ORG. Reprinted with permission; p. 482 © 2005 Ask Jeeves, Inc.

These images are © 2006 Corbis: p. 93, p. 124, p. 201, p. 220, p. 235, p. 247, p.263, p. 280, p. 445, p. 470, p. 529

These images are © 2006 Getty Images and the named photographers: p. 13 Arthur S. Aubry, p. 23 David Perry, p. 34 Image100, 41 Photolink/F. Schussler, p. 54 Chase Jarvis, 58 Michael Saint Maur Shell, p. 61 Brand X Pictures, p. 61 Stockbyte, p. 67 PNC, p. 113 David Oliver, p. 115 Anthony Harvie, p. 128 Teo Lannie, p. 139 Brand X Pictures, p. 140 Image Source, p. 145 Hisham F. Ibrahim, p. 152 Steve Dunning, p.169 Photodisc Collection, p. 202 Brand X Pictures/Photo 24, p. 231 Brand X Pictures, p. 242 Digital Vision, p. 249 Photolink/C. Lee, p. 259 David Oliver, p. 267 Jeremy Woodhouse, p. 278 PhotoDisc, p. 284 DougMenuez, p. 293. Tim Barnett, p. 321 Tom Le Goff, p. 324 Stockbyte, p. 327 Sam Roberts; Sam Roberts; Mediaimages, p. 331 Stockbyte, p. 344 Ryan McVay, p. 345 Barbara Penoyar, p. 347 Lawrence M Sawyer, p. 348 Image Source, p. 435 Ryan McVay, p. 452 Matthius Tunger, p.455 F64, p.457 Digital Vision, p. 464 Manchan, p. 486 Peter Mason, p. 494 Jim Boorman, p. 525 Manchan, p. 534 David Fischer

These images are © 2006 JupiterImages Corporation and the named photographers: p. 31 Rubberball, p. 121 Andrew Sarnecki, p. 154 Thinkstock, p. 159 Comstock Images, p. 214 Brakefield Photo, p. 222 Big Cheese Photo, p. 238 Oliver Furrer, p. 343 Thinkstock, p. 346 William Sallaz, p. 479 Comstock Images, p. 521 Bananastock, p. 537 Imagesource, p. 542 John Lund/Sam Diephuis

Book photo on p. 256 © 2006 Photos.com

The following images were made by Mark Fairweather and are © 2006 Sebranek, Inc.: p. 7, p. 76, p. 105, p. 150, p. 157, p. 205, p. 270, p. 300, p. 314, p. 334, p. 467, p. 472, p. 474, p. 491

The following images were made by Chris Krenzke and are © 2006 Sebranek, Inc.: p. 21, p. 369, p.375, p.381, p. 395

A

Quotations (cont.)
    integrating, 491, 492, 513
    long, 297, 492
    in MLA style, 505
    MLA style for, 510, 513, 514, 515
        attributive phrases for, 514
        in-text citations, 526
    omission from, 292, 299–300, 493
    of passages, 296
    plagiarism and, 485
    plunking, 488
    punctuation of, 296–297
    quotation marks with, 296–297
    within quotations, 297
    shifts in, 266
    showing poetry lines in, 300
    showing the end of, 495
    as support, 77, 114
    when to use, 462
Quote, quotation, 159

R

Race, respectful language for, 144
Rambling sentences, 129
Rationality, critical thinking and, 12. *See also* Logic
Ratios, colons with, 289
Readability
    typefaces and, 173–175
    visuals for, 177
Reading
    active, 4–6
    aloud, 4
    annotation in, 5
    checklist for critical, 10
    critical thinking and, 3–10
    evaluating texts in, 7
    mapping in, 6
    outlining in, 6
    visual images, 20–21
    writing responses to, 8
    writing summaries and, 9
Real, very, really, 159
Reasoning. *See also* Argumentation
    by analogy, 31
    argumentation and, 27–44
    cause and effect, 30
    critical thinking and, 11–13
    deductive, 14, 30

from definition, 31
developing, 35–37
evaluating while reading, 7
from indicators, 30
inductive, 14, 30
in persuasion, 30–31
selecting inductive or deductive, 35
skills in, 13
Reason why, reason . . . is because, 160
Rebuttals, 38
Reciprocal pronouns, 205
Recommendation-request letters, 417
Recommendations, evaluation and, 17
Recordings
    APA reference entries for, 575
    MLA works-cited entries for, 542
Redesigning, 16
Red herrings, 41
Redundancy, 98, 140
Reference works
    APA style for
        reference entries, 569
    in libraries, 472–473
    MLA style for
        in-text citations, 525
    MLA works-cited entries for online,
        539
    research with, 448
References, parenthetical. *See*
    Parenthetical citations.
References pages. *See also* Works-cited
    entries (MLA)
    APA style for, 548, 549, 565–576
    CSE/CBE format for, 582, 583, 585
Reflection
    personal essays and, 360, 361
    on readings, 7
    responses to texts and, 8
Reflexive pronouns, 203, 204
Refutations, 38
Regardless, irregardless, 160
Regular verbs, 331–332
Relative clauses. *See* Dependent clauses
Relative pronouns
    in adjective clauses, 248–249
    closer look at, 207
    combining sentences with, 124
    list of, 204
    rambling sentences and, 129
    as sentence subjects, 255

Revising, Editing, and Proofreading Symbols

ab	do not abbreviate, **313-316**
ad	adjective/adverb error, **221-224**
agr	agreement problem, **257-260**
ambig	ambiguous wording, **270**
avoid	this should be avoided
awk	awkward expression
cap (≡)	capitalize, **301-306**
case	error in case, **206-207**
cf	comma fault, **279-286**
choppy	choppy style, **124**
coh	coherence, **111, 115-116**
concl	weak conclusion, **42**
coord	faulty coordination, **262-263**
cs	comma splice, **262**
d	diction, **133-148**
def	define
details	add details, **76, 125**
dm	dangling modifier, **268-269**
doc	documentation, **494-495**
frag	sentence fragment, **236, 261**
gen	be more specific, **208**
gram	grammatical error, **197-226**
inc	incomplete, **125, 270**
intro	weak introduction, **74-75**
irr	irregular verb error, **216-217**
ital	italics (underscore), **298-299**
lang	slang/jargon/cliché, **142-143**
lc (∅)	use lowercase, **301-306**
logic	not logical, **40-43**
mm	misplaced modifier, **268**
ms	manuscript form, **104**
nc	not clear, **270**
nonst	nonstandard language, **271**
num	numbers error, **311-313**
p	punctuation, **275-300**
?	questionable idea, **40-43**
pass	inappropriate passive, **126**
pro ref	pronoun reference, **203**
ramb	rambling sentence, **129**
rep	repetition, **99**
RO	run-on sentence, **263**
shift	shift in tense/person, **264-265**
sp	spelling, **307-310**
ss	sentence structure, **337-338**
stet	let it stand
sub	faulty subordination, **342**
sum	summarize, **9**
support	add evidence, **36-37**
sxt	sexist, **146-147**
t	tone, **29**
ten	wrong verb tense, **212-213**
thesis	thesis unclear or missing, **63-67**
trans	weak transition, **115-116**
TS	topic sentence, **112-113**
u	unity, **111-113**
use	usage/mixed pair, **149-162**
vary	add variety, **130-131**
vague	vague statement
voice	inconsistent voice, **88, 266**
w	wordy, **140-141**
wc	word choice, **97-99**
ww	wrong word, **149-162**
∥	not parallel, **267**
∧	insert word/s
∧,	insert comma
∨'	insert apostrophe
∨"	insert quotation marks
¶	begin paragraph
ℓ	delete
x	find and correct error
#	insert space
⁀‿	close up space
∼	transpose

CONTENTS